TRI-STATE HEROES
OF '45

TRI-STATE HEROES
OF '45

Together With A Year
in the Life of a
West Virginia Farm Family

RUPERT PRATT

MILL CITY PRESS

Mill City Press, Inc.
2301 Lucien Way #415
Maitland, FL 32751
407.339.4217
www.millcitypress.net

Paperback ISBN-13: 978-1-6312-9915-5
Ebook ISBN-13: 978-1-6312-9916-2

DEDICATION

This book is dedicated to the
men and women of the United States,
and especially to those from the Tri-State area
of West Virginia, Ohio, and Kentucky, who served
in the armed forces during World War II
and those who supported them.

TABLE OF CONTENTS

ACKNOWLEDGMENTS

I OWE DEBTS OF GRATITUDE TO SEVERAL PEOPLE. FOREMOST IS GLENNA Morrison, my mother, whose diary of 1945 led to the creation of this volume. Others are: Barbara Woodrum Harvey, a longtime friend who spent many hours assisting in the gathering of information; Dave Curry, Cabell County, West Virginia Library Assistant, whose friendly help was invaluable; Louie Hutchinson, Betty Keyser Hutchinson, Rachel Midkiff Harbour, and Sonja Rounds for the donation and verification of historical material.

I must also mention friends from my "Monday Lunch Bunch" who nudged, questioned, and advised during the lengthy writing process. Thank you, Tom and Nancy DeVito; Shirley Saccocio; Bob and June VanBuren; Audrey Meyer; Joan Thuotte; June McGarry; Bill Holman, and Clarence Mosher.

My family's support was invaluable. I appreciate your mostly "hands off" but "we're here" attitude. Greg and Jon, Purvesh and Bobbi, Lizzie, Nathan, and Andy, I love you all.

There are also those from 1945, relatives, friends, newspaper people, folks mostly unknown and unheralded who contributed not only news of the time, but also the little personal stories about Tri-State members of the armed forces. My work has been one of resurrection. This book, I happily admit, exists because many hands produced it.

INTRODUCTION

THE FINAL YEAR OF WORLD WAR II WAS A TIME OF ENORMOUS HISTORIC
events: Bombers and fighters of Allied Forces darkened the skies over Germany and destroyed key military and industrial sites while ground forces from East and West enclosed a staggering Nazi regime; a weary president died and an able one stepped into his difficult position; the monster who had set the world aflame perished by his own hand; the war in Europe ended when the Germans in Italy were trapped against the Alps and a final Allied thrust overpowered a decimated German heartland; prisoner-of-war camps were emptied and the gates of Nazi concentration camps were thrown open, releasing populations of dissidents and persecuted minorities, mostly Jews; the difficult and competitive process of occupying and dividing Nazi territory began; American troops left Europe for the United States or to the intensified Pacific theatre; the United Nations Charter was established; a battered and hungry Japan finally bowed after atomic bombs were dropped on her cities; the Allied occupation of Japan began, and finally, to the thunderous celebration of our war-weary country, the troops started coming home. Many made it for Christmas.

I turned twelve that year. I was aware, obliquely perhaps, of foreign and domestic problems, but in truth I enjoyed a carefree lifestyle on our little farm at Salt Rock, West Virginia, a rural and safe place. Events affected me certainly, but my energy, along with other boys my age, turned toward acting out what we understood of the situation. We did our homework about instruments of war, especially airplanes; we filled the air with popular fighters and bombers. Flying Fortresses, Thunderbolts, and Spitfires zig-zagged over imagined war zones, killing the enemy with frightful fury. My own hastily scribbled cartoon strips depicted bitter dog fights over battlefields and oceans. It was the child's way of survival.

Time and maturity bring us to appreciate our past and treasure what mattered to our parents and grandparents, whether ideals or "things" handed down or discovered in their effects after their passing.

My mother was Glenna Adkins, who became Glenna Pratt, and later Glenna Morrison. After her death in 1978, I placed saved letters and other mementos in boxes, resolving to sort through them later. I soon forgot and it was several years before I rediscovered her diary of 1945.

Mother was a prolific letter writer, but to my knowledge she never kept a record of her daily activities any time except that year and a tiny portion of 1946. Her entries were simply brief accounts of her own comings and goings within family and community. She seldom made editorial comment or ventured opinion.

The pages on which she wrote were part of a combination tear-off calendar and writing tablet pasted onto a red cardboard backing. The composite was meant to hang on the wall. The tablet sheets, thin and inferior in quality, are now brittle and the pencil

1

writing has faded. I made digital copies and careful transcripts of each page.

I also kept a diary for several years. My leatherbound book was a 1945 birthday gift from Eddie Harbour, my friend, classmate, and member of the large Harbour family down in the village of Salt Rock. I hadn't looked at it for many years, but soon saw that it covered the same period as Mother's diary, the exception being January 1 through March 3; I had not started writing until March 4. For the most part my writing was as emotion-free as hers.

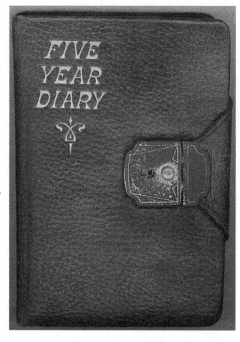

Had we thought our words would ever be read by others, I'm sure we would have been more inclusive of events, explained more, and been careful with spelling and grammar. Mother's writing was usually clear of problems, whereas my mistakes were glaring. I debated whether to "clean up" our jottings, but in the end decided to publish them as written. I did exclude some recordings, especially mine where they were repetitive, such as, "I went to school today."

The diaries form a framework for this book, but the mundane affairs of our family were far overshadowed by that year's world, country, and local events, many of which I recorded alongside the diary entries. Nevertheless, I soon realized that the emphasis must be on the military service of Tri-State men and women.

The *Huntington Herald-Dispatch* and its evening edition, the *Huntington Herald-Advertiser* brought not only world and local news to the area, but also included the publication of two daily columns, "In the Service" for the *Herald-Dispatch* and "With the Colors" for the *Herald-Advertiser.* Those columns carried nearly identical real-life mini-stories that paid tribute to Tri-State sailors, soldiers, marines, airmen, nurses, and others who served with or supported the armed forces of our country. Those brief accounts ranged from a simple statement of a soldier being home on furlough to announcement of a high award for an act of bravery. I soon realized that those little historical records must be the major focus. With permission of the *Huntington Herald-Dispatch,* I've copied entries, verbatim, from "In the Service" and "With the Colors," except where I corrected obvious typos and sometimes eliminated unrelated or redundant information. Weekday entries are from "In the Service" and Sunday entries are from "With the Colors." An exception is August where all entries are from "With the Colors." Entries within the columns may not appear in the same order as originally published. There will be some mistakes; my transcripts are from microfilm, not the original newsprint, and some were difficult to read. Endnotes for these mini-stories are unnecessary since all the columns are from the same source and appear within dated sections.

The little stories reveal detail on several levels: Locations of military camps and bases throughout the United States and the world, along with military hospitals, were named in great diversity; servicemen and servicewomen were listed by rank from lowest private to highest ranking officers; family relationships were stated, usually with home addresses; there were numerous awards for bravery, some very high; battle details with place names, airplane and ship names, and other strategic details frequently cast light on events that may never have appeared in any other account of the war. Many of those who gave so much for our country might never have had anything else ever publicized about their service.

Those war years were difficult. Huntington and Tri-State families often had more than one and sometimes several members of a family in the military services, and many gave their lives. Despite the pain, we didn't lose faith in God, nor faith we would win in the end. Churches overflowed. I recall with wonder the full pews at Salt Rock Methodist Church and the impressive attendance at Wednesday night prayer meetings.

If you were alive in 1945, you have your own memories of that period, good and bad. If this book conjures up bad memories, I apologize. For those of you who were not yet born, or too young to remember, I hope *Tri-State Heroes of '45* enlightens about events of that last year of the war and our place in it. It is also my hope that our diaries present a keyhole glimpse at the commonplace lives of those of us who both endured and celebrated that extraordinary year.

Rupert Pratt 2020

January

WINTER QUIET, TIME FOR HOPE

WINTER HAD SETTLED ON THE LAND; IT WAS A TIME IN OUR RURAL SET-
ting when the cows came home early, the chickens hardly ventured from their roosts, and our activities were mostly indoors. It was a quiet time as well, and I acted out my limited views of world
situations through my creation of stories and cartoons. For adults there was necessary work laced
with introspection and feelings of uncertainty about the war. Looking back on it now, I believe it
was raw courage and faith that bolstered our belief that all would end well. Nurturing hope, we
managed and, as our diary entries show, all was not doom and gloom in our lives.

I have no idea why Mother choose to start a diary. She had enough to do around the house and farm. I'm happy she did, however, for her record shines a light on a year of the mundane activities of our family. Her use of past tense in the first entry indicates she didn't start writing on this date, but more likely on January 4. There are other indications throughout the year that she entered more than one day at a time. I may have also after my initial diary entry on March 4.

> Glenna: [Monday] *January 1st 1945 – Snow. Cold. I washed a big washing and cleaned the house up good. We bought a pig from Danny Keyser. It weighed 102 lbs. at 20¢ costing $20.40 in all. We made sausage that night.*

As much as I wanted to keep my comments about diary entries to a minimum, I couldn't resist the temptation to sometimes clarify or elaborate, especially when they resurrected my own memories of the time.

That being the case, my first clarification is about family: The "we" in Mother's entry was our immediate family of three. My stepfather,

Dawson Morrison, married my mother when I was five years old. My biological father, Bessen Rupert Pratt (I was told no one used his first name), died in December 1932, three months before my birth.

Rupert

Dawson & Glenna

Dawson was raised on a farm two miles north of Salt Rock. He was an incredibly hard worker, fun-loving, and not above a practical joke on selected friends. Stout in frame, he was one of the physically strongest men I have known. At the time he was working a rotating shift at American Car & Foundry Company in Huntington and catching only a few hours' sleep at home before attending to farm duties. His patience with me helped develop skills and qualities Mother alone could not. I addressed him simply as "Dawson." My sons would later call him "Grandpa Dawson."

That already-butchered pig was a great way for a farm family to start the year, although such a purchase was not normal procedure for us since we raised our own pigs. On this New Year's Day, the aroma of cooking ham and sausage must have filled our little house. Smell is the sense most easily resurrected, which may account for my occasional whiff of long-ago kitchen scents.

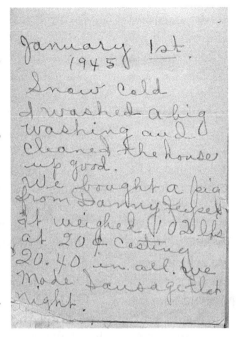

I think it appropriate that this first newspaper entry, a correction from a previous *Huntington Herald-Dispatch* column, is about someone we knew: "The Rev. Horace E. Midkiff of Huntington, who served more than 20 years in the Army, was a staff sergeant, not a first sergeant in his last tour of duty in Hawaii. He is a cousin of Justice of the Peace Ezra M. Midkiff of Huntington, not a brother."[1] (Horace Midkiff, recently discharged from the Army, was our pastor at Salt Rock Methodist Church.)

In addition to news from Mother's kitchen and dispatchs from the theatres of war, sports were of great interest, perhaps a necessary diversion. Duke Ridgley's "Diamond Dust" column appeared regularly in the *Huntington Herald-Dispatch* and was about much more than baseball. "Duke" covered all sports with a direct creative style that earned respect from area readers. A veteran of World War I, he supported service men and women with sincere passion. His column, presented in his own picturesque style, was still running in 1950 when I was a senior at Barboursville High School. I've included his logo in this first of several excerpts from Duke's "Diamond Dust" columns:

"University of Mexico Plays Marshall Tosses Thursday. . . . Coach 'Crafty Cam' Henderson's Thundering Herd will face the strong University of Mexico City Thursday evening on the hardwood lumber at the popular Seventh Avenue Arena, meaning—of course—Arena Gardens. This will be the first gander the Huntington fans have had at the green and white snipers since they embarked on their holiday jaunt through the East, where they distinguished themselves by turning in one of the most successful road-trips in Marshall's basketball history." Duke also mentioned that the St. Joseph Fighting Irishmen were playing the Huntington Pony Express at Arena Gardens on Thursday.[2]

The logo for "In the Service," included in the first column entry below is, except for size, an exact copy of the one at the top of each column in the *Huntington Herald-Dispatch*. The *Huntington Herald-Advertiser* column, "With the Colors," had a different logo. After this date I will simply preface each column with "In the Service" or "With the Colors."

Private George I. Roberts, husband of Mrs. Beulah Roberts, 1428 Charleston Avenue, and son of Mrs. Clara Roberts, 404 Thirty-first Street, has been transferred from Camp Atterbury, Ind. to Fort McClellan, Ala. for infantry training. He is a Central High School graduate and was employed by the Owens-Illinois Glass Co. as a machinist prior to entering the Army.

Miss Frances Woodyard, daughter of Mr. and Mrs. F. C. Rice, 711 Sixth Avenue, has enrolled in the Cadet Nurse Corps. Miss Woodyard is studying nursing in a Pittsburg hospital. The Cadet Nurse Corps is a source of nurses for the armed forces.

Private First Class William W. Webb, son of Mrs. Lilyan Webb of Huntington, has received the Bronze Star Medal "for heroic achievement" in action last June in New Guinea. Serving with a medical detachment as company aid man, he was constantly exposing himself to enemy fire...

Claude Wilmer Stewart of Huntington, [a] Central High School and West Virginia University graduate, has been promoted to major in the Army Air Forces, the War Department announced yesterday.

The War Department also reported Technician Fifth Grade Meredith Lilly of Milton, serving overseas with a field artillery unit, has been awarded the Bronze Star Medal.

Captain Naseeb S. Tweel, son of Mr. and Mrs. Sid G. Tweel, 1016 Ninth Avenue, is awaiting reassignment at an AAF redistribution station at Richmond, Va. He received the Distinguished Flying Cross and Air Medal with three Oak Leaf Clusters while serving 30 months in the European theatre as an aerial navigator.

Staff Sergeant Dwain C. Gillespie, 1827 Fourth Avenue, is undergoing processing at a redistribution center at Asheville, N.C. after serving for 35 months overseas with the 150th Infantry. His wife is with him.

Corporal Clyde A. Murray, son of Mr. and Mrs. Ira Murray of Kenova, who suffered fractured arms while in action in France, is recovering in an English hospital.

Ensign and Mrs. Lewis M. Wilcox are visiting his mother, Mrs. Ferol Wilcox, 2122 Tenth Avenue after completing a communications course at Harvard University. Brothers in the service are Private James E. Wilcox, Boca Raton Field, Fla., and Gunner's Mate Robert Wilcox, on duty in the Pacific.

Seaman First Class William O. Curley, son of Mr. and Mrs. Jack Curley, 630 ½ Eighth Avenue, has returned to the Armed Guard Center at New Orleans, La. after four months aboard a merchant ship.

WAC Private Gladys W. Ketter, 1112 Fifth Avenue, has been transferred from Des Moines, Ia. to Wright Field, O.

Jack W. Spalding, son of Mr. and Mrs. E. R. Spaulding, 210 Marcum Terrace, has been promoted to corporal at his Marine Corps station in the Pacific. He has served overseas for 11 months.

On leave, on furlough, are Marine Private First Class John T. Curnutte Jr., husband of Mrs. Mary Curnutte and son of Mr. and Mrs. John T. Curnutte, 312 Division Street; Seaman Second Class Verlin E. Wells, husband of Mrs. Lorraine Wells of Barboursville Route 2; Army Private John Flowers, son of Mr. and Mrs. George D. Flowers, 2485 Third Avenue, and Motor Machinist's Mate First Class Thomas J. Kea, son of Mrs. Wilbern Kea Sr., 931 Eighth Avenue.

Army Sergeant C. L. Cummins returned to San Francisco last Sunday after spending a 30-day furlough with his parents, Mr. and Mrs. C. S. Cummins, 518 Seventh Avenue. Sergeant Cummins recently returned after three years' service in the South Pacific.

Glenna: [Tuesday] *January 2nd 1945 – I cooked for the school. Only had 43 that day. We served spinach, pinto beans, onions, bread and butter, and prunes. That night I ironed.*

Mother must have staggered under the load of managing house and farm, yet incredibly, she took on this part-time job preparing lunch for Salt Rock school children in the old school building across the road from Salt Rock Methodist Church. That location was used because our new school building on Madison

Creek Road, built in 1939, had a cafeteria still under construction. Children were bussed on cold or wet days and walked in good weather. The old wooden structure was empty except for a basement kitchen equipped for feeding classes. Many food items, blocks of cheese, big jars of peanut butter, and margarine with food coloring were government issue. She had discretion to include leftovers in the next day's lunch. Today's laws covering food service would likely force a quick shutdown of such an operation.

I'd been in first grade in 1939 in the old school until Christmas vacation, when the entire school population moved to Madison Creek Road. Miss Velma Matthews was my teacher and T. E. Walker was the principal. Sometime after 1945 the building was torn down and the remnant basement walls were soon vine-covered. A house sits on the site now.

In the war world, U.S. naval vessels going to Luzon came under attack by kamikaze pilots.[3] American B-29 bombers, based near Calcutta, attacked a railroad bridge and other targets in an area near Bangkok, Thailand.

Glenna: [Wednesday] *January 3rd – I cooked for school. Had peanut butter sandwiches, boiled potato, onions, bread and butter, and green beans. Club meeting that night here.*

That meeting was probably a quilting club event; she traded quilting patterns with other women. Nearly thirty quilts are scattered among my family members, many of those made by my paternal grandmother, Hattie Pratt.

Glenna: [Thursday] *January 4th – Cooked for the school. Served Pinto beans, boiled ham, raw apple, onion, bread and butter.*

The U.S. Navy was making concentrated air attacks on Formosa.

Glenna: [Friday] *January 5th – Cooked for the school. Served meat loaf, cabbage salad, boiled potato, bread and butter, and apple. Maggie Childers died in the early morning. Pretty day. Sunny.*

The lunches were nutritious, somewhat balanced, and not unlike fare children had at home. Some recipes were work-intensive. Preparation for a pot of pinto beans meant "looking" them, to remove small stones, overnight soaking, and then boiling for several hours.

"IN THE SERVICE":

Machinist's Mate First Class Theodore R. Spaulding and Machinist's Mate Second Class Melvin O. Plymale of Huntington were among the first Seabees to land in the Philippines shortly after General Douglas MacArthur's forces invaded Leyte in October. Both men have been with the Naval Construction Battalion for 18 months and served for 10 months in New Guinea.

Private First Class Charles Wolford, husband of Mrs. Freedith Wolford, 302 Bridge Street, has arrived safely at a station in the South Pacific. He is a motor mechanic with a Marine division.

Sergeant Russell D. Moore, son of Osley D. Moore, 5787 Ohio River Road, is an administrative specialist in the quartermaster section of an Air Transport Command base in France.

Private Jack L. Ferguson of Huntington and Private Walter Parsons of Big Creek, W. Va. are serving with an engineer regiment of the Seventh Army in the Southern Saar region of the European theatre.

Forrest D. Jarrell, whose wife resides at 64 West Sixth Avenue, has been promoted to corporal with the Army Military Railway Service in India. He helps operate the Bengal & Assam Railway.

Private Elmon Bledsoe of Barboursville Route 1 and Private First Class Steve F. Galsti of

Rossmore are with engineer troops attached to the Sixth Army Group in the European treater.

Private Anna Marie Bolling [502 Ninth Avenue] has been transferred from Fort Des Moines, Iowa, to a WAC detachment at Esler Field, La.

Sergeant Harold L. Ferguson of Fort Gay Route 1 is a radio operator with the 34th Cavalry Reconnaissance Troops attached to the Fifth Army in Italy.

Private Edward C. Mayo, son of Mrs. Mary Mayo, 1927 Jefferson Avenue, an MP with the 34th (Red Bull) Division of the Fifth Army in Italy, has been promoted to corporal.

Sergeant Charles A. Osborne, 3222 Chase Street, is serving in Italy with a 15th Army Air Force Flying Fortress group which was served turkey and trimmings on Christmas. The same outfit dined on goat stew Christmas Day, 1942, in Algeria.

Ensign Richard S. Bowers, who has been on sea duty with the Maritime Service, is spending a leave with his wife, Mrs. Blanche S. Bowers, [elsewhere listed as his mother] 334 Thirty-first Street.

Major Harry C. Brindle, husband of Mrs. Sara Gibson Brindle, 1570 Washington Boulevard, led the 88th Cavalry Reconnaissance Squadron, the first unit of the Sixth Armored Division to enter German territory in Lieutenant General Patton's Third Army drive. He is a Marshall College graduate and former employee of the International Nickel Company.

Lieutenant Charles E. Hoscar, who served 22 months in Puerto Rico, is spending a leave with his grandparents, Mr. and Mrs. Alpheus Kirkland of Third Avenue.

Radioman First Class James E. Heenan, son of Mrs. D. V. Stuff of Ironton, formerly of Huntington, is on leave here after 27 months of duty in the Pacific aboard a sub-chaser. He is visiting an aunt, Mrs. E. L. Zilhman, 340 West Sixth Avenue.

Seaman Anne E. Colebaugh, daughter of Mrs. Teresa Arpp, 316 Twenty-fifth Street, has been promoted to petty officer third class at her WAVES station in Memphis, Tenn. She has qualified as a parachute packer.

Marine Corporal James A. Moore, son of Mr. and Mrs. W. C. Moore of Kenova, has been granted a 30-day leave after 26 months in the South Pacific.

Sergeant Harrison L. Bailey, who had been listed as missing in action since September 11, is a prisoner-of-war in Germany, according to word received by an aunt, Mrs. Oliver Burchette, 2935 Third Avenue.

Corporal Mildred Hager, daughter of Mrs. Adeline Hager, 1831 Madison Avenue, is a cook with the First Troop Carrier Command at George Field, Ill.

Glenna: [Saturday] *January 6th – Cleaned the house, baked a cake, Cloudy.*

News stories sometimes brought the war closer. One such story reports that 150 German prisoners were put to work in the mess hall at Fletcher Hospital in Cambridge, Ohio.[4]

In the Pacific, American B-29s bombed Tokyo again.[5] Carrying the war to Japan's homeland was a great boost to American morale. Nevertheless, it was only a prelude to what was coming.

"IN THE SERVICE":

Staff Sergeant Fred E. Griffith, husband of Mrs. Almita Mae Griffith 226 ½ Fourth Avenue, was promoted to second Lieutenant December 10 in Germany, his wife has been informed. A veteran of six years' service in the Army, Lieutenant Griffith has been in Germany four months with an infantry unit. He is the son on Mrs. Goldie O'Meara of Milton.

Seaman Clifford Jarrell, serving in the Navy while on leave from the Huntington police department, has returned to Boston after visiting his wife, Mrs. Nora Mae Jarrell, and three children at their home, 2448 First Avenue. A member of the police department since January, 1941, Seaman Jarrell was on sea duty for two months in the Atlantic aboard a destroyer escort.

Sergeant George W. Hirby, 1917 Ninth Avenue, is a member of a military police platoon attached to the 82ⁿᵈ Airborne Division in the European theatre...

Huntington airmen who arrived in Italy for duty with the 15ᵗʰ Air Force are Second Lieutenant James L. Johnson, 317 Thirteenth Street, a B-29 pilot; Second Lieutenant Erskine H. Hatfield, 410 Bridge Street, a bombardier, and Corporal Cecil Frost, 1928 Twelfth Avenue, serving in the refueling section of his bomber group.

Technician Fifth Grade Thomas R. Watson of Culloden is serving with a signal company attached to the 15ᵗʰ Air Force...

Private First Class Harvey H. Wintz, son of James Wintz of Huntington Route 2, has been promoted to corporal with the 88ᵗʰ Division with the Fifth Army in Italy. He is a mechanic.

Second Lieutenant Bernice M. Plymale, daughter of Mrs. Shirley Plymale, 3022 Hughes Street, is an Army nurse assigned to a station in Italy. A former member of the nursing staff at the Veterans Hospital here, she was commissioned in November 1942, at Fort Knox, Ky. and served in North Africa prior to her present assignment.

Private First Class Stephen Gumber, 217 Buffington Street, was one of 17 American infantrymen who escaped a German trap in France. After six days in a cellar in a French home, a 45ᵗʰ Division attack finally liberated the men.

Staff Sergeant Edward V. Lee, son of Mr. and Mrs. Leonard Lee, 3010 Auburn Road, was nose gunner of a Liberator bomber operating in the Central Pacific which recently helped sink three Japanese freighter-transports in the Haha Jima area. He is a Vinson High School

graduate and has been in the Central Pacific since last June.

Private Floyd R. Blankenship of Hinch, Mingo County, has been awarded the Bronze Star for gallantry in action, the War Department announced last night.

Corporal Clyde A. Murray, son of Mrs. Ira Murray of Kenova, who was wounded in the battle of Brest, France, has been returned to this country and is a patient at Finney General Hospital, Thomasville, Ga.

Storekeeper Third Class Oliver F. Johnson, assigned to a Seabee station at Jolliet, Ill., is spending a leave with his wife at 140 Wilson Court.

First Lieutenant Paul E. Eschbacher, son of Mr. and Mrs. Otto Eschbacher of Wayne, who was wounded slightly while serving with the First Army in France, recently was visited by his wife, First Lieutenant Marguerite Eschbacher, an Army nurse in southern France. When his wife learned that he was hospitalized in Paris, she obtained a four-day pass to visit him. It was the first time they had seen each other for 9 months.

Glenna: *January 7ᵗʰ Sunday – Went to Sunday School at 10: o'clock. Went to Mrs. Childers' funeral at 2 o'clock. Awful muddy and cloudy.*

Maggie Childers was buried in the Gill Cemetery across the river from the school.

"WITH THE COLORS":

Private Ralph W. Lewis, husband of Mrs. Elsie Lewis of Overlook Drive, is stationed in Camp Blanding, Fla. for his basic training, having been transferred from Camp Atterbury, Ind...

Private Gloria Gable, WAC, who spent the holidays with her parents, Mr. and Mrs. Paul Gable of 226 West Fifth Avenue, has returned to her station at Washington, D.C.

A son and a daughter of Mrs. Bernice Rohrbaugh, 2105 Jefferson Avenue, have recently earned petty officers' ratings in the naval service. Henry T. Rohrbaugh, serving on an LST in the Pacific, has been promoted to electrician's mate third class, and his sister, Yeoman Third Class Helen Rohrbaugh, received her rating in the WAVES at her station at San Diego, Calif. ...

Lieutenant John M. Baysden, USN, has returned to his base after spending a five-day leave with his mother, Mrs. Addie H. Baysden, and sister, Miss June Baysden, 1805 Twelfth Avenue.

Fireman First Class William O. Charles, son of Mrs. Addie Charles, 1632 Madison Avenue, has been promoted to petty officer third class at an advanced naval base in the Pacific. He is a crew member of an LCT (landing craft, tanks). His wife and two children live with his mother.

L. E. Wise, petty officer third class, has returned to his base after spending a leave with his wife, Mrs. Rita Wise, 2724 Fifth Avenue. While on furlough he also visited his parents, Mr. and Mrs. Homer Wise, 409 Fifteenth Street.

Private Raymond McKenzie, son of Mrs. Hester A. McKenzie of Barboursville, a member of the 'Wildcat' Infantry Division, has been awarded the Combat Infantryman Badge for exemplary conduct and skill against the enemy. The "Wildcat" Division recently invaded the Southern Islands of the Japanese-held Palau group.

Second Lieutenant Paul Hite is Link training officer at Avon Park Army Air Field, Fla., a final phase training base for Flying Fortress combat crews. He is the son of Mr. and Mrs. Elza Hite, 1014 Jefferson Avenue. His wife, Mrs. Blanche O'Brien Hite, makes her home in Sebring, Fla.

Corporal and Mrs. William K. Williams have returned to Oklahoma City, Okla. after spending 15 days with Corporal Williams' parents, Mr. and Mrs. Russell Williams of Third Avenue...

Private Earl M. Traylor, stationed at Camp Sibert, Ala., spent Christmas with his wife and daughter of Russell, Ky. on a 15-day furlough. Private Traylor is the son of Mr. and Mrs. J. W. Traylor, 433 East Road.

Private Thomas B. Frye, a member of the base unit, Army Air Field, Pratt, Kan., is currently spending a furlough at his home, 1887 Rear Doulton Avenue.

Lieutenant Gladyce M. Venable, Army Nurse Corps, is stationed with a field hospital unit somewhere in Holland. Lieutenant Venable was graduated from the McMillan Hospital in Charleston. She is the sister of Mrs. Charles A. Price, 1558 Washington Boulevard, and Mrs. Claude Jackson Park, 2571 Collis Avenue.

Private John W. Grubb, who is stationed at Fort Benning, Ga., has made his fifth jump and is now qualified as a parachutist. He is spending a 10-day furlough with his wife, Mrs. Dorothy Grubb, and son, Ronnie Lee, of 36 West Fourth Avenue.

Sergeant Mike Buncick, former chief inspector for the Zenith Optical Co. here, has been granted an honorable discharge from the Army and will return to Huntington to resume his association with Zenith...

Glenna: [Monday] January 8th – Washed. Cleaned house. Cloudy.

"IN THE SERVICE":

First Lieutenant Donald V. Peters, son of Mr. and Mrs. Sam Peters of Huntington, who is credited with destroying five enemy planes while flying a P-47 fighter plane in the European area for 12 months, is now stationed at Mitchel Field, N.Y. He flew 89 missions and has been awarded the Distinguished Flying Cross with two Oak Leaf Clusters, the Air Medal with three Oak Leaf Clusters and the European ribbon with three battle stars. A brother, Yeoman First Class Francis W. Peters, is serving with the Navy in the South Pacific.

Private Henry T. Lewis of Huntington has been assigned to an Army medical clearing company in the Netherlands East Indies. He trained at Camp Stewart, Ga. and went overseas last May.

Forrest B. Langdon, son of Mr. and Mrs. Forrest Langdon, 2774 Latulle Avenue, has been promoted to staff sergeant at the Army Ground and Service Forces Redistribution Station at Camp Butner, N.C.

Private Lee M. Lyons, 1318 Jefferson Avenue, has received the Army Good Conduct Medal with the American Infantry Division in the Southwest Pacific. A veteran of 15 months overseas, he is a telephone and teletype operator. Private Lyons is entitled to wear a battle star on his Asiatic-Pacific theatre ribbon for combat service at Bougainville.

Glenna: [Tuesday] *January 9th – Ironed, mended. Cloudy.*

Huntington: "Commencement exercises for 23 Marshall College students will be held January 27 while exercises for 159 graduates of Central, East, and Douglass High Schools will be held next week. Senor class sermons for all three high schools will be delivered Sunday." Mrs. Veta Smith, college secretary, proclaimed it the smallest mid-year graduation class in Marshall history.[6]

In the Pacific, Americans landed on Luzon, the central island of the Philippines. Kamikaze attacks on Navy ships increased.[7]

"IN THE SERVICE":

Lieutenant Richard H. Cartwright, son of Mr. and Mrs. R. H. Cartwright, 1333 Fourteenth Street, flew one of three P-38 fighter planes that supplied air cover in the rescue of 11 Army Air Forces men from a Japanese-held island in the Philippines. Shot down in raids on Japanese position in the Philippines, the rescued AAF crewmen represented three B-24 bomber crews and a fighter pilot. They were flown out in a Navy Catalina plane. Lieutenant Cartwright has been serving in the Pacific for 11 months.

Corporal Lowell E. Legge, son of Mr. and Mrs. E. J. Legge of Huntington Route 2 has been graduated from the AAF Flexible Gunnery School at Laredo, Tex. and has won his aerial gunner's wings...

Sergeant Lyle Fraley, husband of Mrs. Ruth Fraley and son of Mr. and Mrs. C. B. Fraley of Lynn Route 1, helps prepare meals for 2,000 men at an Eighth Air Force station in England... A brother, Private James L. Fraley, is serving in the South Pacific.

Miss Marguerite Asher, a graduate of Marshall College, has arrived in Hawaii to serve the armed forces as an American Red Cross recreation worker... Miss Asher was principal of the Sunnyside School in Mason County and attended Point Pleasant schools before her graduation from Marshall.

Private First Class James L. Wallace. son of Mr. and Mrs. Frank Wallace of Sixteenth Street Road, has been transferred from Baltimore to the 548th Signal Base Company at Camp Monmouth, N.J...

Fred A. Hurt, American Red Cross field director and 1935 Marshall College graduate, has arrived in France. Before his assignment overseas, Mr. Hurt served with the Red Cross at Camp Howze, Tex. and Camp Claiborne, La. His wife resides in Beckley.

Private Fuller S. Richardson, son of Mr. and Mrs. Grover C. Richardson of Six, W.Va., who was wounded in France, recently spent a leave with his parents. Now in Lawson General Hospital in Atlanta, Ga., he had served as a scout in an infantry rifle squad after going overseas last June... Brothers in service are Staff Sergeant Woodrow Richardson and Technical Sergeant Wiley M. Richardson, who served 35 months in Panama.

Rush E. Elkins, son of Mrs. Winnie Elkins of Man, W.Va., a navigator on a B-24 bomber based in Italy, has been promoted to first lieutenant. He arrived overseas last July and has participated in 20 combat missions.

Police Inspector Don Maynard was notified yesterday by Army officials that a brother, Corporal Frank Maynard, is seriously ill in a hospital in England. Husband of Mrs. Ruth Maynard of Huntington, Corporal Maynard has served for nine months overseas, including tours of duty in France, Belgium and Germany.

Second Lieutenant Roy Wallace, husband of Mrs. Lilly Wallace, 2816 Cottage Street, [and son of Mrs. Bertha Wallace, 2525 Artisan Avenue] has been awarded the Air Medal for meritorious achievement as a Flying Fortress pilot with the 15th AAF in Italy.

Private First Class Woo Yon Chee, 523 Ninth Street, has arrived at the Ashville, N.C. Army redistribution station for reassignment after 20 months in the Northwest Service Command.

Staff Sergeant George W. Kaneff, son of Mr. and Mrs. G. N. Kaneff, 1856 Marshall Avenue, has received a second Air Medal for achievement as a nose gunner aboard a Liberator bomber in the European theatre. He has been overseas for 10 months.

Captain Roger W. Bussell, husband of Mrs. Jeanne E. Bussell, 1311 Huntington Avenue, has received the second Oak Leaf Cluster to the Air Medal for meritorious achievement aboard a Flying Fortress based in England. He is the son of Mrs. Richard J. Bussell, 1211 Eighth Street.

Sergeant Devore Murdock Jr., son of Mr. and Mrs. Devore Murdock of Chesapeake, recently participated in his first mission when his Flying Fortress took part in a large-scale assault on Nazi marshalling yards at Darmstadt, Germany. He is a gunner.

Sergeant James M. Bailey Jr., husband of Mrs. Mary Maxine Bailey of Ceredo, has been decorated with his third Oak Leaf Cluster to the Air Medal for a number of missions in the European theatre. He is a gunner on a Flying Fortress.

Technical Sergeant Henry C. Reid, son of Mrs. Ida Reid, 573 Norway Avenue, has received the Expert Infantryman Badge in the Central Pacific theatre.

Joseph M. Krantz Jr., son of J. M. Krantz of Raceland. Ky., has been promoted to corporal at Walla Walla Field, Wash., where he is assigned to a combat crew as a gunner.

Corporal Jules H. LeBlanc, nephew of Otto E. LeBlanc of Huntington, has been awarded the Good Conduct Medal at an Engineer base depot in France.

Private Clinton F. McCallister, son of Mr. and Mrs. Cecil Delmer McCallister of Yawkey, Rout 3, has been transferred from Camp Atterbury, Ind. to Camp Robinson, Ark.

Private First Class Dewey Hughes of Huntington, wounded in action October 28 in Holland and now a patient in a hospital in England, has been awarded the Purple Heart. His mother is Mrs. Elsie Hughes of Vancouver, Wash., formerly of Huntington. Two brothers in service are Corporal Hurley Hughes and Private Charles F. Hughes of Huntington.

Staff Sergeant Frank R. Marsh, 2744 Orchard Avenue, a member of the Eighth Army Air Force in the European theatre, has received the Distinguished Flying Cross...

Sergeant Earl B. Reynolds, son of Mr. and Mrs. Arvel C. Reynolds of West Hamlin, and who served for six months in the Southwest Pacific theatre, has received the Bronze Star for heroic achievement and the Combat Infantryman's Badge.

First Sergeant William H. Wheatley, 2224 Eleventh Avenue, is serving with a First Tactical Air Force unit based in France. He has been awarded the European theatre ribbon with two battle stars.

Radioman Claude Jackson Park Jr., who was wounded over Guam last July while serving aboard a Navy Avenger plane, is spending a 30-day convalescent leave with his parents in Chesapeake.

Private First Class Wade Duncan Jr. of Thorpe, W.Va., is serving with an Army railway battalion in France.

Petty Officer Second Class Haven Elwood Fetty has returned to his naval station at Norfolk, Va. after visiting his wife at their Oakland Avenue home. He has been in service for 16 months.

Navy Ensign T. J. F. Caldwell has returned to his base in New York City after spending a leave with his mother, Mrs. Dabney Caldwell of Washington Boulevard.

Corporal Charles H. Hardy has arrived in North Africa with an Army Air Forces unit, his parents, Mr. and Mrs. Tilghman Hardy, 319 Adams Avenue, have been advised.

Glenna: [Wednesday] *January 10th – Visited school. Snowing.*

Mother came often to the school, which kept me on my toes. She knew most of the teachers; after graduating from Hamlin High School, she had taught for seven years in one-and two-room schools in Cabell County. A college degree was not required then. She had taken an intensive summer course of study administered by the State and passed a rigorous written test to acquire a third-degree teaching certificate. The 1932–1933 school year was her last year of teaching, broken up by the death of my father in December, and my birth in March. I have all the class registers for "Miss Glenna."

An editorial in the *Huntington Herald-Dispatch* commented elegantly on the return of General MacArthur's troops to Luzon: "... For the Japs,* the battle of Luzon must be—and will be—a show down battle. They will fight as they have fought in every previous engagement, fanatically and to the death and the Americans will out-fight them, as they have in every previous test, giving no quarter and recording the victory only when the enemy forces have been annihilated."[8]

(*Reporters of the time often used words and terms that are now considered racial slurs. To put it in perspective, it was common usage then for feared and hated enemies. I have not edited out the usage in quotes from newspaper articles and columns.)

"IN THE SERVICE":

Staff Sergeant John Dolin of Huntington was one of a group of convalescent soldiers in England who recently visited the Empire Theatre in Nottingham in Nottingham, England...

Private First Class Raymond H. Adkins, son of Mr. and Mrs. Lee Adkins, 2144 Harvey Road recently was wounded seriously in action in the European theatre. A veteran of two years' service overseas. He is now a patient in a hospital at Staten Island, N.Y.

Technician Fifth Grade Frederick E. Wallace, former Huntington Publishing Co, employee, has been cited for "meritorious and outstanding performance of duty as fire direction center computer during the period of September 1 to 6, 1944, in military operations against the enemy in Brittany, France." A sister, Mrs. L. E. Gregory of Wheeling, was informed of the citation given her brother.

WAC Private Frances Goodall of Huntington was instrumental in securing a service club for Lemoore Army Air Field, Calif. A letter she wrote to the commanding officer of the field was approved and steps were taken to convert a large building into a recreation center.

Private First Cass Okey J. Curnell, son of George O. Curnell, 321 West Twelfth Street, has been overseas 14 months and is serving with the 36ᵗʰ Division in Eastern France.

Staff Sergeant William A. Mannix, who was wounded in action October 18 in Holland, has been awarded the Purple Heart, his parents, Mr. and Mrs. P. H. Mannix, 530 Tenth Street, has been advised. A brother, Raymond Mannix, is also serving in the European Theatre.

Sergeant Lawrence E. Copen of Huntington, son of Mrs. Nannie Copen of Switzer, W.Va., has been transferred to AAF Overseas Replacement Depot at Camp Kohler, Calif., where he is assigned to the Ordnance Section.

Glenna: [Thursday] January 11ᵗʰ – Made myself a blouse out of a feed sack. Cloudy.

Commercial livestock feed consisted of chopped grain or other special mixes. The bags of feed, 100 pounds in weight, came in strong cloth sacks imprinted with colored patterns. The sacks were valued for shirts, women's work clothes, and even dresses. Mother saved them in stacks, arranged by pattern. Her old Singer sewing machine turned out many durable creations.

"IN THE SERVICE":

Private First Class Donald (Jack) Adkins, 2536 Sixteenth Street Road, who is a prisoner-of-war, has notified his family that he "is not being mistreated." A son of Mrs. Addie Shy of Pine Bluff, Ark., formerly of Huntington, he stressed in his message that "cigarettes are most important here."

Technician Fifth Grade William L. Bias, who served for 35 months in the Southwest Pacific with the Army Air Forces, is spending a 22-day furlough with his wife, Mrs. Vivian Bias, 142 Maupin Road, and parents, Mr. and Mrs.

W. H. Bias, 1358 Hall Street. Upon his arrival here, he saw for the first time his son, William Everett. A brother in service is Robert Bias, on leave from Navy Pier, Chicago.

Radioman Third Class James W. Dempsey is spending a 30-day leave with his mother, Mrs. Edna Dempsey, 417 ½ Third Avenue, after a year's service in the Pacific aboard a battleship.

William J. Crum, son of Mr. and Mrs. William W. Crum, 2946 Fifth Avenue, has received his gunner's wings and corporal's rating after completing a flexible gunnery course at Yuma Field, Ariz. He is a graduate of Central High School.

Corporal William E. Williams, son of Mrs. E. E. Williams, 1021 Second Street, won paratrooper wings and boots upon completing jump training at the Parachute School at Fort Benning, Ga.

Private First Class Willard Colbert, husband of Mrs. Selma Colbert, 412 Fourth Avenue, has arrived at the Ashville, N.C. Redistribution Station after serving for 34 ½ months in the Southwest Pacific with a Medical Corps unit. He is the son of Mrs. Bertie Colbert of Fourth Avenue.

First Lieutenant Homer P. Davis, son of Mr. and Mrs. G. D. Davis, 845 Jackson Avenue, is attending an officer communications school at Chanute Field, Ill. The former Marshall College student was commissioned and received his pilot's wings in February, 1943, and has served at San Marcos and Houston, Tex.

Corporal William J. Chapman, husband of Mrs. Alice Chapman, 3540 Fourth Avenue, has received aerial gunner's wings at Yuma Field, Ariz. He is the son of Mr. and Mrs. Burl A. Chapman, 219 Fourth Avenue.

Marine Corporal Leo Ferguson, son of Mr. and Mrs. Charles Ferguson, 3506 Crane Avenue, was one of a number of cruiser crewmen who told an Associated Press correspondent about what happens when enemy dive bombers are attacking. "You feel kind of shaky when they're coming down but when you start firing you're too busy to be scared," was Corporal Ferguson's comment.

Painter First Class E. J. Cridlin has arrived home after a tour of duty with the Navy in the European theatre, and a son, Cadet E. J. Cridlin, Jr. of the Merchant Marine, is also spending a leave here after serving in the Southwest Pacific. The former is a son of T. J. Cridlin, 317 West Nineteenth Street, a master painter employed by the Ohio Valley Bus Co.

Lieutenant Tord V. Malmquist, husband of Mrs. Betty Klein Malmquist, 923 Eleventh Street, has received the Bronze Star for "meritorious service" last summer in Italy...

Private James G. Mellert, husband of Mrs. Libbie Mellert, 530 ½ West Ninth Street, is recovering in an English hospital from wounds received in action in France. A brother, Warren S. Mellert, is serving aboard an LCT in the Pacific. They are the sons of Mrs. Jessie Mellert, 525 West Twenty-sixth Street.

Yeoman Second Class Stella M. Keerans, daughter of Mr. and Mrs. J. B. Keerans, 1743 Nineteenth Street, recently was promoted to that rank at the Naval Training Center, Bainbridge, Md. She has been in the WAVES since August, 1943.

First Lieutenant James Taylor, who served in the European theatre and is now assigned to Selma Field, La., is spending a leave at his home, 2577 First Avenue.

Second Lieutenant George E. Gold, son of Mr. and Mrs. John W. Gold, 136 Norway Avenue, has been assigned as a B-24 co-pilot to the 15th Air Force in Italy.

Robert McCoy is spending a furlough with his father, R. W. McCoy of Huntington Route 4.

State Trooper J. Russell Hogg, who has been with the Barboursville detachment of state police three years prior to entering the Navy over a year ago, has received an honorable discharge and is back on duty at the Barboursville post. He served at Yorktown, Va., and along the East Coast aboard a minesweeper.

On leave or furlough are Sergeant Donald B. Nixon, husband of Mrs. Ida Mae Nixon of Huntington; Sergeant Everett R. Smith, husband of Mrs. Juanita Freda Smith, 1848 ½ Eleventh Avenue; Corporal William E. Copley, son of Mrs. W. C. Murray of Huntington; Staff Sergeant David Poulton, paratrooper son of Mrs. C. A. Poulton, 2014 Fourth Avenue; Staff Sergeant James E. Porter, 309 Twentieth Street.

Glenna: [Friday] *January 12th – Cleaned house good. Washed my head. Cloudy and raining.*

Washing, whether of head, body, or clothing, required water. Without indoor plumbing, my job was to keep filled the six buckets on a back-porch shelf. The water came from a thirty-foot-deep rock-lined well across the road on the Irving Lucas family property, where there had once been a house. The water was cold, clean, and plentiful. At some point the Lucas family on Madison Creek Road and my grandparents, Lucian and Jennie Adkins, probably came to an agreement that our family could use the water if we maintained the well. The Harbour family down in the village near the bridge also used the water. Eddie, a son, and my lifelong friend, had a hand-drawn cart with a wooden barrel attached for carrying their water. (His mother, Essie, was a daughter of Irving Lucas.)

"IN THE SERVICE":

(Microfilm for this date was difficult to read, especially the numerals, so copying these entries may have produced mistakes.)

Private First Class Maurice J. Flynn, son of Mrs. Maurice S. Flynn, 539 Eleventh Avenue, and the late Mr. Flynn, was wounded in action recently in Germany and has been awarded an Oak Leaf Cluster to the Purple Heart Medal.

Twice wounded in action, he is now in a hospital in Europe.

Private First Class Leotis R. Meadows, son of Mr. and Mrs. William R. Meadows, 633 Allen Avenue, Barboursville, has received aerial gunner's wings after completing an intensive flexible gunnery course at Harlingen, Tex., Army Air Field.

Aviation Cadet Chester N. Fannin Jr., son of Mr. and Mrs. Chester N. Fannin of Barboursville, has arrived at Perrin Field, Tex. for additional training.

Lieutenant Lowell O. Rice, husband of Mrs. Alma E. Rice, 2104 Seventh Avenue, who was wounded in action in the European theatre while leading an infantry platoon, has arrived at Miami Beach, Fla. for reassignment. He served for 19 months overseas.

Technical Sergeant Ernest D. Wright, husband of Mrs. Hilary Ann Wright, 329 Fourth Avenue, is in Asheville, N.C. for a new assignment after serving for 23 months in the Latin-America area. He wears the American Defense, Good Conduct and American theatre ribbons.

Major Elmer C. Newman, husband of Mrs. Josephine Newman, 122 West Tenth Street, has been chosen to attend an officer refresher course at the Infantry School, Fort Benning, Ga., after serving in Panama since January, 1941. He is the son of Mrs. Sylvia Hawes of Huntington.

Private Carl C. Brunty, husband of Mrs. Clarice Brunty, 1036 Washington Avenue, has returned from the European theatre and is a convalescent patient at McCloskey General Hospital, Temple, Tex.

Private Thomas E. Bryan, husband of Mrs. Ethel Bryan of Huntington, is a patient in Welch Convalescent Hospital at Daytona Beach, Fla. after a six-month tour of duty overseas...

Private First Class Clyde Beveridge , 919 Twelfth Street, is with a Signal Corps unit in Belgium which recently set up a system of communications in record time at one of the most vital of Allied ports on the European continent.

Private Noah F. Keller of Sixteenth Street is at the Asheville Redistribution Station after 23 months of foreign service in North Africa, Sicily, Italy and France. He received the Purple Heart for wounds received in action.

Corporal H. L. Deppner, son of Mr. and Mrs. Henry L. Deppner, 1688 Underwood Avenue, has received his aerial gunner's wings at Yuma Field, Ariz.

Private Adam Allen has arrived in France with an infantry unit, according to a message received by his wife, Mrs. Mary Allen, 519 Twentieth Street.

Photographer's Mate Third Class Lowell E. McComas has reported to the camera repair school at Pensacola, Fla. after spending a brief leave with his wife, Mrs. Maude McComas, [and] daughter, 604 Third Street, Guyandotte.

Baker Third Class Donald Adkins, who served for 15 months in South America, and his wife and two sisters are visiting relatives here.

Corporal Fred J. Butler Jr., brother of Mrs. Mack Thompson, 428 ½ Nineteenth Street, recently was promoted to that rank at his Coast Artillery station in Panama.

Sergeant James H. Lovins, son of Mr. and Mrs. B. B. Lovins, 337 Locust Avenue, recently attained that rank at Miami Beach, Fla. He served for two years with an Army Air Forces ground crew in North Africa.

Private First Class Ivan J. Smith, son of Mrs. Rebecca E. Burns of Scott Depot, has received the Purple Heart for wounds received in action in Germany. A mortar gunner, he has been awarded the Combat Infantryman Badge for exemplary conduct and skill in action.

Howard C. Whitekettle Jr., 1306 Washington Boulevard, is receiving boot training at Great Lakes, Illinois.

Frank Weider of the Army Air Forces is spending a 15-day furlough with his parents, Dr. and Mrs. Don F. Weider, 2961 Merrill Avenue.

Other service men on leave or furlough are Seaman First Class Curtis E. Lear, son of Mrs. John Lear, 1843 Maple Avenue; Seaman Second Class W. M. Miller, son of Mr. and Mrs. J. P. Miller, 2920 Third Avenue; Seaman Second Class Jacob Rone Jr., son of Mrs. Jacob Rone,

1673 Fourteenth Avenue; Sergeant Herbert Mitchell, son of Mrs. E. C. Andes, 348 Adams Avenue; Yeoman First Class Garland Endicott, husband of Mrs. Grace Endicott of Genoa, W.Va., and Seaman First Class Warren A. Reed, husband of Mrs. Virginia Reed, and son of Mr. and Mrs. J. A. Reed of North Kenova, Ohio.

Glenna: [Saturday] *January 13th – Wrote 2 letters for Mrs. Rousey. Cloudy and raining.*

Mrs. Lou Rousey, an elderly lady, lived in a house beside the post office. Mrs. Rousey's eyesight was poor and Mother often wrote letters for her.

In local sports news, the Marshall College basketball team defeated Murray State College 58 to 54, with Bill Toothman scoring seventeen points. And "In a nip-and-tuck finish the Fighting Irishmen of St. Joseph High School nosed out the Williamson Wolfpack 28-to-25 in a driving finish on the home floor of the men from Mingo." Also, "Coming from behind in the last half, Coach Paul Thompson's Vinson Tigers defeated Wayne 36–30 last night in a Southwestern Conference basketball game played at Wayne."[9]

The war in Europe was much in the news: A major Red Army offensive in East Prussia had begun against a much-weakened German Army.

"IN THE SERVICE":

Lucien Randolph Sammons, son of Mr. and Mrs. F. C. Sammons, 127 Ricketts Place, is attending the Army Coast Artillery School at Fort Monroe, Va. A civil engineer in civilian life, Captain Sammons is a graduate of Virginia Polytechnic Institute. His wife is residing at Fort Rodman, Mass. while he is in school.

Lieutenant E. G. Gibson Jr., Marine Air Group 23, as mess officer at a station in the Pacific was in charge of a Christmas dinner arrangements and menu which included two delicacies probably never before served in that area—fresh corn on the cob and strawberry shortcake. Lieutenant Gibson is the son of Mr. and Mrs. E. G. Gibson, 1015 Euclid Place.

Private First Class Henry K. Warth, son of Common Pleas Judge H. Clay Warth, who was taken prisoner April 9, 1942 in the fall of Bataan in the Philippines, has notified his father that his "health is good" and that he has received a package from his family... Other Huntington men imprisoned by the Japanese in the Philippines are Frank E. Becker, civilian internee, at Los Banos Camp; Seldon W. O'Brien, civilian internee at Santo Tomas, Manilla; Private Clarence E. Simms and Private Farley B. Hall.

Private Roy Thomas Jr., who has recently returned after serving for 18 months overseas as a radio operator mechanic gunner with the Tenth Air Forces, is visiting his mother, Mrs. Roy Thomas, 2009 Tenth Avenue and wife, Mrs. Gladys Thomas, 2222 Fourth Avenue. Private Thomas participated in the invasion of Southern France and the battle of Rome and was awarded the Air Medal after completing 16 missions over occupied territory...

Radioman Claude Jackson Park, son of Mr. and Mrs. C. J. Park of near Proctorville, O., has returned to the U.S. Naval Hospital at San Diego, Calif. after spending a 30-day leave with his parents. A veteran of 15 months' service in the Pacific, he is scheduled to undergo an operation for the removal of shrapnel.

Private Herman A. Preston, husband of Mrs. Dorothy Preston, 1685 ½ Eleventh Avenue, who was injured in the South Pacific when a captured Japanese bomb dump exploded, is a patient at the Army Air Forces Convalescent Hospital, Fort Thomas, Ky. A son of Mr. and Mrs. Arthur Preston of Wayne Route 2, he was hospitalized three months in New Guinea and was a patient at Newton D. Baker Hospital,

Martinsburg, W.Va. prior to his transfer to Fort Thomas.

Seaman First Class Earl E. Nelson, husband of Mrs. F. B. Nelson, 1228 Seventeenth Street, is a patient at a naval hospital in New York after serving for seven and a half months overseas.

Sergeant Edwin M. Turley, son of Mrs. T. W. Turley, 921 Tenth Street, is now stationed at the Santa Rosa Air Field, Calif. He recently was married to the former Miss Betty Woodring of Sterling, Colo.

Corporal Raymond Callicoat, husband of Mrs. Helen M. Callicoat, 805 Marcum Terrace, is a member of an Air Service Command depot in England...

Gunner's Mate Third Class Harlan C. Whaley, son of Mrs. James Nicely of Huntington, is spending a 30-day leave with his mother and brother, T. E. Whaley, and sister, Mrs. Sarah Moore of Spring Valley Drive. He will return to San Francisco January 19.

Technical Sergeant Galen B. Queen has returned to Atlanta, Ga. after spending a furlough with his parents, Mr. and Mrs. W. D. Queen of Gallipolis, O. A brother, Staff Sergeant Clifford E. Queen, is serving in France.

Sergeant Robert P. Van Ness, husband of Mrs. Vancel Van Ness of Huntington, has arrived safely in India...

Lieutenant Fred E. Griffith, 226 ½ Fourth Avenue, was elevated to that rank from staff sergeant recently after he took over a communications platoon in Germany when its commanding officer was killed. In a press announcement released by the 84th Infantry Division, Lieutenant Griffith was lauded for keeping a vital communications system in operation through four days of battle in Germany.

Staff Sergeant Willard Dickerson of Huntington Route 4 has arrived at Asheville, N.C. for reassignment after serving for 35 months in the Caribbean area with an infantry mobile force division.

Corporal Isaac Lerner, son of Mr. and Mrs. Louis Lerner, 404 West Tenth Avenue, has been promoted to sergeant with a raider group on Saipan.

Glenna: [Sunday] *January 14th – Went to Sunday School at Salt Rock M. E. Church. Ezra Woodall is reported missing in action. Charles Ray reported missing in action. Went to church Sunday night. Had a good meeting. Cloudy and raining.*

Ezra Woodall and Charles Ray were later listed as prisoners of war in Germany. After the war, Mother and I visited Ezra and his wife in Salt Rock. He was thin as he recovered from his ordeal.

Frank Pittman, in a *Huntington Herald-Gazette* article reported, "Sam Snead, colorful Hot Springs, Va. Golfer who is leading money winner in the current professional Winter tour, tonight [January 13] said he would quit the circuit at the finish tomorrow of the Phoenix Open. Snead was discharged three months ago from the Navy because of a back injury and the ailment has bothered him the past two days. He shot a 69 yesterday and slipped to a 75, four over par, today."[10]

"WITH THE COLORS":

Seaman First Class Paul Phillips Jr., son of Mrs. Laura Phillips of Fort Gay, W.Va., has returned to his station at Norfolk, Va. after spending a week-end leave with his mother.

Lieutenant Betty Davis, daughter of Mrs. Ruth Davis, 735 Sixth Avenue, is serving at an evacuation hospital in Belgium with the U.S. Army Nurse Corps.

Water Tender Third Class Shannon E. Kitchen is spending a few days leave with his parents, Mr. and Mrs. Wilford Kitchen, 2436 First Avenue. His brother, Private First Class Stanley D. Kitchen, is somewhere in France.

Corporal Cecil Dishman was seriously wounded in action Dec. 23, according to word received from the War Department by his parents, Mr. and Mrs. Cass Dishman of Huntington Route 4.

Private First Class Earl C. Blake, son of Mr. and Mrs. Whirley W. Blake, 2767 Riverview Avenue, has been awarded the Infantry Combat Badge while serving with an armored infantry battalion somewhere in France...

Aviation Student James G. Nichols, son of Carl Nichols, 2686 Fifth Street Road, has just completed his basic flying training at the Merced Army Air Field, Calif. He will now proceed to Army advanced flying school...

Herbert Lee Nutter received his junior grade lieutenancy Dec. 19. He is chief navigator of a flotilla and is serving somewhere in the South Pacific. Before entering the Navy, Lieutenant Nutter was the assistant coach at Barboursville High school. [Mr. Nutter was my assistant football coach at Barboursville in 1948.]

Private Robert M. Gearhart, son of Mr. and Mrs. C. F. Gearhart, 636 Fifteenth Street, is stationed in France with the infantry and is attached to a division of General Patton's Third army.

James I. Black has recently been promoted to staff sergeant. He is an aerial engineer and gunner in a 15th Air force Flying Fortress squadron operating from an advanced base in Italy. Sergeant Black, who is credited with three combat missions, has taken part in aerial attacks on enemy installations in Germany and Austria, His wife, Mrs. Dorcas Y. Black, lives at 3304 Fourth Avenue.

Corporal William Demmler, Barboursville, has played a part in the Rome-Arno campaign since Jan. 22, 1944, according to an announcement from a Twelfth Air Force headquarters that he is now authorized to wear an additional battle star on his European-Middle East-Africa theatre ribbon... His mother, Mrs. Bessie L. Demmler, lives in Barboursville.

Roy C. Dillon, son of Mrs. Ida E. Dillon, 1625 Washington Avenue, has been promoted ...

to technician fifth grade, according to the commanding officer of the 16th Group Army Service Forces Training Center, Camp Claiborne, La.

Private Clifton D. Ellis, who was wounded in France Aug. 29, and for which he was awarded the Purple Heart and the Bronze Star, is convalescing in an Army hospital in England, according to word received by his mother, Mrs. Myrtle M. Ellis. 1257 Twenty-sixth Street.

Major Richard E. East, infantry, recently visited his grandmother, Mrs. M. C. Cochran, 519 Ninth Avenue, en route to receiving orders for reassignment. Major East has just completed a ten-weeks' course for staff officers at the Command and General Staff School, Fort Leavenworth, Kan.

Roy E. Turner, who came overseas with the first American fighter group to arrive in Europe in this war, now has served more than 30 months in the European-African-Middle Eastern theatre... Sergeant Turner is an armorer on a P-38 type airplane in the oldest squadron in his group. He is the son of Mr. and Mrs. C. J. Turner, 344 Oney Avenue.

Private First Class Berton H. Locey left Jan. 7 for Fort Jackson, S.C. after spending a 15-day furlough with his sisters, Mrs. Jerry Johnson and Mrs. Clarence Parker of Huntington, and with his uncle and aunt, Mr. and Mrs. R. S. Johnson, and his brother, Mr. C. A. Locey of Russell, Ky. Another brother, Cobern F. Locey, is a private first class, with the U.S. Army somewhere in England.

Private Buford C. Bryan, son of Mr. and Mrs. Homer P. Bryan, 1847 Maple Avenue, and Private Paul P. Adkins, son of Pharoah Adkins of Prichard Route 2, have been awarded the Bronze Star for heroism in action with a front line medical battalion in France.

Cecil Roach Jr. of 1527 South Third Street, Ironton, O. has been promoted [to] ... captain in the USAAF.

First Lieutenant William E. McCoppin, P-51 Mustang fighter pilot, who shot down a Nazi ME-109 in aerial combat in November, has been awarded a third Oak Leaf Cluster to the air Medal... He is the son of Mr. and Mrs. G. T. McCoppin, 2641 Collis Avenue.

Glenna: [Monday] *January 15th – Washed a big washing. Cloudy.*

Glenna: [Tuesday] *January 16th – Ironed. Cloudy. Dawson got his call to be examined for the Army. Millard Adkins's boy reported killed in the foreign field. We bought two pigs. Cold, snow.*

As the war dragged on, older men were drafted for service. Several years earlier, Dawson had fallen from a bridge under construction at Barboursville and was impaled by a metal rod, leaving a horrendous scar on his abdomen. That injury alone probably made him ineligible for military service.

Amon Adkins, referred to in Mother's diary entry, was killed on Christmas Eve, 1944, when a German U-boat sunk the SS *Léopoldville* off the coast of France. An account of the sinking of this troop transport is in *The Sea Hunters: True Adventures with Famous Shipwrecks.*[11] Detailed information about Amon Adkins is on the West Virginia Division of Culture and History website. The information was up-to-date in May, 2020. (http://www.wvculture. org/history/wvmemory/vets/adkinsamon/ adkinsamon.html)

In addition to the mini-stories in the regular daily columns, the newspapers published other stand-alone articles about Tri-State service members and I have reproduced several, beginning with this one:

The Distinguished Flying Cross, the Air Medal with nine Oak Leaf Clusters, the Purple Heart and a Presidential Unit Citation with one cluster have been awarded Technical Sergeant Albert Tyree, son of Mr. and Mrs. D. A. Tyree of Milton, who has

returned home after two and one-half years overseas. A radio-gunner on a B-26, he was credited with downing three Japanese Zeros on his first mission as a member of the Fifth Air Force... The Purple Heart was awarded for wounds he received in France last May 29. During a mission over occupied France, he was wounded again and hospitalized in England. He was a graduate of Milton High School, where he played football for four years before entering the service December 1, 1939.[12]

In Europe, the United States First and Third Armies linked up following the Battle of the Bulge and Soviet troops laid siege to Budapest.

"IN THE SERVICE":

Second Lieutenant James H. Rusk, husband of Mrs. Joanne Rusk, 302 Twelfth Avenue, has been assigned as a B-17 navigator to the veteran 457th Heavy Bombardment Group based in England. He entered the AAF in 1943...

Corporal John W. Beckley, whose parents reside in Prichard, has been graduated from the AAF Flexible Gunnery School at Laredo, Tex... He is now qualified as a combat crew member after six weeks of intensive training.

Second Lieutenant George W. Long Jr., son of Mr. and Mrs. G. W. Long of Southside, Mason County, has been assigned as a fighter pilot with the 359th Fighter Group of the Eighth Air Force in the European theatre...

Private first Class Edgar (Mickey) Davis, whose wife and mother reside in Huntington, is serving in the Pacific with the Marine Corps. He is well known in sports circles of this area, having participated in boxing tournaments here.

Aubrey T. Carpenter, who served for 28 months in the South Pacific with the Navy Construction Battalion, has returned to his base in California after a 30-day leave in Huntington. He visited his mother, Mrs. A. A. Johnson, and sisters, Mrs. E. C. Johnson and Mrs. L. D. Crouch.

Private First Class Lindsey G. Lambert of Kenova, son of Harrison W. Lambert of Louisa, Ky, is serving at a station hospital in Italy. He served for 14 months in World War I and has been in service for 27 months during the present war.

Corporal Walter R. Sparks, husband of Mrs. Elizabeth Sparks, 408 Smith Street, is scheduled to go overseas soon as an aerial gunner on a B-24 Liberator bomber. A son of Benjamin Sparks of Barboursville, he is now stationed at Davis-Monthan Field, Ariz.

Seaman Second Class Madeline Sarver, daughter of F. B. Sarver and the late Mrs. Sarver of Huntington, is expected to arrive here January 29 on leave. She has been assigned to Washington with a WAVES unit after completing boot training at Hunter College, New York City.

Staff Sergeant G. A. Kitchen, son of Mr. and Mrs. G. A. Kitchen, 311 West Eleventh Avenue, left last night for Richmond Va. for reassignment after spending a 30-day furlough with his parents. He served for 32 months in the China-Burma-India theatre as an aerial gunner.

Infantry Private William G. McCaffrey, husband of Mrs. Garnet McCaffrey of Huntington, has been awarded the Air Medal for volunteering on four occasions to drop supplies from an artillery liaison plane to troops isolated near Metz, France. The son of Mrs. Mary Depriest, 1211 Nineteenth Street, sat behind the pilot and dropped supplies while the aircraft never exceeded 50 feet above the ground. They were continually exposed to machinegun and small arms fire.

Seaman First Class John Edward McGirr Jr., assigned to the U.S. Naval Air Station at Alameda, Calif., is spending a leave with his wife, Mrs. Mary Lynne McGirr.

Private First Class Jesse C. Templeton, son of Mr. and Mrs. F. J. Templeton of Milton, is

assigned to an engineer unit which recently set a record by repairing a bridge in Belgium which had been demolished by a buzz bomb.

Staff Sergeant Robert L. Lindsey, husband of Mrs. Lola Lindsey, 2137 Third Avenue, recently attained that rank serving with the 102nd Infantry Division in the European theatre.

First Lieutenant Arty J. Franzello, a Marshall College graduate has been assigned to duty at the Army Air Forces Overseas Replacement Depot at Camp Kohler, Calif., where he is commissary sales officer. After his graduation from Marshall, Lieutenant Franzello taught in Lewisburg, W.Va. schools.

Glenna: [Wednesday] *January 17th — Mended everything. Made myself an apron. Have an awful cold in the head. Weather cloudy.*

A government favorable to the Communists was installed in Warsaw.[13] During this time, and soon after the war, Russia took every opportunity to acquire new territory under communism.

"IN THE SERVICE":

Sergeant Alva V. Lewis, husband of Mrs. Ruby Lewis, 2216 Tenth Avenue, and son of Mrs. Alta Lewis, 528 Eighth Street, has been awarded the Bronze Star Medal, He entered the service last February and has been overseas since last August 13.

Corporal Sam J. McCoy, husband of Mrs. Elaine McCoy of Shoals, who is serving with the Third Army in Belgium has been awarded the Good Conduct Medal... Corporal McCoy is a son of Mrs. Prudence McCoy and the late George McCoy.

Quartermaster Third Class William M. Gibson has written his mother, Mrs. Fanny Gibson, 912 Monroe Avenue, about his experiences when his ship ran into a typhoon recently in the South Pacific. A veteran of action at Midway, in the Coral Sea, and at Guadalcanal, he related that he had been "in quite a few tough spots, but this was the worst" in describing his impression of the typhoon.

Corporal Lloyd J. Hamlin, son of Mr. and Mrs. E. J. Hamlin, 439 Smith Street, has been promoted to sergeant at an English Air Force station ... where he is serving as a photographic technician.

Seaman First Class Richard Carroll Strong, son of Mr. and Mrs. William Strong of Burlington, O., who recently completed training at Gulfport, Miss. has been assigned to an armored guard unit and is now at sea.

Captain Robert H. Irvin, son of Mr. and Mrs. J. E. Irvin, 1851 Maple Avenue, recently arrived at Miami, Fla. in an Air transport plane after serving for 19 months in the China-Burma-India theatre as a C-47 pilot. A former school teacher, he was awarded the Distinguished Unit Citation while stationed in the CBI area.

Ralph M. Kuhn, son of Mr. and Mrs. G. C. Kuhn of Salt Rock, recently was promoted to technician fifth grade at Assam, India, where he is serving with a trucking company. He has been overseas for 10 months and has received the Presidential Citation, Distinguished Unit Badge and the Asiatic-Pacific ribbon.

Second Lieutenant Robert A. Mayes, who recently received his wings after graduating at the Army Air Forces Navigation School, San Marcos, Tex., is spending a leave with his father, Howard G. Mayes, manager of the Huntington-Ironton-Chesapeake Airport. A brother, John William Mayes, is in the Navy, and a sister, Miss Elizabeth Mayes, is in cadet nurse training at Chicago.

Lieutenant William A. Moore, son of Mr. and Mrs. M. F. Moore, 2263 Fifth Avenue, is home on leave after serving in England and France as a fighter pilot with the Ninth Air Force. He received the Air Medal with four Oak Leaf Clusters, the European theatre ribbon with two Bronze Stars and a Presidential Citation. He will report this week to Valley Forge General Hospital.

Private James A. Turley, 638 Seventh Avenue, is serving with the 398th Infantry regiment, 100th Division, of the Sixth Army in France.

Captain Claude W. Burger Jr. of Huntington is attending the Adjutant General's School at Fort Sam Houston, Tex. A brother, Private Joe A. Burger, who is assigned to Camp McClelland, Ala., is ill at his parents' home here after he was stricken en route to Huntington on furlough.

Machinist's Mate Third Class John E. (Jack) Hemp, son of Mr. and Mrs. M. E. Hemp Sr., 1125 Eighth Avenue, returned here Monday night after serving for 17 months in the South Pacific. Machinist's Mate Hemp previously served for two years in the same area and is a survivor of the USS *Lexington*. He wears the Pacific theatre ribbon with nine stars for major battles. A brother, Lieutenant Mervin E. Hemp Jr., is with the Air Forces in New Guinea.

Glenna: [Thursday] *January 18th – Our sixth year anniversary. Cold still bad. Nearly sick. Visited Mrs. Rousey and wrote a letter for her. Sunshine part of the day but cold and muddy.*

The mud of my boyhood sticks to my memory with nearly the same tenacity it had to my shoes then. Roads and lanes were unpaved except for State Route 10 running through Salt Rock. Madison Creek Road, heavily traveled, had a bed of crushed stone. Our lane from there had winter mire that sucked at shoes and boots. Mother made us scrape our footware clean before we entered the house; we kept tools on the porch for that purpose. I sometimes walked on tiptoe to cut down on my cleanup time.

Sampling of college basketball scores: Penn State 53-West Virginia 27, Western Kentucky 48-Morehead 36, Louisville 74-Evansville 53, American U. 76-Loyola 35, Colgate 55-Syracuse 52, Army 48-Columbia 31.

"IN THE SERVICE":

Warrant Officer W. T. Ellis has left for Tampa, Fla. after spending a leave with his parents, Mr. and Mrs. W. L. Ellis, 1201 Jefferson Drive. He is a veteran of six years naval service in the Pacific and at Tampa will be assigned to a ship which was recently launched.

Aviation Radioman First Class Claude Jackson Park Jr., son of Mr. and Mrs. C. J. Park of Proctorville Route 1, who was wounded in action during the occupation of Guam, has received the Purple Heart at the Naval Hospital at San Diego, Calif. A brother has been lost at sea.

Private John A. Stapleton of Chesapeake and Private First Class Robert L. Buschur of New Weston, O. were with a reconnaissance unit which patrolled 25 miles beyond the front lines on Eastern Luzon in the Philippines, according to an Associated Press dispatch yesterday.

Captain Charles D. Hodges, whose wife and two children reside at 726 Gill Street, recently attained that rank in Italy where he is assigned to General Mark Clark's staff. He is the son of Mr. and Mrs. Ernest Hodges, 732 Gill Street.

Staff Sergeant John M. Collins, 2901 Merrill Avenue, has returned to this country after flying 50 missions as a Liberator bomber gunner in the European theatre. He was awarded the Air Medal with three Oak Leaf Clusters, the European theatre ribbon with three battle stars and a Presidential Citation.

James T. Ward Jr. is spending a leave with his parents at 1335 Ninth Avenue after graduating as honor man of his recruit training company at Great Lakes, Ill. He was nominated by fellow trainees and chosen by his company commander.

Cook Third Class James A. Owen, husband of Mrs. Wilma Owen of Kenova, has been overseas for eight months and is serving aboard an LCT in the Mediterranean theatre.

Private Howard D. Boon, husband of Mrs. Audrey O. Boon, 813 Seventh Street, has been transferred from Camp Atterbury, Ind. to the Field Artillery Replacement Training Center at Fort Sill, Okla.

Corporal Hobert Patton of the Army Air forces is visiting relatives on Huntington Route 1.

Sergeant Clarence Wiley, husband of Mrs. Doris Grant Wiley of Huntington and son of Mr. and Mrs. C. H. Wiley of Eighteenth Street, has arrived in England with an Army Air Forces unit.

Lieutenant Russell F. McCallister has arrived in England with a field artillery outfit according to word received by his wife, the former Miss Betty Fox. Mrs. McCallister is residing with her parents, Mr. and Mrs. Carl V. Fox, 1714 Crestmont Drive.

Private Elmo Gooch, son of Mr. and Mrs. Henry Gooch of Huntington, has received his paratrooper wings and boots at Fort Benning, Ga.

Ray Holley has notified his parents, Mr. and Mrs. James H. Holley, 719 Thirty-first Street, that he is well and safe in France. He has been overseas since last August.

Private First Class Vernon Belling [?], 324 Washington Avenue, has received the Good Conduct Medal in India, where he has served since June 28, 1943.

Glenna: *January 19—Rainy and muddy. I cleaned the house, baked a pumpkin pie.*

Area war casualties continued, as reported in the following two articles: "Machinist's Mate First Class Bud Clarence Hall, 22, previously reported missing in action, is now listed as dead, the Navy notified his mother, Mrs. Lenorah Hall, 420 Thirteenth Street. A member of the Navy since July, 1940, he is survived by his mother, three sisters, Misses Ann and Selma Hall and Mrs. Ervin Cremeans, and three brothers. Paul,

Hillman and Corporal Strother (Todd) Hall. The latter is serving in France."[14]

"Ensign Samuel Marsh Jr., son of Mr. and Mrs. Samuel Marsh of East Liverpool, O., formerly of Huntington, died December 29 when his Navy plane crashed at sea, his parents have been advised. Surviving in addition to the parents are the widow, Mrs. Edith Marsh of Minneapolis, Minn.; a sister, Miss Henrietta Marsh; a brother, George Marsh, Fort Knox, Ky., and maternal grandmother, Mrs. George Day of Huntington."[15]

"IN THE SERVICE":

Mrs. Goldie Oman of Milton, who had received no word for 17 months from her son, Woodrow M. Griffith, a prisoner in Japan, has received a letter from him acknowledging receipt of a gift box. "Do not worry as I will make out," he wrote his mother. Mr. Griffith had been in the Army nine years prior to the Japanese attack in the Philippines and was captured in May, 1942. A brother, Lieutenant Fred E. Griffith, is in the European theatre.

Technical Sergeant Arthur E. Holliday, husband of Mrs. Vivian L. Holiday, 414 Twelfth Street, is a patient at Woodrow Wilson Hospital at Staunton, Va. He has been awarded the Purple Heart with Oak Leaf Cluster after he was twice wounded in action, the Combat Infantryman Badge and Good Conduct Medal. Sergeant Holliday participated in action at the Anzio Beachhead in Italy and in the invasion of France. He is the son of J. S. Holiday of Coal Grove, Ohio.

Private Ernest B. Seay, veteran of 31 months service in the China-Burma-India theatre is spending a 30-day furlough with his mother, Mrs. Maude Seay, 1330 Fourth Avenue...

Sergeant Harry E. Brumfield, son of Mr. and Mrs. A. S. Brumfield, 911 Adams Avenue, is an orthopedic wardmaster in an Army hospital in England. He helps in the care and treatment of battle casualties from the European area.

Seaman First Class Sydney J. Snair of the Coast Guard, son of Mrs. G. N. Vernon, 1647 Washington Avenue, has participated in five major invasions in the Pacific during the past 11 months, He saw action in the amphibious attacks on the Marshall Islands, Emirau, Guam, Peleliu and the landing in the Philippines.

Technician Third Grade Asa C. Eddy, son of Mr. and Mrs. A. R. Eddy, 1702 Seventh Avenue, has received the Bronze Star for meritorious achievement while serving with an Army Signal Corps unit in the European theatre.

Captain John H. (Jack) Cassells, son of Mr. and Mrs. J. C. Cassells, 1004 Eleventh Avenue, is spending a leave here after flying 86 missions as a fighter pilot with the Ninth Air Force in the European area. He was awarded the Distinguished Flying Cross with 10 Oak Leaf Clusters and the European theatre ribbon with two battle stars. The Marshall College graduate will report to Miami, Fla. for reassignment at the expiration of his leave.

Technician Fifth Grade Cecil V. Sowards, son of Mrs. Leuvenia Sowards, 319 North Cedar Street, has been awarded the Combat Infantryman Badge while serving with the 80th Infantry Division in France.

Lieutenant Walter J. Galloway. Son of Mr. and Mrs. Joseph M. Galloway of Hamlin is at Miami Beach, Fla., for reassignment. He flew 50 missions as navigator on a B-24 bomber and received the Air Medal with four Oak Leaf Clusters.

Glenna: *January 20th Saturday – Half cloudy, half sunny. Dawson got his notice and deferment for 6 Mo. President F. D. Roosevelt inaugurated 4th term.*

Harry Truman was sworn in as Vice President. Many, because of the president's health conditions, believed Truman would become president.

In Europe, the Red Army advanced into East Prussia and in the Pacific the Liberty Ship *John A. Johnson* was sunk by a Japanese submarine. It was reported that the Japanese "frenzied crew shouted and danced on its deck and poured machinegun bullets at the helpless survivors."[16]

"IN THE SERVICE":

Private First Class Okey D. Pack, a prisoner of the Japanese since the fall of Bataan is in "excellent health" according to a message received from him by his parents, Mr. and Mrs. L. M. Pack of Huntington. Formerly interred in the Philippines, he is now imprisoned in Japan. He is the nephew of Mrs. Emma Fulton of Huntington. [After the war it was disclosed that the Japanese often gave false information to families about their prisoners.]

Private First Class Joseph E. Noll, son of Mr. and Mrs. H. L. Noll of Chesapeake, has been promoted to technician fifth grade with an ordnance armament maintenance battalion with the Fifth Army in Italy.

Seaman First Class Corbet K. (Corky) Black, son of Mr. and Mrs. R. J. Black, 2988 Third Avenue, and his cousin, Seaman First Class Erva W. Cooper, son of Mr. and Mrs. Floyd Cooper of Milton, have returned to this country on leave after serving together through many engagements in the Pacific with the Coast Guard. They are sons of twin sisters.

Chief Warrant Officer John H. Hoff Jr., husband of Mrs. Frieda Hoff, 1508 Norway Avenue, has arrived at Miami Beach, Fla. for reassignment after completing a tour of overseas duty with the AAF.

Private First Class Robert B. Watts of Camp Campbell, Ky. and WAC Private Helen E. Watts of Cincinnati recently visited their mother, Mrs. Addie Watts, 2020 Seventh Avenue.

Private First Class Paul O. Butler, who served a year in North Africa, has arrived in Italy, according to word received by a sister, Mrs. Mack Thompson, 428 ½ Nineteenth Street.

Storekeeper Second Class Victor Miller has left for Portland, Ore. after spending a leave with his wife and two daughters at 630 ½ Eighth Avenue. He is a son of Mr. and Mrs. Guy Miller of Proctorville, O.

Aviation Radioman First Class S. S. Willey, 616 Eleventh Street, has returned to this country after a tour of duty in the Pacific where he flew numerous missions aboard a Martin Mariner.

Major Paul G. Davis of Lexington, Ky., son of Mr. and Mrs. C. W. Davis of Huntington, is at a redistribution station at Miami Beach, Fla after serving with the AAF overseas.

Private William L. McComas, 1150 Seventeenth Street, is with the 235th Engineer Combat Battalion which was the first unit to bridge the Serchio River below Viareggio, Italy.

Technician Fourth Grade Adrian Puryear, 414 Eighth Avenue, and Staff Sergeant Preston A. Collier, 4502 Auburn Road, were members of an engineer boat regiment which has been inactivated in Italy after winning many commendations for its activities in helping supply the Fifth Army.

Sergeant Joseph Billups of Prichard has received his fourth battle star following his unit's participating in the Rome-Arno phase of the Italian campaign.

Private First Class William C. Herold, son of Mr. and Mrs. Moser B. Herold of Alexandria, Va., formerly of Huntington, has been awarded the Bronze Star for heroism in evacuating wounded men at Leyte while he was subject to enemy fire. He is scheduled to receive the Purple heart for wounds received in action in the Philippines.

Private First Class Jack Saunders, whose parents reside at 1709 Franklin Avenue, will be interviewed tonight over the British Broadcasting Corps System's program, "American Eagle in Britain." The program may be heard in this country over the Mutual Broadcasting System.

Glenna: [Sunday] *January 21st – Dawson and I went down to his mother's, stopped at Elsie's and Ben Nida's on our way back. Sunny day.*

Dawson's parents, Calvery and Nanny Morrison, had seven living children. By 1945 all had left home and his father was deceased. His mother lived alone except when daughter Ocie, a nurse, came home. The boys were Freer, Dallas, John, Dawson, and Drewie. Girls were Lois Cordial and Ossie Roth.

"Elsie" was Elsie Midkiff. Roy and Elsie lived in Salt Rock above the intersection of River Road and Route 10. Without an automobile, we walked the two miles to the Morrison farm. We knew everyone along River Road (Apple Maps lists it as "Guyan River Road") and stopped often to chat. The Nida family lived closest to Route 10 on a farm that had once belonged to Elijah Adkins, my Grandmother Adkins's father. Other families along River Road were Surgeons, Eli and Willie Morrison, Whites, Joe and Ercie Dick, Albert and Marie Queen, and Roy and Georgia Smith. We farmed sections of the Morrison farm and walking the route was a frequent occurrence.

January 22: Mother made no diary entry this day.

"IN THE SERVICE":

Miss Sallee Childs, daughter of Mr. and Mrs. William A. Childs, 33 Fairfax Court, who is a civilian employee in the Navy Department in Washington, has been designated co-sponsor of a new LSM (landing ship, medium). A ceremony is scheduled for next Saturday in New York City, and a dance will be held that evening in the Red Cross Auditorium in honor of crewmen from 12 LSMs and the ship's sponsors. Miss Child's brother, Lieutenant William A. Childs Jr., is serving in the Army.

Receiving their initial naval indoctrination at the U.S. Naval Training Center at Great Lakes, Ill., are Richard Williams, son of Mrs. Louise B. Williams, 1123 Twelfth Avenue, and William E. Stewart, son of Mr. and Mrs. E. L. Stewart of Huntington Route 1.

Private Carl Irving Estler, husband of Mrs. Nellie Jane Estler, 915 Tenth Street, has arrived at Camp Wolters, Tex. for basic infantry training.

Private Charles M. Maddox, husband of Mrs. Ruby Adkins Maddox of Salt Rock Route 1, has been transferred from the Army Ground Forces to the Army Air Forces at Pope Field, N.C. He is a son of John Maddox, Gallipolis, O., Route 2.

Sergeant Alva Bailey of Huntington is serving with a unit in Southwest China which is using equipment flown into China to be used to help open the Burma Road supply route for Allied fighting forces.

Captain Clark M. McGhee, son of Mr. and Mrs. E. F. McGhee of Hurricane, can now wear the third Oak leaf Cluster to the Distinguished Unit Badge. His fighter plane unit in Italy recently became the first AAF outfit in the Mediterranean theatre to be cited four times by War Department general orders. An operations officer, he is a graduate of Hurricane High School and Marshall College.

Army Chaplain Daniel B. Churton of Columbus, O., former Huntington resident and graduate of Marshall College, is serving with combat troops overseas.

William S. Moody, mess attendant second class, U.S. Navy, is visiting his mother, Mrs. Carrie Carr, 512 Rr 11th Avenue.

Glenna: [Tuesday] *January 23rd – Ironed everything. Gaynelle got her notice she was sued for divorce. Man came to sell Papa and Mama a house in Huntington.*

Gaynelle, Mother's younger sister, had a troubled marriage to Selva Wiley, then an officer in the Navy. They had lived in Lincoln County with their son, Howard LaDonne, but Gaynelle finally gave up trying to save her marriage and moved back to Salt Rock with Don. They lived with my grandparents down the lane by the school.

It might have been stress that prodded my grandparents, Lucian and Jennie Adkins, to buy a house in Huntington. The six-room Salt Rock house, with Gaynelle and Don, my Uncle Cline and his daughter, Shelby Jean, living there was crowded.

Two more area families received tragic news: "Sergeant Omer J. Perdue, 22, son of Huntington's "Infantry Mother," Mrs. E. E. Purdue, 527 Elm Street, [she had five sons serving in the armed forces] and Lieutenant Wayne Sullivan, 24, son of Mr. and Mrs. D. C. Sullivan, 526 Second Street, have been killed in action, the parents have been notified by the War Department."[17]

Homefront help was much-needed: Sylvania Electric Products Inc. in Huntington established a "victory shift" for high school students to help the company meet production schedules of critical war material. The plant Manager, W. H. Lamb, said the special program was "designed for high school students 16 or older. They will work from 4:30 to 8 P.M., five days a week."[18]

"IN THE SERVICE":

Sergeant James E. Atkinson, 22, son of Mrs. Georgia A. Atkinson, 1121 ½ Ninth Street, was slightly injured in action December 23 in Luxembourg, the War Department has advised his mother. He has been overseas since last May and has been serving with an infantry unit of Lieutenant General George S. Patton Jr.'s Third Army.

Flight Officer Milton D. Ward Jr., son of Mr. and Mrs. Milton D. Ward. 732 Jefferson Avenue, has been graduated as a B-24 bomber pilot at Fort Worth, Tex. Army Air Field...

John H. Burke, 430 Eleventh Avenue, has been graduated from the Transportation Corps School at New Orleans, La., and has been commissioned a second lieutenant. He served with the Engineer Corps in Iran from November 1, 1942 to August 28, 1944. Lieutenant Burke is a graduate of Central High School and was employed as a clerk by the Chesapeake & Ohio Railway Co. prior to entering the Army.

Staff Sergeant Forrest B. Langdon, son of Mr. and Mrs. Forrest Langdon, 2774 Latulle Avenue, will attend the Army Special Services School at Washington and Lee University. He served for 31 months in the Panama Canal Zone and has been assigned to Camp Butner, N.C.

Sergeant Robert G. Bushea, son of Mrs. A. F. Monroe, 1473 Edwards Street, has been promoted to staff sergeant at an army Air Forces base in the South Pacific. He has been commended by his commanding officer for "tireless effort and unassuming way of doing things" in connection with a special duty engineering project.

Second Lieutenant Charles L. Edmondson, husband of Mrs. Dorothy Jean Edmondson of Logan, and other members of his bomber crew escaped injury when their aircraft. loaded with bombs, was crash landed in England, an Eighth Air Force announcement disclosed yesterday.

Staff Sergeant William A. Wilson, son of Mrs. Rebecca James of Prichard, has been awarded the Air Medal at a 15th Air Force station in Italy. He is a tail gunner on a Liberator bomber.

Staff Sergeant Frank R. Marsh, son of Mrs. E. G. Marsh, 2744 Orchard Avenue, has arrived at Miami, Fla. for reassignment after flying 30 missions as a B-17 gunner in the European area. He received the Distinguished Flying Cross and Air Medal with three Oak Leaf Clusters.

Seaman Second Class Ora Mae Mann, daughter of Mr. and Mrs. Lee Mann, 2422 Collis Avenue, has been assigned to a WAVES detachment in Washington. A brother, Motor Machinist's Mate Fred Mann, is in the submarine service.

Private George L. Douglas, and Private Elmo Summers, step-brothers, 652 Thirty-first Street, met in Paris and spent Christmas together, they wrote their parents here.

Master Sergeant John W. Houston, 1247 Eleventh Avenue, son of Mr. and Mrs. William H. Houston of Huntington, recently attained his present rank with an Army Air Forces unit in France.

January 24: There was no diary entry.

Reported killed in action in Belgium on January 1 was Sergeant Edwin J. Fraley, 27, son of Mr. and Mrs. Cecil Fraley of Miller, Ohio. Other surviving family members were "a brother, Paul J. Fraley of Sharples, W.Va., and six sisters, Mrs. Dean Barrett and Mrs. Wilma Fraley of Huntington, Mrs. L. J. Hivon of Vallejo, Calif., and Mrs. Hugh Gilliam, Mrs. Clyde Stout and Mrs. Milton Evans of Miller."[19]

"IN THE SERVICE":

Corporal Charles Lee Beckett, son of Mr. and Mrs. George A. Beckett, 1517 Seventh Avenue, repairs and adjusts guns used on Flying Fortresses operating from an Eighth Air Force base in England. He is a graduate of Central High School.

James H. Jacobs, son of Mr. and Mrs. Henry Jacobs, 2051 Madison Avenue, has been commissioned a second lieutenant after completing the officer candidate course at the Infantry School, Fort Benning, Ga.

Sylvester R. Bischoff of Huntington has been promoted to sergeant at Tonopah Army Air Field, Nev. He is a graduate of Central High School and attended the Louisville, Ky. College of Pharmacy and Marshall College.

Corporal Guy D. Tealey, whose wife resides in Chesapeake, O., recently completed an orientation course at an Air Service Command station in England. He is a former employee of the International Nickel Co.

Ensign Selva Wiley is spending a leave with his wife, Mrs. Gaynelle Adkins Wiley of Salt Rock. [This followed the divorce notice received by my Aunt Gaynelle.]

First Lieutenant Harold H. Frazier, husband of Mrs. Olene Frazier of Winfield, W.Va., has been awarded the Distinguished Flying Cross and the Air Medal with five Oak Leaf Clusters while serving as a bombardier with the 12th Air Force in the Mediterranean theatre. He is the son of Mr. and Mrs. Elwood Frazier of Fraziers Bottom and a nephew of Mrs. L. C. Alexander of Barboursville.

Albert C. Myers, 1006 Twelfth Avenue, has been promoted to sergeant with the 55th Medical Training Battalion at Camp Berkeley, Texas.

Romey A. Hensley, husband of Mrs. Norma M. Hensley of Barboursville Route 2, is receiving initial naval indoctrination at Great Lakes, Ill.

First Lieutenant Oscar J. Vinson, husband of Mrs. Kizzie Vinson of Louisa, Ky., has been promoted to captain at an Eighth Air Force station in England where he is serving as a supply officer. He is a veteran of World War I.

Private Greene Kitchen, husband of Mrs. Minnie L. Kitchen, 1210 Twenty-sixth Street, has been transferred from Camp Atterbury, Ind. to Camp Barkeley, Tex.

On leave or furlough are Yeoman Second Class Charles C. Lane, son of Mr. and Mrs. Oscar Lane, 928 Twenty-fourth Street; Private Eugene R. Wray, son of Mrs. Marion Nelson, 2235 Third Avenue; Dominick Lobaldo, husband of Mrs. Alice Lobaldo of Huntington, and Private Herman E. Miller, son of Mr. and Mrs. Ernest Miller of Kenova.

Staff Sergeant Marsh L. Faulkner, husband of Mrs. Eloise Winters Faulkner, 4508 Ohio river Road, has received the Expert Combat Infantryman's Badge while serving with the First Army in Germany. He is the son of Mr. and Mrs. W. L. Faulkner of Ohio River Road.

Marine Sergeant Charles F. Tate, who is spending a leave with his parents, Mr. and Mrs. W. H. Tate, 1031 Twenty-sixth Street, has received a letter of commendation from a general officer of his unit with whom he served for 19 months in the Asiatic-Pacific theatre.

Sergeant Alva V. Lewis, whose wife resides at 2216 Tenth Avenue, and a 91st Division buddy have been commended for evacuating a wounded comrade on the Fifth Army front in Italy. The two soldiers crawled 100 yards to rescue a wounded man although they were subjected to intense cross-fire from a German position.

Lieutenant and Mrs. Cecil F. Crumbley are visiting her mother and Grandmother, Mrs. Lola Tidman and Mrs. Thomas Bishop, 836 Eighth Street. He is assigned to the Chicago Ordinance District.

Lieutenant Frank Qulia, U.S. Army, is visiting his father, Mr. A. J. Qulia of Louisa, Ky., and wife, the former Miss Margaret Robinson, 1229 ½ Eighth Street. Lieutenant Qulia, a former Marshall College student and member of Alpha Kappa Pi fraternity, entered the service three years ago and received his commission this month from Fort Benning, Ga.

Glenna: [Thursday] *January 25th – Went to Huntington. Had my shoes mended.*

Our seventeen-mile trips to Huntington were usually by bus but sometimes by rail. Public transportation in 1945, despite rationing of gasoline, was quite good with buses running between Huntington and Logan every two hours each way during daytime and evening hours. Twice-a-day passenger trains also ran between the two cities.

The OPA (Office of Price Administration) declared that ration stamps for meats and fats would expire four months from date of issue, and sugar stamp numbers in use would expire

February 28.[20] The OPA rationing system. was complex and changing almost daily.

Soviet troops liberated Auschwitz concentration camp, which held nearly 3,000 inmates, a great many near death.[21] (The full extent of Nazi regime brutality was yet to be revealed as the Allies advanced.)

In the Pacific, American Navy planes bombarded Iwo Jima in preparation for an invasion.

"IN THE SERVICE":

Private First Class Harold L. Hagaman, son of Mr. and Mrs. Homer P. Hagaman Sr., 624 South Terrace, is serving with an armored battalion with the Seventh Army in France. His wife and two daughters reside on Washington Avenue...

First Lieutenant Homer P. Hagaman Jr., husband of the former Miss Frances Logan, 226 Twelfth Avenue, has arrived safely in India with an Army Signal Corps unit... He attended Marshall College and was employed by the Western Electric Co. prior to entering the Army in 1942.

Private Proctor Middaugh, husband of Mrs. Lorene Middaugh of Weeksbury, Ky., who has been serving with the Third Army in the European theatre, is a patient in a hospital in England... A son of Mr. and Mrs. Proctor Middaugh, he was employed by the Koppers Coal Co. in civilian life.

Sergeant Delbert Chapman, son of Mr. and Mrs. Morris Chapman of Milton, has been cited as "one of the outstanding squad leaders" with the 112th cavalry regiment on Leyte in the Philippines. Recently promoted from corporal, Sergeant Chapman has been overseas 30 months.

Seaman First Class Hearl Johnson, son of Mr. and Mrs. Willie Johnson of Salt Rock, has returned to his naval station after spending a brief leave at home. He has been on sea duty for 16 months. A brother, Coxswain Hezza Johnson, has been in the service for 13 months, including nine months of sea duty.

Private George E. Faine, son of Mr. and Mrs. Harry Faine of Wheelwright, Ky., has completed 17 weeks of infantry training at Camp Blanding, Fla. and is being transferred to California.

Ensign S. C. Wiley, assigned to the Naval Training Center at Miami, Fla., is on leave and visiting his father, J. T. Wiley of West Hamlin, and Huntington friends. [Selva appeared to be distancing himself from my Aunt Gaynelle.]

Second Lieutenant Charles Fetter, son of Mr. and Mrs. M. Fetter, 609 Ninth Avenue, has been promoted to first lieutenant at Fort Hayes, O.

John H. Hall, son of Mrs. Laura Hall, 1661 Thirteenth Avenue, has completed deep sea diving training and has been promoted to diver second class in the Navy.

Corporal Frank B. Strickett has returned to Fort Leavenworth, Kan. after spending a 15-day furlough with his mother, Mrs. M. B. Strickett, 1085 Washington Avenue.

Private Lloyd Stickler is visiting his mother, Mrs. Cloie Stickler, 2125 Seventh Avenue, while on furlough from Camp Shelby, Miss.

Technician Fourth Grade Thurman Robinson has been promoted to technician third grade with an engineer battalion in the European theatre.

Seaman Second Class Lewis B. Strathman is visiting his wife and two children at 1621 Sixth Avenue after serving for 16 months in the Aleutians with the Seabees.

Signalman Third Class John Aubra Pratt, husband of Mrs. Jenoise Kimes Pratt of Marcum Terrace, recently attained that rank at his station in New Guinea.

January 26: Mother had no diary entry.

"IN THE SERVICE":

Sergeant Fuveldia C. Maynor, son of Mr. and Mrs. E. D. Maynor, 1320 Fifth Avenue, recently received his aerial gunner's wings upon completing a flexible gunnery course at Harlingen, Tex. Army Air Field. He is a former Marshall College student.

Private Eugene Bailey, husband of Mrs. Vivian M. Bailey, 328 West Eighth Street, has been transferred to the 1524th [?] Service Training Unit, Camp Atterbury, Ind.

Seaman Second Class Erma Frances Miller, daughter of Mrs. Edith Miller, 2647 Guyan Avenue, has reported for duty at the Navy Department in Washington after completing WAVES training at Hunter College, New York City.

Private David S. Clark, son of Mrs. Carolyn Clark, 4728 Auburn Road, has entered the field artillery officer candidate school at Fort Sill, Okla. He is a former Marshall College student.

Sergeant Arville C. Ferguson of Huntington is serving with an air depot group of the 15th Air Force in Italy which has been awarded the Meritorious Service unit plaque for outstanding service in support of combat operations against the enemy...

Grover F. Perry, 415 Fifth Avenue, co-pilot of a Liberator bomber operating from Italy, has been promoted to first lieutenant at a 15th Air Force base.

Private Charles A. Ray, son of W. M. Ray of Shoals, has won his paratrooper boots and wings after completing four weeks of jump training at Fort Benning, Ga.

Chief Torpedoman Richard E. Seale and Radioman First Class James M. Seale, brothers who entered the Navy together in 1935, are visiting their mother, Mrs. Brooks Ferrell Seale, 1012 Chesapeake Court.

Second Lieutenant Joe Sheppe, assigned to Sioux Falls, S.D. with an AAF unit, is spending a leave with his parents, Dr. and Mrs. A. H. Sheppe, 922 West Second Street.

Seaman First Class Milton Supman and Technical Sergeant Ira Supman, sons of Mr. and Mrs. Ira Supman, 510 West Eleventh Avenue, last week end were home together for the first time in three and a half years.

Staff Sergeant Jack W. Porter, husband of Mrs. Frances H. Porter of Huntington and son of Mr. and Mrs. John Byron Porter, 63 Adams Avenue, has been promoted to that rank with an engineer unit in the South Pacific where he has served for the past 14 months.

Thomas J. Sasser Jr., son of Mr. and Mrs. T. J. Sasser, 1142 Spring Valley Drive, has completed a Navy basic engineering course at Great Lakes, Ill.

Lieutenant James R. McCoy, stationed at Lincoln, Neb., is spending a leave with his parents, Mr. and Mrs. V. W. McCoy of Cleveland, former Huntington residents now visiting here.

Seaman Second Class Kenneth H. Lawson, nephew of Mrs. G. A. Zornes, 974 Twenty-seventh Street, is on leave after completing boot training at Great Lakes, Ill. Ten of Mrs. Zornes' nephews are in the armed forces.

Corporal Paul I. Miros, recently assigned to Baer Field, Ind., is visiting his parents, Mr. and Mrs. Mike Miros, 618 South High Street. A brother, Technical Sergeant Mike Miros Jr., is with the AAF in New Guinea.

Lieutenant Arthur Bagby of Portsmouth, O., nephew of Mrs. H. C. Gordon, 1514 Third Avenue, has completed six aerial missions with the Eighth Air Force in the European theatre.

January 27: There was no diary entry.

"IN THE SERVICE":

Mr. and Mrs. Delbert R. Scragg Sr., 2440 Spring Valley Drive, received a telegram from the war department yesterday stating that their son,

Private Delbert R. (Ted) Scragg Jr., U.S. Army, was seriously wounded in action in Germany December 18 and is now hospitalized in France. Private Scragg attended Central High School and was graduated from Buffalo High School prior to entering the service one year ago. He was engaged in business with his father at the Scragg Service Station, Adams Avenue and Thirteenth Street, He has served overseas for six months.

Corporal Carl C. Perdue, son of Mr. and Mrs. Jesse H. Perdue of Ramage, W.Va., is an ammunition worker at an Eighth Air Force Flying Fortress station in England... Prior to entering the AAF he was employed by the Berry Wilson Drilling Co. here.

Serving with truck companies supplying gasoline for front-line vehicles are Sergeant Jack R. Bailey, 1794 Willamson Street; Private James Gibson, 2035 Fourth Street; Private Benjamin Grews, 1193 Seventh Avenue; Private Paul E. Clark, Barboursville Route 1; Private Clifford A. Prillman, Davy; Private Jack C. Cochran, Reed; Private Trey E. Rutherford, War.

Private Ernest Robinson, 1051 Adams Avenue, has been promoted to private first class at the Camp Butner, N.C. Army Ground and Service Forces Redistribution Station.

Major Robert E. Wallace, whose wife and two children reside at 1847 Underwood Avenue, recently was wounded in action in Germany while leading an 84th Infantry Division battalion. A sniper who shot Major Wallace in the left arm later was killed by an American soldier.

Sergeant Thurman T. Cremeans, son of C. C. Cremeans of Branchland Route 1, is recovering in an English Hospital from wounds received when he was struck by shrapnel near Dielgen, Germany. He has received the Purple Heart.

Mr. and Mrs. Willie A. Holley of Milton received the Air Medal with three Oak Leaf Clusters in a ceremony Thursday at Lockbourne Army Air Field, O. for their son, Second Lieutenant Harold R. Holley, who is a prisoner-of-war in Germany.

Technical Sergeant Jesse A. McComas, son of Mr. and Mrs. C. L. McComas, 1442 Sixteenth Street, has been awarded the third Bronze Oak Leaf Cluster to the Air Medal for meritorious achievement while participating in the airborne invasion of Holland.

Second Lieutenant Robert H. Newlon, husband of Mrs. Erma Newlon, 127 West Ninth Avenue, received his commission recently upon graduating from the infantry officer candidate school at Fort Benning, Ga. A technical sergeant prior to entering OCS, he is a son of Mr. and Mrs. C. L. Newlon of the West Ninth Avenue address.

Woodrow H. Booton, son of W. T. Booton, 38 Adams Avenue, also was commissioned a second lieutenant at the Infantry School at Fort Benning. A graduate of Central High School, he was stationed at North Camp, Tex. before entering the officer school.

Second Lieutenant Paul A. Petterson, son of Mr. and Mrs. Peter N. Petterson of Huntington, has been graduated as a bomber pilot at Fort Worth Field, Tex. He was commissioned in June, 1944.

Seaman First Class Billy Joe Patton, who has been overseas for 15 months, is spending a brief leave with his parents, Mr. and Mrs. Herman Lowe of Whitaker Boulevard.

John Samual Keadle of Williamson has been promoted to captain in the army Corps of Engineers...

Staff Sergeant James Madison Simpson Jr., who spent five years overseas with the AAF, has returned from the Philippines to spend a furlough with his wife, Mrs. Jean Simpson, and his parents, Mr. and Mrs. J. M Simpson, 901 Norway Avenue. He will report to Miami, Fla, for reassignment next Friday, accompanied by Mrs. Simpson. A crew chief on a Liberator bomber, Sergeant Simpson was in the United States on furlough over a year ago but returned almost immediately to foreign service. He helped defend Hickam Field, T. H., December 7, 1941, and since has participated in the battles of Peleliu, Leyte, Midway, Wake and the two Coral Sea engagements. He has been in service six years.

Glenna: [Sunday] *January 28th – Went to Sunday school. Stuart & Ruby Hutchinson and children came home with us and spent the day. We had a good time. Sold them $1.10 [worth] of eggs and Rupert's overall pants $1.00. Rain and muddy. Started snowing at dark.*

I loved Hutchinson visits. Billie was a year older than me and Dencil was about my age. Carlotta, their sister, was a few years younger than Dencil. We played in the woods and fields around our farm, enjoying rough-neck adventures.

I'm mystified about the sale of my "overall pants." We didn't call them "jeans" in those days; I suppose they were thought of as a chopped off version of "bib farmer overalls." Maybe I had outgrown them.

"Sergeant Devore Murdock, the only son of Mr. and Mrs. Devore Murdock Sr., was killed in action Dec. 27, it was reported here yesterday. Sergeant Murdock, an aerial gunner, would have been 21 years old on Jan, 14..."[22]

"Private First Class John S. Neel, son of Mr. and Mrs. J. S. Neel of Barboursville, has been awarded the Purple Heart for wounds received in action in France; He is still a patient in a Paris hospital. A graduate of Barboursville High School, he entered the service in August, 1943."[23]

"WITH THE COLORS":

Staff Sergeant James Williams was recently promoted to that rank on Leyte Island in the Philippines. The son of Mrs. James Williams, 1140 Washington Avenue, he has served in the Pacific area for 22 months and participated in two major campaigns. The husband of Mrs. Edna Mae Williams, he has one son, 18 month-old Jimmy, whom he has never seen.

Petty Officer Second Class Richard P. Petit of Huntington is home on leave from his base at Barin Field, Fla...

Private Clifford S. Napier is spending a 15-day furlough with his mother, Mrs. Helen M. Napier, 1418 Fourth Avenue. He will return to his Army Air Base at Malden, Mo.

Aviation Cadet Joe S. Hazelett, son of Mr. and Mrs. H. T. Hazelett, 2161 Spring Valley Road, and Fairfield, O., has been transferred to the Hondo, Tex. advanced navigation school.

Corporal Brady V. Woodard has returned from the European theatre of operations to spend a 30-day leave with his wife and daughter Saundra Kaye. Corporal Woodard has received three major battle stars and one French citation. He is the son of Mr. and Mrs. Edgar Woodard of Milton. His brother, Private Creath L. Woodard, is in active duty in Belgium.

Private Leroy Jenkins, husband of Mrs. Evelyn Jenkins, has been awarded the Purple Heart for wounds received in action in Germany Nov. 2. His wife has been informed by the War Department that he is making normal improvement while convalescing in a hospital somewhere in England. Private Jenkins is the son of Mr. and Mrs. George Jenkins of Milton.

Private R. R. Rose, son of Mrs. Garfield Rose, 213 Fifth Avenue, Guyandotte, is receiving basic training at Fort Sill, Okla.

Private First Class Charles E. Lewis, USMC, has returned to his Quantico, Va. base after spending a 15-day furlough with relatives here.

Private Richard N. Bolling, son of Mr. and Mrs. K. Bolling, 502 Ninth Avenue, is home on furlough. His brother, Private Carl Bolling, is expected to come home over the week end.

Sergeant Roy G. Bruce, son of Mr. and Mrs. W. S. Bruce, Thirty-fourth Street, is spending a 15-day furlough with his parents and wife, Mrs. Mary Jo Bruce of Marcum Terrace. His wife will accompany him when he returns to Fort Sill, Okla.

First Lieutenant Donald L. Ferguson, son of Mr. and Mrs. Walter L. Ferguson, 2502 Collis Avenue, has been assigned to the San Marcos Army Air Field at San Marcos, Tex...

Glenna: [Monday] *January 29th – I washed up everything. Clear and cold with light snow on.*

"After three years in North Africa, Sicily and Italy, Army Sergeant Lawrence Cartmill came home on furlough yesterday [January 28] to learn that his mother, Mrs. Clara Cartmill, 52, of Huntington Route 2, had died in a hospital here 15 minutes before his arrival... Another son, James Cartmill, is with the Army overseas."[24]

The U.S. Third Army crossed the Our River at two points south of St. Vith, and the U.S. First Army fought to within two miles of the German border.[25]

"IN THE SERVICE":

"On leave or furlough are Private Robert Allen, husband of Mrs. Elizabeth Allen of Huntington; Private Cletis F. Diehl, son of Mr. and Mrs. Elza D. Diehl, 3178 Sixteenth Street Road; Corporal Paul D. Pike, son of Mrs. Ida Allen, 513 Third Avenue; Aviation Machinist's Mate First Class Robert Lee Adams, husband of Mrs. Betty Jane Adams of Huntington; Private Wendell Leonard, husband of Mrs. Etta M. Leonard of Huntington; Seaman Second Class Norman R. Elkins, son of Mrs. Rosa Nell Elkins, 639 Buffington Street; Fireman Second Class John R. Hall of Milton; Staff Sergeant Donald B. Johnson, husband of Mrs. Betty W. Johnson, 1621 Poplar Street, Kenova; Seaman First Class William C. Martin, 2902 Sixth Avenue, and Sergeant Frederick L. Murphy, 402 Fifth Street.

Technical Sergeant Donald E. Craig is spending a 30-day furlough here with his wife and relatives after serving for three years in the Southwest Pacific with an Army Air Forces unit. He is the son of Herbert E. Craig of Charleston and the late Lola Mae Smith Craig of Huntington.

Seaman First Class (radioman) Robert E. Arbaugh spent a brief leave in Huntington last week end with his wife while en route to an Eastern base. He stopped over in Washington before arriving here to visit his brother and sister-in-law, Technician Fifth Grade and Mrs. L. Glen Arbaugh. It was the first time the brothers had seen each other for 19 months.

Private Willard C. Hall, husband of Mrs. Mildred L. Hall, Barboursville, Route 1, has completed basic training at Fort Knox, Ky...

First Lieutenant Orville O. Will, husband of Mrs. Hope Will, 96 Oney Avenue, is serving in the Philippines with a medical battalion. A high school teacher in civilian life, he attended Marshall College and Ohio University.

Technician Fifth Grade Curtis E. Maynard, son of Mr. and Mrs. Ollie Maynard of Catlettsburg, is a patient at the Army Air Forces Convalescent Hospital at Fort Thomas, Ky. He served for 11 months in the European theatre as a truck driver and was injured in an accident in England.

Glenna: [Tuesday] *January 30th — Started cooking at school again. Had 35 children. Served rice with raisins, peanut butter Sand. Bitter cold.*

The German ship, *Wilhelm Gustloff*, was sunk by the Soviets.[26]

"Staff Sergeant Walter M. Cremeans, brother of Mrs. Moberley, 1310 Marcum Terrace is missing in action in the Pacific since December 22... A son of the late Mr. and Mrs. Grant Cremeans of Hamlin, Sergeant Cremeans has four brothers in the armed services, all overseas..."[27]

"IN THE SERVICE":

Lieutenant John Douglas Johnson, son of Mr. and Mrs. Clovis D. Johnson of Huntington has completed the four-engine pilot transition course at Hobbs Field, N.H. Completion of the training qualifies Lieutenant Johnson as a Flying Fortress commander.

Seaman First Class Frank Rodriguez, husband of Mrs. Minnie B. Rodriguez, 620 Thirteenth Street, has been graduated from the parachute riggers school at the Naval Air Station, Lakehurst, N.J. Seaman Rodriguez, a former Marshall College student, entered the Navy last April.

Flight Officer Boyd N. Adkins Jr., son of Mr. and Mrs. Boyd N. Adkins of Stiltner, has shot down his second German plane, an Eighth Air Force announcement disclosed yesterday. Flying a Mustang fighter while helping to escort-17's, Flight Officer Adkins chased the enemy aircraft from 36,000 feet to 20,000 feet where a burst of machinegun fire sent the Nazi plane into a violent spin. The Stiltner flier then watched the German plane crash.

First Lieutenant F. Witcher McCullough Jr., son of Mr. and Mrs. F. W. McCullough, 531 Twelfth Avenue, recently attained that rank at New Orleans, La., where he is serving with the Army Transportation Corps. His wife, the former Miss Betty Van Pelt of Huntington and Oak Hill, W.Va., is with him in New Orleans.

Private Robert Samuel Hoffman, son of Mrs. Cynthia Hoffman, 1827 Fourth Avenue, has been assigned to the 250th Military Police Company, Washington, D.C. after serving in North Africa, Sicily and Italy. His wife, Mrs. Inis Hoffman, and two children reside in Proctorville, O. He recently met Sergeant Robert L. Lee, former Huntington newspaperman who is also assigned to the 250th.

First Lieutenant Rex A. Morgan, husband of Mrs. Louise Swan Morgan of Huntington, is an assistant air inspector at an Eighth Air Force station in England. He is a son of R. E. Morgan, 1008 Madison Avenue.

First Lieutenant Charles C. Chapman Jr., son of Mr. and Mrs. Charles C. Chapman, 2636 Guyan Avenue is undergoing pre-combat training with the 452nd Bombardment Group in England. He is a Flying Fortress navigator.

Private Billy B. Embry, son of Mr. and Mrs. S. P. Embry, 923 Tenth Street, has completed armored forces training at Fort Knox, Ky...

Sergeant Richard H. Snyder, 308 West Third Avenue, who served 35 months in the Southwest Pacific with an ordnance unit, has arrived at a redistribution station at Miami, Fla.

Private Ira J. Buskirk of Wayne Route 1 is a member of the 894th Tank Destroyer Battalion which was recently awarded the Croix de Guerre avec Etoile Vermell in recognition of support given French troops on the Italian front.

The War Department announced last night that Technician Fourth Grade Norman L. Johnson, 2720 Highlawn Avenue was one of three West Virginia soldiers who have been awarded the Bronze Star Medal.

Staff Sergeant Simon B. Mazo, who is with the Army at Pecos, Tex., is spending a furlough with his mother, Mrs. Harry Mazo, and his sister, Mrs. Paul Kirsh, 108 Washington Boulevard.

Corporal Frank Maynard, husband of Mrs. Ruth Maynard of Washington Avenue, who was wounded in action in Aachen, Germany, returned to this country Friday and will be transferred to a general hospital... A brother of Inspector Don Maynard of the Huntington Police Department, Corporal Maynard served overseas a year. He was hospitalized in England until recently...

Glenna: [Wednesday] January 31st — Cooked again. Served 48 children. Served soup with hamburgers. Very cold.

The Red Army crossed the Oder River into Germany less than fifty miles from Berlin. In the Pacific, Americans made a second invasion on Luzon.

"... Signalman First Class William Frank Hensley, 23, son of W. M. Hensley, 1914 Tenth Avenue, and Private Basil Crabtree, son of the Rev. and Mrs. Carml Crabtree of Fort Gay Route 1, have been killed in action, the Navy and War Departments have notified the parents..."[28]

"IN THE SERVICE":

Private First Class Paul E. Seay, son of Mrs. Maude Seay, 1330 Fourth Avenue, has been awarded the Bronze Star Medal for heroism in carrying a wounded man to safety in France, his mother has been advised. Private Seay is serving with a front-line medical battalion attached to the Third Army.

Private Willard N. Fudge of Huntington has arrived at Kennedy General Hospital at Memphis, Tenn. where he is being treated for wounds received in action near Metz, France. The Huntington soldier, who served for five months overseas with an infantry unit, was shot by a sniper while his outfit was attacking a small village.

Among those who received ensign commissions after graduating from the Naval Reserve Midshipman's School of Northwestern University at Chicago were Samuel Sampson Jr., son of Mr. and Mrs. Samuel Sampson, 325 Whitaker Boulevard, and Jack C. Templeton, son of T. J. Templeton, 1946 Tenth Avenue.

Second Lieutenant Sam Porter Jr., son of Mr. and Mrs. Sam Porter, 862 Beech Street, Kenova, was co-pilot of a B-29 Superfortress termed by maintenance men as "the worst shot-up Superfortress that ever got home from a raid." The aircraft was attacked by at least 80 Japanese fighter planes while on a recent bombing mission over Tokyo, but none of the

American aircrewmen was injured. Lieutenant Porter is a Marshall College graduate.

Cadet Nurse Orlene Porter, assigned to St. Mary's Hospital here for training, and Corporal Charles W. Porter, serving in Germany, are son and daughter of Mrs. O. T. Wimbish of Russell. Ky. Corporal Porter's wife, Mrs. Gertie Waddell Porter, is a registered nurse attached to the General Hospital, Wilson, N.C.

Private George Swentzel, son of Mr. and Mrs. George W. Swentzel, 2710 First Avenue, is hospitalized in Cherbourg, France after serving with an armored division in France, Belgium, Luxembourg, Holland and Germany.

Sergeant Richard F. Parker, son of Mr. and Mrs. J. W. Parker, 2704 Oakland Avenue, has been awarded the Air Medal in the European theatre, He is a gunner aboard a heavy bomber based in England.

Corporal Troy E. Keesee, recently spent a brief furlough with his wife and two daughters here before reporting to Camp Shelby, Miss...

On leave or furlough are Lieutenant (j. g.) Thomas B. Bartlett Jr., husband of Mrs. Ann Steele Bartlett of Pea Ridge Road; Private Harold H. Sheets, son of Mrs. Julia Sheets of Milton; Seaman First Class Charles Bert Conner, son of Mrs. Vergie Lockard, 357 Smith Street; Corporal Paul D. Pike, son of Mrs. Ida Pike, 513 Third Avenue; Private Dorothy Mills, daughter of Mr. and Mrs. Edmond Mills of Barboursville Route 2; Staff Sergeant Norman D. Cook, son of Mrs. C. E. Cook, 3003 Fourth Avenue; Private First Class Cullen O. Amburgey of First Avenue; Private Richard Bolling, son of Mr. and Mrs. Carl Bolling, 502 Ninth Avenue; Seaman First Class Vaughn Martin of Culloden, and Seaman First Class James E. Simmons, 1026 West Eleventh Street.

February

ALLIES ADVANCE, NAZIS FLEE

Glenna: [Thursday] February 1st – Cooked again. Had 48 children. *Served Hopping John, cheese, raw apples, and rice. 6 below zero weather.*

The U.S. bombed Iwo Jima again, ahead of an expected Marine attack[29] and Ecuador declared war on Germany.

"IN THE SERVICE":

Private Robert Burgess, son of Mr. and Mrs. William Burgess, 1049 Adams Avenue, is a patient in a hospital in England... His wife and daughter reside at 1329 Monroe Avenue.

Technician Fourth Grade Frank Fritz, son of Mrs. Fred Fritz, 3654 Piedmont Road, has arrived at Fort Meade, Md. where he is to receive a rotation furlough after serving for 29 months in the European theatre with a quartermaster unit. First Sergeant Paul H. Webb, who served for 42 months in the Asiatic-Pacific area, has arrived at Fort Meade and will visit his mother, Mrs. Maude Webb of Ranger, W.Va.

Private Harriet P. Harvey, daughter of Mr. and Mrs. George P. Saurborne, 4426 Ohio River Road, has been transferred from Fort Des Moines, Iowa, to Wright Field, Ohio.

Private Ernest W. Cole, husband of Mrs. Della Ohnalene Cole, 138 ½ Norway Avenue, has been assigned as a ground station cryptographer at Dyersburg Field, Tenn. He is a son of Mr. and Mrs. J. W. Cole, 5362 U.S. Route 60.

Seaman Second Class Madeline Sarver, daughter of F. B. Sarver and the late Mrs. Sarver of Beckley, has returned to her WAVES station in Washington after visiting a cousin, Miss Elizabeth A. Barbour, 1601 ½ Eighth Avenue.

Private Henry Ford, son of Mr. and Mrs. Frank Ford of Barboursville Route 1, has received the Purple Heart for wounds received in action in the European theatre. He has recovered and is serving with the military police in Germany. A brother, Private First Class Robert Lee Ford, is with an engineer's unit in the Philippines.

John Thomas Peyton, son of Mr. and Mrs. John Thornburg Peyton of Barboursville, is scheduled to be graduated as an AAF lieutenant tomorrow at exercises at Moore Field, Tex. A graduate of Woodrow Wilson High School at Beckley, W.Va., he attended Marshall College. Cadet Peyton is a nephew of Attorney T. W. Peyton of Huntington.

Lieutenant (j. g.) Richard S. Bowers, son of Mrs. Blanche Bowers, 334 Thirty-first Street, last week attained that rank at his Merchant Marine station in New York. A former Marshall College student, he returned to this country last December after a tour of duty in the Mediterranean and North Atlantic. A brother, James W. Bowers. enlisted last week in the Merchant Marines.

First Lieutenant Charles F. Spencer, son of Mr. and Mrs. J. L. Spencer, 302 Eighth Avenue, has returned to this country after completing 64 combat missions as a bomber pilot in the Mediterranean theatre. He was a member of the Anderson-Newcomb Co. advertising staff prior to entering the AAF.

Captain Delbert L. Gibson, son of Mr. and Mrs. J. E. Gibson of Ona, who flew 60 missions as a 12th Air Force squadron navigator, has returned home on leave.

Receiving naval indoctrination at Great Lakes, Ill. are William F. Leep, son of Mr. and Mrs. R. J. Leep, 4156 Four Pole Road; Donald L. Howell, husband of Mrs. Elouise E. Howell, 4350 Ohio River Road; Wilber E. Justice, husband of Mrs. Helen Justice, 1324 Fifth Avenue, and Leo E. Meadows, son of Laban Meadows, Huntington Route 1.

Private Cortland A. Rockwell, son of Mrs. Frances Rockwell, 1802 Fifth Avenue, has received the Combat Infantryman's Badge for exemplary conduct in action in France. His wife, Mrs. Harriett Rockwell, resides at Hartford, W.Va.

Corporal William E. Rowe, son of Mrs. Cora Rowe, 337 Buffington Street, has qualified as rifle marksman at Fort Bragg, N.C. He is a former Ohio Valley Bus Co. driver.

Hospital Apprentice First Class Kent M. Keller, son of Mr. and Mrs. Arch Keller, 436 Twelfth Avenue, is serving in the Solomon Islands. He participated in the invasion of France and was home on leave before going to the Pacific.

Flight Officer Wilbur H. Barker, son of Mr. and Mrs. John W. Barker, 410 Twelfth Avenue, has arrived at Rosecrans Field, Mo. for an advanced course in pilot training. His wife and children reside at 1114 Ninth Avenue.

Second Lieutenant James H. Lambert, 315 Highland Street, has been awarded the Bronze Star Medal... He was one of nine West Virginia infantrymen decorated.

Glenna: [Friday] February 2nd – Cooked again. Had 54 children and 3 teachers. Served meat loaf, slaw, and boiled potato.

Weather cold and clear, zero at early morn. Groundhog saw its shadow.

My northern friends think southern West Virginia is near the tropics and are surprised there is sometimes harsh weather, even snow. The reality is that the extremes can be severe. I remember winter days below zero and summer days of 100 degrees or higher.

The Sixth Ranger Battalion and Filipino guerrillas, rescued 513 "gaunt and ragged men, mostly American survivors of the Bataan 'Death March' and Corregidor."[30] In a related article in the *Huntington Herald-Dispatch*, Mrs. Boyce Hall of 601 Seventh Avenue rejoiced at having received word that her son, Private Farley B. Hall, was one of the 513 rescued after almost three years imprisonment. Another area man, Seaman Second Class William Gerald Worley of Ashland, Kentucky was also among the rescued.[31]

"IN THE SERVICE":

Marine Sergeant William A Nance, Son of Mr. and Mrs. Russell Nance, 321 St. Louis Avenue, recently received the Purple Heart for wounds received while serving as a tail gunner aboard a bomber over New Ireland in the Pacific.

Sergeant Harold J. Clagg of Milton Route 2, has been awarded the Purple Heart for wounds received in action December 10 in Germany. A machinegun squad leader with the Third Army, Sergeant Clagg previously received the Combat Infantryman Badge for exemplary conduct in action. He is the son of Mr. and Mrs. T. E. Clagg of Milton Route 3.

Captain Robert E. Hatton, husband of Mrs. Julia Anne Hatton of Catlettsburg, has returned to this country after serving as a staff officer with a Marine Corps dive bomber squadron in the South and Central Pacific. He is a graduate of Matewan, W.Va. High School and Marshall College.

Marine Corporal Samuel A. Midkiff Jr., son of Mrs. Neva Midkiff, 2812 North Staunton Road, recently was promoted to that rank in the Pacific. He participated in the Marianas campaign.

Ensign William Haskell Tidman, whose wife and daughter reside at 836 Eighth Street, has been promoted to lieutenant (j. g.). He has served for more than a year as commander of a Navy patrol yacht in the Pacific.

Gunner's Mate Second Class Orville Lee Wintz, son of Mr. and Mrs. James G. Wintz, 6145 Ohio River Road, has entered the advanced Naval Training School at San Diego, Calif. He received five Bronze Stars for participating in major battles in the South Pacific during 21 months of sea duty. A brother, Private First Class Charles T. Wintz, is on duty in Italy. His father served two years with the Rainbow Division in France in World War I.

Private Blaine Vititoe, veteran of three years' service in the Pacific theatre, is visiting his parents, Mr. and Mrs. Joe Vititoe of Ona, and will report soon to Miami, Fla., for a new assignment.

Corporal Hobert E. Dawson, grandson of Mr. and Mrs. S. A. Davis, 47 A Street, is in a hospital in France after receiving wounds in action. He has been overseas for 17 months and has been awarded five Bronze Stars for participating in major battles.

Marine Sergeant Mack Herndon, assigned to Cherry Point, N.C., arrived yesterday to spend a 15-day leave with his parents, Mr. and Mrs. John W. Herndon, 1101 Ninth Avenue.

Private Robert L. Templeton, husband of Mrs. Irene Templeton, 339 Singer Terrace, has been awarded the Combat Infantryman Badge for action in Italy. He is a member of the 361st Regiment of the 91st Division in the Fifth Army.

Sergeant Alva V. Lewis, husband of Mrs. Ruby J. Lewis, 2216 Tenth Avenue, also a member of the 361st Regiment, has been awarded the Bronze Star for heroic achievement on the Fifth Army front. He was a private at the time of the action for which he was decorated and is now an assistant squad leader.

Private First Class Paul L. Morrison and Private Henry Morrison, sons of Mr. and Mrs. Irving Morrison of Barboursville, recently were reunited in England after a two-year separation.

Captain Martin B. Roush, husband of Mrs. Sarah Louise Roush, 949 Madison Avenue, when not piloting a torpedo plane on anti-submarine patrols in the Guam area, practices his hobby of carpentry. He and his buddies built a clubhouse with all the comforts of home. Two years ago, Captain Roush was credited with scoring a direct hit on a Japanese battleship in the South Pacific.

Glenna: *February 3rd Saturday – Washed, cleaned the house good. Baked a cake. Moderating some.*

Allied bombing continued to decimate Berlin. The Nazis seemed unable to face defeat.

"IN THE SERVICE":

Private First Class Jack Lee Howe, son of Mrs. Mary Howe, 69 Adams Avenue, who has served the past two years with an infantry unit in the Southwest Pacific, is now hospitalized in Hawaii. His mother was informed that Private Howe will be returned to this country following his release from the hospital. He has been in the Army for three years.

Earl Click, son of Mr. and Mrs. J. M. Click, 529 Tenth Street, has returned to his station after spending a leave with his parents. A veteran of four years' service in the Navy, he was one of the first Huntington service men reported missing in action. He graduated recently from stenography school at Sampson Naval Base, N.Y.

Private Lester Swann, son of Eustace Swann, 1934 Twelfth Avenue, has been awarded the Philippines Liberation ribbon by the commanding officer of his infantry division. Previously awarded the Asiatic-Pacific ribbon and the Expert Infantryman Badge, Private Swann has been overseas for more than a year.

Lieutenant and Mrs. R. W. Donaldson, son of Mr. and Mrs. J. Harold Donaldson, 1375 Thirteenth Street, has returned to San Bruno, Calif. after visiting his parents. He was serving aboard a ship in the vicinity of Manila when it was taken by the Japanese.

Private First Class William (Tiny) Bowen of Huntington and a lieutenant recently drove their jeep out of range of German artillery fire by moving every 40 seconds and then taking cover. They had discovered that the enemy barrage was resumed every 40 seconds and drove their jeep between shelling.

Marine Sergeant William J. Paul, 749 Third Street, recently received the Purple Heart somewhere in the Pacific after suffering wounds when struck in the right arm by three fragments of a Jap mortar shell.

Private Jean Leith, 411 Bridge Street, is serving at Wright Field, O. as an Airwac. After receiving an honorable discharge from the WAC, she enlisted again last October.

Private Howard Beheler recently wrote his father, Sergeant Harry Beheler of the Huntington Police Department, that he had visited the sergeant's brother, Claude Beheler, in the Marianas. Private Beheler is in the Army Air Forces and his uncle is with a Seabee unit.

Captain David T. Myles of Barboursville is scheduled to attend the full track vehicle course at the Field Artillery School, Fort Sill, Okla. He is the son of Mrs. Amanda C. Myles of Winchester, Virginia.

WAC Private Sarah Adkins, 4760 Route 60, who has a son serving overseas with an infantry unit, recently was promoted to private first class at Pyote Field, Tex. Her son, Private Elmer M. Adkins, was transferred from the AAF to the infantry. A sister, WAC Private Mary Blevins, is stationed at Spence Field, Ga.

Corporal William H. Stepp Jr., son of Mr. and Mrs. William H. Stepp of Kermit, W.Va., has been promoted to sergeant with the AAF in the European theatre. He is a radio operator-gunner aboard a Flying Fortress operating from England.

Staff Sergeant Gilba A. Kitchen Jr., son of Mr. and Mrs. Gilba Kitchen, 311 West Eleventh Avenue, who served for 31 months in the China-Burma-India theatre, is in Miami, Fla. for reassignment.

Technical Sergeant Paul L. Eastridge of Mann, W.Va., commanded an infantry platoon which was instrumental in repulsing a German counter-attack and resulted in American troops moving into Ludweiler, Germany on December 9.

Glenna: *February 4th Sunday – Stayed at home. Cooked dinner. Had green beans, potato salad, corn, peaches, and fruit nut cake. Rupert writing on his story, Dawson has an awful cold. Ever Bias buried in Shelton Cemetery at West Hamlin. Rain, sleet.*

The beans, corn, and peaches would have been home-grown and canned the previous summer. Potatoes were stored in our cool and dry cellar back of the house on the bank of Buckhorn Creek. The cellar was approximately eight by twelve feet, walled with stones and covered by a tin roof. Rough wooden shelves held glass canning jars.

"Rupert writing on his story" surprised me. I started to write at an early age, but assumed my pastime went unnoticed.

There was a brief reference for "Ever Leona Bias Gill wife of B. S. Bias" on "The West Virginia Division of Culture and History" website.[32] The information was up-to-date in May, 2020.

The *Huntington Herald-Advertiser* published the War Department list of names of sixty-six West Virginians killed in action. Some area men listed were, Private Okey L. Blankenship, Huntington; Private First Class Lawrence Church, Panther; Private First Class Morland H. Floyd, Lesage; Private First Class Edwin J. Morgan, Huntington; Private First Class George W. Davis, Point Pleasant.[33]

Also, in the *Huntington Herald-Advertiser*: "First Lieutenant James F. 'Teensy' Hensley, 23, son of Mr. and Mrs. Fred C. Hensley, 440 Washington Avenue, has been missing in action since Jan. 15, over Germany... Pilot of a P-47 Thunderbolt fighter plane, Lieutenant Hensley went overseas last March and was based subsequently in England, France, and Belgium. A graduate of Huntington High School and a former Marshall College student, Lieutenant Hensley was well known in local athletic circles, having been a Golden Gloves lightweight champion and a basketball player with the Pony Express."[34]

Roosevelt, Churchill, and Stalin began discussion at the Yalta Conference about conducting the final phases of the war and the eventual division of Europe.[35]

"WITH THE COLORS":

Corporal Jack H. Moore, son of Mr. and Mrs. William E. Moore, 2542 Third Avenue, is a member of the small advance unit that established one of the newest Seventh Air Force bases in the Marianas Islands. A teletype operator with a heavy bombardment group, he has served overseas for two years and four months without leave.

Seaman First Class William M. Tawney, who has been serving on an LST (landing ship, tanks) in Atlantic and Mediterranean waters for the past eight months, has arrived here to spend a 30-day leave with his wife, Mrs. Norma Louise Tawney and two children, 706 Thirty-first Street, and his mother, Mrs. Norah E. Tawney, 287 Roby Road. A veteran of several of the European invasions, he will report to Norfolk, Va. February 20 for reassignment.

Seaman First Class Irma F. Miller, daughter of Mrs. Edith Miller, 2627 Guyan Avenue, was called home from her Washington D.C. station last week because of the death of a grandmother, Mrs. Christiana Chirgwin...

Ensign Robert B. Drexler, son of Mr. and Mrs. Arthur A. Drexler, 908 Ninth Avenue, is spending a 10-day leave with his parents while en route to Norfolk, Va. for assignment to active duty after completing an aerial communications course at Harvard University, Boston, Mass. A Marshall College graduate, he served as regimental commander at the Boston school...

Robert A. Gesner, seaman first class (gunner's mate), son of Mr. and Mrs. Mort Gesner, 2843 Collis Avenue, was home on a five-day leave after graduation from gunnery school, Pontiac, Mich. Seaman Gesner left Thursday for Shoemaker, Calif, for further training.

Staff Sergeant William Mitchell has been missing in action in France since Jan. 6. He is the son of Mr. and Mrs. M. Lawrence Mitchell of Kenova, and husband of Mrs. Sybil Mitchell of Huntington.

Captain Clark M. McGhee has been awarded the Bronze Star for "Heroic and Meritorious achievement" at a 12th AAF P-47 Thunderbolt base in Italy where he serves as operations officer. He is the son of Mr. and Mrs. E. F. McGhee of Hurricane, W.Va.

Members of a Railway Operating Battalion serving in France include Private First Class Hollie P. Wess, 1046 Sixth Avenue; Private Paul E. Notter, 2655 Guyan Avenue; Private Norman F. Bexfield, 2839 Overlook Drive, and Sergeant Jack E. Crites, 455 ½ Seventh Avenue of Huntington, and Corporal Howard A. Butts, Martinsburg; Corporal Larry L. Lloyd,

Montgomery, and Private Eustace A. Chadwick, Whites Creek.

Major Edwin G. Hundley, in command of the War Department's Regional Office 9 for Dependency Benefits at San Francisco, Calif. was promoted from the rank of captain Jan. 25. A former Huntington attorney, he is the son of Mr. and Mrs. T. E. Hundley of Huntington. Major Hundley and his wife reside at Palo Alto, Calif.

Staff Sergeant Robert G. Black, 212 Pine Street, is entitled to wear the Distinguished Unit Badge, He is serving with an A-20 Havoc, 47th Bombardment Group in Italy...

Private Robert C. Wilmink, 705 Jackson Avenue, is now stationed at Chanute Field, Ill. and is studying advanced electronics and radar. He recently completed his training in the Army Air Forces as a radio mechanic at Truax Field, Madison, Wis.

Second Lieutenant George E. Gold is a co-pilot of a B-24 Liberator with a 15th Air Force bomber group... He is now authorized to wear the Distinguished Unit Badge with one bronze cluster. He is the son of Mr. and Mrs. John W. Gold, 136 Norway Avenue.

Private First Class Richard Stewart has been missing in action since Jan. 11, according to word received from the War Department by his wife, Mrs. Anna Fay Stewart, 1845 College Avenue. Prior to his entrance into the service last June, Private Stewart was employed by the American Car & Foundry Co.

Flight Officer Frank Darwin McLaughlin received his appointment and silver pilot's wings Thursday upon graduation from Moody Army Air Field, Ga. He is the son of Mr. and Mrs. J. T. McLaughlin, 5743 Pea Ridge Road.

First Lieutenant Donald Sprouse, son of Mrs. Stella Sprouse of Fourteenth Street, has been assigned to bombardment instructors' school at Midland, Tex. following a tour of overseas duty with the Eighth Air Force. Other Huntington airmen returned from overseas duty also stationed in that area are Lieutenants Ralph Sudderth, Robert Stalnaker and William Bowen.

Private First Class Elmer E. Mays, 21, son of Paul E. Mays, 509 Bridge Street, has been honorably discharged from the Army for medical reasons at Scott Field, Ill., parent radio school of the AAF Training Command. Private Mays saw action in the South Pacific and has a brother, Paul A. Mays, a sailor, now serving in New Guinea.

Glenna: *February 5th Monday – Cooked for school. Served green beans, dried peaches, bacon bread and butter. Clear and very muddy. Ironed at night. Read where Everett Belomy was killed in Belgium.*

The casualty lists often had names of people we knew: Corporal Everett Bellomy, age 32, was killed November 3, 1944. He is buried in Spears Cemetery, Lincoln County, West Virginia.[36]

"IN THE SERVICE":

Earl Mayo, husband of Mrs. Betty Mayo, 1680 Kessler Avenue, has been promoted to technical sergeant at a troop carrier base in the European theatre where he is a C-47 crew chief. He is the son of Mr. and Mrs. Thomas Mayo, 1601 Arthur Street.

Serving with the 727th Railway Operating Battalion in France are Sergeant Edgar Smith, 3602 Brandon Road; Corporal Bert Hatten of Pritchard and Private First Class Howard E. Moore of Williamson. Their outfit saw service in the Tunisian, Sicilian and Italian campaigns.

Staff Sergeant Charles Christian, who was wounded in action in France has been awarded the Purple Heart at a hospital in England ... according to word received by his mother, Mrs. Mary DeBord Christian, 1259 Jefferson Avenue. He was a member of the Vinson football team and was employed by the Owens-Illinois Glass Co. prior to entering the Army. A brother, Seaman First Class Joe Shelby Christian, has been in the Navy more than two years and is now in the Southwest Pacific area.

Private Mack Hargis, son of Mr. and Mrs. John Hargis of Ranger, W.Va., was wounded in action December 18 in Belgium and is now hospitalized in Belgium... A veteran of nine months overseas service. he has received the Purple Heart, three battle stars and the Good Conduct Medal. His wife and daughter reside at Carbon, W.Va. A sister, Mrs. Obie Cheuvront, lives at 1812 Third Avenue here.

Private Elmer R. Bird, son of Mr. and Mrs. Andy Bird of Hurricane, is serving with an Army Air Forces engineer unit in Italy which supplies airfields with aviation gasoline. His organization operates an important link of the petroleum distribution network used by AAF units in the Mediterranean theatre.

At Keesler Field, Miss., to undergo processing preparatory to aviation cadet training are Private Charles G. Bennett, son of Mrs. Kathleen Bennett, 2539 Third Avenue, and Private Hampton L. Austin, son of Mrs. H. B. Austin, 1401 Washington Boulevard.

Aviation Radioman Second Class Charles R. Johnson, son of Mrs. Anna Marie Johnson, 1606 Eighteenth Street, has returned form a tour of duty in the Pacific, where he was radioman and tunnel gunner aboard a torpedo plane. He participated in strikes against the Marianas, Wake, Okinawa, Jima, Formosa and the Philippines.

Private Jess O. Baker, son of Mrs. Eva Hess of Huntington, has returned to this country after serving for 10 months in the European theatre with an engineer outfit.

Lieutenant Elmer R. Robinson Jr., husband of Mrs. Josephine Pauley Robinson, 229 Bellevue Road, who received the Distinguished Flying Cross with cluster and Air Medal with three clusters, is now on duty at Carlsbad Field, N.M. He is a son of Mr. and Mrs. Elmer R. Robinson, 158 Sycamore Street.

Second Lieutenant Nancy B. Taylor, daughter of Mr. and Mrs. Harvey C. Taylor of Washington Boulevard, has been promoted to first lieutenant at Robins Field, Ga., where she is an administrative officer.

Recipients of the Combat Infantryman Badge are Technician Fourth Grade Barnette D. Bethel, son of Mrs. Helen D. Bethel, 922 Twelfth Street, and Private Roe M. Collins, son of Mrs. Ollie Collins, Barboursville Route 2. They are with the 81st (Wildcat) Infantry Division in the Pacific area.

Private Eva T. Whitehill, daughter of Mr. and Mrs. W. C. Peters of Mullens, W.Va., has been transferred from Fort Des Moines, Ia. to a WAC assignment at Nichols General Hospital, Louisville, Ky.

Private Paul M. Bryan of Huntington and Corporal Oliver C. Kesler Jr. of Hinton are serving with the 337th Field Artillery Battalion in Italy.

Glenna: [Tuesday] *February 6th – Cooked for school. We had baked beans, bread, butter, boiled potato, slaw. Cloudy and very muddy. I wrote to Kanawha County Schools.*

Mother's "Kanawha County Schools" reference resurrected a memory. She frequently talked about returning to teaching, but thirteen intervening years had brought changes to public education in West Virginia. Most one- and two-room schools were gone; consolidation was the norm and the state required more college education for teachers. Sadly, her time had passed, although she may have had difficulty accepting it. Anyway, taking a job in Kanawha County would have taken us from the farm and interrupted our way of life.

The War in Brief: On the Western Front, U.S. troops penetrated the difficult Siegfried Line and two Roer River dams were seized. Russian troops moved to within thirty-two miles of Berlin. In Italy, the Fifth Army recaptured Gellicano, but the Germans still had strong defenses in the Bologna area. On the Pacific Front, 1,350 more allied prisoners were liberated in Manila.[37]

Two more area casualties were reported: "Second Lieutenant William Weller Mossman, 21, son of Mr. and Mrs. Maurice E. Mossman of U.S. Route 60 near Barboursville, and Staff Sergeant Eustace Butcher Jr., 19, formerly of Barboursville, have been killed in action, it was reported yesterday."[38]

"IN THE SERVICE":

Lieutenant Stephen Wolfe, son of Mr. and Mrs. Harry Wolfe, 605 Tenth Avenue, who was wounded at Aachen and was later hospitalized in England, arrived in New York City Sunday night. He telephoned his parents that he would be assigned to a hospital in this country for further treatment and hopes to visit in Huntington soon.

Serving with the 756 Railway Shop Battalion in France are Staff Sergeant Otho B. Triplett, 17 Twenty-fifth Street; Technical Sergeant Charles A. Foster, 1314 Fifth Avenue; Sergeant Norman S. McCallister, 2816 Cottage Street, and Staff Sergeant Grandville S. Fisher of Lavalette.

Private Anna L. Clay, daughter of Mr. and Mrs. V. L. Clay, 2487 Collis Avenue, has been transferred from Fort Des Moines, Ia. to Fort Myer, Va.

Captain Jack Pancake, 2102 Fifth Avenue, recently narrowly escaped injury when Japanese planes strafed within a foot of him in Western Yunnan in China.

Technical Sergeant Paul A. Ross, husband of Mrs. Patsy Ross, 2933 Washington Boulevard, has arrived at a redistribution station at Miami, Fla. after completing 28 missions as gunner-engineer aboard a bomber in the European area. He received the Air Medal with three Oak Leaf Clusters.

Second Lieutenant Joseph F. Hollywood Jr., husband of Mrs. Imogene Hollywood, 523 Ninth Avenue, has arrived at Miami after serving as a B-24 pilot in the European theatre.

Sergeant James V. Fowler. 228 ½ Fourth Avenue is company clerk at an ordnance depot in England. He is a member of the 250th Heavy Automotive Maintenance Company.

William L. Womack, 2976 Third Avenue, a Marshall College freshman and graduate of East High School, has qualified for entrance into the Navy Radio Technical School at Chicago.

Flight Officer Donald S. Stinson, son of W. L. Stinson, 1701 Crestmont Drive, last week received his pilot's wings at Moore Field, Tex.

Paul L. Stotler, 313 West Twenty-second Street, has been commissioned a second lieutenant and awarded pilot's wings at La Junta Field, Calif. He is a Central High School graduate.

Glenna: *February 7th Wednesday Cooked again. Served vegetable soup, slaw, boiled eggs, bread and butter, and onions. Rupert went to club meeting at Dejarnette's that night. Cloudy.*

I was active in the 4-H Club. Scott Dejarnette's home and farm on Tyler Creek Road was about a mile away. Scott had a daughter, Madeline, who was a couple years older than me.

A *Huntington Herald-Dispatch* article reported, "Seaman Joseph Mackey, a member of the U.S. Coast guard and son of Dr. and Mrs. W. K. Mackey of Chesapeake, is missing in action... He is a graduate of St. Joseph's High School and attended Marshall College prior to entering the service." The same article also reported that Lieutenant Edwin Nelson was in Bilibid Prison in the Philippines. His parents, Mr. and Mrs. C. P. Nelson, lived at 1330 Sixth Avenue. The family was "awaiting word concerning his status following the American liberation at that camp." His brother, Captain J. H. Nelson, "was injured in India and is a patient at Walter Reed Hospital."[39]

"IN THE SERVICE":

Miss Doreene Eckley, daughter of Mr. and Mrs. Roy Eckley, 1666 Eleventh Avenue, has been promoted to specialist first class at her WAVES station in Washington. She is assigned to the photogrammetry section of the Navy Department's hydrographic office. She is a graduate of Central High School and Marshall College.

Lieutenant James B. Rich, son of J. B. Rich of Huntington, recently was praised by an Army publication for his courage and leadership despite wounds received in action in the European theatre. After suffering a leg wound, the lieutenant refused to be evacuated until his infantry unit completed an attack on a group of houses...

Hubert C. Hodges has been promoted to captain in the Huntington district office of the U.S. Engineers... Captain Hodges is a graduate of Central High School and has been with the engineers since 1939.

Corporal William J. Kerr, a St. Joseph's High School graduate, has arrived in Dutch New Guinea, according to word received by his parents, Mr. and Mrs. Charles Kerr, 1055 Nineteenth Street.

Mr. and Mrs. J. L. Owens of Kenova Route 1 have received word that their son, Corporal John F. Owens, has arrived safely in the Philippines. He has served for 30 months in the South Pacific. His wife, Mrs. Ruby Owens, resides in Huntington.

Sergeant Harry H. Suiter, son of Mr. and Mrs. John Suiter, 13 Twenty-fifth Street, is enrolled in a B-29 Superfortress remote control turret school at Lowry Field, Colo.

Lieutenant (j. g.) Monte Scott Harkins of Prestonsburg, Ky., is spending a leave with an aunt, Mrs. Iley Browning of Ashland. His mother, Mrs. Scott Harkins, and brother, Donald Davidson Harkins, are with him in Ashland. He served overseas for 19 months and participated in action at the Anzio and Salerno beachheads in Italy.

Glenna: *February 8th Thursday – Cooked again. Had pinto beans, bread, butter, onions, corn, and oranges. Snowed all day. Very muddy.*

Bill Click (Cabell County Agriculture Agent) in his column "Plan Your Garden," recommended planting new varieties like "Mary Washington Asparagus, Detroit Red beets, Copenhagen Market cabbage, and Danvers Half Long carrots."[40]

The *Huntington Herald-Dispatch* reported, "A Liberty ship launched at Jacksonville. Fla., has been named for James H. Counts, formerly of Lincoln County, who served in World Wars I and II. He served in the present war with the Merchant Marine until his death two years ago. His ship was torpedoed by a German submarine and Mr. Counts was awarded posthumously the Mariner Medal for heroism."[41]

Area men reported killed in action: Private First Class Millard Jordan of Huntington, Corporal Henry Kelso formerly of Huntington, Staff Sergeant Ralph A Daniels of Wayne, Seaman Second Class James Raymond Finley of Huntington. Sergeant Paul N. Haas of Ironton, Ohio was killed in a train wreck in France.[42]

Missing in action: Private Stannard Carlyle Adams of Guyandotte and Lieutenant Robert Elkana Harrold of Huntington.[43]

Paraguay declared war on Germany.

"IN THE SERVICE":

Lieutenant Max E. Weeks and Private William F. Weeks, sons of Mr. and Mrs. E. F. Weeks, 1213 Fourth Avenue, have trained at 10 Army camps. A brother, Robert L. Weeks, is serving in the Philippines. Lieutenant and Private Weeks expect to hold a reunion soon at Alexandria, Va., where the latter is stationed.

Warrant Officer and Mrs. Richard Holtzworth have returned to his station after visiting their families here. He has been in the Navy for more than six years and served a tour of duty in the Southwest Pacific. Warrant Officer Holtzworth is a son of Mr. Charles J. Holtzworth and his wife is a daughter of Mr. and Mrs. Allen Thompson. The Navy officer and his wife are graduates of Central High School.

Lieutenant and Mrs. Paul Ross Shawver and daughter Sandra are spending a leave here from Fort Monmouth, N.J. Lieutenant Shawver is a son of Mr. and Mrs. M. R. Shawver, 1320 Ninth Avenue, and Mrs. Shawver is a daughter of Dr. and Mrs. E. M. Burkhardt, 1934 Eighteenth Street.

Private Charles P. Miller, husband of Mrs. Betty Dailey Miller of Huntington, has completed a 12-weeks general surveying course at the Engineer School, Fort Belvoir, Va. A former employee of the International Nickel Co., he is a son of Mrs. Eva Miller, 506 Bridge Street.

First Lieutenant Owen C. Martin, an Army chaplain and former pastor of the Westmoreland Methodist Church, was in Huntington yesterday en route to a new assignment. His wife and three children are residing in Severn, Md.

Glenna: *February 9th Friday – Cooked again. Had bread and butter, meat loaf, cabbage salad, potatoes. Gaynelle came up and helped me. Weather fair and warm. O.P.A. dropped eggs from 55 to 38 cents.*

Mother sold butter and eggs, so O.P.A. pricing mattered to her.

In local sports, Coach H. C. (Twenty) Lantz's Huntington East Highlanders defeated the Barboursville Pirates, coached by Jackson Stover, 42–21 in a very physical basketball game.[44]

The British 26th India Division captured Ramree Island, an important Japanese Base.[45]

"IN THE SERVICE":

Staff Sergeant John D. Greig, husband of Mrs. Dorcas D. Greig, 2547 Collis Avenue, has been awarded the Bronze Star Medal at a 15th Air Force station in Italy for meritorious and outstanding services as an administrative clerk. He has served with his squadron in North Ireland, England, Algeria, Tunisia, Sicily, Corsica and Italy. Sergeant Greig is a son of Mr. and Mrs. Arthur D. Greig, 317 Wilson Court.

Lieutenant Charles F. Shearer, son of Mr. and Mrs. C. H. Shearer, 2136 Eleventh Avenue, is serving in England with a signal battalion. He is a graduate of Central High School and Georgia School of Technology. Lieutenant Shearer received his commission ... at Fort Monmouth, N.J. He has been in the service for two years.

Private First Class Chesley B. Payne, husband of Mrs. Florence Payne of Fort Gay, was one of a group of combat casualties to arrive at the general hospital at Camp Butner, N.C. He served for six months in the European theatre with an infantry unit. A brother, William W. Payne, is now in the European area.

Private First Class Clifford Effingham, husband of Mrs. Bernice Effingham of Huntington, is a ward attendant at the Regional Hospital, Fort Knox, Ky. A son of Mrs. Ervin Effingham, 239 Davis Street, he was a machinist for the Owen-Illinois Glass Co. prior to entering the Army.

Glenna: *February 10th Saturday – Weather bright and warm until 3:30. Rain that night. Washed a big washing. Cleaned up everything. Papa and Dawson worked on hog pen until noon. Rupert and Shirrell had a fight.*

Shirrell Porter, a couple years older than me, lived on the next farm up Lyle's Branch. His father, Gilbert Porter, was a successful farmer with several sons and one daughter. The "fight,"

as I recall, consisted of dancing around in a circle and punching each other on the shoulder until we finally shook hands and walked away. The reason for the confrontation is long forgotten. Sherrill remained a good friend.

Huntington has called itself "A City of Churches." On this Saturday, the newspaper section "Services in Churches Sunday," listed sixty-eight area churches. (An unofficial number of Huntington churches at that time was 110.) The denominations listed this day were Baptist, Christian, Christian Scientist, Church of God, Congregational, Free Methodist, Fundamental, Lutheran, Methodist, Nazarene, Pilgrim Holiness, Presbyterian, and United Brethren.[46]

Church-related: "The Huntington Council of Church Women has adopted plans for the enlargement of the Eighteenth Street Mission program ... Churches affiliated with the council will provide speakers and other talent, drawn from voluntary workers for a worship period... The Rev. A. R. Young, pastor of Emmanuel Methodist Church, will conduct the devotional

services tomorrow at 3:15 P.M. The committee in charge includes, Mrs. J. S. Weaver, chairman, Mrs. Joe Lusk, Mrs. W. J. Mott and Mrs. Harry C. Criser."[47]

The *New Revised Standard* version of the Bible was finally complete and ready for publication under the official approval of forty-four Protestant denominations.[48]

Glenna: *February 11ᵗʰ Sunday – Didn't go to Sunday School. Mrs. Rousey came up. Drewie was here. We went to church that night. Mr. Scragg preached... Clear and windy.*

I think she was referring to the weather and not to Mr. Scragg's sermon.

Drewie Morrison, Dawson's younger brother, lived in Logan. His executive job with a gas company required frequent travel to Huntington. He often visited his mother and us.

Five area men were reported killed in action. Four were from Huntington: Private First Class Richard L. Nibert, Private First Class Clinton L. Smith, Private First Class Richard M. Hedrick, and Sergeant Charles A. Davis. Sergeant James F. Milum of Kenova was also killed.[49]

"WITH THE COLORS":

Aviation Cadet Robert E. Frazier, son of Mr. and Mrs. H. P. Frazier, 1606 Chestnut Street, Kenova, has reported to the Army Air Field at Greenville, Miss., for flight training.

While defending a building from a German counter-attack with his infantry unit in Luxembourg, Private First Class Donald L. Rice, 24, of 1243 Eighteenth Street, was wounded in the right shoulder. He is now recovering in an Army station hospital in England, where he has been awarded the Purple Heart... Private Rice is the son of Mrs. Mary H. Stephenson. He was employed by the E. W. Mootz Bakery before entering the Army.

Lieutenant Clarence S. Nelson has been assigned to the George Field Troop Carrier Base for instruction in troop transport. He is the son of Mr. and Mrs. Clarence S. Nelson Sr.

Seaman First Class Clifford Brammer has returned to New York for reassignment after spending a 15-day furlough here with his family at 3507 Third Avenue.

Private Willard C. Hall, son of Mr. and Mrs. C. J. Hall of Barboursville, has returned to a new assignment at Fort Meade, Md., after spending 12 days with his family.

Staff Sergeant Johnny Johnson, son of Stan Johnson, 219 West Second Street, is serving in England as an engineer with a combat battalion.

Private Jimmy Graham, son of Mr. and Mrs. J. E. Graham of Huntington, was home on furlough last week from Camp Roberts, Ark. A rifleman, he will report to Camp Ward, Calif., this week.

First Lieutenant William Dugan Steinbrecher, son of Mr. William Steinbrecher of Guyandotte, received promotion to that rank from second lieutenant recently in Luxembourg.

Private Clifton D. Ellis, son of Mrs. Myrtle Ellis, 1257 Twenty-sixth Street, who was wounded in action in France and was confined to an army hospital for five months because of his wounds, has been released from the hospital and is serving as a military policeman in Wales.

Seaman First Class Marian F. Forester, daughter of Mr. and Mrs. Raymond Forester, 1425 Third Avenue, has returned to her station at Vero Beach, Fla., after a seven-day leave spent here with her parents.

Glenna: *February 12th Monday – Cooked again. Had peas, cheese, and cabbage. Clear weather but awfully muddy.*

A desperate German government had begun drafting women sixteen through sixty years of age.[50]

Peru declared war on Germany.

"IN THE SERVICE":

Among those serving with a maintenance company of the 712th Railway Operating Battalion in France are Private Cecil Mobley, 1329 Monroe Avenue; Private First Class John R. Stennett of Hinton and Private Loren L. Hatten of Kenova.

Kenneth N. Gallaher, husband of Mrs. Violet R. Gallaher of Huntington, has been promoted from second to first lieutenant with a medical corps unit in the Panama Canal Zone.

Private Reva Lee Courts, daughter of Mr. and Mrs. Lonnie E. Turley of Hamlin, is stationed at the Pine Bluff, Ark. Chemical Warfare Arsenal. Her husband, Private Percy Courts, is stationed at Fort Story, Va., and a brother, Private Willie R. Turley, is in the European theatre.

Glenna: *February 13th Tuesday – Cooked for school. Served salmon casserole, soup, bread and butter. Put the pigs in their new pen.*

Thirty-six people were killed and 200 were injured by tornadoes in Mississippi and Alabama.[51]

Allied forces bombed Dresden, Germany. In the Pacific, American planes continued bombing runs on Corregidor and Bataan.[52]

"IN THE SERVICE":

Private First Class Olen Vance is spending a leave in Huntington after serving for 27 months in the Southwest Pacific theatre with a paratrooper unit. Now visiting a sister, Mrs. Ruth Whited, 328 Bernard Street, he will report ... to Miami, Fla. His wife, Mrs. Betty Vance, will accompany him to Miami.

Seaman First Class Fred C. Morris has returned to Brooklyn, N.Y. after visiting his wife, Mrs. Bessie Morris, 1326 Fourth Avenue, and his parents, Mr. and Mrs. C. R. Morris of Eleventh Avenue. He returned recently from a tour of duty in the European theatre.

Seaman First Class Claude U. Barbour recently spent a leave with his wife, the former Miss Jean Scott of Huntington, and his patents, Mr. and Mrs. F. U. Barbour, 426 Ten-and-a-half Street. He served for eight months in the European area and participated in the invasion of Normandy.

Fireman First Class Herbert M. Irby, son of Herbert M. Irby, 826 Twenty-first Street, is serving with a Seventh Fleet PT boat patrol which recently destroyed four enemy coastal freighters in a running night battle in the Central Philippines. He has been in the Southwest Pacific area for eight months and has participated in 22 combat patrols in the New Guinea and Philippines areas.

Seaman First Class Emmett W. McNeely of the Coast Guard, 230 Indiana Street, is serving at an advanced Coast Guard war base in the Pacific, where he helps service vessels moving men and material to forward combat positions.

Technical Sergeant Charles L. Durfee, husband of Mrs. Betty Durfee, 2636 Guyan Avenue, has been assigned to duty as a combat radio instructor in England after participating in more than 30 major bombing attacks with the Eighth Air Force. He holds the Air Medal with four Oak Leaf Clusters.

Corporal Hobert E. Dawson, son of Mrs. Ethel Workman of Huntington, is a patient at Stark General Hospital, Charleston, S.C., after 18 months service in the European theater. He received the Bronze Star, Purple heart, European theatre ribbon, Combat Infantryman Badge and Good Conduct Medal.

Corporal Hansel H. Adkins, son of Mr. and Mrs. John B. Adkins, Branchland Route 1, recently completed an orientation course at an Air Service Command station in England. [Hansel is the son of my great uncle, John B. Adkins.]

Second Lieutenant Guinn B. Helmick, husband of Mrs. Laura Mae Helmick, 628 Thirteenth Street, has been promoted to first lieutenant at an Eighth AAF bomber station in England. He is a Flying Fortress navigator.

Corporal Albert A. Wright, son of H. V. Wright of Third Street, Ceredo, has been promoted to sergeant with a Flying Fortress unit in England. He is a ball turret gunner.

Major Charles L. Stafford, husband of Mrs. Yvonne Stafford, 708 West Sixth Street, who is a fighter pilot in the European theatre [and who] shot down a German ME-109 and flew 85 missions, is in Miami Beach, Fla. for reassignment. A son of Mr. and Mrs. Charles F. Stafford of Covington, Ky., Major Stafford received the Distinguished Flying Cross, the Air Medal with three Oak Leaf Clusters and the Distinguished Unit Citation.

Private Charles W. Jones, husband of Mrs. Edith Mabel Jones, 1009 Twenty-sixth Street, has arrived at Camp Wolters, Tex. for a heavy weapons course in infantry training.

Sergeant Artemis H. Cobb, husband of Mrs. Kathryn Cobb of Buffalo, W.Va., has received the Combat Infantryman Badge in Italy.

Private First Class Fred Z. Rust, husband of Mrs. Nannie Rust, 203 Thirty-third Street, is serving as a barber at a hospital in England.

Corporal Newton B. Parker, husband of Mrs. Mary Lee Parker, 821 Seventh Street, and Corporal Leonard C. Bruce, 1229 Adams Avenue, have arrived in England with a Strategic Air Force unit.

Second Lieutenant Clyde Harold Dempsey of Williamson Route 1 has been promoted to first lieutenant...

Glenna: *February 14th Wednesday – Cooked again. Served cookies, kale, boiled eggs, bread, butter, and apples. Beautiful day with some wind. Arnold Morrison's house burned down. Nettie helped me with the dishes.*

Arnold Morrison was one of Dawson's distant cousins. The house was located about two miles north of Salt Rock within the big bend (Henchman Bend) of the river. Salt Rock had no fire department, so the result of this fire was a total loss.

Nettie Bias was my fifth grade teacher at Salt Rock Elementary. She had been Mother's teacher years before. I remember her as strict, but effective. She had a positive influence on my teaching career.

A Huntington soldier, Private Lloyd D. Corum, who had received the Purple Heart for wounds in action in France on October 5, was wounded a second time on January 21. He was in a hospital in the European theatre. His wife, Mrs. Macil Corum, lived at 613 Baltimore Street. He was a nephew of Miss Katherine Taylor of Huntington.[53]

"IN THE SERVICE":

Private First Class George P. Fotos, son of Mr. and Mrs. C. P. Fotos, 610 Twelfth Avenue, has been graduated as an aerial gunner from the Army Air Forces Flexible Gunnery School at Laredo Field, Tex...

Corporal George C. Seager, husband of Mrs. Drewcilla Seager, 1250 Fourth Avenue, is serving with the Army somewhere in India. He is the son of Mrs. Mabel Seager of the Fourth Avenue address...

Members of the 51st Evacuation Hospital staff in France include Corporal George E. Hensley, 243 Adams Avenue, ward attendant, and Sergeant Vernon J. Barrett of Dehue, ward master.

Private First Class Mervin C. Ellis of Hurricane has been awarded the Bronze Star for heroic achievement action in Italy. He voluntarily made his way to the company command post to secure help while intensive enemy fire blasted about him. Private Ellis is with the 34th (Red Bull) Division.

Seaman Second Class Carl Bechdolt, son of Mr. and Mrs. Paul Bechdolt, 418 Thirtieth Street, is attending a Navy physical education instructor school at Bainbridge, Md., after completing boot training...

Ship's Cook Third Class James Austin Owens, whose wife and son reside in Kenova, is serving in Italy after tours in Africa, Italy and Southern France.

Serving at the 238th General Hospital in France are Private William E. Hibbard, 617 ½ Eighth Street; Second Lieutenant Vera J. Barlow, Gary; Second Lieutenant Louise C. Haga, Kimball; Second Lieutenant Audrey E. Volker, Logan, and Private Thomas R. Hatfield, Mount Gay.

With the 55th Medical Battalion in France are Corporal Samuel S. Grose of Welch and Private First Class Ancil Adkins of Williamson.

Private First Class Paul B. Brammer, 3129 Fifth Avenue, has received the Combat Infantryman Badge in Italy. He is with the 88th (Blue Devil) Division.

Staff Sergeant Walter H. Mays, son of W. A. Mays of Barboursville, has received the Bronze Star Medal for meritorious service performed last fall in Southern France. According to a citation, he was "leader of a wire construction team and by his initiative and untiring devotion to duty led his team under the most adverse conditions so that they were able to provide superior wire communications from the Seventh Army" to a corps. A brother, Radioman Second Class Shelby Mays, is serving with the Navy in the Aleutians.

Seaman First Class J. E. Baker, husband of Mrs. Lida Jane Baker, 2912 Marcum Terrace, recently returned to the Armed Guard Center at New Orleans, La. after two months at sea as a member of a Navy gun crew and is now in the South Pacific.

Second Lieutenant William Robert Woefel, son of Mr. and Mrs. George H. Woefel, 412 West Twenty-fourth Street, recently received his commission and aerial wings at San Marcos Field, Tex.

Scheduled to receive boot training at Great Lakes, Ill., are William Wise, 1623 Crestmont Drive; George Young, 1423 Seventh Avenue; James Burnette, 233 Eleventh Avenue, and Lindell Stiff, 449 Seventh Avenue.

Glenna: *February 15th Thursday – Cooked again. Served Scotch stew, slaw, and apples. Very warm day for winter.*

The War Department and the War Production Board called for stepped-up production of ammunition, heavy artillery, and tanks. Spare parts were so scarce that tanks, cranes, and trucks in good working condition were sometimes stripped to get parts.[54]

Venezuela, another "come lately" country, declared war on Germany and Japan.

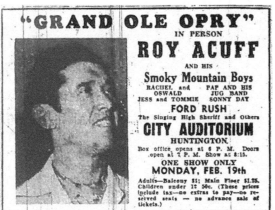

Glenna: *February 16th Friday – Cooked again. Served meat loaf, cabbage salad, kale, orange bread, and butter. Red hen died. Cool and cloudy.*

The death of a "red hen" does not at first seem important, but Mother's flock of laying hens was important to her, economically and emotionally. Some died of old age and some were killed by foxes; she mourned the death of every one.

In the Pacific, American naval vessels bombarded Tokyo and Yokohama. Our paratroopers, along with Philippine troops, landed on Corregidor Island in Manila Bay.

The Tri-State area continued to suffer agonizing losses of men and women in battle: Lieutenant Mervin E. Hemp Jr., an Army Air Force cargo pilot and son of Mr. and Mrs. M. E. Hemp of 1125 Eighth Avenue, Huntington, was reported killed in the Pacific on February 10. James Orr, formerly of Proctorville and Ironton died January 31 of wounds received in Germany.[55]

"IN THE SERVICE":

Private Benjamin T. Maynard was wounded slightly in action January 30 in Belgium, according to a message received from the War department by his mother, Mrs. Stella Maynard, 234 Staunton Street.

Sergeant Clyde W. Keeney, husband of Mrs. Wanda R. Keeney, 3421 Norwood Road, recently observed his first anniversary of service with a troop carrier unit at a base in the European theatre. He is the son of Mr. and Mrs. Edward B. Keeney of Barboursville Route 2.

Seaman First Class James F. Hickman, husband of Mrs. Naomi Hickman, 705 Baltimore Street, and three of his wife's brothers are serving overseas. Mrs. Hickman's brothers in service are Seaman First Class Daniel Boster, husband of Mrs. Fay Boster, 3911 Fourth Avenue; Machinist's Mate Third Class Jonathan Boster and Private David Boster, husband of Mrs. Betty Boster of Baltimore Street.

Sergeant Mabel Musick, daughter of Mrs. Kansas Musick of Matewan, W.Va., who has served in the Women's Army Corps since September, 1942, is now on duty in Paris, France with a signal battalion.

Staff Sergeant Luther P. Swentzel, son of Mr. and Mrs. G. R. Swentzel of Huntington, has returned to his station at Eglin Field, Fla. following an emergency leave because of the death of an uncle, Isaac C. Prince of Beckley.

Private First Class Artie B. Huntley, husband of Mrs. Louise Huntley, 518 First Street, has returned to this country after receiving wounds in action in Luxembourg. He is the son of Mr. and Mrs. A. B. Huntley of Gallaher Street. His wife is awaiting call to active duty with the WAC.

Staff Sergeant Clyde H. Workman, son of John Workman, 1638 Adams Avenue, has arrived at a redistribution station in this country after serving in the China-India-Burma theatre.

Glenna: *February 17th Sat. – Washed and cleaned the house.*

In the *Huntington Herald-Dispatch*: "Major William S. (Billy) Bowen, 30, son of Mr. and Mrs. French Bowen [French was a retired city detective and a personal friend of my grandfather Adkins.], 1612 Thirteenth Avenue, was killed when a transport plane he was piloting was shot down by Japanese anti-aircraft fire over central Luzon..." The crew members all died in the crash. They had just dropped supplies to American troops.[56]

"IN THE SERVICE":

Second Lieutenant Charles Marshall Scott, who is a prisoner of the German government, has advised his parents, Mr. and Mrs. Charles B. Scott, 257 Gallaher Street, that he is in good health and that they "should have no worries about him." The letter was dated last December 17.

First Lieutenant Don Beirne Burns, son of Mrs. B. Beirne Burns, 1026 Eleventh Street, was recently promoted to that rank with a medical corps unit at a general hospital in England.

A veteran of 10 months foreign service, he is a Marshall College graduate and was employed by the Owen-Illinois Glass Co. before entering the Army. His wife, the former Miss Rose Gullett, resides in Columbus, Ind.

Second Lieutenant Erskine H. Hatfield of Washington, D.C., son of Mr. and Mrs. T. F. Hatfield, 410 Bridge Street has ... been awarded the Air Medal by the commanding general of the 15th Air Force. As a liberator bombardier, he has flown many missions in the Mediterranean and European theatres.

First Lieutenant Hubert Cline Hodges, 1424 Seventh Avenue and Harry White of Point Pleasant have been promoted to captain, the War Department announced last night.

Sergeant Simon A. Osborne, nephew of Mrs. Bessie Andes, 48 Adams Avenue, has been awarded the Philippines Liberation ribbon by his infantry unit in the Philippines campaign.

Corporal Albert Allen, formerly of 1129 Eleventh Avenue, is serving with a combat MP outfit attached to the 43rd Division in the Philippines.

Corporal Don Taylor of Pikeville, Ky., has arrived in Italy, where he will be assigned as an aerial gunner in a 15th Air Force unit.

Earl E. Hopkins, son of Mrs. Lula Hopkins of Huntington, has been promoted to private first class with an Army Air Forces unit in Italy.

Corporal Edward L. VanHoose, son of Mrs. Orin Keyser, 324 Marcum Terrace, has been promoted to sergeant with a signal corps unit in Luxembourg. He has been overseas for eight months.

Master Sergeant William Edward Green, son of Mrs. Jessie Green, 1908 Artisan Avenue, is at a redistribution station at Atlantic City, N.J. after eight months of service in the Asiatic-Pacific theatre.

Aviation Radioman Third Class Charles H. Bellamy, son of Mr. and Mrs. D. C. Bellamy of Kenova, has completed an aircrew course at Jacksonville Air Station, Fla.

Corporal John Kellan, husband of Mrs. Evelyn Kellan of Apple Grove, who served with the infantry in the Southwest Pacific, has enrolled in a Spanish class while a patient at an AAF convalescent hospital in Miami Beach, Fla.

First Lieutenant James L. Johnson, 317 Thirteenth Street, a Liberator Bomber pilot with the 15th Air Force in Italy, has received the Air Medal "for meritorious achievement in aerial flight while participating in sustained operational activities against the enemy."

Sergeant Lawrence W. Laishley, son of Mr. and Mrs. Charles G. Laishley, 1851 Sixth Avenue, is a clerk with a veteran Liberator bomber group overseas. He has been on foreign duty for six months.

John W. Courts Jr. of Milton, who has been awarded the Distinguished Unit Badge by the 15th AAF in Italy, has been promoted to staff sergeant. He is a ball turret gunner.

Private Millard F. Keyser, son of Mrs. Molly Keyser of Salt Rock, has been promoted to private first class with the 715th Railway Operating Battalion in the Mediterranean theatre.

Glenna: *February 18th Sun. – Didn't go to Sunday School. Aunt Lina Childers died.*

Perlina Ann Childers was eighty-nine years old.[57] "Aunt" and "Uncle" often designated an older person who might not necessarily be a relative.

"Far-reaching and important changes in Huntington's political, economic, cultural, social and public welfare fields were proposed yesterday by the Chamber of Commerce planning council as post-war projects for the city..." Council members Max K. Jones and Homer Gebhardt, co-chairman, and Walter A. Buchanan, managing director of the Chamber of Commerce, were looking beyond the war. Among several proposals were formation of a city-manager form of government and the building of an "adequate' airport."[58]

The *Huntington Herald-Advertiser* ran an article about teachers fighting for living wages. The beginning monthly salaries in 1945 for teachers with three years of college was $99.16 with a top salary of $114.16. The highest salaries came with a master's degree, which had a beginning salary of $117.91 and a top of $132.91.[59]

"Staff Sergeant Raymond M. Holley, 20, was killed in action in Luxembourg while serving with the infantry; the son of Mr. and Mrs. James H. Holley, 719 Thirty-first Street, he was first reported missing in action until official confirmation of his death; other survivors include two brothers, Orin Lee and James H. Holley, three sisters, Mrs. Romona Vuncannon of Texas, Mrs. Violet Smith, 1801 Fourth Avenue, and Miss Lahoma Holley, 719 Thirty-first Street."[60]

"WITH THE COLORS":

William N. Trumbo, third class petty officer, who recently spent a 10-day leave with his parents, Mr. and Mrs. G. R. Trumbo of 2778 Guyan Avenue, has returned to his base at the United States Naval Air Station, Memphis, Tenn.

Private First Class Charles O. McGinnis was wounded in action January 22 on Luzon, according to word received by his wife, Mrs. Blondena McGinnis of Culloden, W.Va. Private McGinnis is the son of Mr. and Mrs. S. F. McGinnis of Culloden.

Private First Class Glenn A. Lucas is on furlough from Fort Jackson, S.C., and has accompanied his wife, Mrs. Gladys B. Lucas, here where they visited her parents, Dr. and Mrs. S. T. Walker. Private Lucas is now at Morgantown visiting his mother, Mrs. Edna Lucas Baker.

Sergeant Robert F. Dundas is stationed in the Netherland East Indies with the 13th Air Force, He is a radio operator and gunner on a B-24 Liberator bomber which had been participating in bombing attacks over enemy-held territory in the Philippines. He is the son of Mr. and Mrs. A. E. Dundas of 1832 Charleston Avenue. His wife, Mrs. Lillian Denny Dundas, resides at 216 Oakland Avenue. His brother,

Private Paul E. Dundas. is with the infantry in France.

Technical Sergeant Morris W. Bailey, son of Mr. and Mrs. Lunsford B. Bailey, Route 2, Huntington, is a member of a B-26 Marauder group which has been commended by General Patton for its successful and daring attacks on key cities in the German Roer Valley. Sergeant Bailey is a veteran of more than 50 combat missions. He is a radio operator and gunner.

Private First Class Harold F. Ayers, 1641 Charleston Avenue, has been awarded the Bronze Star Medal for gallantry in action during the German counter-attack in Luxembourg.

First Lieutenant John Thomas, son of Mr. and Mrs. Lector Thomas, 317 Sixth Avenue, has been "loaned" to the Ferrying Division of the Air transport Command at Greenwood, Miss. for 30 days of transitional training. On the completion of this temporary duty of ferrying planes and training, he will return to his home station at Coffeyville, Kan.

Captain Holt Lester, 604 Fifth Avenue, was promoted to that rank recently, the war Department announced yesterday...

Glenna: *February 19th Mon. – Cooked again for school. Had buttered peas and carrots, cheese, bread, butter, and apples. Everett Walker's baby died.*

Americans, while cautious, believed the war in Europe was near an end. A February 18 AP article from Paris stated that a "great Allied storm was gathering in the West," and Field Marshall Montgomery declared, "We now come to the 'last and final round' in which knockout blows will be aimed 'from more than one direction.'"[61]

General MacArthur, fulfilling his promise to return to the Bataan peninsula, was met there with great fanfare.

Our War Department seized strike-bound, American Enka Corporation in Asheville, North Carolina, because it was "impeding the war effort."[62]

"Private Garnet Gene Baker, 22, son of Mr. and Mrs. Leslie Baker of Branchland Route 1, has died of wounds received on Leyte November 24... A Wayne High school graduate, he is survived by the parents, two brothers in the Navy and two sisters at home."[63]

"IN THE SERVICE":

Private Roy E. Barrett, son of Mrs. Tom Barrett of Chesapeake, O., was wounded in action February 2 in Germany... He had been overseas less than a month.

Serving with a Psychological Warfare Branch unit in Italy is Private First Class Joseph V. Thompson, husband of Mrs. Pearl T. Thompson, 2958 Piedmont Road, and son of Mrs. Robert J. Thompson of Wayne. His outfit strikes at enemy morale by disseminating news through newspapers, leaflets, radio and sound trucks.

Seaman Second Class Alfred Marvin Atkins, son of Mrs. Dorothy W. Atkins, 1220 Enslow Boulevard, has been promoted to seaman first class at Melville, R.I. where he is undergoing PT boat training.

Mrs. Frances Hageman, 226 Twelfth Avenue, is studying occupational therapy at the Army Service Forces school at Richmond, Va.

Corporal Clair S. Smith of Shoals is a member of a bomber maintenance crew in England which serviced "Hell's Angel Out of Chute 13." a Flying Fortress which recently completed 100 missions without a turnback.

First Lieutenant Frederick F. Shriner, son of Mrs. V. V. Shriner, 603 Trenton Place, has been awarded the Oak Leaf Cluster to his Air Medal for exceptionally meritorious service as a P-51 fighter plane pilot in the European theatre.

Second Lieutenant Ralph Staley, son of Mrs. Minnie Staley of Kenova, is in Ashville, N.C. for reassignment after 33 months in the

Southwest Pacific with an Army Service Forces unit attached to infantry.

Mrs. Katherine E. McMahon, 401 Eleventh Avenue, an American Red Cross worker, recently sailed from England aboard the *Larkspur* which carries 600 American casualties. The ship is a former German cargo vessel redesigned for the Army Transportation Corps.

Private James C. Lilly, son of Mr. and Mrs. O. S. Lilly, 2838 Park Avenue, has been assigned to the Second Provisional Troop Carrier Group at Pope Field, N.C.

With a Fifth Army tank battalion in Italy are Private John W. Chatterton, son of Mrs. Ada L. Chatterton, Huntington Route 1, and Private First Class Irvin Crum of Chapmanville.

Private Frederick W. Maier, 319 Twenty-fifth Street, has been awarded the Combat Infantryman Badge by the commanding officer of the 350th Regiment of the 88th (Blue Devil) Division in Italy.

Private Vivian E. Adkins, daughter of Mr. and Mrs. Garnet Adkins, 1032 Twenty-fifth Street, has been promoted to private first class with a WAC organization at Muroc Army Airfield, Calif. She is serving as a cook.

Staff Sergeant James M. Bailey Jr., husband of Mrs. Mary M. Bailey of Ceredo, has received his fourth Oak Leaf Cluster to the Air Medal after participating in more than 25 missions in the European theatre as a Flying Fortress gunner. He is a son of Mr. and Mrs. James M. Bailey of Ceredo.

Glenna: *February 20th Tue. – Cooked again. Burt Lucas's wife died.*

Mary J. Lucas was sixty-three years old. Her parents were James Parsons and Nancy Boothe.[64] Her husband, Burt Lucas, may have died before her.

The Milton basketball team defeated Guyan Valley 43 to 34 and Barboursville won over Buffalo 62 to 18.[65]

Coal mine accidents were frequent. In Logan County, Bert Rollins, general foreman of the Amherst Coal Company, was killed at Amherstdale and Alexander Huchock was killed in a slate fall at the Island Creek Coal Company Holden Mine 22.[66]

Killed in action were Private First Class Oscar Messinger, husband of Mrs. Lorena Messinger, 704 West Third Avenue and Private First Class Ernest T. Parker, son of Mrs. Elizabeth Parker of Kenova.[67]

In Europe, the Red Army approached Berlin and the Allies broke through the Siegfried Line to reach the Rhine River. Americans bombed Nuremberg.[68]

"IN THE SERVICE":

Sergeant Robert E. Molter, a Flying Fortress tail gunner and son of Mr. and Mrs. Earl C. Molter of 1664 Eleventh Avenue, was forced to bail out over the Frankfort rail yards in the middle of an artillery barrage. He was the assistant manager of the Keith Albee Theatre before joining the AAF in 1943.

Charles L. Maynard, son of Mr. and Mrs. McKinley Maynard of Glenhayes, has been promoted to sergeant from the rank of corporal at an Eighth Air Force bomber station in England.

Promotion of Carl C. Perdue, son of Mr. and Mrs. Jesse H. Perdue of Ramage, from corporal to technician fourth grade has been announced at an Eighth Air Force B-17 station in England.

Carpenter's Mate First Class Harry Charles Lang, Seabees, USNR, is spending a 30-day furlough with his mother, Mrs. Lelia W. Lang, 818 ½ West Ninth Street, after two years of service in the Southwest Pacific.

Motor Mechanic W. K. Hinshaw, who has returned to the United States after 18 months of submarine duty in the South Pacific, is spending a leave with his parents, Mr. and Mrs.

C. W. Hinshaw, 320 Norway Avenue. He will report to an Eastern submarine base March 1.

Glenna: [Wednesday] *February 21ˢᵗ – Cooked again. Served potato salad, boiled eggs, kale, bread and butter. Robbie Beckett's child died.*

"IN THE SERVICE":

Private First Class Charles P. Corn, son of Mr. and Mrs. James Corn, 119 West Third Avenue, was wounded in action February 5... Private Corn has been overseas for five months.

The Silver Star for gallantry in action has been awarded a former Huntingtonian, First Lieutenant Elbert L. Bias, son of Mr. and Mrs. E. D. Bias of Washington...

Corporal Hosea M. Alley, son of Mr. and Mrs. Moses G. Alley of Clothier, W.Va., has received a medical discharge from the U.S. Marine Corps after seeing service in the Asiatic-Pacific area.

Private First Class Woodrow Arthur, a member of an infantry outfit, is visiting his parents, Mr. and Mrs. Lee Arthur, 2148 Johnstown Road, en route to Fort George Meade, Md.

Private First Class Chalmer A. Templeton of Barboursville, a medical technician, and Private Leonard D. Holt of Fort Gay, a truck driver, are stationed together at the 95ᵗʰ Evacuation Hospital with the Sixth Army Group in France.

Technician Fourth Grade Samuel Biern Jr., son of Mr. and Mrs. Biern of Park Hills, has been assigned as a photographic laboratory technician with the Allied Commission in liberated Italy. Before entering the service in October, 1942, Technician Biern was a student at Columbia University in New York. He joined the Allied Commission and arrived in Italy in April, 1944.

Three Huntington men, members of the famed Eleventh Heavy Bombardment Group of the Seventh Army Air Force, have been commended by Major General Robert W. Douglass Jr., commanding officer, for their part "in the campaigns which have taken a large section of the Pacific from the enemy's hands." ... The men are Corporal Robert H. Owens, son of Mr. and Mrs. A. D. Owens, 301 Eighth Avenue; Corporal Jack H. Moore, son of Mr. and Mrs. William E. Moore, 2542 Third Avenue, and Technical Sergeant Herman D. Doss, son of Mrs. G. B. Doss, 215 Richmond Street.

Corporal A. W. Mills Jr., son of Mr. and Mrs. A. W. Mills, 4318 Hughes Street, has completed advanced training at the San Bernardino Air Base in California and has been assigned to the Air Transport Command as engineer on a B-25 bomber. He is stationed at San Diego, Calif.

Captain Joseph C. Riley of Chesapeake, O. has been promoted to that rank ... in the Army Air Forces, it was announced by the European Division of the AAF Air Transport Command.

First Lieutenant Val S. Griffiths, husband of Mrs. Betty White Griffiths, 524 Seventh Street, has returned to Huntington after 16 months service as an Eighth Air Force pilot of a B-24 Liberator bomber. Lieutenant Griffiths has been awarded the Distinguished Flying Cross and the Air Medal with four Oak leaf Clusters. He will report to Miami Beach, Fla. March 4 for a period of rest and reassignment.

Lieutenant Richard B. Douglass, son of Mrs. J. P. Douglass, 534 Sixth Avenue, has gone to Williams Field, Ariz. where he is an instructor, after completing a five-weeks course in advanced flying at Lockbourne Field, Columbus, O. His wife, the former Miss Barbara Scherffius, is accompanying him.

Lieutenant Clarence S. Nelson Jr., son of Mr. and Mrs. Clarence S. Nelson, 2768 Emmons Avenue, has returned to George Field, Ill. after spending a short leave with his parents.

Private Carl L. Boling Jr., son of Mr. and Mrs. C. L. Boling, 502 Ninth Avenue, has completed a 12-weeks course in map reproduction at the engineers' school, Fort Belvoir, Va.

Third Mate John Hunter Cravens, U.S. Merchant Marine, left last night for his base in California after spending several days with his mother, Mrs. E. E. Cravens, 1003 West Fourth Street. Third Mate Cravens recently returned from an eight-months tour of duty that took him around the world.

Glenna: *February 22ⁿᵈ Thur. – Cooked again. Served Lima beans, slaw, bread, butter, and onions. Very windy.*

An area hero was making a great change in his life:

Miss Glennis Dickhouse of Oroville, Calif., and Captain Charles E. Yeager, ranking West Virginia air ace, will be married Monday at 2 P.M. at the home of Captain Yeager's parents, Mr. and Mrs. Hal Yeager of Hamlin." It was to be a quiet ceremony performed by the Rev. W. A. Debarr, pastor of the Hamlin Methodist Church, in front of a few relatives and close friends. "The bride-elect is the daughter of Mrs. Phyllis M. Dickhouse of San Diego, Calif. Miss Pansy Lee Yeager of Huntington, sister of the flyer, will be maid of honor, and Mr. Yeager will be best man for his son." The article goes on to say, "Captain Yeager, a pilot of a P-51 fighter plane with the Eighth Air Force, recently returned from the European theatre where he destroyed 12 German planes in the air and damaged three... He wears the Silver Star, Bronze Star, Air Medal with six Oak Leaf Clusters, Distinguished Flying Cross and Purple Heart.[69]

"Theatres and other amusement places turned on their lights and gas heaters at 7 P.M. last night to end a 48 hour gas-out as moderating temperatures brought mild rains to all but one corner of West Virginia." Several Huntington movie houses also reopened; two used heat from sources other than gas and some even operated without heat.[70]

In Italy, the Fifth Army captured steep Monte Belvedere near Bologna, and in Germany, General Patton's U.S. Third Army captured several towns.[71]

Glenna: *February 23ʳᵈ Friday – Cooked again, served boiled eggs, potatoes, slaw, and oranges. Weather fair and windy.*

"The Huntington tobacco market yesterday closed the books on the best burley season in 25 years from the viewpoint of the farmers. Sales during the 1944–45 season, which opened on December 12, totaled 5,778,765 pounds for $2,448,084.07, a season average of $42.38."[72] I can't help wondering how newsworthy this would be today.

The USS *Henry Bacon* was sunk in the Artic Sea by the *Luftwaffe*.[73]

In the Pacific, U.S. Marines moved across Iwo Jima despite fierce Japanese opposition. [Marines raised the American flag on Mount Suribachi.] In Italy, the U.S. Fifth Army captured many prisoners as they advanced over difficult terrain near Bologna.[74]

"IN THE SERVICE":

Petty Officer Second Class Charles C. Lane has been visiting his parents, Mr. and Mrs. Oscar Lane, 926 Twenty-fourth Street. He recently returned after serving for 19 months in the European area where he participated in four major engagements with the Navy.

Private First Class Bertram E. Edwards, son of Mr. and Mrs. C. R. Edwards of Proctorville, has returned to Oakland, Calif. after spending a 45-day furlough with his parents. Private Edwards returned to the United States recently from New Guinea where he received eye injuries. He was graduated from Proctorville High School in 1941 and was valedictorian of his class. Mr. and Mrs. Edwards have three other sons in service, all of whom have been overseas more than 25 months. They are Lynal Edwards, in the Philippines; Harold Edwards, in the Dutch West Indies, and Willie F. Edwards, in India.

Private First Class Circhel M. Leadmon, son of Mr. and Mrs. Claud Leadmon, 2121 Third Avenue, has returned to this country on furlough after 19 months in the Asiatic-Pacific area with the infantry. After his furlough he will return to Camp Gruber, Okla.

Private First Class Harry E. Combs, stepson of Mrs. Catherine Combs of Kenova, is home on a 30-day furlough after 28 months in Panama. He will report to New Orleans, La. for reassignment.

Private Shirley Adkins, 23, son of Mrs. Louise Adkins, 2924 Eighth Avenue, who twisted his leg when he fell into a German foxhole in the Huertgen Forest and was wounded by shell fragments when going to an aid station, is now recovering in the 97th General Hospital in England. Before entering the Army in 1943, Private Adkins was employed in railway work here. A brother, Russell, is in the Navy.

Gerald L. Billups, son of Mr. and Mrs. W. T. Billups of Prichard, has completed a naval training course at Tufts College at Medford, Mass. and will leave for further service in the Navy.

Private Charles K. Oppenhelmer, son of Mr. and Mrs. Walter Oppenhelmer, 5 Willow Glen, and Private First Class Clint O. Gore of Chapmanville, are serving together with the headquarters and service company, Allied Force Headquarters in the Mediterranean theatre...

Seaman First Class Vivian Elaine Ross of the WAVES, who was recently in Huntington spending a leave with her parents, Mr. and Mrs. Harold C. Ross of Ninth Avenue, has left for Washington where she will be stationed. Her father is assistant industrial commissioner of the Chesapeake & Ohio Railway Co.

Private First Class George C. Henderson, who served for 16 months with the infantry in the Asiatic-Pacific area is spending a furlough in Huntington and Polkadotte, O.

Arthur E. Creuch, son of Mr. and Mrs. A. C. Creuch, 735 Seventh Avenue; Alfred L. Campbell, son of Mr. and Mrs. R. L. Wilkes, 3430 Eighth Street Road; James C. Edwards, son of Mrs. Clara Edwards, 1936 Buffington Avenue; Howard L. Fulton, husband of Mrs. Dulcie Fulton, 1413 Fifteenth Street, and Charles Bledsoe, son of Mr. and Mrs. W. T. Bledsoe, Barboursville Route 1, are receiving their initial training at the Great Lakes Naval Training Station.

Staff Sergeant William Trippett, 4746 Bradley Road, has completed a six-day course in cooking of dehydrated foods at the bakers and cooks' school at Fort Sheridan, Ill.

Technical Sergeant Charles E. Stanley, 1549 Beech Street, and Private First Class Lee Roush of Point Pleasant, have been awarded the Silver Star Medal for action with the Seventh Army in France.

Private Eugene White, 19, son of Mr. and Mrs. Ogie V. White, 1045 Twenty-eighth Street, and Roscoe Dingess Jr., son of Mr. and Mrs. Roscoe Dingess of West Hamlin, have reported to Camp Wolters, Tex. to begin basic training as infantrymen.

Steward First Class Comkolane [?] Gray, husband of Mrs. Marion Gray, 16[?] Ninth Avenue, is spending a nine-day leave with his family. He is head commissary [?] of his unit at Norfolk Naval Training Station, Norfolk, Va.

Staff Sergeant Eldon Douglas Brandenburg, son of Mrs. Lois Brandenburg, 210 Norway Avenue, has arrived at an Army hospital in New York from overseas where he became ill. His brother, Andrew Ion Brandenburg, also ill after 18 months duty in the South Pacific, is assigned to a naval hospital in California.

Major Thomas G. Stevenson, veteran of 31 months' overseas duty, is spending a leave here with his wife at the home of her parents, Mr. and Mrs. V. E. Benhoing of Huntington, Route 4.

Glenna: *February 24th Sat. – Washed, cleaned house, ironed that night. Rupert went to town with Don and Gaynelle. Weather sunshiny and warm.*

Trips to Huntington with my mother, and sometimes with my aunt and cousin, were common occurrences. Sometimes I went alone, catching a bus in Salt Rock, getting off at the bus station on Second Avenue, and reversing the procedure on my return. My in-town routine varied little. I browsed awhile in the Lincoln Bookstore on Ninth Street and ate lunch at one of the "five and ten" stores. I was always careful to save enough money for a movie. Today's child does not have that freedom of movement, and with good reason.

In Italy, U.S. mountain troops and the Brazilian expeditionary force took Highway 64 from the Germans. Other Brazilian troops captured Monte Castello while the Americans took Monte Della Toraccia,[75] and in a "Joyride of Destruction," fleets of RAF heavy bombers "hammered" Germany's traffic centers and rail lines."[76]

"IN THE SERVICE":

Sergeant James P. Peters, son of Mr. and Mrs. Rufus M. Peters of Ceredo, a member of the Ninth Air Force in France, is attached to the 391st Bomb Group ... Known as the "Black Death." The group won battle honors for "outstanding performance of duty against the enemy from December 23 to December 6," in which combat crew members fought magnificently despite overwhelming odds, and men who were wounded remained at their posts and continued firing, and aircraft shot out of the sky went down with their guns still blasting at the enemy.

Promotion from private to private first class has been announced at an Eighth Air Force P-51 Mustang fighter station in England for Omer E. Baker, son of Mr. and Mrs. William L. Baker, 1565 Beech Street.

Sergeant George (Jack) Morrison, son of Mrs. Virginia Morrison of Chesapeake, has been promoted from corporal at an Eighth Air Force Service Command station in England.

Marion W. Hatfield, son of Mrs. Lucian M. Hatfield of Prichard Route 2, has been promoted to private first class at Fort Knox, Kentucky.

For leadership demonstrated as a private during a strafing attack on his gun section by German air forces, Edwin M. Burke, son of Mrs. Cora Burke of Kenova, has been promoted to corporal at a Ninth Air Defense Command unit in France. In his promotion, Corporal Burke skipped the rank of private first class.

Technical Sergeant Charles W. "Bill" Bowles, son of Mr. and Mrs. E. E. Bowles of San Diego, Calif., formerly of Huntington, is spending a furlough with his brother, Eber Bowles, 3117 Merrill Avenue. A veteran of 30 months in the South Pacific and England, he has been awarded the Flying Cross, the Air Medal with seven Oak Leaf Clusters, the Presidential Citation, and four battle stars.

For "meritorious achievement in accomplishing with distinction many hours of meteorological reconnaissance operations," Technical Sergeant James D. Copen, 20, son of Mrs. Eloise D. Copen, 1328 ½ Fifth Avenue, has been awarded the fourth Oak Leaf Cluster to his Air Medal. Sergeant Copen is a radio operator on a B-17 Flying Fortress [operating from England] that makes long range weather reconnaissance missions over the North Atlantic.

Technical Sergeant John H. Beckner, son of Mr. and Mrs. B. O. Beckner, 2552 Third Avenue, an engineer and top turret gunner on a B-17 Flying Fortress of the 100th Bombardment Group, part of the Eighth Air Force's Third Air Division in England, has received the Air Medal and four Oak Leaf Clusters.

Corporal James I. Hensley, husband of Mrs. Betty Ann Hensley, Barboursville Route 1, and son of Mrs. Anna L. Hensley of Salt Rock, recently joined the 467th Bomb Group of the

Eighth Air Force in England to fight as a gunner on a B-24 Liberator bomber.

The Navy has advanced James Irving, son of Mrs. James Irving, 1023 Eleventh Avenue, from ship's cook third class to ship's cook second class.

Private Marion T. Baisden, son of Mrs. Nettie Hodge, 1941 Third Avenue, has been admitted to Moore General Hospital, Swannanoa, N.C. for treatment after serving in the European theatre.

Corporal Lake E. Crawford, husband of Mrs. Lucille Crawford, 1252 Fourth Avenue, was member of one of the first Ninth Air Force Service Command quartermaster truck companies to arrive in France. He formerly was employed as a truck driver by the Try-Me Transfer Co. here.

Technical Sergeant William J. Bias of Columbus, Ind., son of Walter Bias, 728 West Eighth Avenue, was the top scorer as a member of the 458th Bombardment Group, base pistol team, which recently won the Eighth Air Force championship in England. He turned in 96.83 points out of a possible 100.

Technical Sergeant Mennis B. Keyser, son of Mr. and Mrs. Delbert Keyser of Stollings, and Eighth Air Force turret maintenance man,

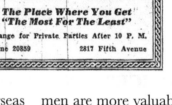

recently completed one year's service overseas with the 452nd Bombing Group.

The Air Medal has been awarded Staff Sergeant William H. Stepp, son of Mr. and Mrs. William H. Stepp for meritorious achievement during Eighth Air Force bombing attacks.

Harold M. Saunders, son of Mr. and Mrs. Everett W. Saunders, 529 Buffington Street and Robert Fry of Salt Rock, Route 1, are receiving recruit training at the Great Lakes, Ill. Naval Training Station.

Lieutenant (Junior Grade) Martin Richards, son of Mr. and Mrs. P. L. Richards of Dayton, O., formerly of Huntington, has been promoted to ensign at Corpus Christi, Tex. where he is serving as an instrument flight instructor in the Naval Air Corps.

Glenna: *February 25th Sun. – Went to Church and Sunday School. Had Lord's Supper. Larry Gill and Marion Nida came home with Rupert. Milo and Maxine came. Aunt Amy was here awhile. Weather very pretty.*

Amy Fry was my Grandfather Adkins's sister. Arnold and Amy Fry lived in Logan County. Their son, Forest, served in the Navy during the war.

Eddie Harbour, Larry Gill, and Marion Nida were fifth grade classmates and my best buddies. Marion has been dead many years and Ed passed away a few years ago. Larry died in the spring of 2017. For many years, Ed, Larry, and I reconnected at our frequent Barboursville High School reunions and picnics.

The war affected all areas of our lives, even sports. Cleveland Indians' manager, Lou Boudreau, wanted 4F rejected baseball players to be eligible to play baseball. He said, "... The army and Navy don't want them. The factories do. Someone in Washington will have to decide whether those men are more valuable in the war plants or on the baseball fields."[77]

Corregidor was recaptured after ten days of fighting.

Turkey declared war on Germany.

"WITH THE COLORS":

Private Leroy Jenkins, son of Mr. and Mrs. George Jenkins of Milton, W.Va. is recuperating at Nichols General Hospital, Louisville, Ky. from wounds received in action Nov. 2 in Germany. His wife, the former Miss Evelyn Daily, has gone to Louisville to visit Private Jenkins. Prior to entering the service in January,

1944, Private Jenkins was employed by the Blenko Glass Co.

Private Keith J. Hamlin was seriously wounded in Iceland, Feb. 13, according to word received by his wife, Mrs. Helen Hamlin of 2970 Eighth Avenue. He is the son of Mr. and Mrs. Tom C. Hamlin of Chesapeake, O. A brother, Corporal Charles Hamlin, is overseas.

Robert B. Engle, serving with the U.S. Navy in the Pacific, has been promoted from radioman third class to radioman second class. He is the son of the Rev. and Mrs. J. D. Engle of Salem, W.Va.

John C. Lockhart Jr., son of Mr. and Mrs. John C. Lockhart Sr., of 2742 Highland Avenue, has been promoted ... to seaman second class. He is serving in the Pacific with the U.S. Navy.

Seaman First Class J. D. Henson has returned to Seattle, Wash. for reassignment after spending a 15-day leave with his parents, Mr. and Mrs. J. D. Henson of Chesapeake, O. He has served eight months in the Pacific with the U.S. Navy as a radioman.

Mr. and Mrs. Joseph O. Yates Sr. yesterday received a message from their son, Technical Sergeant Joseph Yates Jr., stating that he is fighting with American forces in Belgium. He has been overseas four months. Before entering the Army two years ago he was a student at Virginia Polytechnic Institute.

Lieutenant (Junior Grade) Robert W. Gutzwiller ... holder of the Silver Star and veteran of nearly two years fighting in the Pacific as commanding officer of an LCI (landing craft for infantry), arrived at the West Coast of the United States yesterday and will be home this week, according to his parents, Mr. and Mrs. E. J. Gutzwiller, 322 Twenty-seventh Street; a cum laude graduate of Marshall College, he was a star outfielder for the Huntington Aces and Jewels baseball teams.

Sergeant Jimmy Thornton Jr. was wounded in action Jan, 22 in Luxembourg, according to word received from the War Department by his parents, Mr. and Mrs. J. P. Thornton

of Hurricane, W.Va. His wife, Mrs. Naomi Thornton and son Billy live in Milton, W.Va.

Second Lieutenant Charles (Sonny) Allen, son of Mrs. G. F. Allen, 310 North Boulevard West, is home on leave from his station at Richmond Army Air Base, Va., where he serves as a ground officer. He had previously been flight instructor there.

Baker Third Class Sherman Dickson, son of Mr. and Mrs. Walter Dickson of 207 Buffington Street, is now serving aboard an amphibious attack transport in the Pacific. Two brothers in the service are Boatswain's Mate Second Class Edmund L. Dickson, serving in the Pacific, and Corporal Luther H. Dickson, USMC, now stationed at Cleveland, O.

Private First Class Donald E. Taylor, son of Mrs. C. L. Taylor, 2940 Fifth Avenue, has returned to his station at Camp Gordon Johnston, Fla., accompanied by his wife, the former Miss Garnet Gaines of Huntington...

Seaman First Class Lewis B. Strathman, U.S. Navy, has returned to his base at Camp Parks, Calif., for reassignment after spending 30 days here with his parents, Mr. and Mrs. L. G. Strathman of Pea Ridge Road and his wife Mrs. Gussie Strathman, and two children, Billy Ray and Judith Ann, at 1621 Sixth Avenue. Seaman Strathman spent 16 months in the Aleutian Islands.

Glenna: *February 26th Monday — Cooked again for the school. Served pinto beans, slaw, onions, bread and butter. Rain poured all day.*

Clearly, we could not have managed without onions. Easy to grow and harvest, and delicious in most main dishes, they remain a staple in our diet.

There were advances on all fronts: 500,000 incendiary bombs were dropped on Berlin[78] while U.S. forces moved to within fifteen miles of Cologne. In Italy, the 10th Mountain Division was twenty-nine miles from Bologna, and in the

Pacific, three Marine divisions captured parts of the Iwo Jima airdrome.[79]

Syria declared war on Germany and Japan.

"IN THE SERVICE":

The promotion of Shelby A. Harbour Jr., 25, from staff sergeant to technical sergeant has been announced by a U.S. Troop Carrier Forces headquarters in Europe. The husband of Mrs. Lucille Harbour, 1401 Fifth Avenue, Sergeant Harbour helped service troop carrier planes and gliders that took part in the First Allied Army's surprise invasion of Holland.

Seaman First Class Ruth Perry, WAVES, formerly of 1116 Twenty-fifth Street, is stationed in Charleston, S.C.

Corporal Leonard H. Wiley of Logan is a member of a field artillery headquarters in charge of all administrative and operational control of field artillery units in the French Alps...

Technical Sergeant Lester L. Bryant, son of Mr. and Mrs. Lee Bryant, 402 West Twenty-seventh Street, is a member of a signal service group responsible for the communications facilities throughout the Mediterranean theatre of operations. The 977th Signal Service Company ... participated in invasions of Sicily, Corsica, Elba, Italy and Southern France.

Corporal Carl E. Sturgeon, 29, son of Mr. and Mrs. Harrison Sturgeon of Edgarton, was recently awarded the Good Conduct Medal [He later received the Air Medal.] at a base of the Fifteenth Air Force in Italy. A radio operator-gunner on a B-24 bomber, Corporal Sturgeon arrived overseas early last December.

Technician Fifth Grade Robert B. Jones, son of Mr. and Mrs. William B. Kinzer, 426 Eleventh Avenue, is serving with the 958th Signal Service Company in Italy.

Staff Sergeant Robert E. Harper, husband of Mrs. Louise H. Harper, 1139 Monroe Avenue, wounded three times in the European Area, has spent the past 15 day in Huntington and at his home at Harman, W. Va. He returned to the United States January 4 and was sent to the Foster General Hospital at Jackson, Miss, where he was stationed for two weeks prior to his furlough. He has been awarded the Purple Heart Medal and two Oak Leaf Clusters.

Corporal Lawrence Pack of Fort Gay is in a quartermaster truck company which takes supplies to fighting units of the 44th Anti-Aircraft Artillery Brigade. Landing in Southern France on D-plus-1, Corporal Pack helped supply troops in the advance toward Germany until assigned to his present duty along the France-Italian border.

Second Lieutenant Henry J. Ramey Jr., who was commissioned an aerial navigator at Selman Field, Monroe, La. last week, is spending a furlough with his parents, Mr. and Mrs. H. J. Ramey, 1368 Thirteenth Street.

Private First Class Hugh C. Cregger, son of Mrs. Flossie Cregger, 1008 Madison Avenue, is serving with a radio unit of the Third Marine Division now fighting on Iwo Jima, his mother said yesterday. A graduate of Central High School and a former Marshall College student, Private Cregger was previously stationed on Guam.

Private First Class William C. Tyree of Lesage, was graduated last week from the Army Air Forces Flexible Gunnery School, Laredo, Army Air Field, Laredo. Tex...

Technical Sergeant Peter P. Fink, husband of Mrs. Georgia E. Fink, 227 Oakland Avenue, has been awarded the Air Medal for meritorious achievement, He is with the Fifteenth Air Force in Italy.

Thomas L. Clark, son of Mr. and Mrs. George Clark of Chillicothe, O., formerly of Huntington, is in basic training at the U.S. Naval Training Station, Great Lakes, Ill.

The Good Conduct Medal has been awarded Sergeant Dock [?] Hensley, son of Mr. and Mrs. John T. Hensley, 808 Thirty-first Street, at the Romulus Army Air Field, Romulus, Mich.

John Gus Martin, 802 ½ Tenth Street, is one of seven West Virginians who have been promoted to the rank of lieutenant, the War Department announced yesterday. Lieutenant Edward Howard of Huntington was listed among officers ordered to active duty.

Glenna: *February 27th Tues. – Served dinner to 44 children. Had eggs, boiled potatoes, kale, onions, bread and butter. Cold and snowing.*

The Reverend W. R. Napier from Bargersville, Indiana, was conducting revival meetings at the Pilgrim Holiness Church at Crown City, Ohio, and Pastor Oma Williams announced that services would start at 7:45 p.m.[80] Revival meeting by area Christian churches were a fixture of the place and time, but the war seemed to have accelerated their occurrence. Salt Rock Methodist Church would hold three revival services in 1945. I have vivid memories of those meetings.

"Captain and Mrs. Charles E. Yeager, who were married yesterday at Hamlin, will be honored by scores of friends at a public reception Thursday night in the Hamlin High School auditorium." The article described the wedding itself and said that the businessmen of Hamlin had given the couple a sterling silver set while the businessmen of West Hamlin had given them a silver set as well. Mrs. Yeager, daughter of Mrs. Phyllis M. Dickhouse of San Diego, California, met Captain Yeager in Oroville, California near his station. Captain Yeager, a graduate of Hamlin High School, received his commission at Luke Field, Arizona, in March 1943. Mrs. Yeager was to reside with Captain Yeager's parents while he returned to duty.[81]

"The U.S. Weather Station reported last night that the Ohio River probably will reach Huntington's 50-foot flood stage by tomorrow morning." Meteorologist Leroy Stone did not predict a crest for Huntington since there was a forecast for more rain. The river was rising all the way to Pittsburgh.[82]

"Iwo Jima's captured southern airfield was put to American use for the first time Monday while doughty U.S. Marines advancing up to 400 yards captured an important hill overlooking most of the remaining Japanese positions."[83]

Glenna: *February 28th Wed. – Served dinner to 37 children and one teacher, Mrs. Matthews. Raining awfully hard in early morn. Evening bitter cold. Awful thunder and lightning about 6 A.M. — We served custard, baked Lima beans, bread and butter.*

Accumulated paychecks for sixty-eight Army nurses held prisoner in the Philippines for three years averaged $6,500 apiece, minus allotments to families. The highest-ranking officer's check was for $12,000. One of the nurses was Ruby G. Bradley of Spencer, W.Va.[84]

"IN THE SERVICE":

First Sergeant Clifford C. Lipton, Parachute Infantry, who served at Bastogne, Belgium, received the Bronze Star Medal for heroic achievement, his wife, the Former Miss Jo Ann Eckley, 1666 Eleventh Avenue, was notified yesterday... His mother, Mrs. C. C. Lipton, resides at 107 Belford Avenue. Sergeant Lipton received the Purple Heart last June for wounds received in Normandy. He has participated in the battles of Normandy, Holland and Belgium. A Central High School graduate, he also attended Marshall College and was employed by the International Nickel Co.

Private First Class Walter F. Smith Jr., with the 10th Mountain Division, has arrived safely in Italy, his parents, Mr. and Mrs. W. F. Smith, 1655 Sixth Avenue, were notified yesterday.

Fireman First Class James Lee Pennington, son of Mr. and Mrs. G. O. Pennington, 1213 Seventh Street, is on a 30-day leave here after serving for 15 months with the Navy in the South Pacific. Mr. and Mrs. Pennington have two other sons in the Navy, Pharmacist's Mate First Class G. O. Pennington, Norfolk, Va., and Pharmacist's Mate Second Class R. M. Pennington with the amphibious forces in the Pacific.

Petty Officer Floyd F. Smith of Wayne is with the Seabees on Iwo Jima, his wife said yesterday. His wife, five children and parents, Mr. and Mrs. O. J. Smith, live at Wayne.

Machinist's Mate second Class Cesco H. Barnett has returned to San Diego, Calif. after spending an eight-day leave with his wife, the Former Miss Ruth Cooper, and their two children in Huntington. The son of Mrs. Alice Barnett, 932 Twenty-fourth Street, he has a brother, S. L. Barnett, serving with the Navy at Newport, Rhode Island.

Corporal Douglas C. Grove, who recently returned from service in the Army Air Forces in Europe, is spending a furlough with his mother, Mrs. W. F. Grove, 1635 Twelfth Avenue.

Sergeant Charles L. Tyree, stationed at Sheppard Field, Tex., is visiting his parents, Mr. and Mrs. C. L. Tyree, 1131 Sixth Avenue.

Technician Fifth Grade Haskell B. Hysell, stationed at Long Island, N.Y., is spending a furlough with his wife, Mrs. Jewel Hysell, 2118 Harvey Road.

Private Pat H. Trogdon, 29, husband of Mrs. Eula Mae Trogdon, Huntington Route 4, has been released from a U.S. Army hospital in England to return to duty in Germany. Private Trogdon was struck by a small arms bullet near Aachen December 26 while serving with an infantry unit. He entered the Army March 21, 1944.

Corporal William Holbrook, son of Mr. and Mrs. William A. Holbrook, 559 West Third Avenue, has arrived in the Philippines with a field artillery battalion. Overseas since January,

1943, Corporal Holbrook has served in Hawaii and New Guinea.

F. Raymond Jackson, husband of Mrs. Maxine Jackson, 287 Gallaher Street, has been promoted to the rank of sergeant in the South Pacific where he is serving with the Marines. Sergeant Jackson has been in service for two years and overseas for one year.

Private First Class Arthur O. Keyser of Salt Rock has arrived at the Air Forces redistribution center, Miami, Fla. following 28 months of duty as an aircraft welder in the European and China-India-Burma theatres. He is a son of Lon M. Keyser of Salt Rock.

Master Sergeant Frank Windsor Martin, son of Mrs. Ruth G. Martin, 434 Seventh Avenue, at headquarters of an Army corps in Holland where he is chief clerk of G-4 Section.

Private Marjorie Henson, mother of Miss Ethel Hubbard, 403 West Sixth Street, is a medical technician with the Women's Army Corps at DeWitt General Hospital, Auburn, Calif.

Private Brady Perry, 1828 Rural Avenue, has arrived at the AAF redistribution center at Miami after serving for 26 months in the Aleutian Islands.

Chaplain Thomas J. Eastes of Huntington and Louisville, Ky., son of the Rev. Harold Eastes of Man, W.Va., former pastor of Tucker Memorial Baptist Church, is a front-line chaplain with the 127th Infantry Regiment of the 32nd Infantry Division in the Philippines. Chaplain Eastes, overseas for nearly three years, accompanied his troops during bitter fighting along the Driniumor River in New Guinea and in the jungle mountains of Leyte, and more recently on Luzon, living with them in fox holes. A dispatch from the Philippines yesterday told of Christian services conducted by the chaplain in the thick underbrush of the dripping slopes of Leyte,' only a few hundred yards from enemy machine guns. His wife and five-year-old daughter, Emma Jo, reside in Louisville. [The Rev. Thomas J. Eastes died in 1985 in Perry, Ohio, at age seventy.]

March

WELCOME SPRING, HIGH WATERS

GLENNA: MARCH 1ST THURSDAY – SERVED DINNER AGAIN TO 52 *children and 3 teachers. Had salmon, slaw, and potatoes. Weather pretty. That night we went down to Arnold Morrison's.*

Mother had a special connection to Arnold Morrison's family. Virginia Lee Morrison had been her student at Walnut Grove School and appears on her register for the 1931–1932 school year.[85] When twelve-year-old Virginia Lee contacted septicemia, or blood poisoning, Mother visited her and held her in her arms, where she died. The website *Ancestry* has Virginia Lee Morrison's parents listed as Arnold Brooks Morrison and Roxie Paralee Morrison. Virginia Lee's recorded death date is December 20, 1933.[86] Mother could not speak of her without crying.

An announcement came that Turkey and Egypt were attending the planned United Nations conference in San Francisco, bringing the number of countries participating to forty-four.[87]

"IN THE SERVICE":

Technician Fifth Grade John F. Pieraccini, son of Frank Pieraccini of Huntington, was recently promoted from private to his present grade. He is in the 23rd Tank Battalion of the Seventh Army's 12th Armored Division in France.

Seaman First Class William C. Johnson, son of Mr. and Mrs. Roy Johnson, 2917 Third Avenue, has returned to duty in the South Pacific after spending a short leave here with his parents. His brother, Private First Class Garland Johnson is stationed in the Aleutian Islands.

Major Orville F. Bakhaus, husband of Mrs. Earleen Bakhaus, 1338 Charleston Avenue, has been promoted to that grade ... somewhere in the European area. Major Bakhaus is attached to the Ordnance Department of the Army.

Lieutenant (j. g.) Donald Williams, 625 Sixth Avenue, was recently promoted to that rank and is home on leave from the Pacific. Mrs. Williams resides at that Sixth Avenue address and his parents are Mr. and Mrs. Cecil Williams, 1825 Ninth Avenue. Lieutenant and Mrs. Williams will leave tomorrow for the West Coast where he will be reassigned.

Private James Ratcliff, son of Mr. and Mrs. A. G. Ratcliff of Wayne Route 1, has been awarded the Purple Heart Medal for wounds received in action in Belgium December 17. A brother, Private First Class George Ratcliff, husband of Mrs. Cora Blair Ratcliff of Prichard, is with an engineer unit of the Army in England.

Private Kessel L. Barker, 521 ½ Eighth Street, has been transferred from the Women's Army Training Center, Fort Des Moines, Ia., to Camp Atterbury, Ind., for duty at Wakeman General Hospital.

Private Adam Allen, husband of Mrs. Mary Allen, 519 Twentieth Street, is undergoing treatment for frozen hands at an Army hospital in

Europe after serving with the infantry in France and Belgium...

Seaman Second Class Clyde B. Ross, son of Mrs. Sadie Ross, 2 ½ Washington Avenue, is spending a nine-day leave with his family. His wife and child reside at the Washington Avenue address...

Private George W. Howard and his son, Private Alfred E. Howard of Monaville, W.Va., who entered the Army a few weeks apart, are stationed at the Fort McClellan, Ala., Infantry Replacement Training Center.

Captain Wyatte J. Gay of Milton and all of his crew were saved after they bailed out of their stricken B-29 over the China-Burma-India air route recently. The son of A. L. Gay, Chesapeake & Ohio Railway Co. employee of Huntington, Captain Gay is the husband of Mrs. Wanda M. Gay and the grandson of Mrs. M. E. Justice of Milton.

Glenna: *March 2ⁿᵈ Friday – Cooked again. Served hamburgers, raisins and Lima beans. Rain poured all day.*

Charleston, West Virginia: "Twenty-seven West Virginia Negro high school basketball teams start a chase tomorrow for the 1945 state championship ..."[88] This was a state championship for Black schools. Segregation is a dark time in our history and a blight on our otherwise moral society. It would take several more years to achieve school integration. Douglas High School was Huntington's Black high school. Even under the handicap of segregation, Douglas maintained a high standard for teachers, curriculum, sports, and the arts.

"IN THE SERVICE":

Boatswain's Mate Second Class Richard M. Mautz, son of Mr. and Mrs. Albert F. Mautz

of Kenova, is spending a 30–day leave with his parents after serving for two years with the Seabees in the South Pacific. Mate Mautz was graduated from Ceredo-Kenova High School and attended Marshall College where he was pledged to Phi Kappa Nu fraternity. His brother, Machinist Mate Third Class Virgil Mautz is with the Navy in the Southwest Pacific and another brother, Private Lloyd Mautz is with the Army in Utah.

A telegram, the first personal message of any kind since December, 1943, was received Wednesday by Mr. and Mrs. Boyce Hall, 601 Seventh Avenue, from their son, Private Farley B. Hall, who was liberated January 30 when American Rangers and Filipino guerrillas stormed into a Japanese prison camp on Luzon. The message stated that he was well and hoped to be home soon. Private Hall was taken prisoner when Corregidor fell.

Corporal Walter A. Lusk Jr., son of Mr. and Mrs. Walter A. Lusk, 2514 West Ninth Street, and Sergeant Donald C. Swann, son of Mrs. Alice Swann, 818 West Ninth Street, recently arrived in England...

Technician Fifth Grade William E. Booth, son of Mrs. Nancy Booth, 1220 Monroe Avenue, is attached to the 92ⁿᵈ Chemical Composite Company in Italy...

Private First Class Sherman Murphy, son of Mrs. Emma Murphy, 529 North High Street, has been promoted to sergeant with the Fifth Army in Italy. Murphy is a cook with an infantry unit.

Glenna: *March 3ʳᵈ Saturday – Went to town. Bought a sheet, Rupert [a] shirt [and] pants, cooking pan for Arnold, Rupert a birthday cake. The 5 o'clock bus left us and we stayed in town until 10:15 o'clock. We went to the show. Saw "Frenchmen's Creek" at the Keith Albee. Got home at 11:30 very tired and Rupert very sick. Weather cloudy.*

The "Keith Albee" was the largest and classiest theatre in Huntington. It still is.

Mother buying a cake was rare. She must have felt pressed for time.

Glenna: *March 4th Sunday – Day before Rupert's birthday. We had him a dinner. Gaynelle, Don, and Jean were here. Later in the day Nona Gill and children came. After dark washed out a few clothes. Weather pretty and sunshiny.*

Howard LaDonne (Don) was five years younger than me. Shelby Jean (Jean) was about Don's age. Deedy and Nona Gill were Larry Gill's parents. Larry, whose name appears many times in my 1945 diary, had a brother, Raymond, and a sister, June. The Gills lived across the river from the school.

MARCH 4

19[4] *Sunday, 1945*
Dear Diary,
I had a birthday dinner
today and had a dandy cake.

Rupert: *Sunday, March [4], 1945 Dear Diary, I had a birthday dinner today and had a dandy cake.*

This was my first entry in my new leather-bound five-year diary, a birthday gift from Eddie Harbour. I began each entry with "Dear Diary," as transcribed here, but will omit that salutation from this point on.

Mother also gave me a pair of new dress shoes. I climbed the cherry tree out by the lane and scuffed the leather. She was not pleased.

War deaths kept bringing grief to Tri-State families: The War Department announced names of five Huntington area men killed in action: Private First Class Amon Adkins, husband of Mrs. Catherine Adkins; Corporal Joseph Akers, Kenova; Private First Class Joe Butler, Holden; Private First Class Fred C. Scaggs, Logan; Staff Sergeant George N. Gibson, husband of Mrs. Anyce V. Gibson, Huntington; Private Glen E. Thompson, son of Mrs. Beatrice Thompson, Huntington. Also: Prisoners of war: Private William Aliff, husband of Mrs. Virginia Aliff, Guyandotte; Private Nicodemus Estep, Paynesville; Private First Class Hubert R. Mash, Premier: Private First Class Golden R. Miller, Logan.[89]

Finland declared war on Germany.[90]

"WITH THE COLORS":

Lieutenant (j. g.) Robert W. Gutzwiller, who returned last week from naval duty in the Pacific area, is spending a leave with his parents, Mr. and Mrs. Everett S. Gutzwiller, 322 Twenty-seventh Street. Lieutenant Gutzwiller was awarded the Silver Star recently.

Promotion of Edna J. Carter, daughter of Mr. and Mrs. W. F. Knapp of Huntington to the rank of corporal in the Women's Army Corps, was announced yesterday by the commanding officer of Morrison Field, West Palm Beach, Fla., where she is stationed.

William Lewis Harvie, 21, 1416 Boulevard Avenue, was commissioned an ensign in the Naval Reserve and designated a naval aviator recently at the Naval Air Training Base, Pensacola, Fla...

Private F. J. Rider, whose wife resides at 527 ½ Eighth Street, is a member of a unit which supplies food to U.S. soldiers all over the India-Burma-China theatre of war.

Ensign William E. Prout, of Russell, Ky., former Marshall College student, who has returned to the United States from several months of sea duty with a motor torpedo boat squadron, has been presented with the Presidential Unit Citation at San Diego, Calif.

For meritorious achievement while piloting a B-17 Flying Fortress over Germany and enemy occupied Europe, First Lieutenant Harold D. Johnson, 25, 1852 Eleventh Avenue, has been awarded an Oak Leaf Cluster to his previously won Air Medal at an Eighth Air Force Bomber station in England. Lieutenant Johnson is a former Marshall College student.

Sergeant James R. Meredith, son of Mr. and Mrs. E. B. Meredith of Kenova, has returned to this country after 12 months in the European area with the Transportation Corps. Sergeant Meredith is temporarily being treated at Stark General Hospital, Charleston, S.C...

The promotion of Russell E. Chappell, son of Mr. and Mrs. J. Chappell, 395 Smith Street, to the rank of first lieutenant has been announced by Ninth Air Force headquarters in France where he is stationed as an administrative officer. Lieutenant Chappell, who entered the Army in September 1936, has held every enlisted grade from private to first sergeant. He later was appointed a warrant officer and was commissioned a second lieutenant in April, 1943. He has been overseas a year.

Paul Clifford Singleton, son of Mrs. Maude Singleton, 143 Third Avenue, was recently promoted to master technical sergeant in the Marine Corps at Camp Pendleton, Oceanside, Calif...

Lieutenant Donald Malcolm of Buffalo, W.Va., a graduate of Marshall College and former member of the Big Green basketball team, is home on a 10-day leave after serving for a year aboard a destroyer in the Caribbean area, he will report to Boston for reassignment.

Lieutenant Henry F. Fricker of New York, a Marshall College graduate, is a patient at the U.S. Naval Hospital, Corona, Calif., where he is undergoing treatment for leg wounds received in action with the Marines in the South Pacific last October. He returned to the United States in January.

Private Fred B. Lind, son of Mrs. Gladys Lind of Huntington, who was wounded in action in Italy, is a patient in a Portsmouth, Va. hospital.

The Bronze Star for heroic achievement near Ormoc, Leyte, has been awarded Technician Fifth Grade Charles V. Sword, son of Mr. and Mrs. T. R. Harshbarger, 1934 Buffington Avenue. A truck driver in an anti-tank company, Technician Sword volunteered on two occasions to serve as litter bearer when he learned the rifle companies of his unit could not evacuate their men.

Glenna: *March 5th – Rupert's birthday. He went to school as usual. I cooked again for school. Had potatoes, slaw, and peanut butter sand. Raining this morning and clear in evening. We went to Arnold Morrison's a few minutes and took their pan. I ironed some before going to bed.*

Rupert: *Today is my birthday and I was 12.*

The Ohio River in Huntington crested at 55.2 feet, but more predicted rain caused worry.[91]

A desperate German government began drafting sixteen-year-old boys.[92]

"IN THE SERVICE":

Staff Sergeant Jamison T. Pyles, son of Mrs. Martha Pyles, 1313 Maple Street, Kenova, now stationed at the Army Air Forces Convalescent Hospital, St Petersburg, Fla., will be heard in an interview tonight at 7:30 P.M. over WSAZ. Sergeant Pyles was an engineer-gunner on a B-17 from October, 1943 to June, 1944. He has the Distinguished Flying Cross and Air Medal with five Oak Leaf Clusters and is credited with shooting down three German fighters on his 28th mission.

William F. Draper, son of Mr. and Mrs. G. E. Draper, 334 Elaine Court, a member of a veteran troop carrier group in Italy, has been promoted to sergeant. Since being overseas

WELCOME SPRING, HIGH WATERS

Sergeant Draper has been awarded two campaign stars to wear on his theatre ribbon.

Technical Sergeant Elmer B. Reeder of Hamlin has been assigned to Eagles Pass Army Field, Texas, after serving as an operations officer of the 882nd Airborne Engineer Aviation Battalion, Fifth Air Force. Sergeant Reeder helped build the American air base at Finschafen, New Guinea after its site was taken from the Japanese. He served in the South Pacific theatre for seven months.

Staff Sergeant John H. Sayre, son of Mr. and Mrs. Hubert J. Sayre, 2946 North Fifth-seventh Street, is currently assigned to the AAF Redistribution Station No. 4 at Santa Ana Army Air Base in California. A radio technician with the Fifth Air Force in the Asiatic Pacific theatre, Sergeant Sayre wears the Distinguished Unit Citation.

Glenna: *March 6th Tuesday – Raining again. I served kale greens, eggs and rice, and bread and butter to 45 children and 2 teachers. Awfully windy at night and cold. River rising fast.*

Rupert: *The river is rising fast and is already awful high. It has rained all day. Today was a school day.*

The Guyandotte River, or simply the "Guyan," is an old river that has over millennia dug a deep channel 150 miles long from southern West Virginia. Steep hills along its course feed fast-flowing water during extended periods of rainfall. The river and its feeder streams rise quickly and can be destructive in force. The Guyandotte River flows into the Ohio River and is the boundary between the city of Huntington and town of Guyandotte at that point. (Guyandotte is a part of the city of Huntington.)

In Eastern Europe, Romania established a strong pro-Communist government.[93]

Part of an AP article titled, "Little Nations Seek Security" stated, "Invitations to the World Security Conference went out today to 39 United Nations amid signs that smaller nations will strive to limit the authority of the big powers." Poland, because its new government was not yet in place, was the only nation not invited to the conference scheduled to begin on April 25 in San Francisco.[94]

"IN THE SERVICE":

Private First Class Bruce Pauley, 232 Guyan Street, was one of a crew of five men who, although their ammunition-laden trailer glider was forced down near Ghent, Belgium, in the Allied invasion of Holland, got their badly-needed load through to the front after a 200-mile hitch-hiking trek through Holland, Belgium and France. The glider unit, a part of the 327th Glider Infantry Regiment, was in [the] charge of Sergeant Carl R. Green of Troy, N.C.

Technical Sergeant James D. Copen, 20, son of Mrs. Elloise Copen, 1328 Fifth Avenue, was recently awarded his third Oak Leaf cluster to the Air Medal at an Eighth Air Force Aerial Reconnaissance Station in England... Prior to entering the Army in February, 1943, he was a student at Central High School.

An administrative clerk at the headquarters of the 13th AAF Service Command in the Southwest Pacific, Hugh W. Douthitt, son of Mr. and Mrs. Carl C. Douthitt, 315 Eleventh Avenue, was recently promoted to the rank of staff sergeant. Sergeant Douthitt is a graduate of Central High School and attended Marshall College.

The promotion of Walter A. Lusk Jr., 20, son of Mr. and Mrs. Walter A. Lusk, 2514 Smith Street ... to sergeant took place recently at an Eighth Air force Bomber Station in England where the Huntington man is attached to the 398th heavy bombardment group as armor-er-gunner on a B-17 Flying Fortress.

Staff Sergeant William R. Smith, son of Mrs. Lou B. Smith, 2223 West Fifth Street, was recently promoted to that rank at an Eighth Air Force Fighter Station in England where he is serving as a mechanic in the motorized equipment shop.

Private James Lilly, son of Mr. and Mrs. O. S. Lilly of Huntington, has been assigned to the Sedalia Army Air Field, Warrensburg, Mo., installation of the First Troop Carrier Command.

Corporal Leo Arthur, Army Air Forces veteran of the Japanese attack on Pearl Harbor, has arrived in Huntington on his first furlough since the outbreak of the war. He is visiting his parents, Mr. and Mrs. E. F. Arthur, 2435 Tenth Avenue, and his brother, Patrolman Oman Arthur of the Huntington Police Department.

Major H. Brown McGrew returned Saturday to Washington where he is stationed with the Ordnance Department after spending several days with his wife, Mrs. Marie McGrew, and daughters, Betty and Nancy, 1417 Boulevard Avenue.

Sergeant George R. Lewis, husband of Mrs. Alice M. Lewis, 1808 Marcum Terrace, serving with the 157th Infantry Regiment of the Seventh Army in France, is credited with destroying a German position during an enemy counterattack on the Seventh Army front. Sergeant Lewis' company was under concentrated small arms fire. Then Lewis rushed to the spot where the fire was originating, returning the fire of the Nazis. Lewis' buddies, inspired by his example, rushed ahead, too, and the German position fell and the counterattack was repulsed.

Glenna: *March 7th Wednesday – Didn't cook today. River high and school turned out.*

Rupert: *River is high but slowly falling. There wasn't any school today because of the backwater.*

The floods, most prevalent in spring and sometimes in fall and winter, force water to back up into the many winding creeks and streams that feed the Guyandotte River. When the Ohio River floods, it causes further backup. Backwater covers roads and halts traffic, sometimes for days. When I attended Marshall College in the early fifties, I lived at home. When backwater kept me from going to Salt Rock, I stayed in Guyandotte with my grandparents, Alie and Hattie Pratt. Huntington built a floodwall in 1940 after the city endured several major Ohio River floods, including the disastrous 1937 flood. The wall encircles the entire city and has paid for itself many times over.

"IN THE SERVICE":

First Lieutenant Roy L Huddleston of Huntington has been assigned as a training officer to the new First Tactical Air Force in France. Composed of American and French tactical combat units, the new air force is operating in advance of the U.S. Sixth Army Group on the Western Front.

Seaman First Class Frank Perkins, son of Mr. and Mrs. Frank Perkins, 334 Thirty-fifth Street, was a member of the Navy gun crew aboard the merchant ship *Cape Constance*, which ... shot down two Japanese planes during the Leyte invasion...

Petty Officer Second Class C. E. Wetherall, with the Seabees in Guam, was recently promoted to that rank. His wife and daughter reside at 920 Twenty-third Street.

Motor Machinist's Mate Third Class Robert C. Traub, 334 Highland Street, was aboard the LCI *514*, a veteran of six campaigns in the Mediterranean theatre, when she returned to the United States recently for overall. Mate Traub's ship, an infantry landing craft, was in the campaigns of Tunisia, Sicily, Salerno, Anzio, Normandy and Southern France.

Sergeant Ernest Murray, husband of Mrs. Lucille Murray of Barboursville, is a tank commander and gunner in the European theatre.

He holds the Good Conduct Medal and the European Theatre of Operations ribbon.

Motor Machinist's Mate Second Class William C. Craig and Private First Class Charles E. Craig of the Army, sons of Mr. and Mrs. W. C. Craig Sr., 412 Homestead Place, are serving in the South Pacific.

Captain Emmitte S. Harrison Jr., now stationed at Tampa, Fla., an AAF flight commander, and Mrs. Harrison are spending a furlough with his parents here. Captain Harrison, a former member of The *Herald-Dispatch* news staff, had several months' service in England and participated in a number of missions over Europe.

Ernest W. Hazelett, son of Mr. and Mrs. Robert A. Hazelett, 1922 Seventh Avenue, has been promoted to the grade of private first class in a unit of the 316th Troop Carrier Group of the First Allied Airborne Army.

Technician Fourth Grade Eugene Mayenschein, whose wife, Mrs. Iris Augusta Mayenschein and two daughters, Mary Lou and Iris Eugenia, live at 2908 Marcum Terrace, is now chief storekeeper for his engineer equipment company on Guadalcanal. He is the son of Mrs. Sadie Mayenschein, 2561 Collis Avenue.

First Lieutenant William A. Wimmer, son of Mrs. William N. Wimmer, 521 Sixth Street, has been promoted to that rank with the Ninth Army in Germany.

Major George J. McTigue , son of Mrs. Marguerite K. McTigue, 422 Holswade Drive, and husband of Mrs. Martha Bobbitt McTigue, 2104 Wiltshire Boulevard, has been promoted to that rank with the Air Transport Command of the Army Air Forces in China.

Clarence William Bradley, son of Mr. and Mrs. William Bradley and husband of Mrs. Geneva Rose Bradley, 1901 Buffington Avenue, has been graduated from the Naval Air Technical Training Center at Norman, Okla., where he has been studying for aviation machinist's mate.

Captain Wyatte J. Gay, a Superfortress pilot with the 20th Bomber Command's "Hellcat" group, had been awarded the Air Medal for outstanding and meritorious achievement while participating in operational and combat flights from India and China bases. He is the son of A. L. Gay of Huntington...

Sergeant Edgar E. Edwards, youngest son of Mr. and Mrs. Homer H. Edwards of near Hamlin, was recently promoted to that rank from private in Germany where he is serving with the Seventh Army. A brother, Corporal William H. Edwards, is serving with the Army Air Forces overseas. Another brother, Private James H. Edwards, has been a prisoner of the Japanese since the fall of Corregidor. His parents have learned that he has been moved from the Philippines to Tokyo Camp, Japan.

Glenna: *March 8th Thursday – Didn't work at school today. I sewed some on a dress for myself and fixed the legs of Don's pants. Weather cool.*

Rupert: *Most of the backwater has gone down. There wasn't any school today.*

A German V-2 rocket killed more than a hundred people in London's Smithfield Market.[95]

In Italy, the U.S. Tenth Mountain Division reported an advance of five miles in the Apennines southwest of Bologna, to within twenty miles of the city. They took 1,200 prisoners.[96] The surrender of large German units was occurring with greater frequency.

"IN THE SERVICE":

Major Carl E. Frisby, 32, whose wife and daughter, Betty Lou, reside at 2650 Fourth Avenue, has been promoted to that rank as a regular Army officer on the staff of General MacArthur. Major Frisby, who has been overseas for a year, was promoted on recommendation of the general.

Private First Class Earl C. Meek, U.S. Marine Corps, participated in the invasion of Iwo Jima, his mother, Mrs. W. Arch Leap, 1649 Charleston Avenue, and wife, the former Miss Edna Mae Shamblin, 2781 Cedar Grove Court learned yesterday... He is a graduate of Central High School and went overseas last September.

Technician Fifth Grade L. M. Arthur, who served 41 months with the Army Air Forces in the Central Pacific, has arrived in the United States on Furlough. He is the son of Mr. and Mrs. E. F. Arthur, 2435 Tenth Avenue...

Corporal Joseph Thomas, 1921 Fifth Avenue, has arrived at the Army's Oliver General Hospital at Augusta, Ga. and is now a patient there after serving overseas with the field artillery.

Private Everett Wray, son of Mr. and Mrs. W. L. Wray, 816 Twelfth Street, is a member of the 764th Railway Shop Battalion in France. Private Wray was formerly a Huntington Publishing news carrier.

Private First Class Olen Vance, husband of Mrs. Betty Marie Vance, 328 Benard Street, has returned after 27 months of service in the South Pacific and is now being processed through the Army Ground and Service Forces Redistribution Station at Miami Beach, Fla. Private Vance served as a radio operator with the parachute infantry and has been awarded the Combat Infantryman Badge. He entered the armed forces in July, 1940.

Glenna: *March 9th Friday – I didn't work at school again. I washed a big washing. Weather sunshiny but cool.*

Rupert: *We thought there wouldn't be any school today and it was so late when mother found out there that she didn't cook for the school.*

"IN THE SERVICE":

Sergeant H. S. Queen, son of Mrs. Emma Queen of Gallipolis, O. is a mechanic with a service group motor pool of the 12th Air Force Service Command in Italy. He served in North Africa and holds the Good Conduct Medal and the European-African-Middle East campaign ribbon with two battle stars.

Ward Cornett Jr. of the Navy is spending a leave with his parents, Mr. and Mrs. W. L. Cornett, 30 West Sixth Avenue.

Captain George T. Aldridge, son of Mr. and Mrs. John E. Aldridge, 5787 Ohio River Road, and husband of Mrs. Margaret B. Aldridge, 2428 Collis Avenue, has been assigned to a veteran troop carrier group of the 12th Air Force... Before joining the AAF, Captain Aldridge was a student at Marshall College.

Private E. E. Fannin, son of Mrs. Lilly M. Fannin, 445 Camden Road, a member of the 12th Armored Division of the Seventh Army in France, has been awarded the Combat Infantryman Badge. Overseas for three months, his unit is one of the newest on the front of Lieutenant General Patch's Army group.

Flying in a B-25 Mitchell bomb group, Second Lieutenant James E. Conley, 24, of Louisa, Ky., has flown his first combat mission as a bombardier. Lieutenant Conley, who left for overseas duty in January, flew with his twice-cited B-25 group against rail lines leading to the vital Brenner Pass. He is with a 12th AAF group in the Mediterranean theatre.

Technical Sergeant Philip L. Appeldorn, son of Mr. and Mrs. Henry Appeldorn, 1814 Eighteenth Street, is an engineer-gunner with 391st Marauder Bomb Group which has just been awarded the War Department Citation for its attacks against the enemy during the German Christmas counter-attack.

Private Roy W. Ward, 21, of Ivydale, W.Va., has reported for duty with Headquarters squadron of the veteran "Service Commando" Group in the China Air Service Command...

Private First Class Clyde Smith of Verdunville, W.Va., who is serving with the 35th Infantry Division in France, has been awarded the Silver Star by the commanding general of the division...

Mr. and Mrs. J. T. King of Eleventh Avenue have learned that their son, Lieutenant Edward A. King of the Army, and his wife, the former Miss Mildred Mobley of Hillsboro, Tex., an Army nurse, were reunited recently in the South Pacific after two years' separation. They had not seen each other since their marriage in Texas. Lieutenant King is now stationed in the Philippines and his wife, also a lieutenant, has been assigned to another station with the Nurse Corps.

First Lieutenant Elmer R. Daniels Jr. of Mount Hope, W.Va., a former Marshall College student and husband of the former Miss Janice Nida of Huntington, has arrived in the United States after five months of duty in the Pacific as a radar officer with the Marine Corps. Mrs. Daniels left yesterday to join her husband. Private First Class Kenneth Nida, her brother, is an AAF gunner and mechanic at Van Nuys, Calif.

Private First Class Paul E. Harshbarger, son of Mr. and Mrs. Ed Harshbarger of Huntington Route 1, has returned to the United States and is undergoing treatment at Fitzsimmons General Hospital, Denver, Colo. after serving for 18 months overseas with a Ranger battalion.

Private George Bonecutter, 715 Fifth Avenue, brother of Ernest Bonecutter of Chesapeake, O., has arrived at the Army Redistribution Station, Asheville, N.C. after 27 months in the South Pacific with an infantry division.

A reunion of two former schoolmates, Seaman First Class Harold E. Ramsey, son of Mr. and Mrs. Walter Ramsey, and Private Robert L. Ford, son of Mr. and Mrs. Frank Ford, all of Barboursville Route 1, took place recently in the Philippines.

Glenna: *March 10th Saturday — I ironed everything and mended. Weather very pretty.*

Rupert: *I visited a boy friend today. His name is Larry Gill. I had a good time.*

Each Saturday the newspaper printed announcements of area Sunday services: Fifteen Baptist, thirteen Methodist, four Christian, one Church of God, and one Christian Science church posted notices on this day.[97]

"IN THE SERVICE":

William Price Stewart III, 19, son of W. P. Stewart Jr., 2865 Collis Avenue, is a member of the 32nd class of aviation cadets to graduate from Columbus Army Air Field near Columbus, Miss. tomorrow. He will receive a commission as a second lieutenant in the Army Air Forces. Stewart entered pilot training in January, 1943 after studying at Marshall College.

Technician Fourth Grade Frank Fritz, 27, husband of Mrs. Martha Fritz, 3654 Piedmont Road, has returned to the United States and is being processed through the Army Ground and Service Forces Redistribution Station at Miami, Fla. where his next assignment will be determined. Sergeant Fritz served for 29 months as a machinic in Europe and was awarded the European theatre campaign ribbon with three battle stars.

Private First Class Nick Caldwell of Lesage has been awarded the Combat Infantryman Badge for participation against the enemy on the Fifth Army front in Northern Italy.

Private First Class Charles E. Corns, who was wounded in action in Europe recently, has been awarded the Purple Heart medal...

Private William C. Varney, 201 Eighth Avenue; Private First Class Ernest C. Vanover, Lorada; Corporal Carl C. Stout, Canebrake; Corporal Cleo Harris, Delbarton; Sergeant Carl Varney, Meador; Corporal Alonzo Totten,

Varney, and Private Carl McCoy, Williamson, are members of the 81st Mechanized Calvary Reconnaissance Squadron, probing German defenses before Italy's Po Valley.

Private First Class William D. Perkey, son of Mrs. Goldie Perkey, 37 West Fifth Avenue, who was wounded in Germany on February 28, is in a hospital overseas, where his condition is improving.

In a letter written from a foxhole on Iwo Jima received yesterday by his mother, Mrs. W. Arch Leap, 1649 Charleston Avenue, Private First Class Earl C. Meek, told her that at the time of its writing he was sitting beside Private John Wolfe, son of the Rev. and Mrs. Frank E. Wolfe, 1050 Jackson Avenue. Private Meek is the husband of the former Miss Edna Mae Shamblin of Huntington.

Glenna: *March 11th Sunday – Went to Sunday School and to church that night. The revival started. Bro Sullivan is helping Bro Midkiff. Mrs. Rousey was here all Sunday evening. Beautiful day.*

Rupert: *My eyes were hurting today. I didn't go to sunday School*

The Ohio River flood was still front-page news. An article by Hugh Maxwell reported, "Falling at the rate of almost a half-inch an hour, the raging Ohio River, beyond flood stage locally for nine days, was heading back into its banks last night. The river at 11 P.M. had dropped approximately a foot from its crest of 59.1, reached at noon Friday."[98]

Even in wartime the arts flourished: "Members of the graduating class of Wayne High School will present a three-act-farce, "Too Many Relatives," Thursday at 2 P. M. and Friday at 8 P. M. at the school; the play is being directed by Miss Gladys Robinett and Wayne Plymale of the faculty; cast ... Freda Fry, James Mitchell, Joanne Bunn, Vernon

Berry, Ruth Dickerson, James Justice, Frances Hollister, Flora Ross, Bill Ketchum and James Ferguson."[99]

William Frye, in an AP article from London, wrote of an incident at the Remagen Bridge, saying that a "spectacular air battle" had put to flight German dive bombers trying to knock out the bridge. Frye said that Thunderbolts of the Eighth Air Force spotted six Messerschmitt 109s, escorted by five Focke-Wulfe 190s, heading for the bridge over which the Americans were moving men and equipment. "In a savage pass, the Thunderbolts shot down one dive bomber, one Focke Wulfe escort, and then in a swirling battle forced the others to jettison their bombs and scatter."[100] A fine account of the entire battle at the Remagen bridge in Germany is *The Bridge at Remagen*, written by Ken Hechler, Marshall College professor and later congressman from West Virginia.

Glenna: *March 12th Monday – Milo's birthday, He is 33. I cooked again for the school children. We served potatoes, slaw, and peanut butter sand. Beautiful day. I went to church that night. Preacher preached on Honor thy father and thy mother.*

My Uncle Milo was a gentle, unassuming man who visited us almost daily to pick up milk and exchange news. If he wasn't in a hurry, he let me "drive" his Model A Ford down to Madison Creek Road, a treat that had started with sitting between his legs and steering, but eventually learning to use the clutch and shift gears. Milo worked for the county all his working life, driving a road-grader on dirt back-roads that needed constant care. Maxine, his wife, as affable as Milo, endeavored to teach me the more delicate qualities of life, such as the proper way to set a table. Milo and Maxine lived over a mile away, over Salt Rock Hill, on property across the road from the Hutchinson homestead.

Rupert: *I went to school today but the teacher sent me home because of my bad eyes.*

I don't recall that problem, but I do remember getting poison ivy in my eyes several times during my childhood, and this may have been one of those times. There were also periodic outbreaks of pinkeye at school.

Huntington, a river town (as well as a railroad town), was fertile ground for river tales. An interesting article, "Rivermen Save Tom Sawyers," appeared this day in the *Huntington Herald-Dispatch*:

Taking a chapter from Tom Sawyer, two Huntington boys [about twelve] attempted to travel from Proctorville to Chesapeake on two small and flimsily constructed rafts early yesterday and were rescued from almost certain drowning in the swiftly-moving Ohio River by deckhands of the towboat *Sam B. Suit*. Evidently fearful that their parents would learn of their foolhardy venture, the boys declined to identify themselves, accepted hot coffee and money for the bridge toll, and hurried across the river to Huntington—and homes which narrowly escaped tragedy.[101]

"IN THE SERVICE":

Colonel Charles V. Bromley Jr. of Huntington, husband of Mrs. Elizabeth W. Bromley of Lexington, Ky., has been awarded the Bronze Star Metal for "aggressive leadership" in handling the troops of his command during action on the Seventh Army Front...

Edward L. VanHoose, with a signal depot company in Luxembourg, has been promoted to the rank of staff sergeant according to ... his mother, Mrs. Orin Keyser, 324 Marcum Terrace. Sergeant VanHoose has been in the Army 30 months and overseas for ten months...

Sergeant Clifton V. Johnson, son of Mr. and Mrs. William Johnson, 1606 Eighteenth Street, is an automotive mechanic with the 391st

Marauder Bomb Group in France which has been awarded the War Department Citation for its attacks during the German counter offensive in December.

Private First Class Oscar P. Langdon, son of Mr. and Mrs. Van Langdon of Chesapeake, O., is expected to arrive at his home this week for a furlough after serving for eight months overseas.

Corporal Hersey F. Roberts of Sweetland is with the 98th Ordnance Company of the Sixth Army Group in France.

Private Cedric E. Perry, son of Mrs. Essie Perry, 147 Third Street, has arrived in the United States after a seven-month tour of duty in the Asiatic-Pacific area.

Technical Sergeant Walter Felty of Huntington is head of a platoon with the 14th Armored Division of the Seventh Army in France which has two members who recently captured 32 Nazis.

First Lieutenant Val S. Griffiths, son of G. R. Griffiths, 45 Roland Park, and Mrs. Virginia Griffiths, 534 Seventh Street, has arrived at Miami Beach, Fla. for reassignment with the AAF after completing 30 combat missions in Europe. He was awarded the Distinguished Flying Cross and the Air Metal with four Oak Leaf Clusters.

Men from the Huntington area who are serving together with the 445th Ordnance Company of the Seventh Army in France include Corporal James D. Bunton, Rear 2764 Third Avenue; Corporal Jesse B. Maynard, 234 Staunton Street; Corporal Hiter D. Melton, 152 Wilson Court; Corporal Arnold L. Layne, 1516 Seventh Avenue; Private First Class Hayes D. Charles Thacker, and Staff Sergeant John H. Thacker, Whites Creek.

Glenna: *March 13th Tuesday – I cooked again for 44 children and 1 teacher. Served pinto beans, rice, and oranges. Weather very pretty. I went to revival meeting again.*

Rupert: *My eyes are still bad. I didn't go to school. I helped Mother cook for the school.*

In his "How's Your Garden" column, W. D. Click advised, "Wild onions are thriving now and will soon be multiplying at a rapid rate both at the roots and on top if they are not disturbed..."[102] Wild onions were a nuisance because cows' milk picked up the flavor. A wild onion patch grew on the face of the hill above our barn and it became my spring job to pull them up.

The *Huntington Herald-Dispatch* took notice of declining river levels: "Transportation schedules returned to something near normal here last night as the Ohio River dropped below the 53-foot level and more than a dozen gates in the Huntington flood wall system were opened to traffic. The Ohio Valley Bus Company resumed operations directly to Ashland, although there was a detour at Catlettsburg. The Ohio River Bus Co. is expected to resume runs between Huntington and Point Pleasant this afternoon. The first Baltimore & Ohio train in nearly a week ran between Kenova and Pittsburg yesterday."[103]

The Lend-Lease Act was reauthorized for the last time by the U.S. House of Representatives.[104] The Act gave aid to the Allies during the war, mostly in the form of materials.

Marines and Navy men wounded on Iwo Jima were being transported to Oahu hospitals at the rate of 250 a day.[105]

Two Huntington soldiers were reported killed: "Staff Sergeant Raymond Schoenbaum, son of Mr. and Mrs. Emil Schoenbaum, 107 West Tenth Avenue, and Staff Sergeant Dean Lahue, previously reported missing, son of Mr. and Mrs. Paul D. Lahue, 1034 West Sixth Street." Both men were graduates of Huntington High School. Raymond Schoenbaum, 31, attended Marshall College. Dean Lahue, 23, was a graduate of Marshall and DePaul University.[106]

"IN THE SERVICE":

Clifford T. Nelson, husband of Mrs. Wanda Nelson of Harts, W.Va., recently was awarded the Silver Star for gallantry in action on the Fifth Army Front in Northern Italy and at the same time was promoted from corporal to sergeant. After protecting the rear and flanks of a combat patrol which had engaged the enemy, Nelson was ordered to withdraw. Unwittingly, he moved into a minefield and was wounded when he stepped on a mine. Realizing that an outcry would hinder the withdrawal, Nelson remained silent in spite of the intense pain. A flare lighted the area and when two German machineguns opened up on the patrol, he engaged them with his rifle. After the patrol had reached safety, Nelson dragged himself through the intense machinegun and mortar fire. He waded through an icy mountain stream and reached American outposts five hours later.

Private First Class Arnold O. Walker, husband of Mrs. Carrie Walker of Bob White, W.Va., was admitted to O'Reilly General Hospital at Springfield Mo., recently for treatment for battle injuries.

Sergeant Elizabeth Gross, daughter of Mr. and Mrs. Alfred Gross, 706 West Fifth Street, recently visited Rome with a contingent of WACs stationed in Italy.

Sergeant Lester L. Johnson, son of Mrs. Georgia B. Johnson, 417 West Fifth Avenue, who has been on foreign duty for 28 months, is an armorer in an ordnance supply and maintenance company of the 13th AAF Service Command in the Southwest Pacific.

Technician Fifth Grade Daniel A. Gooch, 32, son of Mrs. Orpha Gooch, Huntington Route 2, was one of seven enlisted men who recently received a group citation for "heroic action beyond the call of duty" in extinguishing a blazing ammunition truck which threatened the lives of 130 hospital patients on Luzon in the Philippines. He is a member of the 115th Medical Battalion, 40th Infantry Division.

Second Lieutenant Charles Thomas Williams of Huntington, who was awarded a battlefield commission and presented with the French Croix de Guerre for action with the Fifth Army in Italy last year, is spending a furlough with his grandmother, Mrs. W. A. Williams, 709 Fifth Avenue...

Staff Sergeant Willie Esque, 32, son of Mr. and Mrs. James Esque, Barboursville Route 2, recently added a second battle star to his theatre of operations ribbon... He is an aircraft mechanic for a photo squadron at an Eighth Air Force Aerial Reconnaissance Station in England.

Marine Lieutenant Jack Chapman, former Marshall College basketball star from Logan, and his wife, the former Miss Betty Bartram of Huntington, are spending a leave here.

Ensign S. W. "Buster" Wylie of Collis Avenue, who graduated from midshipmen's school in New York last week, is spending a leave in Huntington. He will report to San Francisco for assignment to duty.

Jess O'Quinn, U.S. Navy, son of Mrs. Beatrice O'Quinn of Matewan, W.Va., was one of the first to hit the beach in a Seventh Fleet amphibious action less than ten miles from Subic Bay, above Manila.

Boatswain's Mate Second Class Harold E. Sellards, son of Mr. and Mrs. R. P. Sellards, 1941 Third Avenue, is serving with the Navy in the Pacific. He has been overseas for 18 months.

Captain Joe Kail, son of Dr. and Mrs. I. J. Kail of Whitaker Hill, has been awarded the Bronze Star Medal for action with the Seventh Army combat engineers in France.

———————————————

Glenna: *March 14th Wednesday – I cooked again for the school. Children had hamburgers and soup. Beautiful day. Papa and Mama moved a load of their furniture to town. Rupert went along and helped.*

Rupert: *I didn't go to school today. I helped my grandmother and grandfather move.*

My grandparents' furniture was moved by a neighbor with a truck. I'm certain they bought the Huntington house because they found their Salt Rock home too crowded. The Salt Rock house was built by my mother in 1935 and my earliest memories are from there. When Mother married Dawson Morrison in 1939, we traded houses with my grandparents. That house eventually belonged to Cline Adkins, then to his daughter, Shelby Jean Adkins Bryant. After she sold it, the new owners moved it across the river to a lot near the intersection of Tyler Creek Road (Apple Maps now lists it as "McComas Road") and Route 10.

Massive bombing of Japan's cities and ports continued.[107]

War correspondent Ernie Pyle, respected for high quality writing and his close contact with service members, observed what GIs were doing in their spare time on one Pacific island: "... The coral sea bottom inside the reef around these islands abounds with fantastic miniature marine life, weird and colorful. Soldiers make glass-bottomed boxes for themselves, and wade out and just look at the beautiful sea bottom. I've seen them out there like that for hours, just staring at the sea bottom. At home they wouldn't have gone to an aquarium if you'd built one in their backyards. Pleasures are all relative. Joy is proportional. Why don't I shut up?"[108]

There was more tragic news in our area: Mrs. Ethel Fuller, 928 Eleventh Street, learned that her twenty-year-old son, Private First Class Robert A. Hatfield, had been killed in action in Burma on February 4. He was in the China-India theatre for about a year. He was an honor student at Central High School and attended Marshall College before enlisting. "Surviving besides his mother, a teacher at Emmons School, are two uncles, Corporal Charles D. Fuller, wounded recently in Germany, and Private First Class Selbert Fuller, with the Army in France, and his grandparents, Mr. and Mrs. A. W. Fuller of Ceredo."[109]

———————————————

"IN THE SERVICE":

Aviation Cadet Robert Lewis Jones, 3645 Hughes Street, has been commissioned a second Lieutenant on completion of training at the Army Air Forces pilot school, Moody Field, Ga.

Private Verlin J. Arthur, who recently completed infantry training at Camp Blanding, Fla., returned to Camp Meade, Md., yesterday after spending several days here with his wife, Mrs. Ruth Thelma Arthur, and daughter, Gloria Jean, 3065 Eighth Street Road. He is the son of Mr. and Mrs. Brady Arthur of the Eighth Street Road address.

Pharmacist's Mate and Mrs. Jack Nichols of Huntington, who left for his station in California last Thursday, have arrived at San Diego, Calif., where they will reside. Mrs. Nichols is the former Miss Betty Arrington, daughter of Mr. and Mrs. T. E. Arrington, 2574 Fourth Avenue.

Corporal Carl Herndon, who is stationed with the Army at Camp Wolters, Tex., is visiting his parents, Mr. and Mrs. John Herndon, 1101 Ninth Avenue.

Corporal Robert E. Vass, son of Mr. and Mrs. Frank E. Vass, 327 Wilson Court, recently arrived at a U.S. Strategic Air Force station in England.

Lieutenant Elvin L. Hinerman, USNE, 2215 Eleventh Avenue, and one of his two sons in service are now overseas. Lieutenant Hinerman is chaplain on a ship in the South Pacific, while Pharmacist's Mate Second Class Jack E. Hinerman is with the Marine Corps in the same area. Apprentice Seaman Walter F. Hinerman is in boot training at the Great Lakes Naval Training Center. Lieutenant Hinerman formerly was pastor of the Beverly Hills Methodist Church.

After serving in Holland with a troop carrier service wing mission, Sergeant Denver D. C. Davis, 2765 Collis Avenue, has returned to his former base in England. He has been overseas for 18 months.

Cline A. Clary of Huntington, former personnel clerk of the U.S. Engineers here, was recently promoted to the grade of sergeant at the headquarters of the Army Air Forces in the India-Burma theatre. His wife, Mrs. Elsie Caldwell Clary, and small daughter, Linda Marie, live at 323 Thirty-first Street, He is the son of Mr. and Mrs. L. O. Clary of Marion, O.

Corporal Roy V. Castle, former employee of the Appalachian Electric Power Co. here, and son of Mr. and Mrs. Roy Castle of North Kenova, O., an Air Forces crewman, has completed 100 missions over enemy territory, 52 over Italy and 48 in the China-Burma-India theatre where he is presently stationed. He is the brother of Mrs. Eloise Adkins, Mrs. Nina Volckmann and Miss Betty Castle of Huntington and is a graduate of Chesapeake O. High School.

Private First Class Joseph B. Hicks of Davy Route 2 and Corporal Elwood P. Lawhorn of Milton have been cited for their heroism in the face of enemy fire recently when their outfit, the 185th Regiment of the 40th Division penetrated into the Cabusilan Mountains of Central Luzon. Private Hicks was commended for crawling down a steep ledge, and while exposed completely to Japanese fire lowered a demolition charge to seal an enemy cave.

Glenna: *March 15th Thursday — I cooked again for school children. Served Lima beans, slaw, and apples. Went to church again that night.*

Rupert: *I didn't go to school today. I helped mother cook for the school.*

A report from Stockholm, said to be from a neutral traveler from Hamburg, reported that the Nazis had opened a new campaign against Jews still in Germany; Jews married to Germans had been ordered to the ghetto, to the Reslendsradt (Terezin) in Czechoslovakia, or to other designated concentration camps.

In other news, "German prisoners asserted that mountain hideouts in Germany and Austria were jammed with German Army deserters and insisted the Gestapo was carrying out threats to kill the families of men taken prisoners without being wounded. Prisoners said German officers' treatment of men was becoming markedly more severe."[110] Except for the most diehard, the Germans had to know the end was near. Officers, watched closely by their superiors, were threatened by death if they did not remain loyal. Those same superiors, accountable for war crimes, probably laid their own plans for escape to neutral countries; time has shown that many did, some to South America.

"Private First Class John R. Wass Jr., 19, U.S. Marine Corps, was killed February 19 on Iwo Jima, the Navy has notified his widow, the former Miss Marguerite Brooks, 1658 Thirteenth Avenue... Private Wass entered service December 14, 1943, and went overseas last May. A former employee of the Huntington News Agency, he is survived also by his parents, Mrs. Vida Newcomb and John R. Wass of Huntington, and an aunt, Mrs. Lewis Gibson of this city, with whom he made his home."[111]

"IN THE SERVICE":

Seaman First Class Calvin Morris, son of Mr. and Mrs. Calvin R. Morris of Eleventh Avenue and husband of Mrs. Bessie Morris, 1326 Fourth Avenue, recently received a certificate of merit for completing a course in anti-aircraft gunnery at the Naval Training School in New York.

Second Lieutenant Phillip H. Crofts, son of Dr. and [Mrs.] W. H. Crofts, 1540 Madison Avenue, pastor of the Open Door Baptist Church, and recently assigned to the Atlanta, Ga. Army Service Forces Depot. Before entering the Army, Lieutenant Crofts was merchandising manager for the J. C. Penny Co. at Portsmouth, Ohio, and traveled extensively in Hawaii, Japan and China.

Coxswain Paul Dixon, son of Mr. and Mrs. Manford Dixon of Wheelwright, Ky., is spending a 30-day with his parents and brother, Glenn Dixon, and two sisters, Mrs. Overton Wiley and Mrs. Georgie Woods. Coxswain Dixon was overseas for 28 months serving in Australia and other parts of the Pacific. Two other brothers in service are Private William T. Dixon in Holland and Sergeant Carl Dixon in France.

Private First Class J. M. Wysong, whose wife, Mrs. Frances Wysong, and son James, reside at 910 Monroe Avenue, is serving with the Fourth Marine Division on Iwo Jima...

Private First Class Walter C. Hammond of Ashland recently completed a year's service overseas with the 452nd Bombardment Group's Sub Depot Detachment in England. He is a member of the Third Air Division which was cited by the President for its England-to-Africa shuttle bombing of a Messerschmitt aircraft factory at Regensburg.

Arthur A. Palmer, son of Mr. and Mrs. T. A. Palmer of North St. Petersburg, (Fla.) was recently promoted to the rank of private first class at a headquarters station of the 15th Air Force Service Command in Italy. He is a graduate of Central High School and a former student at Marshall College where he majored in journalism.

Staff Sergeant John W. Courts Jr., 22. son of Mr. and Mrs. J. W. Courts, 1352 Washington Avenue, Milton, has been awarded the Air Medal at 15th Army Air Force Headquarters in Italy. Sergeant Courts is a ball turret gunner on a Liberator bomber.

The promotion of Newton B. Parker, 25, husband of Mrs. Mary Lee Parker, 821 Seventh Street, to sergeant has been announced at an Eighth Air Force Station in England. He is a tail turret gunner with a B-17 Flying Fortress unit.

Braxton K. McDonie of Huntington has been promoted to the rank of staff sergeant in the Army Air Forces at Stout Field, Indianapolis, Ind., headquarters of the First Troop Carrier Command.

Aviation Machinist's Mate Second Class Jack Leaberry, U.S. Navy and his brother, Aviation Student Ernest F. Leaberry, USAAF, are visiting their mother, Mrs. E. F. Leaberry, 315 West Twenty-second Street.

Allan Scott Perry, 2850 Third Avenue, has been appointed a cadet midshipman in the U.S. Merchant Marine Academy, Kings Point, Long Island, N.Y., with current assignment as midshipman, U.S. Naval Reserve.

Staff Sergeant Guy T. Tooley of Chesapeake, O., has won the Air Medal for meritorious achievement as a ball turret gunner on a B-17 Flying Fortress participating in Eighth Air Force attacks on German targets.

Corporal Charles Hardy, son of Mr. and Mrs. T. W. Hardy, 319 Adams Avenue, is an aerial gunner with the 15th Air Force based in Italy.

Glenna: *March 16th Friday — Served dinner again to school children. Had cabbage salad, apple, eggs, and potatoes. Beautiful day. Very warm. Rupert went home at noon sick from school. Papa and Mama moved their final load to Huntington to stay. I went to revival again.*

Rupert: *I went to school a hafe day. Then I was sick and the teacher sent me home.*

From London: "Comdr. T. J. Keane, U.S. Naval officer, disclosed that 25 per cent of the men under his command had married Northern Ireland girls."[112]

An unofficial British statement disclosed that German peace feelers had been conveyed through a third party, but were rejected. Also, the Swedish newspaper *Aftontidningen* "asserted tonight there were rumors that similar German proposals had been made to Russia."[113]

Killed in action: "Private First Class Woodrow W. Adkins, 32, husband of Mrs. Evie Adkins of Yates [West Virginia]."[114]

"IN THE SERVICE":

Serving with the Sixth Army Group in France from this area are Private First Class Hiram E. Potter, Kenova; Private First Class Art Cooke, Salt Rock; Staff Sergeant Homer H. Albright, Westfield; Captain Icia M. Perry, Army Nurse Corps, Huntington; Sergeant Herman Adkins, Ceredo, and Corporal Roscoe H. Penix, 65 Twenty-fifth Street.

After serving for a year, Seaman First Class Donald Lee Hughes is visiting in Huntington. The sailor is spending a 30-day leave with his parents, Mr. and Mrs. J. M. Hughes, 3016 Sixth Avenue.

Private First Class Paul J. Mayo, husband of Mrs. Elizabeth M. Mayo, 1304 Third Avenue, and son of William O. Mayo, 320 East Second Street., was recently awarded the Combat Infantryman Badge for action on the Fifth Army front in Northern Italy. Serving in Company G, 85th Mountain Regiment of the 10th (Mountaineer) Division, Mayo was a member of a raiding patrol which accomplished its mission without a casualty, returning with German prisoners and enemy material.

Corporal Harrison Jenkins, Husband of Mrs. Opal Maddox Jenkins of near Hamlin, has been awarded the Good Conduct Medal and the European and African-Middle Eastern Medal in Italy. He has also won two Bronze Stars and four overseas ribbons. Enlisting in 1942, Corporal Jenkins has been overseas for 25 months. He is the son of Mrs. Zena Collins of Milton Route 2.

Staff Sergeant Jesse Adkins of Huntington is a member of the First Battalion of the 143rd Infantry Regiment which recently won military acclaim for its capture of Rohrwiller, France...

Private First Class Hatten Adkins, who recently returned from overseas duty, is spending a furlough with his father, N. Adkins of East Lynn.

Electrician's Mate Third Class Lanty Harold Damron, stationed at the New London, Conn., submarine base, is spending a leave in Barbourville with his parents, Mr. and Mrs. R. A. Damron.

Seaman First Class Albert J. Jarvis, husband of Mrs. Lucille Jarvis, 2469 Collis Avenue, is serving with the 149th Infantry Regiment which won its way through the jungle-covered slopes of Zig-zag Pass along Highway 7 on Bataan Peninsula in the drive launched recently by the 38th Division, now known as the "Avengers of Bataan."

Seaman First Class A. Wayne Thompson, a survivor of the *Tasker H. Bliss*, is spending a leave in Huntington with his wife and two children after 18 months in the Pacific. He enlisted in the Navy in 1942 and has participated in nine invasions. He is the son of James H. Thompson of Spring Valley Drive and a brother of Mrs. Cecil Hite of this city.

Lieutenant Abe Forsythe Jr., 821 First Street, who was rescued at sea when his plane was shot down in the Leyte battle, is spending a 15-day leave in Huntington with his family.

Glenna: *March 17th Saturday – I washed and cleaned the house. Rained nearly all day. Went to church again that night. Jaruel Porter was saved.*

Rupert: *I am better today. I am writing a book which I hope can be published.*

That book publication didn't work out, despite my aspirations, although some of my classmates enjoyed my creations—or pretended to. I still have several of those youthful manuscripts, bound with cardboard covers and decorated with my artwork.

Two West Virginia soldiers, listed by the War Department as among military personal arriving in San Francisco after their liberation from Philippine prisoner-of-war camps, were

Corporal Wilson R. Mouser, Route 2, Box 12, Buckhannon, and T-5 Ralph E. Moore of Squire, McDowell County. In Germany, three miles from the Rhine River, Metropolitan Opera Star Lily Pons sang "Ava Maria" to a GI audience in a barn auditorium.[115]

Glenna: *March 18th Sunday – I didn't go to church or Sunday School. Stayed home and fixed a grand dinner. Had chicken and dressing, custard pie, cake, peaches, corn, green beans, potato salad, and sweet potatoes. Dawson, Rupert, and I went to the revival meeting again. Lee Chambers was saved that night. Rev. Midkiff came home with us and stayed all night.*

Rupert: *I went to sunday school today. We had a baked hen for dinner.*

The Reverent Horace Midkiff served more than one church, so Salt Rock Methodist did not have his services every Sunday. It was not unusual for him to stay overnight in homes of church members, especially when revival meetings were in progress.

Lieutenant Woodford W. Sutherland, a 1939 graduate of Marshall College and a B-24 [Number 13] pilot, gave his parents, Mr. and Mrs. G. W. Sutherland of St. Albans [West Virginia] an extraordinary account in a letter: "... I was forced to land my B-24 at midnight on the ocean. I am proud of the results, the entire crew of 11 escaped uninjured. It was the first time that a B-24 was ditched at sea in the nighttime without someone being killed. After getting all the gear we needed out of the plane we sank her and paddled our rafts to an island about five miles away. We got there at 5 A.M. The entire village of natives turned out to welcome us. The chief took us to his 'palace,' and fed us royally on fish, rice, and yams. We broke out all our emergency rations and distributed them among the natives. We gave one woman a parachute which delighted her. After we finished eating, the chief took us to another island and a larger village in outrigger canoes. We were really given a tremendous welcome at the big village." Lieutenant Sutherland went on to say, "A message was sent to our base and a big seaplane was dispatched for us. More than 180 of the natives went down to the shore to see us off. Before rowing out to the plane, we gave the natives everything we had, including guns, knives, shoes, shirts, and other things, as our way of thanking them for their wonderful hospitality."[116]

General Eisenhower broadcast a warning to German civilians and foreign workers in the Frankfurt-on-Main and Mannheim-Ludwig-Shafen areas that those sectors would be "heavily bombed."[117] Thirty Allied aircraft were lost in the heavy bombing of German cities.[118]

Glenna: *March 19th Monday – I cooked for the school again. Had 33 children. Very pretty day. Didn't go to church that night. I ironed until 10:30 o'clock.*

Rupert: *I went to school today. I helped Mother after school.*

I believe Mother was tired; understandable since she cooked for the school, went to evening church services, and managed endless home chores.

On the Western Front, the Remagen bridge collapsed, the pounding of Berlin continued, the U.S. Third Army neared a junction with the U.S. Seventh Army, and the U.S. First Army extended its hold on the Rhine River area. In the Italian campaign, two German ships were sunk by the British off Corsica, and an Italian patrol wiped out a German stronghold near Imola. On the Pacific Front, U.S. planes hit vital targets on Japan's Kyushu Island and Superforts bombed Nagoya.[119] Also in the Pacific, there were heavy *kamikaze* attacks on the American aircraft carriers *Essex, Wolf, Enterprise,* and *Franklin,* with many causalities.[120]

Radio Tokyo reported that, by order of the cabinet of Premier Kuniaki Koiso, all schools, collages, and universities in Japan, except for first grade, would be closed for a year; students and teachers were to be mobilized for war work and food production.[121]

"IN THE SERVICE":

Nineteen-year-old Thomas Lee Harbour, son of Mr. and Mrs. E. W. Harbour of Milton, a Coast Guard machinist's mate, was a crewman on a Coast guard manned assault transport that participated in the invasion of Iwo Jima. Mate Harbour, a 1942 graduate of Milton High School, set ammunition ashore in the midst of intense fire and for several days braved a heavy surf and concentrated gunfire to bring casualties off the landing area. He enlisted two years ago and participated in the invasion of Normandy and Southern France.

Lawrence C. Rutherford Jr., son of Mrs. Mabel V. Rutherford, 1134 Sixth Avenue, recently received a commission as second lieutenant and bombardier's wings at the San Angelo, Tex. Army Air Field...

After completing a tour of duty with the Eighth Air Force, First Lieutenant Charles W. Penhorwood, 245 High Drive, has been assigned to the San Angelo field as an instructor. Lieutenant Penhorwood completed 30 missions in a B-24 and has been awarded the Air Medal with three Oak Leaf Clusters and the European ribbon with four bronze stars. A graduate of Central High School, he attended Marshall College for three years and enlisted in the AAF in May, 1942.

Private First Class Carl Gillispie, son of Mrs. Nettie Gillispie of Dunlow, W.Va., was promoted to that rank with the Fifth Army in Italy where he is a litter bearer of the 109th Medical Battalion, 34th "Red Bull" Division.

A dispatch from the Fifth Army in Italy yesterday reported that Corporal William J. Byus, son of Mrs. Elvis Byus, 78 Oney Avenue, was returning to this country on furlough. Member of a staff section in the 19th Combat Engineer Regiment, Byus has been overseas for 30 months and has seen service in the Algerian, Sicilian and Italian campaigns.

Private First Class Fred W. Maier of Huntington, carrying a tommy gun, was one of 20 men on combat patrol who engaged the Germans recently ... in Italy, killing one Nazi and neutralizing a German machinegun nest. The men are members of the Second Battalion of the 350th "Battle Mountain" Regiment of the 88th "Blue Devil" Division. Private Maier's wife, Ann, daughter, Sharon, three months old, and mother, Mrs. Mildred Maier, live at 319 Twenty-fifth Street.

Corporal James J. Pavis, son of John Pavis of Thirteenth Street, has joined the veteran 21st Infantry Regiment of the 24th "Victory" Division in the Philippines...

Seaman First Class Charles W. Lambert, brother of Mrs. Charles A. Boothe, 1828 Bungalow Avenue, and the only West Virginian on a minesweeper which sank off the coast of Luzon recently, is spending a 30-day leave with his mother, Mrs. Minnie V. Lambert of Ferrelsburg, W.Va.

Private First Class Charles L. Martin, husband of Mrs. Phyllis Martin, 600 Charleston Avenue, is with the 337th "Wolverine" Regiment with the Fifth Army in Italy. In the Army for six years, Martin holds the Bronze Star for heroic achievement in action.

Glenna: *March 20th Tuesday – I cooked again for school. Had only 38. Went to church that night. No one saved. Papa and Mama came up and stayed all night.*

Rupert: *I went to school today. I had an earache today.*

Carpenter's Mate First Class D. D. (Mac) McNeely, a Huntington Seabee, was killed in action on Guam March 9... He had been overseas for two years. Before entering the service, Mate McNeely was employed by the Higginbotham Construction Co. of Charleston. A graduate of Central High School, he was the husband of Blanche Lee, daughter of Mr. and Mrs. A. S. Lee, 247 West Sixth Avenue. Besides the widow, he is survived by two sons, Charles and Richard McNeely, both in the Army Air Forces; the mother Mrs. Alice McNeely, 628 West Division Street, and a sister, Mrs. Harry Kindt of Ashland.[122]

From the Rhine Bridgehead: "Two P-47 pilots came over here expecting to fly Thunderbolts in combat but today they are on errands of mercy." The pilots, Lieutenant Pete Gray, 200 Walnut Street, Huntington, and Lieutenant Bob Geyer of Xenia, Ohio, were assigned "little" L-Is and given the job of picking up wounded near the bridge where they had to find their own landing fields.[123]

"IN THE SERVICE":

Marine Private First Class Russell D. Perry, son of Mr. and Mrs. C. E. Perry of Milton, is with the Third Marine Division on Iwo Jima. Private Perry attended Milton schools before entering the service three years ago. He has been overseas for nine months. His wife and daughter reside in Harrisburg, Pa.

Fireman John W. Leith, 21, 1701 West Fifth Avenue, and Seaman James R. Mosser of Kenova are serving aboard a fleet oiler of the Pacific Fleet Service Force. Their craft participated in three major offensives in the Pacific and was the last oiler to refuel the USS *Princeton* three days before the aircraft carrier was sunk.

Among the first of Huntington area soldiers to return from the Philippines is Sergeant Clarence Hicks of Milton. He served for 39 months in the Pacific area, and is en route to his home via Washington, D.C.

George L. Winkler, turret gunner and aerial engineer on a 13th AAF B-25 Mitchell bomber in the Netherlands East Indies and Philippines, has been promoted to sergeant. Son of Mrs. Elizabeth Boster, 346 Marcum Terrace, he has flown 25 missions and has received the Air Medal.

For wounds received in action in Belgium last December 17, Private James Ratcliff of Wayne Route 1, has received the Purple Heart. The son of Mr. and Mrs. A. J. Ratcliff is with a tank destroyer unit. His brother, Private First Class George Ratcliff, is in England.

Elsie M. Talbert, daughter of Mr. and Mrs. A. L. Ross, 247 Springdale Avenue, has been promoted to private first class at the Santa Maria, Calif., Army Air Field. Her husband, Garland J. Talbert, is with the Army in France.

Servicemen on leave or furlough include Private First Class George C. Henderson, 212 ½ Eighth Avenue; Corporal James Cook, husband of Mrs. Gladys Cook and son of Mr. and Mrs. J. E. Cook, 1208 Tenth Avenue; Sergeant W. T. Atkins, guest of Friends; Corporal Price W. Hall, Medical Corps, husband of Mrs. Rena K. Hall and son of Mr. and Mrs. Claude Kemp, 2713 Fourth Avenue; James F. Duty, U.S. Naval Air Force, husband of Mrs. Jaqueline Duty, 528 West Twenty-Sixth Street; Private First Class G. W. Mellert Jr., Army Air Force, son of Mr. and Mrs. G. W. Mellert Sr., 1905 Madison Avenue; Lieutenant (j. g.) A. W. Kendall, husband of Mrs. Agnes Fern Kendall, 347 Adams Avenue, and Private First Class Frederick E. Ryne, Marine Corps, son of Mrs. E. S. Ryne, 3716 Crane Avenue.

Glenna: *March 21ˢᵗ Wed. – Rained all day and turned to snow at night. I cooked again. Had only 27 children and one teacher. Didn't go to church that night.*

Rupert: *I went to school today. After school I helped Mother.*

"Diamond Dust": "Scoople ... 'Babe' Ruth's leg, the one on which they operated, is doing fine. Now the other knee is aching.; Mayor LaGuardia of New York will start the baseball season at the Yankee Stadium this year by throwing out the first gambler. H-mmmm; I am told that Harrisburg, Ky. has a woman basketball coach. Yet, some of the critics say they are afraid the boys won't take orders from a lady. Since when, fellows, since when; Adolph Rupp, the 'Mr. Basketball' of Kentucky Uni., was an eye-witness to the Logan-Huntington tete-a-tete at Arena Gardens. 'Now I can die happy,' smiled Adolph, 'I've seen everything.' P. S. His team is also nicknamed 'The Wildcats.'"[124]

Other sports news: In Charlotte, NC, Sammy Snead and Bryan Nelson, "the two top men in golf, wound up all square today [March 20] in a see-saw 18 hole playoff for first place in the $10,000 Charlotte Open golf tournament." They were both three under par at 69.[125]

Two area service men had been wounded in action, one on Iwo Jima and the other in Germany. "They are Private First Class J. M. Wysong, U.S. Marine Corps, husband of Mrs. Frances Burly Wysong, 910 Monroe Avenue, and Private First Class Heron M. Adkins of Branchland. Private Wysong, who went overseas in November is under treatment in a Naval hospital in the Pacific after his evacuation from Iwo. He has three children, James, Linda, and Robert, who reside with their mother at the Monroe Avenue address. Private Adkins, the son of Isaac Adkins, was wounded February 28. He entered the Army in October, 1942 and went overseas last April."[126]

"IN THE SERVICE":

Sergeant George Lewis, husband of Mrs. Alice M. Lewis, 1808 Marcum Terrace, has been awarded the Silver Star for gallantry in action. He is serving with the 157ᵗʰ Infantry Regiment of the 45ᵗʰ Division of the Seventh Army.

Corporal John Hager is spending a 30-day furlough with his parents, Mr. and Mrs. John Hager Sr., of Kenova, before returning next week to his station at Fort Bliss, Tex.

Seaman Second Class Velma L. Blake, daughter of Mr. and Mrs. A. C. Blake, 148 Fourth Avenue, has completed her basic training and indoctrination course at the Naval Training School in The Bronx, N.Y., and has received orders to report for duty at San Diego, Calif. Before enlisting in the service she was employed as a bill clerk at National Biscuit Co.

Glenna: *March 22ⁿᵈ Thursday – Cooked again. Went to revival that night. Ruth Johnson Smith was saved at work that day. Fair weather.*

Billy S. Queen, a radio technician with the 99th Division, was killed in action in Belgium on December 17. His mother was Mrs. Mary Queen of Crum, W.Va. A member of Crum Baptist Church, he graduated from Wayne High School and attended Marshall for eighteen months before he entered the Army.[127]

"Private First Class Charles Ray, reported missing in action in Luxembourg since December 23, is a German war prisoner, his parents, Mr. and Mrs. Baxter Ray of Salt Rock, reported yesterday after receipt of a card from him. He wrote that he is well."[128]

"IN THE SERVICE":

Corporal Glenn Tabor of East Lynn is serving with the Seventh Army in France as a messenger. He also has seen action as a courier in Tunisia, Sicily and Italy. He wears the Purple Heart for wounds received in Italy. His father, L. B. Tabor, lives in East Lynn.

Promotion of Captain John R. McCarthy, son of Mr. and Mrs. S. N. McCarthy, 819 Second Street, to the rank of major has been announced in a Fifth Air Force dispatch... Overseas since July, 1943, Major McCarthy has been awarded the Air Medal with two Oak Leaf Clusters and the Asiatic-Pacific ribbon with one campaign star. He is a graduate of Marshall College and attended the University of Cincinnati and the University of Minnesota.

Private Simon A. Osborne of Huntington, participant in the battle for Purple Heart Hill on Luzon, has been promoted to the rank of sergeant as assistant squad leader. He has been overseas for 15 months and holds the Good Conduct Medal, Combat Infantryman's Badge and Asiatic-Pacific ribbon with two stars.

A member of an infantry unit of the Thunderbird Division in France, Frank B. Cummings, 22, son of Mrs. Urna Cummings of Branchland, recently was promoted from corporal to sergeant. Sergeant Cummings division is credited with 365 days of actual combat since it took part in the invasion of Sicily. He entered the service in March, 1943, and went overseas in November, 1944.

Mr. and Mrs. H. R. Griffith, 1901 Madison Avenue, have returned from Columbus, O., where they received the Air Medal their son, Sergeant Thomas M. Griffith, was awarded for meritorious achievement in heavy bombardment missions over Europe. Sergeant Griffith is a prisoner of Germany.

Private Verlin Davis, son of Mr. and Mrs. Basil Davis, 1664 Thirteenth Avenue, has been awarded the Purple Heart for wounds received in action in Germany, according to a War Department message. He is a member of the 94th division. A twin brother, Private Vernon Davis, is with the Army Engineers in the Philippines.

Assistant supply sergeant at an Army General Hospital in Paris is Forest B. Kuhn of Salt Rock. Sergeant Kuhn's wife, Marjorie, lives at Omar and is employed by the West Virginia Coal & Coke Co.

After experiencing three weeks of air attacks in the port of Antwerp, Belgium, in a voyage as a member of a Navy gun crew aboard a merchant ship, Seaman First Class Donald Atkins has returned to the Naval Armed Guard Center in New Orleans. A farmer at Wayne before enlisting in June, 1943, he is the husband of Mrs. Arletta Atkins, 1544 Monroe Avenue.

Glenna: *March 23rd Friday – Lovely day. I cooked for the school again. Old Brownie came fresh. Had a pretty heifer calf. Went to revival meeting again. The Travis Choir from West Huntington came and the Cotton Choir from Midkiff came too.*

Rupert: *I went to school today. We had a test.*

"Old Brownie" was a fixture of my boyhood and youth. We usually had two milk cows, but Old Brownie was the tenured one. She went through her "dry" period every year and produced a calf in the spring.

President Roosevelt and his highest advisers took a night off to dine with capital newspapermen at the 22nd annual dinner of the White House Correspondents Association, held at the Slater Hotel, which followed a wartime pattern adopted after Pearl Harbor—a non-ration menu of "fruit, fish, chicken (no butter for rolls), ice cream and coffee." The article listed the guests: "Members of the cabinet; the Earl of Athlone, governor general of Canada; general of the Army George C. Marshall, chief of staff; Fleet Admiral Ernest J. King, commander-in-chief of the Fleet; Fleet Admiral William D. Leahy, the President's personal chief of staff, and Lieutenant General A. A. Vandegrift, commandant of the Marine Corps." Entertainment was provided by the *Columbia Broadcasting System.* Bob Trout was master of ceremonies and entertainers were Jimmy Durante, Garry Moore, Fannie Brice, Georgia Gibbs and Danny Kaye.[129]

In the Pacific, air raids began against Okinawa to prepare for an eventual American landing.[130]

"IN THE SERVICE":

Staff Sergeant Charles W. Withrow, 3608 Third Avenue, will be heard tonight at 8:45 P.M. over WSAZ in an interview recorded in the Mediterranean theater. Lieutenant Vick Knight, widely known radio producer, also will be on the program, speaking from the Western front.

Christine Fruth, ward nurse in the 38th Evacuation Hospital in Italy, has been promoted from second to first lieutenant. She is the daughter of Mr. and Mrs. Christopher Fruth of Mason. Two brothers, Carl and Ralph, also are in the service, both stationed in the United States.

Staff Sergeant Charles Hughes is home on furlough visiting his parents, Mr. and Mrs. J. T. Hughes, 1639 Seventh Avenue. He has completed 31 months duty in Italy and at the conclusion of his stay will report to Fort Meade, Md.

Corporal Walter D. Nunley, son of Mr. and Mrs. W. D. Nunley, 405 Cavell Court, is serving overseas with the Crusaders, veteran medium bombardment unit of the 13th AAF, which is attacking Japanese installations in the Netherlands East Indies. He is a ground station operator. Prior to that, Corporal Nunley was radioman in the crew of a sea rescue craft, which participated in 67 rescues of airmen forced down.

Promotion of Russell T. Maynard, 918 Chestnut Street, Kenova, pilot in a B-24 Liberator of the 15th Air Force overseas, to the rank of first lieutenant has been announced.

Technician Fifth Grade Harold Shannon, son of Mr. and Mrs. Dock Shannon, 1719 Walnut Street, Kenova, has completed 21 months of service in France.

Sergeant Lowell H. Beckley, 24, son of Mr. and Mrs. Paul D. Beckley of Prichard, has flown his 35th combat mission in the Italian theater as nose gunner on a B-24 Liberator of the Fifth Army Air Force. He holds the Air Medal with one Oak Leaf Cluster. A brother, Harold, is serving in the South Pacific and another brother, John, is training with the Air Force.

Glenna: *March 24ᵗʰ Saturday – Pretty day. I washed and that night went to meeting. Papa and Mama came up.*

Rupert: *I wanted to go to town today but couldn't. I helped mother.*

My grandparents' visits back to Salt Rock were frequent. They had never lived in the city and were homesick during their entire city-living experiment.

A *Huntington Herald-Dispatch* article titled "College Acts To Meet Acute Shortage Of Rural Teachers" stated, "Twenty-five students who will graduate from high schools here in June will be registered at Marshall College for a five-week intensive training period in preparation for rural school teaching next fall, Dean Ottis G. Wilson of Marshall announced yesterday." Superintendent Olin C. Nutter said, "Although no teachers with emergency certificates have been needed in Cabell County, there is an acute need in other areas for rural school teachers."[131]

In Germany, Montgomery's troops crossed the Rhine River at Wesel.

Easter DeButante Exclusive

Navy Blue or Black Calfskin Toeless Pump

7.95

D'Orsay flatterer that "goes with everything" . . . smartly simple for dressy clothes — or with tailored. High graceful heel. . .
—main floor.

Anderson Newcomb

"IN THE SERVICE":

Mr. and Mrs. Leslie R. Miles, 118 Shockey Drive, have received a letter from their son, Marine Corporal John Miles, dated March 16 from Iwo Jima, the date the island was announced as having been secured by Marine fighting forces. The message indicated their son was well and in good health. Another son, Private Leslie R. Miles Jr., is serving in Europe with a combat engineer battalion.

Electrician's Mate Third Class George W. T. Brandt Jr., husband of Mrs. Wanda Brandt, 2713 ½ Emmons Avenue, is serving aboard an LST with the Navy in the South Pacific where he recently took part in the invasion of Iwo Jima. He has been at sea for seven months... A brother-in-law, Technician Fifth Grade Jesse O. D. Lewis, son of the late O. D. Lewis and Mrs. Thomas Bostick of Ironton, O., is with the Army in Italy, after two years overseas, including action in Sicily and North Africa.

Sergeant Clyde "Ikie" Napier has returned to his station at Hondo Army Air Base, Tex., after a 15-day furlough with his parents, Mr. and Mrs. W. F. Napier, 1217 Monroe Avenue. He enlisted June 20, 1942.

Corporal Floyd E. Smith has been awarded the Good Conduct Medal at the Ontario Army Air Field in California where he is a technical supply clerk. His parents, Mr. and Mrs. Harry F. Smith, reside in Chesapeake. His brother, Kimball Lee Smith, is serving with the Navy.

Private Joseph E. Wallace, 351 Smith Street, is serving with the Seventh Army in Europe in an infantry regiment.

Seaman Second Class Chester Pierce is seriously ill at the Naval base hospital, Great Lakes, where he was operated on for a ruptured appendix. he recently returned from 34 months overseas duty and spent a leave with his mother, Mrs. Mary Bailey of Wheelwright, Ky.

Private Willard C. Hall is now serving with the Seventh Army in France. He is the husband of Mrs. Mildred L. Hall of Barboursville.

Staff Sergeant Charles W. Withrow, 3608 Third Avenue, was heard over WSAZ at 8:45 P.M. Saturday in a recorded interview from the Mediterranean theatre.

William H. Forester, with the U.S. Army in the Central Pacific, has recently been promoted to the rank of first lieutenant. His parents, Mr. and Mrs. J. H. Forester, reside at 246 Eighth Avenue. His wife, the former Miss Moyce Morgan, resides at 424 Washington Avenue.

Lieutenant (Junior Grade) Roy E. Huston, USN, is spending a leave with his wife, the former Miss Ellen Frances Burnett of Kenova, W.Va., after 11 months of overseas duty. Lieutenant and Mrs. Huston are visiting his mother, Mrs. Elizabeth G. Huston, 6190 Rosalind Road, and Mrs. Huston's parents, Mr. and Mrs. Oren Burnett of Kenova, W.Va.

Bob Perry, cook (second class) arrived home last night to spend a leave with his parents, Mr. and Mrs. Frank Perry, 1650 Washington Avenue. He is stationed aboard a destroyer.

Private First Class Floyd A. Pennington, son of Mrs. Ida Pennington of Midkiff, and Private First Class Earl Bates, son of James Bates, 24 ½ West Fourth Avenue, have been awarded Combat Infantryman Badges while serving with the Rainbow Division.

Lieutenant David Fox Jr., a bombardier-navigator with the 12th AAF based in Corsica, was recently wounded in action. His father, David Fox of Southwood Heights, recently has news of his recovery following an operation which was performed by Major T. Ewen Taylor, Huntington physician and friend of the airman.

Sergeant Earl B. Reynolds of West Hamlin has been admitted to the Woodrow Wilson General Hospital at Staunton, Va. for wounds received in action in the South Pacific. A veteran of ten months overseas duty, he wears the Bronze Star.

First Lieutenant Erskine C. Chapman, 2636 Guyan Avenue; Captain Paul W. Bonham, 902 West Second Street; Major Frank H. Preston Jr., 600 Lower Terrace; Private Basil N. Bentley of Milton; Sergeant Charles B. Morris and Private John J. Hall, both of Matoaka, are members of the bridge builders of an engineer regiment, following the advance of the U.S. Seventh Army troops, which has opened approximately 600 miles of supply lines from the Riviera to the Rhine.

Glenna: *March 25th 1945 Sun. – I joined the Salt Rock M. E. Church. Jaruel Porter was baptized in Tyler Creek. Others who joined the church were Edith Porter, [Florence] Nida, Jaruel Porter, and myself. It was a beautiful day. The revival meeting closed that night. John Porter was renewed.*

Rupert: *Mother moved her membership from the Baptist church to the Methodist.*

Mother had joined a Baptist church in the area when she was younger, but had attended Salt Rock Methodist Church for several years.

On the lighter side: "Candidates for Carnival Queen to be chosen at the annual Junior Carnival March 29 at Wayne High School are ... Hope Sellards, junior; Virginia Adkins, senior; Beulah Adkins, sophomore, and Betty Jo Bowen"[132]

"The Barboursville churches will begin the commemoration of Easter this week, with a service on Good Friday, at the Pilgrim Holiness Church, from 12 to 3 P.M. Ministers taking part will be: the Rev. J. H. Sherwood, pastor of the Pilgrim Holiness Church; the Rev. Ira Lyons, of Steele Memorial Methodist Church; The Rev. John Sassaman of the Baptist Church; The Rev. A. E. Tullah, of the First Methodist Church;

the Rev. C. A. Slaughter, and the Rev. Ivy Yoak, retired ministers of the Methodist Church. The theme will be: 'The Seven Last Words of Christ.' On Easter Sunday at 7 A.M. a sunrise service will be held in the high school auditorium with all churches in the community participating."[133]

"WITH THE COLORS":

First Sergeant Charles E. Goodall, son of Mr. and Mrs. Iven C. Goodall of Chesapeake, O., has been cited by Major General Raymond S. McLain of the Ninth Army for "outstanding performance of military duty." Sergeant Goodall "actively aided by engineer operators such as mine lifting, road building and bridge construction," the citation said, "the rapid advancement of armored divisions, infantry divisions and cavalry groups through France, Belgium, Holland, and into Germany."

Private Orville W. Vance, former A & P store manager, is spending a furlough with his wife, Mrs. Eva Vance, and son Gary at 2804 Cottage Street...

Private First Class Jack L. Saunders, paratrooper in England, recently was interviewed in a radio broadcast from a BBC station. He wears the presidential citation for a combat jump on D-Day when he landed in Europe with combat engineers to lay mines, barbered wire, booby traps and do general engineering work. A former employee of Appalachian Electric Power Co. in Huntington, his home is at 1709 Franklin Avenue.

James C. Lilly has been promoted to the rank of private first class while serving with the Second Provisional Troop Carrier Group, Pope Field, N.C. He is the son of Mr. and Mrs. O. S. Lilly, 2838 Park Avenue.

Samuel L. Hogsett, overseas eight months, has been promoted to the rank of sergeant while serving in the European theatre of operations. He is the son of Mr. and Mrs. Morgan Hogsett of Glenwood, W.Va. and the husband of Mrs. Virginia Hogsett, 1109 Madison Avenue.

Staff Sergeant Harold L. Goodall, who holds the Purple Heart and Air Medal with an Oak Leaf Cluster, has arrived at Miami Beach, Fla. for reassignment. As a B-17 radio operator and gunner, he flew 16 missions in the European theatre before being wounded in combat. He is the son of Mrs. O. W. Goodall, 305 Thirty-second Street, and the husband of Mrs. Edna Goodall, Texas, Md.

Second Lieutenant Barr Sinnett Jr. has arrived at Bradley Field, Conn. to train in a P-47 Thunderbolt fighter plane. Mrs. Sinnett, the former Miss Ina Mae Davis, joined him there last week. They plan to live in Windsor Locks, Conn. Lieutenant Sinnett is the son of Mr. and Mrs. Barr Sinnett of 1525 Seventh Avenue.

Donald Plant, seaman second class, has returned to Great Lakes, Il. for eight weeks basic engineering training. He has been visiting his parents, Mr. and Mrs. C. R. Plant of Renton, Wash., formerly of Huntington.

Lieutenant Colonel Robert E. Wallace, 1847 Underwood Avenue, is home on a 21-day leave, recuperating from wounds received Nov. 30 while commanding an infantry battalion in action at Lindern, Germany. He will return to Oliver General Hospital, Augusta, Georgia.

Glenna: *March 26th Monday – I cooked for school again. Somebody had broken into the old school house and took some things. A pretty day.*

Rupert: *I went to school today. After school I helped Mother.*

"Diamond Dust": "This column has Spring fever today. It may be because Normantown nosed out the Logan 'Wildcats,' 50–49 in a photo finish for the West Virginia basketball championship Satt'y., at Morgantown. So—a snappy salute to the winner, Normantown, and five stars ***** to the losers, Logan's gallant 'Wildcats.' . . .Normantown, with a total population of 300 souls, and Logan with a proud population of 6,000 citizens, are the two smallest towns ever to tee off against each other for the cage classic of the Mountain State. If population is all that it takes to win basketball tournaments, Huntington and Wheeling—not Logan and Normantown—would have met in the World Series at the WVU Field House, brother-r-r-r. Moral: It only takes five boys to make a basketball team." Later, in the same column, Duke, seemingly unable to let go of the subject, says, "The big song hit in Normantown, W.Va. today is: 'Oh, what a beautiful morning' and at Logan, 'Surrey With the Fringe on Top.'"[134]

An article in the *Huntington Herald-Dispatch* hailed the merits of a Huntington soldier: "The Croix de Guerre for exceptional services rendered in the liberation of France has been awarded Major Harry C. Brindle, 32, of Huntington by General Charles de Gaulle, president of the provisional government of France, according to word received by his wife, Mrs. Sara Gibson Brindle, 1570 Washington Boulevard. At the same time, Mrs. Brindle learned her husband was recently awarded the Bronze Star Medal for meritorious achievement as commanding officer of a task force charged with penetrating the Siegfried Line, and a Certificate of Merit in recognition of 'conspicuously meritorious and outstanding performance of military duty.'" Major Brindle, a native of Martinsburg, West Virginia, attended Marshall College and worked at the International Nickel Company before he entered the service in January 1941. He had been overseas since November 1943. His three children live with his wife in Huntington.[135]

"IN THE SERVICE":

Helping to halt a Japanese banzai charge to wrest a hill from a stiffly resisting Nipponese forces in the Philippines, was the manner in which Private First Class Audie Ramey of Branchland passed his twenty-first birthday. He is the son of Mrs. Lettie Ramey, has been overseas for 11 months and was a former coal miner. His brother James is serving with a Navy Construction Battalion in the Philippines.

Three Huntington men are among the enlisted personnel at a Superfortress base in the Marianas whose efforts have made it possible for the giant bombers to strike regularly at Japan. They are Staff Sergeant William L. Cremeans, son of Mr. and Mrs. Clayton Cremeans, 2905 Third Avenue; Sergeant Everett A. Williams, husband of the former Nora E. Roach, 3037 Third Avenue and son of Mr. and Mrs. Jesse Williams, 3012 Sixth Avenue, and Corporal Doyle E. Smith, son of Mr. and Mrs. James C. Smith, 1814 Fifth Avenue.

Major Charles S. Rife, thoracic surgeon, son of Dr. J. W. Rife, 1701 Chestnut Street, Kenova, is a member of the staff of the Fifth Army's Ninth Evacuation Hospital... This veteran medical unit has been providing expert treatment for the Fifth Army wounded and ill all the way through the Italian campaign.

Private Joseph Wallace, 351 Smith Street, has been assigned to the 399th Infantry Regiment of the 100th Infantry Division and is now serving in eastern France...

Private First Class William J. Childers, son of Mrs. W. J. Childers, 1222 Charleston Avenue, a member of the famous Rainbow Division, has been awarded the Combat Infantryman Badge.

Private First Class Ernis L. Keener of Huntington, a member of the 151st Infantry [Attached to the 38th Division on Bataan. He fought in the battle of Zig-Zag Pass.], served on the selected guard of honor for General Douglass MacArthur when he returned to Corregidor. He is the husband of Ruth W. Keener, 3615 Fourth Avenue, and has been overseas for 15 months in the Central and Southwest Pacific.

Now stationed at Tinker Field at Oklahoma City is Staff Sergeant James Hazelett. His wife and daughter live at 838 Washington Avenue, He is sergeant of the guard for a base unit.

Seaman First Class Dorothy May Smith, daughter of Mrs. A. A. Smith, 219 Eighth Avenue, has been graduated from the U.S. Naval Training School at Stillwater, Okla. She has been assigned to active duty at the Navy radio station in Norfolk, Va.

Corporal Wardie L. Swann, 101 North Walnut Street, has been awarded the Good Conduct ribbon at Morris Field at Charlotte, N.C.

Sergeant Arthur W. Smith, son of Mr. and Mrs. Charles Smith, 1310 Fifteenth Street, has been promoted to the grade of staff sergeant in an infantry training battalion at Camp Croft, S.C.

Promotion of Jack C. Beckett Jr., 20-year-old aerial gunner on an Eighth Air Force B-17 Flying Fortress, from corporal to sergeant has been announced. Sergeant Beckett is the son of Mrs. Agnes V. Bias, 1343 Fourth Avenue.

After 33 months' continuous service in Australia, New Guinea and the Netherlands East Indies, Corporal William Leroy Bias, son of Mr. and Mrs. William H. Bias, 1358 Hall Street, and husband of Mrs. Vivian McCorkle Bias, 142 Maupin Road, is returning home under the personal rotation program.

Glenna: *March 27th Tuesday — A lovely day. I cooked for school again. Viola Morrison came up and helped me wash dishes.*

Viola, one of Arnold Morrison's daughters, was also one of Mother's former students at Walnut Grove School.

"IN THE SERVICE":

Private Kenneth J. Moore, 1225 Third Avenue; Staff Sergeant Denver E. Short of Davin, W.Va., Private Charles Earnest of Lorado, W.Va., and Corporal Foster M. Sisk of War, W.Va., are members of the 101st Airborne Division on the Western Front, whose acting commander, Brigadier General Anthony C. McCauliffe when asked to surrender by the Germans, answered, "Nuts."

Corporal Leonard E. Barber, son of Mr. and Mrs. L. E. Barber, 1601 Doulton Avenue, has been awarded the Bronze Star medal for bravery in action with an antiaircraft unit of the U.S. Third Army in Germany. He also holds the Good Conduct medal and the European campaign bar. He is a former city employee and before entering the Army in 1943 was employed by the Huntington Cab Co.

Technician Fifth Grade Ora J. Grady of Riddle, W.Va., with the 308th Combat Battalion in Germany, has been awarded the Bronze Star Medal. He was cited for "displaying outstanding courage and devotion to duty" as a jeep driver during the severe combat and difficult terrain from December 10 to 25. His mother is Mrs. Maude Kate Grady.

Private First Class Haspel R. Mooney, U.S. Army, was wounded this month in Germany, his parents, Mr. and Mrs. R. L. Mooney, 401 Vinson Road, were notified yesterday... He entered the service four years ago and has been overseas since last year.

Corporal William E. Rowe, Army Air Forces, has arrived in Brazil, his mother, Mrs. Cora Rowe, 537 Buffington Street, learned yesterday. Corporal Rowe was a driver for the Ohio Valley Bus Co. before entering the service. His wife resides at Big Creek, W.Va.

A member of the famous Rainbow division since last September, Private Robert B. Sanford, 26, of Barboursville, has been advanced to the rank of sergeant in the 232nd Infantry in France. His wife, Mrs. Leon Sanford, and son, Steven D. Sanford live at Barboursville.

Lieutenant Henry S. White, USNR, of Matewan, W.Va., has returned from a tour of combat duty as pilot of fighter planes based on one of the Navy's big carriers in the Pacific.

As a member of the squadron of Air Group 2, he flew a Hellcat on 20 missions while taking part in strikes against Formosa, Okinawa, the Philippines, Hongkong, and French Indo-China. Son of Mrs. Mary White, the 29-year-old flier attended West Virginia University and Marshall College.

Glenna: *March 28th Wed. – I cooked for school again. Weather is very pretty. Went to prayer meeting that night. Church is being fixed up.*

Argentina declared war on Germany.

"IN THE SERVICE":

Second Lieutenant James R. Green, son of Mr. and Mrs. Warren Green, 1417 Sixth Avenue, has been awarded the Air Medal for meritorious achievement as pilot of a P-47 Thunderbolt plane based in Italy in attacks on enemy installations and communications. Overseas since October 1944, he has flown 41 missions as a member of the veteran fighter group which first adopted the P-47 for low level bombing and strafing. Lieutenant Green enlisted December 11, 1942 and received his commission April 15, 1944 at Foster Field, Texas.

Corporal Frank L. Chambers, son of Mrs. F. W. Schneider, 1304 Ninth Avenue, recently received a Battle Participation Star for the German campaign. He also wears stars for the Normandy and Northern France campaigns, as well as the

Distinguished Unit Citation presented for work in the Invasion of France on D-day. He arrived overseas in May, 1944.

Eight Huntington applicants for the Navy's new combat air crewman's program have been transferred to Washington where they will be given final examinations for acceptance, the Navy Recruiting Station announced. They were Jack H. Aldridge, 325 Hughes Street; Carl J. Fulks, 1024 Jefferson Avenue; John S. Sowards, Pikesville, Ky.; Charles M. Wilkerson, Huntington; Eugene S. McVey, Third Avenue and Eighteenth Street; Billy G. Hite, 210 Baer Street; Robert M. Davis, Route 4, Huntington, and Allen B. Maxwell, 5693 Ohio River Road.

As a member of the Army Transportation Corps in England, Corporal Archie C. Malcolm, 4813 Beadley Road, has been overseas for three and one-half years. Arriving in Iceland in August, 1941, his unit has since served in Iceland, Southern England and France... Private Otis Marshall of Wayne also is [in] a member battalion.

Award of the Combat Infantryman Badge to Staff Sergeant Donald N. Weiseman, 22, 1223 Tenth Avenue, for exemplary conduct in action with the 17th Airborne Division, has been announced. Son of Mrs. Frederica Weiseman of the Tenth Avenue address, he is a machine gun section leader with a glider infantry company.

Private First Class Eugene O. Leighty, son of Mr. and Mrs. Edward Leighty, 2838 Fourth Avenue, now is entitled to wear two gold stripes for serving overseas for more than a year. He is an ordnance specialist in a 15th Air Force B-24 Liberator Bomb group that has completed more than 150 bombing missions from Italy.

Returning from an overseas hospital a few days ago, Private Lloyd Duncan is visiting his family at Chesapeake, O., Route 1 on a 21-day furlough. He was wounded last November 21 in Germany while serving with the 30th Infantry Division and will return to Billings General Hospital at Fort Benjamin Harrison, Ind. for further treatment. He is the husband of Mrs. Crystal Duncan and father of two children, Carol and Donnie. His parents are Mr. and Mrs. Oscar Duncan.

The Bronze Star for meritorious service has been presented [to] Captain Edward W. Knight Jr., whose parents live at 923 Madison Avenue. He is commander of Company B, 329th Engineer Combat Battalion in Germany.

Captain Robert C. Rosenheim, son of Mrs. W. S. Rosenheim, 411 Tenth Avenue, and the late Dr. Rosenheim, has been promoted from a first lieutenant at headquarters of the Second Air Force at Colorado Springs, Colo...

Mrs. Pauline Stiltner Thornburgh, 1537 West Fifth Avenue, has received a Purple Heart award from her husband, Private First Class Hugh Warren Thornburgh. He was wounded in action in Germany last November 2.

Private First Class A. B. Huntley Jr., son of Mr. and Mrs. A. B. Huntley Sr., 146 Gallaher Street, is in the Oliver General Hospital at Augusta, Ga... He was wounded in Luxembourg last November 1 while serving with the Third Army.

Private Carl Turner, whose wife, Pauline, and three sons live at 145 Gallaher Street, is serving with the Thirty-second Division on Luzon in the Philippines.

Vivian E. Ross, seaman first class, USNR, daughter of Mr. and Mrs. H. C. Ross, 640 Ninth Avenue, has reported for duty at the Bureau of Ordinance in Washington. She received her recruit training at the Naval Training School in New York City.

Glenna: *March 29th Thur. – I cooked for school for the last time. I'm quitting this job. Showers this morning.*

Rupert: *Hot lunch ended today. I went to school today*

It's easy to detect some disdain in Mother's declaration, justified considering her work load.

War fronts: On the Western Front, the British Second Army advanced nearly unopposed toward Berlin, and the U.S. Third joined the First Army at Giessen. In other U.S. Division actions, "Fourth Armored, drives 27 miles north from Honan; Fifth Infantry, mops up in Frankfurt; Sixth Armored, drives beyond Frankfurt; Ninth Armored, races toward Frankfurt from First Army sector; 30th Infantry, breaks into Duisburg; 35th, gains in Ruhr mop up, captures Hoten; 79th, mops up in Duisburg; 87th, advances east of Boppard area; 90th crosses Main between Frankfurt and Hanau; 313th, enters Holten." On the Pacific Front, the U.S. captured the Japanese-held city of Cebu in the Philippines and long-range search planes sunk four freighter-transports off Saigon.[136]

"IN THE SERVICE":

Private First Class Brent H. Warren, with the Fourth Marine Division on Iwo Jima, was wounded on the eighteenth day of battle, his mother, Mrs. Gladys Warren, 1226 Eighteenth Street, was notified yesterday. The letter stated that Private Warren was in an Iwo Jima hospital after suffering shrapnel wounds from a Jap hand grenade.

Mrs. Arnold Davis, 1312 Fifteenth Street, has received a telegram from her brother, Staff Sergeant Waitman B. Childers, that he is in the states for a furlough after 42 months overseas with the Third Army. Sergeant Childers, son of Mrs. Laura Childers of Lavalette, served in Iceland, France and Germany.

Lieutenant and Mrs. David W. Arnett have returned to his Army Air Force base at Winfield, Kan. after visiting his parents in Martinsburg, W.Va., and her parents, Dr. and Mrs. J. C. Wells of Beverly Hills [Huntington]. Mrs. Arnett was formerly Miss Anne Virginia Wells.

Corporal George Baylous, son of Mrs. Calvin Baylous, 2483 Third Avenue, sings bass in the choir of the 88th (Blue Devil) Infantry Division Headquarters on the Fifth Army front in Northern Italy...

Announcement of the promotion of Frank W. Martin ... to master sergeant ... in Germany. Master Sergeant Martin, son of Mrs. Ruth G. Martin, 434 Seventh Avenue, has served in England, France, Belgium and Holland.

Gunner's Mate Third Class John W. Cooney has returned to New York City after a four-day leave [with] his mother and other relatives in Kenova. He is assigned to Army transport and recently returned from France and England.

Seaman Second Class Robert. L. Casey is home visiting his wife. Mrs. Charlene Casey, 714 Lucian Street. He is stationed at Sampson, New York.

Sergeant Clarence Hicks is visiting his mother, Mrs. Oscar Hicks of Milton.

John Armstrong of the Navy is visiting his parents, Mr. and Mrs. H. F. Armstrong of Barboursville. He is stationed in Columbus, O.

Corporal George K. Dillman of the 20th Air Force, stationed on Saipan as B-29 ground crewman is home on a 21-day furlough. He is the son of Mrs. C. R. Dillman of Huntington. After completion of his furlough, Corporal Dillman will report to Miami Beach, Fla. for reassignment.

Ensign Ernest J. Thabet Jr., USNR, who is spending a leave with his parents, Mr. and Mrs. E. J. Thabet, 1211 Washington Avenue, has as his guest Ensign Gerald Tomlinson, USNR, of Seattle, Wash. Both Ensign Thabet and Ensign Tomlinson were commissioned and awarded their naval wings last week at Pensacola, Fla. At the completion of their leave the officers will report to Sanford, Fla. Naval Air Station for operational training.

Lieutenant (j. g.) Robert L. Brown was promoted March 1 to that rank while serving on a landing ship in the Pacific, his wife, the former Miss Vivian Black of Lesage, was notified yesterday. Lieutenant Brown, a Marshall College graduate, has a daughter, Kathie Sue, born last October, whom he has never seen.

Glenna: *March 30th Friday – We cleaned the [church] house up. Several helped. It was a pretty day. Good Friday.*

Rupert: *There wasn't any school today. I helped clean the church house.*

"IN THE SERVICE":

Private First Class William E. Davidson, husband of Mrs. Ethel Davidson, 214 Division Street, and son of Mrs. Ella J. Garten of Clifton Forge, Va. has been awarded the Bronze Star for heroic achievement in Belgium last January 8 when he was sent into enemy territory during a heavy snowstorm to obtain information. According to a citation from Major General L. S. Hobb, Private Davidson and his four companions returned with data which was of valuable assistance to his unit. Private Davidson is the father of two children, Tommy and Peggy, and was employed by the International Nickel Co. before entering the Army. He has been overseas for six months.

Mrs. Rufus Elliott of Huntington has received a card from her son, Private Richard A. Elliott, who wrote he is a prisoner-of-war in Germany. He had previously been reported as missing in action since December 9. A member of the Army Medical Corps, Private Elliott entered service Jan. 17, 1944 and went overseas last August.

Private Benjamin T. Maynard, son of Mr. and Mrs. James Maynard, 234 Staunton Street, has been missing in action in Germany since March 13, the War Department had advised the parents. He was serving with the Ninth Army. He was employed by the Huntington Furniture Corp. before entering the Army about two years ago.

Led by Lieutenant William B. Taylor, USNR, 620 Trenton Place, Torpedo Unit 41, with Admiral Halsey's Third Fleet from the time of the Palau invasion through strikes at China in January, has returned to Norfolk, Va. for leave and reassignment...

Second Lieutenant Charles A. Hodge, son of Mr. and Mrs. C. A. Hodge, 717 Sixth Avenue, and husband of Mrs. Wanda Hodge of Slaton, Tex. has been assigned to the San Marcos Army Air Field, an AAF navigation school. A veteran of six combat missions, he wears the Distinguished Unit Citation with one Oak Leaf Cluster and the Air Medal with two Oak Leaf Clusters.

Lieutenant Richard Cartwright Jr., 1333 Fourteenth Street, piloted a P-38 Lightening on a recent 13th AAF Fighter Command strafing sweep of Formosa... The sweep was made by the "Fighting 13th Vampire Unit." ...

Staff Sergeant Joe D. Sullivan, son of Mr. and Mrs. C. O. Sullivan, 1739 Sixth Avenue, is a member of the 557th Fighter group of the Eighth Air Force in England... He is in the intelligence section of a squadron.

Corporal Donald L. Chapman, son of Mr. and Mrs. F. R. Chapman, 905 ½ Twenty-eighth Street, and his brother-in-law, Seaman Second Class Andrew T. Quinn, Seabee, husband of Mrs. Lois Quinn, Rear 904 Twenty-eighth Street, were reunited recently in Hawaii.

Ensign William Clifton Wagoner, 21, son of Mr. and Mrs. W. L. Wagoner of Barboursville, received his commission as an aviator in the Naval Reserve and was awarded wings at recent graduation exercises at the naval air training base at Pensacola, Florida. [Bill Wagner would later marry Frances Paugh, one of my Salt Rock Elementary School teachers. He once buzzed Salt Rock School in a small plane. He later owned a grocery store in Barboursville, across the street from the junior high school.]

Glenna: *March 31st Saturday – Rupert went to town. I cleaned the house and baked a cake...*

Rupert: *I went to ~~school~~ town today. I saw a good show*

On the sports front: "Skinny, spindle-shanked Willie Pep, who is in a class by himself as a featherweight boxer, today entered a fairly exclusive class of World War II veterans. Pep, who signs his checks 'William Papaleo,' received a medical discharge from the Army authorities at Fort Devens, Mass., [it was] announced today. He left the Navy after seven mouths of service."[137] (Pep held a discharge from two branches of the armed forces in the same war. The Navy had earlier discharged him because of a punctured ear drum.)

"IN THE SERVICE":

Private First Class Richard M. Hedrick, son of Mrs. Maryetta Hedrick, 2052 Fourth Avenue, has been awarded the Bronze Star Medal posthumously for heroic action in France, the War Department has advised the mother, who will be presented with her son's medal. He was killed last September 29. Private Hedrick's citation praised him for rescuing a wounded officer of his mechanized cavalry unit under heavy enemy fire and then returning to his machine gun post to continue the fight.

Private Billy Templeton, son of Mr. and Mrs. Reed Templeton of Chesapeake, O. has been promoted to private first class in the 70th Division of the Seventh Army in Germany. He has been awarded the Combat Infantry Badge. Private Templeton has been in the Army for about a year and overseas since last December. Brothers in the service are Corporal Jack Templeton with the Army in India, and Corporal Julian C. Templeton, U.S. Marine Corps, in the Pacific.

Boatswain's Mate Second Class Wallace G. Jefferson of Barboursville, was among the men of the amphibious Navy who helped carry American soldiers across the Rhine River.

Private John W. Meadows, son of Mr. and Mrs. Emil Meadows of Glenwood Route 2, recently played dead to avoid death or capture by the Germans while serving with the Fifth Army in Italy. He was a member of a three-man patrol caught in heavy German fire, They rolled into a ditch and the Germans looked at the "bodies" and then departed.

Seaman Johnny William Jones, son of Mrs. Rosie Jones, 4548 James River Turnpike, Elbert Harmon Jr. of Northfolk and Van Marcum of Accoville are among West Virginians serving aboard the old battleship USS *Pennsylvania* which was sunk at Pearl Harbor and is now back in the Pacific.

Private First Class Harry A. Chinn of Huntington Route 3 is a member of the famous Mars Task Force fighting the Japanese in Burma...

Private First Class Robert M. Fleeshman, 415 Ninth Avenue, is a member of the staff of the 117th Evacuation Hospital with the Sixth Army Group in France...

Sergeant Marion G. Terry, 1923 Virginia Avenue, is a member of the 805th Tank Destroyer Battalion which has fought through the Winter as artillery from a ridge overlooking the Po Valley in Northern Italy. [This seems incomplete as it is unclear whether they took artillery fire or gave it.]

Corporal Welford R. Pygman, son of Mr. and Mrs. Chlovis C. Pygman, 1360 Hall Street, recently received the Purple Heart Medal at a ceremony of the 538th Quartermaster Battalion in France. He was wounded last June 7 but continued to lead his squad...

Private First Class Dale Johnson of Huntington is at Moore General Hospital at Swannanoa, N.C. for rest after two years' service in the South Pacific. He was with the Army Medical Corps on Guam, Leyte and Luzon.

Corporal Drexel Dyer, 1733 Doulton Avenue, is serving with an Army Engineers unit in Belgium, working with Belgian allies who haul supplies by barge. He formerly was employed by the Ohio River Dredging Co. and the Wilson Sand & Supply Co.

Corporal Oswald Peters, who has just completed an advanced course of radar at Boca Raton Field, Fla., arrived in Huntington yesterday to visit his sister, Mrs. L. J. Marshall of Green Oak Drive...

Corporal Richard Perry, son of Mr. R. J. Perry of Salt Rock, was recently promoted to that rank at Camp Plauche at New Orleans, La. where he is stationed with the Army Transportation Corps. Corporal Perry has served in the Army for 14 months.

April

ROOSEVELT, TRUMAN

GLENNA: APRIL 1ST SUNDAY – EASTER. THE CHURCH WAS BEAUTIFUL
with the new seats and polished floor. Lucian Stevens preached for us. Had an egg hunt for the children. Lovely day but cool.

Rupert: *Today is Easter. I went to Sunday school. There was a Easter egg hunt. I found 4 eggs.*

Ernie Pyle's writing brought touches of the human element to the brutal world of war. In hindsight, I find this day's elegant column especially poignant since his voice would soon be silenced. He described a makeshift house built on an island for Lieutenant Colonel John H. Griffith by his men as being "wonderfully comfortable," then spoke poetically of the sea, fifty feet away. "Before you is only the curve of the lagoon, and the pounding of incessant rollers on the reef a hundred yards out, and the white clouds in the far blue sky. Several times a day sudden tropical showers drench and cool the place."[138]

United States troops, 60,000 strong, landed on Okinawa.[139]

A Barboursville family received dreadful news: "Private First Class Billy Gwinn was killed in action in Germany March 14, his sister, Mrs. John Jefferson of Barboursville, has been informed by the War Department; enlisting in the service last August he was sent overseas January15 and served with the 39th Division of General Hodges Army; in addition to Mrs. Jefferson, he is survived by another sister, Mrs. K. B. Harlan also of Barboursville and a brother, Private First Class John L. Gwinn with the First Cavalry in Manila."[140]

"WITH THE COLORS":

F. M. Plymale, aviation machinist's mate first class, of Huntington is stationed at a naval air base in the Marianas. He has been overseas 13 months, including 10 at Eniwetok in the Marshall Islands. He is the nephew of Miss Ruth Plymale of Huntington. His wife and daughter are living with Mrs. Plymale's parents at Palatka, Fla.

Serving on Iwo Jima with the U.S. Marines is Corporal Paul Frazier, according to word received by his wife, Mrs. Rachael Frazier of Kenova. Corporal Frazier has been overseas 26 months and participated in the Bougainville and Guam campaigns...

Chaplain John W. Hollister is with an armored division moving toward Berlin, it was reported yesterday. The chaplain is a member of the West Virginia Conference of the Methodist Church and was minister of the Milton Methodist Church before entering the services. Chaplain Hollister formerly taught at Morris Harvey College and was associate pastor of the Johnson Memorial Methodist Church. His wife [Blanche M. Hollister] and three children are residing in Wayne. [He was about forty-five years old at the time. Rev. Hollister died in 1988.]

Sergeant Max Whitley, son of Mrs. Zoe Whitley, 2527 Third Avenue, who returned from overseas duty to be assigned to Sedalia

Army Field, Warrensburg, Mo., has been notified that his troop carrier group in Europe has been awarded the Distinguished Unit Citation. He was a member of this group which participated in the initial phases of the European invasion, delivering paratroopers and glider infantrymen to their assigned areas.

Private First Class Sidney Christy, son of Orlando Christy of Huntington, who served 37 months as a cook ... in the American theatre of operations, has returned to Miami Beach, Fla. for a period of rest and reassignment processing...

Private First Class Cledas O. Moreland, son of Mr. and Mrs. Luther Moreland, 1928 Eleventh Avenue, recently celebrated his 21st birthday in Germany, where he is serving with the Ninth Army.

First Lieutenant Merideth Price Wiswell, son of Mrs. M. P. Wiswell, 530 Fifth Street, has been assigned to duty at the ATC Army Air Base, Fairfield, Calif. He is a graduate of Huntington Central High School, 1937, and Washington and Lee University, 1941...

Glenna: *April 2nd Monday – I washed. Irene Donahoe and her son Bernard from the Army came to see us that night. Rain in the evening.*

Rupert: *I went to school today. Mother washed today. Mother's cousin and her son visited in the evening.*

I'm not sure if the kinship with Irene Donahoe was on my grandfather's or grandmother's side of the family, but visitations back and forth were frequent. Cleve Donahoe, Irene's husband, was a carpenter. He built Mother's house in 1934 and would build our new house in 1951.

An AP article from London titled, "Britain's Unwed Mothers Pose International Problem," stated, "Illegitimate babies, born in increasing numbers in a Britain crowded with Allied soldiers, are beginning to cry loud enough to be heard in international legislative halls." The article went on to say that U.S. and Canadian governments would be asked to provide financial aid for the children "who have arrived at the rate of more than six in every 100 births in 1943, latest year for which figures are available."[141] (Our boys were quite active—in many ways.)

"IN THE SERVICE":

Gunners Mate First Class Carl Collins, U.S. Coast Guard, of Ashland, is serving at a Coast Guard base in the Pacific which helps facilitate the movement of battle-bound sea traffic. The unit with which Collins serves is credited with breaking up four sabotage attempts during the past year. He is the son of Mr. and Mrs. Marion Collins of Ashland.

Overseas assignment awaits Corporal H. B. Adkins, son of Mr. and Mrs. J. S. Adkins, 117 Ninth Avenue, who has completed his required phases of combat training at the Mountain Home Army Air Field, Mountain Home, Idaho, as a radio operator on Liberator bombers.

Technician Fourth Grade Cecil T. Burchett, son of Mrs. T. J. Burchett of Huntington Route 4, has been awarded the Good Conduct Medal at Fort George G. Meade, Md. He has been in service for four years and is an Army cook.

Glenna: *April 3rd Tuesday – I ironed nearly all day and mended everything. Cloudy and windy. Mrs. Almeda Keyser died at midnight.*

Rupert: *I went to school today. Mother ironed today.*

Seventy-seven year old Almeda Keyser was the wife of Charles Lee Keyser. Her parents were Elisha Dial and Mary Hatfield.[142]

The National Collegiate Football Rules Committee reported rule changes: "Forward passing will be permitted anywhere behind the line of scrimmage and a second successive out-of-bounds kickoff will be put in play by the receiving team on the kicking eleven's 40 yard line." There were also these changes: a substitute could report to any official on the field; the elbow-block was made illegal, and none of the center's body could extend beyond the forward point of the ball. Another change in rules was the allowance of a kickoff from a tee.[143]

Boxing was popular and often in the news. On this day Duke Ridgley wrote, "The $75 question in the boxing world is: 'What kind of shape is Joe Louis in?' I think he's in tip-top shape. Joe has had a long lay-off. His timing may be bad, but—if he can get down to 210 pounds, Billy Conn—nor anybody else—doesn't have a Chinaman's chance against 'the Shuffler.' P. S. My guess is that Conn won't be on his feet at the finish."[144] (They finally fought in 1946 in the first-ever televised boxing match, in which Lewis knocked Conn out in the eighth round.)

Washington appointed General MacArthur and Admiral Nimitz to command land and sea forces for the Allied invasion of Japan.[145]

"IN THE SERVICE":

Lieutenant (j. g.) Lawrence W. Thompson, USNR. former Marshall College student and member of Alpha Kappa Pi fraternity, is missing in action in the Pacific, his parents, Mr. and Mrs. E. M. Thompson of Chattaroy, W.Va., were notified Saturday. He holds the Air Medal and Distinguished Flying Cross with Oak Leaf Clusters. A Hellcat pilot on a carrier that won fame in the invasion of Southern France, Lieutenant Thompson recently wrote that he had participated in the Iwo Jima battle

and was preparing to come home. He has three brothers overseas and another brother at Marshall College." (Lieutenant Thompson, according to *West Virginia Archives and History*, died on April 27, 1945 when his aircraft lost power on takeoff from the deck of an aircraft carrier and was "cut in two by the ship.")

Fireman First Class Lewis M. Warmsley and Shipfitter Third Class Hobart P. Swartwood, brothers-in-law, recently held a reunion at Pearl Harbor after two years separation. Fireman Warmsley is the husband of Mrs. Betty Warmsley, 338 Washington Avenue and the son of Mrs. W. T. Waldon, 1909 Eleventh Avenue. He has been on sea duty since August, 1944. Shipfitter Swartwood, whose wife and son reside at Ceredo, is the son of Mrs. Rhoda Swartwood, 412 Tenth Street. He has served with the Seabees for the past 16 months and was stationed at Pearl Harbor when his brother-in-law's ship docked there.

Sergeant Thurman T. Cremeans, who recently returned to this country after ten months of overseas duty, is spending a 21-day furlough with his wife, Mrs. Cuma Cremeans and daughter, Dorcas Ellen, of Branchland. Sergeant Cremeans served with the 90th Division and fought through Normandy and France, and was wounded in Germany December 17. He holds the Purple heart and Good Conduct medals. At the end of his furlough, Sergeant Cremeans will return to McGuire General Hospital, Richmond, Va.

Second Lieutenant Albert N. Minton of Huntington, B-17 Flying Fortress navigator, has been awarded his second Oak Leaf Cluster to the Air Medal... The 24-year-old flier is a veteran of more than 15 attacks on objectives in Germany, including two on targets in Berlin. He also participated in the assault at the Baltic port of Swinemunde March 12. His parents, Mr. and Mrs. Emile U. Minton, live at 1303 Ninth Avenue, and his wife, Mrs. Carolyn V. Minton, at 331 West Eleventh Avenue.

Staff Sergeant Harry L. Roberson of North Matewan, W.Va. has been awarded the Army

Air Force Airplane Armorer Technician badge at a Ninth Air Force Bomber base in France. He is the son of Mrs. Alice Roberson of North Matewan.

James Owen Overby, son of Mr. and Mrs. Claude J. Overby, 309 ½ Twenty-first Street, has graduated as a seaman second class from the aviation ordnance school at the Naval Air Technical Training Center at Norman, Okla.

Captain Paul V. Osburn, son of Mr. and Mrs. Thurman Osburn, 418 Thirty-first Street, has been awarded a fifth Oak Leaf Cluster to his Air Medal at an Eighth Air Force bomber station in England.

Willard Woodrow Carico, husband of Mrs. Martha Carico, 259 Springdale Avenue, is a trainee in a ship repair unit at the Boston Navy Yard.

Three Cabell County men are aboard the USS *Pennsylvania,* which is believed to have shot more main battery ammunition at enemy positions than any other ship, more than 11,000,000 pounds. They are James R. McCreery, son of Mrs. W. A. McCreery 3854 Green Valley Drive; William W. Hayes, husband of Mrs. Mabel V. Hayes, 2411 Collis Avenue and Bernard Ray Hunt, son of Mrs. Zelda Lettie Hunt, Barboursville...

Motor Machinist's Mate First Class Ivan D. Long, stationed with the Navy at Norfolk, Va., spent the Easter holidays with his parents, Mr. and Mrs. N. V. Doss, 918 Twenty-third Street.

Glenna: *April 4ᵗʰ Wed. – Mrs. Rousey came up and I wrote a letter for her. Had a rainstorm late in evening.*

Rupert: *I went to school today. We are having a big April shower.*

County Agent W. D. Click warned that apples would suffer heavily if "temperatures drop below freezing tonight as predicted by the Weather Bureau... Peaches, cherries and plums

are far enough along to stand a mild cold spell, but apple blossoms are at their most tender stage of development."[146]

AP report from London: "The Allies hurled 3,000 planes against the dwindling targets of shrunken Germany today, including 1,000 Flying Fortresses and Liberators which blasted submarine building yards at Kief and Hamburg and airfields throughout the Northwestern Reich... Nine bombers and four fighters were missing, but one of the bombers landed safely at Malmoe Airport in Sweden."[147]

The Third Army moved into Central Germany after capturing Kassel, Gotha, and Suhl. The British crossed Weser in a flanking movement on Bremen. The French captured Karlsruhe, and the Seventh Army was 34 miles from Nuremberg.[148]

After the liberation of the Nazi concentration camp at Ohrdruf, an angry General Patton rounded up townspeople to show them the carnage. Elsewhere, German civilians were forced to look at the concentration camps as they were liberated and some civilians were even forced to bury the dead.[149]

"IN THE SERVICE":

Duncan W. Daugherty Jr., 19, son of Mr. and Mrs. D. W. Daugherty, 1702 Sixth Avenue, was a member of the first class to complete the new 20-week navigation curriculum at Hondo Army Air Field, Hondo, Tex. He was awarded his navigator's wings and commission as second lieutenant.

Technician Fifth Grade David Fleming of Huntington, and his step-brother Corporal George B. Fortner, met recently in Germany for the first time since they have been in service and were together for one night. Technician Fleming, whose wife and three-year-old daughter, Linda Lou, reside at 215 Sixth Avenue West, has served for the past six months with the field artillery of the Ninth Army. He has been in service for a year and has two brothers-in-law in the armed forces. They are Corporal Ray S. Amick, with the medical corps in the South Pacific, and Jack H. Brown, who was wounded in Belgium and is now in a Paris hospital. Corporal Fortner, a Huntington resident, is also serving with the Ninth Army somewhere in Germany. Mrs. Fortner lives here.

Aviation Cadet William L. Gibson III has arrived at Camp Atterbury, Ind., his mother, Mrs. Madeline Gibson, 2038 Eleventh Avenue, learned yesterday. Aviation Cadet Gibson, a former member of the Civil Air Patrol here, was inducted last Thursday. His father, Major Gibson, is serving with the AAF in Africa. [There are questions about these family relationships, since other entries list William L. Gibson, son of Madeline Gibson, as William L. Gibson Jr.]

TRI-STATE DISTRIBUTING CO., DIST.—PHONE 22031

Second Lieutenant Buell B. Whitehill Jr., whose wife resides at 1502 Fifth Avenue, assistant public relations officer and assistant special service officer, Fletcher General Hospital, Cambridge, O., has received an overseas assignment and will assist the War Department in collecting historical data of Army units for a complete history of the war.

Private First Class Norman L. Roberts, 20, husband of Mrs. Leola Roberts and son of Mr. and Mrs. William M. Roberts of Huntington Route 3, has returned to a Pacific base after participating in the first American landings on Leyte and Luzon. He was a member of a picked and specially trained group of infantrymen who fired chemical mortars from landing craft in support of assault troops.

Coxswain Howard Lee Davis, son of Mr. and Mrs. William L. Davis of Williamson, is returning to the United States under the Navy's rotation program after serving for 18 months overseas with the Pacific Wing of the Naval Air Transport Service.

Private Wilson Adkins, son of Mr. and Mrs. Enoch Adkins of Branchland, has been made a platoon guide at Camp Fannin, Tex.

Staff Sergeant Robert L. Hunt, son of Mr. and Mrs. Orland Hunt, 958 Washington Avenue, who is serving with the 44th Division of the Seventh Army in Germany, has been awarded the Combat Infantryman Badge.

Private George Smith, husband of Mrs. Mabel Smith, 445 Fourth Avenue, and son of Mr. and Mrs. Lindsey Smith of Kenova, is assigned to the post office of the 85th "Blue Devil" Division on the Fifth Army Front in Italy.

Staff Sergeant Troy E. Clay, husband of Mrs. Lois Clay, Branchland Route 2, has added a seventh bronze battle star on his theatre ribbon. He has participated in the campaigns of Egypt-Libya, Sicily, Italy, France, Germany and is now in Northern Italy at a 12th AAF base.

Lieutenant (j. g.) Virginia Mildred Gonoski, 324 Twenty-ninth Street, has been promoted to that rank at the U.S. Naval Hospital at Long Beach, Calif. where she is on duty with the U.S. Navy Nurse Corps.

Sergeant James E. Michael of Prichard is with the First Army engineers somewhere in Germany. He has been in Europe for two and a half years.

Glenna: *April 5th Thursday – Went to town. Bought two new dresses, shoes, hose, and girdle for myself. For Rupert I got 3 shirts and a pair of pants. Spent $37. Very cold and light snow. Hard freeze that night. Went to see Papa and Mamma.*

It's not only the prices that revive memories, but also the items: Hose? Girdles?

Rupert: *I went to school today. We had a big test.*

The Army was making an urgent appeal for civilian typists and stenographers. Miss Ruth Ware of the Civil Service Commission was scheduled to interview applicants [in Huntington] at the United States Employment Service. "Upon acceptance, they will go to Washington with transportation paid and housing facilities available immediately upon arrival. Both men and women 17 ½ or older are eligible, but Manpower Commission regulations will still apply except in the cases of World War II veterans."[150]

The Allies in Italy launched the Po Valley Campaign.

The Japanese high command ordered its entire Second Fleet to attack U.S. forces off Okinawa.[151]

"IN THE SERVICE":

A set of Barboursville twins met for the first time in 18 months in the battle for Iwo Jima...They are Corporal Clive E. Bowen and Private First Class Clyde M. Bowen, sons of Mr. and Mrs. Foster Bowen of Barboursville Route 2. Corporal Bowen is serving with the Third Marine Division and his brother with the Fifth Division. They last saw each other at San Diego, Calif. They attended Barboursville High School before entering the service.

Warrant Officer (j. g.) James C. Stevens of the 377th Infantry Regiment, son of Mr. and Mrs. C. L. Stevens, 1639 Thirteenth Avenue, and husband of Mrs. Betty Stevens, 1833 Third Avenue, has received a citation for meritorious service between last November and February... Warrant Officer Stevens, who has been in the Army for five years and overseas since last August, is now in Germany. He holds the Combat Infantryman Badge.

Staff Sergeant John L. Bentine, husband of Mrs. J. L. Bentine, 2921 Hughes Street, was recently promoted to that rank in Southern France where he is serving as crew chief of the 393rd Ordnance Company at Marseilles. He went overseas in March 1944 and has received the European-African-Middle Eastern theatre ribbon with one battle star for service in North Africa, Corsica and Southern France.

Sergeant Carl E. Sturgeon, 29, son of Mr. and Mrs. Harrison Sturgeon, Edgarton, W.Va., was recently awarded the Good Conduct Medal at a 15th AAF base in Italy. A radio operator-gunner on a B-24, he arrived overseas last December and has flown more than 19 combat missions. He holds the Air Medal.

Radio Technician Second Class Emmette L. Wright, son of Roy O. Wright, 2019 Eighth Street, is a crewman of a motor torpedo boat in the Pacific.

Sergeant Calvin Porter, 29, son of Mr. and Mrs. Jarrette Porter, 1132 Minton Street, is assigned to the construction engineers at the El Aouina Air Base at Tunis, Tunisia, North African Division of the Air Transport Command. He has been overseas for 22 months and has been stationed at Camp Ataka and Payne Field in Egypt, and Camp Yeargin in West Africa.

Private James W. Lipscomb, 945 Madison Avenue, is now at a replacement center at Camp Gordon, Ga. He is a former Marshall College student.

Private Ufo R. Fisher of Chesapeake, O. has completed her basic training in the Women's Army Corps at Fort Oglethorpe, Ga, and is enrolled in the medical and surgical technicians' course. On completion of the course she will be assigned to the Birmingham General Hospital at Van Nuys, Calif.

Private William D. McGinnis, son of James McGinnis, 611 Bridge Street, is a member of the military police platoon of the 34th "Red Bull" Division on the Fifth Army front in Italy, an outfit which recently completed more than four years of continuous service.

Lieutenant Dee E. Worrell, Army Transport Command pilot, and Lieutenant Rodney E. Worrell, Troop Transport Command pilot, sons of Mr. and Mrs. E. E. Worrell, 812 Third Street, were recently reunited in Africa.

Private First Class Arnold Willis Jr., son of Mrs. Sarah Willis, 2636 Washington Boulevard, who is home on furlough from the Marine Corps base at Camp Lejeune, N.C., spoke at services last night at the First United Brethren Church. Before entering service, Private Willis was active in Huntington church circles.

Glenna: *April 6th Friday – Cleaned the house and stayed at home. Cold and frost that night.*

Along the Ligurian coast in Italy, "American artillery laid down a heavy barrage for several hours before ground forces began their operation."[152] The long hard march from southern Italy to the Alps was near an end. German soldiers there were surrendering in droves.

Japan made fierce *kamikaze* attacks against United States ships during air and naval battles off Okinawa.

"IN THE SERVICE":

Musician Second Class Avie Lake Jr., 26, son of Mr. and Mrs. Lake, 2809 First Avenue, was among six officers and enlisted men on an aircraft carrier to receive commendations, or Purple Heart medals for wounds received in action in the Philippines.

Private John J. Murray, husband of the former Miss Irene Nelson, 2606 Marcum Terrace, was wounded March 17 while serving with the Seventh Army in Germany...

Staff Sergeant James P. Peters, 21, son of Mr. and Mrs. R. L. Peters of Kenova, has been promoted to that rank at a Ninth Air Force base in France. He is a tail gunner of the 391st "Black Death" B-26 Marauder group which was recently cited by the War Department for gallantry.

First Lieutenant Raymond G. Polland, 1931 Washington Avenue, is one of the technicians of the 15th Field Artillery Observation Battalion, which has located more than 4,100 enemy machinegun positions on the Fifth Army front in Italy.

Private First Class Thomas Newsome, USMCR, son of Mr. and Mrs. William H. Newsome, 2978 Winters Road, narrowly escaped death in the recent battle for Iwo Jima when a motor shell fragment pierced the gas chamber of his rifle, according to a shortwave broadcast by Tony Smith, Marine combat correspondent.

Second Lieutenant Charles Cohen, son of Mr. and Mrs. Joseph Cohen of Fifth Avenue, was promoted to that rank recently ... at a station hospital in France where he serves as registrar.

A promotion to staff sergeant was recently awarded Riley W. Lowe, son of Mrs. May W. Lowe, 604 Tenth Avenue. He is serving in Europe.

Gunner's Mate Leonard Barker is expected to arrive in Huntington shortly for a 30-day leave after spending 16 months in the Atlantic and Pacific. His sister, Mrs. Carl J. Mannon of this city, is now visiting him in New York.

Donald H. Greenwell, 18, son of Mrs. O. W. Greenwell, 2223 Adams Avenue, was recently graduated as an electrician's mate from a specialized course at the Great Lakes, Ill. Naval Training Station.

First Sergeant Stuard B. McCaw, 25, son of Mr. and Mrs. William E. McCaw, 215 Division Street, was one of two men from his station to attend a dinner given in honor of U.S. Ambassador Norman Kirk in Italy recently... The other man to receive an invitation was

Sergeant McCaw's commanding officer. He is an instructor in a replacement center and has been overseas about two years.

Colonel Alexander M. Neilson, serving with the Army in the Philippines, was recently awarded the Bronze Star Medal for saving the lives of six service men after their PT boat was wrecked by enemy action...

"William Wagers, son of Mrs. Lucille Wagers, 607 Twelfth Avenue, was recently promoted to staff sergeant from the grade of corporal in Germany where he is serving with the 517th Parachute Combat Team. He also participated in Italy, France and Belgium.

Glenna: *April 7th Saturday – Cool but sunshiny. Everything looks beautiful. 14 years ago today since I married Rupert. Looks like the same day. Sad and full of memories.*

Mother honored my father all through my childhood and youth. Toward the end of her life, and after Dawson's death, she told me that she and Dawson had married with an agreement that, on her death she would be buried beside my father. She faithfully tended Rupert's gravesite at the Porter Cemetery the rest of her life. As a boy, I sometimes helped, and as we worked she told me about the father I never knew.

Rupert: *Nothing much happened today. I work[ed] today.*

"Marine Private First Class Jack W. Shafer, 22, son of Mr. and Mrs. Edward Shaffer of Proctorville, O., was killed on Iwo Jima March 10..."[153]

"Three of Goering's Luftwaffe pilots landed at the Lisbon, Portugal, airport after a flight from Germany in the latest model Junkers 183 bi-motor fighter bomber and told Portuguese authorities "we have fled because we are tired of fighting;"[154]

Twenty-five hundred Japanese sailors died when their ship, the *Yamato*, under attack by American planes, capsized in the East China Sea.[155]

"IN THE SERVICE":

Private Dorothy Ruth Eastham, 301 West Ninth Street, and Jo Anna Holderby, 333 Norway Avenue, are on duty with the Women's Army Corps at William Beaumont General Hospital at El Paso, Tex.

Petty officer Second Class Ward L. Cornett Jr., son of Mr. and Mrs. W. L. Cornett, 30 West Sixth Avenue, was commended by his commanding officer for "meritorious performance of duty."...

... [Through] the untiring efforts of Staff Sergeant Gene Kelly Slutz, Marshall College graduate, a new Tenth Air Force [recreation?] station has been established in Burma. Sergeant Slutz is manager, announcer, commentator, interviewer and master of ceremonies. He has been in service for the past 21 months in the India-Burma theatre and holds the Bronze Star Medal. His wife, the former Jean Ashby Johnson, holds the rank of lieutenant (j. g.) in the U.S. Naval reserve.

Flight Officer W. H. Barker of the Army Transport Command has returned to his base after spending 10 days with his wife and family at 1114 Ninth Avenue. He is the son of Mr. and Mrs. J. W. Barker, 410 Twelfth Avenue.

Charles Thomas Herrenkohl, 23, husband of Mrs. Beulah Cremeans Herrenkohl, 308 Buffington Street, has been advanced to seaman first class and assigned to the photographic reconnaissance training detachment at the Naval Air Facility at New Cumberland, Pa.

Technical Sergeant Francis R. Cooper, 1326 Tenth Avenue, a veteran of the Alaska theatre of war, has arrived at the Scott Field, Ill. Army Air Forces Training Command radio school.

Carl P. Cooper Jr., 60 Adams Avenue, has arrived at the Pearl Harbor Navy Yard to assume his duties as a civilian war worker.

Private Anna Bolling, daughter of Mr. and Mrs. Carl L. Bolling, 502 Ninth Avenue, is now assigned as photographer at Dyersburg Army Air Field at Dyersburg, Tenn.

Flight Officer Carl L. Fox, 2875 Collis Avenue, and Second Lieutenant James Fattaleh, 1013 Monroe Avenue, have been awarded Air Medals somewhere in India.

Lieutenant Colonel Justice M. Chambers, USMC, commander of the famous "Chambers Raiders," is in a hospital in the Marianas after being wounded in action for the third time, most recently in the battle for Iwo Jima. He was previously wounded at Tulagi and Saipan. His parents, Mr. and Mrs. A. F. Chambers, reside at 3137 Brandon Road, and his wife, Joanna and their three children live in Washington.

Seaman First Class Corbet K. Black, U.S. Coast Guard, is serving aboard a Coast-guard manned frigate in the North Pacific. He is the son of Mr. and Mrs. J. R. Black, 2988 Third Avenue.

Corporal Millard G. Rorrer, husband of Mrs. Donetta Rorrer, 142 ½ Washington Avenue, a veteran of the China-Burma-India theatre is undergoing reassignment processing at Miami Beach, Fla.

First Lieutenant Wayne G. Thompson, son of Mrs. R. J. Thompson of Wayne, has arrived home on leave after a year's duty in the South Pacific.

After a year's duty as a Navy torpedo plane pilot, Lieutenant (j. g.) William C. Baumgardner is spending a 30-day leave with his parents, Mr. and Mrs. C. A. Baumgardner, 1502 Charleston Avenue, and his wife, the former Miss Beatrice Woodrum, and three-month old son, William Daniels, 212 Staunton Street.

Sergeant Stanley R. Wilson, son of Mr. and Mrs. Curtis W. Wilson of Chesapeake, O., has been awarded the Bronze Star medal and a citation for services in combat in Italy...

Glenna: *April 8th Sunday – Went to Sunday School then down to Stewart and Rubie's at 4 Pole and spent the day. Went to church that night.*

Rupert: *We visited some friends just outside Huntington. They was the Hutchintons [Hutchinsons].*

Early in my parents' marriage, they were close friends with Stuart and Ruby Hutchinson, so I was destined to become good friends with Billie, Dencil, and Carlotta. Later in life the Hutchinsons had another son, George. Although Billie and Dencil were a grade ahead of me in school, we played football together at Barboursville High School. Carlotta Blue still lives in the Huntington area and Billie lives in California. Dencil passed away in California several years ago.

The large Hutchinson family is prominent in Salt Rock history. Their farmland once covered a wide swath within a loop of the Guyandotte River known as Henchman Bend. I think it appropriate to give a short account of the military service of six Hutchinson family brothers. Three served in the Second World War and three were in the Korean War. Betty Keyser Hutchinson supplied the following briefs:

Three brothers served in the Second World War: Private Ercell C. Hutchinson, U.S. Army, was drafted in April 1942 from his job as postmaster at Salt Rock. He served on a hospital ship that transported war-wounded from Europe to Charleston, South Carolina hospitals; Corporal Richard E. Hutchinson, U.S. Army Air Force, served from December 1941 to August 1945 in the Pacific maintaining B-26 bombers; Sergeant First Class Vernon L. Morrison, U.S. Navy, served from May 1941 to October 1945. Before Pearl Harbor, he served briefly on the USS *Arizona*, but then transferred to the USS *Ranger*. (Both Richard and Vernon were students at Walnut Grove School when my mother was the teacher.)

Three other brothers from the same Hutchinson family served in the Korean War: Sergeant First Class Russell L. Hutchinson, U.S. Navy, served from March 1952 to March 1956 with duty on an LST landing craft; Airman First Class Manford C. Hutchinson, U.S. Air Force, served from March 1952 to March 1956, with time in Korea. After his discharge he attended seminary and became a Methodist minister; Corporal Louie R. Hutchinson requested draft and served in the U.S. Army from March 1951 to March 1953. He served in the 20th Field Artillery 155mm in Hanau, Germany. He is the surviving brother of the six.[156]

There were many other Tri-State families with multiple service members in the Second World War. Notable was the farm family of Mr. and Mrs. Millard Jeffrey, Route 2, Barboursville (Melissa). Several family members serving were: Corporal Thomas M. Jeffrey, Yeoman First Class Opal S. Jeffrey; Seaman First Class Robert Paul Jeffrey; Private Raymond R. Jeffrey; Seaman Second Class Roy L. Jeffrey; Wylie Jack Jeffrey; Vivian L. Jeffrey; and Stacy E. Jeffrey.

I knew some others who served in 1945. The short list is Forest Fry, Roy Fry, Pat Adkins, Bill Harvey, Wed Cremeans, Russell Harbour, and Jim Harbour.

"'Calling All Girls' will be presented by the June graduating class of Huntington East High School in the auditorium Thursday at 8 P. M. under the direction of Mrs. Pauline W. Osborn; the cast ... Connie Isner, Peggy Johnson, Betty Harris, Bertha Sheets, Barbara Ellis, Jane Wheatley, Don Waggoner, Neal Strader, Jim Van Verth, Bob Rapp, Madge Gould, Margaret Curry, and Julius Johnson."[157]

Glenna: *April 9th Monday – Washed that day, Very pretty. Eardie [?] Eplin was buried.*

Ewell Eplin, husband of Mahalia Eplin, died April 7 at the age of forty-one. He was born in Lincoln County, son of Marshall Eplin and Johanna Adkins. He was buried in the Adkins-Little Marion Cemetery.[158]

The Germans executed Dietrich Bonhoeffer, a Lutheran minister and theologian. Bonhoeffer was thought by the Nazis to be associated with the failed plot to assassinate Hitler. His book, *The Cost of Discipleship*, has become a modern classic.

"IN THE SERVICE":

Coxswain Ralph W. Bates has returned to the U.S. Naval Training Station at Newport. R.I. for advanced training after spending a 12-day leave with his mother, Mrs. J. D. Arthur, 1548 Harvey Road, and his wife and son in Washington. Coxswain Bates has served for 29 months in both Atlantic and Pacific areas.

Private Gordon Wooten, 1830 Wiltshire Boulevard, has returned from overseas where he served with the infantry and is now a patient at Oliver General Hospital at Augusta, Ga. He has been in service for two years.

Flight Officer John L. Mitchell, son of Mr. and Mrs. Harry L. Mitchell, 603 Sixth Avenue, a former Marshall College student, is studying at the four-engine pilot school at Roswell, N.M. Army Air Field. He received his pilot wings last month at Douglas Field, Ariz.

Staff Sergeant Okey Clark of Huntington has arrived in the United States after serving for 32 months in Europe. He is expected to spend a furlough here with his parents and sisters who reside at 1106 Jackson Avenue.

Private First Class William E. Frampton, 1738 Third Avenue, was recently promoted to that rank in North Africa where he is serving as a radio maintenance technician.

Private Aubrey D. Norris, 530 Sixteenth Street, and Private First Class Joe DeRossett of Premier are serving with the 693rd Field Artillery Battalion of the Sixth Army Group in Germany...

Private First Class Sharline Reese, daughter of Mrs. T. L. Reese, 2155 Fifth Avenue, who is stationed at Baer Field at Fort Wayne, Ind., has received the Good Conduct Medal. She entered the service in February, 1944.

Private First Class Willis P. Adkins of Branchland Route 1, Private First Class Raymond Coleman of Letart Route 2, Private Virgil Lockard of Newtown and Private Eary Galoway of Stirrat are veterans of 32 months overseas with the Sixth Army Group and have done construction work in England, Algeria, Italy and France...

Sergeant Charles L. Newman, husband of Mrs. Mildred Newman, 817 Twenty-eighth Street, has enrolled in the AAF Training Command's basic airplane and engine mechanics course at Keesler Field at Biloxi, Miss.

Technician Fourth Grade Earl S. Walton, 3323 Norway Road, was graduated last week from a technical and combat training course at the First Signal Radio Maintenance Unit, Robins Field, Ga.

Chaplain Norman R. Lewis was recently promoted to the rank of captain at the Hondo Army Air Field, Hondo, Tex., navigation air base of the AFF Training Command, where he is on duty. He is the son of Mr. and Mrs. R. C. Lewis of Huntington and received his Bachelor of Arts degree from Marshall College in 1937. Before entering the armed forces, he served at the Broadway Baptist Church, Houston, Tex.

Glenna: *April 10th Tuesday – I went to Huntington. Bought Rupert some tennis shoes and a new hat for myself. Weather was beautiful. I came home and ironed that evening. Heard about Vernon Lucas being killed in the war.*

Rupert: *I went to school today. We had a test.*

Vernon Lucas, born in Cabell County in 1921 (son of Mr. and Mrs. Vinson Lucas of Branchland), enlisted May 31, 1943. A member of the 307th Parachute Infantry Regiment, he was killed in the Netherlands on March 24, 1945, and was buried there.[159]

Two area men were killed in Germany: Sergeant Richard H. Dial died March 24 "of wounds received the same day." He was husband of Mrs. Georgia Bias Dial, 402 Clarendon Court, Huntington, and son of Mr. and Mrs. Leo Dial, 1610 Twelfth Avenue; Corporal Paul C. Wheeler, 24, husband of Mrs. Weltha Wheeler of Pea Ridge Road and son of Mr. and Mrs. Walter Wheeler of Sweetland. "Corporal Wheeler, previously reported missing in action on January 10, was killed on that date while serving with the Seventh Armored Division of the Third Army."[160]

American Ninth Army soldiers captured the German city of Hanover.[161]

"IN THE SERVICE":

Staff Sergeant Robert L. Casey, aerial radio operator of 110 Short Street, has been awarded the Air Medal upon completion of 150 hours of operational flight in transport aircraft over the difficult India-China air routes. The award was made for services from November 23 to December 27, 1944.

Staff Sergeant Cyril F. Wilson, 581 Reid Avenue, has been promoted to that grade at Camp Wheeler, Ga.

After returning from overseas service, which included France and England, Clarence Hawkins Jr. of the Navy is spending a leave with his parents in Guyandotte.

Aviation Machinist's Mate Second Class James W. Warfuel, Naval Air Corps, is visiting his wife, Mrs. Lucille R. Warfuel and daughter, Joan, at 2710 Washington Boulevard. He is stationed at Peru, Ind.

Private First Class Henry G. Cremeans Jr., AAF, is spending a furlough with his parents, Mr. and Mrs. H. G. Cremeans Sr. of Twenty-fifth Street. He is stationed at Santa Ana, Calif. after a tour of duty in Europe.

The Purple Heart for wounds received in combat on New Guinea has been awarded Private Joseph Gibson of Huntington... His wife resides at 307 Water Street and his mother, Mrs. Eva Mitchell, lives in West Hamlin. A brother, Corporal Thomas Gibson, is in the Army at Cheyenne, Wyo.

Glenna: *April 11th Wednesday – Beautiful day. I visited the sick Mrs. Smith [and] Aunt Sallie Moore [Sallie Morris?]. That night I went to prayer meeting. Jaruel Porter was our leader. Several were there.*

Rupert: *I went to school today. We had another test.*

Fighting continued on all fronts: Russian troops entered Vienna and liberated the Buchenwald concentration camp. Near Okinawa, *kamikaze* pilots continued heavy suicide missions, causing damage to the *Enterprise* and the *Missouri*.[162]

"IN THE SERVICE":

Sergeant Wilber Gibson of Fraziers Bottom, Putnam County, is a member of a Signal Corps unit which recently received the Meritorious Service Plaque. Before entering the Army in January 1942, Gibson was a glassblower in Huntington.

Sergeant Richard F. Harbour, son of Mr. and Mrs. R. F. Harbour of 1668 ½ Sixth Avenue, has been awarded his fifth Bronze Battle Star, representing the fifth major campaign of the war in which he has participated. He also holds the Presidential Unit Citation. Sergeant Harbour attended Central High School and was employed as a shipping clerk for Strietmann Biscuit Co. before entering the service in November, 1942.

Radio Technician First Class Morris E. Cunningham, husband of Mrs. Bertha E. Cunningham, 3437 Piedmont Road, is with a ship repair unit in training at the Puget Sound Navy Yard. He is a former Marshall College student.

Technician Fifth Grade Ray R. Eplion, son of Mr. and Mrs. Audie A. Eplion, 241 South High Street, has been awarded the Purple Heart. He was wounded during the battle for Bastogne, Belgium. Technician Eplion has returned to duty in Germany.

Private Arthur G. Myers, husband of Mrs. Glenna Myers of Ona, has returned after eight months' duty in Europe and is a patient at Woodrow Wilson General Hospital at Staunton, Va. He participated in campaigns in Holland and Germany.

Private First Class Rocco Narcise, 21, son of Mr. and Mrs. Patsy Narcise, 112 Fifth Avenue, is a member of the Fifth Air Force Troop Carrier headquarters engaged in operations in the Philippines.

Staff Sergeant Newton B. Parker of Huntington has been awarded the Air Medal for meritorious achievement. He is a tail gunner with the Eighth Air Force in England. His wife and two children reside at 821 Fifth Avenue. Sergeant Parker has been overseas since last January.

Glenna: *April 12th Thursday – Lovely day. President Roosevelt died at 3:30 in Warm Springs, Georgia. I worked at the graveyard and picked up and burned trash here at the house.* (This entry, and those for several following days were written in ink, possibly to indicate their importance.)

Rupert: *Our nation morns over the death of President Franklin D. Roosevelt. died at 3 thirty today.*

I heard the news on the radio and went to the cemetery to inform Mother. She cried.

The reins of government changed hands quickly: "President Truman announced tonight [April 12] that the United Nations conference for April 25 will go on as scheduled... Several delegates already have arrived in this country..."[163]

Tornados in Oklahoma left fifty-eight dead and hundreds injured and homeless.[164]

"Private Elza L. Conard, son of Mrs. Eora E. Conard, 824 Twenty-seventh Street, was seriously wounded March 17 while serving with the Fifth Army in Germany [The Fifth Army was in Italy, but there may have been elements of it in Germany at this time.] ... He has been in the Army for about a year and overseas for more than two months."[165]

"IN THE SERVICE":

Private First Class John W. Mash of Point Pleasant is a member of the 372nd Military Police Escort Guard Company attached to the Sixth Army in Germany. This company has transported more than 100,000 Nazi prisoners from the front lines to interrogation pens without the loss of a prisoner.

Bernice M. Plymale of 3022 Hughes Street, an Army nurse stationed at a hospital in Italy, has been promoted to the rank of first lieutenant. She is the daughter of Mrs. Robert Plymale and has been overseas since April 1943.

Technical Sergeant Harry E. Schrader, son of Mr. and Mrs. W. M. Schrader of Barboursville, has been awarded the Oak Leaf Cluster to the Distinguished Flying Cross for extraordinary achievement as an aerial engineer in flights between India and China. Sergeant Schrader entered the Army in December 1940, and has been in the China-Burma-India theatre for 17 months. His wife lives in Allston, Mass.

Sergeant Ruth J. Eddy, the daughter of Mr. and Mrs. A. R. Eddy, 1702 Seventh Avenue, was on the WAC welcoming committee assigned to greet returning prisoners of war liberated in the Philippines when they arrived at San Francisco. The WAC delivered mail and official messages of welcome.

Chester L. Shipe, 1221 ½ Sixth Avenue, has been honorably discharged from the Army after serving with the infantry overseas. He received his medical discharge at Oliver General Hospital, Augusta, Georgia.

Private Harold L. Curry of 2802 ½ Marcum Terrace, has won his private first class stripe. He is an automatic rifleman in the Army.

A. B. Angel, son of Mr. and Mrs. Henry Angel, 609 Hawthorne Way, has been honorably discharged from the Navy. He held the rank of Chief Storekeeper. After enlisting in 1942, he served in the Aleutians. He was returned to the states after being taken seriously ill and has been assigned to a Navy Hospital in the East since. He will resume his former duties as a vice-president of M. D. Angel Co.

Harold F. Smith, son of Mrs. Edith F. Smith of 1824 Midway Avenue, has been promoted on the field of battle to Technician Fifth Grade for outstanding ability, leadership, and initiative shown during the Philippine campaign. Smith, a veteran of the Admiralty Islands, has been overseas since June 1943.

Bronze Stars have been awarded to two Huntington soldiers for outstanding service and meritorious achievement. Staff Sergeant John D. Greig, the son of Mr. and Mrs. Arthur D. Greig, 317 Wilson Court, received his award for action against the enemy at a P-51 Mustang base in Italy. His wife is residing at 2547 Collis Avenue. Sergeant Kermit M. Parker, 1654 Doulton Avenue, won the award as a crew chief in a 15th Air Force Flying Fortress squadron operating from an advanced base in Italy.

Mark Hayton, son of Mr. and Mrs. Ezra Hayton of Prichard, has been advanced to the rank of technician fourth grade. He participated in the invasion of Normandy and the Northern France and the German campaigns.

Private First Class Dennis L. Sutherland, 1120 Eighteenth Street, has been awarded the Bronze Star for extraordinary achievement in Germany. He is with the 30th Infantry Division. [In another entry last name is spelled "Sunderland."]

Louis L. Wilson Jr., son of Mr. and Mrs. L. L. Wilson of Hurricane and formerly of Huntington, has been promoted to the rank of major and placed in command of an AAF fighter squadron on the Western Front. He has been awarded the Air Medal with several oak leaf clusters and the Distinguished Flying Cross. Major Wilson attended Hurricane High and graduated from West Point.

Glenna: *April 13th Friday – I cleaned up the old Meat House. Warm and pretty. Listened all day to the radio telling about the death of President Roosevelt.*

The "Meat House" was also a storage place for tools and farm supplies.

Rupert: *There was no school today. I went to town.*

The world of sports paid respect to Franklin Delano Roosevelt by announcing cessation of all sports activity until after the funeral.[166] President Harry Truman telephoned his mother and brother after taking the oath of office and told them, "I'm terribly busy—you folks probably won't hear from me for some time." He talked to his brother, Vivian Truman, and then to Mrs. Martha Truman, his ninety-eight-year-old mother. The President was concerned because he had heard that his mother refused to meet the press. It was Vivian Truman who kept the press and visitors away. Vivian said, "... Too much excitement might not be good for her."[167]

"For leading a patrol successfully against enemy forces and bringing his men back to his unit position with 'vital information concerning enemy strength and disposition' despite suffering wounds himself, First Lieutenant Edward M. Selfe Jr. was awarded the Silver Star in Germany." Son of Mr. and Mrs. E. M. Selfe of 1049 Fifth Avenue, he served with the 60th Infantry Regiment of the Ninth Division. He had also been awarded the Purple Heart and the Bronze Star.[168]

Chile joined the war against Germany and Japan.[169]

"IN THE SERVICE":

Ossie I. McComas, 21, son of Mr. and Mrs. Roy McComas has been promoted to the rank of technician fifth grade. He is a cook with an airborne anti-aircraft battery in Burma. He has been in that theatre for 14 months.

Corporal John W. Reed of Nolan, son of Mr. and Mrs. Wallace Reed, landed with the 40th Infantry Division on Panay exactly 24 years and fifteen minutes after his birth. He previously had taken part in the invasion at Lingayen Gulf in January.

George N. Sawyer, a corporal with the 90th Infantry Division in Germany, has been awarded an Oak Leaf Cluster to the Bronze Star. His wife, Mrs. Edith L. Sawyer lives at 348 Adams Avenue.

Private Raymond Hines, husband of Mrs. Opal Fraley Hines, 2606 Adams Avenue, has arrived in the European theatre. Before entering

The Style Shop
1005 Fourth Avenue

the service, he was a crane operator for the International Nickel Co.

Private T. D. Murphy has been awarded the Presidential Citation with two Oak Leaf Clusters, according to word received by his parents, Mr. and Mrs. Freeman Murphy of Logan. Private Murphy, a former student at East High school, is a member of the 502nd Parachute Infantry in Europe. A brother, Sergeant Raymond R. Murphy, is attending officer candidate school in Paris, and another brother, Sergeant Clyde Murphy, is with the 359th Engineers in Germany.

Signalman First Class Jack M. Cochran, son of Mrs. Maude Cochran, 416 West Ninth Street, and a shipmate spent Easter Sunday with Mr. and Mrs. Richard Morgan of Long Beach, Calif. Mrs. Morgan is the former Frieda Greer of Huntington.

Photogrammetry Specialist Doreene Eckley of the WAVES will return today to Washington after spending a leave with her parents, Mr. and Mrs. Roy Eckley, 619 Elm Street.

Seaman First Class John W. Hatten, son of Mr. and Mrs. Alva Hatten of Kenova, is safe and well after participating in the action at Iwo Jima. He also took part in the invasion of Guam, Luzon, Saipan and Leyte. He has been in the South Pacific for 14 months.

Technician Fifth Grade Homer L. Chapman Jr., grandson of Mr. and Mrs. James C. Nottingham of Culloden, and Private First Class Ray Altice, son of Mrs. Roxie M. Altice of Lillybrook, W.Va. have been commended as members of the 149th Tank Battalion of the Seventh Army in France...

Captain I. Joseph Kail Jr. and his brother, Major Samuel Goodhue Kail, recently met in the European war zone and spent the Easter week end together. They are the sons of Dr. and Mrs. I. J. Kail of Whitaker Hill.

Private Edgar L. Burns, whose sister Inez Henderson lives at West Hamlin, recently arrived in the European theatre. Before entering the service, Private Burns was a block maker in West Hamlin.

Glenna: *April 14th Saturday – Listened to the radio tell about death of President Roosevelt and arrival of his body in Washington at 10:00 A.M. Funeral was 4 o'clock. I baked some pies. It was a pretty day.*

Rupert: *The President's furnal was today in Washington.*

The opening game of the baseball season in Washington between the New York Yankees and Washington Senators was dedicated to the memory of Franklin Delano Roosevelt.[170]

"Diamond Dust": Duke headed this day's column with the words, "FRANKLIN DELANO ROOSEVELT 1882–1945". Duke went on to say in his unique prose, "For him there is no passing, only farewell. His memory will live as eternally as the stars. He died in a small town way down South in Georgia— Warm Springs. He did his job well until the end. Franklin D. Roosevelt, a man among men, esteemed and loved by all. It was a great life and only weakened after 63 years. The GIs loved him... There is a report in Washington that there is a little black dog, named Fala, at the White House, who can't understand where his Master can be. Ten-Shun... Open ranks, soldiers, sailor, and Marines ... Make way for the litter bearers. A 22 gun salute... The Commander-in-Chief has gone Out to sea."[171]

IRONING BOARDS
Carolina Lumber Co.
204 21st STREET
Route 60—Opposite Nickel Plant

The Allies entered the "Ruhr Pocket" taking prisoners and cutting the resistance in half. A rumor had circulated that the Germans planned to attack New York City with V-2 rockets from U-boats. The Allies launched "Operation Teardrop" to locate the threating submarines.[172]

"IN THE SERVICE":

William Ralph Gothard, serving aboard an LST with the Pacific Fleet, has recently been advanced to the rank of carpenter's mate. Mate Gothard participated in the invasion of Iwo Jima. His wife and children are living in Barboursville.

Aviation Chief Radioman William Thomas Jones has been presented the Gold Star in lieu of a second Air Medal. Chief Jones, now serving with a detachment of the Atlantic Fleet Air Force, distinguished himself last summer in air operations during the invasions of the Mariana Islands. His wife resides at 1122 ½ Fourth Avenue. He is the son of Mr. and Mrs. Don T. Jones, 712 West Fourth Street.

Sergeant Thomas M. Horn of Kermit is a member of the 332nd Engineer General Service Regiment, one of the crack construction outfits of advance section communications zone...

Technical Sergeant John R. Witten, son of Mr. and Mrs. John M. Witten, 1318 Fifteenth Street, has completed three years as chief pharmacist of Darnall General Hospital at Danville, Ky...

Corporal Willie Arthur, husband of Mrs. Florine Arthur of Barboursville, is stationed at an air base in Italy. Prior to his enlistment, Corporal Arthur was employed by Kerr Glass Co.

Private James J. Goode, son of Mr. and Mrs. H. L. Goode, 225 Twenty-third Street, was graduated from the enlisted pack course at Fort Riley, Kan. Private Goode received his basic training at Camp Fannin, Texas, and was formerly a student at Marshall College.

After 24 months of service in the South Pacific, Private Ralph W. Johnson, son of Mr. and Mrs. David Johnson of North Kenova, has arrived at the Air Forces Convalescent Hospital at Fort Thomas, Ky. for therapy, rest and recreation. Before entering the service in March, 1942, he was employed by the Armstrong Products Corp.

Private Donald C. Lycan of Fort Gay has arrived at the Field Artillery Replacement Center at Fort Bragg, N.C. for basic training.

Lieutenant Arnold D. Johnson was recently given a seven-day vacation in England after completing 18 missions over Nazi-held Europe. Formerly an American Airlines mechanic here, Lieutenant Johnson was one of the airmen to provide cover for attacking ground forces in Germany.

Corporal Earl Prince, 221 West Thirty-second Street, has arrived in England... Before entering the Army, Corporal Prince was an inspector at the Owens-Illinois Glass Company.

Ship's Cook Second Class Charles E. Eskew Jr., son of Mr. and Mrs. Earl Eskew of Auburn Road, is home on a 30-day furlough. He has been in the South Pacific for 17 months aboard an LST and took part in five major invasions, He reports to Columbus, O. on April 23.

Glenna: *April 15th Sunday – President Roosevelt's body arrived at Hyde Park where he was buried. Ossie and Mrs. Morrison came up and stayed all day with us. We had a good dinner. It rained and turned cool.*

Rupert: *Today the president was buried in Hyde park in New York on the Hudson river.*

As a teacher in Upstate New York, I helped take several classes on field trips to Hyde Park to visit the Roosevelt home and library.

The British Army liberated 40,000 from the Bergen-Belsen concentration camp.[173]

Radio Tokyo said of the latest B-29 bombing, "It is apparent the enemy carried out such an atrocious action in an attempt to conceal his disappointment over the death of President Roosevelt."[174]

Still more area families received bad news: The "Second son of Mr. and Mrs. James Maynard, 234 Staunton Street, to be killed in action was Private Benjamin T. Maynard who died in action in Germany March 3; previously listed missing in action, he was employed by the Huntington Furniture Co. before entering the service; he had been in the Army more than two years; his brother Private (First Class) Dennis Maynard was killed in Italy; another brother, Technician (Fifth Grade) Jesse Maynard is in France."[175] Also, Mrs. Lola Trippett of University Apartments learned that her husband, Private First Class Roy Trippett had been killed in action over Luzon on February 28. His parents were Mr. and Mrs. Dock Trippett, of 4745 Bradley Road apartments. Private Trippett received his training at Fort Leonard Wood, Missouri. He had been 18 months overseas.[176]

Sometimes there was good news: "Private Clifford Allen Pritt, son of Mr. and Mrs. Henry Pritt, 714 West Sixteenth Street, previously listed missing in action is a prisoner of the Germans, his parents have been informed; he was in the infantry."[177]

Glenna: *April 16th Monday – Very windy. I washed a big washing. Rained real hard about 12 o'clock.*

Rupert: *I was sick today. I didn't go to school.*

"The music department of Douglas High School will present its first annual Spring concert Friday evening, May 4, in the school auditorium... Miss Ruth Stewart of New York City, soprano, will be guest soloist; The concert is being arranged by Miss Hortense Pace, Douglas music instructor."[178]

Hitler ordered the execution all German officers who ordered a retreat. The German transport ship *Goya*, with 6,200 troops on board, was sunk in the Baltic Sea. Allied forces ended the air war over Germany.[179]

"IN THE SERVICE":

Four times previously awarded battle participation credit for troop carrier sorties on the Western Front, Staff Sergeant George R. Trumbo has been presented his fifth bronze battle star. The son of Mr. and Mrs. G. R. Trumbo, 2778 Guyan Avenue, is a member of 436th Troop Carrier Group, which had operated in Northern and Southern France, Normandy, Rome-Arno, and Germany.

Wiley M. Richardson, who is a member of the Infantry Replacement Training Center at Camp Blanden, Fla., has been promoted from technical sergeant to first sergeant. His wife, Mrs. Marian P. Richardson, lives at 1501 Fourth Avenue.

Private First Class Artie B. Huntley, 156 Gallagher Street, has been granted a 15-day furlough from Oliver General Hospital in Atlanta where he is a patient.

Private Tommy L. Collins, 235 ½ Third Avenue, is currently assigned to the AAF Redistribution Station at Santa Ana, Calif. Army

Air Base. Private Collins has returned from the Asiatic theatre after almost three years of duty. He entered the service November 17, 1941.

Corporal Charles S. Miller, son of Mrs. Irie Miller of Nallen, has been awarded the Combat Infantryman Badge for action against the enemy on the Fifth Army Front in Italy.

Glenna: *April 17th Tuesday – I ironed and mended everything. Cool and clear after a hard rain.*

The Huntington flood wall, built five years previously, had "prevented about $7,000,000 of damage" to the city according to the U.S. Corps of Engineers; it had saved Huntington $3,600,000 during the last month alone. The Federal Government had spent about $7,500,000 on the wall. The city spent about $1,500,000 for rights of way and other items incidental to the actual construction.[180]

Edith Gaylord, in an AP article, wrote, "Mrs. Harry S. Truman today [April 16] set forth with quiet determination to do what is expected of her as First Lady... She spent almost an hour and a half with Mrs. Roosevelt and heads of the White House staff... the former President's widow is spending long hours directing the monumental job of packing and removing belongings, to enable the Trumans to move into the White House before the week's end."[181]

"IN THE SERVICE":

Otis Finley Cavendish Jr. has been commissioned a second lieutenant in the Army upon successful completion of the officer candidate course at the Infantry School at Fort Benning, Ga. He is the son of Mr. and Mrs. O. F. Cavendish, 118 West Eleventh Avenue. A graduate of Marshall College, Lieutenant

Cavendish entered the Army in January 1943 and served with the Anti-aircraft artillery.

Billie R. Sherman, daughter of Mrs. Ruth Gilmore, 1838 Maple Street, has been promoted to the rank of private first class. She is a clerk-typist at the Fourth Air Force field at Santa Maria, Calif. Prior to her enlistment in May, 1944, she worked in Baltimore as a beautician.

Brinton O. Gray of Vandalia, O. has been promoted to private first class in a night fighter squadron in Northern Italy. Private Gray formerly lived on West Fifth Avenue and attended Central High School.

These West Virginians, members of an AAF Aviation Engineer Battalion, speeded up the bombings of Tokyo by completing a Superfortress base in the Marianas in the record time of 54 days: Private First Class H. R. Easthman [? Eastman], 1512 Adams Avenue, Technician Fifth Grade A. H. Keifer and Private First Class W. W. Estep of Clendenin.

Private First Class Brilliant J. Huffman is a member of the crack 21st Infantry Cannon Company which is credited with destroying 300 Jap gun emplacements and helping free 2,200 prisoners on the road to manila... His mother is Mrs. Viola Huffman.

Second Lieutenant Henry J. Ramey Jr., son of Mr. and Mrs. H. J. Ramey, 1368 Thirteenth Street, has been assigned to a B-29 Superfortress at Barksdale Field, Ala. He was commissioned a navigator last month in Texas.

Corporal Herschell F. Riggs, son of W. B. Riggs of Prichard, is completing his final stage of training as a member of a B-29 crew at Pyote Army Air Field, Texas. Corporal Riggs graduated from Buffalo High School in Wayne County in 1941.

Staff Sergeant Philip Appeldorn, son of Mr. and Mrs. H. J. Appeldorn, 1814 Eighteenth Street, has been returned to Huntington after completing 61 missions over Europe. He has the Air Medal with 11 Oak Leaf Clusters and has been awarded the Presidential Citation. He entered the service in January, 1941.

First Lieutenant Edward A. Sigler Jr., son of Mr. and Mrs. E. A. Sigler, 1906 Wiltshire Boulevard, is spending a 30-day leave with his parents after serving for 21 months in the South Pacific. A graduate of Marshall College, Lieutenant Sigler was a member of the Marine Group 23, and was awarded the Presidential Citation for action on Guadalcanal. While on Midway, Lieutenant Sigler met an old friend, First Lieutenant Ed G. Gibson of Huntington. After his leave he returns to Cherry Point, N.C. for reassignment.

Glenna: *April 18th Wednesday – Cool and clear. I went down to Dawson's Mother's. Ossie was there. I stopped at Joe and Urcie's [Joe & Ercie Dick] on my way back. Ernie Pyle killed in Japan.*

Rupert: *Ernie Pyle was killed today in the war. A jap shot him.*

Larry Gill, whose uncle had died in the Pacific theatre the year before, was a faithful follower of Pyle's column. I saw Larry that day and he wiped away tears as he talked of Pyle's death.

Two hundred twenty-five thousand surrounded German troops in the Ruhr surrendered to General Walter Model.[182]

"IN THE SERVICE":

Private First Class Clifford Cremeans, son of the Rev. and Mrs. Richard Cremeans of Salt Rock, is with the Army on the Philippine Islands. He has served for 26 months in the Pacific area.

Staff Sergeant Robert W. White, 1320 Mallory Court, is on duty with the 569th Signal Company of the American First Army's 69th Division in Germany. As the company's wire chief, he supervises installation and checking of telephone connections with other units. He was recently near Naumburg, Germany.

Sergeant Mabel M. Musick, daughter of Mrs. Kansas Musick of Thacker, is now stationed in Paris ... with a WAC signal battalion... While in London, she helped train American women who enlisted there. Before enlisting, Sergeant Musick made her home in Thacker with her grandparents, Mr. and Mrs. A. L. Copley. She is a niece of Mrs. J. G. Williams, 520 Fifth Avenue.

Master Sergeant Clifford W. Hutchinson, 515 Eighth Street, is a member of a quartermaster continental advance supply section which recently received the Meritorious Unit Plaque Award for outstanding work in supplying the American Seventh and the French First Armies.

Corporal Lester C. Whittington, son of Mrs. Emma Whittington, 1012 West Fourth Street, has been honorably discharged from the Army. Corporal Whittington, after serving in Africa, Sicily, Italy and Corsica for 23 months, has been assigned to the AAF Regional and Convalescent Hospital near Miami. He wears the European theatre ribbon with three battle stars.

Private Nick Winters, 6 Summit Street, is home on a 10-day furlough from Valley Forge General Hospital at Phoenixville, Pa. During his 21 months overseas, Private Winters was wounded twice. He wears, besides the Purple heart with one bronze Oak Leaf Cluster, the European campaign ribbon with two battle stars and the Combat Infantryman Badge. He served with Patten's Third Army and Hodges First Army.

Private First Class Golden Dick, USMC, son of Mr. and Mrs. H. C. Dick, 2749 Highlawn Avenue, telephoned his mother from San Francisco and said that he expects to be home soon after his release from the hospital there. Private Dick spent 27 months in the South Pacific and participated in a number of battles. He was hospitalized in Hawaii where he was treated for malaria and combat fatigue and later sent to the California hospital.

Alvin E. Spurlock, son of Rev. and Mrs. A. E. Spurlock, 210 Bridge Street, was promoted to the rank of baker third class... He is stationed at the U.S. Naval Air Technical Training Center at Gainesville, Ga.

Mrs. R. T. Early, 1306 Charleston Avenue, has three sons serving in the Army. First Lieutenant William F. Early is quartermaster of a truck company serving his second year in Italy. First Lieutenant Bert H. Early is an Air Force pilot now stationed at Childress, Texas, and Staff Sergeant Robert T. Early is stationed at Camp Lee, Va. All three are former students at Marshall College.

Glenna: *April 19th Thursday – Cool with frost. I cleaned the house, hoed peas, and planted flowers.*

Rupert: *I went to school. I went to a friend and got some books.*

Salt Rock Elementary School in 1945 had only a few built-in bookcases in each room. Reading material was sparse. Some of us had read all the fifth grade fiction books and borrowed books from the sixth grade. I often exchanged reading material with Larry Gill and Marion Nida. I traded something with Marion for a copy of "Return of Tarzan," a sequel to "Tarzan of the Apes," which Mother had given me the previous Christmas. I still have both those books.

Shortly after the war, the Cabell County Library would make a significant change in the lives of county residents with the debut of the Bookmobile. And just a few years ago, Salt Rock received the gift of a public

library across Madison Creek Road from the school. It pleases me that the library was built on land that was part of my Grandfather Adkins' farm.

With the rapid advance of Allied troops in Europe, many prisoner-of-war camps were emptied: The Herald-Dispatch announced that "Lieut. Harold Holley, son of Mr. and Mrs. W. A. Holly of Milton, was among the prisoners whom the Army announced yesterday has been released by U.S. troops from the Langwasser prison camp outside Nuremberg, Germany. Lieutenant Holly, a navigator in the Army Air Forces, was shot down over Frankfurt last May 12."[183]

"IN THE SERVICE":

John L. Whisman, son of Mr. Philip Whisman, 415 Eighteenth Street, has been promoted from private first class to corporal on the Fifth Army front in Italy. He is a battalion store-keeper with an engineer unit.

Private John V. (Jack) Hobbs, 321 Willard Court, recently arrived in the European theatre. Before entering the service, he was a student at Marshall College.

Seaman First Class Robert Jordan is spending a short leave with his parents, Mr. and Mrs. Sanford Jordan, 2905 Auburn Road. He enlisted in the Navy in September 1944. After his leave, he reports to a base at Davisville, R.I.

Sergeant Robert J. Robertson, husband of Mrs. Kathryn L. Robertson of Sharon, Pa., has been assigned to Company E of the Special Training Unit at New Cumberland, Pa. He is the son of Mrs. W. H. Robertson,

2582 Collis Avenue. Sergeant Robertson was a member of the National Guard before entering the service in January, 1941.

First Lieutenant Lee E. Nelson, son of Mr. and Mrs. T. A. Nelson, 2043 Eleventh Avenue, is a member of the communications staff at headquarters of the 13th AAF. He has been in the South Pacific since October, 1943. Lieutenant Nelson's wife is Mary E. Nelson of Miami, Fla.

A hospital unit commanded by Major Clinton L. Border, a former pre-medical student at Marshall College, has been awarded the Fifth Air Force Commendation. Major Border, a graduate of the University of Louisville, remained on duty for 48 hours during a Jap airborne attack at his base in the Philippines. He performed 61 major operations with the aid of only one medical officer and five enlisted technicians. Major Border has been overseas 21 months and has received another commendation for outstanding work.

Brooks D. Anderson has been advanced from first lieutenant to captain at Fort Story, Va., where he is the commanding officer of the Corps of Military Police. Captain Brooks, a former student at Marshall College, has been in the Army for nine years.

Lieutenant William R. "Peg" Taylor, a Navy pilot and commanding officer of VT (N) *41*, was key man in a night search for Japanese fleet units at the San Bernardino Straits in the second battle of the Philippines. Lieutenant Taylor recently spent a 30-day leave with his parents, Mr. and Mrs. E. B. Taylor, 620 Trenton Place.

Private James E. Deal, son of Mrs. Tom Houvouras, 540 Seventh Avenue, is now serving with the Third Army in Germany.

On foreign duty for more than 24 months, Technician Fourth Grade Lester L. Johnson, son of Mr. and Mrs. Manna Johnson, 417 West Fifth Avenue, has been presented with the Army Good Conduct Medal. He is a small-arms weapon repairman with a unit of the 13th AAF Service Command in the South and Southwest Pacific. Sergeant Johnson entered the Army in December, 1941.

Glenna: *April 20th Friday – We went to town and bought $27.75 worth of wall paper. Cool and slow rain at morning.*

Rupert: *I went to school. Mother went to town. She bought me 12 pair of socks.*

Briefs from Last Night's Associated Press Wires reported that actor Gary Cooper was to be awarded an honorary doctor's degree by Grinnell College, which he had attended for two years. Also, Franklin D. Roosevelt's application for his 1945 license tag [Georgia] for the specially built automobile he used at Warm Springs was to be placed in the state archives. On the application, the president listed his occupation as 'executive.' "He paid $1.50 for the tag, asked for no special number and was issued No. A-12610."[184]

"IN THE SERVICE":

Vivian E. Adkins, daughter of Mr. and Mrs. Garnet Adkins, 1032 Twenty-fifth Street, has been promoted to the grade of corporal at Murdo Army Air Field, Calif. Corporal Adkins entered the Women's Army Corps in March, 1944.

Corporal Michael Cozma Jr., son of Mr. and Mrs. Michael Cozma, 703 Twelfth Avenue, is spending a short furlough with his parents and wife, the former Miss Marguerite Rains of McKinney, Tex. Corporal Cozma is with the Army Medical Corps at Fort Lewis, Md.

Private First Class Thomas H. Bottoms of Macon, N.C. whose wife, Mrs. Ruth Pennington Bottoms, resides at 416 West Twenty-seventh Street, played a vital part in the recent battle of Zig-Zag Pass on Bataan. A liter squad leader in the 113th Medical Battalion, he led his men on the field, many times under incessant enemy machine gun and mortar fire to rescue wounded men. His gallantry has brought commendations from his commanding officers.

Private Dora C. Walker of Park Hills has been transferred from the First WAC Training Center at Fort Riley, Kan. where she will serve in a regional hospital.

Sergeant Homer L. Beckley, son of Mr. and Mrs. Charles A. Beckley of Prichard, has been awarded the Good Conduct Medal. A veteran of the Leyte battle, he entered the Army in January, 1942 and went overseas in March, 1944. He is now fighting with the 32nd "Red Arrow" Division on Luzon and holds the Combat Infantryman Badge. His wife, the former Ruth Long, and their son live in Akron, O.

Private First Class John S. Neel Jr., son of Mrs. Harriet A. Neel of Barboursville, has been awarded the Combat Infantryman Badge. He is serving with the 100th Division of the Seventh army in Germany.

Ralph C. Gardner, 3454 Piedmont Road, has received a commission in the field as second lieutenant in the Signal Corps. He has been overseas for 18 months and participated in the North Burma campaign which culminated in the opening of Stilwell Road and land lifeline to China... Lieutenant Gardner holds the Good Conduct Medal, the North Burma bronze campaign star, [and] the Meritorious Service Citation awarded his unit for outstanding work during the course of the campaign.

Private First Class Henry B. Willis, husband of Mrs. Nancy J. Willis of Chesapeake, O., is a member of the 24th Infantry "Victory" Division fighting in the Philippines...

Petty Officer Third Class Lillian R. Eplin, daughter of Mrs. Charlotte Eplin, 696 Popular Street, Kenova, has returned to her station at the University of Kanas, Lawrence, Kan., after spending a leave with her mother.

Fireman First Class Willis Crum of Omar, W.Va. is on the LST *356* which makes shuttle runs across the English Channel with supplies for the Allied forces in Europe. His ship was under enemy attack for seven hours during the invasion of France.

Several men from the Huntington area are members of the 1338th Engineer Combat Group, which is maintaining 67 miles of vital highway feeding the Fifth Army front in Italy. They are Corporal Clyde E. Dunn, truck driver, son of Mrs. Mamie Dunn, 1040 ½ Fourth Avenue; Corporal Eugene D. Church, chauffeur, son of William Church, 429 Third Avenue; Private Carl A. Fitch, truck driver, son of Mrs. Gladys Wallace, 62 A Street; Corporal James E. Athey, armorer, son of Mrs. Viola Burgess, 1019 West Thirteenth Street; Private Edward C. Thomas, orderly, son of Mrs. Anna Thomas, 1033 Sixth Street of Huntington; Private Julius Baisden of Dingess; Corporal Frank Dean, Fort Gay; Private Drewey H. Toler, Justice; Corporal William T. Ward, truck driver whose wife, Private First Class Delcie Ward, lives at 1610 Sycamore Street; Staff Sergeant Ralph G. Smith, motor sergeant, son of Mrs. Rosa Hall Smith, 1119 Pine Street, Kenova; Captain Ralph S. Altman, Williamson; Private First Class Willard J. Cox, Thacker; Sergeant Henry C. Hylton, Switchback and Corporal Russell L. Dick, bridge carpenter, son of Mrs. Urcie Dick of Salt Rock. [Russell Dick was a student at Walnut Grove School when my mother was the teacher. He wired our house for electricity in 1946. I helped him install wire in the dusty attic.]

Glenna: *April 21st Saturday – Cool and cloudy at morning.*

Rupert: *I earned $ .25 working for Roy Midkiff.*

Roy and Elsie Midkiff's property on the hillside above the intersection of Route 10 and River Road was steep, uneven, and full of small shrubs and stones. The lawn was a challenge. The Midkiffs had two children, Lynn and Nannell. Lynn Midkiff was away fighting in the Pacific. Elsie let me read some of his letters. He stayed in the Army after the war and eventually became a helicopter pilot. Nannell Midkiff, about a year older than me, would marry Manford Hutchinson.

"Adolf Hitler remained silent on this, his 56th and darkest birthday ... The once-mighty fuehrer had boasted that he would fight until 15 minutes past midnight. For him, it is now 14 minutes past midnight and the best guess in London was that he had fled—if still alive—to the Bavarian Alps."[185]

Briefs from Last Night's Associated Press Wires reported the following: Princess Elizabeth was to celebrate her nineteenth birthday today; In San Francisco, delegates to the United Nations Security Conference were marveling at the silver dollars they were getting in their change. "'This is the first time I've seen one of these things since I was a little boy,' said one 40-year-old man."[186] (I was amazed, too, when I arrived in Alaska in 1953 and saw that silver dollars were almost as numerous as paper ones.)

Commander James S. Willis, son of Dr. and Mrs. C. A. Willis, 1326 Enslow Boulevard, was killed in the Pacific. A destroyer division commander, he had also been an instructor at the Naval Academy before the war. His wife and daughter lived in Charleston and his son was attending an academy in Massachusetts.[187]

"IN THE SERVICE":

First Lieutenant Charles C. Chapman, son of Mr. and Mrs. Charles Chapman, 2636 Guyan Avenue, has been awarded the 12th Oak Leaf Cluster to his Air Medal. He is a navigator on a B-17.

Private First Cass Russell E. Wise, husband of Mrs. Peggy Robison Wise, 1626 Chestmont Drive, has been transferred from Patton's Third Army to the Eighth Air Force. Wounded in France last November 24, 1944, he is now a member of a B-24 Liberator group. The night before he was wounded, the former automatic

rifleman in the infantry met his cousin, Second Lieutenant Byron D. Meadows, also of Huntington.

Master Sergeant James M. McQuinn, 29, son of Mrs. Dollie B. McQuinn, 550 Second Street, is a ground crew technician who helps make it possible for Eighth Air Force planes to continue their round the clock missions against Germany. Sergeant McQuinn entered the Army in February, 1941.

Walter A. (Tom) Lusk, son of Mr. and Mrs. A. Lusk, 2514 Smith Street, has been promoted to the rank of staff sergeant. He is stationed at an air base in England. A graduate of Central High School and a former student at Arizona State College, Sergeant Lusk was awarded the Air Medal and Presidential Unit Citation.

Sergeant Herman Black [423 West Fifth Avenue], whose sister, Mrs. W. E. Orwig, lives at 1715 Railroad Avenue, is an aircraft armorer with the 12th Air Force in Italy. He wears seven bronze battle stars on his theatre ribbon. Sergeant Black entered the Army in July, 1941.

Captain Roger W. Bussell, 27, husband of Mrs. Jeanne E. Bussell and son of Mrs. Richard J. Bussell, has won his third Oak leaf Cluster to the Air Medal. He is a bombardier on a B-17 and a graduate of Marshall College in 1941.

Charles E. Stanley, 1549 Beech Street, has received a battlefield commission as second lieutenant in Germany. He was a staff sergeant in the infantry.

First Lieutenant Lewis Ansara, 2106 Fifth Avenue, has been commended by General James Doolittle for his teamwork as statistical and classification officer at an air base in England.

Jack C. Beckett, son of Mrs. Agnes V. Bias, 1343 Fourth Avenue, has been promoted from corporal to sergeant at an air base in England.

Sergeant Clarence W. Wiley, 21, son of Mr. and Mrs. C. H. Wiley, 220 Eighteenth Street, has been awarded the Air Medal at a bomber base in England.

Private First Class Martin T. Kitchen Jr., son of Mr. and Mrs. M. T. Kitchen Sr., was recently awarded the Good Conduct Medal at an air base in England.

Staff Sergeant Wilfred F. Stone, whose sister, Mrs. Eloise Camp lives at 3308 Fifth Avenue, is a member of the 403rd Antiaircraft Artillery Gun Battalion attached to the Fifth Army in Italy.

Private First Class William Webb, son of Mrs. Lilyan Webb of Huntington, has been awarded the Bronze Star Medal for heroic achievement in action against the Japanese.

Corporal George K. Dillman, 32, husband of Mrs. Ada Dillman, 1931 Monroe Avenue, has returned from the South Pacific where he served in aircraft supply. He is now at Miami Beach, Fla.

Second Lieutenant George W. Long Jr., son of Mr. and Mrs. G. W. Long of Huntington, has been awarded the Air Medal. He is the pilot of a fighter plane based in England.

Private First Class Regina M. Derda, 1630 Charleston Avenue, is a member of the Airwacs at a base in France.

Corporal William E. Demmler, son of Mrs. Bessie L. Demmler of Barboursville, is an armorer with a B-25 bomber squadron in the Mediterranean Theatre.[188]

Glenna: *April 22nd Sunday – Went to church and Sunday [School]. Mr. Fannin was our speaker that day. Cool all day. We stayed at home.*

C. N. Fannin was a Cabell County educator and Assistant Superintendent of Schools who lived in Barboursville. Donald Fannin, a son, became my good friend although I would not know him until I was in high school. Our friendship has continued to this day.

Rupert: *I went to Sunday school today. Later two school mates went home with me.*

Glenna: *Monday 23rd April – I washed all day. Cool and rainy. Went to graveyard late that evening.*

Rupert: *I went to school today. Nothing happened today.*

I'm certain "nothing" was a relative understanding. My days were filled with activities generated by the school curriculum, home chores, and pursuits of interest. I listened to the radio in evenings, to local and network news, and to the popular fifteen-minute adventure series sponsored by cereal companies. I tried to time my chores so I would not miss those programs.

The Russians finally entered Berlin. Reichs Fuhrer Heinrich Himmler offered to surrender to the Allies but not to the Russians. The offer was refused.[189]

"IN THE SERVICE":

Private Carl R. Turner, son of Mrs. C. W. Chapman of Norway Avenue, was slightly wounded on March 23 while fighting with the 32nd Division on Luzon, according to word received by his wife, Mrs. Pauline Turner, 146 Gallaher Street. Private Turner, the father of three sons, entered the Army in July, 1944, and went overseas last December. He is a former employee of the International Nickel Co.

Maurice E. Hinerman, son of Mr. and Mrs. A. B. Hinerman, 2224 Tenth Avenue, celebrated his promotion to first lieutenant by going hunting in Corsica. Lieutenant Hinerman studied at Marshall College and is married to the former Miss Evelyn Bobbitt. He is a meteorologist assigned to the 12th Weather Region in Italy.

Corporal Harold Morgan, son of Mrs. Ella R. Morgan, 3326 Crane Avenue, is now in the final stages of training as a B-29 crew at Pyote Army Air Field, Texas. He is married to the former Alah M. Leach. Corporal Morgan entered the service in March 1944 and is a tail gunner on his bomber.

William W. Jones, grandson of Mrs. W. F. Hite, 699 Thirteenth Street, has been promoted from second to first lieutenant and awarded the Air Medal. He is an air officer in the field artillery and has participated in campaigns in Belgium and Germany.

Corporal Norman B. Adkins, husband of Mrs. Greta Porter Adkins of Genoa, recently arrived in the European theatre as a member of the Air Forces.

Staff Sergeant James O. Freeman, son of Mr. and Mrs. W. E. Freeman, 918 Fifth Avenue, is at the infantry replacement center at Camp Blanding, Fla. He entered the service in 1941.

Lieutenant Robert E. Booth, 1028 Sixteenth Street, a patient at an Army hospital in China, was recently sketched by Don Barclay, famous artist and caricaturist. Lieutenant Booth is a member of the 14th Air Force.

Technician Fifth Grade Bennie R. Stanley, son of Mrs. Rebecca Stanley of Branchland, has been slightly wounded in action in Germany, according to a message from the War Department received by his wife, Mrs. Olive Stanley. He is with the Ninth Division of the First Army.

Captain Raymond L. Austin Jr., son of Mr. and Mrs. R. L. Austin, 2917 Ninth Avenue, is undergoing primary flight training at the Lodwick School of Aeronautics at Lakeland, Fla. Captain Austin is a graduate of Huntington High School, served overseas for 11 months, participating in 30 missions against Germany. He holds the Distinguished Flying Cross, the Air Medal, and the Presidential Citation.

Glenna: *April 24th Tuesday – Beautiful day. I ironed and mended everything.*

Rupert: *I went to school today. I did more playing than working*

Hitler's generals were ignoring and defying him at every turn. He ordered the arrest of Goering and announced that Himmler was to be shot on sight.[190]

"IN THE SERVICE":

Private First Class Francis Arbaugh recently completed 38 months of overseas duty with the 945th Anti-Aircraft Artillery, which is attached to the 14th Anti-Aircraft Command. He is the son of Mr. and Mrs. Floyd Arbaugh of Barboursville. Private Arbaugh entered the Army in October, 1942. He participated in the Solomons campaign. He was awarded the Good Conduct Medal and is qualified as an expert gunner.

Donald Scites, husband of Mrs. Emma Scites, 4215 Auburn Road, is a member of an armed guard crew on a merchant vessel which has returned to the Armed Guard Center in New Orleans. His ship was under continuous Jap attack at Leyte last December and January. On the return voyage, the vessel fought a hurricane, which he described as "as bad as the Japs."

The following service men and women from the Huntington area are home on leave or furlough: Private Eva J. Whitehill, WAC, 5701 Ohio River Road; Staff Sergeant John H. Sayre, AAF, husband of Mrs. Lynette F. Sayre, 1438 Norway Avenue; Ensign George F. Saurborne Jr., 4426 Ohio River Road; Seaman First Class James Robert McCreevy, son of Mr. and Mrs. W. A. McCreevy, 3853 Green Valley Drive; Private First Class W. M. Pancake, son of Mrs. Delpha Pancake of Milton; Private Culver A. Green, 528 West Tenth Avenue; Seaman Second Class L. P. Cremeans, husband of Mrs. Maxine Cremeans, 1904 Marcum Terrace.

Technical Sergeant Sherman J. Frazier, husband of Mrs. Bonnie R. Frazier, 514 Bridge Street, was promoted to that rank recently as a member of the Fifth Air Force in the Philippines. Sergeant Frazier, an engineer-gunner on a B-26

Mitchell strafer-bomber, has won the Air Medal with one Oak Leaf Cluster. He graduated from Central High School in 1941, and entered the Air Forces in February, 1943.

Private First Class Thomas C. Cochran, 32, husband of Mrs. Elda Marion Cochran, 519 Ninth Avenue, has returned from overseas service... Private Cochran served for 33 months as a rifleman in the European theatre and wears four battle stars on his campaign ribbon, and the Combat Infantryman Badge.

Staff Sergeant Edgar Hoke, brother of William Hoke of Kenova, is a railroad chief in the 689th Ordnance Ammunition Company which daily handles more than 1,000 tons of ammunition. Sergeant Hoke has been in the Army since November, 1942, and landed in Europe nine months ago.

Billy J. Estep, 20, son of Mrs. Bertha Ridenour, 516 Wilson Street, has been promoted to the rank of technical sergeant. He is an engineer-gunner with the 15th AAF in Italy. Sergeant Estep entered the Army in June.1943.

Charles H. Lewis, a motor machinist's mate third class in the Navy, is stationed at the Amphibious Base at Little Creek, Va. He is the son of Milford Lewis of Olive Hill, Ky., and entered the Navy in June, 1942.

Ina B. Spurlock, daughter of Chester A. Spurlock, 2726 Collis Avenue, has been promoted from private first class to corporal in the Air Transport Command's Ferrying Division Headquarters in Cincinnati. She has been in the WAC about a year.

Lieutenant Fred C Griffin of Huntington and Dallas, Tex. has returned to Huntington on leave to visit relatives and friends. Lieutenant Griffin lost a leg in the Battle of the Bulge in Belgium and is recuperating at Walter Reed Hospital in Washington.

Sergeant Richard J. Selfe, son of Mr. and Mrs. E. M. Selfe, 1049 Fifth Avenue, has been awarded the Alaskan Department Certificate of Commendation after 26 months' service in Alaska and the Aleutians.

The Combat Infantryman Badge has been awarded to Private Harry R. Scott, son of Mrs. Corba Scott, 610 Third Avenue, Guyandotte. He is a member of the 75th Division in Germany.

Major Elmer C. Newman, husband of Mrs. Josephine C. Newman, 122 West Tenth Street, has returned to the United States after 36 months with the infantry in the American theatre.

Captain John E. Aldridge of Ohio River Road was reverted to inactive status on Saturday after four years with the Army Ground Forces...

Private First Class Steve Tarkany of Logan and Sergeant Ralph E. Powers, 1725 Eleventh Avenue, are members of the 319th Medical Battalion serving with the 94th Infantry in Germany.

Private First Class Eldora Bias, 547 Sixth Avenue, escaped from a German prison camp with two other infantrymen after two weeks of captivity in the Reich.

Corporal Elden E. Smith, son of George Smith, has arrived at his home near Hamlin after being a prisoner of the Reich for nearly six months. He had been overseas for more than two years. He was freed by the advancing American armies.

Two soldiers from the Huntington area are members of the 343rd Engineer Regiment which helped in the construction of the Seventh Army bridge over the Rhine River. They are Private First Class Marvin W. Justice of Gilbert, and Captain Paul W. Bonham, 902 Second Street.

Glenna: *April 25th Wednesday — Started my round of house cleaning by moving everything out of one room and washing a few windows. Went to prayer meeting that night. Had a fine meeting. Weather warm.*

Two more Huntington men had died in the Pacific. Private First Class Kermit Lowell Bias, 20, USMC, son of Mr. and Mrs. F. W. Bias, 2016 Monroe Avenue was killed February 19 on Iwo Jima, and Private First Class Walter W.

Swann, 27, son of Edgar Swann, 1691 Doulton Avenue, was killed March 19 on Panay Island in the Philippines.[191]

In Europe, the Allies' noose was tightening: The first contact between Soviet and American troops occurred near Torgau on the River Elbe. Belorussian and Ukrainian troops surrounded Berlin.[192] In Italy, U.S. Fifth troops had crossed the Po River while other Allied troops captured La Spezia, Modena, and Ferrara. Forty thousand prisoners had been taken in the Spring offensive and it was reported that "Allied warplanes and armor cut to pieces German troops and transport trapped in pockets back of the swiftly moving Allied troops."[193]

From *Briefs from Last Night's Associated Press Wires:* "The Supreme Soviet, Russia's chief governing body, paid unprecedented tribute to the memory of Franklin D. Roosevelt; In London, members of Commons cheered when the light over Big Ben was snapped on for the first time in over five years."[194]

"IN THE SERVICE":

Private First Class Clyde Stevens, husband of Mrs. Ruth Stevens, 410 Homestead Place, has been awarded the Bronze Star for heroic achievement in action against the Germans in Italy last December. Private Stevens is the son of Mrs. B. W. Stevens, 405 West Third Avenue and has been overseas for 21 months.

Sergeant Steve Rencsok, USMC, a veteran of 33 months in the South Pacific, who was wounded in the invasion of Palau Islands and wears the Purple Heart, served in the honor guard for the late President Roosevelt. Sergeant Rencsok, son of Mr. and Mrs. Dave Rencsok of Fifth Avenue, is now stationed at Quantico, Va.

Assistant Secretary of War John McCloy and Lieutenant General Alexander M. Patch, commander of the Seventh Army, congratulated Major Frank Preston Jr. and Captain Paul W. Bonham, both of Huntington, for rebuilding a bridge in Germany which the enemy had destroyed, and enabling the Seventh Army to pass by. The bridge was rebuilt in record time.

Private First Class Harold Maynard has recently completed his second year overseas. He is the son of Mr. and Mrs. Noah Maynard of Big Creek, W.Va., and is with the 15th AAF in Italy.

Captain and Mrs. Stephan S. Summers of Charleston spent the past week end with Mrs. Stephan's parents, Mr. and Mrs. M. H. Craig of Ona. Captain Summers was on duty in the South Pacific for three years. He enlisted as a private in 1941.

Private First Class Eddie E. White, son of Mrs. Martha Stevens of Accoville, W.Va. has completed two years in the Mediterranean Theatre. He is in Italy with the 15th Army.

Wilford Stone, brother of Mrs. Eloise Camp, 3308 Fifth Avenue, has been promoted from staff sergeant to first sergeant on the Fifth Army front in Italy.

Private Walter F. McClaskey, husband of Mrs. Elizabeth McClaskey, 429 West Tenth Street, has been cited for action with the 86th Mountain Regiment Division and awarded the Combat Infantryman Badge on the Fifth Army front in Italy.

Technical Sergeant William N. Branch, son of W. N. Branch, 831 Ninth Avenue, has reported for duty at the Carlsbad Army Air Field, Carlsbad, N.M. He recently returned from the European theatre where he won the Air Medal with four Oak Leaf Clusters.

Private First Class William Perkey, son of Mrs. Goldie Perkey, 37 West Fifth Avenue, has returned to his outfit with the Ninth Army. He was wounded and awarded the Purple Heart last February and has been recovering in a hospital since.

Private First Class Harvey B. Little of Wilcoe is a member of the 601st Ordnance Base Armament Maintenance Battalion with the Sixth Army Group in Germany.

Private Boyd Gibson, son of Mr. and Mrs. Alex Gibson of James River Road, has returned after 18 months of service overseas and is spending a 30-day leave with his parents. He was wounded in action last December.

Glenna: *April 26ᵗʰ Thursday – Cool day and slow rain at morning. Jean McComas was killed by a train at 5 minutes until 7 o'clock this morning. Essie Harbour, Viola Morrison, and myself went down to Ellis's.*

Rupert: *Jean McComas daughter of Mr. and Mrs. Ellis McComas was killed by a train today.*

Jean McComas' tragic death was a terrible shock to Salt Rock people. A student at Barboursville High School, she was struck while she walked on the railroad tracks from her home toward the Route 10 highway bridge. An often-muddy road paralleled the rails, which may be the reason she walked on the tracks. The southbound train approached her from behind and, apparently, she did not hear it.

"Private First Class Irvin J. LeMaster, 22, son of Mr. and Mrs. D. LeMaster, 4330 Piedmont Road, was killed April 1 in Germany where he was serving with the infantry... Overseas only a month at the time of his death, Private LeMaster had been in service for two years. He was graduated from Vinson High School where he stared in basketball and football. A brother, Private First Class Charles E. LeMaster, the only other survivor, is en route to overseas with the engineers."[195]

The Silver Star Medal was awarded Private Curtis E. Adkins, son of Andrew Adkins, 2915 Overlook Drive for "his action during the construction of a footbridge over a river separating American troops from the enemy. The Germans set up a heavy barrage and American casualties were severe... Private Adkins' actions greatly aided the construction of the bridge and the successful crossing of the river." The medal was awarded while Private Adkins was in Fort Story Convalescent Hospital in Virginia

recovering from separate wounds received near St. Lo, France on July 25 and 28 of 1944.[196]

AP report from Beckley, West Virginia: "President George J. Titler of United Mine Workers District 19 said today [April 25] that he had protested directly to OPA Administrator Chester Bowles against the Office of Price Administration's 'dictatorial attitude' in allocating meat to the coal fields..."[197]

The Chesapeake & Ohio Railway Company announced that twin, two-unit combination diner and kitchen-pantry-dormitory cars would be added for the sections of the eastbound "George Washington," and the westbound "Fast Flying Virginian."[198]

"IN THE SERVICE":

Coast Guardsman Tommy L. Harbour, machinist's mate second class of Milton, participated in the invasion of Okinawa. The son of Mr. and Mrs. E. W. Harbour of Milton, he previously had taken part in the invasions of Normandy and Southern France. He was graduated from Milton High School in 1942.

Lane S. Anderson, motor machinist's mate first class, USCG, husband of the former Helen Eugenia Sindell, 724 Jefferson Avenue, is now serving aboard a Coast Guard-manned LST carrying war material to the front lines of our advancing armies in the Pacific. He is the son of Mrs. J. L. McCluse of Richmond, Va.

Sergeant Roy Ford, son of Mr. and Mrs. James Ford of Hamilton, Ohio, is serving with the military police at the Air Transport Command base at Marrakech, French Morocco, North Africa. A former employee of the Huntington Grocery Co., he went overseas last July and has been stationed at Marrakech since.

Private First Class Paul M. Venoy, son of Mr. and Mrs. L. W. Venoy of Salt Rock, was liberated from a German prison camp on April 2 by advancing American troops. The husband of Mrs. Eltha Venoy, he entered the Army in

October 1943, went overseas last June and was captured in January.

Staff Sergeant Charles Grant Kindle, husband of the former Miss Mary Ellyn Steele, 1660 McGuffin Avenue, was awarded the Distinguished Flying Cross with three Oak Clusters to his Air Medal, at a review at Avon Park, Fla. Sergeant Kindle already holds the Purple Heart, the Bronze Star, the Good Conduct Medal and the European theatre ribbon with two battle stars.

Glenna: *April 27th Friday — Very cool and clear. I have been working on my house cleaning. Rupert is gone to Huntington to visit Papa and Mamma. He went yesterday the 26th.*

Rupert: *I didn't go to school today. I went home with my Grandpa and Grandma Adkins.*

Among the 1,930 sick or wounded troops from the European theatre who disembarked at Camp Patrick Henry, Virginia, were area service members "Technician Fifth Grade Cecil A. Brudine, Amherstdale; Private First Class Thurman Childers, Salt Rock; Private Sherman A. Coulson, 2207½ Third Avenue, Huntington; Private First Class Andrew C. Guella, Roderfield, and Private First Class Charles E. Woodward, Huntington."[199]

Private First Class Charles William Thornburg, nineteen, son of Mr. and Mrs. Charles I. Thornburg of Ridgewood Road, Park Hills, drowned April 25th in a freak accident in a swimming pool at Lake Field, Tempe, Arizona. Private Thornburg was on detached military police duty while he awaited assignment to pre-flight school. "A member of one of Huntington's prominent families, Private Thornburg was born November 2, 1925, and attended Miller School, Cammack Junior High School and was graduated from Central High School in June 1943. He starred in football. Later he attended Marshall College where he was pledged to Phi Tau Alpha fraternity. He was the grandson of C. W. Thornburg, Huntington insurance executive and civic and religious leader and Mrs. Thornburg, who survive in addition to the parents. Their other grandson, Lieutenant Herbert Nash, was lost in aerial combat over Germany last year."[200]

"IN THE SERVICE":

Sergeant John O. Cogar, husband of Mrs. Inez Cogar of Marvis, W.Va. has been advanced to that rank from private first class. He is an infantryman with the 94th Division in Germany, and has participated in the campaign of Northern France and battle of the Siegfried Line in Germany.

William E. Davis, motor machinist's mate third class, son of Mr. and Mrs. W. L. Davis, 15 East Oakland Avenue, has returned to his base at Danville, R.I. after a nine-day leave here.

Sergeant Harold C. Bohl, stationed with the Air Transport Command in Washington, recently spent a three-day furlough with his wife, Sergeant Betty Bohl, a member of the WAC recruiting staff here.

Corporal Don W. Clauson, husband of Mrs. Phyllis Clauson, 2719 Fourth Avenue, has been awarded the Presidential Unit Citation and the Good Conduct Medal at his 15th Air Force station in Italy. He has been overseas for six months.

Train Kills Schoolgirl

Doris Jean McComas, 16, of Salt Rock, was killed instantly yesterday morning when she was struck by a Chesapeake & Ohio freight while walking on the tracks on her way to Barboursville High school. The daughter of Mr. and Mrs. Ellis McComas was a junior in high school and was on her way to meet the school bus, which her father was driving.

Coroner F. X. Schuller said the girl was walking on the eastbound tracks beside a moving Westbound train and apparently did not see or hear the approach of an Eastbound train.

Besides the parents, she is survived by two sisters, Margaret and Lucille, and one brother, David Ellis, all at home.

Funeral services will be held tomorrow at 2 P. M. at the Salt Rock Methodist Church with the Rev. Elijah Stevens and the Rev. Horace Midkiff officiating. Burial will be in the family cemetery near the home. The body is at the McGhee Funeral Home at West Hamlin and will be taken to the residence this afternoon. Classmates will act as flowerbearers at the funeral.

James K. Wilcox, aviation machinist's mate third class, USNR, son of Mrs. Mayme C. Wilcox, 1220 Nineteenth Street, served as turret gunner in a Navy Avenger torpedo-bomber plane based aboard a carrier during a strike at Japan's defenses. He was recently home on leave.

William T. Jones, son of Mrs. W. B. Kinzer, 426 Eleventh Avenue, has been promoted from second to first lieutenant. He is a member of the 42nd (Rainbow) Division in Germany. His wife and son live in Detroit with her family.

Glenna: *April 28th Saturday – Gene [Jean] McComas was buried. Very cool and cloudy. Rupert came home.*

Rupert: *I came home today from Huntington, West Virginia.*

Benito Mussolini and his mistress, Clara Petacci, were executed by Italian partisans.[201]

"IN THE SERVICE":

Robert E. Ellis, 343 West Seventh Avenue, has been promoted from second to first lieutenant in the Third Army in Germany... The promotion of the former Huntington Publishing Co. employee was effective April 1.

Private Lloyd G. Doxey, husband of Mrs. Lloyd Doxey, 625 Sixth Avenue, has been awarded the Good Conduct Medal. He is a member of the 36th "Texas" Division of the Seventh Army in France...

First Lieutenant Harold D. Johnson, 25, son of Mr. and Mrs. H. G. Johnson, 1852 Eleventh Avenue, has been awarded the Oak Leaf Cluster to his Air Medal at a bomber base in England. He is a pilot of a B-17 Flying Fortress with the 91st Bombardment Group.

Radioman First Class Merlin C. (Red) Farris, USN, son of Mr. and Mrs. Clyde Farris, 2721 Oakland Avenue, has been promoted to that rank from second class petty officer in the Mariana Islands. He has been in the Pacific 19 months.

Private Wayne Smith, son of Mr. and Mrs. Wayne M. Smith of Fifth Street Road, has arrived in Belgium. His brother, Alvin, has been in the Army for 26 months and is stationed in England with a repair unit. Another brother, William, is with the 43rd Division on Luzon in the Philippines.

Aviation Chief Ordnance Mechanic Jack Locher, 21, son of Mr. and Mrs. John Locher, 1665 Thirteenth Street, is home on leave after four years' service with the Navy in the South Pacific. He has the Pacific campaign ribbon with seven battle stars, the Presidential Unit Citation and Good Conduct Medal. He will report to the naval base at Jacksonville, Fla., for special training.

Private First Class James Cohen, 25 East Third Avenue, and Corporal Henry T. Lacock, 414 East Second Street, are members of the Sixth Army Group in Germany. They previously were stationed in Italy where they fought with the infantry and were commended by General Mark Clark.

Staff Sergeant Dale E. Ernest, 20, of Thurmond, W.Va. Son of Mr. and Mrs. G. H. Ernest, was awarded the Air Medal at an Eighth Air Force base in England. He is a waist-gunner on a B-17.

Glenna: *Sunday, April 29th – Went to Sunday School and church. I ate dinner with Papa and Mamma at Cline's.*

Hitler and Eva Braun were married in their Berlin underground bunker.

"WITH THE COLORS":

The Silver Star has been awarded Staff Sergeant Earl S. E. Thornton, son of Mr. and Mrs. S. E. Thornton of 1110 Twenty-first Street, for gallantry in action with the 36th "Texas" Infantry Division of the Seventh Army on Dec. 9, 1944, according to an overseas announcement yesterday. He is a former Marshall College student and joined the 34th Division in June, 1944.

Grover Russell Scarberry, 22, motor machinist's mate (first class), USNR, husband of the former Lanier Bowen of Proctorville, O., is at the Atlantic Fleet's Amphibious Training Base, Camp Bradford, Va. preparing for duty aboard an LST. He is a graduate of Rome Rural High School, Proctorville and was previously employed by the E. D. Bager Co. of Huntington.

Staff Sergeant Charles Blair, son of Mr. and Mrs. Charles Blair, 626 Elm Street, engineer on a B-17 Flying Fortress, has been awarded the Air Medal with two Oak Leaf Clusters at an Eighth Air Force Bomber station in England with the 91st Bombardment Group. He is a former Marshall College student.

Seaman (First Class) Robert L. Plymale, aboard his ship in the South Pacific participated in the recent invasion of Iwo Jima. His brother, Seaman's Mate (Third Class) Dwight Plymale is at Okinawa. They are the sons of Mr. and Mrs. C. Plymale of 2112 Twelfth Avenue.

The Combat Infantryman Badge has been awarded Private (First Class) Lester Swann, son of Mr. and Mrs. Eustace Swann, 1923 Twelfth Avenue for participation in the Battle of Zigzag Pass, the battle of Purple Heart Hill and the liberation of Bataan. He is an anti-tank cannoneer in the 151st Infantry Regiment of the 38th Division on Bataan. Private Swann volunteered with 20 others to carry food, water, and ammunition over 4,000 yards of gullies and cliffs to the front lines.

Steward's Mate (Second Class) Joe Shiveley, U.S. Merchant Marine, has arrived home to spend a 30-day leave with his parents, Mr. and Mrs. J. C. Shiveley, 1366 Thirteenth Street, after having served four months and 20 days aboard a merchant vessel in the Mediterranean area including North Africa, Italy and France. A former student at Central High, he enlisted last October.

Private (First Class) Elsie M. Talbert, daughter of Mr. and Mrs. A. L. Ross, 247 Springdale Avenue, a member of the Woman's Army Corps for 13 months, has been awarded the Good Conduct Medal at the Santa Maria Calif. Army Air Field with the Fourth Air Force.

Radioman (Second Class) Lloyd Edward Massie, 23, USNR, son of Mr. and Mrs. J. F. Massie of Fort Gay, has completed a Navy refresher course at Miami, Fla. after returning from duty in Panama, and has been transferred to Norfolk, Va. for training aboard a new destroyer.

Hospital Apprentice (Second Class) Thomas J. Conaty, USNR, was graduated from St. Elizabeth Hospital, Washington, D.C... as a neuro-psychiatric technologist. He and a classmate, Tom Colloway of New Orleans, La. are here spending a three-day leave with the former's parents, Mr. and Mrs. Walter Conaty, 1411 Fifth Avenue. Petty Officer Conaty will serve as a member of the St. Elizabeth Hospital staff.

Frank E. Weider, son of Dr. and Mrs. Don F. Weider, 2981 Merrill Avenue, has been promoted ... to ... sergeant. Sergeant Weider is a radar technician with the 493rd Bomber Squadron in India.

Private (First Class) James B. Humphreys, son of Mr. and Mrs. Gordon Humphreys, 455 Seventh Avenue, has been reported safe in military hands. Previously reported missing on Dec. 20, 1944, he was liberated April 2. Word from Private Humphreys indicated that he was recuperating in an American hospital. He entered the service in June, 1943 and went overseas the following May. He was a member of the Third Armored "Spearhead" Division of the First Army.

Glenna: *April 30th Monday – Cool and rainy in late evening. I washed. News of death of Mussolini.*

Rupert: *News of Mussaloin's death.*

We had not yet heard, but Hitler and his wife had committed suicide in their Berlin bunker.

The Allies took Munich in Bavaria and liberated Dachau concentration camp.[202]

"Private Evertt M. Skaggs, 19, husband of Mrs. Easter M. Skaggs, 20 West Fourth Avenue, was killed in Germany April 15... He is the son of Mrs. Lenny Skaggs, 109 West Third Avenue."[203]

Huntington was ready to celebrate. "At least one person was recovering yesterday from a premature V-E Day celebration Saturday night which completely disrupted traffic in the downtown area as thousands poured into the streets." There were ten arrests for drunkenness.[204]

"IN THE SERVICE":

Private Marion T. Baisden, son of Mrs. Nettie Hodge of Huntington, has been honorably discharged from the Army for physical disabilities. He is a veteran of the Normandy invasion, and the battles for Belgium and Germany. He entered the Army before Pearl Harbor and wears three battle stars on the campaign ribbon, along with the Combat Infantry Badge.

Private First Class Leslie E. Ferguson of Wayne has returned to this country after 33 months in the Mediterranean theatre. He will spend his furlough with his parents.

Private Roy L. Hysell, husband of Mrs. Nannie B. Hysell, 1340 Jefferson Avenue, has been awarded the Combat Infantryman Badge during the battle of Germany. He is a rifleman in the 291st Infantry.

Boatswain Glenn Ervin McCloud has been transferred to the Atlantic Fleet's Minecraft training center at Little Creek, Va. He is married to the former Sadie Swartz of Portsmouth, N.H. His parents, Mr. and Mrs. Melvin B. McCloud live at 3502 Waverly Road.

Sergeant Arthur L. Harrison of Huntington is a radio technician with the 154th Signal Company, attached to the Seventh Army in Germany.

Corporal Harvey H. Wintz, husband of Mrs. Harvey Wintz of Huntington is a mechanic with the 88th Division Quartermaster Company attached to the Fifth Army in Italy.

Private First Class Everett W. Wray, 816 Twelfth Street, is a member of the 764th Railway Shop Battalion in France. They landed in France last August and have been close behind the battling armies ever since.

Sergeant Andy H. Brown, husband of Mrs. Ermalee H. Brown, 2576 Fourth Avenue, has been presented with his fifth bronze battle star since arriving in the European Theatre. He is a member of the 438th Troop Carrier Group and has participated in Northern and Southern France, Normandy, Rome-Arno and Germany operations.

May

VICTORY IN EUROPE

GLENNA: MAY 1ST TUESDAY – COOL AND WINDY. I IRONED AND MENDED
everything. News of Hitler's death.

Rupert: *News of Hitler's death came today.*

I marvel at the casualness with which we commented on the death of the man who plunged the world into war and was responsible for deaths of millions.

Hitler's successor, Admiral Karl Dönitz, quickly established a government in Germany following Hitler's suicide.[205] Goebbels, Hitler's Minister of Propaganda and his wife, Magda, killed their six children and themselves.

Britain had asked for the return of control of the big Bovington airport after the war but the U.S. was showing unwillingness because, "the airport was thought to be important in the redeployment of men, machines and material for the Pacific war."[206]

"For heroic service against Germany from February 23 to March 1 inclusive, Second Lieutenant Fred E. Griffith, husband of the former Miss Almita Wood, 226 ½ Fourth Avenue, has been awarded the Bronze Star Medal..."[207]

"Three Marines from the Huntington area who participated in the Battle for Okinawa were Staff Sergeant Jesse J. Williams Jr., 21, son of Mr. and Mrs. J. J. Williams Sr., of Bradford, Va. and husband of Mrs. Antionette T. Williams of Filbert, W. Va.; Sergeant James W. Hatmaker, 21, son of Jerry Hatmaker, and Corporal Albert J. McCoy, 20, brother of Smith McCoy of Roderfield."[208]

"IN THE SERVICE":

Lieutenant Colonel Charles Johnson, who was recently identified in a news dispatch as the youngest man of his rank to command a battalion, is the son of Mr. and Mrs. Warren Johnson, 2310 Winchester Avenue, Ashland. For several years, Mrs. Johnson was manager of the millinery department of the Princess Shop here. Colonel Johnson led his men in an attack on Tombstone Ridge on Okinawa.

Technician Fifth Grade Walter P. Nease, son of Mrs. Spicie Nease of Ranger, has been wounded in action for the second time but has been returned to duty with the famous Fourth Armored (breakthrough) Division of the American Third Army...

Yeoman Helen Lane, daughter of Mrs. Julius Evans of Henlawson, W.Va. has been assigned to a Coast Guard base in the Hawaiian Islands as a member of the SPARS... Yeoman Lane formerly was stationed in the Jacksonville, Fla. Coast Guard office, military morale division.

Sergeant Roy E. Turner, 344 Oney Avenue, will soon have earned his sixth overseas stripe, representing three years and seven campaigns in the European-African-Middle-Eastern theatres. Sergeant Turner went overseas in June 1942.

First Lieutenant Guinn B. Helmick, 21, of Sandston, Va., husband of Mrs. Laura M. Helmick of Huntington, has been awarded his fifth Oak Leaf Cluster to the Air Medal at a bomber base in England. Lieutenant Helmick entered the Air Force in November, 1941, and has taken part in more than 25 missions against the Nazis.

Corporal Leonard C. Riggs, son of Mr. and Mrs. S. K. Riggs of Genoa, W.Va. is serving with the AAF in Italy. Corporal Riggs has been overseas for 22 months and is on duty with the firefighting platoon at an advanced base.

Private Earl Bloss, husband of Mrs. Rebecca Bloss, 711 Third Avenue, is attached to the 204th Ordnance on Luzon. Private Bloss has been in the Army since June, 1941, and prior to that was in the meat market business.

Private First Class Hiram R. Dean, son of Mrs. Ella Dean of Branchland, recently took part in a night raid into no man's land on the Fifth Army Front in Italy. The raiders returned with five prisoners after knocking out three enemy machinegun nests...

Corporal Paul F. King, son of Mrs. Rheba L. King, 418 Eighteenth Street, is serving with the Fifth Marine Division in the Pacific. He participated in the Iwo Jima invasion. Corporal King entered the Marine Corps in December, 1942.

Staff Sergeant Donald L. Smith of Ceredo has returned to the Army hospital at Camp Pickett, Va. after spending a furlough with his mother, Mrs. Drucilla Smith. Sergeant Smith was wounded twice during his overseas service.

Private First Class Chester W. Webb, 277 Gallaher Street, was wounded in the battle of Iwo Jima when his group ran into heavy Jap fire, according to a Marine Corps correspondent's dispatch.

First Lieutenant George K. Harshbarger, 30, USMC, son of Mr. and Mrs. C. L. Harshbarger of Milton, has returned to the Miramar Marine Air Depot in California from the South Pacific. Lieutenant Harshbarger is an ordnance officer with a fighter-bomber squadron in the Palaus.

Staff Sergeant Earl W. Smith, 21, son of Mr. and Mrs. J. W. Smith, 212 Short Street, is a flight engineer with a Fourth Marine Air Wing in the Marshall Islands. He recently returned to the Air Depot at Miramar.

Sergeants Ernest and Everett Farmer, sons of Mr. and Mrs. S. T. Farmer, 203 South Walnut Street, recently spent 48 hours together in London, the second time they have met in the last four years.

Private First Class Bennie Bowens of Webb, W.Va., son of Mrs. Georgia Bowens, is a member of the 173rd Field Artillery with the Fifth Army in Italy...

First Lieutenant William C. Campbell of Huntington has been awarded the Bronze Star for heroic achievement in action in Germany. Lieutenant Campbell attended Princeton University before entering the Army.

Captain George T. Aldridge, son of Mr. and Mrs. J. E. Aldridge, 5787 Ohio River Road, received his first overseas stripe for completing more than six months service in Italy. The Air Force pilot is the husband of Mrs. Margaret Aldridge, 2428 Collis Avenue.

Sergeant James R. Morgan, son of Mr. and Mrs. Robert Morgan of Guyandotte, is fighting with the 149th Infantry in the central sector of Luzon. He is a squad leader in a rifle company. Sergeant Morgan entered the Army in 1940 when he was only 16.

Technical Sergeant James R. Rimmer, husband of Mrs. Rose Rimmer of Ona, has been awarded the Bronze Star Medal for "outstanding duty in every type of combat against the enemy." He is a member of the 83rd Infantry Division in Europe.

Glenna: *May 2nd Wednesday — We papered ½ of the back room. Cool and cloudy. I went to prayer meeting and led that night*

Rupert: *We papered part of a room. I went to school today.*

"A Guyandotte youth and a former Marshall College student have been killed in battle in Europe, the War Department has notified their parents. They were Private First Class Leslie

Morton Barcus, Jr., son of Mr. and Mrs. L. M. Barcus, 520 North High Street, Guyandotte, and Lieutenant David R. Totten, 24, of Beckley, W.Va."[209]

"Seven men from the Huntington area are listed in the files of the Red Cross here as prisoners of War at Stalag 7-A, a German prison camp which has been liberated. They are: Private First Class Donald E. Adkins, son of Mrs. Addie C. Adkins, 2536 Sixteenth Street; Private Clyde R. Caldwell, husband of Mrs. Elizabeth E. Caldwell, Route, 1, Ona; Private Loren Dean, husband of Mrs. Madge Dean, 1832 Maple Avenue; Sergeant Cecil W. Estep, son of Mrs. Sarah Estep, Route 1, Salt Rock; Private Harold L. Johnson, husband of Mrs. Dorothy Johnson, 1634 Charleston Avenue; Private First Class William Short Jr., son of William Short Sr., 1925 James River. Road; Private Jack Watts, husband of Mrs. Ethel Watts, 1909 Jefferson Avenue; Private Richard A. Elliott; son of Mr. and Mrs. Rufus Elliott, 1667 Gimlet Hollow, has been freed from a German prison camp. He wrote his parents recently he would be home soon and that he is well."[210]

Berlin surrendered unconditionally to Soviet General Vasily Chuikov by German General Helmuth Weidling who was no longer bound by the commands of Joseph Goebbels.

"IN THE SERVICE":

First Lieutenant G. B Richmond, son of J. L. Richmond, 1123 Twelfth Street, has been awarded the Bronze Star Medal for distinguishing himself by heroism last September 21, in the area of Bouzieres-Froldmont, France.

Fern Black Koontz, WAVES, Daughter of Mr. and Mrs. Martin V. Black, 4619 Bradley Road, and widow of Lieutenant Elmer R. Koontz, who was killed in action in Germany, hopes to be a Link trainer operator when she completes her Navy course at Hunter College in New York City. Seaman Koontz has one brother in the Army and three in the Navy.

First Lieutenant Robert H. Martin, 20, a bombardier on a Flying Fortress, has been awarded the fifth Oak Cluster to the Air Medal. He is the son of Mr. and Mrs. Quinn V. Martin of Huntington and a student at Marshall College before entering the service in February 1943. He is a veteran of more than 30 Eighth Air Force missions over Nazi-held Europe.

Private First Class Clifton H. Wallace, 21, son of Mr. and Mrs. J. W. Wallace, 997 Turner Road, was seriously wounded in the neck and one leg by shrapnel in Germany on April 8... He has written that he is recovering in a hospital in France. The U.S. First Army soldier is a grandson of Mrs. Clemma Wallace of Hamlin, Route 1.

Sergeant Edgar Taylor, son of Mr. and Mrs. E. B. Taylor, 620 Trenton Place, has been freed from a German prison camp by American armies. A gunner in the 15th Air Force in Italy, he was captured last August and was one of the 100,000 war prisoners who were marched 400 miles across Germany by their captors last year. He is now in a hospital in England, and according to a letter received by his parents, he is well and "not much worse off from my stay in Germany."

Major Frederick A. Fitch, former instructor of physical education at Marshall College, has been promoted to that rank while serving as an AAF executive officer in New Guinea. He has been there for 30 months. His wife and two children live at 156 Wilson Court.

Major Harry B. Keller of Pittsburgh, formerly of Huntington, has been awarded the Bronze Star Medal for meritorious service. Major Keller is chief of the plans and operations division of the Ninth Air Force in Europe.

Private Marcellus L. Davis, son of Mr. and Mrs. Harland Davis of Hurricane, has returned to the United States after serving for 35 months overseas...

Second Lieutenant Albert N. Minton, husband of Mrs. Carolyn V. Minton, 331 West

Eleventh Avenue, has been decorated with his fourth Oak Leaf Cluster to his Air Medal at an Eighth Air Force station in England. The son of Mr. and Mrs. E. U. Minton, 1303 Ninth Avenue, he entered the service in November, 1942. He is a navigator on a B-17 and has taken part in more than 25 missions.

Corporal William Guthrie, son of Mrs. Eleanor Guthrie of Proctorville, O., Route 1, is an aircraft mechanic with the 31st Air Transport Group in England.

Technical Sergeant James D. Copen, 20, son of Mrs. Eldise D. Copen, 1328 ½ Fifth Avenue, has arrived at the AAF Redistribution Station No. 2 at Miami Beach for reassignment. Sergeant Copen has flown in 42 missions as a radio-gunner in the European theatre and holds the Air Medal with four Oak Leaf Clusters.

Captain John F. Reynolds, 37, son of G. E. Reynolds, 2659 Fifth Avenue, has returned to the United States after 18 months' duty in the European theatre as a supply officer. He is now at a redistribution center in Miami, Fla. Captain Reynolds entered the service in January, 1941.

Technical Sergeant Morris W. Smith and Gunner's Mate Third Class Roscoe E. Smith, sons of Mrs. O. F. Smith, 1510 Norway Avenue, spent Easter Sunday together in Panama, Sergeant Smith is an infantryman and has been in Panama for three and a half years.

John E. Glover, son of Herbert A. Glover, 265 High Drive, has been promoted from second to first lieutenant in the 87th Infantry Division in Germany, where he is aide-de-camp to the commanding general.

Private First Class Arna R. Neal, 1648 Doulton Avenue, is a member of an artillery battery wire crew which braved heavy mortar fire to lay communications wire across a German river after it had been flooded when the U.S. Army Engineers blew up a dam...

Sergeant John P. Cross, son of Mrs. M. V. Cross, 1019 ½ Fourth Avenue, has been awarded the Combat Infantryman Badge. He is a rifle squad leader in the 28th Infantry Division in Germany and participated in the Belgian bulge, Rhineland Colmar and Hurtgen Forest battles.

Glenna: *May 3rd Thursday – Rainy at Morn. Cool. We finished papering the back room.*

Rupert: *We finished a room today. I went to school.*

Major Burtis W. Anderson, USMCR, son of Mr. and Mrs. W. W. Anderson, 136 Woodland Drive, was awarded the Silver Star Medal for "repeatedly performed aggressive acts of individual bravery while leading his company in attack." The action took place on Guam. He was previously awarded the Bronze Star. "Major Anderson graduated from Marshall College in 1941, where he was president of the student body in his senior year. He has returned from the Pacific and is now stationed at Quantico, Va. His wife, the former Miss Mary Pryor of Ashland, is with him."[211]

The Red Army secured Berlin while other Allied forces captured Hamburg and Innsbruck, Austria.[212]

A tragic occurrence: Three German ships, the *Cap Arcona*, the *Thielbec*, and the *Deutschland* were sunk by British planes. Unknown to the British, the ships were under direction of the Red Cross and were carrying rescued prisoners from German concentration camps, mostly Jews. Eight thousand died in the disaster.[213]

"IN THE SERVICE":

Joseph D. Markham, 19, electrician's mate third class, son of John B. Markham Sr. of Logan, helped take his new cruiser into battle for the first time against the Japanese. Guns of the cruiser sent two Japanese bombers crashing into the sea just off the Jap mainland.

Second Lieutenant Abel M. Warren, former member of the 347th College Training Detachment at Marshall College, has been awarded the Distinguished Flying Cross. Lieutenant Warren, a native of Garland, N.C., has completed more than 300 operational hours over the hazardous India-China air lanes.

Russell Edmondson, motor machinist's mate first class, son of Frank Edmondson of Wilsondale, W.Va., has been on active duty aboard a patrol craft in the Pacific for more than 15 months.

Technician Fourth Grade Mildred H. Page, WAC, daughter of Mr. and Mrs. Thomas L. Page, 315 Walnut Street, is home on furlough from Moore General Hospital at Swannanoa, N.C. where she is a medical stenographer. She enlisted in the WAC in December, 1942.

Marine Sergeant Cyrus Lancaster of North Matewan, a veteran of several Pacific engagements including Guadalcanal, has been assigned to the Recruiting Marines Center here.

Lieutenant (j. g.) Clarence E. Morrison, son of Mr. and Mrs. W. B. Morrison of Kenova, is home on leave from Chapel Hill, N.C. He is an instructor in the Naval Pre-Flight School.

Staff Sergeant Dwight D. Messinger, 1721 Charleston Avenue, has been awarded the Air Medal at an Air Transport Command base in India, He is an aerial engineer.

William M. Bryan Jr., seaman second class, son of Mr. and Mrs. W. M. Bryan of West Hamlin, recently spent a nine-day leave with his parents after completing his basic training at Great Lakes, Illinois.

Private John C. Foose, son of Mr. and Mrs. A. M. Foose, 2569 Third Avenue, has been awarded the Expert Rifleman Badge for superior marksmanship at the Infantry Training Center at Camp Fannin, Texas.

Glenna: *May 4th Friday – Cleaned house and stayed at home.*

Neuengamme concentration camp was liberated. Karl Dönitz ordered all U-boats to cease operations. German troops in Denmark, Northern Germany, and The Netherlands surrendered to General Montgomery.

"Private Clyde H. Earls, husband of Mrs. Wanda L. Earls, 1502 Harrison Avenue, was wounded in Germany April 13... Private Earls, who went overseas in January, is hospitalized in Germany and is improving satisfactorily, according to a letter received from him."[214]

"Two Huntington soldiers have come out of German prison camps and are on their way home today ... Private Ray S. Beatty, son of Mrs. Lela Rucker, 405 Thirteenth Street, a prisoner for more than two years ... was released from Stalag 2B on April 14. Sergeant John L. Bays, 419 Sixth Avenue, said in a letter that he escaped ... and that even though he has lost considerable weight he is in fairly good condition. Sergeant Bays, a paratrooper, has been a captive since January, 1944." Also liberated from a prisoner-of-war camp was Sergeant Glenn E. Monk, brother of Arthur E. Monk of Kenova Route 1.[215]

"IN THE SERVICE":

Corporal Eamon E. White, son of Edmond White of Huntington, has been awarded the Bronze Star Medal for heroism and meritorious service with the Army in Europe between last October 1 and December 31. The citation which accompanied the medal praised him for repeatedly volunteering to assist in the removal of casualties and for outstanding performance in planning and moving truck convoys. Corporal White has been overseas since September. A brother, Private First Class Harry White, is serving in Germany.

Corporal Robert S. Sidebottom, who served for 30 months overseas, has left for an Army hospital at Camp Butner, N.C., after spending a 30-day furlough with his parents, Mr. and Mrs.

John Sidebottom of West Hamlin, and his wife, who resides at Marcum Terrace. Two brothers of Corporal Sidebottom are overseas.

Douglas W. Tignor, aviation electrician's mate second class, is visiting his wife, the former Naomi Miller, 2129 Eleventh Avenue, after 20 months in the Pacific theatre where he participated in several major engagements, including the Tarawa action. He and his wife will go the Charlottesville this week to visit his parents, who were formerly residents of Huntington...

James I. Hensley, husband of Mrs. Betty Ann Hensley of Barboursville Route 1, has been promoted from corporal to sergeant at a bomber base in England. Sergeant Hensley is a gunner on a B-24 Liberator bomber and is the son of Mrs. Anna L Hensley of Salt Rock. He entered the service in August, 1943.

Lieutenant (j. g.) Rudd C. Neel, USNR, son of Mr. and Mrs. R. T. Neel, 1505 Sixth Avenue, is spending a 30-day leave with his parents. He has been in the Pacific theatre for 20 months, serving as commissary, communications and executive officer.

Glenna: *May 5th Saturday – Rainy and cool.*

Rupert: *It was rainy and cold today.*

AP sports news from Columbus, Ohio: "Carroll Widdoes, Ohio State's head football coach, who worked side by side with Lt. Paul E. Brown for 12 years, today [May 4] said his former boss ... is 'signing or trying to sign' players who still are eligible for college football." Brown, at the Great Lakes Training Station, but slated to coach at Cleveland in the *All-American Pro League* after the war, denied it. Among those rumored to have been approached by Brown was Joe Whisler, star fullback at Ohio State, Lou Groza of Martins Ferry, Ohio, a place-kicking star, and Hal Dean."[216]

Allied and German officials met in Reims, France, to work out terms of a German surrender. In Prague, partisans rose against the German occupation.[217]

Over a million Germans surrendered on Field Marshall Montgomery's 21st Army Group front.[218]

The following three men were released from German prison camps: Private First Class Everett T. Adkins, son of Mrs. Ethel Adkins, 1131 Minton Street, captured in October and freed from Stalag 2-B on April 14; Corporal Thomas J. Goodwin, husband of Mrs. Marie Lilly Goodwin, 16 Twenty-seventh Street, freed after spending two weeks in a prison camp; Private First Class Lloyd R. Mays of Logan was released from Altengrabow prison camp.[219]

The Pacific war continued: "A savage Japanese air and sea attack on U.S. ships off Okinawa yesterday sank five light American warships and damaged another small surface vessel, for which the Nipponese paid with 54 planes shot down and 15 tiny suicide boats destroyed." Superfortresses continued to bomb Oita and Tachiara airfields on Northern Kyushu, dropping bombs visually from medium altitude. "American carrier planes struck furiously the same day at Japanese air units in the Amami Island group north of Okinawa, downing 96 enemy aircraft for a total of 150 accounted for..."[220]

The U.S. submarine, *Swordfish*, was overdue and considered lost.[221]

"IN THE SERVICE":

Staff Sergeant Robert E. Hall, 25, 101 Eighth Street, has recovered from wounds received last December. He has been at an Army hospital in England, during that time. His wife is Mrs. Ruth E. Hall.

Staff Sergeant Leon P. Clark, son of Sampson H. Clark, 1625 Twelfth Street, has been presented with his fifth Bronze Battle Star since arriving in the European theatre.

Sergeant Clark is a member of the 438th Troop Carrier Group.

Sergeant Arthur H. Schmauck, 25, son of Mr. and Mrs. Arthur Schmauck, 645 Fifth Avenue, is in England undergoing pre-combat training with the 452nd Bomber Group. He entered the Air Forces in October, 1943. [Another entry on June 9th has the last name spelled "Schmauch," and with a different address.]

Ford W. Roberts of Olive Hill, Ky. has been promoted to the rank of coxswain. He is at a Navy base in the Mariana Islands.

Sergeant Paul H. Wilson, son of Mrs. Nan Wilson of Milton Route 2, is a member of the Air Forces Military Police on duty at John H. Payne Field in Cairo. Sergeant Wilson entered the service in December, 1942...

First Lieutenant Frank Blood, 403 Thirteenth Street, participated as a glider pilot in the latest airborne assault on the Wesel area in Germany. He is the flight leader with one of the 435th Troop Carrier Group.

Private First Class Earl W. Albright of Branchland is a member of the 22nd Infantry Regiment of the Seventh Army which drove across the Rhine and pursued the Germans 65 miles east of the river before meeting any organized resistance.

First Sergeant E. M. Swain, 1915 Poplar Street, Kenova, saw action with the Marines on Iwo Jima. He has served in China and Nicaragua.

Private First Class Clyde Yoho Jr. of Ona has been awarded the Purple Heart...

Sergeant Froud Carter, son of Mr. and Mrs. F. G. Carter of Milton, is a section machine gun leader with the Marine Corps and has been awarded the Purple Heart for wounds received on Iwo Jima.

Staff Sergeant Thomas Willis, brother of Mrs. Virgie Gibson of Kenova, has arrived in France. He has been in the Army for more than four years.

Sergeant Ewell F. Shuff, 1361 Madison Avenue, met Coast Guard Commander Jack Dempsey, former world heavyweight champion, aboard a Coast Guard-manned invasion transport shortly before the American landings on Okinawa. Sergeant Shuff's wife and two daughters reside at the Madison Avenue address.

Second Lieutenant George E. Gold, 21, son of Mr. and Mrs. J. W. Gold, 136 Norway Avenue, is authorized to wear a second cluster to his Distinguished Unit Badge. He is a pilot of a B-24 Liberator with the 15th Air Force in Italy.

Corporal Paul E. Frazier, son of Mr. and Mrs. H. G. Frazier of Kenova, took part in the battle of Iwo Jima. Corporal Frazier is married to the former Miss Rachel Frances West of Huntington and was a student at Marshall College before joining the Marine Corps.

Private Russell P. France, son of Mrs. Mary J. France, 642 Adams Avenue, has arrived at the Fairfield Army Air Base, Calif. Private France was wounded on Luzon in March and has received the Purple Heart.

Glenna: *May 6th Sunday – Cline's birthday. Tom Keeny started papering for us. I didn't go to Sunday School.*

Rupert: *Today is my uncle Cline's birthday.*

Mother was on a mission to get the house papered, but I believe she realized the job was more than she and I could manage and hired Tom Keeny to finish it.

"Don't Keep Him Waiting," a three-act comedy, was to be presented by the senior class of Milton High School in the high school auditorium the following Friday. Cast members were Mildred Clark, Faye Jordan, Floyd Ray Stephens, Margaret Swick, Lewis Ball, Flora Belle Dunlavy, Mildred Nicholas, Libby Windsor, Jack Stanley, Beuford Coleman, Jimmy Fugate, and George Woody.[222]

Three more area men were reported killed in action: Private Herschell Campbell, son of Mr. and Mrs. Owen R. Campbell of 337 Twenty-second Street, was killed April

5; Private Walter F. Smith Jr., son of Mr. and Mrs. Walter F. Smith of 1655 Sixth Avenue was killed in Italy on April 17; Private First Class George Chafin, nephew of Mrs. Nora Spaulding, 1554 Madison Avenue was killed March 6 in Germany. Wounded in action, and in an English hospital, was Technical Sergeant Grant Chaffin. Mrs. Chaffin resided at 1418 Jefferson Avenue.[223]

"Two Marines of Huntington who were in the invasion of Okinawa are Corporal Beckett, son of Mr. and Mrs. Morris A. Beckett, 2662 Guyan Avenue, and Private First Class Kenneth W. Chandler, son of Mr. and Mrs. E. S. Chandler, 2807 Elmwood Avenue. Corporal Beckett's brother, Franklin Clark Beckett, fire controlman second class, is a prisoner in Japan. Private Chandler's brother, Sergeant E. S. Chandler, is with the 13th AAF somewhere in the Pacific."[224]

The Allied campaign in Burma ended.[225]

"WITH THE COLORS":

Pharmacist's Mate Third Class Leonard Kincaid, son of Mr. and Mrs. L. M. Kincaid of Barboursville Route 1, is one of four brothers in the armed forces and recently took part in the battle for Iwo Jima, administrating medical aid to wounded Marines. He was previously taken prisoner by the Japanese during the fighting at Saipan, but was freed in the ensuing battle. Two brothers in service are Water Tender Third Class Zernie Kincaid, who was home on leave after 18 months at sea aboard a destroyer, now awaiting reassignment in Rhode Island, and Sergeant Teddy Kincaid, with the Seabees at Providence, R.I. Another brother has been discharged following foreign battle service in North Africa.

Simon A. Osborne, nephew of Bessie Andes, 848 Adams Avenue, is a member of the 38th Division on Carabao Island. After a recent pre-landing bombardment on that island, he and members of his infantry platoon "captured" the sole survivor, a 240-pound hog.

Machinist's Mate First Class Vernon S. Hatcher is spending a leave with his parents, Mr. and Mrs. E. G. Hatcher of 2902 Merrill Avenue.

Radioman Third Cass Bill I. Lyng, son of Mr. and Mrs. Henry I. Lyng of 1610 ½ Third Avenue, is serving overseas in the South Pacific. He is a graduate of East Huntington High School.

Corporal William E. Rowe, son of Mrs. Cora Rowe of 537 Buffington Street, has landed in England with the U.S. Air Force... His wife, Mrs. Donna Rowe, resides at Big Creek.

Machinist's Mate Second Class William W. Priddy, son of Mr. and Mrs. W. C. Priddy of 1107 Adams Avenue, who recently spent a leave with his family, has returned to Norfolk, Va. where he is taking advanced training in mechanics. He has been on duty aboard an aircraft carrier in the Pacific for 14 months. Among some of the battles in which he participated were Tarawa, Wake, Marshall Islands, Yap, Ulithi and the Marianas.

Seaman First Class Joe Peck, son of Mrs. W. Shad Peck, 802 Fifth Street, and the late Mr. Peck, has been home on leave for the past two weeks after several months of sea duty with the U.S. Navy armed guard... A brother, Private William S. Peck Jr., husband of Mrs. Mary Peck, also of the Fifth Street address, is home on furlough after completing training at Camp Fannin, Tex. He has been in the Army two and a half years.

Seaman First Class Jennings B. Parsons, husband of Mrs. Jennings Parsons of 2008 Marcum Terrace and son of Mr. and Mrs. J. H. Parsons of 903 Twenty-eighth Street, is spending a leave here after nine months overseas in the Philippine area.

Russell V. Campbell Jr., quartermaster, third class, after two years in the South Pacific, is expected home soon for a 30-day leave. He is the son of Mr. and Mrs. Russell V. Campbell of 4432 Auburn Road.

Glenna: *May 7th Monday – 2nd room was papered. I washed. Heard rumors of peace in Europe.*

In Reims, France, Germany surrendered unconditionally to the Allies.[226]

"IN THE SERVICE":

Sergeant William C. Sowards, 265 Oakland Avenue, has recovered at the 185th General Hospital in England from wounds received in action in Germany on February 7. He has been released from the hospital for return to duty.

Private Harold Billups is a member of an anti-tank platoon which recently was attacked by German troops at night near Erfelden, Germany. The Germans were held at bay by small arms fire until daylight when a rifle company arrived to scatter the enemy. Private Billups is with the Fifth Infantry Division.

Seaman First Class William F. Braddock, husband of Mrs. Grace Braddock of Martin, Ky., has had a grandstand seat for the invasion of Okinawa as a member of the crew of a battleship of the Pacific Fleet.

... In England is Second Lieutenant Herman Edward Mace, son of Mrs. Thelma Mace, 2020 Fourth Avenue.

Captain Harold Ben Davies, 424 West Fourth Avenue, has been promoted to Major in the Air Technical Service Command. He is stationed at the Bell Aircraft Corp. at Niagara Falls, N.Y.

Corporal Technician Chester E. Spurlock, son of Chester A. Spurlock, 2726 Collis Avenue, has been assigned to the veteran 32nd Division as a battalion air man attached to the Combat Engineers. The 32nd is now on Luzon in the Philippines and Corporal Spurlock's present job is assistant to the battalion surgeon.

Private Herschel Campbell of Huntington was a member of an American patrol which tried three times unsuccessfully to cross the Rhine River before the East bank of the stream was cleared of the enemy. On the last attempt, two in the eight-man patrol were wounded and Private Campbell paddled the unit's rowboat with the wounded aboard back to the Allied side of the Rhine with his hands, despite heavy machinegun and artillery fire. He is with the 12th Engineer Combat Battalion of the Eighth Infantry Division.

First Lieutenant Arthur P. Gough, 333 West Fifth Avenue, was reported clearing the Air Transport Command's Army Air Field at Miami, Fla., en route home after flying 47 missions as a B-24 navigator in the China-Burma-India theatre. He is the son of Mr. and Mrs. A. P. Gough and wears the Distinguished Flying Cross and Air Medal with one Oak Leaf Cluster.

Staff Sergeant John J. Dean, son of Mr. and Mrs. Elba Dean of Wayne, has been transferred from the AAF Redistribution Station at Miami, Fla., to the AAF convalescent hospital at Fort Thomas, Ky. A gunner on a B-24 bomber, Sergeant Dean was wounded on his sixth mission—over Ploesti. He holds the Air Medal, Purple Heart, and Distinguished Unit Citation.

Private First Class Dennis F. Parsons, son of Mrs. Della Parsons of West Hamlin, is with a field artillery unit in the Southwest Pacific. He has been in that theatre for 20 months. His wife, Mrs. Virginia Parsons, resides at Salt Rock.

Second Lieutenant John P. Younger, son of Mr. and Mrs. George Younger of Williamson, has arrived at a U.S. Strategic Air Force station in England.

Glenna: *May 8th Tuesday – President Truman confirmed the story of peace in Europe. It is true. The Germans surrendering and peace come. Pretty day.*

Rupert: *V-E day came in Europe today.*

German troops all over Europe laid down their arms. Hermann Goering, highest ranking Nazi to later be tried at Nuremberg, surrendered to Allied troops.[227] The Soviet Union army hosted a second ceremony, this time with Germany surrendering unconditionally to them. Reich President Karl Dönitz and General Wilhelm Keitel signed for Germany. The Prague uprising ended with a negotiated surrender that allowed German troops to leave the city.[228]

Vietnam was divided in half at the 16th parallel to disarm the Japanese. Chinese Nationalists moved in north of the parallel while the British did the same in the south. Vietnam became a French colony again.[229]

The Navy announced that "2,000 more WAVES each month are now needed to keep pace with the acceleration of the war in the Pacific... Eligible were women 20 to 36 with at least two years of high school and with no children under 18 years of age."[230]

"IN THE SERVICE":

Captain Joseph L. Greene, son of Mr. and Mrs. David Greene of Ninth Avenue, has been promoted to that rank from first lieutenant. After serving overseas three years, Captain Greene is now a surgeon in a California Army hospital. He is a Marshall graduate, attended Western Reserve University in Cleveland and received his M. D. from Johns Hopkins University. His sister, Shirley Grace Greene, WAC, has been promoted from second to first lieutenant at her base in New Guinea, where she has been stationed with the Medical Corps for the past 17 months. She is a graduate of West Virginia University, did graduate work at Ohio State University, and was graduated from Walter Reed Hospital of Dietetics in Washington.

Staff Sergeant Newton B. Parker, 25, husband of Mrs. Mary Lee Parker, 821 Seventh Street, and son of Mrs. Grace S. Parker, 953 Monroe Avenue, has been missing in action over Czechoslovakia since April 19... He was tailgunner aboard a Flying Fortress based in England and had made approximately 30 missions. The former Owens-Illinois Glass Co. employee holds the Air Medal with two Oak Leaf Clusters and has been overseas since last January. He is the father of two children. [Sergeant Parker was a prisoner-of-war.]

Private First Class Arnold L. Ballard, son of Mrs. Shirley Ballard of Huntington, has been awarded a Certificate of Merit for service with the 87th Division of the Third Army in Germany. He was cited for meritorious and outstanding performance of duty from January 1 to April 9. His wife is the former Dixie Cremeans of Huntington.

Sergeant William J. Chapman, Rear 3540 Fourth Avenue, son of Mr. and Mrs. Burl Chapman, 219 ½ Fourth Avenue, recently was promoted to his present rank and is spending a 15-day furlough with his wife and parents. He will return to Savannah, Ga. on expiration of his furlough.

Technician Third Grade Ronald V. (Bud) Waldron, husband of Mrs. Eloise Smith Waldron, 1305 Ninth Avenue, has been freed from a Nazi prison camp... A member of the 106th Infantry Division, he was captured last December.

Edwin C. Dial, 23, gunner's mate second class, 1005 Minton Street, is a member of the Pacific Fleet. Mate Dial is aboard a minelayer.

Private First Class Elizabeth Washington, daughter of Mrs. Mary E. Hilbert of Hamlin, helped to celebrate the WAC's third birthday at the Victorville Army Air Field, Calif.

Aviation Cadet Sebren B. Dean, son of Mr. and Mrs. Levi J. Dean, 2748 Guyan Avenue, formerly a flight instructor at a Texas flying school, has arrived at Perrin Field, Texas, where he will take 10 weeks of flight training that will lead to his graduation as a pilot in the AAF.

Private First Cass Martin Wellman, son of Mr. and Mrs. W. Wellman, 2649 First Avenue, has been awarded the Combat Infantryman

Badge. Wellman participated in the Normandy, Siegfried Line, and other major European campaigns. He is a jeep driver with the 28th Division.

Staff Sergeant Ernest B. Wagers, son of Mr. and Mrs. C. B. Wagers, 269 South Walnut Street, is assigned to an air service Squadron at Tinker Field, Texas. He entered the service in July, 1941 and was formerly employed by the Grocers Wholesale Co. here.

Druery T. Allen, husband of Mrs. Marie Hope Allen, 1536 Eighteenth Street, is stationed at the Naval Air Base at Kaneohe Bay, Hawaii. He was recently advanced to the rating of ship's serviceman second class.

"Lieutenant Oscar L. Price Jr., son of Mr. and Mrs. O. L. Price, 319 Thirty-first Street, recently completed a combat course in the Army's newest attack bomber, the A-26 Invader, at a Mariana Army Field. He enlisted in November, 1942 and won his commission last August.

Staff Sergeant Hugh McGlone, 28, son of Mr. and Mrs. Thomas McGlone of Kenova, is currently assigned to the AAF Redistribution Station No. 4 at Santa Ana Army Air Base, Santa Ana, Calif. He entered the service in January, 1942 and wears five battle stars on his Asiatic-Pacific theatre ribbon.

Dennie C. Perry, former hauling contractor at Accoville, W.Va., has been promoted from captain to major at a depot of the Replacement Training Command in New Caledonia. Major Perry is the husband of the former Miss Elsie Napier, who lives in Accoville.

Private First Class Orville E. McComas, son of Mr. and Mrs. E. V. McComas of Branchland, was seriously wounded in Italy on April 20, according to word received by his parents from the War Department. He has been overseas 19 months.

The Bronze Star has been awarded to First Lieutenant Edward C. Gibbs, 929 Seventh Street, and Technical Sergeant Charles Tutis of Omar, W.Va. The medals were awarded at the same ceremony at a 20th Bomber Command base in India, the War Department announced.

Technical Sergeant Charles E. Gill, son of Mr. and Mrs. Albert Gill of Salt Rock, is an assistant crew chief in charge of all sheet metal work of his unit in the Ninth AAF. Sergeant Gill, now stationed in Belgium, entered the service in June, 1941, and has been overseas for 15 months.

Glenna: *May 9th Wednesday – I started straightening up my house. Very pretty day but cool. Went to prayer meeting that night.*

Mother was methodical. With the papering job finished, she needed to put everything in order.

Rupert: *It is cool today. I went to school.*

In Copenhagen, Denmark, the German cruiser *Prinz Eugen* was turned over to the Allies.[231]

"Soundman Second Class James D. Deskins, 19 year-old son of Mrs. J. L. Backley, 1536 Eighteenth Street and B. F. Deskins of Logan, W. Va. is on a minesweeper with the Pacific Fleet. He has been based on Guam, Saipan and Tinian, and participated in the invasions of Iwo Jima and Okinawa."[232]

"After a three-year separation, two sons of Mr. and Mrs. Thomas Clagg of Milton were reunited recently in Belgium ...Corporal Thurman Eugene Clagg, who has spent 30 months in the European theatre was transferred to ... [the] Third Army where he met his brother, Sergeant Harold Clagg... Both soldiers have received the Order of the Purple Heart..."[233]

"Second Lieutenant Robert W. Shively Jr., 20, 723 Sixth Avenue, scored a pair of victories over the Luftwaffe, destroying one German fighter plane in the air and one on the ground recently near Kassel and Welmar, Germany. A veteran of more than 45 missions, Lieutenant Shively entered the Air Force in August, 1942

139

and holds the Air Medal with six Oak Leaf Clusters."[234]

"IN THE SERVICE":

Corporal Ezra W. Vannatter, son of the Rev. and Mrs. W. M. Vannatter of Barboursville has been awarded an Oak Leaf Cluster to his Distinguished Unit Badge in Italy where he is serving as an ordnance and maintenance man with the 5th Air Force.

Private First Class Stanley D. Kitchen, who had been reported missing in action in Germany since February 23, has been reported safe and well... The message did not say whether he had been liberated from a German prison camp, however. Private Kitchen was serving with the U.S. Seventh Army.

Corporal John E. Herald, 24, son of Mrs. Lena Herald of Crum, has been flown back from his station in the China-Burma-India theatre. Corporal Herald spent 30 months with the Medical Corps in India.

Staff Sergeant Russell Senter, son of Mrs. Hattie C. Senter of the Emmons Apartments, a veteran of two and a half years in the B-B-I theatre, is ready to return to the Far East after spending a 45-day leave with his mother.

Private First Class Theodore A. Martufi, 835 Twelfth Avenue, is a member of an engineer company with the Army in Belgium...

First Lieutenant William W. Jones, nephew of F. E. Hite, 699 Thirteenth Avenue, has been awarded the Air Medal for meritorious achievement in Germany where he has been serving as an artillery liaison pilot.

Seaman Second Class James A. Grass of Huntington is convalescing at the U.S. Naval Hospital at New Orleans after serving overseas on an LST. His wife, Mrs. Bonita Louise Grass, and daughter reside at 412 Twenty-fifth Street.

Private First Class Marion F. Hammonds of Ashland is serving at an air base at Tunis, Tunisia as a military policeman. His wife, Mrs. Mary Catherine Hammonds, and two daughters, Marion Kay and Caroline Hammonds reside at 2143 Central Avenue, Ashland. He is the son of Mr. and Mrs. Oscar Hammonds, also of Ashland.

An aircraft mechanic with the 455th Bombardment Group of the 15th Air Force in Italy, Sergeant Irvin D. Armstrong, 117 West Ninth Avenue, was recently authorized to wear the bronze Oak leaf Cluster to the Distinguished Unit Badge when his group was cited "for outstanding performance of duty in armed conflict with the enemy."

Hansford McCallister, husband of Mrs. Mae Rose McCallister of Salt Rock, has been promoted to petty officer third class from seaman first class. Petty Officer McCallister entered the Navy in January, 1944.

Major Harry Brindle of Huntington was commander of an infantry force of the Sixth Armored Division in Germany that helped to take a group of towns during the recent drive. Major Brindle's company captured Langfuhr.

Private First Class Jeanne L. Parker, WAC, has been assigned to duty in the Philippines. The daughter of Mr. and Mrs. A. W. Parker, 206 West Eighth Avenue, she was serving with a WAC detachment in New Guinea.

Glenna: *May 10th Thursday — Everett Johnson got killed on motorcycle. Cool. I ironed Monday's washing.*

Rupert: *Everett Johnson got killed today on a motorcycle.*

Everett Johnson was born in 1921, the son of Okey Johnson and Violet Joyce Bias. He was buried in Enon Cemetery near Salt Rock.[235] Betty Kirk of East Lynn, twenty-two years old, was also killed in the accident.[236]

From Sunnyside, Utah: "At least twenty-two miners were killed today [May 9] in an explosion in the Utah Fuel Co. mine here... Eleven bodies have been recovered and six other men have been treated for injuries."[237]

The U.S. High Command announced that 3 million troops in Europe would soon be on their way home—or to the Pacific Theater.[238]

Marshal Gregory [Georgi] K. Zhukov, deputy commander-in-chief of Russian forces, lauded General Eisenhower May 9 as "one of greatest generals of all time, and one of America's outstanding sons."[239]

"IN THE SERVICE":

Vivian W. Shaw of Hurricane has been promoted from second to first lieutenant in the Army Nurse Corps.

Sergeant Irvin D. Armstrong, 117 West Ninth Street, has been awarded a bronze Oak Leaf Cluster to his Distinguished Unit Badge. On a recent mission, his flight downed at least 34 German fighters, while losing only a few B-24 Bombers.

Second Lieutenant Mary K. Casella, 2857 Fourth Avenue, was one of 26 new nurses who will take up their duties at the Newton D. Baker General Hospital at Martinsburg, W.Va.

Private Omer E. Baker, 27, son of Mr. and Mrs. William L. Baker, 1505 Beech Street, is a clerk-typist with the Eighth Air Force in England. He arrived in England about a year ago.

Corporal John B. Bryant of Davin, W.Va. is a member of the fighting 811th Tank Destroyer Battalion which recently knocked out 19 Nazi tanks within a three-day period...

Corporal Robert Hamlin, son of Mrs. Hazel Hamlin of Huntington, has been home on a 60-day recuperative furlough after serving with the Fifth Army in Africa and Italy for more than two and a half years. A holder of the Presidential Unit Citation, he goes back to Camp Meade, Md. before reporting to an overseas station.

Second Lieutenants Dora F. McKee, daughter of Mrs. Esther E. McKee, 1042 Tenth Avenue, and Imogene Ball, daughter of Mrs. Margaret Ball of Bellepoint, W.Va., have arrived at the Billings General Hospital at Indianapolis, where they will take a 30-day basic training course. Lieutenant McKee trained at Chesapeake & Ohio Hospital and Lieutenant Ball at Memorial Hospital.

Glenna: *May 11th Friday – Cool. Cleaned on the house. Gaynelle and Don stayed all night here.*

Rupert: *My aunt and cosin are staying with us tonight.*

Mother and Gaynelle were sisters, and good friends. The physical closeness of our families made seven-year-old Don more like a brother than a cousin. We were devastated four years later when he died in an automobile accident while riding with his paternal grandfather.

With the Australian capture of Wewak from the Japanese, the Allies gained control of all ports in New Guinea.[240]

"IN THE SERVICE":

Pharmacist's Mate First Class Jack M. Stone, U.S. Navy, has returned to Huntington to visit his parents, Mr. and Mrs. J. W. Stone, 330 Seventh Avenue, after 18 months of overseas duty. Mate Stone recently received the Purple Heart for wounds received on Iwo Jima, where he served for 12 days with the Marine Corps. During his transportation from Iwo to a hospital in the Marianas, he met Dr. William Strange, Huntington physician now serving in the Pacific area. Also the holder of the Presidential Citation, Pharmacist Stone has participated in the battles of the Marianas, Saipan and the Marshall Islands. He was graduated from Central High School, attended Marshall College, and was employed by the Chesapeake & Ohio Railway Co. before his enlistment.

A veteran of naval actions on many of the seven seas, Woodrow Wilson Nease, coxswain, USNR, son of Mr. and Mrs. J. W. Nease, 4802 Waverly Road, believes that the invasion of Africa was his most difficult one. He is now serving in the Pacific aboard a light cruiser, and has participated in more than 30 major engagements, including Iwo Jima.

Private James F. Hines, husband of Mrs. Lucille L. Hines, 48 Northcott Court, has been awarded the Good Conduct Medal at the Indiantown Gap Military Reservation, Pa. He entered the service in February, 1944.

Sergeant Hasten Queen, son of Mrs. Ada Queen of Stiltner, W.Va., was wounded in action on Luzon and was awarded the Purple Heart. He has returned to duty with the First Cavalry Division.

Richard E. Haas, husband of Mrs. Garnett Haas of Columbus, O., has been advanced to the rank of motor machinist's mate third class. A former employee of the International Nickel Co. here, he is now serving aboard a destroyer escort in the Atlantic Fleet where he has been for the last 16 months.

Private First Class Howard W. Kennedy, son of Mrs. Frances Kennedy, 506 Third Avenue, has arrived at his destination in the Pacific. Private Kennedy has been in the service two years.

Private First Class Hal P. Dillon Jr., husband of Mrs. Virginia F. Dillon, 821 Adams Avenue, has been awarded the Good Conduct Medal. He is an ammunition handler with the 102nd Infantry Division in Europe.

Sergeant Noel E. Stover, son of Mrs. Minnie Stover of Ameagle, W.Va., has been promoted to that rank... He is with the Third Army in Germany.

Tolbert B. Dean, 528 Eighth Street, a resident of Huntington for 40 years and an employee of the Owens-Illinois Glass Co. for 13 years, will leave this morning for Pearl Harbor where he will be employed by the Navy Department... His son, Private First Class John T. Dean of Huntington, returned recently to this country after 37 months of action in the Pacific with the Marine Corps and is now stationed at New River, N.C.

Now fully recovered from wounds received last November during action in Germany, Private Jack Harris, 20, husband of Mrs. Virginia E. Harris, of Barboursville, has been released from a hospital in England and returned to active duty. The infantryman entered the service in June, 1943.

Staff Sergeant Guy T. Tooley, 27, son of Mr. and Mrs. Wilburn Tooley and husband of Mrs. Mary B. Tooley of Chesapeake, O., has been awarded an Oak Leaf Cluster to the Air Medal at a bomber station in England. Sergeant Tooley is a gunner on a B-17 Flying Fortress.

Coxswain Floyd Halley, USN, husband of Mrs. Eloise Halley of Hamlin, and Private First Class Charles Walford, USMCR, husband of Mrs. Freedith Walford, 302 Bridge Street, cousins, met several weeks ago in the South Pacific. They hadn't seen each other since early in 1944.

Lieutenant Colonel L. T. Ferguson, 2775 Collis Avenue, is spending a few days with his family after serving as an infantry officer in the C-B-I theatre for more than a year. He has been an officer in the regular Army since the last war.

Glenna: *May 12th Saturday – Worked on the house and straightened. Cooked for Sunday. Cloudy all day. Ossie came late that evening. Gaynelle and Don stayed all night.*

Ossie Roth, Dawson's sister, was single and a nurse at the Veterans Hospital in Huntington. She rode a bus home when her schedule allowed. Ossie stopped often to visit with us before walking the two miles down River Road to her mother's house.

Rupert: *I took a long bicycle ride today.*

I had acquired my bike the previous summer from Wink Finley. I liked to coast down quarter-mile-long Salt Rock Hill and make a sharp right-hand turn by the post office onto the path toward home. I reached a fairly high speed at that point. It wasn't the safest maneuver, some good citizen suggested to Dawson, and I received a "talking to."

In the Pacific, Americans endured heavy losses on Okinawa's Sugar Loaf Hill.[241]

"IN THE SERVICE":

Private Thomas Rone is one of three sons of Mr. and Mrs. Jacob Rone, 1673 Fourteenth Avenue, who are serving in the armed services overseas. He is with the infantry in Germany. He entered the Army last September and has been overseas since last February. Private Rone formerly was employed in a shipyard in Baltimore. One of his brothers, Private First Class William Rone, is with an Army signal corps unit in the Philippine Islands. He was a student at Central High School before enlisting two years ago. William has been on overseas duty for a year. Another brother, Fireman Second Class Jacob Rone Jr., is serving with the Navy in the Pacific theatre. Before entering the service last October, Fireman Rone was employed by the International Nickel Co. here. He left in February for overseas duty.

Now recovered from wounds received last December during action at Bastogne, Private French McClung, 22, 1405 Sixteenth Street, has been released from an Army hospital in England and is ready for active duty. The infantryman entered the armed forces in December, 1942.

Captain Thomas William Harvey Jr., son of Mrs. T. W. Harvey, 1127 Twelfth Street ... is now stationed in Washington after serving as an Air Forces pilot in the Pacific for several months. He is residing in Alexandria, Va. with his wife, the former Miss Fan Downey of Huntington, and their two-year-old son.

Private First Class George Bryant of Huntington is a member of the 84th Infantry Division in Germany...

Private First Class Everett C. Westfall, husband of Mrs. Mary Westfall of Proctorville, O., took part in the Battle of the Bulge at Bastogne... He is a member of the 907th Glider Field Artillery attached to the celebrated 101st Airborne.

Private First Class Morry Riter, son of Mr. and Mrs. David Riter, 1015 West Fifth Street, has been given the Purple Heart for wounds suffered last February with the combat engineers in Germany...

Staff Sergeant Dewey J. White, son of Mr. and Mrs. Dewey White of Miller, O., has arrived at Camp Atterbury, Ind. reception center prior to coming home on furlough. He is a veteran of 13 months in the European theatre.

William Thompson, 23, of Holden, has been promoted to the rank of boatswain's mate third class while serving aboard a patrol gunboat in the Atlantic Fleet.

Jack Cornett, 19, son of Mr. and Mrs. W. L. Cornett, 30 West Sixth Avenue has been promoted to the rank of radioman third class while serving on a destroyer in the Atlantic Fleet. His brother, Ship Serviceman Ward L. Cornett, is also in the Navy.

Flight Officer Herbert Muncy, son of Mr. and Mrs. B. R. Muncy, 2734 Latulle Avenue, participated in the aerial assault in Germany which paved the way for the ground forces. He is a glider pilot and took part in the D-Day invasion for which his squadron was given the Presidential Citation.

Master Sergeant L. T. Cassel, son of Mr. and Mrs. W. M. Cassel of Wayne County, was recently given his second bronze battle star for his participation in the Normandy campaign. Sergeant Cassel is an airplane inspector at the Seventh Photographic Group in England. His brother, Private First Class Richard Cassel, has received the Purple Heart for wounds received at Anzio. He is a member of the Seventh Army and has been overseas for two years.

The promotion of Elwood L. Kelley, 21, son of Mr. and Mrs. S. J. Kelley of Salt Rock, from corporal to sergeant has been announced at an Eighth AAF Base in England. Sergeant Kelley is a radio operator on a B-17 Flying Fortress.

Glenna: *May 13th Sunday – Stuart and Ruby and children came up and stayed all day with us. We had baked chicken. Dawson and Stuart went to Carlie Cremeans' funeral at Greenvale. That night we all went to church at Salt Rock. Mr. Fannin from Barboursville delivered the sermon. Abner Adkins got killed in mines.*

Rupert: *Some of our friends came and stayed all day.*

Hutchinson visits were special. I remember the sequence of events on those Sundays after church: Billie, Dencil, and I played in the yard while the dinner (midday) table was set. After dinner the three of us ventured farther out to play games on our hill, or on surrounding hills until exhaustion set in and we returned home for a second dessert before their departure, or in this case to another church service.

It was near the end of the school year. H. D. Hazelwood, principal of Douglas High School, announced scholarship winners to Kentucky State College. "Music scholarships were awarded Alma Moses and Lenora Lewis, with basketball and football scholarships going to Donald Greer and Eddie Gill."[242]

Barboursville High School: "An impressive ceremony was held Tuesday, V-E Day in the high school auditorium. A medal sent by Sergeant George Everett Surgeon, a former student and outstanding athlete stationed in Panama, was presented to the outstanding athlete of this year in memory of Sergeant Surgeon's close friend Joe Nelson, who lost his life on Iwo Jima. Cecil

Stephens, having been voted the outstanding athlete of Barboursville High School, received the medal from Everett's sister, Miss Elizabeth Surgeon, a student in the high school."[243] Joe Nelson's family owned the lumber yard and store in Barboursville near Route 60. (A personal note: The Nelson family set up an annual "outstanding athlete" award to honor their son. I was privileged to receive the *Joe Nelson Athletic Award* in the spring of 1951, my year of graduation from Barboursville High School.)

"WITH THE COLORS":

Aviation Machinist's Mate Second Class Charles L. Mullens, son of Mr. and Mrs. Landon Mullens, 1216 Jackson Avenue, who has served in the Pacific area for three years as a mechanic and gunner, has returned home to spend a leave with his parents. He will leave for the west coast May 24 for reassignment to duty.

Dallas Queen of Wayne recently was promoted from the rank of captain to major at Army Peninsular Base Headquarters in Italy... He is the husband of Mrs. Opal Queen of Wayne and is the father of two children...

Staff Sergeant George Keneff, 20, son of Mr. and Mrs. George Keneff, 1856 Marshall Avenue, is assigned to the AAF Redistribution Station at Santa Ana, Calif. after completing 32 missions as a gunner on a B-24 Liberator bomber in the European theatre. He holds the Air Meal with four Oak leaf Clusters.

Also at Santa Ana is Sergeant Enslow S. Plumley, 27, son of Elisha S. Plumley, 1688 Fourteenth Avenue, an intelligence specialist with the Fifth Air Force. He wears the Asiatic theater ribbon with 10 battle stars.

Carlos Marsh, USMC, who has served with the Marines in the Pacific for two years, including the Bougainville and Iwo Jima campaigns, has returned to the United States and will visit with his father, the Rev. C. H. Marsh, pastor of the

Methodist Church at Omega, O. The Marine is a former Huntington resident.

Sergeant Frank Selbert, son of Mrs. Bertha Selbert, 424 Main Street, and Private John W. Price of Fort Gay, W.Va., have arrived at the Army's Ashburn General Hospital, McKinney, Tex. from overseas. Sergeant Selbert served in England, France and Germany. Private Price served in Hawaii and at Saipan.

Technician Fifth Grade Virgil Meddet, 1236 Fourth Avenue, has reported to the Camp Kilmer (N.J.) Reception Center on his way home from the European theatre where he has served for 12 months.

Private Michael Foley of the U.S. Army has been released from a German prison camp, his mother, Mrs. Kate Foley of 1410 Beech Street, Kenova has been informed. Private Foley was reported missing in action Dec. 16, 1944. His wife and three-year-old son reside in Pensacola, Fla.

Mrs. Mamie Snyder of Milton has received a telegram from the War Department that an enemy propaganda broadcast from the Japanese government carried a message from her son, Private Ralph J. Roberts, that he is well. Private Roberts, who was captured in the fall of Corregidor, is now a prisoner-of-war at Osaka, Japan.

Staff Sergeant Clifford Swann Jr. of Milton has been promoted to that grade in the Palau Islands where he is serving with the Army Air Force. He has been awarded the Air Medal for aerial operations against the enemy from July 2, 1944 to Feb. 13, 1945, and Oak Leaf Clusters for additional bombing missions since that time.

Harlow Warren Denny, petty officer, third class, U.S. Navy, husband of Mrs. Freda Runyan Denny of 2314 ½ Marcum Terrace, and son of Mr. and Mrs. Homer Denny of 2317 Fifth Avenue, has been promoted to his present rating ... after serving 16 months in the Pacific theatre of war.

Corporal Charles Hardy, son of Mrs. Ella Black Hardy of 319 Adams Avenue, was slightly injured in Italy sometime in April. Corporal Hardy was a waist-gunner on a B-17 bomber.

Lieutenant (j. g.) W. R. Taylor, son of Mrs. E. B. Taylor of 620 Trenton Place, will leave for the coast today after spending a week's furlough here with his family. Lieutenant Taylor just returned from the Pacific where he was in charge of a squadron in the U.S. Naval Air Force.

Private First Class Robert S. Halley Jr., son of Mr. and Mrs. R. S. Halley, 1947 ½ Third Avenue, was wounded in action in Germany April 23. Private Halley previously served in France and 32 months in the Panama Canal Zone. He has been in the military service five years.

Corporal Emery Waugh, husband of the former Miss Jean Adams, 2145 Fifth Avenue, has been promoted ... at his station in the Pacific. His wife is employed in the offices of the Appalachian Electric Power Co. here.

Isabell Smith of Proctorville, O., was among 50 Red Cross workers who arrived in England recently to serve as staff assistants.

Private First Class Clyde Yoho Jr., USMC, son of Mr. and Mrs. Clyde Yoho of Ona, W.Va., was chosen as honorary guard at the christening of the USS *Tarawa* May 5 at Norfolk, Va. Private Yoho has received the Presidential Citation for taking part in the invasion on Tarawa. He was wounded June 23, 1944 on Saipan.

Sergeant Joda D. Evans Jr., son of Mr. and Mrs. J. D. Evans of Neal, has been liberated from a prison camp in Munich, according to a message from the Red Cross. Sergeant Evans was a waist gunner on a B-17 bomber and was reported missing in action July 19, 1944. Mr. and Mrs. Evans have two other sons in the service, and another one, Lieutenant Fred Gordon Evans, pilot of a B-17, was killed in action August 12, 1943 when his plane was shot down over Gilsenkerchen. Private Clifford Evans is with General Patton's Third Army in Europe, and Staff Sergeant Robert H. Evans is stationed at Camp Perry, O., after serving 31 months in Alaska and in the Aleutian Islands.

Lieutenant (j. g.) William C. Baumgardner, son of Mr. and Mrs. Craven A. Baumgardner, and husband of the former Beatrice D. Woodrum of Huntington, has been granted a leave after a four-months tour of duty as a torpedo plane pilot in the Pacific. He took part in 63 thrusts against the Japanese on Leyte, Mindore, Luzon and Iwo Jima.

Leotis R. Meadows, son of Mr. and Mrs. W. R. Meadows of Barboursville recently was promoted from private first class to corporal at March Field, Calif. He is a waist gunner on a B-24 bomber.

Glenna: *May 14th Monday – I washed. Pretty day.*

Rupert: *I was sick today. I came home from school.*

Gold, currency, and looted art were discovered in a salt mine in Austria, hidden there by the Germans.

American B-29 bombers hit the Japanese city of Nagoya. Fighting in the southern Philippines continued.[244]

Glenna: *May 15th Tuesday – I ironed all day. Very warm.*

Rupert: *It was warm today. I went to school.*

"Ironed all day. Very warm." Washing and ironing took a lot of time, especially since Mother was a "clean freak." We got dirty on the farm. I still have Mother's irons, the kind heated on the stove and captured with a wooden-handled "gripper."

"Mother's Day was a red letter day for Mrs. Etta McDaniel of Chesapeake, O., who received a Mother's Day greeting Sunday from her son, Private Herbert H. McDaniel, who was reported missing in action January 20, and for his wife and daughter who received a telegram saying he had returned to his outfit in France and was safe..."[245]

"IN THE SERVICE":

Mr. and Mrs. Alka Slone of West Hamlin has received a letter from a soldier who credited their son, Clifford Slone, with saving his life after a German shell had severed one leg at the knee during the battle at the Remagen bridgehead across the Rhine River. "It was our fourth day of fierce fighting across the Rhine," wrote Private First Class Roy L. Dodge of Lancing Mich., "that a German shell came in on us, severing my leg just at the knee. Your brave son saved my life by endangering his life in the shellfire and dragging me to safety where he stopped my bleeding and bandaged my wounds." Private Dodge is a patient at Percy Jones Hospital at Battle Creek, Mich.

Second Lieutenant Joseph R. Holcomb of Roanoke, Va., grandson of J. W. Spessard, 2810 Collis Avenue, has been missing in aerial action over Germany since April 26, his grandfather has been advised. Lieutenant Holcomb is a P-51 Mustang fighter-bomber pilot. He holds the Air Medal with Oak Leaf Cluster.

Seaman First Class Billy F. Martin of Vinton, O. is serving aboard the USS *Platte*, a Navy oiler in the Pacific. The *Platte* has been in action in almost every major engagement from the Aleutians to Guadalcanal to the recent attacks on Tokyo.

The Purple Heart has been awarded to Private First Class Walter Glen Jeffers, son of Mrs. Cora E. Jeffers, 1916 Fourth Avenue and husband of Mrs. Sherma L. Jeffers, 1947 ½ Fourth Avenue. Private Jeffers was wounded in Germany while serving with the 302nd Infantry last February.

Richard H. Preston, husband of Mrs. Helen Preston, 974 Twenty-seventh Street, has been advanced to the rank of staff sergeant. He has been in the Army for five years, and overseas for nine months, [and is] now serving with the 17th Airborne Division in Germany.

Firemen First Class Ira Finley Graham, 4249 Sixteenth Street Road, has returned to the United States after nine months of sea duty in the Pacific. Fireman Graham wears three battle stars, which include the invasions of Iwo Jima and Okinawa. His mother left last week to see her son in California.

Lieutenant Carter W. Wild, USNR, husband of the former Miss Peggy Dunbar, 236 Fifth Avenue, has returned to the United States after several months sea duty in the Pacific.

Lieutenant and Mrs. Chauncey Hicks left yesterday for Boise, Idaho after spending eight days here with Mrs. Hicks parents, Mr. and Mrs. V. E. Silvey of Bedford Avenue, and his parents, Mr. and Mrs. Clarence Hicks of Chesapeake. Lieutenant Hicks, formerly stationed in California, has been assigned to the Army Air Forces at Boise.

Technician Fifth Grade William T. Ward, son of Frank Ward of Barger Hill, Kenova, is reported en route home via the Air Transport Command's Miami Army Air Field after serving for two years in the Mediterranean theatre with the Army Engineers. He was in the landings at Salerno. His wife, Mrs. Delcie Ward, resides at 1610 Sycamore Street, Kenova.

Sergeant Leonard E. Mullen, 28 West Third Avenue, was decorated last Friday with the Silver Star for gallantry in action at Cherbourg last June 24. Sergeant Mullen received his medal at Moore General Hospital at Swannanoa, N.C., where he is a patient. Sergeant Mullen has served overseas for 19 months in North Africa, Sicily, England and France. He received the Purple Heart for wounds received at St. Lo, France in July, 1944. The infantryman, who singlehandedly disposed of a German machine gun nest, also wears the Presidential Citation and the Combat Infantryman Badge. He is married and has one child.

First Lieutenant Harold E. Ward, 3215 Bradley Road, has returned to the United States after 24 months in the Pacific and European theatres. He is the wearer of the Silver Star, the Purple Heart with one cluster, the Presidential Unit Citation with one cluster and the Combat Infantryman's Badge. He is now at Stark General Hospital at Charleston, S.C.

Flight Officer Hassel L. Miller, 23, a fighter pilot, has been assigned to the "Flying Tigers" fighter group of Major General C. L. Chennault's 14th Air Force in China. He is the son of Hassel Miller of Madison, W.Va., and was a student at Marshall College before entering the AAF in February, 1943.

Howard R. Washington, 27, pharmacist's mate first class of Barboursville has been assigned to the USS *Cabell*, a cargo transport. He has been in the Navy for almost five years and was at Pearl Harbor on December 7, 1941. Mate Washington served 19 months' patrol duty in the Pacific and was stationed at several naval hospitals throughout the United States.

Glenna: *May 16th Wed. – Mamma, Papa, Milo and Maxine came. Showers. Went to prayer meeting that night.*

Rupert: *My Grandpa and Grandpa came up today from Huntington.*

My grandparents were showing increasing signs of discontent with their new environment.

British destroyers sunk the Japanese cruiser *Haguro* in the Malacca Strait.[246]

Glenna: *May 17th Thursday – Rainy all day. I stayed by myself. Worked on house cleaning.*

Rupert: *I went to school today. It rained all day.*

American forces captured Manila's Ipo Dam after three days of bombing.[247]

"IN THE SERVICE":

Sergeant Hansel H. Adkins, 22, son of Mr. and Mrs. J. B. Adkins of Branchland, is a tail gunner on a B-17 Flying Fortress with the

Eighth Air Force. The former Barboursville High School student participated in many raids against the Germans and had several narrow escapes, including a crash landing in Belgium. He is a holder of the Air Medal. [His father, John B. Adkins, was my Grandfather Lucian Adkins' brother. Sonja Rounds, daughter of Hansel's sister, Hattie Mason, added to the story: After Hansel's plane crash-landed and he was scurrying to hide, Belgium farmers confronted him with pitchforks, thinking he was a German wearing an American uniform, something they sometimes did to uncover Belgium patriots. Once the farmers believed him, one took him into his home where the family hid him for three weeks while he recovered from injuries and planned a route back to the Americans. Hansel corresponded with the Belgium family for many years afterward.]

Staff Sergeant Jay Blankenship, son of Mrs. Irvin Blankenship of Wayne, is now appending a 21-day furlough with his parents after a two-year tour of duty with the Air Forces in the China-Burma-India theatre. Sergeant Blankenship has been in the AAF for four years.

Staff Sergeant Wilbur E. Lynch, 19, son of Mr. and Mrs. E. A. Lynch of Walton, W.Va., has been awarded the Oak Leaf Cluster to his Air Medal for meritorious achievement during an Eighth Air Force attack on Germany. The Flying Fortress tail-gunner entered the AAF in December, 1943. His wife, Mrs. Jean E. Lynch, lives at 1718 Washington Avenue in Huntington.

Private Harry Marks Jr., son of Mr. and Mrs. Harry Marks, 2456 Third Avenue, has been wounded twice in action in Europe and has been awarded an Oak Leaf Cluster to his Purple Heart. His wife and son reside at the Emmons Apartments.

Arnold L. Walker, 20, son of Mr. and Mrs. Arnold Walker of Salt Rock, was recently promoted from corporal to sergeant at an Eighth Air Force base in England. Sergeant Walker is currently undergoing pre-combat training in England as the enlisted bombardier on a B-17 bomber.

Staff Sergeant Albert A. Wright, 20, son of H. V. Wright of Ceredo, has been awarded his second Oak Leaf Cluster to the Air Medal for meritorious achievement during attacks on Nazi airfields and railroads. He entered the AAF in May, 1943, and is a ball-turret gunner on a B-17 with the Eighth Air Force.

Staff sergeant Leroy E. Eckley, son of Roy Eckley, 1666 Eleventh Avenue, was recently awarded the Air Medal at an Eighth Air Force bomber base in England. Sergeant Eckley has participated in many attacks against Germany as a tail-gunner on a B-24 Liberator. He entered the AAF in December, 1943. His wife, the former Lucretia Porter, and son live at 639 Eighth Avenue.

Staff Sergeant Clarence W. Wiley, 21, son of Mr. and Mrs. Clyde Wiley, 220 Eighteenth Street, has been awarded an Oakleaf Cluster to his Air Medal. Sergeant Wiley is a tail-gunner on a B-17 Flying Fortress with the Eighth Air Force. His wife, Mrs. Doris L. Wiley, resides at 1865 Marshall Avenue.

Sergeant Bill Copley, son of Mr. and Mrs. Wayne Copley of Dunlow, W.Va., has been awarded the Air Medal in the Eighth Air Force, Sergeant Copley is an engineer-gunner on a B-17 Flying Fortress and entered the Air Force in April, 1942.

Petty Officer USN and Mrs. Franklin C. Kelly and their son, James G., are the guests of Petty Officer Kelly's parents, Mr. and Mrs. A. J. Kelly, 531 Fifth Avenue. Petty Officer Kelly is stationed at San Diego, Calif, and entered the Navy before Pearl Harbor.

Staff Sergeant Melvin Dickman, 2483 ½ Third Avenue, is serving with the "Headhunters" Squadron of the AAF in the Philippines. He has been overseas for about six months.

Chief Yeoman La Vern Miller, husband of Mrs. Hilda B. Miller, 2651 Collis Avenue, is home on a 20-day furlough after serving in the Pacific for 28 months with a Naval Construction Battalion. He will report to Columbus, O. June 10 for reassignment.

Technician Fifth Grade Henry G. Wintz, son of Mrs. Ina Wintz, 1669 Eleventh Avenue, is serving with the Air Technical Service Command in Europe.

Staff Sergeant Kenneth G. Russell, USMC, a veteran of 28 months in the Pacific with the Third Marine Division, has arrived in California and is expected to visit his mother, Mrs. Dora Russell of Marcum Terrace, soon.

James B. Christian, seaman second class, son of Mr. and Mrs. W. V. Christian, 2714 Highlawn Avenue, has completed submarine school course at New London, Conn., and is training for an electrician's rating there. His wife, the former Miss Wanda Haskins of Huntington and their two small daughters are living at New London.

Glenna: *May 18th Friday − I went to Huntington. Got Rupert shoes, window blinds, paint, and oil cloth. Went to see Papa and Mamma. Ate dinner with them. Cold and misty rain.*

Dinner? A bit of colloquialism: We never ate "lunch" at home. The midday meal was "dinner." "Lunch" was food in a bag or pail you carried somewhere away from home. The evening meal at home was "supper." And speaking of "evening," that was the designation for the time that extended from noon to sundown. After that it was "night."

Rupert: *Mother went to town today.*

U.S. Marines captured Sugar Loaf Hill on Okinawa and ended a costly ten-day battle.[248] (How costly would only later be realized.)

"IN THE SERVICE":

Second Lieutenant Ralph H. Hall, son of Mr. and Mrs. George B. Hall of Tampa, Fla. and husband of Mrs. Kathleen Hall, 519 Thirteenth Street, has been awarded the Air Medal for meritorious achievement in action against the Germans. Lieutenant Hall is a navigator on a B-17 Flying Fortress and a former student at Marshall College. He entered the AAF in 1943.

Captain Rush E. Elkins of Man, W.Va., has completed more than 33 combat missions against the Germans. He is squadron navigator in the 451st Bombardment Group with the 15th Air Force in Italy.

Captain Howard Rosenheim, son of Mrs. W. S. Rosenheim, 411 Tenth Avenue, and the late Dr. Rosenheim, former managing director of the Huntington Chamber of Commerce, has been promoted to Major in the Army Air Forces. He is chief of the planning branch of the Air Technical Service Command at Wright Field, Dayton, O.

Lieutenant (j. g.) J. M. Baysden, husband of Mrs. Addie Baysden, 1806 Twelfth Avenue, helped take his ship into battle for the first time recently against the Japs. His cruiser was credited with downing two Jap planes and one probable.

R. W. Clay, seaman first class, son of Mr. and Mrs. Van Linden Clay, 2487 Collis Street, is serving aboard an Essex class aircraft carrier in the Pacific...

Flight Officer James M. Gibson, son of Mrs. Susie McDenie, 2108 Ninth Avenue and husband of Mrs. Juanita Gibson of Fifth Avenue, is now on duty with the Air Transport Command in the Middle East, flying from Casablanca to Karachi, India.

Walter D. Roush, seaman first class, son of Mr. and Mrs. Earl E. Roush of Middleport, O., is aboard an aircraft carrier in the Pacific.

Private James E. Canter of Huntington is stationed in Germany with the field artillery. He landed in Normandy 10 days after D-Day last June and has been awarded the Bronze Star and the Good Conduct Medal. He wears three battle stars and is a former employee of the International Nickel Co.

First Lieutenant Edward George, son of Mrs. Charles George, 439 Sixth Avenue, has been promoted to that rank ... at Camp Atterbury, Ind. where he is stationed as administrative officer.

Private Charles R. Hedger, son of Mr. and Mrs. E. C. Hedger, 1206 Ninth Avenue, is spending a 10-day furlough with his wife, the former Miss Mary Rhodes...

Chief Petty Officer Charles Hagaman, son of Mrs. Blanch Marks, 2456 Third Avenue, has been promoted to that rank at New York City where he is awaiting a sea duty assignment.

Private First Class Kermit McGinnis, son of Mr. and Mrs. B. C. McGinnis, 333 Eleventh Avenue, recently spent a week in London on convalescent leave from a general hospital in England.

Seaman Clinton Jackson Earl, who served for 29 months in the South Pacific, is visiting his parents, Mr. and Mrs. W. R. Earl, and wife and daughter, of Highlawn Avenue.

Lowell H. Beckley, 24, son of Mr. and Mrs. Paul D. Beckley of Prichard, has been promoted to staff sergeant after completing more than 40 missions with the 15th AAF in Italy. He holds the Air Medal and two Oak Leaf Clusters.

Staff Sergeant Denver Martin, 21, son of Mr. and Mrs. R. L. Martin of Branchland, recently returned from the European theatre where he was a gunner in the AAF. He is now stationed at Las Vegas, Nev. Army Air Field. He wears the Air Medal with three Oak Leaf Clusters.

Captain Paul V. Osburn, 22, husband of Mrs. Betty Jo Osburn, 413 Thirty-first Street, has been awarded the sixth Oak Leaf Cluster to his Air Medal. He is a navigator on a B-17 and recently completed his second tour of combat duty in Europe.

Glenna: *May 19th Saturday – I painted my clothes box and did other things about my spring cleaning. Cool and clear. Milo and Maxine were here. They are moving to Mrs. Lewis.'*

Milo and Maxine lived on Roach Road across from the Hutchinson farm. I don't remember circumstances of their move, but Maxine's father had died recently, so Maxine may have wanted to be with her mother in West Hamlin. They were not there long.

Rupert: *My friend came here today. He was Marion Nida.*

Although our relationship was sometimes contentious, Marion and I were good friends. In later life he owned a gas station in Salt Rock. On one of my visits to Salt Rock while Mother was still alive, and about twenty years since I had seen Marion, I stopped at the station for gas. It was a time when gas station owners cleaned windshields and checked the oil. Marion didn't recognize me. He filled the tank, checked the oil, and sprayed and wiped the windshield. As he walked away, I pecked on the glass and pointed to an imaginary spot he missed. He dutifully cleaned it again. I found another spot and continued the deception for a couple more times before he threw down his wipe cloth in disgust. After I revealed myself, we had a good laugh and a hearty reunion.

Briefs from Last Night's Associated Press Wires: "A gigantic staging area capable of processing up to 15,000 Pacific-bound American soldiers daily for the Marseille port of embarkation is being prepared in Southern France; Hollywood – Jim and Marian Jordan, better known as Fibber McGee and Molly, today became grandparents for the first time. Their daughter, Katherine, wife of Lt. Adrian Goodman, Navy doctor, gave birth to a six-pound girl."[249]

Four more Huntington soldiers are home after liberation from German prison camps. They are, Staff Sergeant John L. Bays, son of

Mr. and Mrs. C. M. Bays, 419 Sixth Street; Technician Third Class Ronald V. (Bud) Waldron, son of Mrs. Bess Waldron, 1106 Fifth Avenue; Private First Class Ray Beatty, son of Mrs. Lela Rucker, 405 Thirtieth Street; Private First Class Everett Tucker Adkins, son of Mrs. Ethel Adkins, 1131 Minton Street. Freed, but awaiting transportation to the United States Private are, First Class James M. Donohoe Jr., son of Mr. and Mrs. J. M. Donohoe, 1427 Seventh Avenue; Corporal Norman Le Master, son of Mr. and Mrs. B. E. LeMaster, 2558 First Avenue; Staff Sergeant Gerald L. Honaker, son of Mr. and Mrs. J. C. Honaker, 412 Thirtieth Street; Staff Sergeant William G. Mitchell, husband of Mrs. Sibyl Mitchell, 1034 Seventh Street and son of Mr. and Mrs. Lawrence Mitchell of Kenova; First Lieutenant Charles M. Pace, 510 Washington Boulevard, whose wife, Mrs. Allie Loo Pace lives in Omaha.[250]

"IN THE SERVICE":

Electrician's Mate Third Class Roy Eugene Holley, who served for 28 months with the Navy in the Pacific theatre, has returned to duty at Seattle, Wash. after spending a 21-day leave with his mother, Mrs. Grace Vance, and his sister, Mrs. Ruby Kirk, 214 Short Street.

Private Lawrence Ferguson Lakin, son of Mr. and Mrs. J. S. Lakin of Fort Gay, is at Letterman General Hospital in San Francisco recovering from wounds received in action on Luzon on March 18. He is a paratrooper and expects to be assigned to a hospital near his home. Private Lakin is a graduate of Fort Gay High School and a member of the Future Farmers of America.

Corporal Tony J. Magariello, son of Mr. and Mrs. Anthony Magariello, 2808 Highland Court, has been awarded the Air Medal for meritorious service as radio operator-gunner of a Mitchell medium bomber with the 13th AAF

in the Philippines. He is a veteran of more than 31 missions.

First Lieutenant Orville O. Will, husband of Mrs. Hope Will, 96 Oney Avenue, and Corporal James H. Smith, husband of Mrs. Alma Smith, 4321 Siders Avenue, recently saw action with the 38th Division in the battle of Zig-Zag Pass, Bataan and the Zambales Mountains campaigns in the Philippines. Corporal Smith, who has been overseas for 16 months, was highly commended for individual bravery and courage under fire. Lieutenant Will, also a veteran of more than 16 months in the Pacific, wears the Asiatic-Pacific Ribbon with one campaign star and the Philippine Liberation ribbon with one battle star.

Marion E. Thackston, 29, son of Mrs. Pauline Thackston, 2916 Staunton Road, crewman on a Seventh AAF Liberator pounding Jap bases, has been promoted to sergeant.

Private Juanita M. Bartram, daughter of Mr. and Mrs. Earl W. Norris, 40 Burlington Road, recently left Fort Des Moines, Ia. for technical training at William Beaumont General Hospital, El Paso, Texas.

Captain John H. Flournoy, 29, 1007 Seventh Street, is responsible for the coordination for all activities at a hospital in England where he is serving as administrative manager. He joined the Army in January, 1942.

First Lieutenant Francis M. Lambert, husband of Mrs. Margaret Lambert, 820 Thirteenth Avenue, recently piloted his Liberator bomber on a hair-raising photographing mission against Jap installations in Borneo. Although his plane was hit at 700 feet and several men were wounded slightly, he successfully completed the task and returned to his base.

Staff Sergeant Jay Holbrook of Chesapeake, O. recently obtained his release from the Army after compiling more than the necessary 85 points.

Clyde Taylor of Kenova has arrived in San Francisco from the Pacific where his ship was sunk in the Okinawa campaign.

Private Fred Painter, 20, son of Mr. and Mrs. Fred Painter Sr., 348 West Twenty-fifth Street, has returned to this country after serving with the infantry in Europe for 15 months. He wears the Purple Heart and four battle stars on his campaign ribbon.

Glenna: *May 20th Sunday – Went to church and Sunday School. Bill Vernatter preached. I was sick that morning. Sunday night Jaruel Porter and Velma came down and stayed a long time.*

Rupert: *I went to Sunday school. Today I came home before church.*

"Captain Richard Wilkinson, 32, of Walden, N.Y., pilot in the U.S. Army Air Force, who was critically injured at 3 A.M. yesterday when he and two non-commissioned crewmen bailed out of a bi-motored army "Boston Bomber" near Hurricane, W.Va., was reported 'improving' last night at St. Mary's Hospital." Captain Wilkinson underwent emergency operation shortly after admission. Other crewmen, Staff Sergeant F. R. Gaines of Asheville, N.C. and Technical Sergeant H. S. Heller of New York City had only cuts and bruises. The plane was traveling from New Jersey to Cincinnati when it crashed on the Donald Patterson farm, 26 miles east of Huntington.[251]

Cecil W. Estep, son of Mr. and Mrs. Hirom Estep of Salt Rock, who was taken prisoner January 30, 1944, while serving with the Fifth Army, came home after 14 months in a German prison camp. Other news of area men include: "Private Carter E. Harrison, whose wife resides on Chesapeake Street, was wounded in action and captured while serving with a Fifth Army tank division as radio operator; Mrs. Fleming Suiter, the former Miss May Gillett of Rome, O., received a telegram Friday from her husband, Lieutenant Fleming W. Suiter, who had been a prisoner of the Germans since Nov. 29,

1943. He was in Stalag Luft I in Barth, Germany, on the Baltic coast and was liberated by the Russians on May 2. His wife believes he is somewhere in France and is encouraged by his words saying he is both 'fit and well.' He is the son of Mr. and Mrs. R. W. Suiter of Chesapeake."[252]

"WITH THE COLORS":

Technician Fourth Grade Ed D. Hoback, son of Mr. and Mrs. L. S. Hoback, 1925 Jefferson Avenue, and husband of Mrs. Betty Hoback of Sistersville, W.Va., is a tank driver with the 775th Tank Battalion fighting the Japanese on northern Luzon. He is a former aircraft mechanic for Fairchild Aircraft at Hagerstown, Md. A tank platoon sergeant in the same battalion is Staff Sergeant Granville M. Fisher, son of Mr. and Mrs. H. F. Fisher, Route 4, Milton, whose wife, Mrs. Opal Fisher and their one-year-old son Harry, live at the same address.

Private Nicholas Winters, son of Mrs. Sophia Winters, 6 Summit Street, has arrived at Valley Forge General Hospital, Phoenixville, Pa., for treatment of shrapnel wounds ... sustained in action in Belgium while serving as a rifleman and scout with the First Infantry Division... Private Winters served 21 months overseas in England, France, Belgium and Germany. He is a former Central High School student and was a sheet metal worker and aircraft mechanic in civilian life.

Private First Class James M. Lambert, son of Mrs. Inez S. Lambert, 341 Fifth Avenue, has been awarded the Combat Infantryman's Badge for action in Germany with the 49th Armored Infantry Battalion, Eighth Armored Division.

Private Cecil E. Sexton of Coal Grove, O., was discharged from the U.S. Army yesterday at Camp Atterbury, Ind. under the Army's adjusted service rating plan.

The Good Conduct Medal has been awarded Private First Class Chester L. Carrico, 23, son of Edward T. Carrico, 1319 Fourth Avenue, at the Miami, Fla. Ground and Service Forces Redistribution Center... He recently returned to the United States from the Mediterranean theatre where he served 28 months, and was wounded last July 7 near Rome...

Sergeant Robert L. Bills of the 802nd M. B. Battalion in Egypt was recently promoted to that rank. He is the brother of Mrs. James Smith, 512 Buffington Street, Guyandotte. Sergeant Bills has been in Egypt 33 months.

Navy Chaplain Charles W. Duling will be guest speaker at 11 A.M. today at the Highlawn Baptist Church, it was announced by Dr. W. C. Reeves, pastor. Chaplain Duling has been serving with a convoy in the Pacific. Prior to that, he had been with a convoy in the Atlantic, Iceland and Greenland.

Survivor of a U.S. destroyer sunk off the coast of Okinawa, during the invasion of that island, Radarman First Class Eddie D. Cregut Jr., 19, son of Mr. and Mrs. E. D. Cregut of 1509 Seventh Avenue, has written that he is well and safe following his experience.

Glenna: *May 21st Monday – I washed. Very pretty day.*

Churchill called for general elections, the first in many years.[253]

"IN THE SERVICE":

Lieutenant (j. g.) George Clinton Martin, USNR, a native of Huntington, son of Mrs. Inez May Martin of Parkersburg, W.Va., has been awarded the Distinguished Flying Cross for heroism and extraordinary achievement during operations against Japanese forces in the Philippines area. He has been listed as missing in action since last November 14, the date on which he distinguished himself in Mindoro Strait.

Gunner's Mate Second Class William Paul Vance, 22, son of Mr. and Mrs. W. P. Vance, 1179 Norway Avenue, and husband of the former Miss Madelean Napier of Huntington was recently commended by his commanding officer for helping rescue an American flyer from drowning in rough water alongside his destroyer in the Atlantic. The flyer was unconscious when Mate Vance leaped overboard and held him up until help came. Young Vance has been in the Navy for five years and holds the Presidential Unit Citation, the American theatre ribbon and the European-African-Middle Eastern theatre ribbon with one battle star.

Seaman First Class Don C. Ferguson, U.S. Coast Guard, of Huntington mans an anti-aircraft gun aboard a Coast Guard-manned LST in the Pacific. His tank landing ship is helping in island invasions... Seaman Ferguson's home is at 1618 Thirteenth Avenue.

Second Lieutenant John D. Johnson, son of Mr. and Mrs. Clovis D. Johnson of Huntington Route 2, will soon complete a course in combat flying at the Alexandria La. Army Air Field. He is pilot in a Flying Fortress crew trained by the Third Air Force...

Wounded in the left shoulder while his unit was firing on German tanks near an autobahn super-highway in Germany, Sergeant George W. Nelson, 26, son of Mr. and Mrs. Andrew C. Nelson, 1346 Fourth Avenue, is now recovering at the 68th General Hospital in England. He was awarded the Purple Heart.

A reunion took place recently in the South Pacific when Seaman First Class Paul E. Kesselring of West Hamlin, met Seaman First Class William L. Meade, son of Mrs. Ruth Hatfield of Branchland, W.Va., after a separation of more than three years. Seaman Meade is a cousin of Mrs. Kesselring, who resides with her parents, Mr. and Mrs. W. M. Bryan of West Hamlin.

Staff Sergeant Bryan B. McComas, son of Mr. and Mrs. S. W. McComas, 638 ½ Fourth Avenue, has reported at Santa Ana Calif. for reassignment after spending a 21-day leave with his parents. The B-24 waist gunner recently returned from England after completing 35 missions over Germany. He holds the Air Medal with five Oak Leaf Clusters. A brother, Private First Class William McComas, U.S. Marine Corps, was wounded on Okinawa and has been awarded the Purple Heart.

Glenna: May 22nd Tuesday – I ironed and patched. Mrs. Rousey came up. I wrote a letter for her.

Rupert: Marion Nida and I have become the Twin Blackies, or secret Detectives. We wore masks and clokes.

The masks were left over from Halloween, and cloaks were probably feed sacks substituting for the capes of comic book heroes. The high hill between his house on River Road and mine became a rendezvous point, a land of fabricated mysteries and imagined killing fields.

"Diamond Dust": "Making Whoopeeee: WELL, WELL, WELL, the guys and gals out at 8th Street Tech are going to paint the town a turkey red for a few minutes this morning. Yes-sire-e-e, they are going to stage a 'colossal' parade—and a victorious one—through the business section of West Virginia's largest city, celebrating the track and field triumph of Coach McCoy & Co., Sat'y at Laidley Field... Max Schmeling. The German heavyweight says he was given a raw deal by the sports writers of the U.S. when he was in this country ... It makes me feel sick at the 'tummy' to read of a Nazi talking about a square deal... Schmeling is a bum who associated with a bigger bum— Herr Hitler."[254]

"IN THE SERVICE":

Technician Fifth Grade William H. Trautner, husband of the former Miss Fannie M. Elswick of Williamson, has been awarded the Bronze Star for heroic conduct in action with the 508th Parachute Infantry in Germany last January. The son of Mr. and Mrs. William Trautner of Gurnee, Ill., he was employed here before entering the service in November, 1943.

First Sergeant Lloyd D. Barbour is visiting his parents, Mr. and Mrs. J. H. Barbour, 534 ½ Eighteenth Street. He recently returned to the United States after a tour of duty with the Fifth Air Force in the South Pacific...

Private William H. Parker, son of Mrs. Frank Parker of Kenova, is now spending a 14-day furlough here from Fort Knox, Ky... His brother, Seaman Second Class Elmer Parker, is serving in the South Pacific.

Corporal Thomas D. Dearnell, 21, son of Mr. and Mrs. Elbert Dearnell of Kermit, has been awarded the Air Medal for action during a bombing raid on the Axis with the 15th AAF. He is an engineer-gunner on a B-24 Liberator and has been overseas since last December.

Private Lloyd G. Keaton, 2522 Ninth Avenue, and Private Earl Day of War, W.Va., are members of the Sixth Army in Germany. The 753rd fought in Sicily, Southern France and at Salerno.

Oscar L. Lewis, seaman first class, husband of Mrs. Thelma I. Lewis of Chandler's Branch, is serving aboard a battleship which took part in the pounding of Okinawa prior to the land invasion.

Technician Fifth Grade Alvin M. Cyrus, 28, son of Mrs. Rose Chandler, 1037 Seventh Avenue, has returned to the United States after serving for 31 months in the C-B-I theatre...

Private First Class Walter F. Paul, husband of Mrs. Hazel Paul, 812 Twenty-fourth Street, is serving with the 27th Infantry Division in the Ryukyu Islands...

Flight Officer Elby H. Cross Jr., son of Mr. and Mrs. E. H. Cross, 184 Gallaher Street, received his wings recently upon graduation from Childress, Tex., Army Air Field as a bombardier-navigator. He is now ready to join an Army Air Forces combat team for duty in the Pacific. Flight Officer Cross was a member of the 30th class to receive wings at Childress.

Private First Class Sidney Arden Floyd, U.S. Army, has been assigned to a military police unit in England after recovering from a gunshot wound in the leg received in France last October when a 14-year-old German boy fired at the soldier, according to word received here. Private Floyd is the son of Mrs. Helen Floyd of Sixth Street, and the late E. B. (Scotty) Floyd.

Private First Class Ernie L. Keener, 1216 Thirteenth Street, is a member of a rifle company of the 151st Infantry which was recently cut off from all communications in the jungles of Luzon. The company existed five days on a diet of berries and roots before finally making contact with a base patrol. Private Keener entered the Army in January, 1941, and has been overseas for 17 months.

Stanley Wright, 22, seaman first class, USNR, of Louisa, Ky., has taken part in three campaigns aboard a minelayer. A veteran of the Iwo Jima and Okinawa battles, he entered the Navy in March, 1943.

Staff Sergeant Donald J. Smith, 3602 Brandon Road, was in a party of six volunteers under command of First Lieutenant John D. Marks, noted New York song writer, which captured two captains, two lieutenants, and 36 enlisted German soldiers in a recent two-day clean-up on the Western Front. They are members of the Seventh Army in Germany.

Glenna: *May 23rd Wednesday – I washed the furniture covers. Mowed at the graveyard. Very pretty day.*

Rupert: *Me and Marion went on a protoling trip this evening as the twin blackies.*

Those clandestine escapades normally played out after a few days and we went on to some new adventure. Sometimes, I picked up the heroes we (mostly me) had dreamed up and incorporated them into my cartoons and written stories.

Events in Germany were escalating: Heinrich Himmler committed suicide while in British hands. General Eisenhower ordered the arrest of all German military leaders.[255] British forces captured and arrested what was left of the Flensburg government members formed by Reich President Karl Dönitz after the suicides of Adolf Hitler and Joseph Goebbels.[256]

The war in the Pacific was continuing. There was heavy bombing of Yokohama, an important Japanese port and naval base.

An article in the *Huntington Herald-Dispatch*, titled "Army to Present Femoyer's Medal at Mass Here May 30," is presented here in its entirety because the Nation's highest military honor deserves special attention.

The Congressional Medal of Honor awarded posthumously to Second Lieutenant Robert E. Femoyer of Huntington will be presented at a mass at St. Joseph's Catholic Church at 11 A.M. next Wednesday—Memorial Day. The Rt. Rev. Monsignor James F. Newcomb, St. Joseph's pastor, said yesterday he had been advised by Army officials of the arrangements for the presentation. When the War

Department announced the award, it said the medal would be presented to the Flying Fortress navigator's mother, Mrs. E. P. Femoyer, formerly of Huntington and now of Jacksonville, Fla. The 23-year-old officer, believed to be the first Huntingtonian and one of the fewest West Virginians ever to receive the nation's highest decoration, fought off death for three hours, November 2 to navigate his shell-torn Flying Fortress home from deep inside Germany, thus saving his eight fellow crewmen. Lieutenant Femoyer died a half hour after the crippled bomber landed at an Eighth Air Force base in England. Miss Nancy Gibson, daughter of Mr. and Mrs. E. G. Gibson, 1015 Euclid Place, fiancé of the lieutenant, said last night that Lieutenant Stanley Ferbank of Worchester, Mass., the bombardier on the aircraft, telephoned her last week from Atlantic City in an attempt to learn the date of the ceremony so that he might attend. Monsignor Newcomb reported he was informed of arrangements for the presentation by Lieutenant Colonel W. W. Van der Wold, who said that an AAF officer would arrive in Huntington by plane Tuesday to make final arrangements. An AAF Catholic chaplain, high in rank, will make the presentation. The ceremonies will be open to the public.[257]

Private Willie E. Brown, 1158 Jackson Avenue, recently joined the 435th Troop Carrier Group in the European theatre. A former infantryman, Private Brown has been overseas more than 19 months.

Private James E. Aliff, husband of Clara M. Aliff of Huntington, has returned from Europe after eleven months service. He participated in three major battles and was awarded the Purple Heart, He is now at the Wilson General Hospital at Staunton, Va.

Benjamin P. Greenhill, seaman first class, son of Mrs. Harriett Greenhill of Lawson, Ky., is serving aboard a battleship that has been pounding Okinawa with 1,500-pound shells.

G. O. Pennington, pharmacist's mate first class and his wife, Faye Pennington, are spending a 10-day leave with his parents, Mr. and Mrs. G. O. Pennington, 1213 Seventh Street. He is stationed at the Norfolk Naval Air Base.

First Lieutenant Robert S. Graham, 750 Twelfth Avenue, who for the past three and a half years has been with the AAF, will be reverted to inactive status on June 14, it was announced yesterday by the Camp Atterbury Public Relations Office.

Private First Class Charles W. Early, son of Mr. and Mrs. C. H. Early, 719 Sixth Avenue, has been transferred from Mitchel Field, N.Y. to Wilson General Hospital at Staunton, Va. He was wounded in action in Germany with the 95th Division.

Private First Class Robert E. Crickmer, 735 Thirteenth Street, is a member of a port battalion which was recently awarded the Meritorious Service Plaque in the China-Burma-India theatre.

"IN THE SERVICE":

Technical Sergeant Earl Mayo, 1601 Arthur Street, has recently been awarded the Oak Leaf Cluster to his Air Medal. Sergeant Mayo is an aerial engineer on a C-47 and has been in the European theatre for more than 20 months.

Glenna: *May 24th Thursday – Pretty day. I painted the white chairs.*

Rupert: *I went to school today. I found out that I was getting propoted.*

Obviously, my promotion didn't depend on my spelling ability. Some things don't change much; my spell-checker comes often to my rescue.

"Logan County coal miners stopped work as a protest against meat shortages... The striking men blamed both the shortage and 'the fact that what meat came in was unfairly distributed.'" U.S. Senator Harley M. Kilgore (D-W.Va.) sent a telegram that promised increased meat allotments into West Virginia.[258]

"IN THE SERVICE":

Second Lieutenant Jack L. Hagan, son of Mr. and Mrs. Charles H. Hagan, 1526 Sixth Avenue, has been presented with the Air Medal at a B-24 Eighth Air Force base in England. As co-pilot of a bomber, Lieutenant Hagan has taken part in many raids against the Reich, including such strongholds as Berlin, Munster, and Dortmund.

First Lieutenant Val S. Griffiths, son of Mr. and Mrs. G. R. Griffiths, 45 Roland Park, has reported for duty ... at Langley Field, Va. Lieutenant Griffiths entered the service in January, 1942, and served in the European theatre for 16 months where he won the Distinguished Flying Cross and the Air Medal with four Oak Leaf Clusters.

Fireman Second Class Frank E. V. Carper, son of Mr. and Mrs. E. V. Carper formerly of Huntington who are now living in Norfolk, Va., is visiting his aunts, Mrs. A. M. Bias, 225 Davis Street and Mrs. Demma Bess, 735 Tenth Avenue. Fireman Carper was injured in action in the Pacific and is now attached to a hospital in New York.

Private First Class George L. Fuller, brother of Charles E. Fuller, 704 Thirteenth Street, was one of the Camp Maxey, Tex. soldiers praised this week for aid given during the recent tornado which took 83 lives and destroyed much property in Antlers, Okla.

Private First Class Roy E. Fudge of Huntington was among seven men whom the War Department recently honored at Finney General Hospital, Ga. by presenting them with awards for combat service. He received the Combat Infantryman Badge.

Staff Sergeant Lemon C. Nimmo, husband of Mrs. Mary E. Nimmo, 2124 Seventh Avenue, is stationed at an air depot in England. He was employed by the Standard Ultramarine Co. here before entering the service in June, 1943.

Flight Officer George R. Burgess, son of Mrs. Monta T. Burgess of Wayne, is serving with the Air Transport Command in India. he was a flight instructor at Union City, Tenn. before entering the service last August.

Captain Elmer E. Ours, 95 Kings Highway, a C-47 pilot, was recently awarded the third Oak Leaf Cluster to the Air Medal in the European theatre, Captain Ours has been overseas for more than 20 months.

Frederick F. Shriner, 23, a P-51 Mustang pilot, son of Mrs. V. V. Shriner, 603 Trenton Place, has been promoted from first lieutenant to captain at an Eighth Air Force station in England. A former student at Marshall College, Captain Shriner was an aircraft inspector with the Glen L. Martin Co. before entering the Air Force.

Private First Class Florence A. Smith of Lesage is stationed at an air depot in England and was recently commended for her work. She is the daughter of Mrs. Dona Smith and has been overseas for about a year.

Sergeant Charles L. Newman, husband of Mrs. Mildred Newman and son of Mrs. Maggie Davis, 817 Twenty-eighth Street, is spending a 15-day leave here while en route to a new station at Hondo Army Air Field, Tex. He is a veteran of two and a half years in the Central Pacific with the 38th Infantry Division.

Lieutenant (j. g.) Thomas Hazapis, husband of the former Miss Carol Bond of Huntington, has been awarded the Bronze Medal for meritorious service in performance of his duties as diving officer of a submarine. His sub is credited with sinking 25,000 tons of enemy shipping. Lieutenant and his wife are now living in Portsmouth, N.H. where he is stationed as an instructor.

Glenna: *May 25th Friday – Pretty day. I painted the door of the living room.*

Rupert: *We had a picknic for our school today.*

"Pharmacist's Mate Third Class Lewis Shirley Fisher Jr. of Huntington has been awarded the Silver Star Medal posthumously by the Navy for gallantry in action on Peleiu Island last September 22, when he was mortally wounded while administering first aid to injured comrades under heavy Japanese fire. Although wounded himself ... he was administering first aid to a wounded Marine when cut down by machine-gun fire. The son of Mr. and Mrs. L. S. Fisher, 1206 Jefferson Avenue, died October 1."[259]

"IN THE SERVICE":

Corporal Leonard C. Bruce is now on duty in a unit of the Army Air Forces in France, his parents, Mr. and Mrs. C. E. Bruce, 1229 Adams Avenue learned this week. Corporal Bruce went overseas in January after entering the service in March, 1942.

Staff Sergeant Wetzel Hay, son of Mr. and Mrs. Wetzel Hay Sr. of Wayne, is completing his training on a Liberator bomber at the Pueblo Army Air Field, Colo. He is an armorer-gunner of his crew and entered the service in August, 1941.

Melvin Paul Suffron, 20, pharmacist's mate third class, USNR, of Chesapeake, son of Mr. and Mrs. Stanley C. Suffron, has been granted leave from his station [at] the Atlantic Fleet's anti-aircraft center at Price's Neck, R.I.

Lieutenant Carl F. Fisher, 25, USNR, patrol boat commander, will spend the week with his parents, Mr. and Mrs. C. C. Fisher of Spring Valley Drive. Lieutenant Fisher is stationed at Norfolk, Va.

Bennie B. McCloud, 18, seaman second class, is stationed at the Amphibious Training Center at Little Creek, Va. His brother, Private First Class James McCloud, is in an Army hospital at Jackson, Miss. They are the sons of Mr. and Mrs. J. E. McCloud, 724 Eloise Street.

George E. Schultz, 20, son of Mr. and Mrs. O. J. Schultz, 2774 Elwood Avenue, has been advanced to machinist's mate third class while serving aboard a destroyer in the Atlantic Fleet. He wears the American and European-African-Middle Eastern ribbons.

Hoke Smith, 36, machinist's mate first class, son of Mr. and Mrs. Darius Smith, 621 Seventeenth Street, is now stationed at Norfolk, Va. He is a veteran of the European and Pacific theatres and is the husband of the former Charlotte Ward of Miami, Fla.

James L. Scaglion, radioman first class, husband of Mrs. Charlotte Scaglion, 417 ½ Twentieth Street, is serving aboard a Navy oiler in the Pacific and took part in the invasions of Iwo Jima and Okinawa.

Technician Fourth Grade Miriam W. MacRae of the Huntington WAC recruiting station will be in charge of a convoy of WACs leaving next Tuesday from Fort Hayes, O. for Fort Des Moines, Ia.

Flight Officer Milton "Lefty" Ward, son of Mr. and Mrs. M. D. Ward of Jefferson Avenue, is spending several days with his parents en route from Westover Field, Mass, to his new base at Hobbs Field, N.M.

Wilber E. Winegar, husband of Mrs. Hilda M. Winegar, 1824 Seventh Avenue, was recently promoted to staff sergeant at his base in the Pacific. Sergeant Winegar entered the Army in April 1942 and went overseas about six months ago.

Glenna: *May 26th Saturday – Rainy and muddy. I painted the doors and the floor of back bedroom. Cephus Duty died.*

Joe Cephas Duty was born February 18, 1911 and died May 25, 1945. He was the son of Robert Duty and Myrtie Anise Smith. He had two sons, Robert and Esau Jackson. He was buried in Powell Cemetery at Hamlin, West Virginia.[260]

Rupert: *I worked in the corn field today.*

Mother's comment about "rainy and muddy," and mine about working in the corn-field seem at odds. They are not; I was "thinning" the field corn. At planting time, the hand-held corn planter dispersed about a half-dozen grains of corn at a time. The problem was that most of the grain germinated and the hill required thinning. We accomplished that while the ground was wet, which meant sometimes working in the rain.

Except for tobacco, corn was the most work-intensive crop we grew. "Old Fred," a black mild-mannered Morgan Horse crossbreed, was our power plant. To prepare the soil there was the sequence of turning, harrowing, dragging, and laying off. After planting and thinning there came cultivating and hoeing. There was great relief when the corn was "laid by." Old Fred was probably relieved as well. Our relief was only temporary, however, for in the fall the plants had to be cut and the ears shucked and placed in the crib to dry. Field corn was used to feed cattle and grind into meal. We sold the larger portion.

Glenna: *May 27th Sunday – Clear and hot. I went to church and Sunday School. Lucian Stephens preached. That evening I went to the church cemetery with Mrs. Rousey to decorate. Saw Alma Johnson and her mother, Luther Creagor and his wife, and Ralph (?) Gill.*

Frankfurt on the Main, May 26: "General Eisenhower opened his new headquarters here today in the huge sprawling I. G. Farben building..."[261]

"Private First Class Benjamin H. Thompson, son of Mr. and Mrs. Everett Thompson, 2523 Twelfth Avenue, died of wounds received in Germany May 2 while serving with the 82nd Airborne Division as a paratrooper; Private Thompson had served in Africa, Sicily, Italy, Iceland, England, France, Holland and Germany."[262]

"Staff Sergeant Max Crawford, son of Mr. and Mrs. A. G. Crawford of Lesage, has completed his missions in Europe and has returned to the Santa Ana, Calif. Air Base after spending a 21 day furlough with his parents; he was a top gunner on a B-24 Liberator with the Eighth Air Force, based in England."[263]

"WITH THE COLORS":

Major Henderson O. Webb Jr., husband of Mrs. Christine V. Webb of 1029 Tenth Street, was awarded the Bronze Medal for meritorious achievement in Belgium and France. He is stationed with the 1111th Engineer Combat Group, III Corps.

Private First Class Leo K. Garrett, son of Mrs. Dorothy Garrett of Hurricane, has been awarded the Good Conduct Medal. Private Garrett entered the service in August, 1943, and is serving with the Fifth Army in Italy.

Private Gilbert Garrett, husband of Mrs. Betty Garrett of 407 Sixteenth Street, has been cited by the 362nd Infantry Regiment of the Fifth Army's 91st "Power River" Division and awarded the Combat Infantryman Badge for actual participation in combat against the enemy in Italy.

Private George T. McCoppin Jr., husband of Mrs. Ruth Dietz McCoppin, 2053 Eighth Avenue ... returned to his outfit in the 11th Infantry on V-E night when he learned for the first time of the German surrender... A brother, First Lieutenant William E. McCoppin, 2641 Collis Avenue, a veteran of more than 60 combat missions as an Eighth Air Force Mustang pilot, has completed instructor's school at Waco, Tex. and has arrived at his new station, Aloe Army Field, Texas.

Staff Sergeant Duncan R. Kerr, stepson of Mrs. Elizabeth Kerr of Huntington, and son of Donald R. Kerr of Detroit, is to be sent home from a hospital in France where he has been confined for the past four months following service with General Patton's Seventh Army... He entered the Army in 1942 and was sent overseas last September.

Aviation Cadet Daniel B. Wheeler has returned to Matagorda Island in the Gulf of Mexico, off the coast of Texas, where he is stationed after spending a 20-day furlough with his wife, Mrs. Lorena Wheeler, and sons of 4281 Four Pole Road.

Coxswain Perry Orville Wilks, U.S. Navy, who has been on active duty in the Pacific for 20 months participating in the invasions of Saipan, the Philippines, Iwo Jima and other islands, has arrived home to spend a 30-day leave with his parents, Mr. and Mrs. Perry Wilks, and his sister of Chesapeake, O. The holder of the Silver Star for gallantry in action, the Bronze Star and the Presidential Citation, he has been in the U.S. Navy two years and will return to San Francisco at the end of his leave. Private William V. Wilks, a brother of Coxwain Wilks, is serving with the U.S. Army infantry in the Philippines. Another brother, Carroll E. Wilks, who was recently honorably discharged after serving overseas with the Navy Air Corps as a radio operator, is attending Ohio State University under the legislation providing education for discharged veterans.

Gunner's Mate Second Class Earl Edward Dorsey, who returned from active duty with the U.S. Navy in the South Pacific area, arrived in Kenova last week to visit his parents, Mr. and Mrs. Lee Dorsey of Sycamore Street.

Glenna: *May 28th Monday – I washed all day. Fair.*

With exception of the Pacific Ocean, wartime shipping rules ended. Shipping could return to pre-war conditions.[264]

"Chester N. Fannin Jr., 19-year-old son of Mr. and Mrs. C. N. Fannin, 677 Water Street, Barboursville, has received his pilot wings and appointment as a flight officer in the Army Air Forces upon completion of his twin-engine advanced training at the Pampa, Tex. Army Air Field. His father is an assistant superintendent of Cabell County Schools."[265]

"IN THE SERVICE":

Private First Class Earl Pace, 421 Nineteenth Street, has been promoted to sergeant in the Eighth Infantry Division in Germany...

Ensign Robert R. Phillips, 315 Tenth Avenue, is co-pilot of a Navy search plane which recently attacked Japanese radar installations on Shimushu Island in the Kuriles.

Seaman Second Class Charles L. Joyce, 1801 Bungalow Avenue, and Aviation Radioman Second Class Charles Pyles Jr. of Huntington Route 4 are serving aboard a heavy cruiser of the Pacific Fleet which has been bombarding Okinawa.

Thomas Elwood Christian, mailman third class, is serving at the Fleet Post Office in Pearl Harbor. He is the husband of Mrs. Joyce Christian, 1535 Spring Valley Drive.

Private First Class Mona Kean, daughter of Mr. and Mrs. Newell B. Kean, 28, Pogue Street, is working as a photographer at San Marcos Army Air Field at San Marcos, Tex.

Eugene Kelly Slutz, former Huntington radio announcer and sports commentator, has been promoted to technical sergeant at headquarters of the 10th Air Force in Burma where he is station manager of the 10th's radio station.

He has been awarded the Bronze Star Medal for his radio work in the Army.

Corporal Charles L. Beckett, son of Mr. and Mrs. George Beckett, 1517 Seventh Avenue, is a member of the computing gunsight department of an Eighth Air Force Service Command station in England. He has been awarded the Computing Gunsight Technician badge for outstanding work.

John Edward McGirr Jr., son of J. E. McGirr, 2210 Fourth Avenue, has been promoted to aviation machinist's mate third class at the Naval Air Station at Alameda, Calif. where he is assigned to the operations department.

Private First Class Marvin C. Threlkeld, son of Mr. and Mrs. R. A. Threlkeld, 828 Ninth Street, is a member of a 151st Infantry mortal platoon which was recently commended ... for its speed and accuracy in delivering mortar fire in the Zambales Mountains on Luzon.

Berkie W. Bias, machinist's mate second class, husband of Mrs. Maxine Bias, 1104 Sixteenth Street, is on duty with a ship repair unit at the Naval Repair Base at Algiers, La.

Thaddeus K. Kauffelt Jr., son of Mr. and Mrs. T. K. Kauffelt, 1329 Sixth Avenue, has been promoted to staff sergeant at a 21st Bomber Command base on Tinian Island in the Pacific. He is a gunner aboard a Superfortress which has been attacking Japan.

Private First Class Virgil Brumfield Jr., son of Mr. and Mrs. Virgil Brumfield and husband of Mrs. Mary Brumfield of Huntington Route 2, has been awarded the Combat Infantryman Badge for action with the 43rd (Winged Victory) Division on Luzon. He has been overseas for 32 months and participated in four campaigns.

Glenna: *May 29th Tuesday – Ironed, baked a cake, made potato salad. Rainy and bad.*

Rupert: *School was out for the summer today.*

Fighting broke out in Syria and Lebanon as nationalists demanded freedom from French control.

Glenna: *May 30th Wednesday – Memorial Day. Clear and pleasant. Mamma, Papa, Gaynelle, Don, and Jean ate dinner with us. We decorated Rupert's grave about 3 o'clock. Dawson went to his mother's to set out tobacco plants.*

Tobacco plants were started from seed in a cheesecloth-covered bed in January. Corn takes a long time, but tobacco season lasts all year and is highly work-intensive. I didn't work in the tobacco patch until a year or two later.

Rupert: *Today is Decoration Day.*

"The Purple Heart has been awarded posthumously to Marine Private Don D. Moreland... Private Moreland, son of Mrs. Anna L. Moreland, 1214 1/2 Third Avenue, died of wounds received in action on Iwo Jima. A former employee of the Huntington Publishing Co., he entered the Marine Corps in January, 1943." He was one of six sons on active duty in the armed forces. The other sons: "Captain Karl Moreland is with the infantry in France; Sergeant Marion Moreland, AAF, is in England; Private Alonzo Moreland is an infantryman at Camp Hood, Texas; Private Lyle E. Moreland, an infantryman at Camp Gordon, Ga., and Apprentice Seaman Lewis H. Moreland is at Great Lakes, Ill."[266]

"IN THE SERVICE":

Private First Class Claude Hatfield of Huntington is a member of a 60 mm mortar team of the Seventh Infantry Division now fighting on Okinawa. Private Hatfield's team recently scored three direct hits on a Jap machine gun stronghold, wiping it out completely.

Sergeant Charles D. Fuller, son of Mr. and Mrs. Anthony W. Fuller of Ceredo, was recently promoted from Corporal with the Fifth Armored Division in Germany. Sergeant Fuller, a tank commander, holds the Purple Heart.

Master Sergeant S. G. Oswald, 2923 Washington Boulevard, celebrated V-E Day at the AAF Service Command in Italy. He is a member of the Air Supply Division...

Boatswain's Mate Wallace G. Jefferson, 19, son of Mr. and Mrs. John Jefferson of Barboursville, a veteran of three years in the Navy, took part in the amphibious action on the Rhine by transporting the advancing troops across the river into the heart of Germany. He is now home on a furlough after 22 months of sea duty...

Staff Sergeant Arden Queen, son of Mr. and Mrs. J. A. Queen of Mercerville, O., was recently honorably discharged from the Army on the point system after almost four years of service, 38 months of which was spent on Pacific islands... His brother, Jack, is a private first class in the Army and is presently stationed in the Philippines.

Robert W. Shively Jr., 20, 723 Sixth Avenue, has been promoted from second to first lieutenant at a Ninth AAF base in Germany. Lieutenant Shively is a veteran of more than 65 missions as a P-51 fighter pilot and is credited with destroying two German planes, one in the air and one on the ground.

Mrs. Fern Black Koontz, seaman second class, of Huntington, recently finished her indoctrination course at Naval Training School for WAVES in the Bronx, N.Y. A former employee of Sylvania Electric Products Inc., she enlisted in the WAVES after her husband, Lieutenant Raymond Koontz, was killed in action in Germany. Four brothers are in the service.

Glenna: *May 31st Thursday – Beautiful day. I varnished chairs. Rupert has cold. We set out sweet potato plants.*

Rupert: *I have a cold today.*

"IN THE SERVICE":

Word has been received from Fukuoka, Japan, from Private First Class Okey D. Pack of Hamlin, who is being held there as a prisoner-of-war, according to his parents, Mr. and Mrs. L. M. Pack. Private Pack has been a prisoner since the fall of Corregidor in May, 1942. The card received was dated October 11, 1944 and he said he was in good health. He is a brother of Mrs. Shirley Lawson of Huntington. [That's three years as a prisoner of the Japanese. It's hard to imagine what horror our captured service personnel endured.]

Private Robert E. Carter, 25, husband of Mrs. Helen B. Carter, 815 Adams Avenue, is at the AAF Convalescent Hospital at Fort Thomas, Ky. The son of Oxford Carter, 517 Washington Boulevard, he served in the European theatre for nine months as a clerk.

Dorothy M. Mills, daughter of Mr. and Mrs. Edmond Mills of Barboursville, has been promoted from private to private first class at Patterson Field, O. where she is a member of the WAC.

Leonard L. McLeod, son of Mrs. Rosa McLeod, 1219 Eighth Avenue, has been advanced to the rating of storekeeper second class at the Naval Ammunition Depot at Puget Sound Bremerton, Wash.

Ralph Holt, seaman first class, is a veteran of four Pacific engagements aboard the now-famous USS *Franklin*. He was injured aboard that carrier last October and was hospitalized at San Diego, Calif. until about a month ago. He is now at the Naval Air station at Anacostia, D.C. His wife and child live in Huntington.

June

OCCUPATION OF GERMANY, UNITED NATIONS CHARTER

GLENNA: JUNE 1ST FRIDAY – CLEANED HOUSE. CLOUDY.

Rupert: *It was cloudy all day.*

Weather is a topic that begins many conversations. Near the surface in our thoughts, it's quick to leap to our tongues. Our diary entries echo that importance.

With the European front closed, efforts were ratcheted up in the Pacific: "Osaka, Japan's second largest city was set ablaze today (Friday, U.S. Time) by 3,200 tons of incendiaries dropped by at least 450 Superfortresses making the second daylight strike on prime mainland targets in 72 hours." The B-29s were escorted by 150 Mustangs.[267] Twenty–seven of the Mustangs were lost because of bad weather while on the route to Osaka.[268]

"IN THE SERVICE":

Private Robert E. Klein, 21, son of Mr. and Mrs. H. S. Klein, 1347 Thirteenth Street, is recovering in a hospital in England from wounds received in action in Germany. He is a graduate of Central High School and was a medical student at the University of Cincinnati before entering the Army on December 7, 1942.

Private First Class Dennis L. Sunderland, husband of Mrs. Dorothy Sunderland, 1120 Eighteenth Street, has been awarded the Bronze Star for heroic action during the campaign in Northern France. He is a member of the 30th Infantry Division. [Another entry for this soldier spells last name as "Sutherland."]

Lieutenant Richard H. Cartwright Jr., 1333 Fourteenth Street, recently took part in a long-range fighter sweep over Formosa as a P-38 fighter pilot of the 13th Air Force. The 12 planes on the 2,000-mile flight were credited with shooting down one Japanese bomber, extensively damaging enemy transport and damaging a costal vessel. Every plane got safely back to base in the Philippines.

Frank Whisman, 22, of Culloden, aviation machinist's mate second class, has returned from a recent tour of duty in the Pacific aboard a baby flattop. The Navy carrier took part in the invasions of Palau, Leyte, Mindoro, Luzon, Okinawa and Leyte Gulf. Machinist Whisman attended Milton High School.

Coast Guardsman Joseph Edwards, seaman first class, 928 Eutaw Place, is on duty in the Pacific aboard a Coast Guard-manned LCI. Seaman Edwards is a veteran of the invasion assaults on Normandy.

Corporal Harold Conrad, husband of Mrs. Della Conrad of Milton and son of Mr. and Mrs. Ernest L. Conrad of Milton, is a member of the 38th Ordnance Medium Maintenance Company in Italy. He also served with the 88th Division in Italy and was awarded the Purple Heart, the Combat Infantryman's Medal, and the Mediterranean theatre ribbon with two battle stars.

Master Sergeant Thurman F. Fry, son of Mr. and Mrs. H. F. Fry of Stiltner, W.Va., is stationed at an Eighth Air Force base in England. Sergeant Fry graduated from Wayne High School in 1938 and entered the Army in December, 1941. He has been in the European theatre for more than two years.

Private First Class Robert L. Simms, son of Mr. and Mrs. J. H. Simms, 2560 First Avenue, received the news of the German surrender at an air force base in Italy. Private Simms, who has been overseas for 30 months joined his buddies for a full day of celebration.

Charles H. Gibson, 23, son of Mrs. Susie McDenie, 2108 Ninth Avenue, is an Air Transport Command pilot at John H. Payne Field, Cairo, Egypt.

Charles H. Hardy, 23, son of Mr. and Mrs. T. W. Hardy, 319 Adams Avenue, has been promoted from corporal to staff sergeant at a 15th AAF base in Italy. Sergeant Hardy, a waist gunner on a Flying Fortress, joined the Army in January, 1942 and has been overseas since last December.

Private First Class James T. Hetzer, son of Mr. and Mrs. T. A. Hetzer, 1809 West Fifth Avenue, is a member of an entertainment group which has been touring the fighting fronts in Europe. Private Hetzer formerly operated a dance school and theatrical agency here. His wife, Mrs. Elouise Hetzer, is also on an entertainment tour.

Private First Class John Adams Jr., son of Mr. and Mrs. John Adams Sr., 310 Staunton Street, is a member of the 60th Air Service Group of the 15th AAF in Italy. He entered the Army in January 1943 and went overseas a year later.

Andrew C. Camp, 33, boatswain's mate second class, a former Huntington contractor, is at the amphibious training base at Camp Bradford, Va. He is the son of J. M. Camp, 2806 Fourth Avenue and a veteran of the invasions of Sicily, Salerno and Normandy...

Corporal Raymond A. Bostic, 22, son of Mrs. Edith Fletcher, 507 North High Street, is recovering in a hospital in England from wounds received in action in Germany. He has been awarded the Purple Heart.

Corporal Paul T. Miros, son of Mr. and Mrs. Michael Miros, 618 High Street, has been awarded his fifth bronze battle star. He is a member of the 438th Troop Carrier Group in the European theatre.

First Lieutenant Charles Chapman, son of Mr. and Mrs. Charles C. Chapman, 2636 Guyan Avenue, a navigator of a B-17, has been awarded his fourteenth Oak Leaf Cluster to the Air Medal at an eighth Air Force bomber base in England. Lieutenant Chapman entered the AAF in October, 1940.

Technical Sergeant Sherman J. Frazier, husband of Mrs. Bonnie R. Frazier, 514 Bridge Street and son of Mr. and Mrs. Fred L. Frazier, 3730 Riverside Drive, is on his way home from the Philippines where he served with the 13th AAF as a gunner on a B-25 strafer-bomber. He graduated from Hurricane High in 1941 and entered the service in February, 1943.

Second Lieutenant John H. Baker Jr., son of Mr. and Mrs. John Baker of Peach Creek, W.Va.is a pilot assigned to the Mellaha Air Base at Tripoli.

Huntington soldiers who are members of the Second Bombardment Group of the 15th AAF in Italy include Technical Sergeant James I. Black, 3304 Fourth Avenue, aerial gunner; Sergeant Wilber C. Mills, 4648 Piedmont Road, mechanic; Sergeant Kermit M. Parker, 1654 Doulton Avenue, and Corporal Charles H. Hardy, 319 Adams Avenue, waist gunner.

Corporal Technician Walter A. Hogsett, 238 ½ Fifth Avenue, overseas for 35 months with the 815th Engineer Aviation Battalion, will soon be on his way home from the Mediterranean theatre.

Captain Ira J. Kail Jr. has arrived in New Orleans from Germany and is on his way to Huntington to visit his wife and son. Captain

Kail was a member of the 86th Division of the Seventh Army.

Seaman First Class Kelsie R. Biggs has returned to New York after spending a furlough with his mother, Mrs. Helen Biggs of Huntington. Brothers in the service are Dennie B. Biggs, aviation machinist's mate third class, in the Pacific, and Orville D. Biggs, with the 34th Infantry Division in the Philippines.

Corporal Virgil I. Allen, husband of Mrs. Nellie Allen, is spending a furlough here after a year with the 13th Infantry Division in Europe. He holds the Bronze Star.

Staff Sergeant Lowell H. Beckley, 24, son of Mr. and Mrs. Paul D. Beckley of Prichard, has been awarded the Good Conduct Medal. He has been in the European theatre for more than a year and holds the Air Medal with two Oak Leaf Clusters.

Navy Lieutenant J. B. Russell of Portsmouth, O., recently promoted from lieutenant (j. g.), is in Hawaii after completing 82 combat missions against the Japs. A pilot of a torpedo bomber, the former football star at Marshall College holds the Navy Cross, the Purple Heart, and the Air Medal. His wife and daughter live in Miami, Fla.

Glenna: *June 2nd Saturday – Painted windows. Rain. News that Johnny Childers was killed.*

Rupert: *Johnny Childers was reported killed today.*

"Private John T. Childers, 26, son of Mrs. Noma Lee, 817 Sixth Avenue, and the late Tilmon Childers of Branchland, was killed May 1 on Okinawa Island... In service 21 months ... he was with the 77th Field Artillery. Surviving are his mother, eight sisters, Mrs. Elmer Gue of Branchland, Mrs. Hersel Ross of Salt Rock, Mrs. Lovell Gibson and Mrs. Kermit Gue of Huntington, the Misses Ladoskia, Kathryn and

Janet Childers, stationed at Ashford General Hospital at White Sulfur Springs, W. Va. with a WAC medical detachment, and two brothers, Arnie Childers of Logan and Elson Childers of Branchland."[269]

"IN THE SERVICE":

Captain Howard Bowles Jr. of Barboursville is in charge of a group of Nazi SS troops who have been ordered to clean up the former hideout of Adolf Hitler at Berchtesgaden. Captain Bowles has been with the 101st Airborne Division since D-Day last June 6.

Second Lieutenant William J. Hatch, son of Mrs. Charles Hatch, 529 Twelfth Street, has been awarded the Air Medal at a base in England. Lieutenant Hatch is a pilot of a B-17 Flying Fortress.

Floyd J. Workman of Huntington is among the civilian workers at the Pearl Harbor Naval Yard.

Captain Delbert L. Gibson, son of Mr. and Mrs. Jess E. Gibson of Ona, has been assigned to the San Marcos Army Air Field, Texas as a navigator instructor. Captain Gibson served with the Eighth Air Force in Europe for a year and a half where he won the Distinguished Flying Cross, the Air Medal with seven Oak Leaf Clusters and three battle stars on his campaign ribbon.

Private First Class Edgar Scott, son of Mrs. Kate Mullins of Wayson, Ky., who has been freed from a German prison camp, is on his way back to the United States according to a telegram received recently by his mother.

After 32 months duty in Egypt with the Army Air Forces, Technical Sergeant William L. Chapman, 30, 310 Twenty-first Street ... [is] en route home on furlough.

Herbert D. Arthur, seaman first class, son of Mr. and Mrs. Lloyd Arthur of Ona, is serving at the Naval Air Station at Honolulu.

John J. Hall, fireman second class, son of Mrs. John R. Hall of Milton, a veteran of the invasion of Southern France, is now stationed at the Navy amphibious base at Little Creek, Va.

Cecil R. Gooch, 20, son of Mr. and Mrs. Oliver Hall of Milton, has been advanced to motor machinist's mate third class at a naval base in the Western Carolinas.

Major John F. Wilkes, formerly a chemist for the Chesapeake and Ohio Railway Co. here, has been promoted to that rank ... in Washington, D.C. where he is stationed. He is the husband of the former Miss Helen Ferguson of Huntington.

Ralph W. Patrick, husband of the former Miss Charmaine Dotson, 1835 Hall Avenue, has been promoted to gunner's mate third class at the Atlantic Fleet's antiaircraft training center at Shell Beach, La.

Machinist's Mate Third Class Charles F. Collins, husband of Mrs. Ruth Collins, 322 Twenty-second Street, recently spent a furlough with his wife and daughter prior to transfer to overseas duty with the Navy Seabees.

First Lieutenant William Blackwell is spending a 15-day furlough here with his wife and daughter after 20 months service in India where he was an aide to Brigadier General Neyland.

Brady Thompson, electrician's mate second class, 1353 Hall Street, was on the destroyer escort USS *Robert I. Payne* when she [the ship] recently represented the Navy at the formal surrender of eight German submarines at Londonderry, Northern Ireland.

Glenna: *June 3rd Sunday – Went to Sunday School. Cold and cloudy. Drewie and Gladys came that evening and ate supper.*

Rupert: *I still have a cold today. I went to Sunday school today.*

I had bouts with hay fever and it was sometimes difficult to tell the difference.

Vatican City: Pope Pius XII expressed hope that Germany "can rise to new divinity and new life." He also warned that postwar Europe is endangered by a "tranny no less despotic than those for whose overthrow men planned."[270]

Manila: American Forces, under aerial and naval support, landed on Mindanao Island at Lauyon, seventy-five miles south of Davao the capital, in a move to encircle and exterminate isolated Japanese garrisons. There was light opposition and the troops quickly moved inland.[271]

"Boatswain's Mate (First Class) Edward C. Ellis, son of Mr. and Mrs. Walter Ellis of Proctorville, O. was killed in a plane crash in the Pacific theatre May 5..."[272]

"WITH THE COLORS":

Private (First Class) Harry C. Gray, 407 ½ Bridge Street, has arrived at Asheville, N.C. Redistribution Station after 35 months in the South Pacific with the 37th Infantry Division. He participated in the Solomon Islands campaign and has been awarded the Purple Heart with an Oak Leaf Cluster, Combat Infantryman's Badge and the Good Conduct Medal. His father is Charles S. Gray, 1937 Fourth Avenue.

Yeoman (Second Class) Stella Keerans, daughter of Mr. and Mrs. John B. Keerans, of 1743 Nineteenth Street, and Aviation Machinist's Mate (Second Class) Ruby Hutchinson, daughter of Mrs. Delta Hutchinson of Buffalo have arrived at Pearl Harbor for duty.

Staff Sergeant Kenneth G. Russell, USMCR, a former member of the football team at Huntington high school, has arrived to spend a 30-day furlough with his mother, Mrs. Dora Russell, 2204 Marcum Terrace, after spending 28 months in the South Pacific. He took part in campaigns at Guadalcanal and Guam while serving with the Third Service Battalion of the

Third Marine Division. Two brothers in service are Pharmacist's Mate (Second Class) Don Russell and Quartermaster (First Class) Robert Russell, both in the Navy.

Sergeant Clifford Slone, son of Mrs. Bertha Slone of West Hamlin, has been awarded the Bronze Star for gallantry in foreign fields of battle. Sergeant Slone, who is with a U.S. medical detachment in Germany, has been overseas eight months.

Private Harold L. Johnson, whose wife resides at 1634 Charleston Avenue, has been returned to U.S. military control after being a prisoner of the Germans...

Robert Gartin, water tender (third class) has received a commendation for participation in amphibious operations in the Philippines, with all landings on D-Day... [He] "acquitted himself with honor under numerous enemy air attacks in which his ship brought down three Jap planes and assisted in shooting down others." The invasions included those at Leyte, Luzon, Palawan, Mindanao, [and] Cebu Islands.

Corporal Charles J. Blair, son of Mrs. Kathryn Blair, 62 Elm Street, has been awarded the Air Medal for meritorious achievement as a B-17 Flying Fortress gunner over German targets in Europe. He is a member of the 91st Bombardment Group and attended St. Joseph's High School.

Private (First Class) William E. Davidson, 214 Division Street, was recently awarded his first Battle Star while fighting in Germany [30th Infantry Division]. Other awards he has received include the Purple Heart, the Bronze Star, and the Combat Infantryman's Badge.

Corporal George C. Mosby has just returned to Boca Raton Field, Fla. after spending 11 days with his parents, Mr. and Mrs. Howard Mosby of Shoals, W.Va. Corporal Mosby will resume his radar training which he began in Sept., 1944. He entered the Army Air Force in August, 1943.

Private (First Class) Wayne E. Halfhill, son of Mr. and Mrs. R. C. Halfhill, 420 Eighth Avenue, has been promoted ... at the Marine Corps Air Station , Cherry Point, N.C. He was an apprentice machinist at the International Nickel Co. before joining the Marine Corps. His wife, Mrs. Elaine Legg Halfhill, resides at Bern, N.C.

Private Roy Allen, husband of Mrs. Virginia Allen of 2043 Fourth Avenue is a patient of the 32nd General Hospital in England... Allen has served in England, Scotland, France, Belgium and Germany as a cook with the First Army. He has been in the service 21 months and overseas for six months.

Sergeant Taylor V. Thacker, USMC, son of Mr. and Mrs. Era Fox of Kenova, Route 1, has been graduated from Machine Gun School at Camp LeJeune, N.C.

Private (First Class) Mildred Mays, USMCWR, daughter of Mr. and Mrs. E. Mays, 3404 Third Avenue, has been promoted to the rank of corporal at the Marine Barracks, Quantico, Va.

Corporal Othal Azel Blake Jr., son of Mr. and Mrs. O. A. Blake, 211 Short Street, who has served overseas 29 months with the Marine Corps aboard three aircraft carriers and one battleship at various times, has arrived in the United States to spend a furlough with relatives. He was a crew member of one of the carriers from whose decks the first carrier-based planes hit Japan last January. He was a welder in civil life and his wife resides in Providence.

Private (First Class) Luther J. Warren Jr., son of Mr. and Mrs. Luther J. Warren Sr., 1114 Sixteenth Street, who was stationed at Camp Pendleton, Calif., has been awarded the Purple Heart for machine gun bullet wounds in the right shoulder sustained in action on Tinian Island July 31, 1944. He served overseas with the Fourth Marine Division in the Marshall Islands campaign and at Saipan before Tinian. He was a front line radio operator with a rifle company and returned to the United States last September. He was married to Miss Evelyn Nason of Los Angeles April 19, and is awaiting new assignment...

Corporal Jack Frost of the Army Air Forces has returned to the United States from a B-29 base in Italy. While overseas he was awarded the Distinguished Unit Citation with one Oak Leaf Cluster, four Battle Stars and the Good Conduct Ribbon. After spending a 30-day furlough with his wife, Mrs. Faye Nester Frost and son David, he will report to Fort Meade, Md. For reassignment.

Glenna: *June 4th Monday – I washed. It was real cold.*

Rupert: *It was cold outside today.*

Troops were coming home from Europe in great numbers. Over 10,000 European war veterans had already arrived in New York aboard the *Monticello*, the *LeJeune*, and the *Santa Margarita*.[273]

"IN THE SERVICE":

Aviation Radioman Second Class Charles Pyles Jr., 826 Vernon Street, was aboard the plane of Lieutenant Robert W. Gabel of Sioux Falls, S.D. when the Navy pilot landed his small observation ship in heavily mined waters off Okinawa to rescue an American flyer shot down by antiaircraft fire. Radioman Pyles spotted the missing flier and covered the area with a machine gun while the rescue was effected. Lieutenant Gabel last December received the Navy Cross for rescuing two fliers off Tinian.

Yeoman First Class William Wallace, son of Mrs. Grace Jobe, 1313 Center Street, Barboursville, is on duty at the Atlantic Fleet Operational Training Command at Norfolk, Va. He wears the American theater ribbon, the European-North African-Middle Eastern ribbon with one battle star for the invasion of North Africa, and the American Defense ribbon

and Good Conduct Medal. Yeoman Wallace has been in the Navy since 1938.

Captain Paul V. Osburn, son of Mr. and Mrs. Thurman Osburn, 415 Thirty-first Street, and Staff Sergeant Clarence W. Wiley, son of Mr. and Mrs. Clyde H. Wiley, 220 Eighteenth Street, are serving in the veteran 306th Bomb Group of the Eighth Air Force. Both are former Marshall College students. Captain Osburn holds the Distinguished Flying Cross with one Oak Leaf Cluster and the Air Medal with six Oak Leaf Clusters for his 50 daylight bombardment missions over Germany as Flying Fortress navigator. His wife, Mrs. Betty Jo Osburn, lives at 413 Thirty-first Street. Sergeant Wiley has flown as a tail gunner on 27 missions and holds the Air Medal with three Oak Leaf Clusters. He is the husband of Mrs. Doris L. Wiley, 1865 Marshall Avenue.

Private Forrest N. Rice, son of Mr. and Mrs. Fred Rice, rear 2112 Seventh Avenue, has returned to the United States after serving with the Army in the Philippines for six months. He is in a hospital in California.

Machinist's Mate Second Class George W. R. Trainer and Cecil A. Hewitt, who were formerly baseball rivals in the same Meigs County, O. sandlot league are now shipmates aboard a battleship in the Western Pacific. Mate Trainer is the son of Mrs. Ethel Shively, of Vinton, O., and Mate Hewitt is the son of Mrs. Alta Dyke of Langsville, O.

Corporal Ferdinand J. White, 330 Davis Street, is serving as a surgical technician in the surgeon's office of a combat engineer group of the 11th Corps on Luzon.

Sergeant Lee R. Clayton Jr., son of Mrs. L. R. Clayton, 6 Hills Court, is a member of the 276th Coast Artillery Battalion's championship basketball team which recently won the base title at its station in the Southwest Pacific. He played forward.

Private Verlin J. Arthur, 3065 Park Hill, is a member of the staff operating a rest and recreation center for troops of the XXIII

American Army Corps in the village of Esch in Luxembourg.

Millard Jackson Galloway of Proctorville, O. has been advanced to boatswain's mate second class aboard a destroyer of the Atlantic Fleet. He is the son of Mrs. I. G. Galloway of Proctorville and husband of the former Miss Wanda Moore of Proctorville.

Technical Sergeant Earl Mayo, 1610 Arthur Street, is serving with the 435th Troop Carrier Group in Germany, hauling in supplies and carrying out liberated prisoners of war. He is an aerial engineer on a C-47 transport plane.

Sergeant Clair S. Gothard, 743 Central Avenue, Barboursville, is cook in charge of the preparation of all patient's special diets at the 55th General Hospital in England. He is the son of Mrs. Mary S. Gothard.

First Lieutenant James C. Wall, 611 Fourteenth Street, Private First Class John A. Patterson, 926 Seventh Avenue, and Private Lloyd K. Smith of Berwind are members of the 995th Signal Service Company which has installed and operated a communications system in a large Belgian port. Before the war in Europe ended, they were subjected to numerous V-bomb attacks.

Private First Class Ted Wilson, 424 Fourth Street, is a patient at the AAF Convalescent Hospital at Fort Thomas, Ky, after serving for 14 months as a military policeman in the Southwest Pacific.

Private First Class Lowell Nicholls of Salt Rock, a railroading veteran with more than two years of service in Iran to his credit, has been flown back to the United States ... and is now at Miami, Fla.

Sergeant Charles E. Hager of Bidwell, O., a former student at Marshall College, has been awarded the Air Medal with one Oak Leaf Cluster at the base of the 25th Bomb Group (Reconnaissance) in England.

Captain Carroll R. Ogden, husband of Mrs. Mae Y. Ogden, 11 Fairfax Court, and professor of English at Marshall College before entering the Army more than three years ago, is attending the Army Education Staff School in Italy for training which will help him guide the educational program for soldiers overseas.

Glenna: *June 5th Tuesday – Cool and clear. I ironed and mended.*

Rupert: *It's cold again today. I still have a slight cold.*

Farm Agent W. D. Click called on Huntington men with farm experience to help Cabell County farmers: "Mr. Click directed his appeal especially to men employed in retail stores which close Wednesday afternoon during the summer and those who have free time on Saturdays..."[274]

San Francisco: A United Nations charter provision was approved on June 4... "A compact 11-member Security Council would serve as the instrument of a new world league in bringing unruly nations into line and preventing the eruption of war in the future." Armed forces, directed by top military experts, would enforce it.[275]

Five hundred B-29 bombers dropped incendiaries on the Japanese city of Kobe,[276] and the Navy announced the loss of the destroyers *Morrison* and *Luce* off Okinawa, with heavy casualties.[277]

"IN THE SERVICE":

Captain Frederick W. Schoew of Huntington was promoted to that rank from commander last Saturday at the Norfolk, Va., Naval base, according to a telegram received yesterday by his mother, Mrs. F. L. Schoew of the Hotel Frederick. Captain Schoew is a veteran of the World War I and is engaged in ordnance work at Norfolk.

Private First Class Calvin E. Saul, son of Mrs. July A. Saul of Yawkey, W.Va., has been awarded the Bronze Star Medal for heroic action against the Japs on Mount Matabs, Luzon, last March 28. Private Saul is a member of the 51st Field Artillery of the Sixth Infantry Division, holder of the record for continuous combat in the Pacific Theatre.

Private James T. Taylor, husband of Mrs. Vesta Taylor, 1934 Sixth Avenue, has received the Combat Infantry Badge for participation with the 151st Infantry Regiment in action against the enemy on Luzon. Private Taylor attended Barboursville High School and entered the Army in October, 1944, going overseas two months ago.

For Meritorious service in connection with military operations against the Germans, technician Fifth Grade Gerald P. Woodrum, son of Mr. and Mrs. P. D. Woodrum, 212 Staunton Street, has been awarded the Bronze Star Medal. Corporal Woodrum is with the 378th Infantry Division and is married to the former Miss Juanita Tackett, who resides in Raleigh, N.C.

Staff Sergeant Richard J. Penhorwood, husband of Mrs. Marion Penhorwood, 223 Sixth Avenue, has been awarded the Air Medal for meritorious achievement as a gunner with the Twentieth AAF in the Pacific. Sergeant Penhorwood received the award for participating in low altitude incendiary raids against Japan.

Private E. O. Bryant has been assigned to a new Army station after spending a furlough with his wife and son at their home, 2145 Eighth Avenue... He expects to go overseas soon.

The War Department yesterday announced the promotion of Robert Lee Smith, 143 Olive Street, and John L. Thomas, 316 Sixth Avenue, from second to first lieutenant.

Technician Fourth Grade Norman L. Coleman, 108 Richmond Street, is serving with the 724th Railway Operating Battalion in France.

Second Lieutenant William M. Forman [22], son of Mrs. Hattie Foreman, 819 Vernon Street, recently won his silver wings and commission as a flying officer in the AAF at the Big Spring, Texas Bombardier School. [He went to Boca Raton Army Air Field.]

David B. Stombock, son of Mrs. Alma B. Stombock, 201 Nineteenth Street, has been promoted ... to private first class in the 276th Signal Heavy Construction Company. Private Stombock went overseas last August and participated in the Leyte and the Luzon campaigns.

Private First Class Harold M. Bartram, husband of Mrs. Doris Bartram, 218 ½ Twenty-first Street, is a convalescent patient at the Ashburn General Hospital at McKinney, Tex. Private Bartram is a veteran of many European campaigns.

Corporal Avnel E. Childers, 31, son of Mrs. Oscar Childers of Barboursville, has been given the Combat Badge recently in the Philippines campaign with the 40th Infantry Division. Corporal Childers is an ambulance driver in the 115th Medical Battalion and has been overseas for more than 33 months, participating in several major campaigns.

Glenna: *June 6th Wednesday — Cool and mostly cloudy. I painted kitchen floor.*

Rupert: *It was cloudy today.*

The Rev. Martin Niemoeller, a Lutheran pastor who had been a U-boat commander in the First World War, and who had attacked Nazism from the pulpit in 1937, was released by American troops after eight years in Nazi camps. Niemoeller said at a press conference that "the German people like to be governed and live under authority... It might be true that Germans are incapable of living under a democracy."[278]

"IN THE SERVICE":

Thomas D. Dearnell, 21, son of Mr. and Mrs. Elbert Dearnell of Kermit, an engineer-gunner on a B-24 Liberator, was recently promoted to staff sergeant at a 15th AAF base in Italy. Sergeant Dearnell entered the AAF in June, 1943, and went overseas last December and has taken part in many bombing attacks.

Lieutenant Donald R. Hart, brother of Mrs. Tennyson Bias, 1221 Washington Boulevard, has been awarded the Bronze Star Medal for heroic achievement in combat against the Germans in Italy last April 23. Lieutenant Hart entered the Army in December, 1942, and went overseas last January. He attended Marshall College in 1940–41.

Private First Class Milford D. Charter Jr., son of Mr. and Mrs. M. D. Charter, 2842 Third Avenue, is stationed at Regensburg, Germany, where he guards prisoners of war. Private Charter is with the 243rd Field Artillery Battalion of the Third Army and was formerly attached to a medical unit. His brother, Private Richard L. Charter is stationed at Camp Robinson, Ark.

Corporal William F. Demmler, son of Mrs. Bessie L. Demmler of Barboursville, is attending classes offered by the Army's information and education program in Italy where he is studying radio and telephone. Corporal Demmler, an armorer with the AAF in Italy, went overseas in November, 1943 and participated in the North African and Italian campaigns.

Captain Ira J. Kail Jr. of Huntington has returned here for a 30-day leave after 26 months of fighting in Italy and France with an engineer battalion. Captain Kail is a graduate of Ohio State University and entered the Army three days before Pearl Harbor. His brother, Major Goodhue Kail, is in Europe with an airborne unit.

Seaman First Class Gay H. Gilpin, son of Mrs. G. A. Ramey, 2816 First Street, has arrived here after 18 months duty in the South Pacific.

Lieutenant John M. Vest, son of Mrs. John Vest, 40 Twenty-seventh Street, has been promoted ... to first lieutenant while serving as a platoon leader with the 75th Infantry Division in Germany.

After completing 40 missions as a B-24 gunner in the Pacific, Staff Sergeant Clifton E. Temple, 26, 2971 Sixth Avenue, has arrived at AAF Redistribution Center at Miami. Sergeant Temple holds the Air Medal with six Oak Leaf Clusters.

First Lieutenant Jack C. Schurman, son of Mr. and Mrs. C. R. Schurman, 93 Twenty-seventh Street, was recently awarded his third Oak Leaf Cluster to the Air Medal for his part in the dropping of supplies to the trapped 101st Airborne Division at Bastogne, Belgium, last December. Lieutenant Schurman is a pilot on a C-47 and entered the service in June, 1942.

Glenna: *June 7th Thursday – Cool-rainy. I cleaned the cabinet.*

Rupert: *I worked a little in the corn today.*

"Speculation that Cabell County might have to undertake financing of the Huntington airport project developed last night when City attorney Maxwell W. Flesher declared that in his opinion it would be legally impossible for the city to float a bond issue of the size needed... Other West Virginia cities have found themselves in a similar situation, including Charleston, where Kanawha County is financing a new airport."[279]

Film of Buchenwald and Bergen-Belsen concentration camps were shown to civilians in the Western Allies' occupation zones.[280]

London, June 6: "Moscow newspapers published maps today indicating that Russia would occupy approximately half of Germany... "A British Foreign Office spokesman said the American, British and French occupation zones were 'under discussion,' ... but there was no indication when their boundaries would be decided upon."[281]

"IN THE SERVICE":

For volunteering to cross an untried bridge to see if it was mined, without the benefit of a mine-detector, and successfully completing the task, Sergeant Walter E. Robinson, son of Mrs. Mattie E. Robinson, 640 First Street, was awarded the Bronze Star Medal. His wife and child live in Oakland, Calif.

Captain Frank H. Pearman, AAF, son of Mr. and Mrs. Hale Pearman, 2851 North Staunton Road, has arrived home after being honorably discharged from the Air Forces. Captain Pearman is a veteran of 48 missions with the Eighth AAF against the Nazis and holds the Distinguished Flying Cross with one Oak Leaf Cluster, the Air Medal with five Oak Leaf Clusters and five battle stars on his campaign ribbon. He also holds the Presidential Unit Citation. Captain Pearman totaled 126 discharge points and is believed to be Huntington's highest point man.

The Bronze Star Medal has been awarded to Sergeant James H. Monnig, husband of the former Miss Mar A. Hall of Huntington, for meritorious service, his parents, Mr. and Mrs. L. J. Monnig, 1712 Third Avenue, have been informed. Sergeant Monnig attended St. Joseph's High School and was with the 85th Infantry Division in Italy.

Second Lieutenant Charles H. Reckard, son of Mrs. Lois Reckard, 1445 Washington Boulevard, has been named aide to Brigadier General Vincent J. Meloy, commanding general of Truax Field, Wis. Lieutenant Reckard, a former physicist at the International Nickel Co., has been stationed at several air fields throughout the country...

Orville L. Wintz, 20, gunner's mate second class, son of Mr. and Mrs. Gilbert Wintz of Huntington, has arrived at a naval base at Norfolk, Va. for training for duty aboard a new destroyer of the Atlantic Fleet. He is a veteran of the Pacific theatre.

Samuel W. Trowbridge, 24, of Gallipolis, O., has completed two years aboard a destroyer escort of the Atlantic Fleet where he attained the rating of radioman second class. He wears the European-African-Middle Eastern theatre ribbons.

Charles F. Craft, 25, carpenter's mate second class, 169 Oakland Avenue [Son of Mrs. Fred W. Craft and husband of Mrs. Dixie Lee Craft], is stationed at a naval base at Weymouth, Dorset, England. A former employee of the Huntington Furniture Corp., he has been overseas for 15 months.

Aubrey C. Bryant, seaman first class, recently observed his 34th birthday aboard a heavy cruiser in the Pacific...

Corporal Thomas McDowell, husband of Mrs. Perla McDowell, 2601 Adams Avenue, is serving with the Marines on Guam as a truck master. Five days after D-Day on Guam, he went ashore with $140,000 in silver coin for the American forces.

Now at an Army staging area in France awaiting shipment back to the United States is Sergeant Carl I. Adkins, husband of Mrs. Thelma Adkins, 1634 Sixth Avenue. Sergeant Adkins wears three battle stars on his campaign ribbon and has been overseas for 16 months. He is a member of the Second Armored Division and has been in the Army since February, 1941.

Glenna: *June 8th Friday – I went to Huntington. Sunny in evening. Went to the show and saw "God is My Co Pilot."*

Rupert: *I went to town today. I got a Tarzan book and went to the show.*

Boston, June 7: "Swashbuckling" General George S. Patton Jr., arrived home to a "screaming welcome... He jumped from a huge Army transport plane straight into the arms of his waiting wife." Mrs. Patton told reporters later that Patton had expected to die fighting the Germans.[282]

"Diamond Dust": "(It was the late Irvin Cobb who once said: 'Until you got to Kentucky and with your own eyes behold the Derby, you ain't never been nowhere and you ain't never seen nothin.') The captain of this column is still whooping things up for Pot-O-Luck as the Derby winner. Bet your $$$ on the Warren Wright ace and you'll have an easy time paying off the mortgage on the old homestead, at Milton-on-the-Mud River... Horse racing is called the 'sport of kings.' Money will be king tomorrow at Churchill Downs. The Kentucky Derby is the most famous of all races, due to a southern gentleman by the name of Col. Matt Winn. The Derby is more than 'just a horse race'—it's play day for society and politics and gambling men."[283] (Hoop Jr., ridden by Eddie Arcaro, won the 1945 Kentucky Derby.)

"IN THE SERVICE":

Technical Sergeant Lewis A. Miller Jr., son of Mr. and Mrs. Lewis A. Miller of Huntington and Miller, O., has been promoted to that rank from corporal at his Army base at Naples, Italy. He is a veteran of the North African and Italian campaigns.

Captain Andrew Faller, son of Mr. and Mrs. Harold Faller, 208 Twenty-eighth Street, has been promoted to that rank from first lieutenant. He enlisted in the Air Forces in December, 1941, and is a veteran of several Pacific campaigns, having been overseas more than two and a half years.

Private First Class Luther M. Honacker, son of Mrs. Sarah Honacker of Berwind, is a member of the 172nd Smoke Generating Chemical Co., which screened the gathering Fifth Army that pounced on Bologna during the Allied offensive which resulted in the unconditional surrender of all enemy forces in Italy.

Coast Guardsman Jack B. Lilly, yeoman first class of Ashland, is serving aboard a Coast Guard-manned troop transport in the Atlantic which has been carrying supplies and material to help defeat Germany. Yeoman Lilly is a veteran of 36 months of sea duty.

George W. Wechsler, seaman first class, USCG, of Catlettsburg, is serving aboard a Coast Guard-manned troop transport which is engaged in bringing home the victorious American Armies from the European Theatre. Guardsman Wechsler has had 14 months of sea duty in both the Atlantic and Mediterranean theatres.

Donald W. Smith, son of City Electrician W. Z. Smith, has been honorably discharged from the Coast Guard where he served as a chief petty officer... He has accepted a position in the personnel section of the Reconstruction Finance Corps in Washington.

Ensign William L. Spurlock Jr., son of Mr. and Mrs. W. L. Spurlock of Chesapeake, O., recently graduated from the U.S. Naval Reserve Midshipmen's School at Northwestern, University. A former student at Marshall College, he joined the Naval Reserve in December, 1941, and is stationed at Miami, Fla. where he is undergoing advanced officer training.

Sergeant Luther Smith, son of Mr. and Mrs. Lindsey Smith of Kenova, recently marked his second anniversary of overseas duty. He was employed by the Tri-State Cleaning Co. before entering the service in April, 1942, and is now a mess sergeant at an air depot in Italy.

Billie E. Nelson, 21, boatswain's mate second class, husband of the former Miss Betty Jane Simons of Huntington, is at the Naval Training Station at Norfolk, Va., where he is training for duties aboard a new destroyer of the Atlantic Fleet.

Private Jack Huffman, son of Mr. and Mrs. C. C. Huffman, 2668 Collis Avenue, is stationed at Fort Wood, Mo. where he recently won the sharpshooter's medal. His brother, Private Ferrell Huffman, is stationed at Camp Barry, Calif.

Private George A. Caudill, husband of Mrs. Aleen Caudill of Huntington, is a member of the 172nd Smoke Generating Chemical Company which took part in the knockout blow against the Germans in Italy.

Corporal Lyle Bradley, 505 West Ninth Avenue, has returned to the United States after serving with the 173rd Field Artillery in Italy where he participated in several major campaigns.

First Lieutenant George E. Gold, 21, son of Mr. and Mrs. J. W. Gold, 136 Norway Avenue, has arrived at the Charleston, S.C. port of embarkation en route home

for a 30-day furlough. Lieutenant Gold served with the 15th AAF in Italy where he won the Air Medal with two Oak Leaf Clusters and four battle stars to his campaign ribbon.

Corporal Dean L. Stidham of Huntington is serving in the South Pacific with the Marine Corps Women's Reserve, and was pictured in the June issue of the marine magazine in a boxing bout with a sister marine.

Glenna: *June 9th Saturday – Rainy part of the day. I cooked all day.*

Rupert: *I played with Marion Nida today.*

Marion visited often, and sometimes I went to his house. At other times we met on the hill to the south at an old unused tobacco barn visible from our house. Zeke, Marion's younger brother sometimes joined us as we pursued our grand adventures.

Fred Betts of Huntington, along with three fellow merchant seamen, were back on American soil after four years as prisoners of Germany.[284]

"IN THE SERVICE":

Sergeant Arthur H. Schmauch, 25, son of Mr. and Mrs. Arthur Schmauch, 2774 Guyan Avenue, is a radio operator-gunner on a B-17 Flying Fortress of the Eighth AAF which is now engaged in flying Allied prisoners back to their native countries. Before he entered the service in October 1943, he was employed by the Chesapeake & Ohio Railway Co., here. [Another entry on May 5th spells the last name "Schmauck," and with a different address.]

Waldo W. Smith, 28, of Prestonsburg, Ky. has been promoted to lieutenant, USNR, at the Naval Training Station, Newport, R.I. Lieutenant Smith has served for 25 months in the American, Pacific and Philippine theatres and wears the Bronze Star Medal for heroism in action in the Pacific.

Lieutenant (j. g.) William K. Gibson Jr., son of Mr. and Mrs. W. K. Gibson, 104 Washington Boulevard, is piloting a carrier-based Navy plane in the Pacific and has taken part in several recent strikes against the Japanese. He formerly was a student at the University of Pennsylvania.

Robert O. Ellis Jr., son of Mr. and Mrs. R. O. Ellis, 1108 Jefferson Avenue, was commissioned an ensign in the Naval Reserve and designated a naval flyer recently at the air training bases at Pensacola, Fla. He attended Marshall College for four years and was active in college athletics.

Lieutenant Charles W. Ferguson III of Wayne is completing final stage [of] training as a member of a B-29 Superfortress crew at Pyote Army Air Field, Tex. He is the son of Circuit Judge and Mrs. C. W. Ferguson and transferred from the Navy Air Corps to the Army in 1942. Lieutenant Ferguson is the radar observer on his bomber.

The 21st Bomber Command has announced the award of the Air Medal to Lieutenant Louis O. Gadeke, 2748 Highlawn Avenue, pilot of a B-29 Superfortress based on Tinian Island.

Private Silas Gibson of Huntington has returned to the United States and is now a patient at McCloskey General Hospital at Temple, Tex. He was wounded in the right leg by a hand grenade while fighting with the infantry against the Germans in the Rhine sector.

Sergeant Carrol F. Wood, 31, son of Mrs. F. L. Wood, 1221 Washington Avenue and husband of Mrs. Helen G. Wood, 2848 Fourth Avenue, is a turret specialist with the Eighth AAF in England.

Two Huntington airmen have been awarded the Air Medal for exceptional meritorious service during combat operations over Continental Europe, at an Eighth AAF base in England. They are Second Lieutenant William T. Pinson, 27, husband of Mrs. Marguerite E. Pinson, 2006 Marcum Terrace, a pilot, and

Second Lieutenant William J. Hatch, 25, 529 Twelfth Street, a co-pilot. Both men arrived overseas last March 21.

Staff Sergeant James A. Freeman, son of Mr. and Mrs. Willard Freeman, 1241 Jackson Avenue, has won the right to wear the boots of the Army paratrooper after completing four weeks of jump training at Fort Benning, Ga.

Private First Class Florence A. Smith, daughter of Mrs. Dona Smith of Lesage, is stationed at an air depot at Warrington, England.

Sergeant George V. Black, son of Mrs. Mabel M. Black, 4619 Bradley Road, is a member of the combat support wing of the Air Service Command in England.

Sergeant M. R. Quinlan, son of M. I. Quinlan, 1012 Ninth Avenue, has arrived home to spend a 30-day furlough after 27 months in England with an Army radar unit.

Private First Class Joseph C. Wheeler, 705 West Sixteenth Street, a member of the headquarters staff of General Courtney C. Hodges, U.S. First Army, has returned to the United States for a 30-day furlough before returning to active duty. The First Army is preparing for operation in the Pacific.

Private First Class Clyde W. Howell, 2512 Third Avenue, recently spent a 15-day furlough with his wife and daughter. He is stationed in Colorado.

Willie W. Brown, husband of Mrs. Dossie E. Brown, 1158 Jackson Avenue, has been promoted ... to private first class with the 435th Troop Carrier Group in Europe. He is a squadron cook.

Technical Sergeant E. C. Nicolls, son of Mr. and Mrs. E. E. Nicolls of Salt Rock, has returned to the United States after serving for 22 months with the 15th AAF in Italy. He is spending a 30-day furlough with his parents.

Glenna: *June 10th Sunday – Pretty day. Had Home Coming at the church at*

Salt Rock and big dinner. Manford Paugh was buried.

Manford H. Paugh, born about 1862, fathered children whose families were prominent in Salt Rock history. His wife was Nancy Dillon.[285] His obituary had appeared in the June 7 *Huntington Herald-Dispatch*.

Rupert: *I went to an all day meeting today and ate my fill.*

"All-Day Meetings," or "Homecomings," were church events for warm weather. After regular church service the men brought out tables and set them under the trees where the women loaded them with baskets of food brought from home. Fried chicken, hams, beef roasts and pork dishes, along with vegetables, were followed by an amazing assortment of desserts. Even during that time of severe food shortages, those spreads were exceptional. Preachers, quartets, and invited guests performed their specialties all afternoon while children played outside the church. Those annual events provide pleasant memories for me.

Guam: "The U.S. 10th Army [June 10] tightened a noose Saturday on a doomed pocket of Japanese on Okinawa's southwest coast while the only other Nipponese force, backed into a rugged escarpment, was pounded from sea, air and land with a tremendous bombardment." The Japanese had lost 67,703 troops killed, and there were still about 15,000 resisting, according to the AP report.[286]

"Emperor Hirohito directed the Japanese yesterday (Saturday) to hand over virtually all its powers to the war cabinet, which will rule by decree in an effort to cope with what Premier Kantaro Suzuki called 'the most critical situation in the history of our nation.'" Premier Suzuki rejected unconditional surrender and said that Japan's only choice was "to fight to the last."[287]

MANFORD H. PAUGH—Eighty-three years old, of Sixteenth Street Road, died at his home yesterday at 1:15 P. M. of a heart attack. Funeral services will be conducted Sunday at 2:30 P. M. at the Susie Chapel Church of God by the Rev. Frank Wolfe, the Rev. Charles Johnson and the Rev. Ernest Turner. Burial will be in Susie Chapel Cemetery. The body will be taken from the Cavendish Funeral Home to the residence at 10 A. M. today. Mr. Paugh was born in Wetzel County, W. Va., on June 8, 1861, a son of the late Archibald and Nancy Grose Paugh. He came to Huntington when 14 years old, and was a farmer at his Sixteenth Street Road residence for 25 years. He was a member of the Susie Chapel Church of God. Surviving are the widow, Mrs. Nannie Dillon Paugh; three sons, Leonard Paugh of Huntington, William Paugh of Salt Rock and Joseph Paugh of Mason City, W. Va.; seven daughters, Mrs. Ola Vaughn of Louisville, Ky., Mrs. Callie Hutchinson of Salt Rock, Mrs. A. A. Nash of Barboursville, and Mrs. Della Adkins, Mrs. Delena Stroud, Mrs. Fred Johnson and Mrs. Sam Byrd of Huntington; two sisters, Mrs. Alphens Kirkland of Huntington and Mrs. Rachael Cauliflower of Huntington and 52 grandchildren and 20 great grandchildren.

"WITH THE COLORS":

Among the survivors from United States warships sunk by enemy aerial action off Okinawa was Seaman (First Class) Emerson Burgess of Barboursville.

Private Ralph Blevins, son of Mrs. Madeline Blevins, 514 Hagan Street, has been awarded the Combat Infantryman's Badge for action with the 42nd "Rainbow" Division of the Seventh Army in France. He volunteered for service when the United States entered the war and has been overseas for three years.

Private Clifton D. Ellis, son of Mrs. Myrtle Ellis, 1257 Twenty-sixth Street, who was with the military police during V-E Day in France, is now in Military Police training there.

Private Ted Houvouras, son of Mr. and Mrs. Nick Houvouras, 201 ½ Eighth Avenue, returned yesterday to Storrs, Conn. where he is a civil engineering student with an Army specialized training unit at the University of Connecticut. He spent a seven-day furlough here with his parents. He is a graduate of Huntington Central High School and the West Virginia University.

Sergeant John R. Scott Jr., son of Mr. and Mrs. J. R. Scott of 2532 Third Avenue, is with the 304th Infantry now stationed with the Army of Occupation at Altenburgh, Germany.

First Lieutenant Tom Hagan, son of Mr. and Mrs. W. T. Hagan of 524 Twelfth Street, after 22 months with an airborne anti-aircraft machine gun battery attached to the Sixth Air Force in New Guinea, has arrived home. He will spend a 30-day leave with his parents and his wife, the former Miss Charlotte Nix of Logan, and their 14-month-old son, Thomas Marion, whom he saw for the first time upon his arrival home... Lieutenant Hagan wears the Asiatic-Pacific campaign ribbon with one battle star...

Private (First Class) Charles L. Bandy, son of Mrs. Samantha Bandy, 1512 Seventh Avenue, is stationed with the 32nd Infantry Division in Northern Luzon. He is entitled to wear the American Defense Ribbon, the Army Good Conduct Medal, the Asiatic-Pacific theatre ribbon with two battle stars and the Philippine Liberation Ribbon with one battle star. Prior to his entry into the Army, he was employed as a machine operator for the Tent and Awning Co.

Sergeant Anna O. Spurlock, daughter of Mr. Emory Osburn of 2616 Orchard Avenue, was recently awarded the Good Conduct Medal. She is stationed at Patterson Field, O., where she is assigned as a driver. She entered the armed Forces in March, 1943.

Private Orville D. Biggs, 1236 Fourth Avenue, has been commended for his heroic efforts at attempting to rescue a fellow soldier from drowning. Though his efforts to resuscitate the drowned man failed, Biggs' courage at the risk of his own life won high praise. He is a mortar man with the 24th Infantry Division on Mindanao.

Second Lieutenant Walter B. Henderson Jr., son of Mr. and Mrs. Walter B. Henderson Sr. of Huntington, is completing his training on a Liberator bomber at the Pueblo, Colo. Army Air Base...

Private (First Class) Matthew Wagner, brother of Mrs. Sara M. Gold, 517 West Third Avenue, is serving with a ground unit of the Army Air Forces in the South Pacific. He has been overseas more than a year.

Glenna: *June 11th Monday – Church Vacation School started. Hard rains all day.*

Rupert: *The church bible school started today. Mother is a teacher.*

Glenna: *June 12th Tuesday – Went to Church Vacation School. Ironed and mended. Cloudy.*

Rupert: *I went to Vacation Bible School today.*

London, June 11: "All the pomp and ritual of the ancient walled city of London will be revived tomorrow for General Eisenhower who will be given honorary freedom of the old city and presented with the sword carried by the Duke of Wellington who beat Napoleon at Waterloo." Eisenhower flew in from Frankfurt on the Main, Germany. An informal dinner was planned at the Dorchester Hotel, site of his headquarters in 1942.[288]

Japanese soldiers on Okinawa's Oroku Peninsula were committing suicide in great numbers.[289]

"IN THE SERVICE":

Staff Sergeant Robert F. Dundas, husband of Mrs. Lillian Dundas, 1832 Charleston Avenue, a radio-operator with the 13th AAF in the Philippines, has been given the Air Medal at an advanced Philippine base. Sergeant Dundas went overseas last December.

Navy Lieutenant William Chambers has arrived in Huntington from Washington to spend a leave with his wife and son, and will leave later this week for a new assignment at Jacksonville, Fla. He is a former Huntington Publishing Co. staff photographer.

Private First Class Regina M. Derda, 1630 Charleston Avenue, celebrated the third anniversary of the Women's Army Corps at St.

Germainen-Laye, France. She is stationed at a U.S. Strategic Air Forces base in France.

Sergeant Thaddeus N. Blakely, son of Mr. and Mrs. Walter Blakely, 1516 Ninth Avenue, is stationed at the army redistribution center at Camp Butner, N.C. He is a veteran of 36 months in the Pacific theatre where he served as a demolition man. His brother, Sergeant Walter Blakely Jr., is serving in Europe.

Technician Fifth Grade Hubert Sunderland, son of Mr. and Mrs. Edgar Sunderland of Culloden, is also at the Camp Butner redistribution center after serving 26 months in the China-Burma-India theatre.

Private First Class Willie C. Pauley, son of Mrs. Martha Pauley, 1828 Oak Street, Kenova, has been awarded the Purple Heart for wounds received in action against the Japs near San Mateo, Luzon, on April 13. Private Pauley is a member of the Sixth Infantry Division.

Coxswain Robert S. Mathews, son of Mr. and Mrs. W. H. Mathews, 3641 Hughes Street, and husband of the former Miss Elnora Long of Huntington, has been appointed ship's photographer aboard the USS *Memphis* in the Atlantic Fleet. Coxswain Mathews has been in the Navy since July, 1942.

Private James H. Lowe has returned to his station at San Antonio, Tex. after spending a 20-day furlough with his mother, Mrs. E. E. Christian, 1615 ½ Charleston Avenue, and his wife and baby, who also live at the Charleston Avenue address. He is a member of the Army Air Forces.

Corporal Shirley E. Lively, son of Mrs. Lydia M. Lively of Kitts Hill, O., has received the Purple Heart for wounds received in action last January 26 against the Japs at Cauringan, Luzon. Corporal Lively is a member of the Sixth Infantry Division and has been in other battles before being wounded.

Sergeant Vernon L. Cremeans, son of Mr. and Mrs. Ernest A. Cremeans, 4438 Siders Avenue, is serving with the 1002nd Engineer Forestry Battalion in the Philippines. Before entering the Army in March, 1943, Sergeant Cremeans worked with his father in refrigeration repairs here. He has been overseas since October, 1943.

Corporal Clarence Howell Jr., son of Mr. and Mrs. Clarence Howell of Milton, has been serving in the Philippines with the aviation engineers. He is assigned to headquarters as an administrative clerk. He graduated from Milton High School and worked for the Blenko Glass Co. before entering the service.

First Lieutenant Charles H. McCulloch, 108 Oney Avenue, has been assigned to duties in the Truax Field, Wis. operations office. He was formerly stationed with the AAF Training Command Field at Sioux Falls, S.D.

Bill A. McMillen, 21, seaman second class, 629 Sixth Avenue, husband of the former Miss Amelia F. Hunt of Hampton, Va., has completed training at the torpedo boat repair training unit at Melville, R.I., and will join a torpedo boat tender.

Seaman First Class E. Wright, 35, USNR, of Route 2, Huntington, is serving aboard the USS *Bennett*, a destroyer in the Pacific theatre, and recently took part in the battle for Iwo Jima.

Captain Lucian Harrison, who served for several months in the Southwest Pacific with the Army engineers, has gone to Morgantown, W.Va. after spending part of a convalescent leave with an uncle, C. O. Harrison, 2802 Third Avenue.

Staff Sergeant James F. Wilks, husband of Mrs. Faye Wilks, 1451 Third Avenue, has been awarded the Presidential Unit Citation ribbon for outstanding service as a member of the 36th Armored Infantry Regiment in Germany.

Seaman First Class William M. Tawney of Huntington is now serving aboard a destroyer escort of the Atlantic Fleet after duty in the amphibious forces. He participated in the Anzio landing in Italy and the invasion of Southern France.

Sergeant First Class Clarence Webb, on furlough from Morrison Field at West Palm Beach, Fla., is visiting his wife, Mrs. Dorothy Webb of Huntington.

Sergeant Clarence Elsey, son of Captain and Mrs. Phil C. Elsey, 501 Ninth Avenue, has been transferred from Indiantown Gap, Pa. to Camp Beale, Calif.

Private Earl D. Henry, son of Mr. and Mrs. William Henry, 430 Twenty-second Street, has been promoted to private first class in the 774th Railway Grand Division, a unit of Allied Force Headquarters in the Mediterranean theatre, where he is serving as a general clerk. He has been overseas for 25 months and wears the Mediterranean ribbon with one battle star.

Serving as an assistant crew chief at a Fifth Air Force base in the Philippines is Sergeant Raymond B. Moser, son of Mr. and Mrs. William Moser, 624 Sixth Street. His Liberator bomber recently made its 100th mission, with a Japanese air force base on Formosa as the target.

Glenna: *June 13th Wednesday – Clear-hot. I finished painting the floor.*

Rupert: *I went to the Bible school again.*

Transportation Director J. Monroe Johnson announced that, due to battle-bound troops from Europe moving to western embarkation points, "Fifty per cent less Pullman space and 10 to 12 per cent fewer railroad coaches would be available for civilian travel in August and thereafter, ... but if necessary, we'll ration."[290]

"IN THE SERVICE":

Huntington sailors receiving their naval basic training at the Great Lakes Training Center are: Paul E. Ramsey, 23, husband of Charlene Ramsey, 2404 Jefferson Avenue; Robert A. Shy, 30, husband of Avanel M. Shy; Luther R. Brown, 28, husband of Louise Brown, 1530 Fourth Avenue; Jeanne M. Bond, 25, husband of Ruth N. Bond, 1621 Jefferson Avenue;

and Clarence D. Floyd, 24, husband of Birdie F. Floyd of Huntington Route 1.

Private First Class James M. Donohoe Jr., son of Mr. and Mrs. J. M. Donohoe, 1428 Seventh Avenue, who was recently liberated from a German prison camp, is back in France awaiting passage home...

Private First Class Stanley D. Kitchen, son of Mr. and Mrs. Wilford Kitchen, 2426 First Avenue, a former member of the Seventh Army who was captured by the Germans and later liberated, is home for a 60-day furlough. He will report to a redistribution center in Florida for reassignment.

Corporal John Ross, husband of Mrs. Lucille Ross of Milton, is spending a furlough with his wife after serving 27 months in Alaska with the 714th Railway Operating Battalion.

Lieutenant Commander Charles R. (Buzz) Gebhardt, 31, son of Mr. and Mrs. Grover C. Gebhardt, formerly of Huntington and now of Beckley, W.Va., is mentioned in the article "Twenty Thousand Headaches Under the Sea." by Pete Martin in the June 16 edition of the *Saturday Evening Post*. The article exploits some of the hair-raising adventures aboard an American submarine in the Pacific war. Commander Gebhardt, the nephew of Mr. and Mrs. E. S. Gebhardt, 2227 Ninth Avenue, attended Marshall College for two years and is a graduate of the Naval Academy at Annapolis.

Technical Sergeant Herman D. Doss, son of Mrs. G. B. Doss, 215 Richmond Street, has returned to the United States after serving for 31 months in the Pacific with a heavy bombardment group of the Air Forces. He entered the Army in October, 1940 and is married to Mrs. Nettie L. Doss of Oklahoma City, Okla. He wears the Good Conduct Medal and three battle stars on his campaign ribbon.

Technician Fifth Grade Edward Koehler, son of Mrs. Inez Koehler, 13 Northcott Court, and husband of Mrs. Sadie Koehler, 1750 Eleventh Avenue, and Private Roy Fisher of Liberty, W.Va., have traveled over 6,000 miles in two years with an airfield-building aviation engineer battalion in the Mediterranean theatre. They are now at an AAF Engineer Command base in Italy.

Marvin Rice, 21, son of Mr. and Mrs. Oscar Rice of Louisa, Ky., a co-pilot on a Liberator bomber, has been promoted ... to first lieutenant at a 15th AAF base in Italy. He entered the AAF in January, 1943 and arrived in the Mediterranean theatre last November.

Private First Class John P. Ratcliff, son of Mr. and Mrs. John A. Ratcliff of Stonecoal, W.Va., an armorer, is preparing for combat duty aboard a B-29 Superfortress at Pratt, Kas. Army Air Field. Private Ratcliff was a student at Kermit High School before entering the service.

Technical Sergeant Don E. Craig, husband of Mrs. Kathleen Craig of Huntington, has arrived at his new base in the Philippines. He served for three years with an AAF repair squadron in Australia before returning home for a furlough and reassignment.

First Lieutenant Jack L. Hagan, son of Mr. and Mrs. C. H. Hagan, 1626 Sixth Avenue, a co-pilot of a B-24 Bomber, has returned home for a 30-day leave after eight months in the European theatre. He wears the Air Medal. His brother, Charles H. Hagan Jr., USNR, will graduate from the Medical College of Virginia this week.

Glenna: *June 14th Thursday – Finished partnighting [?] the chairs. Mended and made muffins. At night an awful storm of wind and lightening.*

Rupert: *I am still going to the Bible school.*

Los Angeles, June 13: "Shirley Temple passed another milestone in her fabulous career today—she graduated from high school... Among the congratulators was Shirley's boss, Producer David O. Selznick, who said he thought he could fix it so she could go to college. Shirley's fiancé, Sgt. John George Agar, was unable to attend the graduation. Shirley was 16 in April."[291]

San Francisco, June 13: "The longest and perhaps bitterest battle of the United Nations Conference ended today in defeat for small powers and the sealing of Big Five veto control over peace-enforcement mechanism of a new world league." The smaller countries wanted to prevent Britain, Russia, China, France and the United States from having veto power over peaceful settlement of disputes.[292]

Former Nazi foreign minister Joachim von Ribbentrop was arrested in Hamburg.[293]

"IN THE SERVICE":

Technical Sergeant Howard E. Martin, son of Mrs. Nellie Astes of Milton, has been awarded the Bronze Medal by Major General C. E. Hurdis, commander of the Sixth Infantry Division, for heroism in action against the Japs on Luzon last March 15.

Seaman Second Class Fern B. Koontz, daughter of Mrs. Mabel M. Black, 4619 Bradley Road, has reported for duty with the Navy Department in Washington.

A veteran of many early naval engagements in the Pacific, James E. Heenan, 21, radioman third class, 340 West Sixth Avenue, has been transferred to an aircraft carrier in the Pacific. His mother, Mrs. Ruth T. Stuff, lives in Williamson, W.Va.

Walter W. Chapman, 28, fireman second class, formerly of Huntington and now of Sanford, Fla., who served in the engineering division of an Atlantic Fleet destroyer, has been transferred to Norfolk, Va. for further training.

First Lieutenant Robert A. Kopp, son of Mr. and Mrs. A. A. Kopp, 452 Ninth Avenue, is spending a short leave here with his parents and wife, Mrs. Florine Kopp. Lieutenant Kopp, a graduate of West Virginia University, has been in the Army for more than four years and is now stationed at the Military Police School at Fort Sam Houston, San Antonio, Texas.

Private First Class Herman L. Adkins, 1900 Sixteenth Street, supervises 15 civilians in fly and insect work in connection with the sanitation section of the Manila city health department.

Technician Fifth Grade John Queen, son of Mrs. Hillie Perchu, 313 ½ Third Avenue, has arrived at the Ashburn General Hospital at McKinney, Tex. after serving as an infantryman in Europe. He has been awarded the Purple Heart.

The Combat Infantryman Badge has been given to Private First Class Kenneth H. Smith, husband of Mrs. Dorothy Smith, 1315 Jefferson Avenue, now serving with the 151st Infantry of the 38th Division on Luzon.

Private Steve C. Stapleton of Proctorville, O. has been awarded the Purple Heart for wounds received in action in Italy last April 30, according to his wife who resides in Proctorville with their two children.

Staff Sergeant Donald N. Weiseman, son of Mrs. Frederica Weiseman, 1223 Tenth Avenue, a member of the 17th Airborne Division of the Ninth Army, was present at the capture of Franz von Papen, Nazi diplomat, and four other high ranking officers of the defunct Third Reich.

Seaman Second Class Phillip J. Lester, son of Mr. and Mrs. Max E. Lester, 604 Fifth Avenue, is spending a 12-day furlough here from his Naval Construction Battalion at Camp Endicott, R.I.

The Bronze Star for heroic achievement in action against the Germans has been awarded to Technician Fourth Grade Norman P. Bromley, son of the Rev. Norman P. Bromley, pastor of the First Congregational Church, and Mrs. Bromley. Technician Bromley wears the Purple Heart and two battle stars on his European theatre ribbon and is a member of the Seventh Army.

Glenna: *June 15th Friday – Finished Church Vacation School. Had a picnic. Rained at 2 o'clock.*

Rupert: *The bible school is over today. We had a picnic.*

"IN THE SERVICE":

Wallace Reynolds, 19, son of Mr. and Mrs. Marshall Reynolds, 1614 Thirteenth Avenue, recently received his Navy aircrewman wings upon successful completion of flight combat training at the Naval Air Station at Fort Lauderdale, Fla. He is a graduate of Barboursville High School and his wife, Betty Jo Reynolds and their child live at Salt Rock.

Corporal Cumberland Clark, 3710 Brandon Road, is a member of a Signal Company of the Seventh Army's Twelfth Armored Division which made a historic dash to the Rhine rolling through the German Army in the final days of the war.

Seaman First Class John C. Allen has arrived at his base in the Philippines and his brother, James E. Allen, machinist's mate second class, has arrived at San Francisco after serving for two years in the Pacific. They are the sons of Mrs. Edley H. Allen of Barboursville. [When I was at Barboursville High School, the football exploits of the Allen brothers were still discussed.]

First Lieutenant Henry C. Pearman, AAF, son of Mr. and Mrs. Hale Pearman, 2852 North Staunton Road, has been spending a leave here from Biggs Field, Tex. where he is a bombardier instructor, The officer and his wife, Mrs. Dorothy Pearman, will return today to Texas.

James H. Farrell Jr., 26, husband of the former Miss Betty A. Blair, 4802 Auburn Road, has been advanced to the rating of specialist artificer first class at the U.S. Naval Air Station, Quonset Point, R.I. He is a former employee of the Chesapeake & Ohio Railroad Co. here and attended Marshall College.

Lieutenant William C. Bockway, 30, of Charleston has reported to the Naval Training Station at Newport, R.I. The son of Mrs. Frank Bockway, 101 Twelfth Avenue, he is a veteran of 20 months in the South Pacific. His wife, Mrs. Mildred Bockway and child live at Beckley, W.Va.

Coxswain Frederick Adkins, 32, son of Mr. and Mrs. W. F. Adkins of Branchland and brother of Mrs. Princess Clagg and Rose M. Adkins, 603 ½ Washington Avenue, is home on a 30-day leave after 14 months on duty in the Bermuda Islands.

Billy L. Stidd, husband of Mrs. Imogene Stidd, 529 Roby Road, was recently promoted to the grade of corporal at an AAF ordnance depot in Italy. He wears the Good Conduct Medal and two battle stars on his campaign ribbon.

Private First Class Harry K. Roberts, son of Mrs. Helen Carroll, 2025 Seventh Avenue, and husband of Mrs. Gertrude Roberts of Twenty-fifth Street, is recovering at a hospital in the Mariana Islands from burns received in action on Okinawa.

Glenna: *June 16th Saturday – Patched paper. Rupert went to town and stayed until Monday. Clear day until night. Big storm.*

Rupert: *Me and Cline are whitwashing today. In the evening I went home with my grandpa and grandma.*

General Montgomery's Headquarters, Germany, June 15: German Foreign minister Joachim von Ribbentrop, "who knew thousands of Nazi secrets," was questioned by Allied military experts... "The once-dapper foreign minister, generally credited with having 'sold' Hitler on the idea that he could invade Poland without interference from Britain, was identified to British authorities by his sister, Frau Doctor Marie Jenke, also taken into custody..."[294]

Glenna: *June 17th Sunday – Stayed at home and rested all day. That night went to church. Bro. Sullivan preached. A big storm came.*

Rupert: *I went to the movies today and saw Red Ryder and Little Beaver.*

New Orleans, June 16: A move was underway to allow returning veterans "the right to compete in intercollegiate athletics at the institution of his choice rather than restrict him to play for the school he previously attended." Rufus C. Harris, president of Tulane University, summed up the thinking: "Many veterans have acquired new outlooks which will cause them to desire to change their pre-war plans for their life work..."[295]

It's interesting to hear the thinking of members of Hitler's inner circle as to why they were defeated. In this AP article from the Twelfth Army Group Headquarters, Germany on June 16, Reichsmarshal Hermann Goering gave these factors as leading to Germany's defeat: "Hitler's ignorance of the uses of airpower; the unreliability of the Italians in the Mediterranean; the destructive force of U.S. long-range heavy bombers, and the overall supremacy in European waters of the British home fleet..." Goering said he had urged Hitler to take Gibraltar [the failure to do so is considered a fatal mistake by the Allies.], "but Hitler could not see it and went into Russia instead."[296] The view of Field Marshal Ernst Busch was that Germany's greatest weakness was that "we were too thinly spread in manpower and equipment on the Russian front where our men were terribly slaughtered."[297]

In the Pacific, U.S. troops attacked the last stronghold on Okinawa.[298]

"WITH THE COLORS":

Private First Class Howard R. Thompson, son of Mrs. Minnie McNeely, is with the 25th Armed Engineers Battalion of the Ninth Army somewhere in Germany. Enlisting in August, 1940, he now holds the Good Conduct Medal, the Pre-Pearl Harbor medal and the Purple Heart.

Private Mary Elizabeth Mooney, daughter of Mr. and Mrs. Joseph A. Mooney of 331 South Boulevard, is spending a 15-day furlough with her parents. She is stationed at Boca Raton Field in Fla.

Private (First Class) Richard G. Backus, son of Mr. and Mrs. W. M. Backus of 810 Sixth Street, is home on a 60-day furlough. Just released from a German prison camp, Private Backus arrived in Boston last Sunday. He served with the 102nd Division of the Ninth Army.

Private (First Class) Donald (Jack) Adkins of 2536 Sixteenth Street, arrived home June 14 after serving overseas 20 months with the 88th Division as scout patrol in Italy and being interred since Sept. 21, 1944 in a German prison camp. Private Adkins, the son of Mrs. Addie Shy of Pine Bluff, Ark., will report to Miami, Fla., after a 65-day furlough.

Aviation Machinist's Mate (Third Class) William Howard Smith, 1824 Midway Avenue, and Fire Controlman (Third Class) Robert Downey, 526 West Tenth Avenue, are serving aboard an aircraft [carrier?] in the Pacific ... following a period of rest at one of the Navy's "recreation islands."

Gunner's Mate (Second Class) George Francis Butts, 940 Eleventh Avenue, has been granted a leave from Newport, R.I., where he is stationed with the Atlantic Fleet's Anti-Aircraft Training Center at Price's Neck. His wife is the former Miss Elaine Bennett of Jermyn, Pa.

Chief Petty Officer Charles W. Hutchinson, son of Mr. and Mrs. C. W. Hutchinson, 538 Adams Avenue, has been promoted to ...

quartermaster (first class) in the Pacific, where he is serving aboard an ammunition cargo ship. He has been on sea duty for the past three years and was transferred last November from the Atlantic to the Pacific.

Petty Officer (Third Class) Cecil Paul Varney is spending a leave with his wife, Mrs. Joanne Varney of 1121 Fifth Avenue. He is stationed at Quonset Point, R.I. as a gunnery instructor.

Aviation Machinist's Mate (Second Class) J. Fred Rardin, son of Mr. and Mrs. F. M. Rardin of 3575 Sixteenth Street, has returned from 20 months of active service in the Pacific theatre and is now stationed at Beeville, Tex. He recently spent a 21-day furlough in Huntington.

Wearing the Purple Heart for wounds received on Iwo Jima, Petty Officer (Third Class) Hilbert A. Moore of Culloden, has arrived home after several months service in the Pacific theatre where he participated in five major battles. Saipan and Okinawa campaigns were those in which Petty Officer Moore saw combat action.

Glenna: *June 18th Monday – I washed. Rained all day. At night Milo and Maxine came.*

Rupert: *I came home today. I read all evening.*

Local well-known businesses were in the news: The Huntington Land Company was purchasing the Emmons Apartments at the Southeast corner of Third Avenue and Twelfth Street, conveyed by Arthur S. Emmons and Margarita Emmons, his wife. Mr. Emmons had inherited the apartment building from his uncle, Arthur S. Emmons, who built them. The Emmons building was erected in 1911 and the Emmons Jr. in 1925. Jointly they contained ninety-four apartments. B. L. Wilson, B. C. McGinnis, and C. C. McGinnis owned the Huntington Land Company.[299]

At the San Francisco United Nations Conference, Secretary of State Stettinius strived for completion of the charter by Saturday when President Truman was scheduled to address a final session.[300]

"IN THE SERVICE":

Aviation Radioman First Class William H. Hensley, 1719 Poplar Street, Kenova, and Radioman Second Class Lan J. Kirk, 2144 Third Avenue, have returned to this country after a tour of combat duty in the Pacific with one of the Navy's land-based search plane squadrons. They participated in strikes on the Marianas, Bonins, Volcano Islands, Carolines and Palau, and saw action over the Philippines, Formosa and the Japanese-held China coast. Their plane is credited with sinking 13 enemy schooners and junks. Radioman Hensley is the son of Mrs. Ezra Ellis of the Poplar Street address, and Radioman Kirk is the son of Mr. and Mrs. Chester Kirk of the Third Avenue address.

Machinist's Mate First Class Vernon S. Hatcher, son of E. G. Hatcher, 2902 Merrill Avenue, has begun his sixth year of naval service aboard a ship of the Atlantic Fleet. He was on a light cruiser for 22 months and aboard a light escort vessel for 33 months in European waters.

Private Thelma G. Irvin, WAC, of Pt. Pleasant, has been assigned to the Army Air Field at Great Falls, Mont. after receiving her certificate as a medical technician at the station hospital at camp Hood, Tex. Her husband, Corporal John R. Irvin, is with an antiaircraft unit in the Philippines. — Private Jo Anna Holderby, WAC, of Huntington, also has received her certificate as a medical technician at Camp Hood and has been assigned to the Orlando, Fla., Army Air Base.

Miss Ida Jo Mullins and Mrs. John E. Bissnette, doing war work as employees of Sylvania Electric Products, Inc., have five brothers in the Armed forces, They are,

Lieutenant John Mullins Jr. and his twin, Private James Mullins, in Germany; Corporal Charles Mullins, in Germany; Corporal Clyde L. Mullins, on Luzon, and Private Sam Mullins, Fort Knox, Ky. Their parents are Mr. and Mrs. John Mullins Sr. of Pikeville, Ky. [How unusual is it to name one twin Jr.?]

Seaman First Class Clarence A. Estep, son of Mrs. Jennie E. Estep of Main Street, Catlettsburg, is serving aboard a Coast Guard-manned troop transport in the Atlantic. He formerly was a meat cutter in an Ashland A&P store. His wife, Mrs. Billie Estep, resides in Bayonne, N.J.

Radioman First Class Dennis Coleman of Empire, Ore., son of Mr. and Mrs. Marion Jones, 1844 Charleston Avenue, is at the Naval Training Station at Norfolk, Va. for training for duty aboard a new destroyer of the Atlantic Fleet. He has served in both the Atlantic and Pacific theatres.

Fireman First Class Clayton C. Browning, son of Mr. and Mrs. George Browning, 702 Sixth Avenue, and Fireman First Class Karl L. Stewart, son of Mr. and Mrs. Charles Stewart, 1846 Sixth Avenue, are serving aboard the Aircraft carrier USS *Hancock* which on February 15 set a record of 71 Japanese planes downed, 19 probably downed and eight destroyed and 12 damaged on the ground during a strike in the Tokyo area, The carrier also participated in the preliminary bombardment of Okinawa, sinking 10 ships and destroying 22 Jap aircraft, and industrial and chemical plants.

Glenna: *June 19th Tuesday − I ironed, mended, and [did] several kinds of work. Pretty clear day.*

Rupert: *Marrion broke up the Twin Blackies. But I've not give up yet.*

A "falling out" with Marion was not an unusual event. As usual, we soon made up.

Washington, June 18: "Dwight David Eisenhower came home in triumph today and captured the hearts of wildly cheering Americans who like their heroes mighty but plain. It was the first time the five-star had set foot on American soil since he led the Allies to victory over the European Axis..."[301]

This is an interesting story that will no doubt be told down through the families for a long time: "A former Barboursville school teacher who fought across Europe with General George Patton's Third Army has kept his promise to his mother—to liberate a brother whose flying Fortress was shot down during the first great raid on Schweinfurt, Germany on October 14, 1943. When he left for the Army in 1944, Lieutenant Ross W. Smith told his mother, 'I will open Ken's gate.' He referred to the gate on the prison camp where his brother, Staff Sergeant Kendall W. Smith, a ball turret gunner, was held. Lieutenant Smith fought with a combat engineer unit, was wounded twice and won the Bronze Star Medal and a battle-field commission. Shortly before V-E Day, the Russians overran Stalag 17-B and it appeared the lieutenant would not be his brother's liberator after all. On May 2, however, Third Army troops entered Branau, Austria, Hitler's birth-place, and in a woods nearby Lieutenant Smith and others found 4,100 American airmen who had been moved from Stalag 17-B by the Germans in the path of the Russian advance. Sergeant Smith was among them. Later the sergeant wrote his mother, Mrs. Albert Smith of Roseville, O.: 'When I saw him (Lieutenant Smith), I can sincerely say it was the nearest to paralysis I have ever encountered. It isn't often one can be liberated by his own brother. I guess we are both so excited we can't realize it yet.' The liberation marked the brothers' first meeting since they said, 'So Long,' at Camp Forrest, Tenn. in 1942."[302]

"IN THE SERVICE":

Melvin J. Johnson, seaman first class, son of Mrs. Ella Johnson, 1405 Seventh Avenue, recently graduated from the aviation ordnance school at the Navy Technical Training Center at Norman, Okla.

Private Franklin H. Spears, son of Oscar Franklin, 3016 Sixth Avenue, has been assigned to the 32nd Infantry Division now on Luzon. Private Spears is the husband of Mrs. Odna M. Spears of Norfolk, Va.

Watertender Third Class Vincent M. Davis, a former employee of the Chesapeake and Ohio Railway Co. here, is on duty with the Hawaiian Sea Frontier, a unit of the Fleet.

A marine identified as Private First Class Gilbert E. Bailey of Huntington was pictured on page one of a recent edition of the *New York Herald-Tribune*. He was shown attempting to free a mud-mired vehicle on Okinawa.

Staff Sergeant Roy E. Berry and Seaman First Class Charles Berry, sons of Mrs. Bessie Berry of Huntington, recently met in the Netherlands East Indies for the first time in three years. Sergeant Berry has been in the Army for three years and had spent 30 months overseas. Seaman Berry has been in the service for 16 months, many of them spent overseas. His wife, Mrs. Willa Berry, and daughter, reside at 238 Twenty-sixth Street. Another brother, Seaman First Class James H. Berry [see below], has served in the Pacific.

Seaman James H. Berry, who is home on leave from Okinawa Island waters, was honored recently with a dinner given by Mr. and Mrs. W. J. Ross of Barboursville. He has been in the Navy for 23 months, and during 11 months of Pacific service participated in the invasion of Palau, Leyte, Mindoro, Luzon and Okinawa.

Private First Class Lester Swann, son of Mrs. Eustace Swann, 1934 Twelfth Avenue, is a member of the 38th Division of the Sixth Army on Luzon where he is engaged in the hazardous task of carrying supplies through the mountains.

Lieutenant James L. Foster, son of Mrs. C. D. Foster, 643 Tenth Avenue, is serving at the Naval Air Station at Kaneohe, Hawaii, in a carrier aircraft unit. He was formerly stationed on Midway.

Private First Class Donald L. Pelfrey, son of Mr. and Mrs. Basil Pelfrey of Route 4 Huntington, has been given the Combat Infantryman Badge after seeing action with the 32nd Infantry Division on Luzon. Private Pelfrey, who also wears the Philippines Liberation ribbon, went overseas last February.

Glenna: *June 20th Wednesday – Pretty day. Canned peaches. Milo and Maxine began fixing the little rooms up to live in.*

Rupert: *My aunt and uncle moved into a little house behind ours today.*

The "little house" was a two-room building with a covered front porch. The building was so close behind the main house that it required only a couple of steps to go from porch to porch. One of the rooms had become a hideaway for me, and as much as I loved Milo and Maxine, I felt put-out. I'm not sure why they moved in, but it may have been because Milo was renovating their house. In any event, the arrangement lasted only a few weeks.

New York: Dwight D. Eisenhower, at the last of several dinners to honor him, said, "Peace is an absolute necessity to this world. The nations cannot stand another world catastrophe of war... We cannot be isolated from the world."[303]

"IN THE SERVICE":

Sergeant Mike Cortellesi, son of Mrs. Emma Cortellesi of War, W.Va., a veteran of 28 months overseas, has been awarded the Bronze Arrowhead Medal for the assault landings on Leyte and Luzon. Sergeant Cortellesi fought through the New Guinea and Admiralty Island campaigns and wears three battle stars on his Asiatic-Pacific ribbon. He is a member of the 592nd Engineer battalion and is now on Luzon.

First Lieutenant Betty J. Davis, ANC, daughter of Mrs. Ruth Davis of Sixth Avenue, has been promoted to that rank at a hospital in France... Lieutenant Davis wears the Purple Heart for wounds received when a hospital in which she was working was bombed last January. She has been overseas for 15 months.

Second Lieutenant Charles E. Manilla, 19, son of Mr. and Mrs. Anthony Manilla, 1704 Sixth Avenue, has been awarded the Air Medal for meritorious achievement at an air base in England. He is a graduate of St Joseph's High School and entered the service in August, 1943.

Captain Matthew Freed, husband of Mrs. Louise Freed, 2527 First Avenue, a medical officer in the 314th Medical Detachment of the 89th Infantry Division, captured a Nazi Officer who came into his tent for treatment by removing the Nazi's belt, making it necessary for the German to use his hands to hold up his pants. The medical detachment was weaponless at the time.

Curtis E. Click, electrician's mate third class of Olive Hill, Ky., is serving aboard a battleship in the Pacific which took part in the bombardment of Okinawa.

Charles E. Ray, 20, seaman first class, son of Mr. and Mrs. Baxter Ray of Salt Rock, was wounded by shrapnel during a Jap bombing in the battle for Okinawa. He is now recovering at a Navy hospital in San Diego, Calif. He is a veteran of the invasion of France and had been in the Pacific for five months.

Corporal John (Jack) Neale, son of Mr. and Mrs. Eugene L. Neale, 1306 Washington Boulevard, has been awarded the Presidential Unit Citation for extraordinary heroism in helping his outfit, the 563rd Signal Air Warning Battalion establish a forward battalion director post in the Mont St. Mihiel [Michel?] area of France last summer... On the citation was written: "Corporal Neale—For your part in making this citation possible, my heartiest thanks." The note was from Captain Thomas J. Slattery, Corporal Neale's commanding officer.

Seaman Second Class Lawrence E. Might, USNR, son of Mr. and Mrs. Clarence Might of Middleport, O., is serving aboard the USS *Nevada*, a battleship in the Pacific.

Private Wallace A. Ford, son of Mr. and Mrs. James H. Ford of Park Hills, has been discharged from the Army at Westover Field, Mass. so that he may enter the U.S. Military Academy at West Point, N.Y. Private Ford was in the Air Forces for three years and holds a congressional appointment to the academy.

Private First Class Belvin T. Hendrick, 25, son of Mr. and Mrs. W. H. Hendrick, 122 Edison Court, and Private First Class James B. Workman, 29, husband of Mrs. Thelma Workman of Fort Gay, recently arrived at LaGuardia Field, N.Y. by Air Transport Command plane from the European theatre. Private Hendrick, a military policeman has two battle stars and Private Workman, a medical corpsman, wears one battle star.

Sergeant Charles E. Ward, 4751 Bradley Road, is serving with the 12th Field Artillery, which, with four 155 MM howitzers, put 24 German 88 MM guns out of commission in a 40-minute duel, a short time before the collapse of Germany.

Private First Class Edward C. Mayo, son of Captain C. C. Mayo of the Huntington fire department and Mrs. Mayo, 1927 Jefferson Avenue, has arrived in Florida by plane from the European theatre...

Private Abe Adkins of Branchland and Private Hugh Ferrell, 8 ½ Northcott Court, are members of the 38th Infantry Division of the Second Infantry Division and have been awarded the Combat Infantryman Badge for conspicuous achievement against the enemy in Germany.

Glenna: *June 21st Thursday – Very pretty day. I waxed two rugs and worked in the garden.*

Rupert: *Milo and Maxine are getting settled down.*

The formation stage of the United Nations Charter was near completion. The charter was to "bring into being, when enough governments ratify it, an international league empowered to settle disputes peacefully or to use armed might to prevent war or aggression."[304]

U.S. troops captured the port of Aparri on the island of Luzon in the Philippines.[305]

"IN THE SERVICE":

Private First Class William G. McCaffrey, son of Mr. and Mrs. T. A. Depriest, 1850 Twelfth Avenue, has been awarded the Bronze Star Medal for meritorious service during the 95th Division's combat activities in the European theatre.

Second Lieutenant Charles M. Scott, who was a prisoner in Germany for six months, is coming home soon, he said last night in a telephone conversation with his parents, Mr. and Mrs. C. B. Scott, 257 Gallaher Street. He has arrived in Norfolk, Va., and will go to Fort Meade, Md., before coming to Huntington. Co-pilot of a B-24 bomber, Lieutenant Scott was taken prisoner after his plane was shot down over Germany. [Lieutenant Scott "was one of three crew members saved when their bomber was shot down by German fighter planes November 26. He was held near Barth, Germany, where he was a fellow prisoner of Lieutenant Robert Cavendish of Huntington... Lieutenant Scott said he lost little weight, but only because of Red Cross parcels. The Germans gave each prisoner one-seventh of a bread loaf and a bowl of watery soup each day."[306]]

Corporal Harry E. Danford Jr., son of Mr. and Mrs. Harry Danford, 923 Eleventh Avenue, is an automotive mechanic with the 3471st Ordnance Medium Maintenance Company which repaired 63 vehicles in one day shortly before V-E Day.

The Combat Infantryman Badge was awarded Technician Fifth Grade Verlin L. Boyd, son of Mrs. Bessie L. Boyd, 609 Roby Road, who fought with the Seventh Armored Division in Europe.

Technician Fifth Grade Mack D. Thompson, son of Mrs. Viola Thompson of Hamlin, is en route home after 31 months in Italy and North Africa with a unit of the AAF Engineer Command. After a furlough, he will report for reassignment.

First Lieutenant Robert R. Mahan, son of Mr. and Mrs. C. E. Mahan of Ashland, has been awarded the Oak Leaf Cluster to the Distinguished Flying Cross for extraordinary achievement with the 15th AAF in Italy. He is a bombardier on a B-17 Flying Fortress.

Roy E. Harris, 21, gunner's mate second class, son of Mr. and Mrs. Ollie Harris of Olive Hill, Ky., is serving aboard a destroyer of the Atlantic Fleet. He wears the Presidential Unit Citation and the European-African-Middle Eastern theatre ribbon with a battle star.

Navy Lieutenant Everett A. Kamp, USNR, of Pleasanton, Calif., a pilot whose wife lives in Huntington, was shot down during the battle of Okinawa by flak and was rescued from the ocean by an old school chum, whom he hadn't seen for seven years.

Seaman First Class Burton H. Mott Jr., son of Mr. and Mrs. B. A. Mott, 820 Thirteenth Avenue, is home on leave after a 10-month tour of duty with a Navy blimp squadron in South America.

Private First Class Donald A. Baker, husband of Mrs. Helen Baker of Midkiff, W.Va., has been awarded the third Oak Leaf Cluster to the Purple Heart at an Army hospital in Paris. He received the first wound on Bataan early in the war by a Jap bayonet. He was discharged from the Army in April, 1942, but was recalled the following December and sent to Europe. He landed in France on D-Day with the 29th Division and fought in every major battle afterward. A brother, Sergeant Ralph Baker, is with the Seventh Army in Germany and another one, Seaman First Class Duffy Baker, is with the Seabees in the Pacific.

Stephen D. Pauley of Park Hills was recently commissioned a second lieutenant in the Army after completing an eight weeks course at an infantry Officer Candidate School in the European theatre. Lieutenant Pauley was one of the outstanding enlisted men chosen for the intensive infantry training school.

Major Samuel G. Kail, husband of Mrs. Mary M. D. Kail of Dallas, Texas, and son of Dr. I. J. Kail, 522 Tenth Street, was recently appointed assistant to the assistant chief of staff, G-3 division air ground liaison officer of the 13th Airborne Division in France.

Louis W. Workman, 27, seaman second class of Russell, Ky., is completing his first year with the Navy and has already participated in four major engagements in the Pacific, including the Iwo Jima and Philippine campaigns.

First Lieutenant Charles L. Quitmeyer, 1040 ½ Sixth Avenue, Corporal Brady D. Burger, Branchland, and Sergeant Phillip M. Easley of

Peach Creek, are members of the 569th Field Artillery Battalion of the 15th Army, one of the American armies occupying defeated Germany.

First Lieutenant Carl M. Persinger, son of Mr. and Mrs. J. E. Persinger, 403 Ninth Avenue, was recently assigned to Operations Division of Camp Stoneman, Calif. His wife, Mrs. Avanelle Persinger, and daughter, reside at 1040 Madison Avenue.

First Lieutenant Carl B. Ballengee, 1919 Twelfth Avenue, is a veteran of the 30th Infantry Division which fought across Europe after D-Day last year, compiling an impressive number of victories.

Staff Sergeant Johnny U. Johnson, 219 West Second Street, is with the 381st Engineer Construction Battalion of the 15th Army which ... has been busy rebuilding the damaged roads and bridges along the Army supply routes in the Reich.

Private Nolice W. Bowen Jr., husband of Mrs. Thelma Bowen of Huntington Route 1, has been awarded the Purple Heart for wounds received during the Battle of Germany. He is a clerk in the provost marshal's office of the 15th Army.

Lieutenant Cary M. Smarr of Monel Park is a Second Battalion motor officer with the 309th Infantry of the 79th Division...

Second Lieutenant William H. Butcher of West Hamlin has been ordered to active duty by the War Department...

Corporal George J. Selvey Jr., son of Mr. and Mrs. G. J. Selvey, 821 Eleventh Avenue, is serving with the 12th AAF and has seen action in Africa, Italy and France.

John F. Fain, son of Mrs. Maude Fain, 1706 Williams Avenue, has been promoted to technician fifth grade with the 15th Air Force Service Command in Italy.

Staff Sergeant Charles Hardy, 23, 319 Adams Avenue, has been awarded the Air Medal for meritorious achievement as a waist gunner with the 15th AAF in Italy.

Glenna: *June 22nd Friday – I mowed the graveyard. Very hot all day.*

Rupert: I *worked in corn today. it was very hot.*

Paris, June 21: "The Germans guessed the place, strength and approximate time of the Allied invasion of Normandy, but were fooled in their expectation that a second stronger thrust would come farther north." That information was disclosed through questioning of Colonel General Gustav Jodi of the Nazi high command by a Supreme Headquarters intelligence officer. Jodi also said that the Allied invasion of North Africa was a complete surprise.[307]

Okinawa was finally secure.[308] It was the costliest Allied operation of the war. 12,281 American and 110,000 Japanese soldiers died.[309]

"IN THE SERVICE":

Arvel A. Mullins, 33, gunner's mate third class, son of Mrs. Alice Yeager of Branchland, was recently commended by his commanding officer for his part in recent naval action. He is aboard a destroyer in the Pacific and was employed by Commercial Motor freight here before entering the Navy in February, 1943.

Second Lieutenant James E. Conley of Louisa, Ky. has been awarded the Air Medal at a 12th AAF station in Italy for his work in the bombing of the Brenner Pass rail line last March. Lieutenant Conley is a bombardier on a B025 bomber.

Private First Class Edward E. Morrison, son of Mr. and Mrs. C. S. Morrison of Myra and husband of Mrs. Christine Morrison of West Hamlin, has returned to the states after 12 months in the European theatre where he served as a gunner in ground forces. He wears three battle stars on his ribbon.

Staff Sergeant Robert W. White of Huntington is with the 569th Signal Company of the 69th Division of the First Army which held off an entire German garrison for an hour and a half when they entered the city of Weissenfels to establish Signal Corps communications. They were finally aided by the arrival of an infantry company which cleared the town.

Corporal June D. Dilley, 2626 Third Avenue, has been given a certificate of Merit by his commanding officer for meritorious and outstanding performance of duty as a member of the signal section of a large port headquarters. He is now stationed in France after 15 months duty in England after going overseas in December, 1943.

Technician Fourth Grade Robert R. Ferris, 3329 Willard Court, is one of the specialists with the Services of Supply of the Army in China. This unit repairs and replaces equipment worn out along China's highways.

Frank W. Roberts, coxswain, son of Mrs. Gertrud Roberts of Olive Hill, Ky., is stationed at a naval base in the Mariana Islands where planes are groomed to deliver knockout blows against Japan.

Edgar May, gunners mate third class, son of Mr. and Mrs. Waldeck May of Route 1, Huntington, is at the Naval Armed Guard Center, Treasure Island, Calif. awaiting assignment to a gun crew board a merchant ship.

Private First Class Sylvin S. Fuller of Long Branch, and Technical Sergeant Walter G. Francis Jr., son of W. G. Francis Sr. of Logan have been freed from German prison camps.

Technical Corporal Tommie Webb, son of Mrs. Mattie Webb of Williamson, is a member of the 21st Engineer Aviation Regiment which has built many air fields in Europe. He has been overseas for more than two and a half years and served in Africa and Italy, and has three battle stars on his campaign ribbon.

Sergeant Jack McClure, who served with the Army in Panama for 18 months, is spending a furlough with his parents, Mr. and Mrs. D. C. McClure, 216 Nineteenth Street. From here he will go to Fort Benning, Ga. to enter officer candidate school.

Private First Class Carl Adkins, son of Mr. and Mrs. J. W. Adkins of Huntington, has been assigned to Casablanca with the Air Transport Command's North African Division.

Glenna: *June 23rd Saturday — Very hot and sunny. Mamma and Papa came up. I didn't work much. Went and took flowers to Rupert's grave.*

Rupert: *I worked in corn again today.*

London, Saturday, June 23: Moscow radio announced that agreement had been reached by Polish groups meeting in Moscow on the formation of a Polish government.[310]

"IN THE SERVICE":

The following three entries should be read as a group:

Fireman First Class Jacob Rone Jr., 26-year-old son of Mr. and Mrs. Jacob Rone, 1673 Fourteenth Avenue, helped rescue some of the men trapped when the aircraft carrier USS *Franklin* was severely damaged by a Japanese bomber last March, his mother reported yesterday. He wrote her that his destroyer had served in the escort for the carrier during a strike on Japan and when the *Franklin* was hit he and others went aboard the big vessel to help bring to safety men trapped below deck.

Serving on the same destroyer which has fought the Japs over 200,000 miles of the Pacific, is Gunner's Mate Marion C. Sweney, 28, son of Mr. and Mrs. A. Ross Sweney, 309 West Ninth Avenue. The vessel has been in action from Wake Island to Okinawa. She shot down three enemy planes off Bougainville, and during assaults on Saipan, Tinian and Guam she accounted for two twin-engine Jap bombers.

A third Huntington aboard the destroyer is Seaman Second Class Hugh J. Evans, 25, 159 Cedar Street, son of Mrs. Kathryn Drown Evans and nephew of Mrs. J. T. Roach, 649 South Terrace. All three men were employed by the International Nickel Co. before entering the service. They have been in the far Pacific since last February.

Sergeant Wilford Hamm, son of C. E. Hamm, 321 Thirteenth Street, served with the Third Army in France and Germany and received the Bronze Star Medal for gallantry in action. He has been overseas for about six months with the 70th Infantry Division.

First Lieutenant George Dugan, husband of Mrs. Betty Dugan, 1026 Eleventh Street, has been awarded the Combat Infantryman Badge for exemplary performance against the Japs on Luzon. He has been in the Army since 1941 and has served in New Guinea, Morotai Island, and in the Netherlands East Indies. Lieutenant Dugan is with the 136th Infantry of the 33rd Division.

Private First Class James J. Adkins, son of Mr. and Mrs. A. F. Adkins of Wayne, has been promoted to corporal at the 81st Air service Squadron headquarters in Italy.

Private First Class George E. Mills, 913 West Twelfth Street, received the Combat Infantry Badge for outstanding performance of duty with the 103rd Infantry Division of the Seventh Army against the Germans.

Private First Class Orin E. Adkins, 1220 Enslow Avenue, is at the Halloran General Hospital in New York City recovering from wounds received in action last April in Germany. His brother, Seaman First Class Marvin Adkins, is with a Navy PT boat squadron in Miami, Fla.

First Lieutenant James G. Perry Jr., son of Mr. and Mrs. J. G. Perry of Logan, who spent two years in a Nazi prison camp, is home and is visiting his sister, Mrs. Thomas D. Wagers, 2703 Third Avenue. Lieutenant Perry was a pilot on a B-17 Flying Fortress and was shot down over Kiel, Germany on his fourth mission.

Private First Class Judge Stevens of Huntington is serving with the 99th Division of the First Army which drove across the Siegfried Line into Germany.

Boatswain Mate First Class W. E. Jones, son of Mr. and Mrs. M. P. Jones, 1844 Charleston Avenue, is spending a 30-day leave with his parents after 28 months in the South Pacific where he participated in several major engagements, including the Philippines campaign. His brother, Radioman First Class Dennis Jones is stationed at Norfolk, Va.

Corporal Tommy F. Midkiff, son of Mr. and Mrs. W. J. Midkiff, 1305 Eighth Avenue, is spending a 30-day furlough here after 15 months in England with the Eighth Air Force. He served with the 786th Bomber Squadron, the first to bomb Berlin.

Corporal Norman LeMaster, who was captured by the Germans in the second hour of the Battle of the Bulge, has returned to Huntington after spending four and a half months in German prison camps. Attached to the 99th Division of the First Army, he was liberated last April 29. While in the various camps, Corporal LeMaster met several local men by writing "Huntington, W.Va." on the back of his coat, he said. Although he described the prison treatment "fair," he stated that meeting Huntington men such as Technical Sergeant Malcolm Henshaw and Staff Sergeant William R. Lewis, was the only "bright spot" in his prison life. His parents, Mr. and Mrs. B. E. LeMaster, his wife, the former Miss Mildred Meadows and five-months-old daughter, Julia Kathryn, reside at 2558 First Avenue.

Glenna: *June 24th Sunday — Went to Church and Sunday School. Very hot.*

Rupert: *Mother and I went to Sunday school today.*

San Francisco, June 23: Fifty nations approved the United Nations charter. Formal approval was scheduled for Monday.[311]

"WITH THE COLORS":

Wounded in Germany while serving as a pathfinder with the 82nd Airborne Division, Private Gordon D. Wooten Jr., former Pony Express basketball star, is spending a 30-day furlough with his parents, Mr. and Mrs. Gordon Wooten at 1830 Wiltshire Boulevard. He will return to Lawson General Hospital, Atlanta, Ga. next month for further treatment of shrapnel wounds of the leg and hand. Private Wooten entered the Army May, 1943 and served on the cadre staff at Camp Croft, S.C., for a year before going overseas in June, 1944. He attended the University of Tennessee at Knoxville, and was a member of the varsity basketball squad following his graduation from Huntington Central High School. He was a member of the First Allied Airborne Army organized in Europe, and trained to become a paratrooper at Lester, England. His first combat jump was made last September 17th in Holland.

Private (First Class) Earl Rex Arix, veteran of 29 months overseas duty, has reported to Washington D.C. for reassignment following a 30-day furlough with his parents, Mr. and Mrs. Charles Arix of Branchland. Stationed with the Marines in the Pacific war zone, Private Arix has served in Samoa, Guadalcanal, Hawaiian Islands, Cuba, the Panama Canal Zone and the Marshall and Marianna Islands. He wears eight major battle stars representing the landing on eight beach heads. Private Arix has three brothers serving with the U.S. Army. They are Private (First Class) Paul Arix, stationed in Italy and Corporal Robert Arix and Corporal Charles Arix Jr., both stationed in the Philippine Islands.

Private (First Class) William T. Rose, son of Mr. and Mrs. C. E. Rose, 2982 Third Avenue, was injured in action on Luzon June 6, his parents have been informed. He attended Huntington Central High School.

Flight Officer Homer Duncan, son of Mr. and Mrs. C. R. Duncan, 4825 Auburn Road, arrived home for a furlough after being a prisoner-of-war for eight months in Germany. He was liberated on May 15 and will report to Fort Meade, Maryland on August 23 for reassignment.

Flight Officer Forrest B. Young, 3805 Auburn Road, a former Marshall College student, has returned from the European War theatre where he fought in England, France, Belgium and Holland. He was a prisoner-of-war in Germany for six months and holds the British Distinguished Flying Cross.

One of 17 West Virginians named on the Army's list of liberated prisoners of war in Germany was Private Gene H. Emrick, husband of Mrs. Frances P. Emrick of 537 Washington Avenue...

Fireman (Second Class) William C. Skeens Jr., son of Mr. and Mrs. Clinton Skeens of Ceredo, has arrived overseas and is serving aboard a destroyer somewhere in the Pacific.

Lieutenant (j. g.) Frank Booth Jr. has been assigned to the Naval Hospital at Jacksonville, Fla. for a year of internship following his graduation from the Medical College at Richmond. He is the son of Mr. and Mrs. Frank Booth of 522 First Street. His wife, the former Miss Edna Lynn Williams of Huntington, will join him in August.

A veteran of World Wars I and II is Corporal Arnold Christian, husband of Mrs. Lulu Dyer Christian of Clarksburg, W.Va., who was recently discharged from military service. He has been visiting relatives in Huntington. Corporal Christian served with the 59th Infantry and took part in several major battles in the First World War.

Ensign John E. Scheifly, who has been visiting his parents, Mr. and Mrs. Luke Scheifly of Enslow Boulevard ... will go to Pearl Harbor for reassignment. Ensign Scheifly has been specializing in radar.

Sergeant Richard Dial, husband of Mrs. Georgena Dial of 402 Claredon Court, who was killed in action in the European theatre, has been awarded the Purple Heart posthumously...

Mr. and Mrs. W. A. Scott of 658 Marion Court received word yesterday that their son, Private Leonard Scott, had arrived in New York on Friday after two years in the European theatre of war.

Sergeant Joe Precce, son of Mr. and Mrs. W. M. Z. Precce of 429 Brandingwood Avenue, was recently awarded the Purple Heart and promoted ... to corporal while serving with the 157th Infantry of the 7th Army in Germany, He has been in the Army 20 months and served overseas 15 months.

Private Carroll L. Howell, son of Mrs. Iris Force, 2213 Jefferson Avenue, has been graduated from the Curtiss Technical Training School at Buffalo, N.Y., and is qualified as a skilled technician on the C-46 airplane.

Mrs. Eva T. Whitehill, 5701 Ohio River Road, a member of the WAC, has been promoted from the rank of private to that of corporal... She has been stationed at Nichols General Hospital, Louisville, Ky. Her daughter, Mrs. Betty Sue Beach, has returned from the naval station of her husband, S. Conway Beach Jr., former Huntington musician who has gone overseas.

First Lieutenant George Dugan, husband of Mrs. Betty Dugan of 1026 Eleventh Street, has been awarded the Combat Infantry Badge for exemplary performance of duty in action against the Japs on northern Luzon. Previously he has been awarded the Expert Infantry Badge, given for meeting the highest standards of the American infantry. He is also authorized to wear the Good Conduct Medal, the Asiatic-Pacific Ribbon and the Philippine-Liberation Ribbon with battle stars.

Glenna: *June 25th Monday – I washed. Very hot.*

Rupert: *Its very hot today.*

Moscow, June 24: "Adolf Hitler's personal Swastika flag was dragged over the cobblestones of Red Square and hurled into a muddy gutter today after Marshall Georgi K. Zhukov, in a victory speech, said the Red Army was the most powerful in the world, but that Russia must not become 'conceited or complacent.'"[312]

Emergency aircraft landings on recently acquired Iwo Jima was reported to have already saved thousands of lives.[313]

Glenna: *June 26th Tuesday – I ironed. Very hot. Rupert went to West Hamlin that night. Maxine's brother Earl came home.*

Rupert: *I went to West Hamlin today.*

I remember that evening. Earl Lewis had been in Germany and the family sat around the dining room table, listening as he talked about his war experiences. Maxine's younger brother, Delano, was a year or two older than me.

San Francisco, June 25: Final approval was given the United Nations Charter.[314]

"IN THE SERVICE":

Private First Class Herman H. Lucas, 25, son of Mrs. Rosa Lucas of Salt Rock, has been awarded the Purple Heart for wounds received while fighting with the 147th Infantry in the Pacific. He entered the Army in September 1941, and has been in six major island engagements since May, 1942.

Technical Sergeant Robert F. Dundas, husband of Mrs. Lillian Dundas, 216 Oakland Avenue, a radio operator and gunner with the 13th AAF, has been awarded the Air Medal for meritorious achievement against the Japs in the

Philippines. He entered the Army in October, 1943 and has been overseas since last December.

John B. Preston, yeoman second class, of Louisa, Ky, has served aboard a Seventh Fleet cruiser for more than four years and has taken part in about 30 engagements with the enemy.

Tony J. Magariello, son of Mr. and Mrs. Anthony Magariello, 2808 Highlawn Court, has been promoted to sergeant with the 13th AAF in the Philippines. Sergeant Magariello, a radioman-gunner on a Mitchell bomber, has been overseas since last October and has taken part in 32 bombing missions.

Lieutenant Robert Allman, son of Mr. and Mrs. H. B. Allman of Kenova, a B-26 navigator, was awarded the Air Medal while serving with the 42nd bomb wing in France. He has been overseas for three months and completed 10 missions against the Germans. He holds the Distinguished Unit Badge.

Corporal Earl R. Vest Jr., husband of Mrs. Anna Frances Vest, 1203 Jefferson Avenue, is stationed with the Air Forces in New Guinea and is assigned to a supply section of a service group whose chief function is to keep the planes in flying condition. He was employed by the War Department before entering the service in February, 1943, and has been overseas for 31 months.

... Richard E. Neal, son of Mr. and Mrs. A. R. Neal, 1648 Doulton Avenue, is busy with a transportation section of an Eighth Air Force fighter station in England. He was a student at Central High School when he entered the Army in February, 1943.

Corporal Raymond A. Callicoat, husband of Mrs. Helen M. Callicoat, 806 Marcum Terrace. is stationed at the Second Base Air Depot, Blackpool, England, where he is helping repair thousands of flight instruments for use against the enemy in the Pacific. He joined the Army in July, 1943, and has been overseas for 21 months.

Corporal Charles L. Beckett, 1517 Seventh Avenue, glimpsed Japan of tomorrow when he recently flew in an Eighth Air Force bomber over the charred ruins of once-great German cities. Corporal Beckett has been on duty at an aerial repair depot for the past three years.

Technical Sergeant Billy J. Estep, 20, 516 Wilson Street, an engineer-gunner with the 35th Liberator Bombardment Group of the 15th AAF, will return to the United States soon...

Frank B. Gray, son of Charles S. Gray, 1937 Fourth Avenue, has been promoted ... to staff sergeant at a Ninth AAF Service Command base in Germany. He has been in the European theatre for two years.

Technical Sergeant General W. Deerfield, husband of Mrs. Louise Deerfield of Huntington, was recently assigned as chief clerk of operations and training of the redeployment section of the Far Eastern Air Forces in the Philippines. Sergeant Deerfield has four brothers in the Marine Corps, all in the South Pacific.

Private First Class Hughbert Stapleton, a former coal miner from Whitman, W.Va., was recently promoted to that rank and awarded the Combat Infantryman Badge after seeing action with the 33rd Division on Luzon... He is [now] with the 136th Infantry Division and is a veteran of several major battles, including the Morotai Island campaign.

Master Sergeant Weldon T. Allen, son of Archie Allen of McComas, W.Va. is fighting with the Red Raiders, Fifth Air Force Bomber unit in the Philippines, and recently acquired a much prized saber from a Jap captain after a patrol skirmish on the island.

Second Lieutenant James Fattaleh, 1013 Monroe Avenue, a co-pilot with the Air Transport Command, has been awarded the Distinguished Flying Cross at his base in India upon completion of 300 operational [missions]...

First Lieutenant Cara E. Crews, daughter of Dr. and Mrs. A. W. Crews, 2118 Holswade Drive, is an Army flight nurse attached to an evacuation unit headquarters at Memphis, Tenn. She is a graduate of the University of Virginia.

Major Burtis W. Anderson, son of Mr. and Mrs. W. W. Anderson, 136 Woodland Drive, is spending a week's leave here from his base at Quantico, Va. He is accompanied by his wife, the former Miss Mary Pryor of Ashland.

Sergeant Charles O. Osborne, son of Mr. and Mrs. Walker Osborne, 1616 Edgewood Drive, a veteran of 33 months with the 15th AAF in Italy, has returned to Fort Meade, Md. after completing a 45-day furlough here.

Seaman First Class Charles C. Howes of Man, W.Va., was aboard the USS *Franklin* last March 19 when she was hit by a Japanese dive bomber off the coast of Japan.

Winford R. Bazemore, son of Mr. and Mrs. Ray Bazemore of Lesage, W.Va., was recently advanced to the rank of signalman third class aboard a destroyer in the Atlantic Fleet. He enlisted in the Navy in October, 1943, and wears the European-African-Middle Eastern theatre ribbon.

After spending two years in Iceland, Private First Class Charles C. Satterfield is visiting his mother, Mrs. H. A. Satterfield, 1105 Sixth Avenue.

Staff Sergeant William V. Lemley, 24, son of Mrs. G. D. Lemley, 1103 ½ Sixteenth Street, was recently awarded the Purple Heart for wounds received on Luzon. He is now spending a 30-day furlough here after three years' service in the Pacific.

The Standings

NATIONAL LEAGUE

YESTERDAY'S RESULTS

Cincinnati at Boston, rain.
Others not scheduled.

STANDINGS

	W	L	Pct.	GB
Brooklyn	37	22	.627	---
St. Louis	33	25	.569	3½
Pittsburgh	32	27	.552	5
New York	33	28	.541	5
Chicago	29	25	.537	5½
Boston	28	28	.500	7½
Cincinnati	24	30	.444	10½
Philadelphia	16	48	.250	23½

AMERICAN LEAGUE

YESTERDAY'S RESULTS

New York 5, St. Louis 4.
Others not scheduled.

STANDINGS

	W	L	Pct.	GB
Detroit	35	22	.614	---
New York	34	23	.596	1
Boston	30	27	.526	5
Chicago	31	28	.525	5
Washington	27	28	.491	7
St. Louis	25	30	.455	9
Cleveland	23	31	.426	10½
Philadelphia	20	36	.357	14½

Rupert: *Mother went to prayer meeting. I didn't go.*

San Francisco: June 26: "President Truman left San Francisco, stopping in his native Missouri to visit family. He will hand to the Senate at Washington on Monday the finished United Nations charter..."[315]

Manila, June 27: The Australian Ninth Division forces took back the Borneo oil fields Sunday, capturing Miri, whose "300 oil wells have been blazing under the Japanese torch for the last three weeks."[316]

Three hundred seventy-three American sailors died in a kamikaze attack on the USS *Bunker Hill.*[317]

Briefs from Last Night's Associated Press Wires: Simla, India: "Indian political leaders and British Viceroy Lord Wavell reached 'certain provisional conclusions' on British proposals for extending the self-government of India ..." In Louisville, Governor Ellis Arnall of Georgia said that "economic equality for the Negro is a right which should not be denied him." A report from Bad Tolz, Germany said that a group of American and German scientists had gone to the Bavarian Mountains where they found Germany's entire radium supply, 21.8 grams valued at $2,000,000."[318]

Home is Staff Sergeant William H. Smith, 23, son of Mrs. Maxine Smith of Bridge Street.[319]

"IN THE SERVICE":

Glenna: *June 27th Wednesday – I painted some. Very hot. Went to prayer meeting that night.*

Lieutenant Colonel Earl L. Mullineaux, son of Mrs. A. A. Mullineaux, 814 Seventh Avenue, a former Huntington garage owner and truck sales agent, has returned to the United States after serving in the Pacific for 18 months with the Fifth Air Service Group.

Private Charles F. Holtash, 19, son of Dr. and Mrs. Frederick Holtash, 923 Charles Court, received the Purple Heart Medal for wounds received in action against the Japs on Okinawa last month. He is recovering in an Army hospital in the Pacific.

Curtis J. Roane, 24, boatswain's mate second class, son of Mr. and Mrs. C. J. Roane of West Hamlin, is at the Naval Training Station at Newport, R.I. preparing for duty aboard a heavy cruiser. A veteran of three invasions, he enlisted in the Navy in October, 1940, and wears a silver star and three bronze stars on his European and Mediterranean theatre ribbons.

Private Carl R. Turner, 28, husband of Mrs. Pauline H. Turner, 146 Gallaher Street, is at an Army hospital in San Francisco recovering from wounds received on Northern Luzon while fighting with the 32nd Infantry Division. He entered the Army last July and has been overseas since December.

Second Lieutenant William W. Butcher, husband of Mrs. Madalyn Butcher, 1212 Eighth Street, has been awarded the Purple Heart Medal for wounds received in combat against the Japanese in New Guinea last July. Lieutenant Butcher is recovering at Deshon General Hospital at Butler, Pa.

Private First Class George E. Faine, son of Mr. and Mrs. Harry Faine of Wheelwright, Ky., was wounded on Okinawa while fighting with the 96th Infantry Division. Private Faine entered the Army 10 months ago and went overseas last March.

Sergeant Norman P. Hazeldine, son of Mr. and Mrs. Henry Hazeldine, 657 South Terrace, a former Marshall College student, was recently promoted to that rank at Camp Gruber, Okla.

Second Lieutenant Ernest J. Baker, 25, husband of Mrs. Alice M. Baker, 424 First Street, has joined Company B of the 97th Signal Battalion in Germany as a radio-link officer. Lieutenant Baker joined the Army in September, 1940, and finished officer candidate school last October.

First Lieutenant Russell L. McCallister, husband of Mrs. Betty F. McCallister, 1714 Crestmont Drive, recently received a promotion to that rank while serving with the 180th Field Artillery of the 26th "Yankee" Division in Czechoslovakia. He went overseas last December and wears three battle stars on his campaign ribbon.

Seaman Second Class Alan B. Maxwell, son of Mr. and Mrs. Hugh L. Maxwell, 5693 Ohio River Road, is spending a seven-day leave here form the Naval Air Technical Training Center at Memphis, Tenn. He is a former student at Marshall College and worked for the *Herald-Advertiser* before entering the Navy.

Private First Class John David Lubin was wounded in action in the Philippines, according to word received yesterday by his mother, Mrs. Dora Lubin, 239 Fifth Avenue. Private Lubin, a member of the 124th Infantry Division, has been in the Army almost two years and overseas for about 15 months.

Glenna: *June 28th Thursday – The hottest day so far. I finished my painting.*

Rupert: *Mother painted the porch today.*

"IN THE SERVICE":

Captain William F. Sawyer, son of Mr. and Mrs. William Sawyer of Ashland, has been assigned to the flight section, headquarters Air Technical Service Command at Wright Field, O. Captain Sawyer entered the Army in November, 1941 as an aviation cadet and obtained his pilot wings in May, 1942. He is a veteran of 30 missions over Germany where he won the Air Medal with five Oak Leaf Clusters and four battle stars.

Second Lieutenant Joseph O. Matthews, 20, son of Mr. and Mrs. O. W. Matthews, 501 Madison Avenue, was wounded early this month while fighting with the Marines on Okinawa. Lieutenant Matthews joined the Marines while a student at Yale University and went overseas last November.

Sergeant Paul Baumgardner, son of Mr. and Mrs. J. W. Baumgardner, 743 ½ Washington Avenue, has returned home on furlough after three years in the Pacific. A veteran of the New Georgia and Bougainville campaigns, he wears the Purple Heart for a hand wound received while helping drive the Japs from Manila.

Raymond L. Hensley, 19, of Barboursville has been promoted to the rank of watertender first class aboard a destroyer of the Atlantic Fleet. He entered the Navy in July, 1942, and has served on anti-submarine duty in the Atlantic between Brazil and Africa and convoy duty to England.

Private Jack L. Pinson, son of Mr. and Mrs. Freelin Pinson, 2006 Marcum Terrace, is spending a 30-day furlough here. He is a veteran of 30 months duty in North Africa, Sicily, Italy, and France and he wears five battle stars.

The Purple Heart for wounds received against the Germans has been presented to Technician Fifth Grade Fred Clary, husband of Mrs. Addie Clary, 404 Simms Street, at Maguire General Hospital at Richmond, Va. where he is a patient. Corporal Clary was fighting with the Infantry when he was wounded in Germany last March 5.

Private First Class Allan L. Desmond, 20, and Staff Sergeant William C. Desmond, 27, sons of Mr. and Mrs. H. L. Desmond, 1534 Third Avenue, recently met in the Philippines after a two-year separation. Private Desmond is with an AAF photo technician unit and his brother is with a heavy bomber group.

The War Department announced yesterday that Lieutenant Warrington Austerman of Huntington has been ordered to active duty.

Three sons and two sons-in-law of Mr. and Mrs. Shirley Stewart, 1171 South Jefferson Avenue, are serving in the war. They are Harvey Stewart, a Merchant Marine veteran of the Pacific; Private First Class Charles Stewart, with the 38th Infantry Division in the Pacific; Private Curtis Nicely, at Fort Sill, Okla; Seaman First Class Wilton Stewart, a veteran of Pacific action, and Private First Class Gid Hampton, with the 70th Infantry Division in Germany.

Hospital Apprentice Second Class Thomas J. Conaty and Ensign Robert C. Conaty, sons of Mr. and Mrs. W. J. Conaty, 1411 Fifth Avenue, are spending leaves here with their parents. Ensign Conaty will return to San Francisco to be assigned to a ship in the Pacific Fleet, and Apprentice Conaty will return to Washington where he has been stationed for several months.

Private Nick Dalmer Jr., son of Nick Dalmer of Fourteenth Street, fought with the 126th Anti-aircraft battalion at Antwerp, Belgium, which helped to destroy 259 Nazi flying bombs. His battalion was visited at one time by the Queen of Belgium.

Private First Class Charles B. Morrison, 1045 Ninth Avenue, and Private First Class Henry F. Fields of Kimball are members of the 508th Military Police Battalion which is playing the "Watch on the Rhine" role with the 15th Occupation Army in Germany...

Private First Class Ray A. Chapman, son of Louis Chapman of Ona, has been assigned as a maintenance specialist at Camp Baltimore, France, first of the Army's redeployment camps to be set up in Northeastern France.

Glenna: *June 29th Friday – Very hot and sultry. Maclk(?) Joe died a day before.*

Rupert: *I have a pain in my side. I can't work today.*

Kansas City, June 28: President Truman demanded that the United States be the first to ratify the United Nations charter, which he said was necessary for the United States to live with the "world as a whole."[320]

"IN THE SERVICE":

Marine Private First Class Dollman W. Dailey, 22, son of Mr. and Mrs. Leonard Dailey of West Hamlin, recently returned to the United States after seeing action on Iwo Jima and Okinawa. He enlisted in the Marines in October, 1942, and is now at San Diego, Calif.

Private Norman Russell, son of Harvey Russell of East Lynn, a veteran of 25 months in the Pacific with the Army Medical Corps, is now at the Redistribution Station at Camp Butner, N.C. Private Russell wears the Bronze Star Medal and the Good Conduct ribbon.

Corporal Robert E. Lowe. 20, USMCR, son of Mr. and Mrs. Ervin Lowe of Kenova, has charge of a Dobermann Pinscher dog when his Marine platoon goes on patrol on Okinawa.

Corporal James H. Kitchen, 19, son of Mr. and Mrs. J. S. Kitchen, 1200 Enslow Boulevard, was recently graduated from an advanced communications course at Boca Raton Army Air Field, Fla.

Lawrence Evans, 30, ship's serviceman third class, son of Mrs. Alma Barnhart of Russell, Ky., is serving aboard a destroyer escort in the Pacific after a long tour of duty in the Aleutians.

Marine Gunnery Sergeant John R. Coffey, son of Mrs. Mary Coffey of Barboursville, was recently promoted to that rank ... at Camp Pendleton, Oceanside, Calif. Sergeant Coffey is a Guadalcanal veteran and has two brothers in the Army overseas.

Howard E. Boster, husband of Mrs. Bettie M. Boster, 658 Marion Court, has been advanced to the rating of Machinist's mate second class at the Naval Air Station at Kaneohe Bay, Hawaii.

Charles Peyton Jr., 20, seaman first class, son of Mrs. Mary Peyton of Milton, is at the Naval Armed Guard Center at Treasure Island, San Francisco. Seaman Peyton is a veteran of a year's duty in the Pacific and has been in the Navy for 18 months.

Three sailors from the Huntington area are serving aboard the destroyer USS *Healy* which has cruised in Pacific waters for 100,000 miles in the last year and a half without suffering any damage or loss of a man through enemy action. They are Edward V. Hillery, seaman first class, Raysal; Ernest H. Elkins, radioman second class, 1214 Twenty-fifth Street, and Herman Trent, watertender first class, Logan.

Seaman First Class Otho Bowman of Lesage has reported to the Naval Armed Guard Center at Treasure Island after serving for 16 months as a member of a gun crew of a merchant ship.

Eddie Mac Hunter, seaman first class, son of Mrs. Marie Hunter, 916 West Third Street, is attached to the Navy Yard Supply Depot at Pearl Harbor...

Tilden A. Winters Jr., fireman first class of Branchland, fought aboard a destroyer-escort which took everything the Japs could throw at her during the early stages of the Ryukus campaign and came up scarred, but still punching.

Jack Cogar, a French horn player in the U.S. Army band, is now home on leave after touring more than a dozen countries of Europe at the request of General Dwight D. Eisenhower. Musician Cogar, the son of Mrs. T. J. Cogar, and brother of Mrs. C. H. Wilson, 1116 West Third Street, has been in the Army since October, 1941.

Leonard H. Barker, 24, gunner's mate third class, son of Virgil W. Barker, 1628 Seventh Avenue, has arrived at the Naval Training and Redistribution Center at Shoemaker, Calif. for reclassification and further assignment. He has been in the Navy for three and a half years and is a veteran of Sicily, where he underwent five days of continuous bombing...

Sergeant Hairson Bailey, 24, 2935 Third Avenue, has returned to the United States after serving for 43 months as a battalion wire chief in the European theatre. He is at the Army

Ground Service Station Forces Redistribution station at Miami Beach, Fla.

Staff Sergeant Carroll W. Zirkle, 1622 Doulton Avenue, has been awarded the Bronze Star Medal for outstanding service during the military operations against the Germans from February to April 21.

Glenna: *June 30ᵗʰ Saturday – Hot. Done nothing much.*

Rupert: *I tried to get Mother to go in swimming, but she wouldn't.*

My grandparent's land extended down a steep bank to the Guyandotte River. At that time of year the river was shallow, seldom above my waist. I loved to swim there but wasn't allowed to go alone.

July

SUMMER HEAT, POTSDAM SUMMIT

GLENNA: JULY 1ST SUNDAY – WENT TO SUNDAY SCHOOL. RESTED ALL *day. Hot.*

Rupert: *I went to Sunday school today.*

Heat waves were often accompanied by high humidity, making it even more oppressive.

This Associated Press report presented the shortage of eggs as a national concern: "Slowly but unmistakably eggs are becoming as scarce as the ham that used to go with them... The pinch is growing tighter in all sections, accentuated by the meat shortage which has stepped up the table demand for eggs as substitute."[321] With a flock of laying hens we had no shortage of eggs. Pork was not a concern either, but beef was scarce.

Charleston, June 30: "West Virginia's population has dropped approximately 200,000 in the past four years, from a 1940 total of 1,901,000 to 1,715,000 in 1944, Health Commissioner J. E. Offner reported today." He said the decrease was largely due to the absence of service members, but noted that the birth rate had also dropped.[322]

Chungking, June 30: "Generalissimo Chiang Kai-Shek's soldiers reoccupied Linhai, on the China coast 380 miles northwest of American-invaded Kume Island and reached the French Indo-China frontier at Chungchingfu and Malungschai."[323]

"WITH THE COLORS":

Corporal Jack A. Moore, 24, son of Mr. and Mrs. W. E. Moore, 2542 Third Avenue, is spending a 45-day furlough with his parents after 33 months in the Pacific. He will return to Seattle, Wash. for embarkment on July 15. He has fought in Guam, Marshall, Gilbert and Hawaiian Islands.

Petty Officer (First Class) Bob Russell, son of Mrs. Dora Russell of Marcum Terrace, is spending a 30-day leave with his family before returning to his station at San Francisco. He has spent 19 months in the South Pacific aboard a mine-sweeper. Petty Officer Russell has two brothers in the service, Carpenter's Mate (Third Class) Don Russell and Staff Sergeant Kenneth Russell.

First Lieutenant Leland W. Bagby Jr., son of Mr. and Mrs. Leland W. Bagby Sr. of 1513 Third Avenue, has returned to the states by B-17, which he flew back from the European Theatre of Operations. He holds the Distinguished Flying Cross, the Air Medal with three Oak Leaf Clusters, a Battle Star and a Presidential Citation. His wife is the former Miss Juanita Chadwick of Huntington.

Corporal Elliot C. Christopher, son of Mr. and Mrs. Robert Christopher, has arrived home on a 15-day furlough from Seaside, Ore., where he is now stationed with the U.S. Air Force.

First Lieutenant Frederick L. Lester, 23, son of Mr. and Mrs. M. E. Lester, 604 Fifth Avenue, was recently promoted to the rank of captain while serving as a chemical officer with the Eighth Air Service Group in New Guinea, where he has been serving for the last

11 months. He has two brothers also in the service, Captain M. H. Lester, who is with the U.S. Engineers at Fort Belvoir, Va., and Seaman (Second Class) P. J. Lester, with the Seabees at Camp Endicott, R.I.

Gunner's Mate (Third Class) Joseph F. Shepard, who has been spending a 22-day leave with his parents, Mr. and Mrs. C. L. Shepard, 2205 Fifth Street and his wife, the former Miss Ruth Starkey, 328 Thirteenth Street, will return to New York today for reassignment. Gunner's Mate Shepard has been in the Navy 23 months and wears the American, European-African Middle Eastern and Asiatic-Pacific ribbons.

Electrician's Mate (Second Class) George W. Hayes was recently promoted to that rank while serving aboard an LST in the South Pacific. He is the son of Mr. and Mrs. P. M. Hayes of 928 Twenty-seventh Street, and the husband of Mrs. Eloise Hayes of 1713 Franklin Avenue.

Sergeant David M. Baker, son of Mr. and Mrs. Nathan Baker of 66 Oakwood Road, is home on a delay en route to his new station at Harlingen, Tex.

Electrician's Mate (Second Class) Ralph Robinson, husband of Mrs. Charlotte Robinson of 431 Sixteenth Street Road, has just returned to the U.S. Navy receiving station for reassignment after spending a 21-day furlough with his wife. Overseas six months, Electrician's Mate Robinson has fought on Iwo Jima, Okinawa and the Philippines.

Private (First Class) James Lambert, son of Mrs. Inez Lambert and grandson of Mr. and Mrs. J. A. Holder, 341 Fifth Avenue, arrived in Huntington yesterday morning to spend a 30-day leave with his family. He was wounded in March while serving with the American forces in the European Theatre of Operations...

Master Sergeant Lee M. Baumgarner will return to Manchester, N.H. next week after spending a furlough with his wife's parents, Mr. and Mrs. S. E. Sibley of 608 Twelfth Avenue. Sergeant Baumgarner is the son of Mrs. A. L. Baumgarner of Huntington.

Sergeant Simon A. Osborne, nephew of Mrs. Bessie Andes of 848 Adams Avenue, is a member of the 38th "Cyclone" Division...

Major Clyde E. Wagner of Huntington was among the officers from the American Fifth Army and the British Eighth Army who were guests of the First Scottish Brigade, 56th British Regiment, at a retreat ceremony and formal dinner.

Coxswain Charles Estep, 21, son of Mrs. Mabel Estep of 2032 Jefferson Avenue, is in the Pacific with an amphibious force which participated in the invasion of Okinawa. His brother, Seaman (Second Class) Robert Estep, a paratrooper, was wounded in Germany and holds the Purple Heart.

Glenna: *July 2nd Monday – I washed. Very hot.*

Rupert: *I mowed the lawn today.*

Sections of our lawn had tough crabgrass. In hot and wet summers, the lawn was mowed at least once a week to prevent a return to forest. Our lawnmower, an iron beast of a machine, was propelled by leg power alone—mine. Heat aside, the job was difficult. I still occasionally dream of racing to get that lawn finished while sidetracked into some other unavoidable task.

"Nearly 600 Superfortresses, largest fleet yet sent against Japan, spilled a record 4,000 tons of fire bombs on Nippon's greatest naval base and three other cities teeming with important war industries."[324]

"IN THE SERVICE":

Seaman First Class Carl Melvin Rice, son of Mr. and Mrs. Millard E. Rice of Point Pleasant, has arrived at the Naval Training Station at Norfolk, Va. to train for duties on a new destroyer of the Atlantic Fleet. He wears ribbons for the American theatre; the Asiatic-Pacific theatre, with three stars; and the Philippine Liberation with two stars. He has been in the service for 23 months.

Corporal Frank Grant, son of Mr. and Mrs. Frank P. Grant, 1140 Tenth Avenue, is at the camp Butner, N.C., redistribution center for a two weeks stay prior to reassignment. He served 21 months in the Asiatic theatre of war with the engineers.

Private First Class Albert J. Jarvis, husband of Mrs. Lucille Jarvis, 2417 Collis Avenue, and son of Mr. and Mrs. Okey A. Jarvis of 56 B Street, is a member of a heavy machine gun crew of the 38th Division on Luzon, having served 17 months overseas in Hawaii, New Guinea and Luzon with the 38th Division, the "Avengers of Bataan."

Richard H. Cartwright Jr., son of Mr. and Mrs. R. H. Cartwright, 1338 Fourteenth Street, has been promoted to the rank of Captain in the Thirteenth Army Air Force in the Philippines. Pilot of a P-38 Lightening with the redoubtable Vampires Squadron, ... he has flown more than 100 combat missions involving 350 flying hours. He holds the Air Medal with two Oak Leaf Clusters; the Navy's Distinguished Flying Cross; and a letter of commendation from Lieutenant General George C. Kenny ... in recognition of a devastating strike at oil-rich Balikpapan, Borneo last October. A former employee of the International Nickel Company here, Captain Cartwright is a graduate of Central High School.

Thomas T. Dingess, son of Mr. and Mrs. J. M. Dingess, 311 West Fifth Avenue, has been promoted to the rank of private first class in an aviation engineer battalion on Okinawa.

Private Melvin C. Lockhart, son of Mr. and Mrs. Ray M. Lockhart, 3928 Fourth Avenue, has been assigned to the 32nd (Red Arrow) Infantry Division on Luzon and is a member of a mortar section.

Bobby Traylor, son of Mr. and Mrs. J. W. Traylor, left this week for the Great Lakes Naval Training Station at Great Lakes, Ill. after enlistment... He has three brothers in service: James, with the Navy at Fort Pierce, Fla.; Corporal Jack E. with the Army in India, and Private First Class Earl, with the Army in Hawaii.

Seaman Second Class Martin Lewis Cogan, son of Mr. and Mrs. Bruce G. Cogan of Russell, Ky., is in training at the Atlantic Fleet's Naval Training Station at Newport, R.I. for duty with a new heavy cruiser's gunnery division. His wife is the former Vivian Elkins of Ashland.

Chief Radio Technician Charles Edward Hagaman, husband of Mrs. Maxine Smith Hagaman, and son of Mr. B. F. Hagaman, 4500 Siders Avenue, and a former assistant manager for the A & P Tea Co., is a member of one of the fleet's destroyer crews.

Electrician's Mate Second Class Ardrey Vernon Peyton, husband of Mrs. Virginia Marie Adkins Peyton, 911 Sixth Avenue, and formerly of Logan, is on his way to a special temporary assignment at the electrician's mates classification center at the Navy Yard in Philadelphia. A former member of the crew of a flagship of the Atlantic Fleet, he has been in the service over three years.

Seaman Second Class Lowell Lewis is at Puget Sound Navy Yard, Bremerton, Wash., with a ship repair unit stationed there. A graduate of Ceredo-Kenova High School, Seaman Lewis is a son of John F. Lewis of Kenova and is the husband of Mrs. Mildred Lewis of Wayne.

Staff Sergeant Ira C. Beheler, son of Mr. and Mrs. Maxie G. Beheler, 1421 Beech Street, has been awarded the Good Conduct Medal at a Fourth Air Force installation at Salinas, Calif.

Guthrie Monroe Clonch, son of Mr. and Mrs. Leslie L. Clonch, 2860 Thornburg Road, and husband of the former Rose Mae Tabit of Montgomery, W.Va., has been advanced to the rank of yeoman second class aboard a submarine of the Atlantic Fleet. A graduate of Central High School, he is a former employee at the International Nickel Company.

Glenna: *July 3rd Tuesday – I ironed. Rupert went home with Papa and Mamma. Cool.*

Rupert: *I went home with my grandma and grandpa today.*

Advance units of American troops, veterans of the war, entered Berlin, "the rubbed German capital, in a triumphal march…" Hundreds of British, Canadian and French troops were expected to enter the "once-proud capital of Hitler's shattered empire…"[325]

Mackinac Island, Michigan, July 2: "Harold E. Stassen told a news conference today that 'we are facing a basic reorientation of our entire foreign policy' and if the United States follows a course of wise world leadership it will be possible to go 50 years without a war."[326] (How miserably we failed Stassen's vision.)

Private Clarence E. Simms, nephew of Mrs. Nonie Hemplle, 321 Elaine Court, was reported killed, and Private James W. Reynolds of Hamlin was reported as wounded.[327]

"IN THE SERVICE":

Alex Morris, boilermaker third class, 118 Olive Street, and William H. Pearman Jr., fireman first class, of Welch, are serving aboard the oldest destroyer in the Navy, the USS *Allen*. The *Allen* is a veteran of World War I and is referred to as "Gracie" by crewmen. It is now on duty in the Hawaiian Sea Frontier.

Second Lieutenant Carl E. Gutzwiller, 22, son of Mr. and Mrs. E. J. Gutzwiller, 322 twenty-seventh Street, won his wings and commission in the Army Air Forces last Saturday at Hondo, Tex. He is a graduate of Marshall College and entered the AAF in December, 1943. The navigator worked in a New England shipyard before going into service.

Major Edward Kime, husband of Mrs. Dorothy Kime, 1518 Holderby Road, has arrived at the Ground Forces Redistribution Station at Camp Butner, N.C. after serving in the European theatre for 35 months. He is a veteran of the campaigns in Normandy, Northern France, and Germany.

Sergeant Paul S. Keenan, 22, son of Mr. and Mrs. T. Keenan, 1618 Van Buren Avenue, has arrived in London for a seven-day leave from his base on the continent. He is a member of the First Ranger Battalion, and expects to spend his leave visiting in Bristol.

Private Oscar W. Johnson, son of Mr. and Mrs. Herman Johnson, 1688 Sixth Avenue, and husband of Mrs. Anna Mae Johnson, same address, is stationed at the Ground Forces Redistribution Station at Camp Butner, N.C., after serving for 28 months in the South Pacific as a dental technician.

The War Department announced yesterday the promotion of Ernest George Tweel, 1433 Fifteenth Street, from second to first lieutenant.

Technician Fifth Grade Charles W. Anderson, son of Mr. and Mrs. E. J. Anderson, 409 Seventh Avenue, was awarded the Bronze Star Medal for gallantry in action as a medical aid man in Europe. The medal was presented to the former employee of Owen-Illinois Glass Co. during a ceremony in Germany.

Technician Fifth Grade Cumberland Clark, son of Mrs. Arona Clark, 3710 Brandon Road, is with the 152nd Armored Signal Division…

John S. Hall Jr., son of Mr. and Mrs. John S. Hall, 6011 Pea Ridge Road, recently enlisted in the Navy and left last Saturday for the Naval Training Station at Sampson, N.Y. for basic training.

Glenna: *July 4th Wednesday – I picked blackberries and made 21 pints of berries all by myself.*

I usually helped with berry-picking; it was an activity I enjoyed. Later, as a teenager, I picked berries to sell. Blackberry thickets covered the lower section of our pastureland and the berries were of a high quality. The Morrison farm down River Road also had blackberries in abundance. I could easily pick five gallons a day on either farm.

Rupert: *I went to the show today and saw "My Friend Flica."*

Briefs from Last Night's Associated Press Wires: General George S. Patton left for Europe to resume command of the Third Army; In Fairbanks, Alaska a WAC was burned to death and ten other WACs, four soldiers, and two civilians were injured in a barracks' fire at Ladd Field; A Navy plane crashed at Burgaw, North Carolina with no known survivors."[328]

The Wayne County, West Virginia Board of Education announced a "shift of positions.": State Senator C. H. "Jackie" McKown was named principal of Crum Grade and Junior High Schools; M. J. Robinett, former county superintendent, was assigned principal of Wayne High School; Fred Carey was appointed superintendent; Dr. Fenton T. West was named principal at Vinson High School; Caleb Smith named principal of Buffalo High School; Robert Campbell, a former teacher at Barboursville Junior High School, was appointed assistant superintendent; Julia Haws was assigned the principalship of the Kenova Grade School, succeeding Mrs. Louise Hutchinson; Julia Adkins was appointed acting principal of Fort Gay High School, filling in for Illiff West, who was in the service; Claude Asbury was appointed Director of Attendance, Henry Williams appointed business manager, and Sam Herald was appointed superintendent of transportation.[329]

"IN THE SERVICE":

Sydney J. Snair, seaman first class, a veteran of 11 Pacific invasions, has been assigned duty with the Coast Guard in the 13th Naval District at Seattle, Wash. after spending a 30-day furlough with his mother, Mrs. G. N. Vernon, 1647 Washington Avenue. Seaman Snair has been in the Coast Guard 27 months, recently taking part in the Okinawa landings.

Private First Class Marvin C. Threlkeld, son of Mrs. Lillian Threlkeld, 826 West Ninth Street, a veteran of the battles for Zig-Zag Pass and the liberation of Bataan, has been awarded the Purple Heart Medal for wounds received in action against the Japs on Luzon. He is a member of the 151st Infantry of the 38th "Cyclone" Division and has recovered from his wounds and returned to duty with his company.

George W. Hazelett, husband of Lillian L. Hazelett of Huntington, was recently promoted to staff sergeant at a U.S. Troop Carrier base in France. Sergeant Hazelett is a crew-chief of a C-47 Skytrain in the 439th Troop Carrier Group and wears the Air Medal and the Presidential Unit Citation.

James G. Duvall, 26, son of Mr. and Mrs. G. A. Duvall, 1143 Ninth Avenue, has received his wings and commission as a second lieutenant in the Army Air Forces at the Hondo, Texas Army Air Field. He trained as a navigator. His wife, Mrs. Dorothy J. Duvall, lives at 628 Eighth Avenue.

Also graduated as navigators at Hondo were Second Lieutenant Joseph Hazelett, 19, son of Mr. and Mrs. H. H. Hazelett, 2161 Spring Valley Drive, and Flight Officer Samuel O. Wilkes, 20, son of Mr. and Mrs. S. O. Wilkes, 525 ½ West Eleventh Avenue, and husband of Mrs. Estella J. Wilkes of the same address.

Private First Class Hal P. Dillon Jr., son of Mr. and Mrs. H. P. Dillon, 821 Adams Avenue, has arrived in London from the Continent to spend a seven-day leave in England. Private Dillon, who fought with the 102nd Infantry Division, plans to spend his leave visiting London.

Currently stationed near Nurnberg, Germany, is First Lieutenant William D. Steinbrecher, son of W. M. Steinbrecher, 235 Main Street, serving as a utilities mess officer with the Ninth Air Force Tactical Air Command Headquarters.

Staff Sergeant Ollie C. Hale, 50, brother of Mrs. Erie Luther, 4822 Piedmont Road, a veteran of more than 29 years in the Army, is now stationed at Sioux Falls Army Air Field, S.D. Sergeant Hale completed more than 60 missions against the enemy while stationed with the AAF in the Pacific theatre.

Corporal Raymond W. Bertram, 29, son of Mr. and Mrs. W. E. Bertram, 2754 Emmons Avenue, holder of the Silver Star Medal, served with the First Armored Division in Italy for 14 months. During almost a year of fighting, he engaged in four major battles and is now at an Army rest camp in Florence, Italy.

Private First Class Clyde Hunt of Rocky Ford, Colo., grandson of Mr. and Mrs. Floyd Hunt, 1049 Fourteenth Street, is in Huntington on a 60-day furlough after two years duty in Italy with the Army. Private Hunt was awarded the Bronze Star Medal for heroic achievement in February, 1944.

Sergeant Lawson S. Henley Jr., son of Mrs. L. S. Henley Sr., 1529 Fifth Avenue, has returned to Lexington, Va. after spending a furlough here with his mother and wife, the former Miss Vivian Sexton. He is training at the Special Military Affairs School at Lexington and will be assigned to an Army general hospital following his graduation July 11.

Corporal Thomas J. Rainey, who served for 25 months with the Twelfth Air Force in Africa, Sicily and Italy, is spending a 19-day furlough with his father, T. H. Rainey, 811 Seventeenth Street. Corporal Rainey is now attached to the Third Air Force at Coffeyville, Kan. His brother Corporal Ralph G. Rainey, is also attached to the Third Air Force and is stationed at McDill Field, Fla.

Glenna: *July 5th Thursday — Rained some. Went to town and brought Rupert back.*

Rupert: *Mother came down today. We shopped and come home on the train.*

Berlin, July 4: "The American flag was raised over Berlin today... Berlin lay in ruins... The capital's sullen, subdued people lined up for food and labored in long work-lines... Old glory went up beside the red flag of the Soviet Union."[330]

"IN THE SERVICE":

Private First Class Leo Womack, son of W. M. Womack of Hurricane, recently arrived at the U.S. Army Hospital at Camp Pickett, Va., where he is undergoing treatment for wounds sustained in the European theatre. An artilleryman and a veteran of eight months overseas, he was wounded last March in the Battle of the Rhine River.

Private First Class George E. Murdock, 1500 Rugby Street, is serving with the 274th Infantry Regiment of the 70th Infantry Division in Germany. Private Murdock, who worked at the Norfolk Navy Yard before entering the Army, serves as a regimental photographer and took many historical pictures during the fighting in France and Germany.

Lieutenant Frank W. Porter, son of Mr. and Mrs. G. A. Porter of Kenova recently completed a year of duty as welfare and recreation officer at the U.S. Naval Supply Depot at Exeter, England. Lieutenant Porter was athletic director of Ceredo-Kenova High School before entering the Navy in 1942. His son, Frank W. Porter Jr. is in his second year at the U.S. Military Academy.

Don Richards, 18, seaman second class, of Shively, W.Va. is a second loader aboard a warship off Okinawa. He is a veteran of the Iwo Jima campaign in which his ship bombarded Jap shore installations in the days prior to the invasion.

David A. Hartley, 20, fireman first class, son of Mr. and Mrs. E. D. Hartley, 703 Buffington Street, is now at the Melville, R.I. Naval base, training for duty aboard a PT boat in the Pacific. A former employee of the Huntington Precision

Products, he is the husband of the former Miss Eva R. Villers, 724 Maple Court.

Major David C. Boy Jr., son of Mr. and Mrs. D. C. Boy of Holswade Park, is spending the week here with his wife and parents. He has been director of administration at Godman Field, Fort Knox, Ky., and is being transferred to another post.

Clarence W. Knapp Jr., 22, seaman second class of Richmond, Va., husband of the former Miss Elma Rose Cox, 1809 Twelfth Avenue, is serving aboard a seaplane tender which has just returned to the States with naval aviation personnel who operated from England. Seaman Knapp has been in the Navy for three years and served in the Atlantic for 18 months.

Recently flown from overseas in Air Transport Command planes to the ATC's Miami Army Air Field were five more battle-tested soldiers from the Huntington area. They were Sergeant Floyd T. Hazelwood, 22, Ashland, W.Va.; Private First Class Paul E. Winters, 22, Branchland; Staff Sergeant Arnold Johnson, 30, Huntington; Private Frank E. Hall, 25, Pageton, and Sergeant Berman A. Summerfield, 28, Wilsondale.

Glenna: *July 6th Friday – I cleaned the house, made pickles. Uncle June came here and stayed all night. Wiles came and stayed with Cline. They caught a ground hog next morning.*

Junius Adkins (Junie/June) was another of my Grandfather Adkins' brothers. A barber, he and his family lived in Huntington. Besides Wiles, his other children were daughter Maxie Erby and son Patrick Adkins.

Rupert: *I read a book all day today.*

My authors were Zane Grey, Edgar Rice Burroughs, and a few other popular adventure writers. I still have several of those old books on the top shelves of my bookcases.

Action in the Pacific was intensifying: Fighter planes from Iwo Jima hit airfields near Tokyo; Aircraft from Okinawa raided the island of Kyushu, and Naval planes hit rail tunnels and bridges on Korea's main lines to Manchuria.[331]

"IN THE SERVICE":

Private First Class Paul Badgett, son of Mrs. Ona Baggett of Rush, Ky., has been awarded the Bronze Star Medal by the commanding general of the Sixth Infantry Division for heroism in action against the Japs at Cabaruan, Luzon, last January 20.

Private First Class Donald B. Hagley, 24, son of Mr. and Mrs. L. Hagley of Lesage, is home on a 45-day furlough after 35 months in the Pacific where he participated in the battles of Leyte and Okinawa. Private Hagley entered the Army in July, 1942, and reports to Camp Meade, Md., August 14.

Captain Hunter C. Kincaid, son of Mrs. Anne J. Kincaid, 2623 Washington Boulevard, and husband of Mrs. Betty A. Kincaid, 928 Eleventh Street, served as a dental surgeon in the medical section of the 62nd Wing, a fighter-bomber component of the 12th AAF in Italy. Captain Kincaid served overseas for more than 30 months.

Kenneth E. Flesher, 3805 Hillside Drive, has been promoted ... to corporal with the 32nd Division in Northern Luzon. Corporal Flesher entered the Army in October, 1944, and has been in the South Pacific for three months.

Walter H. Smith, 20, pharmacist's mate third class, nephew of Miss Myrtle Paynter of Olive Hill. Ky., is serving aboard an LST in the European theatre. He has been in the Navy since August, 1943.

Major Kyle K. Fossum, husband of Mrs. Jessi H. Fossum, 235 South Walnut Street, has arrived in the United States after seven months' duty with the Finance Department in France. Major Fossum, who entered the Army three years ago as a private, expects to be sent to the Pacific after a furlough here and in Minneapolis, his home, and further training.

Corporal Basil Porter of Ceredo was recently advanced to that rank ... as a member of the 313th Field Artillery of the 80th Infantry Division in Europe.

Corporal Vivian W. Cook of Huntington is at the Army Air Forces Redistribution Station, Miami, Fla. for reassignment after completing a tour of duty as a medical technician in Europe.

Private Elsie Childers, daughter of Mrs. Norma Childers of Huntington, was recently promoted to the rank of technician fifth grade at the Ashford General Hospital at White Sulphur Springs, W.Va. Technician Childers has been in the WAC since last February.

Glenna: *Saturday July 7th – Very hot. I didn't work much.*

Rupert: *My Uncle and another Man killed a groundhog. I went in swimming today.*

Wartime rationing affected more than private households. A *Huntington Herald-Dispatch* article titled, "New Ration Totals Force Further Meat Curtailment in Restaurants," said in part, "Three hotels will continue to serve meals as usual with what food is available. According to A. L. Watts, assistant manager of the Hotel Prichard, Leo Ree, steward at the Hotel Frederick, and Sidney Hayes, manager of the Hotel Governor Cabell, there will be few changes in the present eating arrangements except for reduced amounts of rationed food... Morris Bailey, owner and manager of Bailey's Cafeteria, 408 Ninth Street, said that he was contemplating a return to two meatless days each week such as was instituted early in the war."[332]

Six hundred Superfortresses raided five Japanese war production centers on Honshu Island.[333]

Generalissimo Chiang Kai-Shek pledged that China would bear "the main burden of battle against the enemy on the Chinese mainland."[334]

Nineteen former German prisoners of war from the Huntington area recently passed through a Recovered Allied Military Personnel camp in France on their way back to the United States. They were Private First Class Warren R. Whitt, Buffalo; Private First Class Damon F. Young, Branchland; Private Hubert Gore, West Hamlin; Private First Class Ray S. Allison, Coalwood; Private First Class Garland E. Ball, Kenova; Private First Class Will W. Chaney, Dehue; Private First Class Doyle Hughes, Woodville; Private First Class Dewie Isbell, Asco; Private First Class Carl J. Osburn, Lavalette; Private First Class Charles W. Ray, Salt Rock; Private First Class Roy M. Smith, Ranger; Private Rogers Kennedy, Logan; Sergeant Pete Thomas, Kimball; Second Lieutenant Charles M. Scott, 257 Gallaher Street; Private First Class Frank K. Hager, 702 Jackson Avenue; Private William Aliff, 313 Bellvue Road; Private Harry L. Bailey, 1101 Railroad Avenue; Private James T. Carter, 625½ Fifteenth Street, and Private Reathel E. Hargis, rear 111 North High Street.

"IN THE SERVICE":

Private Charles Wallace, 32, son of the late Mr. and Mrs. Henry Wallace of the East End, arrived in Huntington Tuesday night from the Nichols General Hospital at Louisville, Ky. on a 30-day furlough. He was wounded in Germany April 9. He was in the invasions of North Africa, Italy and Normandy with the Amphibious Engineers of General Patch's Seventh Army."

Master Sergeant Clifford W. Hutchinson, 24, husband of Mrs. Billie M. Hutchinson, 808 ½ Third Avenue, has arrived at Miami, Fla. by plane after serving for 33 months in Europe.

Radioman Second Class Allan R. Diehl, son of Mr. and Mrs. I. R. Diehl, 2548 First Avenue, is spending a 30-day leave here after 16 months aboard a sun-chaser in the European theatre. His brother, Ensign Donald E. Diehl, a Navy pilot, is also home.

Seaman First Class Richard C. Strong, son of Mr. and Mrs. William Strong of Burlington, O., a veteran of the European theatre, left yesterday for New Orleans, La. for reassignment after a furlough.

Private First Class Alvin D. Smith, son of W. M. Smith, 2320 Fifth Avenue, is an aircraft technician at the Second Base Air Depot at Blackpool, England.

Lieutenant (j. g.) Woodford W. Sutherland, son of Mr. and Mrs. G. W. Sutherland and nephew of Mrs. C. A. Crouch, 2702 Highlawn Avenue, is home on leave after duty in the South Pacific as a pilot of a Navy B-24.

Captain James R. Backus, 810 Sixth Avenue, is a liaison officer between the 1137th Combat Engineer Group and the XII Corps in Europe.

Sergeant and Mrs. James R. Clark and their small son, formerly of Huntington, have been visiting Mr. and Mrs. C. H. Stroud here for the past week. Sergeant Clark was a prisoner of Germany for more than three months.

Lieutenant Colonel Harry C. Brindle, 1522 Washington Boulevard, was one of 26 officers and enlisted men of the Sixth Armored Division who were cited by General de Gaulle and awarded the Croix de Guerre...

Second Lieutenant Charles A. Scrivner, son of Mrs. Frances C. Scrivner, 1928 Fifth Avenue, is at the Gulfport Army Air Field, Miss., where he will be assigned to a Superfortress.

Wetzel C. Davis, 20, storekeeper third class, is home on a 30-day furlough after 20 months in the South Pacific. Storekeeper Davis is the son of Mr. and Mrs. Earsel Davis, 122 North High Street.

First Sergeant James E. Legg, 409 Water Street, Staff Sergeant Willard G. Roush Jr., Letart, and Corporal Denver R. Slone, West Hamlin, are serving with the 82nd Airborne Division in Germany.

Seaman Second Class William E. Stewart, son of Mr. and Mrs. E. L. Stewart of Four Pole Road, is now in the Philippines. Seaman Stewart has been in the Navy since January, 1945, and his brother, Corporal Eyster L. Stewart Jr., has been serving in the Philippines for 20 months.

Eight brothers and sisters of Private First Class Randall L. Fisher, 33, a veteran of the 82nd Airborne Division and many friends will gather at the home of Mr. and Mrs. G. T. Brown, 915 Eutaw Place today and tomorrow for a reunion and a welcome-home for Private Brown. Private Brown was a prisoner of Germany for almost a year.

Glenna: *July 8th Sunday – Went to Sunday School. Rested all day. Revival started that night.*

Rupert: *I went to sunday school. After Sunday School Jerry Lynn Adkins and I went in swimming.*

Jerry Lynn Adkins was the son of Eron (Jerry) and Evelyn Coffman Adkins. (Eron was distantly related to my grandfather Adkins. The large Adkins family had settled early in what is now Cabell County and the name is one of the most common in the area.) Jerry and I became friends in grade school while they lived in Salt Rock, and I remained friends with him and his sister, Myrtle Ellen, after they moved to Huntington.

Jan Ciechanowski, outgoing ambassador of Poland, stated that Russia was "imposing on Poland 'a government and a political, social and economic system alien to her.'"[335]

Neuwied, German: An Army raid discovered a cache of European art works. The paintings included some owned by Lady Astor that were seized early in the war by the Germans in Antwerp as they were being moved to England from the Astor castle at Hoffmansthal, Austria. Among the find were works by Rembrandt, Van Dyke, and Hoffman. The most valuable was said to be "Professor in His Study" by Van Dyke.[336]

"Lieutenant Robert L. Dickinson, USAAF, of Tucson, Ariz. and Huntington, who recently returned from the European theatre of war is the guest of his grandmother, Mrs. Robert L. Hutchinson of Sixth Avenue; he was joined here this week by his mother, Mrs. A. H. Dickinson and brothers Bert and Tommy and sister, Mrs. Richard Dillworth and children Lora Helen and Dickie of Tucson; he was a fighter pilot and completed 90 missions, received the Presidential Citation, 11 Oak Leaf Clusters and 140 points; he will remain in Huntington."[337]

"WITH THE COLORS":

Private (First Class) George Lee Naylor arrived home last week to visit his mother, Mrs. Marjorie Naylor of 218 Sixth Avenue. He has the Combat Infantryman Badge, a Presidential Unit Citation and the ETO ribbon with two battle stars. Between January and V-E Day Private Naylor fought with the 15th, Ninth, First and Third Armies and once had his gun holster shot off his hip by German shell fire. He will report to Ft. Bragg, N.C. to train for Pacific warfare.

Aviation Ordinance (Third Class) Dewey Earl Midkiff, son of Mr. and Mrs. W. B. Midkiff of 4738 Ohio River Road, is spending a 24-day leave with his parents after serving 25 months overseas duty with a patrol bombing squadron. He has completed 60 missions and will at the end of his furlough report to Memphis, Tenn. for reassignment. His brother, Wilbern Midkiff, seaman (first class), is with a construction battalion in the Philippines.

Petty Officer Dwight F. Plymale has been sent to a rest camp in Hawaii after serving two and a half months at Okinawa. His brother, Robert L. Plymale, seaman (first class), has been sent to Manila, where the ship on which he is serving is being repaired. He served at Iwo Jima and Okinawa. They are the sons of Mr. and Mrs. Camden Plymale, 2112 Twelfth Avenue.

Private (First Class) Charles E. Crawford, who has been stationed with the 174th Station Hospital in the Netherlands East Indies, has arrived home after 37 months overseas to spend a 45-day temporary duty furlough with his parents, Mr. and Mrs. E. C. Crawford, 3813 Hillside Drive. He has been in the Army 41 months and will return to his overseas post at the end of his furlough. His sister, Private (First Class) Jessie F. Crawford. WAC, is also home on furlough from her station at Hammer Field, Calif.

Private Leo E. Oiler, who has been spending a 15-day furlough with his parents, Mr. and Mrs. H. E. Oiler of Pea Ridge Road, will leave Monday for Albuquerque, N.M. where he will be stationed with the Second Air Force...

Staff Sergeant Walter M. Sperry of 717 Jackson Avenue was recently promoted to that rank while serving with the 1362nd Military Police Aviation Corps stationed in India. Sergeant Sperry has been overseas for almost two years. His wife and son reside at the Jackson Avenue address. Before enlisting he was an employee of the Owens Illinois Glass Co.

Following processing at Indiantown Gap Military Reservation, Pa., Private (First Class) Lawrence Ross Jr., son of Mrs. Maybel Ross of 1329 Adams Avenue, will depart on a 30-day furlough prior to redeployment. Private Ross entered the Army in June 1943 and served a year overseas with the Engineers, where he participated in three major campaigns.

A veteran of 18 months overseas, Private (First Class) Joseph H. Nichols arrived yesterday at the Presque Isle Army Air Field aboard an Air Transport Command plane of the North Atlantic Divisions "fleet." Private Nichols is the husband of Mrs. Betty Nichols, who resides at 2048 Fourth Avenue.

Corporal Raymond A. Beaman and Staff Sergeant Gordon W. Beaman, sons of Mr. and Mrs. O. W. Beaman of 858 South High Street, were united in the South Pacific after a three-year separation. Corporal Beaman has been overseas 11 months with the Army Air Forces. His wife, Mrs. Genevieve Beaman and daughter are residing in Huntington. Staff Sergeant Beaman has been overseas 25 months with the

Marines. He holds the Purple Heart for wounds received in action.

Glenna: *July 9ᵗʰ Monday – I washed. Very hot. Went to the revival that night.*

Rupert: *Mother washed today.*

Briefs from Last Night's Associated Press Wires: Rome: The Italian cabinet voted to recognize the new Polish government in Warsaw. Washington: "Radio, 'by its very nature must be maintained as free as the press,' President Truman said in a letter made public today by *Broadcasting Magazine*."[338]

An American soldier, Private First Class Clarence Bertucci, 23, of New Orleans, Louisiana, shot and killed eight sleeping Germans and injured twenty others at a prisoner-of-war camp at Ogden, Utah.[339]

"IN THE SERVICE":

Aviation Machinist's Mate Second Class David C. Smith, son of Mrs. Maud E. Smith, 2105 James River Road, and a former student at East High School, has returned from a 12-month tour of duty in the Atlantic, where he served as Navy plane captain and top turret gunner. He is a veteran of 51 combat patrols with Patrol Bombing Squadron 105.

Staff Sergeant Walter A. (Tom) Lusk Jr., son of Mr. and Mrs. Walter A. Lusk, 2514 West Smith Street, has arrived in Huntington after serving as a gunner on a B-17 in the European theatre. The Eighth Air Force veteran will spend a 30-day furlough with his parents.

Private First Class William C. Smith Jr., son of Mr. and Mrs. William C. Smith Sr., Route 3, Fifth Street Road, has been awarded the Combat Infantryman's Badge for service with the 43ʳᵈ "Winged Victory" Division on Luzon

in the Philippines. During 32 months overseas he had participated in four campaigns: Guadalcanal, Northern Solomons, New Guinea and Luzon.

Sergeant Joda D. Evans, son of Mrs. J. D. Evans, Kenova, has returned to the United States after 13 months overseas in the European theatre of operations. He is now at Stark General Hospital, Charleston, S.C. Sergeant Evans, a graduate of Buffalo Valley High School, received the Purple Heart while serving overseas with the Army Air Forces.

Seaman Second Class Samuel R. Adkins, son of Mose Adkins, Logan, is an ammunition passer aboard a destroyer in the Pacific. A veteran of the Okinawa campaign, he has a brother, Private First Class Raymond Adkins, with the Army. Seaman Adkins enlisted in the Navy in October 1944.

Fireman First Class Frank W. Pinson, son of Mrs. Mary Pinson, Kenova, is serving aboard a minesweeper of the Atlantic Fleet. A graduate of Ceredo-Kenova High school, he formerly worked for the Owens-Illinois Glass Co. in Huntington. He wears the American Theater ribbon.

Gunner's Mate Second Class James Francis Quickle of Pliny, W.Va., while resting from the Okinawa campaign at an advanced base in the Western pacific, recently assisted voluntarily in sorting mail with a group of his buddies. The mail had accumulated at the base because of a lack of shipping space.

Gunner's Mate Third Class Basil Linville, son of Mr. and Mrs. Ott Linville, Monaville, W.Va., is at the Naval Training Station, Newport, R.I. He has seen action in the Pacific and European areas since his enlistment in 1941.

Earl Robert Wheeler, husband of Mrs. Georgia Hutchinson Wheeler, 1911 McVeigh Avenue, has advanced to the rank of electrician's mate third class, aboard a destroyer escort of the Atlantic Fleet.

Gunner's Mate Third Class Truman Workman, son of Mrs. Ellen Workman, Fort Gay, W.Va., has returned to the Naval Armed

Guard center, New Orleans, La. after 14 months at sea on a Navy tanker which covered 100,000 miles, visiting a total of 47 different ports in the Atlantic, Pacific, and Indian Oceans. He is a graduate of Fort Gay High School and a former employee of the Carnegie-Illinois Steel Co., South Charleston.

Glenna: *July 10th Tuesday – I ironed and mended everything. Went to revival that night.*

Rupert: *I went to West Hamlin today.*

The "birds and bees" were flying and buzzing full-time in post-war Germany. There was speculation among British troops that the non-fraternization policy might soon be lifted. German girls seemed willing to fraternize. Venereal disease had nearly doubled since crossing the Rhine.[340]

At Fort Douglas, Utah, Private First Class Clarence V. Bertucci, 23, of New Orleans admitted killing German prisoners of war by "spraying .30-caliber machine gun bullets through their tents, killing eight." Twenty other prisoners were wounded in the attack. Bertucci declared that he was not sorry about what he had done.[341] (This incident had international implications. Bertucci was later declared insane and sent to a mental hospital.)

"IN THE SERVICE":

Staff Sergeant Claude E. Duty, son of Mr. and Mrs. George Duty of Culloden, W.Va., is serving with an amphibious tank company in Germany and is also a veteran of the North African and France fighting. He has been in the Army for almost five years.

William Thompson Jr., gunner's mate second class, USN, son of Mr. and Mrs. William Thompson Sr., of Olive Hill, Ky., has been transferred from his carrier to attend a course in gunnery and electric hydraulics at Washington, D.C. He is a veteran of the operations at Leyte, Lingayen, Palau, Iwo Jima, and Okinawa.

Aboard a Coast Guard-manned troop transport, Private First Class Walter M. Tackett of Catlettsburg, Ky. recently returned to an East Coast port from the European Theatre of Operations...

R. O. Robertson Jr., 222 Holswade Drive, was recently commissioned an ensign in the Naval Reserve after graduating from the midshipman's school at Fort Schuyler, N.Y. Ensign Robertson was graduated from Huntington Central High School and received naval training at Princeton University, University of Pennsylvania, pre-midshipmen's school at Asbury Park, N.J., and Fort Schuyler.

Clifton C. Alley, husband of Mrs. Edna Mae Alley, 1748 Jefferson Avenue, has been graduated from the aviation metalsmith school at the U.S. Naval Air Technical Training Center, Norman, Okla. Seaman First Class Alley was employed by the Owens-Illinois Glass Co. until entering the service in January, 1944.

First Lieutenant David Fox, 24, son of Mr. and Mrs. David Fox of Southwood Heights, Huntington, arrived at the Charleston, S.C. port of embarkation on July 4 en route home for a 30-day furlough. Lieutenant Fox, who entered the service in August, 1942, wears the Air Medal with three Oak Leaf Clusters, the Purple Heart, and the Presidential Unit Citation with a Cluster. He has been overseas since last November with the 15th AAF in Italy.

Glenna: *July 11th Wednesday – Cool. I mowed at the graveyard, then helped Papa and Momma peel 4 bu of peaches. Didn't get to go to church.*

Rupert: *I peeled peaches down at My Grandpa's today.*

Although they still resided in Huntington, the Salt Rock house remained "Grandma and Grandpa's." Home-canning of peaches was normal procedure. We had a few peach trees but the best peaches came from the southern states and were sold by the bushel at two Salt Rock stores.

Mar-Del-Plata, Argentina, July 10: "A 700-ton Nazi U-boat which apparently had cruised the Atlantic for 18 weeks surfaced today inside the Mar-Del-Plata breakwater within sight of a few startled Argentines and surrendered to the commandant of this submarine base."[342]

London announced "that all waters of the Atlantic, Caribbean, the Baltic, North Sea, White Sea, Mediterranean, Black Sea and Red Sea were now safe from attack by enemy forces, though parts were still dangerous because of mines."[343]

President Truman, aboard the Cruiser *Augusta*, sailed toward Potsdam, site of the "Big Three" meeting with Prime Minister Churchill and Premier Stalin.[344]

Fort Douglas, Utah: The eight German prisoners of war machine-gunned by an American Army private were to be buried Thursday "with a protestant funeral service and under a volley from U.S. Army riflemen." A few fellow German prisoners at the Salina camp would be allowed to attend the funeral, but could not display Swastikas or other Nazi emblems.[345]

There was a new problem for United States Army legal and welfare authorities—"what to do with Australian girls finding their marriages to American soldiers vanishing along with their husbands." Many American soldiers returning to the United States sought divorces unrecognized by Australia.[346]

Washington: Secretary of State Grew brushed aside Japanese "vague peace feelers" with words to the effect that the United States "is interested only in the enemy's unconditional surrender."[347]

"IN THE SERVICE":

Private First Class John W. Cartwright, 20, son of Mr. and Mrs. W. D. Cartwright, 318 Thirteenth Street, who was wounded on Iwo Jima, has just finished a 30-day furlough here and has reported to the Navy's General hospital at Charleston, S.C. Private Cartwright, a marine since April 1942, wears the Purple Heart and the Chesapeake Bay Commendation for bravery for saving the lives of three other marines.

Sergeant William R. Archer, 28, husband of Mrs. Myrtle Archer, 1001 Eleventh Avenue, landed on the beaches during the assault phase of the invasion of Leyte and Okinawa. Sergeant Archer is a battalion sergeant major with a combat engineers company. He entered the service in September 1943 and was an accountant at Archer Flowers, 534 Tenth Street, before enlistment.

Flight Officer Carl L. Fox, a co-pilot, 2875 Collis Avenue, and Staff Sergeant Dwight D. Messinger, an aerial engineer, 1721 Charleston Avenue have been awarded the Distinguished Flying Cross upon completion of more than 300 hours of operational flight in transport aircraft over the difficult China-India air routes. Both fliers are stationed at an Air Transport Command base in India.

David S. Clark, 4720 Auburn Road, has been commissioned a second lieutenant of field artillery following graduation from Field Artillery Officer Candidate School, Fort Sill, Okla. Lieutenant Clark is the son of Mrs. Carolyn Clark and a former student at Marshall College.

Private Ray R. Rose, 213 Fifth Avenue, Guyandotte, is now spending a furlough here from Fort Sill, Okla., visiting his mother and friends.

Lieutenant and Mrs. Cecil F. Crumbley are visiting her mother, Mrs. Lola Tidman, and grandmother Mrs. Thomas Bishop, 836 Eighth Street, while Lieutenant Crumbley is on leave from his Army ordnance post in Chicago.

Robert H. Morgan, 38, 1008 Madison Avenue, has been advanced to the rating of storekeeper first class, USNR, at the Naval Air Station, Alameda, Calif. Storekeeper Morgan has been in the Navy since January 1942 and recently completed a tour of duty aboard a battleship.

Harold A. Taylor, 624 Sixth Avenue, was recently advanced to the grade of ship's serviceman second class, USNR, aboard a light cruiser in the Pacific.

Cecil Simms Jr., pharmacist's mate, USNR, son of Mrs. Anna M. Simms, 226 Fourth Avenue, recently received a medical discharge from the Navy after three years of service. He served eight months in the Pacific and took part in the invasions of Iwo Jima and Okinawa.

Glenna: *July 12ᵗʰ Thursday – Cool and mostly cloudy. I cleaned the house up. That night went to the revival meeting.*

Rupert: *I picked beans today.*

"Fifteen Negro selectees reported from Logan [West Virginia] yesterday for their pre-induction examination. they were: James Moak, Logan; Andrew Dulin, Omar; William Hensley Jr., Williamson; James W. Roberts Jr., Yolyn; and Robert Hunter, Whitman; all from Board No. 1. Ernest Hill, Macbeth; George T. Cook, Stirrat; Thurmond Coleman, Logan; Willie Billups, Omar; and Atha L. Beatty, Mt. Gay; from Board No. 2. John Calvin, Taplin; Edgar A. Motely, Sharples; Arthur P. Barner, Crites; and James E. Means, Lorado."[348]

President Truman decided not to talk with Prime Minister Churchill before the Big Three meeting in Potsdam. Churchill went sailing and spent most of the afternoon painting on the deck of the small sardine fishing vessel. His daughter, Mary, "spent the day beside the Bay of Biscay as usual in a red bathing suit. Mrs. Churchill, although suffering from an infected toe and a broken tooth, both incurred during her vacation, spent the morning walking around the grounds of their chateau."[349]

"IN THE SERVICE":

Second Lieutenant Elmer E. Howard, 1940 Fourth Avenue, has been awarded the Air Medal for his part in one of the first Superfortress raids at the heart of Tokyo, Japan. Lieutenant Howard is a member of the 73ʳᵈ Bomber Wing Command at Saipan and has since participated in many raids over the Jap homeland.

Staff Sergeant John Sollazzo of West Hamlin, and Private First Class Robert W. Adkins, son of C. L. Adkins of Lavalette are returning home from Europe with the Eighth Infantry Division, which fought in the battles of Normandy, Brest and Hurtgen Forest in Germany. The Division accounted for 316,187 German prisoners during their 10 months of action. Both Sergeant Sollazzo and Private Adkins are members of the 13ᵗʰ Infantry Regiment and both wear the Purple Heart and the Combat Infantryman's Badge.

Soon to fly in a combat theatre of operations in a B-29 Superfortress ... is Staff Sergeant Frank E. (Ted) Brooks, son of Mr. and Mrs. Charles Brooks of Huntington. Sergeant Brooks is an aerial gunner on the Superfort. Before entering the AAF, he was employed by the Owens-Illinois Glass Co. as a machinist.

The promotion of Rex A. Morgan, 34, son of R. E. Morgan, 1008 Madison Avenue, squadron adjutant at an Eighth Air Force base in England, from first lieutenant to captain, has been announced by Lieutenant Colonel E. B. Maxwell, commanding officer of the 94ᵗʰ Bomber Group.

Ensign Gerald L. Billups, son of Mr. and Mrs. W. L. Billups of Prichard, W.Va., graduated from the U.S. Naval Reserve Midshipmen's School at the University of Notre Dame, South

Bend, Ind., last Monday... Approximately 730 men received commissions.

Howard C. Whitekettle Jr., son of Mr. and Mrs. H. C. Whitekettle, 1306 Washington Boulevard, recently graduated from an electrician's mate course at the Great Lakes Naval Training Station, Chicago.

First Lieutenant Norma V. Moore of Kenova was recently promoted from a second lieutenant in the Army Nurses Corps...

Walter S. Moore Jr., 1559 Holderby Road, was commissioned an ensign in the Naval Reserve last July 7, at the U.S. Naval Training School at Cornell University, Ithaca, N.Y. Ensign Moore was in a class of 175 graduates.

Lieutenant Delos E. (Deacon) Parsons, USNR, son of Mr. and Mrs. W. S. Parsons, 1639 Sixth Avenue, has arrived in Huntington for a 30-day furlough after 22 months in the South Pacific aboard an LST, during which time he took part in seven major campaigns. He is accompanied by his wife, the former Miss Jean Branham of this city, who joined him on the West Coast last May.

Glenna: *July 13th Friday – Cool and pleasant. Went down to Mrs. Morrison's and picked berries and canned 17 quarts. We went in bathing in the river. I didn't go to church that night.*

Rupert: *I picked berrys today. My boy friend Jerry Lynn Adkins came up to stay till sunday.*

"IN THE SERVICE":

Seaman First Class Carroll J. White, 18, USNR, son of Mr. and Mrs. George P. White, 321 West Ninth Street, is serving in the Pacific Theatre aboard a Navy LST ship and recently took part in the Okinawa campaign. Seaman White attended Central High School and has been in the Navy since April 1944.

Captain Paul W. Bonham, husband of Mrs. Edna Bonham, 902 West Second Street, was recently awarded the Bronze Star Medal for a display of "engineering skill of the highest order and marked ingenuity" in the construction of a railway bridge over which supplies were moved during the critical months of fighting during the European struggle. Captain Bonham, a member of the combat Army Engineers [343rd Engineer Regiment], entered the service in May 1942.

Private First Class Paul E. Seay, a wearer of the Silver Star Medal, was recently honorably discharged from the Army, after almost five years of service. Private Seay served more than three years overseas and took part in the action in Northern France, the Rhineland, Ardennes and Germany. He is the son of Mrs. Maude Seay, 1330 Fourth Avenue.

The Purple Heart was presented to Sergeant Frank S. Seibert, 424 Main Street, recently by Lieutenant Audie Murphy of Farmersville, Texas, the most decorated man in the American Army, The presentation was made at the Ashburn General Hospital, McKinney, Texas, where Sergeant Seibert is now a patient.

Private Maurice J. Flynn, 21, son of Mrs. Maurice Flynn, 539 Eleventh Avenue, is now spending a 30-day furlough here, after 10 months in Europe as a member of the 95th Infantry Division. He entered the Army in December 1943 and wears the Purple Heart.

Two sons of Mr. and Mrs. Charlie McClellan of Branchland, W.Va. are now serving in the U.S. Army. Private Verlin E. McClellan, who entered the Army in October, 1942, is now fighting on Luzon in the Philippines. Technician Fifth Grade Gerald McClellan is stationed at Camp Livington, La., where he is attached to the camp hospital. He has been in service since March, 1942.

Sergeant Clyde J. Steele, son of Mr. and Mrs. C. L. Steele, 1425 Stewart Avenue, has just completed his second year as a member of the Eighth Air Force in England. He is with the 65th Fighter Wing.

Private Clyde V. Henderson, 27, husband of Mrs. Freda M. Henderson, 4727 Bradley Road. recently graduated from the AAF Training Command's eight-week radio repair course at Truax Field, Madison, Wis.

Private Samuel A. Davidson, husband of Mrs. Doris E. Davidson, 2725 Riverview Avenue, has been awarded the expert Infantryman Badge after completing a rigorous course of training at the Camp Blanding, Fla. Infantry Replacement Training Center.

Marine Second Lieutenant John R. Perdue, son of J. W. Perdue and husband of Mrs. Ann Katherine Perdue, 1608 Jackson Avenue, has been assigned as officer in charge of the radio station at Camp Lejeune, N.C. Lieutenant Perdue enlisted in January, 1937 and since then has served 18 months sea duty and 16 months with the Marine Third Division at Bouganville and Vella Lavella.

Charles A. Burns, 19, coxswain USNR, son of Mr. and Mrs. Landis Burns of Midkiff, W.Va., is at the Naval Training Station, Norfolk, Va. to train for duties aboard a new destroyer in the Atlantic Fleet. He has a brother, Cecil Burns, 25, in the Army, and another, George Burns, a gunner's mate second class in the Navy.

Technical Sergeant John W. Poindexter, 339 Sixth Avenue, now at Westover, Mass., will arrive at Fort Meade, Md. next week where he will be discharged from service. Sergeant Poindexter now has 109 service points.

Gary Carlos Deihl, 28, son of Mrs. Tillie Deihl, 908 Eleventh Street, recently won silver and gold wings and the rating of aviation machinist's mate third class, on completing an intensive operational course at the U.S. Naval Air Station, Jacksonville, Fla. The new mechanic and aerial gunner in the Navy entered the service in December, 1943.

Sergeant Russell H. Adams, son of Mr. and Mrs. K. A. Adams, 262 Gallaher Street, is now stationed at the AAF combat training crew base, Avaon [Avon ?] Park, Fla. He recently received his promotion to sergeant.

Private First Class Jack W. Evans, USMCR, is recovering from wounds received on Iwo Jima at the Naval Hospital at San Diego, Calif. He is the son of Mrs. Agnes Evans, 1911 Fifth Avenue, and he entered the Marines in August 1944.

Glenna: *July 14th Saturday – Rainy and cool – Lavonia Pratt came up and stayed all day. She brought Emogene's boy (Jimmy Porter) with her. Jerry Lynn Adkins was here too. Went to revival.*

Rupert: *Me and Jerry and my cousin Jimmy played all day.*

Jimmy Porter, one of my first cousins, was a few years younger. My father had two brothers and five sisters. His brothers were Ausley and Maxwell. Rupert, the oldest, married first and I became the oldest Pratt grandchild. Rupert's sisters were Olga Keesee, Emogene Porter, Mary Harvey, Elizabeth Cremeans, and Lavonia Fry. My father's two brothers have been dead many years, but, as of this writing, three of the sisters are still living. Olga died in 2012 at 100 years of age and Emogene passed away in 2017 at 103.

"The weekly bird walk of the Huntington Bird Study Club will be held tomorrow morning at the David Fox property. Members and others interested in bird study are to meet at the Eighth Street bridge a 7 A.M."[350]

Guam: A 138 miles-per-hour typhoon crippled at least twenty-one ships of Admiral William F. (Bull) Halsey's Third Fleet. Most vessels were repaired quickly. Admiral Halsey also broke radio silence to report that a 1,000-aircraft force of the U.S. Third Fleet had bombed Hokkaido and the northern Honshu islands. He said that "342 enemy planes and four ships [were] destroyed or damaged and 15 airfields smashed."[351]

Washington, July 13: The United States acknowledged and took responsibility for the sinking by an American submarine of the Japanese relief ship, *Awa Maru*, traveling under an Allied safe conduct guarantee. The U.S. informed the Japanese government that "disciplinary action is being taken."[352]

"IN THE SERVICE":

Corporal James H. Smith, husband of Mrs. Alma Smith, 4321 Siders Avenue, was recently given the motor vehicle driver and mechanics badge for careful driving and excellent upkeep of his vehicle, as a member of the 113th Medical Battalion on Luzon. Corporal Smith entered the Army in April 1941, has been overseas for 17 months and wears three battle stars on his campaign ribbon.

Kenneth R. Huffman, gunner's mate third class, son of Mrs. Huffman of Russell Ky., has been a member of the Hawaiian Sea Frontier, a unit of the fleet assigned to keep the sea lanes clear of enemy fleet units, for the past 18 months. He entered the Navy in December 1942.

Walter Lee Mullins, 19, son of Mr. and Mrs. Robert Mullins of Tram Ky., has advanced to seaman first class, USNR, while serving aboard a destroyer-escort in the Pacific. He entered the Navy in October 1943 and has been [in] action in the Luzon, Iwo Jima, and Okinawa campaigns.

Overseas 53 months and stationed in the Midway Islands since the Navy's historic victory there in 1942 is Strother Staley, boatswain's mate second class, husband of Mrs. Viola Staley, 2112 Jefferson Avenue. Bos'n Staley enlisted in the Navy in November 1940 and before that he was a farmer.

First Lieutenant Nancy C. Deardorff, USMCR, daughter of Mr. and Mrs. H. C. Deardorff, 523 Tenth Avenue, was recently promoted to that rank at the Marine Corps Air Depot, Miramar, San Diego, Cal., where she is assistant post exchange officer. She enlisted in May, 1943 and took her officer training at Camp Lejeune, N.C.

Lieutenant Walter L. Diddle, 21, son of Mr. and Mrs. N. S. Diddle, 3120 Fifth Avenue, has arrived at the Boca Raton, Fla. Army Air Field, a technical school of the AAF training command, for assignment on the base.

[Lieutenant] Robert J. Snider, son of Mr. and Mrs. C. W. Snider, 909 Ninth Street, has graduated from the AAF Administrative Officer Candidate School at Maxwell Field, Ala...

Sergeant William H. Toler of Commerce Avenue is stationed at a peninsular base in Italy as a member of the 384th Port Battalion, which supplies the Fifth Army Air Corps ground crews and naval elements in the Mediterranean Theatre.

The War Department announced yesterday the promotion of Captain Barrner M. Hill, 1735 Eleventh Avenue, from first lieutenant.

Sergeant Arthur Herndon, 29, USMCR, son of Mr. and Mrs. J. H. Herndon, 1101 Ninth Avenue, has arrived in the Pacific Theatre, He enlisted in the Marines in September, 1943 and trained at Parris Island, S.C. and Cherry Point, N.C.

First Lieutenant Grover F. Perry, son of Mrs. Laura Perry, 976 Washington [Avenue], has graduated from an intensive course in transition flying at the Palm Springs Army Air Field, Cal.

Petty Officer Third Class Kermit Gue, 26, USN, 2326 West Fifth Avenue, husband of Mrs. Thelma Gue of that address, was recently promoted to that rating at his base in Hawaii.

Eugene F. Salyers, 19, aviation ordnanceman third class, USNR, husband of Mrs. Hope Salyers, 1103 Washington Avenue, has returned to the United States after a tour of duty with Patrol Bombing Squadron 209 operating from naval bases in Central America and the Caribbean.

Coast Guard Seaman First Class Leonard Hartz, son of Mr. and Mrs. S. K. Hartz, 1205 Charleston Avenue, and a member of the Huntington Fire Department, is visiting at his home, 3638 Piedmont Road. In the Coast Guard since September 1943, he is in the map and chart drafting room at the base in Philadelphia.

Sergeant James H. Monnig, husband of Mrs. Alyce Monnig, 1625 Douton Avenue, was recently awarded the Bronze Star for meritorious service in support of combat operations with the Fifth Army in Italy. Sergeant Monnig is a clerk in the 85th "Cluster" Division Battle Casualty Division.

Glenna: *July 15th Sunday – We canned 26 quarts of peaches that day.*

Rupert: *I didn't go to Sunday school today. Jerry went home.*

Britain turned on its night lights after nearly six years of blackouts.[353]

In Germany, the non-fraternization rule was relaxed with the general approval of American troops. A German girl said, "... I don't see where there will be any real difference since American soldiers have been promenading with Fräuleins since the day they arrived."[354]

Guam: July 15: U.S. Navy battleships shelled the city of Muroran on the coast of Hokkaido, more than 250 miles north of the scene of the recent fleet bombardment of Honshu.[355]

"WITH THE COLORS":

Lieutenant (Junior Grade) William C. Baumgardner, Navy pilot, son of Mr. and Mrs. Craven A. Baumgardner, 1502 Charleston Avenue, left Huntington yesterday to return to his station at the Jacksonville Fla. Naval Air Station, where he expects to receive overseas duty orders. He spent a 10-day leave in this city with his wife, the former Miss Darlene Woodrum of Guyandotte, and young son,

William D. Baumgardner, who returned here with him from Jacksonville, where they had been residing for the past few months. Lieutenant Baumgardner returned to the United States last spring from the Pacific where he flew Navy combat planes in several campaigns, including those of Iwo Jima and the Philippines.

Metalsmith (Third Class) David I. Dick is spending a 30-day leave with his parents, Mr. and Mrs. D. R. Dick of 277 Gallagher Street after serving 18 months overseas.

A veteran of 30 months service as a chief of section in the European theatre of operations, Staff Sergeant Basil R. Ross, 29, arrived at the Presque Isle Army Air Field yesterday aboard an Air Transport Command plane of the North Atlantic Division's Snowball fleet. Sergeant Ross is the son of Mr. Alex Ross of Barboursville.

Aviation Ordnanceman (First Class) William Anderson, 22, son of Mr. and Mrs. Edwin H. Anderson of Huntington and formerly of Charleston, is the fifth Cabell County serviceman to survive the sinking of the USS *Bunker Hill*. Anderson said that he was in the second of three groups into which the crew of the *Bunker Hill* was divided for the purpose of leaves. Other survivors of the ship from Huntington were in the first group.

Technical Sergeant William C. Crouch, son of Mr. and Mrs. Clyde A. Crouch, 2702 Highlawn Avenue, who has been spending a 15-day furlough with his parents, will return to his station tomorrow morning at Camp Roberts, Calif. He is a former Marshall College student and was employed by the local Associated Press Bureau before entering the Army December, 1942.

Private George I. Roberts, son of Mrs. Clara Roberts, 404 Thirty-first Street, is serving with the U.S. Army Infantry Division somewhere in the Philippines. Entering the Army Dec. 7, 1944, he received his training at Fort McClellan, Ala. Before entering the service he was employed by the Owens-Illinois Glass Co.

His wife, Mrs. Beulah Roberts, and son reside at 1428 Charleston Avenue.

Storekeeper (Second Class) Victor Guy Miller was recently discharged from the naval hospital at San Diego, Calif. He has served three and a half years with the Navy. His wife and three daughters reside at 630 ½ Eighth Avenue.

Staff Sergeant Fayette Maynard of Ceredo, and Technician (Fifth Grade) Lester Shuff, 1535 Harvey Road, are returning home from Europe with the Eighth Infantry Division which accounted for 21 times its own weight in Germans by taking 316,187 prisoners during 10 months of combat. Sergeant Fayette [Maynard] took part in four major Central Europe campaigns and was awarded the Good Conduct Medal, the Combat Infantryman's Badge and the Purple Heart. Technician Shuff participated in the campaigns in Normandy, Northern France and the Rhineland.

Returning from service outside the United States, Technician (Fourth Grade) Peter C. Beseler, husband of Mrs. P. C. Beseler, 111 Walnut Street, is being processed through the Army Ground and Service Force Redistribution Station at Miami Beach, Fla., where his next assignment will be determined.

First Sergeant Wiley M. Richardson, a veteran of 54 months in the American theatre of operations, received an honorable discharge from the Army at Camp Blending, Fla. He is the husband of Mrs. Marian Richardson [daughter of Mr. and Mrs. R. C. Arbaugh] of 1501 Fourth Avenue.

Private Garrett Hash, son of Mr. and Mrs. O. T. Hash, and husband of the former Miss Pauline Miller, all of Barboursville, has returned to Camp Mead, Md. after spending a furlough with his family.

Glenna: *July 16th Monday – I washed. Cool and cloudy.*

Rupert: *I read all day today.*

Berlin, July 15: "President Truman and Prime Minister Churchill arrived in Germany to join Premier Stalin for historic talks it was hoped would shorten the Pacific war and decide the world's fate for years to come."[356]

"IN THE SERVICE":

Corporal Grayson T. Osborne, son of Mrs. Martha Osborne, 233 Gallagher Street, has been awarded the Good Conduct Medal at the Oklahoma City Air Technical Service Command. A veteran of 29 months overseas service, who participated in four campaigns, Corporal Osborne was formerly stationed at Charlotte Air Base, N.C.

Private First Class Sherman L. Curry, 2017 Eighth Avenue, a veteran of 21 months overseas, is now at Camp Norfolk Assembly Area. Also at the Camp Norfolk Assembly Area is Private First Class Robert L. Adams, Barboursville, a veteran of 23 months overseas.

First Lieutenant Gerald B. Howes, Huntington, is executive officer of "Dog" Battery of the 777th AAA Battalion which led the anti-aircraft men during their 10 months of combat with the Sixth Armored Division in Europe.

Private Elmer H. Dean, Genoa, W.Va., a veteran of five months as a rifleman in the European Theatre of Operations, who wears the Combat Infantryman's Badge and the European campaign ribbon with one battle star, has returned from overseas and is now being processed through the Army Ground and Service Forces Redistribution Center at Miami Beach, Fla.

Seaman Second Class Robert P. Melvin, Russell, Ky., is aboard the USS *Fletcher* in the Pacific... Yeoman First Class Ray V. Allen, Eleanor, W.Va., is aboard the same ship.

Captain Ralph H. Cook, son of Mrs. Rebbeca Cook, Logan, has received the Oak Leaf Cluster to the Bronze Star Medal denoting meritorious service in European Theatre operations. He is headquarters commandant in the 330th Regiment of the 83rd Infantry Division.

Corporal Lewis Reede, son of Mrs. Octavia Reede, Lex, W.Va., has been awarded the Bronze Star for heroic achievement in action on January 3, 1945, in the vicinity of Bastogne, Belgium, where the enemy succeeded in overrunning his quarter-ton truck and trailer, containing three .50 caliber machine guns and ammunition. The McDowell County soldier voluntarily went forward under intense fire and retrieved the guns and ammunition which later proved instrumental in repelling a strong enemy arrack, the citation said.

Glenna: *July 17th Tuesday – Cool. I ironed and mended everything.*

Rupert: *I stayed at home this day. It's cool today.*

Conspiracy theorists were at work. A *Chicago Times* dispatch from Vincent DePascal, a Montevideo correspondent, reported, ... "I am virtually certain Adolf Hitler and his wife, Eva Braun, the latter dressed in masculine clothes, landed in Argentina and are on an immense, German-owned estate in Patagonia..." The pair was said to have landed from a German submarine.[357]

"IN THE SERVICE":

Private Glen E. Osburn, son of Mr. and Mrs. Wayne Osburn of East Lynn, W.Va., is a member of the 299th Engineer Combat Battalion, which was recently given the Presidential Unit Citation for successfully completing their assigned work under heavy enemy fire, during the battle of the Rhine. Private Osburn also received the Good Conduct Medal, ETO ribbon and five battle stars in addition to the citation. Private Osburn has been in service for two years, and has a brother, Corporal Jay K. Osburn, serving with the Army on Okinawa. Private Osburn is now stationed at Nuremburg, Germany.

The Bronze Star was awarded to Commander William H. Groverman, 36, USN, of Huntington and Covington, Ky., by Admiral Jonas H. Ingram, commander of the Atlantic Fleet. The medal was given for meritorious service during 14 months duty with the Atlantic Fleet.

First Lieutenant Arthur P. Gough, 333 West Fifth Avenue, a veteran of 12 months in the China-India-Burma Theatre, has reported to Ellington Field, Texas, where he will undergo a refresher course for navigators returned from combat.

Robert K. Flanagan, son of Mr. and Mrs. R. K. Flanagan, 1556 Sixteenth Street, received his wings and commission as a navigator in the Army Air Forces last Saturday at the Selman Army Air Field, Monroe, La...

Also commissioned Last Saturday at Selman Field as a navigator ... was James Marshall Hawkins, son of Mr. and Mrs. H. B. Hawkins, 1170 Wiltshire...

Private Ralph W. Lewis, son of C. W. Lewis, 114 North High Street, and husband of Mrs. Elsie Lewis, 120 Perry Street, has been assigned to the 22nd (Red Arrow) Infantry Division on Luzon. Private Lewis entered the Army last December and trained at Camp Blanding, Fla.

Major John H. Zell, USAAF, assistant professor of engineering at Marshall College on military leave, was promoted to that rank ... at the Massachusetts Institute of Technology, where he is now engaged in aeronautical engineering research.

Sergeant Quentin Hazlett, husband of Mrs. Quentin Hazlett, 1754 Madison Avenue, was among the first American ground troops in China. He is a member of the Tenth Air Force gun crew, which mans the highest anti-aircraft gun position in the China-India-Burma

Theatre and protects an important Stilwell road bridge spanning the Mekong River.

Private First Class James T. Stultz of Huntington is now with the 407th Infantry Regiment of the 102nd Division in Europe. He has been in Europe since last September and recently toured the German historical sites and also their infamous concentration camps.

Fireman Second Class Clarence Williams, son of Mrs. C. M. Williams of Chesapeake, O., is serving aboard the battleship USS *Iowa* in the Pacific...

Two Huntington Navy men are serving aboard the USS *Gregory*, which has shot down six Jap planes and engaged in two major engagements since arriving in that theatre last October. They are: Elmer C. Robinson, 24, gunner's mate second class, USN, 2405 Adams Avenue; and Kermit R. Wilson, 24, ship's serviceman first class, USN, son of Mrs. Mary E. Wilson, 167 Davies Street.

Glenna: *July 18th Wednesday – Hot. I went to prayer meeting that night.*

Rupert: *I read all day.*

Potsdam, July 17: As the Big Three held their first official meeting, President Truman was invited to preside. The war against Japan was to be a main concern.[358]

"IN THE SERVICE":

Private Sewell Kingrey, 1931 Doulton Avenue, has been discharged from the Army at Westover Field, Mass. for the purpose of entering the United States Military Academy at West Point, N.Y. Private Kingrey had been stationed at Westover as part of a new pre-cadet training program.

Private First Class John Jorden of West Hamlin, en route home from the European theatre, is now being processed at Camp Atlanta in Northern France. Private Jorden fought with the 13th Armored Division and wears the Combat Infantryman's Badge. Also at Camp Atlanta in France is Private Elijah A. Dial, husband of Mrs. Thena M. Dial, 415 Seventh Street, also a veteran of the fighting with the 13th Armored Division.

Private First Class Donald W. Browning, son of Mrs. Hallie Browning, 1917 Twelfth Street, following service in the combat areas in the Pacific, has arrived at the U.S. Naval Receiving Hospital, San Francisco, Calif., for medical treatment. His wife, Mrs. Iva Browning, lives at 2504 ½ Marcum Terrace.

Sergeant Harold R. Davis, 25, of Westmoreland, a veteran of the Mediterranean theater, has arrived at the Army Air Forces Redistribution Station in Miami Beach for reassignment. He served overseas as a B-24 mechanic.

Wounded at the Ruhr pocket on April 3, Private First Class Charles E. Teschler, son of Mrs. Georgeanna Teschler, 2107 Jefferson Avenue, is "recovering quickly" at the U.S. Army's 201st General Hospital at Verdun, France. He entered the Army in July 1944 and went overseas last February. He has been awarded the Purple Heart. His brother, Max Teschler, is serving with the Navy in the Pacific.

Marine Second Lieutenant James A. McCubbin, 22, of Huntington, recently completed training at the Air Observers Training Center and qualified to serve as "flying eyes" for the ground troops. He was a student at Marshall College before enlisting in the Marines in March, 1942. His father, I. L. McCubbin, lives at Munfordville, Ky.

Flight Officer Milton D. Ward Jr., son of Mr. and Mrs. M. D. Ward, 732 Jefferson Avenue, has entered a streamlined five-week course at the AAF Training Command's B-29 transition school at Roswell Army Air Field, Roswell, N.M. to become a co-pilot.

Private Nathan H. Clay, son of Mr. and Mrs. Walter Clay of Branchland, W.Va., has been given the Expert Infantryman's Badge ... at the Camp Blanding, Fla. Infantry Replacement Center.

Technician Fifth Grade Ira C. Dingess, son of Mr. and Mrs. Ansel Dingess, and husband of Mrs. Virginia Dingess, all of Proctorville, O., is currently stationed at the retribution center at Camp Butner, N.C. He recently returned to the States after 35 months duty in the European theatre where he served as a clerk in the Signal Corps.

Staff Sergeant Clem Meador and Private First Class John A. Meador, sons of Mr. and Mrs. A. M. Meador of Monroe Avenue, recently met for the first time in two years at Vurdeen, [Virden?] France. Sergeant Meador has been in the Army for four years, 12 months of it overseas, and Private Meador has served 20 months in the Army, nine overseas.

Sergeant Clement Hudson, 810 Lincoln Place [is] a member of the 93rd Cavalry Reconnaissance Unit of the 13th Armored Division...

Ensign Donald W. Rice, 20, son of Mr. and Mrs. E. P. Rice, 214 Eleventh Avenue, has been transferred to a sound school at San Diego, Cal. for further training after completing a course at the Navy Training Center, Miami, Fla. He was commissioned last March at the Naval Midshipmen's School, Fort Schuyler, N.Y.

Sergeant John W. Halley, 3722 Guyan Avenue and Private First Class Woodrow L. Thompson, Sweetland, are with the 106th Infantry Division in Wiesbaden, Germany, now on occupational duty with the Fifteenth Army. Sergeant Halley and Private Thompson recently enjoyed three-day passes to Brussels, Belgium.

Glenna: *July 19th Thursday – I went to town to get a pair of unrationed shoes and two cooking pots. Very hot. We went to the*

show and saw "My Pal Wolf." Rode home with Cline and Edith Porter.

Rupert: *I went to town today.*

"Carpenter's Mate First Class Dellifee Dennis McNeely, 45, ... who was accidently killed on Guam last March 9" has had a new athletic field on Guam named "McNeely Field," it was announced by the 59th Naval Construction Battalion. His mother was Mrs. Alice McNeely, 628 West Division Street.[359]

Six hundred B-29 bombers hit the Japanese cities of Choshi, Fukui, Hitachi, and Okazaki.[360]

"IN THE SERVICE":

Lieutenant (j. g.) Aubrey C. Byrd, USNR, son of Patrolman William R. Byrd of the Huntington Police Department and Mrs. Byrd, 814 Roby Road, was recently authorized for the Commendation Ribbon of [by ?] Admiral W. F. Halsey, commander of the Third Fleet in the Pacific. He was cited for "excellent service in the line of a close-in fire support ship on September 18, 1944, during the assault and capture of an enemy held island." Lieutenant Byrd, a graduate of Marshall College, safely guided his ship through waters, known to be mined, to deliver effective rocket fire.

Seaman First Class Warren Reed, USN, son of Mr. and Mrs. J. A. Reed of North Kenova, O., recently arrived in the United States after an extensive tour of duty in the South Pacific. His wife, Mrs. Virginia Reed, and his mother, have gone to San Francisco to be with him. He entered the service in October 1943.

Private Charles William Foster, USMCR, of Ashland, Ky., and Sergeant Marvin Taylor King, USMC, have been wounded in the Pacific theatre, the Navy Department announced yesterday.

Private Verlin E. McClellan, son of Mrs. Marion McClellan of Branchland, has been assigned to Company K, 136th Infantry Regiment of the 33rd Division on Luzon, as a rifleman. He entered the Army in October, 1944.

Elmer C. Robinson, gunner's mate second class, is home on a 30-day furlough, visiting his wife, the former Miss Wanda Miller, and infant daughter, Susan, at 2405 Adams Avenue. Mate Robinson served in the Pacific aboard the destroyer, USS *Gregory.*

James P. McCoy, 24, watertender third class, USN, son of Mr. and Mrs. J. P. McCoy of Huntington, and Lieutenant (j. g.) Harold E. Jackson, USNR, of Milton, are serving aboard the USS *Quincy,* which on July 14 went to the shores of Japan and helped a mighty naval task force hurl dynamite into the Jap homeland...

Private Henry Smith, son of Mr. and Mrs. C. J. Smith of Milton, won the Expert Infantryman's Badge ... at the Infantry Replacement Center, Camp Blanding, Fla. Private Smith is a graduate of Milton High School.

Private Darrell Rice, husband of Mrs. Velva Rice of Wayne is now enjoying a 60-day furlough, after serving in the European theatre where he saw much action.

Rocco Narcise, son of Mr. and Mrs. Patsy Narcise, 112 Fifth Avenue, was recently promoted to corporal in his capacity as an electrician with the headquarters of the Fifth Air Force Troop Carrier Command now stationed on Luzon in the Philippines. Corporal Narcise entered the Army in September, 1943 and has been overseas for the past 15 months.

Lieutenant Ross D. Surbaugh, 22, of Huntington, a veteran of Iwo Jima and Okinawa invasions, has emerged from 150 hours of flying over enemy lines in a battleship based observation plane with a minimum of shooting and yet is indirectly responsible for untold damage to Jap installations at Iwo Jima and Okinawa. Lieutenant Surbaugh won his wings in February 1942 and saw action it the Normandy and Southern France invasions.

Glenna: *Friday July 20th – Very hot. Cleaned up house and went in swimming in the river.*

Rupert: *Hot. I went in swimming today.*

The Duke of Windsor said he "expected to confer next month with his brother, King George, and the British prime minister." The former King Edward VIII, who had given up his throne to marry his American-born duchess [wife], said he "has no plans for either 'a future home, nor occupation.'"[361]

Potsdam, July 19: "President Truman entertained Premier Stalin and Prime Minister Winston Churchill tonight at a state dinner, the first such function of the Big Three Conference now proceeding on a workmanlike timetable..."[362]

"IN THE SERVICE":

Corporal James C. McAllister, a member of the 419th Engineer Company, is spending a 30-day furlough with his parents, Mr. and Mrs. J. E. McAllister, 544 Eighth Avenue. Corporal McAllister returned to the United States last week after serving 22 months in French, Germany and Belgium. At the termination of his furlough he will report to Camp Meade, Md. for reassignment to the Pacific theater of operations.

Private First Class Shelvey E. Johnson Jr., son of S. E. Johnson of Huntington, has been promoted to technician fifth grade while serving with 143rd Ordinance Battalion in France. Corporal Johnson participated in the fighting in Belgium last December and has been in the service since November 1943.

Private Donald H. Esque, 187 Gallaher Street, a veteran of 18 months in the European theater, is now at the Newton D. Baker General Hospital, Martinsburg, W.Va., for treatment. Private Esque served in France and Belgium with the 3204 Quartermasters and the 151st Combat Engineers.

Mr. and Mrs. Lovie Stephenson and Mr. and Mrs. Otho Davis Sr. of Barboursville, have been informed that their sons, Corporal Jack Laverne Stephenson, USMC, and Private First Class Otho Davis Jr. USMC, met on Okinawa. Both of the Marines attended Barboursville High School.

Technician Fifth Grade Brady D. Burger, son of Mr. and Mrs. W. S. Burger of Branchland, W.Va., is now enjoying a 30-day furlough after returning from the European theater, where he served in a field artillery and radio battalion in Germany.

Glenna: *July 21ˢᵗ Saturday — Very hot. Cleaned 4 chickens and baked a cake. Went to see Mrs. Smith.*

Rupert: *We went to see some old people today.*

My definition of "old people" has evolved.

"Diamond Dust": "It does my heart good to see President Harry Truman wearing a cap. When I was a kid up at Milton-on-the-Mud I always wore a cap. They were all the rage. Huntington's champion all-around cap wearer is Gerald Dober. And—I think he's better looking in a cap than Harry Truman. H-mmmm. * * * The $75 question: How much would Tommy Holmes be worth on the open market? A safe guess would be $100,000. I imagine the Yanks would part with that much moola for him. Yet, they once owned Tommy for free. Holmes was with the Yankees in '41, but they had DiMaggio, Keller and Henrich policing the gardens sooo—there was little room for Mr. T. Holmes. * * * Which reminds us, that Danny (The Great) Gardella, who is burning up the NL with the Giants, once starred with Beckley, at Huntington's League Park. Danny is so hot today that he doesn't know his own strength. A great hitter—no field. * * * Pvt. Jack Davis says

the 'Big Three' agreements will not be a case of 'The Potsdam calling the kettles black.'"[363]

Berlin: July 20: President Truman, speaking from the former Kaiser's Palace, said, "We are not fighting for conquest. There is not one piece of territory or one thing of a monetary nature we want out of this war."[364]

"... Mustang fighters raided the industrial heartland of Japan twice on Friday, and Far East Air Force headquarters announced ... that bombers and fighters had riddled the vital Shanghai shipping area with bombs and bullets for the second straight day..."[365]

"IN THE SERVICE":

First Lieutenant Charles E. Pancake, son of Mr. and Mrs. E. M. Pancake of Miller, O., a veteran combat navigator, recently reported to the Ellington Field, Tex., installation of the AAF Training Command. Lieutenant Pancake's wife, Mrs. Lucille M. Pancake, resides at 928 Twelfth Avenue.

Corporal Christine L. Shanklin, daughter of Mrs. C. B. Shanklin, Huntington WAC who was present at the German surrender at Reims, is now stationed at Frankfurt, Germany as receptionist to General Biddle Smith. In a recent letter, Corporal Shanklin stated that she expected to be in Europe for about another year.

Technician Fifth Grade Frank Blevins, son of Mrs. Delphia Blevins, 609 Second Avenue, a veteran of 27 months in the Pacific theatre, is now at the Army Redistribution Station at Camp Butner, N.C.

Seaman First Class Bernard S. Stevens, USN, has returned to the Navy Armed Guard Center, Brooklyn, N.Y. after spending a 21-day furlough here with his wife, Mrs. Virginia Stevens, 640 Sixth Avenue. Seaman Stevens recently completed 17 months sea duty in the Pacific.

Technical Sergeant Raymond Sheppard, son of Mr. and Mrs. W. M. Sheppard of Barboursville, is now stationed at the Army

Redistribution Center, Camp Butner, N.C. He recently returned from the European theatre, where he served 40 months and was awarded the Purple Heart, the Croix de Guerre and the Combat Infantryman's Badge.

Lloyd H. Landau, brother of Bert G. Landau, 418 Twelfth Avenue, was recently promoted from major to lieutenant colonel in the European theatre while serving with the U.S. Control Group of the Allied Military Government. General Mark Clark pinned the insignia of the new rank on his tunic.

James F. Sizemore, aviation machinist's mate third class, USNR, son of Mr. and Mrs. A. H. Gill of Logan, is an aircrewman serving aboard a land-based Navy search plane, which recently destroyed five enemy ships during a single flight over Borneo.

Corporal J. A. Meador, now stationed in France, was recently promoted to that rank ... according to a letter received from him by his wife, Mrs. J. A. Meador, 1661 Thirteenth Avenue. He is the son of Mr. and Mrs. A. Meador of Huntington.

Aviation Machinist's Mate E. D'Arcy Morton of the WAVES was recently promoted to that rank at Barin Field, Pensacola, Fla. She entered the service in January, 1944.

First Lieutenant Max Edwin Weeks, 1213 Fourth Avenue, was promoted to that rank ... according to a War Department announcement. Lieutenant Weeks is a graduate of Central High School.

Major Thomas W. Wolfe, husband of the former Miss Betty A. Bobbitt, was recently promoted to that rank from captain while serving as intelligence officer of a troop carrier group in France.

Glenna: *July 22ⁿᵈ Sunday – Papa's 61st birthday. We had a birthday supper for him. Present were Papa, Momma, Cline, Milo and Maxine, Gaynelle, Don, Rupert, Uncle June, Wiles, Dawson, and myself.*

Rupert: *I went to Sunday school today. In evening had birthday dinner for Grandpa.*

I remember those family gatherings with fondness; there was banter, laughter, and always heated political discussion.

Hamlin, West Virginia: "The Lincoln National Bank of Hamlin revealed that, for the first time in history, it has struck a balance of assets against liabilities exceeding $3,000,000."[366]

Washington, July 21: The Army planned to send more than 2,500 German prisoners of war with mining experience to Europe to help mine coal. The men would remain Allied prisoners of war.[367]

"WITH THE COLORS":

Elbert Hager of Salt Rock, and Albert Rimmer of Barboursville, are receiving their initial Navy indoctrination at the U.S. Naval Training Center, Great Lakes, Ill. Each man will receive a leave after completion of this recruit training.

Machinist's Mate (Second Class) Homer C. Jarrell [21], son of Mrs. Vina Ellis of Moncio, W.Va., has taken part in at least 10 major campaigns and invasions since he entered the Navy in June 1941. He has seen action in the Mediterranean off Algiers and participated in the invasions of Sicily and Palermo. [He became a "two theatre" man aboard a destroyer in the Pacific.]

Recently returning from the South Pacific, Petty Officer (Second Class) Sherman Dickson, USN, is spending a 15-day furlough with his parents, Mr. and Mrs. Walter Dickson of 307 Buffington Street. While serving in the South Pacific he received a Purple Heart for wounds suffered during the invasion of Okinawa.

Corporal Lloyd Keaton, son of Mr. and Mrs. Ellis Keaton of 2522 Ninth Avenue, was recently promoted from the rank of private while serving with the 753rd Tank Battalion in Germany.

Serving in the European theatre for 22 months, Private (First Class) Wayne Damron, brother of Mrs. Jean George, 2853 Fourth Avenue, has returned to the United States. He was awarded the Presidential Unit Citation, the ETO ribbon with five battle stars and the Good Conduct Medal.

Technical Sergeant Thaddeus D. Kauffelt, 20, son of Dr. and Mrs. T. D. Kauffelt Jr., 1329 Sixth Avenue, has been awarded an Oak Leaf Cluster to the Air Medal, ... at a B-29 base at Tinian Island in the Pacific. A B-29 gunner with the 313th Bombardment Wing, Sergeant Kauffelt has been overseas since last January. He has completed 15 combat missions and has returned to his bomber base after a rest period in Hawaii... He is a graduate of St. Joseph's High School and attended Marshall College.

Second Lieutenant George B. Brown, 951 Madison Avenue, is enrolled in a B-29 transition flying school at Maxwell Field, Ala., as a flight engineer, a member of a three-man team which handles the flying controls of the giant heavy bombers.

Private (First Class) William Morrison is currently assigned to the Military Police at an Air Transport Command base near London. He is the [husband] of Mrs. Gladys Morrison of 317 West Eleventh Street.

A former combat engineer with the Army's 36th Division in Europe, Captain Ira Joseph Kial Jr. and his wife, the former Miss Nancy Ferris, are visiting his parents, Dr. and Mrs. I. J. Kail of Whitaker Hill. Captain Kial is en route ... to the Army Service Forces Training Center at Fort Belvoir, Va. for further assignment.

Steward's Mate (Third Class) Billy Jack Newman, son of Mr. and Mrs. J. H. Newman of Route Four, Huntington, is stationed somewhere in the Pacific.

Corporal Arnold Powers, 622 Chesapeake Street, and Private (First Class) Fritz A. Bartram, 218 ½ Twenty-first Street, both members of the 454th Liberator Bombardment Group, and

Corporal Joe Rowsey, 2579 Guyan Avenue, an ordnance technician with the 301st Flying Fortress Bombardment Group for 30 months, are now on their way home.

... Corporal Brinton O. Gray of Huntington is serving as an administrative clerk with the 12th Air Force Night Fighter Squadron in the Mediterranean theatre of operations.

Second Lieutenant Kathleen Neal, daughter of Mr. and Mrs. Elliot Neal of 2620 South Fifth Street, Ironton, O., was recently promoted to the rank of first lieutenant by Lieutenant Colonel Flora Ballard, chief nurse of Fletcher General Hospital at Cambridge, O. Lieutenant Neal enlisted Feb. 1944, and received her basic training at Billings General Hospital, Fort Benjamin, Harrison, Ind. She is a graduate of St. Mary's Hospital and was active in Red Cross work. She is now on leave of absence from her work as a city nurse at Ironton.

Glenna: *July 23rd Monday – I washed. Put flowers on Rupert's grave. Very hot.*

Rupert: *I stayed at home today.*

Paris, July 22: "Marshal Petain [89-year old former Vichy chief of state] was taken in a bulletproof limousine to the Palace of Justice today and lodged in a special apartment beside the courtroom where he is to go on trial for his life tomorrow." His wife joined him there.[368]

Conditions had improved in areas of the Pacific: The U.S. Third Fleet roamed unchallenged over a large sweep of enemy waters and Australian troops landed at the headwaters of Balikpapan Bay without meeting Japanese opposition.[369]

Manila: American troops from the German front, mostly engineering units, arrived in the Philippines... Troops from Italy had arrived the week before. "The men appeared to be in good spirits, but the universal refrain was: 'It wouldn't be so bad if we could have had a little furlough at home on the way out here.'"[370]

"IN THE SERVICE":

Private First Class Virgil Brumfield, husband of Mrs. Mary M. Brumfield, 5223 Pea Ridge Road, has been awarded the Silver Star Medal for gallantry in action against the Japanese at Ipo Dam, Luzon.

Private First Class Ernest Mullins of Matewan, member of Lieutenant General Robert L. Eichelberger's Eighth Army headquarters staff, was recently awarded the Good Conduct medal on Luzon.

Staff Sergeant James H. Rayburn, son of Mr. and Mrs. James H. Rayburn of Barboursville, is a member of the 113th Engineer Combat Battalion, engineers unit of the 38th "Cyclone" Infantry on Luzon.

Private First Class Marvin C. Threlkeld, son of Mr. and Mrs. R. A. Threlkeld, 828 Ninth Street, was a member of a 38th Division mortar platoon on Luzon which eliminated a Japanese strongpoint after artillery shells failed to neutralize the position.

Corporal Clair S. Smith of Shoals, W.Va., is spending a 30-day furlough with his relatives after three years in the Army, two of which were spent in the European theatre.

Mrs. Eulah Mae Dann, daughter of Mr. and Mrs. R. L. Johnson of Branchland, has accepted a civilian position in the Classification and Assignment Division of the Army Ground and Service Forces Redistribution Station at Asheville, N.C.

Seaman First Class William Wallace Hall of Auxier, Ky., has been commended by his commanding officer aboard a Pacific Fleet destroyer for his part in saving an LCT which had caught fire in Leyte Gulf in May.

Boatswain's Mate First Class Charles E. Hall, son of Mr. and Mrs. Troy Hall of Wheelwright, Ky., was aboard the USS *Colorado* for 60 days and nights at Okinawa.

The Fifth Naval District has announced the arrival in Pearl Harbor of Tolbert B. Dean, 528 Eighth Street, a civilian, who will assist in overhaul and repair of ships of the Pacific Fleet.

Private James L. Clay of Huntington has reported to the Medical Department Enlisted Technicians School at Brooke Hospital Center, Fort Sam Houston, Tex. to undergo training as an Army medical-surgical technician.

Private Chester Black of Chesapeake, O. received an honorable discharge from the Army at Crile General Hospital in Cleveland on July 20.

Ensign Edsel C. Varney of Banco, a graduate of Chapmanville High School in the class of 1941, has returned on leave from a tour of duty in the Pacific where he piloted one of the Navy's fighter planes in support of the invasions of Luzon, Iwo Jima, and Okinawa.

Glenna: *July 24th Tuesday – Very hot. I ironed and mended.*

Rupert: *I got a letter from Jerry Lynn. I answered it.*

Potsdam: July 23: Roy Porter, of the National Broadcasting Company, said in a broadcast that some members of the American delegation to the Big Three Conference were leaving for a "new and surprising destination... Who they are and what they will do is another one of those prohibited subjects, prohibited this time by security rather than political significance." (Word about atomic bomb development seems to have been leaked.)

Mondorf, Luxembourg: July 23: Dr. Bohuslav Ecer, Czechoslovak representative on the War Crimes Commission, announced that most war criminal trials would be held at Nuremberg, and would start after September 15. Karl Hermann Frank, "the butcher of Lidice" was to go on trial in Prague about September 1, but it was made clear that, "regardless of the outcome, Frank would be turned back to the United Nations War Crime Commission for re-trial on other charges at Nuremberg."[371]

Paris, July 23: Marshal Henri Philippe Petain displayed French medals on his chest as he went on trial for his life. He stated that he had not betrayed France, but had "prepared the road to liberation." Petain further said, "I sacrificed my prestige for the French people. If I've treated with the enemy, it was to spare you."[372]

B-29 bombers made runs against Osaka and Nagoya.[373]

"IN THE SERVICE":

Corporal Frank Dean, son of Mrs. Mary Dean of Fort Gay, was recently awarded the Soldier's Medal for heroism not involving actual conflict, with the Fifth Army in Italy. Corporal Dean made his way along a mined and booby-trapped road to two American soldiers who had been wounded, gave them first aid, and then led litter bearers back safely through the hazardous route.

Technician Fifth Grade Harley M. Pearson, 2116 Tenth Avenue, is a member of the 397th Infantry of the Seventh Army's 100th Division, which was awarded the meritorious Service Unit Plaque for its superior performance of duty in France and Germany.

Staff Sergeant Clarence Wiley, whose wife resides at 1865 Marshall Avenue, has participated in 33 bombardment missions as a tail gunner on a B-17 bomber and holds the Air Medal with four oak leaf clusters. He has been overseas for seven months. Staff Sergeant Wiley is the son of Mr. and Mrs. Clyde Wiley, 220 Eighteenth Street.

Seaman Second Class Allen J. Cremeans, 18, son of Allen Cremeans Rear 2927 Third Avenue, and Cledith Robson, 31, machinist's mate third class, have reported at the Naval Training Station at Norfolk, Va., to train for duties aboard a new destroyer of the Atlantic Fleet. Machinist Robson, 1926 Monroe Avenue, is a veteran of 23 months in the Pacific theatre.

Lieutenant (j. g.) Charles E. Davis, 29, son of Mrs. Effie Webb, 1667 Twelfth Street, was presented with the Air Medal on July 14 at the Naval Air Station at Lake City, Fla. The medal was presented for meritorious service while participating in aerial flight in the South Pacific. He is the husband of Mrs. Sybil Adkins, 1704 Twelfth Street.

B. B. Bradbury, 19, yeoman third class, has been presented the Purple Heart for wounds received when the destroyer on which he was serving was under fire during the Okinawa campaign. He is the son of Horace B. Bradbury of Mercerville, O.

Lieutenant Donald R. Eastburn, son of Mr. and Mrs. A. E. Eastburn, 940 Eleventh Avenue, ... has left for the Pacific theatre...

Private Clovis Liston, 24, husband of Mrs. Juanita Liston, 1119 Adams Avenue, ... just completed his basic training... He was employed at a shipyard in Wilmington, Del. before entering the service.

Clayton E. Morris, son of Mrs. Trulio Morris, 627 West Division Street, was recently promoted to corporal... He is a cook with the First Armored Division of the Fifth Army in Italy.

Clifford Stevens, machinist's mate first class, son of Mr. and Mrs. Ben Stevens of Olive Hill, Ky., is training at the Naval Training Station at Newport, R.I. for duty aboard an ammunition ship. Machinist Stevens has been in the Navy since 1938 and has served in all the major theatres.

Private Leo Earl, 25, husband of Mrs. Kathryn Earl, 1323 Fifth Street, arrived home last Friday for a 65-day furlough after spending 27 months in a German prison camp. Private Earl, who has been in the Army since November 1941, expects to be discharged at Miami Beach, Fla. after his furlough.

Glenna: *July 25th Wednesday — Very hot. We picked and strung beans. Gaynelle got her divorce from Silvia [Selva Wiley]. I went to prayer meeting that night. Jaruel Porter was the leader.*

Rupert: *I helped pick beans to can.*

"IN THE SERVICE":

Estill D. Arrowood, mailman first class, husband of Mrs. Imogene Arrowood, 421 Second Street, is chief mail clerk at a Navy post office at a station on Midway in the Pacific. He was a letter carrier at the post office here before joining the Navy in July, 1943, and has been overseas for 14 months. His parents are Mr. and Mrs. Albert Arrowood of Offutt, Ky.

Midshipman Stoddard Emmons of the Merchant Marine has arrived here to spend a three-week leave after eight and a half months in the Pacific theatre, where he was wounded in the leg by shrapnel. He is the son of Mr. and Mrs. Arthur S. Emmons of the Emmons Apartments and was on the USS *Hurricane* during the 138-mile-per-hour typhoon which damaged 20 warships last June 5.

Lieutenant Waldron M. McLellon, USN, formerly of Huntington, was recently graduated with a master's degree in civil engineering at the Rensselaer Polytechnic Institute at Troy, N.Y. Lieutenant McLellon is the grandson of J. L. McLellon, councilman here in 1892, and nephew of Mrs. Charles Kitts of North Kenova, O. He was aboard the USS *Oklahoma* when she was sunk at Pearl Harbor on December 7, 1941.

Private Glen Adkins of Chillicothe, O., son of Mrs. Hettie Adkins, 419 Fifth Avenue, a veteran of 32 months overseas, including 10 in a German prison camp, has completed a 60-day furlough and has returned to Miami Beach, Fla.

Staff Sergeant Edward V. Lee, son of Mrs. M. C. Lee. 3010 Auburn Road, was graduated from the AAF Instructor's School at Laredo, Texas. He is now qualified to become an instructor at one of the nation's seven aerial gunnery schools.

Staff Sergeant Francis D. Van Valkenburgh, son of P. K. Van Valkenburgh, 1235 Eighth Street, has started his training as an aerial engineer of the Air Forces at Geiger Field, Spokane, Washington.

Captain Elizabeth Johnston of Union, W.Va., a Marshall College graduate, sailed last week for Europe aboard the German liner *Amerika* in charge of 215 members of the Woman's Corps. Captain Johnston for the past 18 months had been in command of all WACs at Lowry Field, Denver, Col.

Staff Sergeant Frederick V. McCoy, 26, son of Mr. and Mrs. M. G. McCoy Sr., 1868 Marshall Avenue, has arrived here to spend a 30-day furlough. Sergeant McCoy was Huntington's first Army inductee from the Cabell County Board No. 2 in 1940, and saw action in Africa and in the Mediterranean theatre.

Glenna: *July 26th Thursday — Very hot. Hard rain that evening. Papa and Mamma sold their home at Huntington and all their furniture. Rupert went to town to visit Jerry Lynn Adkins. I canned a bushel of peaches and 30 quarts of beans.*

Rupert: *I went to Jerry Lynn's today. Grandpa and Grandma are moving back to the country.*

The move "back to the country" was destined to happen. On more than one of my visits I had heard them complain about the house and neighborhood.

A *Huntington Herald-Dispatch* article reported a ground-breaking for the new Beverly Hills Presbyterian Church at Green Oak Drive and Norway Avenue. "About 80 members, who have been worshiping in Gallaher School, were present for the ceremony preceding the mid-week prayer service. Dr. Charles A. Logan, the pastor, pushed the first wheelbarrow load of dirt off the site. Speakers included Dr. Carl Campbell, an elder, A. L. Campbell, a deacon, and Sam Brown, who presented the plans and specifications for the concrete block and brick veneer building. The War Production Board last week granted priorities for the work. Actual construction will start soon."[374] (Sadly, a January 27, 2020 *Huntington Herald-Dispatch* article announced the closing of this church.)[375]

The Labor Party in Britain took power on this day as Clement Attlee replaced Churchill. Attlee, at the Potsdam Conference, along with Truman and Stalin, warned Japan that if they do not surrender, they will be "utterly destroyed."[376]

The Japanese, still defiant, said in an Associated Press release, "Should America show any sincerity of putting into practice what she preaches, for instance in the Atlantic Charter, excepting its punitive clause, the Japanese nation, in fact the Japanese military, would automatically, if not willingly, (several words missing) follow in stopping the conflict and then and only then will sabers cease to rattle both in the East and in the West."[377]

While at the Potsdam Conference, President Truman learned about the first successful test of an atomic bomb at New Mexico's Alamogordo testing grounds.[378] Also unknown by the public was that critical atomic bomb components were delivered to the bombing base at Tinian by the USS *Indianapolis*.[379]

Glenna: *Friday July 27th – Cleaned the house. Sold 5 hens and went to visit out at Roy Midkiff's. Hot and damp.*

Rupert: *I went to the show with Jerry Lynn. We saw "Son of Lassie."*

Attlee's replacement of Churchill brought reactions: The *Yorkshire Post* said, "In some ways it is nothing less than a grave disaster for the nation to drop Mr. Churchill ... We do not for one moment believe the decision must be regarded as a vote of censure upon his conduct of the war."

From Bombay came, "The general view here in Bombay, India, on the British Labor Party victory was that the new government, like the old, would do little toward advancing independence for India." Clement Attlee's wife, Violet, apprehensive about a move to 10 Downing Street, said, "It's been bad enough running my house at Stanmore during the war... Cooking, as well as everything else these days, takes a lot of doing."[380]

Associated Press: "The United States, Britain and China last night demanded ... that Japan immediately surrender unconditionally or undergo 'prompt and utter destruction.'" The Big Three leaders agreed that "Japan shall be given the opportunity to end this war."[381]

"IN THE SERVICE":

Private First Class Louie Bowen, 40, son of Ora Bowen, 2040 Fourth Avenue, and Sergeant Wallace H. Lett, 26, son of Mrs. Sarah Lett of Huntington, arrived at the Presque Isle Army

Air Field, Maine last Monday for the European theatre. Sergeant Lett served overseas for 36 months in a transportation battalion, and Private Bowen was a water supply man in that theatre for 33 months.

Private First Class Clarence E. Hysell, 22, son of Mr. and Mrs. Eli Hysell, 1523 Madison Avenue, was awarded the Bronze Star Medal for heroic achievement while serving in Germany with the 71st Infantry Division. He entered the Army in April, 1941, and served two and a half years in Panama before going to Europe in May, 1944.

Technician Fifth Grade Lloyd Dempsey, former employee of the Huntington Publishing Co. and son of S. H. Dempsey, 728 Ninth Avenue, is with the 279th Engineers Battalion of the 13th Corps in Germany. His brother, Lieutenant Paul E. Dempsey, was a German prisoner and was freed early in May.

Technician Fourth Grade Bluford Smith, 22, husband of Mrs. Helen V. Smith of High Hat, Ky., has been awarded the Bronze Star Medal for meritorious service while serving with the Third Army in Germany. He entered the Army in February, 1943, and went overseas a year later.

Private First Class Orville D. Owens, son of Mrs. Minnie Owens of Milton, is spending a 32-day furlough with his wife and son at West Hamlin. He served in Germany for 14 months and wears five battle stars on his campaign ribbon.

Private Jacob P. Nicely Jr., son of Mr. and Mrs. J. P. Nicely, 2146 Eighth Avenue, an airborne veteran of the Battle of Bastogne and prisoner of Germany for six months, is home on a 60-day furlough before reporting to Miami Beach, Fla. Private Thurston V. Nicely, 18, his brother, is also spending a furlough home now before reporting to Fort Meade, Md.

Corporal Harold D. Turner, son of Mr. and Mrs. H. O. Turner, 237 Davis Street, is with the Fifth Air Force in the Philippines. He has been overseas for 14 months and wears the Pacific theatre ribbon with three battle stars.

Private James C. Pennington, son of Mrs. Ruby Pennington, 4960 Sunset Drive, is en route home from the European theatre where he served with the 28th Infantry Division. He saw action during the Normandy campaign last summer.

Chaplain O. V. Hitchcock, USNR, formerly of Huntington and now of Florida, was a member of a group of Navy personnel which recently explored the island of Tangoa in the South Pacific. Since his ordination as a minister in June, 1942, he has held three pastorates in Florida.

Corporal Willard V. Adams, 29, son of Mr. and Mrs. E. L. Adams, 927 Ninth Street, has been assigned to the Cazes Air Base at Casablanca with the North Africa Division of the Air Transport Command. Corporal Adams has previously served in England with the 303rd Bomber Group for 32 months.

Technical Sergeant Welden Stewart, son of Curtis Stewart of Jesse, W.Va. is being returned to the United States under the Army point system, it was announced by the 13th AAF headquarters in the Philippines. Sergeant Stewart has been overseas since September, 1942, serving as an airplane mechanic with a P-38 Lightening squadron.

Private First Class William T. Bowen, 2051 Hughes Street, fought across Europe with the 318th Infantry Regiment of the 80th Infantry Division, taking part in the Bastogne counter-offensive last December which stopped the final German offensive of the war...

Private First Class Charles C. Hancock, son of Mrs. H. V. Hancock of Chesapeake, O., was recently released from the Army under the point system. Private Hancock entered the Army in June, 1941 and was overseas for 44 months. His brother, Private James Hancock, was killed a year ago in France.

Glenna: *July 28th Saturday – Rained all day. Papa and Mamma came back home to live. I went to visit Mrs. Rousey.*

Rupert: *We went to the show again. We also played. We saw "Tall in the Saddle."*

A B-25 bomber crashed into the Empire State building on this day.

First Lieutenant Chester Ball, son of Mr. and Mrs. R. Harry Ball of Seth, W. Va., and 1942 editor of the *Parthenon* at Marshall College, is visiting in Huntington, Charleston and Seth on a 30-day furlough from the Army after nearly two years in the European theatre. He wears the Purple Heart with two Oak Leaf Clusters, five battle stars, the Silver Star and the Bronze Star with one Oak Leaf Cluster. An artillery forward observer, Lieutenant Ball was wounded at Metz Luxembourg, and Frankfurt-on-Main. He went to the European continent with the Fifth Division on July 9, 1944, and was in the St Lo break-through and the Third Army's spearhead across France... He said he was most grateful for the fact he had had two years of French at Sherman District High School at Seth, and two years of the same language at Marshall. He found himself in a position to act as interpreter.[382]

"IN THE SERVICE":

Serving aboard the cruiser USS *Guam* in the Pacific are Lieutenant (j. g.) John M. Baysden, 1806 Twelfth Avenue and Electrician's Mate Second Class Joseph D. Markham of Logan. The *Guam* has taken part in nearly six months of continuous action from Okinawa to the Inland Sea of Japan.

Howard F. Thivener, 25, fireman first class, son of Mr. and Mrs. Harry Thivener of Gallipolis, O., is at the Atlantic Fleet's Naval Training Station at Newport, R.I., preparing for a second tour of sea duty. He is a veteran of 16 months duty in the Pacific. His wife, Mrs. Ruth Thivener and young daughter live in Gallipolis.

Sergeant Alfred T. Cantrell, 339 Adams Avenue and Staff Sergeant John B. Bowden, 310 West Eleventh Avenue, will soon return to the United States with the veteran 459th Bomb Group after long service in Italy with the 15th AAF.

Second Lieutenant Effie P. Taylor, 2728 Fifth Avenue [former nurse at Morris Memorial Hospital at Milton], was graduated on Thursday as a member of the 12th class in the basic training school for Army nurses at the Fort Knox, Ky. Regional Hospital. She is the daughter of Mrs. Tressie M. Pickett of Huntington.

Technician Fifth Grade Albert Black, husband of Mrs. Ethel Mae Black of Huntington, Technician Fifth Grade Warren L. Cremeans, son of Mr. and Mrs. Joe Cremeans, 225 Marshall Street, and Private Philip C. Justice, 2663 Chesterfield Avenue, are patients at Newton D. Baker General Hospital at Martinsburg, W.Va. All are veterans of overseas fighting.

Technical Sergeant Harold G. Enos, 40, and his son, Boatswain's Mate Second Class Harold G. Enos Jr., 19, formerly of Huntington, have been together for the last month for the first time since 1941. Both have seen much action and have many ribbons and awards, Sergeant Enos, a veteran of 17 years in the Marine Corps, has been in the Army since 1942 and completed 84 aerial missions in the Pacific. Boatswain Enos joined the Navy in 1941 when he was 15.

The Bronze Star Medal was awarded to Technical Sergeant James R. Hayes, son of Mr. and Mrs. W. S. Hayes, 2411 Collis Avenue, for meritorious service in Europe with the 138th Quartermaster Truck Company. He has been overseas for 33 months and is now in Germany. He has three brothers in the Navy and another in the Army.

Seaman Second Class Robert B. Ball, 17, son of Mr. and Mrs. Frank Ball, 1133 Ninth Avenue, is serving aboard an aircraft carrier in the Pacific as the captain's orderly. He entered the Navy last March and took his basic training at Great Lakes. Ill. He was a senior at Central High School before joining the Navy. The aircraft carrier was recently commissioned and Mr. and Mrs. Ball received an invitation to attend the ceremony in Tacoma, Wash.

Second Lieutenant Kenneth B. Dunham, 1937 Madison Avenue, graduated from the Medical Department Officer Candidate School at Carlisle, Pa. last Wednesday...

Charles O. Gilfilen, 34, son of B. O. Gilfilen of Middleport, O., has advanced to radio technician second class aboard a destroyer of the Atlantic Fleet. He is married to the former Miss Bonita Delancy of Kanauga, O.

Lieutenant (j. g.) Jack Cromwell, USNR, 1702 Third Avenue, and 182 other U.S. Navy men who lost their lives while operating from the Naval Air Station at Dunkeswell, England, had their names inscribed on a memorial dedicated there recently by Fleet Air Wing 7.

Staff Sergeant Earl B. Thornton, son of Mr. and Mrs. S. Thornton, 1110 Twenty-first Street, and Private Roy E. Webb, son of Mrs. Lottie Webb, 1618 Commerce Street, have been awarded the Bronze Arrowhead to wear on their European theatre ribbon. Both are members of the 36th "Texas" Division of the Seventh Army.

Corporal Donald B. Romer, son of Mrs. J. Ben Romer, 619 Tenth Avenue, is scheduled to arrive at Hampton Roads, Va. from Italy. Corporal Romer has been in the service for three years and overseas since last March.

Billy M. Estep, 1131 Sixth Avenue, and Gerald A. Fielder of West Hamlin were sworn into the U.S. Marine Corps yesterday at the recruiting station here.

Glenna: *July 29th Sunday – Went to Sunday School. Warm with showers. Rupert came home from Jerry Lynn's.*

Rupert: *I came home and went to Sunday school.*

Gallup Poll, Princeton, New Jersey, July 28: "Limiting the presidency to two terms—an issue raised during the Roosevelt administration and recently brought up again in Congress—finds the public more evenly divided in its opinion now than a year ago."[383] (The Constitution was amended in 1947 to limit a president to two terms in office.)

Guam, July 29: "... Superfortress task forces today swept six forewarned Japanese cities with firebombs that left more than half the targets enveloped in 'conflagrations...'"[384]

Guam, July 29: "American Third Fleet planes set fire to the Japanese battleships *Haruna* and *Ise* and three cruisers in their strikes yesterday at the Kure naval base ..."[385]

The USS *Indianapolis* was sunk by a Japanese submarine. Three quarters of the crew died over the next few days because of a series of operational blunders. Many died from shark attacks.[386]

"WITH THE COLORS":

Captain David T. Myles of Barboursville, recently joined the First Field Artillery Battalion of the Sixth Infantry Division, now fighting on northern Luzon. Captain Myles' wife, Mrs. Quindora Myles lives at Barboursville.

Private (First Class) Eugene E. Mers, son of Mrs. Perl I. Ferguson of 930 Twenty-Eighth Street, who is a veteran of the 36th "Texas" Division, has been awarded the Bronze Arrowhead to wear on his European Theater of Operations ribbon. The Arrowhead was awarded for participation in the Salerno invasion.

Private Ernest R. Elkins, son of Mr. and Mrs. Ernest Elkins Sr. of 629 Buffington Street, who was wounded in Germany is now in a convalescent hospital at Fort Story, Va.

Staff Sergeant Roy C. White has returned to his home at 790 Vansant Street after serving 14 months in the European Theatre of Operations. He has seen action in Tunisia, Sicily, France, Belgium, Holland and Germany and holds four Bronze Stars, the Purple Heart, Combat Infantryman's Badge and the Good Conduct Medal. Sergeant White has a son, Charles, who is serving somewhere in Alaska.

Currently serving aboard the USS *Mobile*, light cruiser, is Coxswain Woodrow Nease, son of Mrs. Rosa Nease, 4802 Waverly Road. The cruiser which is stationed in the Pacific has dodged a dozen Jap planes and evaded enemy mines, torpedoes and suicide boats in order to move in close and smash more than 350 Jap shore targets near Okinawa.

Returning from the European theatre of operations, where he has spent the past year with the U.S. 13th Air Force, Pfc. Roy J. Elkins spent a 30-day furlough with his mother, Mrs. Bessie Elkins of Kenova. He has returned to Kelly Field, Tex.

First Lieutenant Albert M. Dickerson has been promoted from a second lieutenant at Hill Field, Ogden, Utah. The son of Mr. and Mrs. G. J. Dickerson of 210 Sixth Avenue, he is now attending a school of special training in Denver, Colo.

Private Robert W. Johnson is spending a furlough with his parents, Mr. and Mrs. Emery C. Johnson of Merritt Road, and his grandmother, Mrs. A. A. Keeling. He was awarded the Infantryman's Badge on completion of his basic training at Camp Blanding, Fla.

Captain Naseeb E. Tweel will take courses given to all Air Corps navigators who have returned from battle areas at the Central Navigation School at Ellington Field, Tex., where he has just been assigned. He is the son of Mr. and Mrs. Saied G. Tweel of 1016 Ninth Avenue.

Completing his work in an Officer Candidate School in France, Second Lieutenant Forrest Parsons received his commission. He is the son of Mr. and Mrs. L. A. Parsons of Baker Road and husband of the former Miss Marguerite Adams of Beckley, W.Va. Mrs. Parsons and her young daughter reside with his parents on Baker Road.

Assigned to guard duty with the United States Marine Corps on Saipan is Private (First Class) Howard Kennedy, son of Mrs. Frances Kennedy of 506 Third Avenue.

Glenna: *July 30th Monday — Hot with small showers. I washed. Papa bought two pigs.*

Rupert: *Grandpa bought two little pigs.*

Grandpa did not waste time returning to farm life. His pigs shared the pigpen with the two pigs we had purchased earlier in the year.

San Francisco, July 29: "Warning selected Japanese cities that they are next on the list of B-29 targets was begun 'so that all Japanese people must realize that further resistance is senseless,' Maj. Gen. Curtis LeMay asserted today in a broadcast from Guam."[387]

Japanese officials told their population to eat acorns to prevent starvation.[388]

"IN THE SERVICE":

Enoch J. Dailey, husband of Mrs. Violet Dailey and son of Mr. and Mrs. Henry Dailey of Milton, has been promoted to staff sergeant in the Air Transport Command's Pacific division in the Schouten Islands, Netherlands East Indies. He is sergeant of the guard at his base unit. He has been in the Army for nearly four years and has been overseas for more than a year. He wears a battle star for the New Guinea campaign and the Meritorious Service Unit insignia.

Private First Class Kenneth P. Marcum, son of Mr. and Mrs. Gid Marcum of Dunlow, is en route home from the European theatre with the 28th Infantry Division. The division fought from St. Lo, France, to the Rhine. He wears four battle stars, the Good Conduct Medal and the Combat Infantryman Badge.

Private Kenneth E. Riddle, son of Mrs. Lena M. Riddle, 1231 Wayne Avenue, Kenova, has been awarded the Silver Star Medal for gallantry in action with the Fifth Army in Italy. When his tank was subjected to intense enemy bazooka fire, Private Riddle dismounted, selected a position and guided the tank driver as he withdrew to safety. The citation said his courage undoubtedly saved the lives of his fellow crew members.

Marine Captain Martin B. Roush, who flew 120 missions with a torpedo bomber squadron in the Pacific, is at the Miramar, Calif., Marine Corps Air Station for leave and reassignment after completing his second tour of overseas duty. He is the husband of Mrs. Sara Louise Brunk Roush, 949 Madison Avenue, and son of Mr. and Mrs. O. B. Roush of Washington. Captain Roush has been awarded the Distinguished Flying Cross twice.

Private First Class Howard L. H. Woods, husband of Mrs. Erma Lee Woods, 2311 Jefferson Avenue and Private First Class Grover C. Clark Jr., whose father lives at 2637 Bradley Road, are among the West Virginians in the 31st Infantry Division which recently took part in the longest inland water thrust of the Philippines campaign, driving 80 miles up the Agusan River to deny the Japanese refuge even in the swamps of Mindanao.

Fourteen West Virginians are members of the 6th Medical Battalion which was awarded the Meritorious Service Plaque for outstanding performance of duty "under the most trying and difficult conditions" both in the Dutch New Guinea and Luzon campaigns. They included Cpl. Leslie E. Carter of Barboursville and Pfc. Ray Kirk, Ferrellsburg.

Seaman First Class David Paden, who played baseball at Central High School and elsewhere before the war ... is now driving buses for the transportation department at the Naval Auxiliary Air Station at Los Alamitos, Calif. after serving aboard an attack transport in five major Pacific naval battles...

Private First Class Charles W. Keener, husband of Mrs. Hazeline Keener and son of Mr. and Mrs. W. A. Keener of Holden, is a member of the 96th Signal Construction Battalion which has built a large part of the wire communications linking the China, Burma, and Indian theatres...

Corporal Henderson Ferguson, son of Mr. and Mrs. J. M. Ferguson of Wilsondale, W.Va., whose wife lives in Chesapeake, O., has been assigned to the Air Transport Command's big terminal at Manilla. He is serving as an airplane mechanic.

Fire Controlman Third Class William C. Preston of Olive Hill, Ky. was aboard the light cruiser USS *Mobile* when the ship fought off Japanese suicide planes and evaded torpedoes and enemy suicide boats to move in and shell targets on Okinawa.

Seaman Harold C. Clark of Alkol was aboard the battle cruiser USS *Guam* during six months of continuous action against Japanese targets.

Shelton McDowell, son of Mr. and Mrs. Shelton S. McDowell of Garretts Bend, is receiving instruction in the repair and maintenance of motor torpedo boats at the naval station at Melville, R.I. He served in the Pacific for 17 months.

Watertender First Class Clyde Workman, son of Mr. and Mrs. Wallace Workman of Harts, who is serving aboard a destroyer in the Pacific, recently rounded out five years in the Navy. He was in the Battle of Midway and participated in the campaigns which cleared Attu and Kiska in the Aleutians...

Corporal Robert C. Crickmer, son of Mrs. Vera Crickmer, 1012 Eleventh Avenue, has been awarded the Good Conduct Medal at a port in the China-Burma-India theatre where he is serving as a cargo checker.

Firemen First Class Harry Edward Stafford of Camp Dix, Ky., and husband of Mrs. Althea Burchett Stafford of Olive Hill, Ky., has arrived at the Norfolk, Va. Training Station to prepare for duties aboard a new destroyer of the Atlantic Fleet. He served aboard a destroyer in the Pacific and participated in five major actions.

Private First Class Mary B. Burns, WAC, of Slagle, formerly of Huntington, was recently promoted to that rank at the Lemoore, Calif. Army Air Field. She is the daughter of Adam Burns of Slagle.

Private Walden Lee Adkins, son of Mr. and Mrs. Ezra Adkins, 228 Richmond Street, has served as an orderly at the 106th General Hospital in England...

First Lieutenant Homer P. Davis, son of Mr. and Mrs. G. D. Davis, 845 Jackson Avenue, has been selected for four-engine bomber pilot training and has been transferred to the Liberal, Kan. Army Air Field.

Torpedoman Third Class Harold E. Kirk, son of Mr. and Mrs. Harry Kirk, 505 ½ Thirty-first Street, has arrived at the receiving station of the Naval Training and Distribution Center at Shoemaker, Calif., for reclassification and further assignment. He has been in the Navy for four years and saw action at Ormoc, Mindoro and Luzon in the Philippines.

Glenna: *July 31st Tuesday – Hot. I ironed.*

Rupert: *Stayed at home.*

"IN THE SERVICE":

Charles E. Harless, son of Roscoe Harless, 315 Simms Street, an Army veteran at 16 years of age, has now enlisted in the Navy and is taking his basic training at Sampson, N.Y. He was discharged from the Army last December and has been with the Navy since early June. His father is a veteran of World War I.

First Sergeant Roderick K. Wilson, son of Mr. and Mrs. A. B. Wilson, 2137 Fourth Avenue, a veteran of 42 months in the Pacific, is on his way home for a furlough. Sergeant Wilson participated in the Solomons, Philippines, and Netherland East Indies campaigns.

Private First Class Lyle D. Lusher, son of Mr. and Mrs. E. L. Lusher, 633 Fourteenth Street; Sergeant Robert L. Lovely, husband of Mrs. Evelyn E. Lovely of Huntington,

and Private First Class Jack M. Gillespie, son of Mr. and Mrs. J. M. Gillespie, 13 Twenty-eighth Street, are members of an AAF engineer battalion which has been awarded the Meritorious Service Plaque for building B-29 bases on Saipan.

Lieutenant (j. g.) Donald M. Loudermilk, USNR, son of Mr. and Mrs. J. H. Loudermilk, 408 West Sixteenth Street, was presented a letter of commendation for "excellent service" as a pilot of a fighter plane during the assault on the Palau Islands. Lieutenant Loudermilk is a veteran of 95 combat patrols in the pacific.

Ezra L. Adkins, seaman second class, son of Yadles Adkins of Ethel, W.Va., is serving aboard the light cruiser, USS *Mobile* in the Pacific. The *Mobile* took part in the bombardments of the Jap mainland recently.

Lieutenant (j. g.) Mary Lois Garrett, daughter of Dr. B. D. Garrett of Kenova, and Seaman First Class Colleen Sue Spurlock, daughter of Mrs. W. S. Spurlock, 4728 Ohio River Road, are stationed at Norfolk, Va. Naval Air Base.

Frederick H. Steinbrecher, a veteran of 18 months with the engineers in Germany, has returned to Camp Meade, Md. after spending a 30-day furlough here.

Private First Class Clyde E. Legg, 24, son of Mr. and Mrs. Edward Legg, 1542 Madison Avenue, is in the United States after eight months in Europe as a rifleman. Private Legg wears the Combat Infantryman Badge.

Machinist's Mate Foster Sperry, husband of Mrs. Shirlene Sperry, 925 Jefferson Avenue, was awarded the Purple Heart Medal for wounds received in action against the Japanese in the Pacific. The medal was presented at a naval hospital at Alez Heights, Oahu, Hawaii.

Seaman Second Class Paul Edward Nance, 27, 2630 First Avenue, son of Mrs. Grace Nance of Twenty-fifth Street, has completed basic training at the Navy's submarine school at New London, Conn. and will be assigned to one of the undersea fighters. Seaman Nance attended Central High School and joined the Navy last December...

Sergeant William O. Davis Jr., 23, son of Mr. and Mrs. W. O. Davis, 414 West Tenth Avenue, graduated recently as an aerial gunner at Davis-Monthan Field, Tucson, Ariz. The new B-29 gunner is a graduate of Huntington High School and was employed by the Chesapeake & Potomac Telephone Co. before entering the service in March, 1944.

Master Sergeant Elbert S. Alston, son of Mr. and Mrs. R. D. Alston, 1814 Doulton Avenue, is a member of an AAF ammunition company on Iwo Jima...

Charles W. Foster, seaman second class, Rear 8 A Street, and Bruce C. O'Neal, water-tender second class of Davin, W.Va., are serving aboard the cruiser USS *Birmingham* in the Pacific. The *Birmingham* is a veteran of the invasion of Sicily.

First Lieutenant Paul Hite, 334 Fifth Avenue, stationed at Avon Park, Fla., was recently promoted to that rank... Lieutenant Hite is a B-17 pilot as well as a Link trainer instructor.

Harold L. Persinger, 19, seaman second class, son of Mr. and Mrs. Frank Persinger of Gallipolis, O., is at the Newport R.I. Naval Training Station preparing for duty aboard a new heavy cruiser. He has seen action in the Mediterranean and Atlantic theatres.

Landon L. Riffe, seaman second class of Yatesville, Ky., is serving aboard the USS *Birmingham* in the Pacific theatre.

Ernest W. Stroud, 2899 Fourth Avenue and Charles G. Cole of Barboursville are employed at the Navy yard at Pearl Harbor, T. H., where they are helping repair damaged naval craft.

Hospital Apprentice First Class Katherine Lloyd of East Lynn has been transferred from the Naval Air Station at Ottumwa, Ia. to the Naval Training Station at Shoemaker, Calif.

Private Joan Perry, 20, daughter of Mr. and Mrs. Wirt Perry of Huntington, was sworn into the WAC yesterday here and will leave soon for Fort Des Moines, Ia. for basic training.

Louis O. Gadeke Jr. has been promoted from second to first lieutenant while serving in the Tinian Islands with the 313th Bombardment Wing of the AAF.

Corporal David Cohen, son of Mrs. Sarah Cohen of Huntington was recently promoted to that grade from private first class while serving with the 21st Bomber Command on Guam.

August

ATOMIC BOMBS, JAPAN SURRENDERS

GLENNA: AUGUST 1ST WEDNESDAY – I MOWED AT THE GRAVEYARD. VERY
hot. Went to prayer meeting that night.

Rupert: *I read a book.*

"Dr. J. Trimmer, pastor of the First Baptist Church in Macon, Ga. for the past six years, has accepted a call to the pastorate of the Fifth Avenue Baptist Church here and will assume his duties Sunday, September 16... The call to Dr. Trimmer to fill the pastorate vacated by the resignation of Dr. E. B. Willingham was extended following a special congregational meeting following the morning services at the church last Sunday... Dr. Willingham left here to become pastor of the National Memorial Church in Washington, D.C."[389]

Marshall College was set to graduate eighty-two from summer school, one of the largest classes ever to receive summer diplomas from the school, according to Marshall president, Dr. J. D. Williams. Nineteen would graduate with masters degrees.[390]

Huntington: "Interest was centering anew ... on proposals for a city-county hospital, but city officials, preoccupied with the municipal airport project, remained lukewarm..."[391]

An honor deserved: "Private Willie L. Adkins of Lavalette, W.Va., who was killed while fighting on the Fifth Army front in Italy with the 362nd Infantry Regiment of the 91st ('Powder River') Division, has been awarded the Bronze Star Medal posthumously. The citation accompanying the award related: 'Because of poor

visibility and wet weather, causing the foxholes of the men to fill with water, the fighting efficiency and morale was very low. Adkins encouraged his comrades, killed several of the enemy and showed such coolness and fighting spirit that a fierce counterattack by the enemy was turned back, with 17 killed and many wounded, as well as much enemy equipment being abandoned and our own lines secured. Adkins gave his life for his country and by so doing encouraged his comrades [to] complete their mission,' concluded the citation. His mother, Mrs. Lorena Adkins, lives on Route 1, Lavalette."[392]

"Private (First Class) Dorsey Darrell Elkins, USMCR, the son of Mrs. Hazel V. Elkins, 4445 Bradley Road, who was previously reported missing in action, was wounded, the Navy announced today in its daily war casualties report."[393]

"Lieutenant (Senior Grade) Abe Forsythe Jr., 821 First Street, who was medically discharged from the Navy on July 7 after four and a half years of service, will receive the Navy Cross at the South Charleston Naval Ordnance Plant at 11 A.M. Friday for heroic action as the pilot of a Wildcat fighter plane in the Battle of Leyte Gulf on October 25, 1944... He attacked in the face of intense enemy fire and 'made his runs with courage and audacity.'"[394]

New York, August 1: "The toll in the crash of a B-25 bomber into the Empire State building ... rose to 14 today with the death of Joseph C. Fountain, 47, a National Catholic Welfare Council employee who received third degree burns trying to aid other workers in the office to safety."[395]

Potsdam, August 1: "The Big Three came to an end early tonight of their historic sessions upon which the future peace of the world may possibly hinge."[396]

Jerusalem, August 1: "The Palestine government has been conferring with the British on the problem of readmitting the Germans to their six settlements in Palestine and giving them back their property holdings, which were considerable..."[397]

Darmstadt, Germany: August 1: Verdicts were returned for the ten Germans tried for killing six captured American airmen in August 1944. Seven defendants, two of them women, were sentenced to be hanged and three others faced long prison terms.[398]

"WITH THE COLORS":

Corporal Walter H. Chapman and Private Bruce McCluskey, brother-in-law, met on July 17 on Luzon, where they are members of the Coast Guard Artillery and Cavalry respectively. Corporal Chapman is the husband of the former Miss Wayne Silas of Milton and the son of Mr. and Mrs. E. C. Chapman of Branchland. Private McCuskey is the son of F. C. McCuskey Sr. of Branchland and husband of the former Miss Betty Chapman. The two soldiers had not seen each other for over a year and a half.

Private (First Class) Charles E. Rose, 1916 Madison Avenue, and son of Mrs. Daisie A. Wheeler, 1034 Sixth Avenue, is serving as a postal clerk with the 2628th Postal Directory Company in Caserta, Italy. Private Rose has been overseas 17 months and has seen action with the 143rd Infantry Regiment of the 36th "Texas' Division." He wears the Combat Infantryman's Badge.

Five fighting men from the Huntington area were with the 94th Infantry Division during the breakthrough from the Saar River bridgehead to the Rhine River near Ludwigshafen, Germany. They were Private (First Class) Clarkson E. Green, Accoville; Private (First Class) Joe Maynard, Kirk; Corporal Clifford McCoy, Matewan; Private (First Class) Granvil H. Landers, Scott Depot, and Private (First Class) Harold Hale, 1607 Eighteenth Street.

Private (First Class) Donald LeGrand, 22, a veteran of six months action in the European theatre of operations, is spending a 30-day furlough with his parents, Mr. and Mrs. Claud LeGrand of Perry Avenue. A graduate of Huntington High School, Private LeGrand wears the ETO ribbon with two battle stars for participation in major campaigns, the Good Conduct Medal, and the Combat Infantryman's Badge. He was employed by the International Nickel Co. prior to his entering the service last September.

Private Martin Cunningham of Huntington, a veteran of 12 months in the Asiatic-Pacific theatre of operations where he served in the Transport Corps as a clerk typist and was awarded the European theatre and Asiatic-Pacific theatre ribbons, returned to the United States today aboard a trans-Atlantic plane of the Air Transport Command, landing him at La Guardia Field, N.Y. His wife resides at 524 West Twenty-seventh Street.

Fire Controlman (First Class) Russell K. Adams, son of Mr. and Mrs. Galway Woods, 817 Twenty-fourth Street, and Seaman (First Class) George A. Wyant, husband of Mrs. Mildred F. Wyant, 1320 Jackson Avenue and son of Mr. and Mrs. C. A. Payne, 2778 Latulle Avenue, are serving aboard the USS *Melville*, a repair ship in the English Channel.

Melvin J. Dickman, son of Mrs. Lana S. Dickman, 2483 ½ Third Avenue, has been promoted to technical sergeant in the Headhunters, a crack P-38 outfit of the Fifth AAF in the Philippines.

Private (First Class) Billie R. Sherman, 24, WAC, daughter of Mrs. Tom Gilmore, 1838

Maple Avenue, ... has been transferred from Geiger Field, Spokane, Wash. to the Santa Maria, Calif. Army Air Field. Private Sherman has been serving in the WAC for 16 months.

Private (First Class) Clyde E. Murphey, 657 Thirty-first Street, is en route home with the 2838th Petroleum Distributing Company, which has finished its job of fueling Army vehicles in Europe...

Marine Private (First Class) Samuel M. Jackson, son of Mrs. Ottie Miller, 1212 Third Avenue, was recently promoted to his present rank ... at the Marine Corps Air Station, Cherry Point, N.C... Private Jackson entered the Marine Corps in March, 1944. He is serving as a crash crewman.

Lieutenant Joseph S. Hazelett, son of Mr. and Mrs. H. H. Hazelett, 2161 Spring Valley Road has been transferred to Carlsbad, N.M. for four weeks of training, and from there he will go to Victorville, Calif...

Sergeant Andrew J. Deline, son of Mrs. Mae Deline, 134 Sycamore Street, has been transferred with the 58th Bombardment Wing, a pioneer Superfortress group from the India-China theatres, to the island of Tinian in the Marianas. Sergeant Deline is a sheet metal worker in a maintenance unit.

After spending 13 months in the China-Burma-India theatre of operation, during which time he completed 48 bombing missions. Staff Sergeant O. M. Smith of Logan is an aerial instructor at the Myrtle Beach, S.C. Army Air Field.

Glenna: *August 2ⁿᵈ Thursday – Warm. I went down to Mrs. Rousey's and wrote 3 letters for her.*

Rupert: *I went to the show at West Hamlin. I saw "Meet Dr. Chirstin* [Dr. Christian]."

Maxine visited her mother often, and I sometimes went along. Although the theatre was small,

there was a full crowd. It was a dark night and I remember walking back to the house with Delano, who had a flashlight.

New York, August 2: "The 'Shooting Star' jet-propelled fighter plane which hurtled 555 miles between Dayton, Ohio and New York in 62 minutes, was acclaimed today as the world's fastest plane."[399]

London, August 2: "U. S. headquarters in the United Kingdom said today it was unlikely that British wives of American servicemen could be transported to the United States before next spring."[400]

President Truman, on his way back to the United States, had lunch with King George VI at Plymouth aboard the *H. M. S. Renown.* The king also visited the President aboard the President's ship, the USS *Augusta.* Later, the *Augusta,* with Mr. Truman aboard, left for the voyage home.[401]

The Japanese city of Toyama was destroyed by American bombing.[402]

"Torpedoman's Mate (third class) William Harold Patton, USNR, the husband of Mrs. Frances Evelyn Patton, 2920 Winchester Avenue, Ashland, has been killed in action... The Ashland sailor was previously reported as missing." In the same report was a list of wounded, among them, "Private Robert L Simms, brother of Miss Dorothy P. Simms, Hurricane, W. Va.; Corporal Edwin G. Rose, Route 2, Gallipolis, O.; ... Seaman (first class) Donald Lee Brumfield, USNR, husband of Mrs. Mary Jewell Brumfield, Kenova, W. Va."[403]

"WITH THE COLORS":

Private (First Class) Lester Swann, son of Mrs. Eustace Swann of Huntington and husband of Mrs. Norma Swann of Atlanta Ga., is serving with the 38th Division on Luzon and recently helped to take an important hill near Manila.

Private (First Class) Charles W. Bledsoe, son of Mrs. Nancy A. Bledsoe of Barboursville, a rifleman with the 349th "Krautkiller" Regiment of the Fifth Army in Italy, has been cited and awarded the Combat Infantryman's Badge.

Ship's Serviceman (First Class) Aubrey C. Bryant, whose wife and five children reside at 318 Marcum Terrace, is serving aboard the USS *Quincy* in the Pacific.

Private (First Class) George T. McCoppin Jr. and his brother, First Lieutenant William E. McCoppin, USAAF, are home together for the first time since they entered service in 1943. They are the sons of Mr. and Mrs. G. T. McCoppin, 2641 Collis Avenue. Private McCoppin, husband of Mrs. Ruth D. McCoppin, 2053 Eighth Avenue, returned last week from Europe. Lieutenant McCoppin, who returned in January from England, is en route from Bryan, Tex., where he finished a pilot's instrument course, to Aloe Field, Victoria, Tex. to be a flying instructor. A brother-in-law and sister, Mr. and Mrs. V. S. Harrison, and son, of Charleston, arrived for a visit today.

Second Lieutenant Virginia Lee Garren, the daughter of Mrs. W. C. Garren, 307 Thirty-second Street, is serving as a nurse in India. Lieutenant Garren has two and a half years' service as an Army nurse, with a year and a half overseas. The exact location of her unit was not disclosed by a dispatch from New Delhi, but most of the nurses, it said, are on duty at jungle outposts in the mountainous areas of Assam, India and northern Burma.

Lieutenant Jacqueline B. Clay, daughter of Mr. and Mrs. L. Clay of Barboursville, and Lieutenant Mary B. Earnest, daughter of Mr. and Mrs. W. A. Earnest, 1120 Nineteenth Street, were among the nearly 50 graduates of the Third Service Command Nurses Basic Military Training Center at the Quartermaster School at Camp Lee, Virginia.

Aviation Machinist's Mate (Third Class) William H. Smith, 1824 Midway Avenue, and Fire Controlman (Third Class) Robert L. Downey of West Tenth Avenue, are serving aboard the cruiser, USS *Shangri-La* in the Pacific theatre.

Seaman (First Class) James R. Hull, 18, of Stollings, W.Va., is currently stationed at the Norfolk Naval Training Center, preparing for duties aboard a new destroyer of the Atlantic Fleet. He is the son of Mrs. Ester Williams of Stollings and has just returned to this country after serving for four months in the Pacific aboard a tug boat.

Fireman (Second Class) Everett E. Brown Jr., 30, son of Mr. and Mrs. E. E. Brown Sr. of Kenova, is stationed at the Newport, R.I. Naval Training Station preparing for duties aboard a new auxiliary ship of the Atlantic Fleet. His wife, the former Miss Eileen Warden, and infant daughter, reside at 629 ½ Fourth Street.

Private James Taylor, husband of Mrs. Vesta Taylor, 1934 Sixth Avenue, is fighting with the 38th Infantry Division on Luzon...

Private (First Class) Sidney A. Floyd, son of Mrs. E. B. Floyd, 419 Sixth Street, has been praised ... for his "efficiency, tact, and cooperation" in helping quell a disorder between Scottish military personnel and civilians in Walsall, England on July 7... A member of the military police unit, he served with the infantry in Normandy, Luxembourg, and has been awarded the Purple Heart Medal, the Bronze Star Medal with one Oak leaf Cluster and the Presidential Unit Citation. He was employed by the American Car and Foundry Co. prior to entering the Army.

Private Sherwood S. Hensley who is with a U.S. Railway Battalion in India has been overseas for the past year. He is the son of Mr. and Mrs. Andrew J. Hensley of 2476 ½ Third Avenue... Private Hensley is a graduate of Huntington High School where he was active in sports.

Private (First Class) Maurice E. Webb, 101 South Minton Street, is serving in Kunming, China, with the headquarters unit at the base general depot handling supplies traveling to American and Chinese units fighting the Japanese in the China theatre of operations...

Seaman (Second Class) Sam Haworth, son of Mrs. S. V. Haworth, 1107 West Fifth Street, arrived here today from the Great Lakes Naval Training Station, Great Lakes, Ill. on a 13-day furlough before reporting to the engineering division training station near Providence, R.I., where he will receive instructions for assignment to the Seabees.

Staff Sergeant Wetzel C. Jobe, son of Mr. and Mrs. Fred Jobe [of Salt Rock], is en route to the United States after 13 months in the Pacific theatre of operations as an aerial engineer-gunner with the "Red Raiders," a B24 Liberator unit of the Fifth Air Force Bomber Command, now based in the Philippines. Sergeant Jobe has completed 46 combat missions over New Guinea, the Palaus, Celebes, Halmaharas, Philippines, Formosa and China. A graduate of Barboursville High School, he has been awarded the Air Medal with two Oak Clusters, the Asiatic-Pacific ribbon with three battle stars, the Philippine Liberation ribbon with two battle stars and the Good Conduct Medal.

Glenna: *August 3rd Friday – Cleaned the house and baked a cake.*

Rupert: *I stayed at home today.*

Bluefield, West Virginia, August 3: "Junior J. Spurrier, Bluefield's Congressional Medal of Honor winner, was married quietly last Monday in Pikeville, Ky. to Miss Velma Kathleen Romano, it was announced by her parents, Mr. and Mrs. Domenic Romano of Bluefield."[404]

Dayton, Ohio, August 3: A jet-propelled 'Shooting Star' plane crashed near Brandenburg, Kentucky, and test pilot Major Ira Boyd Jones was killed. The plane was a sister ship of the one that flew from Dayton to New York in a record sixty-two minutes.[405]

"WITH THE COLORS":

Private (First Class) Donald L. Rice, son of Mrs. Mary Stevenson, 1234 Eighteenth Street, an infantry veteran of 12 months overseas duty, is at the Newton D. Baker General Hospital, Martinsburg, W.Va. for treatment. A former member of the 319th Regiment of the 80th Division, he fought in France and Germany and wears the Purple Heart Medal and the Expert Infantryman's Badge.

Private (First Class) Leslie E. Ferguson, son of Mr. and Mrs. Wade Ferguson of Wayne, a veteran of 33 months with the 62nd Air Service Group in North Africa and Italy, has been assigned to the motor pool at the Middletown, Pa., Air Technical Service Command. Private Ferguson entered the service in June 1942 and wears three campaign stars on his campaign ribbon.

Second Lieutenant Beulah L. Fizer, daughter of Mr. and Mrs. H. W. Fizer of Crumpler, W.Va., and Second Lieutenant Virginia L. Garren, daughter of Mrs. W. C. Garren, 307 Thirty-second Street, are Army nurses stationed in India. Lieutenant Fizer has been in the service for three years, more than two years overseas, and Lieutenant Garren has been in almost three years, with a year and a half overseas.

Private (First Class) Donald L. Earl, 1940 Artisan Avenue, is a member of the 168th "Rainbow" Regiment of the Fifth Army's 34th Division. He is stationed near Monte Colle de Tena on the Franco-Italian border.

... Verlin W. Lee, 23, 217 Division Street, has been promoted to the rank of hospital apprentice (first class) and assigned to the U.S. Naval District in San Diego, the Eleventh Naval District announced today. Corpsman Lee, a graduate of Huntington High School, attended Marshall College and the College of Medicine, Cincinnati, O... His wife, Mrs. Dorothea Lee, resides at 525 Thirtieth Street. He has two brothers in the service, Yeoman (First Class)

Ralph A. Lee, USN, and Private (First Class) James F. Lee, in the U.S. Army.

Fireman (Second Class) Hugh E. Norton, 30, USN, husband of Mrs. Edna Mae Norton, 721 Lynn Street, recently completed his training at the U.S. Naval Training Station at Great Lakes, Ill. and is currently stationed in San Diego, Calif... He has two brothers, Private Ralph Norton and Captain Jean Norton serving with the Army overseas, and a sister, Rudelle, a member of an American Red Cross Unit which will soon be sent overseas.

Private William Adkins, 19, son of Mr. and Mrs. G. O. Adkins, 2661 First Avenue, has recently been assigned to the U.S. Signal Corps, 43rd Signal Company, and is attached to the telephone section as a switchboard operator at the 43rd Division headquarters on Luzon. Private Adkins, who graduated from Huntington High School and attended Marshall College prior to his entrance into the service in December, 1944, received his basic training at Camp Blanding, Fla., and embarked from Fort Ord, Calif., for the Pacific theatre last May.

Glenna: *Saturday August 4th – I went down to Mrs. Morrison's and helped cook for the reunion.*

Rupert: *I walked down to Morrisons today.*

The Morrison Reunion was an annual affair at the family farm. That year I cleaned the spring that flowed from beneath the roots of a large beech tree across the road from the house and repaired a rock walkway from road to spring. The spring had once been the family's source of water and a cool place to preserve food. We set up tables under the big tree. The reunions continued for several years after Dawson's mother died, but were held at the 4H camp near Barboursville. The last Morrison reunion I remember attending was with Millie,

about 1975. Our small sons, Gregory and Jonathan were with us.

"The Rev. R. G. Dillard, who has been serving as a teacher at the Seventh Avenue Baptist Church, will begin duties as pastor of the First Baptist Church of Hamlin tomorrow. Mr. Dillard, a speaker at the Hamlin church on July 22, received a call to the pulpit there on Wednesday. He is a member of the Guyandotte Baptist Association."[406]

Bad Tolz, Germany, August 4: "A son of Field Marshal Erwin Rommel declared in a sworn statement today that his father committed suicide as an alternative to a death sentence passed by a people's court 'because he was suspected of complicity in the July 20, 1944 bomb plot on Hitler's life. The statement ... was made by Manfred Rommel, 17-year-old son of the German 'Desert Fox.'"[407]

Manila, August 4: "General MacArthur announced today that he had taken command of the entire Ryukyu Island chain south of Japan—including Okinawa—as a base 'from which a mighty invasion force is being forged' for the subjugation of the enemy."[408]

"WITH THE COLORS":

Private (First Class) Raymond L. Reynolds, son of Mr. and Mrs. W. E. Reynolds of Salt Rock, a member of the 142nd Infantry of the 36th 'Texas' Division, has been awarded the Bronze Arrowhead to wear on his European theatre of operations ribbon for his participation in the Riviera invasion last August.

Private (First Class) Joseph E. Wallace, 351 Smith Street, has recently been awarded the Silver Star Medal for his action in combat prior to V-E Day, while serving with the 100th Division of the Seventh Army in Germany, division headquarters announced today. The award recognized the part Private Wallace played in the division's drive through France and Germany.

Private (First Class) Clinton E. Morrison of Huntington was recently awarded the Bronze Star Medal for heroic achievement in action while serving with the Fifth Army in the Italian campaign. His mother, Mrs. Louise Alley, resides at 333 Fourteenth Street.

Technician (Third Grade) Thomas R. Lyon Jr., son of Mrs. Thomas R. Lyon, 2006 Ninth Avenue, has recently been awarded the Bronze Star Medal for meritorious service against the enemy in the European theatre of operations. He served with the 2nd Medical Battalion in France, Luxembourg, Belgium and Germany, and on one occasion went forward to administer first aid to the wounded although subject to heavy artillery and mortar fire.

Corporal George Eddins, 917 Ninth Street, a member of the 86th Air Depot Group, one of the first Ninth Air Force service units scheduled for redeployment to the United States, is at Camp Detroit in the assembly area command in France.

Private (First Class) Al G. Shires, 20, 1205 Sixth Avenue, was recently awarded the Bronze Star Medal by Brigadier General Jesse A. Ladd, commanding general of the veteran Ninth Infantry Division, for heroic achievement during action in Germany last February. Private Shires, an ammunition bearer in the division's 47th Infantry Regiment, was inducted in May, 1943 and saw action in Normandy, Northern France and Belgium, before entering Germany with the first troops last September. He also holds the Purple Heart Medal for wounds received in Germany.

Glenna: *August 5th Sunday – We went to the Morrison Reunion at Dawson's mother's. Had everything to eat and saw everybody. Nice weather.*

Rupert: *I went to the Morrison reunion.*

For me, the highlight of the reunions was seeing Ramona and Wesselene Cordial, daughters of Dawson's sister, Lois. They came from Springfield, Ohio for a couple of weeks each summer to visit their grandmother.

St. Petersburg, Florida, August 3: "Doctors at the Army Air Forces Don Cesar Convalescent Hospital tonight diagnosed S-Sgt. Joe DiMaggio's stomach disorder as a duodenal ulcer..." Soon to be discharged, he said "He thought he could condition himself for play in a few weeks."[409]

There was discontent about the Potsdam Conference decisions, mainly the sharp division between eastern and western Europe with "Soviet domination of all the eastern European countries ranging from Finland in the north to Bulgaria in the south."[410]

War crime trials were to begin on September 1 at Nuremberg against Germans "who formulated Nazi policy, high military chiefs who executed it, ranking diplomats who intrigued for it, [and] industrialists and financiers who gave it substance." [411]

Guam, August 5: "The old battleship *West Virginia* came back from the grave the Japanese made for her with bombs and torpedoes at Pearl Harbor to thunder terrible vengeance in the Philippines and at Iwo Jima and Okinawa..." She was flying the same flag she was flying at Pearl Harbor.[412]

Although it did not appear in this day's news, an atomic bomb was dropped on Hiroshima, Japan, killing up to 80,000 civilians.

Glenna: *August 6th Monday –I washed and cleaned up everything. Cloudy.*

Rupert: *Don stayed up here almost all day.*

An AP report from Washington gave detailed news about the United States' use of the atomic bomb. "An atomic bomb, hailed as the most terrible destructive force in history and as the greatest achievement of organized science, has been loosed upon Japan," the article said. President Truman declared, "The atomic bomb is the answer ... to Japan's refusal to surrender," and Secretary of War Stimson said it would "prove a tremendous aid in shortening the Japanese war."[413]

The USS *Augusta*, with President Truman aboard, was making record time returning home from the Potsdam Big Three meeting. "Mr. Truman slept until 7 A.M. yesterday, a rare event for him, then attended church services in the forward mess hall below the well deck."[414]

"WITH THE COLORS":

Three men from Huntington and one from Culloden are serving with railway operation units of the Army in India. These units aid in the transportation of material to the Chinese. The four West Virginians are Technician (fifth Grade) Clinton G. McCallister, son of Mrs. Anna McCallister of Culloden; Technician (Fifth Grade) Covy L. Smith, husband of Mrs. Wanda M. Smith, 1340 Hall Street; Technician (Fifth Grade) Charles S. Brown, son of Mrs. C. C. Brown, 918 Thirteenth Street, and Private (First Class) Paul E. Williamson, son of Mrs. L. Mae Williamson, 202 Fifth Avenue.

One Huntington man and one from West Hamlin are serving in Italy with the 2698th Technical Supervision Regiment (Overhead), which was formed to supervise the activities of Italian troops performing essential services of supply tasks in the Peninsular Base Section. They are Master Sergeant Thomas E. Mynes, 812 Twenty-fifth Street, Huntington, and Sergeant Clive Ferguson, husband of Mrs. Anna Mae Ferguson, Box 141, West Hamlin, and son of Mr. and Mrs. James D. Lewis, West Hamlin.

Corporal Charles E. Wilcox, 23, of Huntington, is spending a 30-day furlough with his parents, Mr. and Mrs. E. R. Wilcox, who reside at 102 Richmond Street. A former employee of the C & O shops in Huntington, he entered the service in July 1944, and was shipped to the European theater of operations last October. Corporal Wilcox saw action in Southern France and Germany with the Fifth Division of General Patton's Third Army. He wears the Good Conduct Medal and the Combat Infantryman's Badge. After his brief visit here, he expects to be reassigned to active duty in the Pacific.

Private (First Class) Edward L. Harris, son of Mr. and Mrs. Joe Harris, 2215, Eighth Avenue, a veteran of 36 months in Iceland, England, France, Germany and Czechoslovakia, is a patient at the Newton D. Baker General Hospital at Martinsburg, W.Va. He served with the 495th Anti-Aircraft Artillery Gun Battalion, U.S. Ninth Air Force, and wears the European theatre of operations ribbon with five battle stars for action in major campaigns.

Sergeant William V. Stevens, son of Mrs. Mary Lou Stevens of Spring Valley Road, a veteran of 33 months in the China-Burma-India theatre with the 475th Infantry, landed at LaGuardia Field, N.Y., aboard an Air Transport Command plane. Sergeant Stevens wears the Asiatic-Pacific theatre ribbon with three stars, the American theatre and defense ribbons, the Combat Infantryman's Badge and the Good Conduct Medal.

Staff Sergeant Charles Blair, son of Mr. and Mrs. Charles J. Blair of 626 Elm Street, has reported to Sioux Falls, S.D. for reassignment following a 30-day furlough after serving in the European Theatre of operations. He was stationed with the 401st Bombing Squadron, 91st Bomb Group and completed 18 missions over Germany in a B-17 as a waist gunner. He wears the ETO ribbon with two battle stars, the Good Conduct Medal, the Air Medal with two Oak Leaf Clusters and the Presidential Unit Citation.

Technician (Fifth Grade) Charles E. Smith, son of Mrs. Georgia Smith, 325 West Ninth Street, returned home July 26 after being a German prisoner-of-war for five months. Technician Smith who had been in the service for two years and had served overseas 18 months was with the 12th Army under General

Omar Bradley when he was captured. He was taken prisoner in Belgium December 26.

Technician (Fifth Grade) Jimmie F. Blankenship, 67 Twenty-fifth Street, a supply assistant with the Army Air Forces Engineer Command in Italy, who has been overseas with the 845th Engineer Aviation Battalion, [which] was recently ... awarded the Meritorious Service Unit Plaque.

Corporal Leonard E. Barber, the son of Mr. and Mrs. L. E. Barber, 1601 Doulton Avenue, stationed with the Army in southern Germany, recently spent a 15-day furlough in Nice, France.

Private (First Class) John H. Neace, 101 Broad Hollow Road, Ceredo, W.Va., is serving with the 1786th Engineer Parts Supply Company, which has been helping to maintain the flow of supplies over the supply line through the India-Burma-theatre into China.

Fireman (First Class) Jess Edward Bragg, USNR, husband of Mrs. Mary E. Bragg of Huntington, has returned to Treasure Island, Calif. after two weeks' vacation at the U.S. Naval Rest Center at Sonoma, in the Valley of the Moon.

Captain James S. Klumpp, U.S. Naval Reserve Medical Corps, of Huntington, has asked the Navy to place him on inactive status after four and a half years of active duty, ... Mrs. Klumpp reported yesterday. He is currently stationed at Long Beach, Calif. The Huntington surgeon entered the Naval reserve Medical Corps in February, 1941, and has seen action overseas, including the North African campaign.

Electrician's Mate (First Class) Wilfred E. Whitten, husband of Mrs. Bessie Margaret Whitten, 1718 Third Avenue, recently accompanied Major Manuel Valley, famous guerrilla leader of the Philippines, on a return to the islands and photographed the Filipino leader on the scene of his past victories. He has been serving as a Seabee photographer.

Second Lieutenant James Marion Love of Point Pleasant is assigned to duty as a pilot of a B-17 in training at the Army air field at Dyersburg, Tenn.

Radioman (Second Class) Harold Golden Hazelett, son of Mr. and Mrs. Pearlie Hazelett, 805 Twenty-fourth Street, is convalescing at the U.S. Naval Hospital at the Charleston, S.C. Navy Yard. A graduate of Huntington High School in the class of 1942, he has served 13 months overseas.

Captain Harold M. Parsons, 27, of Charleston, W.Va., a veteran of 18 months service in the Southern Pacific theatre of operations, who is now on a 30-day furlough, recently visited his uncle, Mr. J. Price Miller, who resides at 225 29th Street. Captain Parsons entered the Army a year after the Japanese bombing of Pearl Harbor. A brother, Sergeant Ray A. Parsons, is serving with the Army in the Pacific.

Second Lieutenant Mary M. Earnest, daughter of Mr. and Mrs. W. A. Earnest, 1120 Nineteenth Street, was recently assigned to duty at the Deshon General Hospital at Butler, Pa.

Ship Fitter (Second Class) Ezra Cole Jr., 4242 Waverly Road, is a member of the crew aboard a submarine tender at an advanced Pacific base.

Yeoman (Second Class) Herman Smith is spending a 15-day leave with his mother, Mrs. Sylvia Sexton, 2240 Eighth Avenue, before returning to Vero Beach, Fla. for reassignment. Yeoman Smith served overseas for 36 months.

Electrician's Mate (Third Class) Jack W. Sabo, whose parents, Mr. and Mrs. J. G. Sabo, reside at 1032 Monroe Avenue, and Seaman (First Class) James W. Rose of Olive Hill, Ky., fought during the Okinawa campaign aboard the USS *West Virginia*. The ship was blasted at Pearl Harbor by two bombs and at least six torpedoes and was resurrected and repaired to join the fleet.

Seaman (Second Class) E. H. Turner of Huntington recently completed his training at the U.S. Navy Training Camp, Sampson, N.Y. and has been sent to the Philadelphia Navy yards for further training. His wife, Mrs. Mozell Turner, and son Richard, reside at 501 West Sixth Street.

First Lieutenant David J. McKinney is spending a 30-day leave with his parents, Mr. and Mrs. D. W. McKinney, 2989 Chase Street. Lieutenant McKinney recently returned from the European theatre of operations where he has served two years with the 96th Bomb Group of the Eighth Air Force. He holds four major combat stars and the Presidential Unit Citation with one Oak Leaf Cluster.

Glenna: *August 7th Tuesday – I ironed and mended everything.*

Rupert: *I read today.*

"Dr. Peter Marshall, pastor of the New York Avenue Presbyterian Church, sometimes referred to as the 'President's Church in Washington, D.C.,' will be the first of 10 prominent speakers who will be presented in public assemblies at Marshall College during the coming year."[415]

Guam, August 7: "... from the stunned enemy finally came admission that the terrific new weapon had done damage... The Japanese talked of new 'bombs.' Their use of the plural indicated the blast was so shattering they could not believe only one bomb had struck."[416]

From the local column, "Trends," by DeWitt MacKenzie: "There are two ways of looking at this terrible new power. The happier view is that militaristic-minded nations no longer will dare make war and so expose themselves to annihilation... There's another and less comforting viewpoint ... by an editor colleague of mine... 'You wonder whether man isn't getting too damned smart and won't destroy himself.'"[417]

"WITH THE COLORS":

Technician (Fifth Grade) Lester N. Gibbs, brother of Mrs. J. C. West, 816 Twelfth Avenue, was recently awarded the Bronze Star Medal by Major General Fay Brink Pickett, commandeering general of the Tenth Armored Division in Germany. A water point supervisor of the 55th Armored Engineer Battalion, Technician Gibbs was cited for "heroic achievement in connection with military operations ... at Crailsheim, Germany on last April 10. Exposed to intense enemy artillery fire, he maintained a continuous water supply to forward elements during combat." His wife and children reside in Charleston.

Private Ray S. Beaty, 26, husband of Mrs. Naomi Beaty, 720 Adams Avenue, has recently returned from the European theatre of operations where he served for three years as a rifle man. Private Beaty wears two battle stars on his campaign ribbon.

Technician (Fifth Grade) Charles A. Chapman, husband of Mrs. Faye Chapman, 235 Indiana Street, a veteran of 28 months in the European theatre of operations, arrived at the Presque Isle Army Air Field, Me. last Friday aboard an Air Transport Command plane.

Corporal M. L. Hairston, husband of Mrs. Marie L. Hairston, 909 Eighth Avenue, is among a group selected for service with the recently activated all-Negro military police platoon in the Ledo Assam area of India. Corporal Hairston is the son of Mrs. Manilla E. Shelton, 216 Hendric Street, Detroit, Mich.

Lieutenant John J. Sweeney Jr., son of Mr. and Mrs. John J. Sweeney of Guyandotte, a former Eighth Air Force bombardier in Europe, has reported to Sioux Falls, S.D. for reassignment. Lieutenant Sweeney entered the AAF in June 1943 and wears the Air Medal with three Oak Leaf Clusters. His brother, Seaman (Second Class) Robert F. Sweeney, is stationed at Norfolk, Va.

First Lieutenant Donald W. Sprouse, son of Mrs. Stella Sprouse, 416 Fourteenth Street, recently arrived at the Mountain Home Army Air Field, Idaho, for assignment. He served for several months overseas where he was awarded the Distinguished Flying Cross and the Air Medal with three Oak Leaf Clusters.

Staff Sergeant William J. Cregan, 28, of 1737 Washington Street, is assigned to the Assembly Area Command with the 75th Infantry Division engaged in redeploying American soldiers from Europe. The husband of Mrs. Norma J. Cregan, he is stationed at Camp Atlanta, a redeployment center near Reims, France.

Lieutenant Clarence S. Nelson Jr., son of Mr. and Mrs. C. S. Nelson, 2768 Emmons Avenue, a pilot on a C-47 cargo plane, flew over Huntington Saturday afternoon, flying over his mother's house twice and dipping his plane as a means of identification, his mother reported.

Glenna: *August 8th Wednesday – I canned tomatoes. Went to prayer meeting. I had to lead. I read Rev. 21st chapter. Helped Milo and Maxine string beans after church. Mrs. Strum died.*

Rupert: *I picked beans today.*

It was canning season. Green beans, fresh in summer and canned for winter, were a staple for our table. We had a large bean patch which provided produce to sell, in addition to varieties we grew in our vegetable garden.

"Dr. Harold E. Burdick, 39, research chemist of the Standard Ultramarine Co. of Huntington, who has been 'on loan' to the War Department for the past 26 months, worked on the new atomic bomb, it was revealed today. Dr. Burdick, who left the Standard Ultramarine Co. by War Department request on company leave of absence May 11, 1943, did research on atomic energy in New York, at Grand Junction,

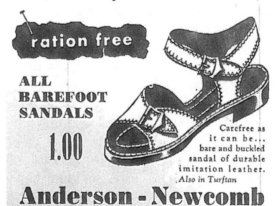

Colo., and at Oak Ridge, Tenn... Dr. Burdick is now at Oak Ridge."[418]

"Flying the swastika under the stars and stripes, two destroyers, the first German surface warships to come to this country since the start of the war, were anchored in Boston Harbor today. The vessels ... were manned by volunteer German crews under American supervision and came by way of the Azores. where they refueled."[419]

President Truman delivered a radio address in which he warned Japan of nuclear destruction if they did not surrender.[420]

The Soviet Union declared war on Japan.[421]

"WITH THE COLORS":

Coxswain Elwood Shelton, 18, Olive Hill, Ky., helps man the depth charge guns aboard a destroyer of the Atlantic Fleet. He wears a bronze star on his American theatre campaign ribbon, signifying the sinking of a German U-boat in the Atlantic waters. A brother, Sergeant Andy Shelton, is serving with the U.S. Army.

Technician (Fourth Grade) Claude F. Selbee, a veteran of 28 months in the European theater of operations, arrived at the Presque Isle Air Field, Me. aboard an Air Transport Command plane. He is the husband of Mrs. Kathryn Selbee of 813 Seventeenth Street.

Machinist's Mate (Third Class) Jonnie L. Adkins, son of Mr. and Mrs. Ottie Adkins, 1610 West Road, has been awarded the Purple Heart for wounds received during the bombardment of the Ligurian coast of Italy. He also wears the Croix de Guerre, awarded by the French government for conspicuous services despite his wounds.

Austin W. Bowers, husband of Mrs. Phyllis Bowers, 2035 Ninth Avenue, is serving aboard the USS *Corduba*, a refrigerated cargo vessel in the South Pacific. He is the son of Mr. and Mrs. E. W. Bowers, 920 Sixth Street, and has been in the Pacific for the past six months.

Apprentice Seaman Donald E. Fligor, son of Mr. and Mrs. James Fligor of Chesapeake, O., is stationed at the U.S. Naval Training Station at Sampson, N.Y...

Second Lieutenant James G. Chapman, 20, son of Mr. and Mrs. W. L. Chapman of Ashland received his pilot's wings and commission in the Army Air Forces last Saturday upon completion of his twin-engine training at the Pampa Army Air Field, Pampa, Tex., a unit of the AAF Central Flying Command.

Sergeant Forest Zimmerman, 333 Highland Street, overseas for more than two years, and Corporal Fred J. White, 333 Davis Street, serving with a medical detachment of the combat engineers, recently met for the first time since they entered the service.

Seaman (Second Class) Eugene Skaggs of Huntington is receiving training in the Seabees at Davisville, R.I. after recently completing initial training at Great Lakes, Ill. Seaman Skaggs, a former East High School student and Chesapeake and Ohio Railway Co. machinist apprentice, recently spent a 15-day leave with his parents, Mr. and Mrs. R. H. Skaggs. While at East High School he played in the band.

Second Lieutenant William Miller of Huntington is spending a 20-day leave of absence at his home, 1915 Doulton Avenue. Lieutenant Miller is stationed at the Dyersburg, Tenn. Army Air Field. Also home on leave is Second Lieutenant Robert A. Mayes, who is stationed at the Army Air Field in Dyersburg.

Two first cousins from Huntington, serving in the Navy, recently held a reunion at a base in the Pacific. They were Radioman Jack Adams, son of Mr. and Mrs. Tim J. Adams, 819 Fourteenth Street, and Radioman Wyatt E. Paugh, son of Mr. and Mrs. W. D. Paugh of Salt Rock. Radioman Adams is aboard a destroyer in the Pacific after two years with the Atlantic Fleet, while Radioman Paugh is aboard a tanker. He has been in the Pacific for 20 months. Mrs. Adams reported that the reunion was arranged when her son learned that his cousin's ship was in port and went aboard the tanker. Radioman Paugh has a brother, Corporal Sterling Paugh, who is serving in the U. S Army. [Both Wyatt Paugh and Sterling Paugh had been students at Walnut Grove School when my mother was the teacher.]

Glenna: *August 9th Thursday — Pleasant day. We made ice cream down at Mamma's. Dawson and Milo got the toilet fixed.*

Our outdoor toilet, a one-holer thirty yards down a path from the house, was accommodating five people. I'm not sure what the "fix" was about.

Rupert: *We made Ice cream.*

"Governor Frank J. Lausche of Ohio told Mayor R. L. Hamilton of Chesapeake and Lawrence County Sheriff Milton B. Rucker of Ironton, O., today that gambling was rampant in their territories and if they fail to act immediately to wipe it out, he, the governor, would use his authority to do so."[422]

"The world's most destructive force—the atomic bomb—was used for the second time against Japan today, striking the important Kyushu Island city of Nagasaki which observed 'good results.'"[423] Japan offered a surrender under terms that they remain sovereign.[424]

"WITH THE COLORS":

Sergeant Charles F. Perry, 26, of Huntington, a veteran of 48 months in the European theatre of operations where he served as a rifleman and was awarded the ETO ribbon with two battle stars, the American theatre and defense ribbons, the Good Conduct Medal and the Combat Infantryman's Badge, returned to the United States today aboard Air Transport Command transatlantic plane, landing at LaGuardia Field in New York City. The veteran and holder of 128 points will visit his wife, Mrs. Anna Perry, who resides at 1116 Twenty-fifth Street.

Electrician's Mate (Third Class) Seward S. Price, son of Mr. and Mrs. S. S. Price of Ona, helped the escort carrier USS *Suwannee* send her planes against the enemy at Okinawa. The *Suwannee's* planes supported the assault troops during the invasion.

A Navy man from Point Pleasant and a Milton man are serving aboard the 2,200 ton destroyer USS *Ingraham,* which recently survived the blast of a Japanese suicide plane off the coast of Okinawa. The crippled ship returned to the United States under her own power for repairs. They are Coxswain Donald M. Swisher of Point Pleasant and Sonarman (Third Class) Floyd E. Powers of Milton.

Seaman (First Class) William J. Sturgill of Amba, Ky., recently served aboard the 2,200-ton destroyer USS *Ingraham* which survived the fury of a Jap Kamikaze attack off Okinawa and came back to the States for repairs, battered and charred, but under her own power.

Private (First Class) Charles Dulfield, 27, of Charleston, a former resident of Huntington, is spending a 30-day furlough with his mother, Mrs. J. C. Shanklin, 825 First Street. Private Dulfield served overseas for a year with general Hodge's First Army in France, Belgium and Germany and was awarded the European theatre of operations ribbon with one battle star, the Good Conduct Medal, the Presidential Unit Citation, and the Bronze Star Medal... He

[is] expected to be reassigned to active duty in the Pacific.

The promotion of Private Howard Triplett of Huntington to the rank of private (first class) was announced today by ... [the] commanding officer of the Pyote, Tex. Army Air Field. Private Triplett, who is the son of Mr. and Mrs. Wilson Triplett of Branchland, W.Va., is married to the former Miss Joan Burns of Clair Shores, Mich. He is assigned to the B-29 Superfortress combat crew training field of the Second Air Force.

Private (First Class) Freelin H. Booten Jr., son of Mr. and Mrs. F. H. Booten, 1650 Twelfth Avenue, is stationed at the Maison-Blanche Airport in Algiers, as a mail dispatcher. He is a graduate of Huntington High School and worked at the Patterson Air Field, Dayton, Ohio as a civilian clerk before entering the Army.

Jairet C. Massie Jr., son of Mr. and Mrs. J. C. Massie of Coal grove, Ohio, has been recently promoted to the rank of staff sergeant with the Air Service Command in Italy. Sergeant Massie has been serving overseas as an aircraft electrician for 18 months. He wears two battle stars on his campaign ribbon for participation in major action.

The War Department announced yesterday the promotion of Paul Hite, 1014 Jefferson Avenue, from second to first lieutenant.

Staff Sergeant James O. Freeman, son of Mr. and Mrs. Willard Freeman, 1234 Virginia Avenue, recently completed nine weeks basic and advanced training at the Communication School at Fort Benning, Ga.

Seaman (First Class) John W. Lawson, 22, 449 Thirteenth Avenue, has returned to the United States from a tour of duty in the Pacific aboard the aircraft carrier USS *Hornet,* which is undergoing typhoon damage repairs.

Glenna: *August 10th Friday – Went to Amanda Strum's burial in Salt Rock Church Cemetery. News came that Japan is willing to surrender four days after atomic bomb was used.*

Rachel Amanda Strum was the wife of F. M. Strum and daughter of Elias Waters and Catherine Watkins.[425]

Rupert: *Rummors of peace.*

London, August 10: "The Stockholm radio said tonight that Japan had handed the Swedish minister of foreign affairs a note to the British, American and Russian governments offering to surrender."[426]

"Japan announced today she is ready to surrender under the Potsdam declaration if Emperor Hirohito can retain his power... Wild celebrations were set off on Okinawa and at other points throughout the Allied world.[427]

Washington, August 10: "President Truman assembled his cabinet in an atmosphere of official expectancy today, but the war raged on in the Pacific as hours slipped by without official confirmation here of a broadcast Japanese surrender offer."[428]

"WITH THE COLORS":

Corporal John H. Medley, son of Mr. and Mrs. Charles Medley of Sidney, W.Va., is en route home from Europe and is at the infantry redeployment center at Oklahoma City. Corporal Medley fought across Europe with the 30th Infantry Division and holds the Purple Heart Medal, the Bronze Star, the Combat Infantryman's Badge, the Presidential Unit Citation, and four battle stars on his campaign ribbon.

Private Aubrey Winston Jr., son of Mr. and Mrs. Aubrey Winston, 1908 Artisan Avenue, is serving with the 766th Engineer Truck Company as a truck driver in the Tacloban area of the Philippines.

Sergeant Charles William Brockmeyer, 22, was killed in an airplane crash on Niihau Island in the Hawaiian group on July 23, the War Department has advised his wife, the former Miss Virginia Harris of Auburn Road. Sergeant Brockmeyer was a graduate of Huntington High School and attended Marshall College before entering the Army in November, 1942. He had formerly been employed by the Western Electric Co. at Kearny, N.J.

Topping off their overseas experience with a trans-Atlantic flight with the Air Transport Command, veterans from West Virginia have arrived at Miami Army Air Field, en route to their homes. From the Huntington area are Sergeant Joe Tweel, 1007 Eighth Avenue, a veteran of 26 months service in the European theatre of operations; Private John P. Kees, 351 Davis Street, nine months overseas service concluded in Italy, and Private (First Class) Woodrow Fannin of Iaeger, veteran of 19 months overseas action.

Corporal Charles A. Smith, son of Mr. and Mrs. E. H. Smith, 413 Olive Street, is stationed at Langley Field, Va. with the AAF Training Command Radar Observers School, where he is serving as a crew chief on a B-17 Flying Fortress.

Sergeant Andrew Platania, son of Mr. and Mrs. John Platania of Brooklyn, N.Y. and husband of the former Miss Marcelina White, 333 Davis Street, was recently promoted to that grade with the 85th Depot Supply Squadron at Beri, Italy.

... in accordance with the Army regulation of releasing all service men with 85 points or more... Those from this area who complied were Technician (Fourth Grade) Frank Fritz, 3664 Piedmont Road and Private Clifford F. Burns of Peach Creek.

... Alex Morris of 118 Olive Street has been promoted to the rank of petty officer (second class). The Huntington Navy man is serving on a destroyer based in the Hawaiian Islands. He has a wife and a daughter, Delores Margaret, living at the Huntington address.

Private (First Class) William N. Spurlock, 333 33rd Street, was recently awarded the

Combat Infantryman's Badge for exemplary conduct under fire during his first experience in action with the 32nd Infantry Division on Northern Luzon...

Seaman (First Class) John W. Kidwell [24] has recently returned to the naval base at New Orleans, La. after spending a 19-day furlough here with his wife and daughter who reside at 2672 Fourth Avenue. He has just returned from a six-months' tour of sea duty [On a naval gun crew aboard a merchant ship] outside the continental United States.

Private Billy M. Austin, son of Mr. and Mrs. Walter M. Austin, 1258 Jefferson Avenue, was recently promoted to private (first class) at an Army base in the South Pacific. Private Austin, who attended schools in Huntington and was a baker for three years before the war, is a machine gunner in the Army.

Glenna: *August 11th Saturday – Nice day. Partly cloudy. Strong talk of peace with Japan. I took flowers to Rupert's grave for his 37th birthday.*

Rupert: *I got a hair cut.*

Uncle Cline was my barber, as he was for all our family members and eventually all of Salt Rock and much of the surrounding area. My grandfather had encouraged him to go to barber school and get a license, but Cline was too busy cutting hair to act on that.

"Lieutenant (Junior Grade) Aubrey C. Byrd, USNR, 814 Roby Road, Huntington, has been presented the Bronze Star Medal, and a letter of commendation with commendation ribbon, for performances as commanding officer of a close-in fire support vessel during engagements with the enemy in the Pacific."[429]

The Ceredo-Kenova Chamber of Commerce sponsored a circulation of petitions to sound out citizens on the merger of Ceredo and Kenova, and H. S. Dudleston, chairman of a consolidated committee, announced that there were enough signatures to bring the proposal to a vote.[430]

Brigadier General Thomas F. F. Farrell, head of the atomic bomb project in the Pacific said, "The world's second atomic bomb, which was dropped on Nagasaki Thursday was so explosive that it immediately relegated to the obsolete the first bomb dropped two days earlier on Hiroshima..."[431]

Washington, August 11: "The Big Four powers agreed today to accept Japan's surrender offer provided ... the Emperor is made subject to the supreme commander's orders."[432]

"WITH THE COLORS":

Stationed in the Midway Islands is Fireman (First Class) Harold L. Back of Olive, Ky., serving as a watch stander.

Private (First Class) Tommy Hayes, son of Mrs. Julie Hayes, North Matewan, W.Va., has been awarded the Bronze Star Medal for heroism against the Japs on Northern Luzon. Private Hayes, a member of a machine gun company of the 33rd Division, also holds the Combat Infantryman's Badge and two battle stars.

Sergeant Paul V. Brumfield, son of Mr. and Mrs. F. B. Brumfield, 4363 Eighth Street Road, a veteran of the 13th AAF in the Pacific, is returning to the United States after serving for 27 months in that theatre.

Flight Officer Herbert Muncy, son of Mr. and Mrs. B. R. Muncy, 2734 Latulle Avenue, has been awarded the Air Medal for meritorious achievement while serving with the Ninth Air Force Service Command Unit in the European theatre of operations. Flight Officer Muncy is the pilot of a troop carrier glider.

Sergeant Tony J. Magariello, 2808 Highlawn Court, has recently been awarded an Oak Leaf Cluster to the Air Medal for meritorious service as radio-gunner in the Philippines with the Thirteenth Air Force. He has flown 50 missions.

Corporal William R. Sweney, son of Mr. A. R. Sweney, 307 West Ninth Avenue, is en route home after 33 months service in the Pacific with the 13th AAF.

Corporal Henry G. Cremeans, son of Mr. and Mrs. H. G. Cremeans, 53 Twenty-fifth Street, was recently promoted to that rank at Luke Field, Phoenix, Ariz., where he is attached to the provost marshal's office. Corporal Cremeans returned to the United States in March after serving 14 months in the European theatre of operations.

Seaman (First Class) Douglas A. Turley of Hartford, W.Va., is one of the survivors of the USS *Drexler*, which was sunk in a 90-day attack by three Jap suicide planes off Okinawa May 28.

Master Sergeant Worthy Evans, son of Mrs. Tava B. Evans, 737 Seventh Street, has been awarded the Meritorious Service Unit insignia at the Miami Beach service base of the Air Technical Service Command. He is the veteran of action in both European and Africa theatres of operation, and wears two battle stars on his campaign ribbon.

Fireman (First Class) Manuel Barcello, husband of Mrs. Rosemary Barcello of Kenova, participated in recent major Pacific actions aboard a destroyer which has been six months in that theatre. It has fought off Formosa, Luzon, French Indo-China, Tokyo Bay, Iwo Jima, Okinawa and Kyushu and has downed four Jap planes.

Private (First Class) Daniel Pridemore, 34, son of Mr. and Mrs. Joson Pridemore of Myra, W.Va., has returned to the United States after serving for 11 months in the European theatre of operations as a rifleman.

Private John R. B. Morrow, USMC, of Huntington, has returned to Camp LeJeune, N.C. after spending a 15-day furlough with his parents, Mr. and Mrs. Robert Morrow, 1103 Ninth Avenue, Private Morrow entered the Marine Corps four months ago.

Corporal Leslie E. Price, son of Mr. and Mrs. J. E. Price, 1832 Washington Avenue, has been presented with the Good Conduct Medal while stationed at Fort Jackson, S.C.

Three West Virginia men recently completed the Army Air Forces B-29 Flight Engineer course at Hondo Army Air Field, Tex., and were awarded the newly adopted flight officer wings of the AAF. From Huntington were Second Lieutenant Eladio Garcia, 1618 Charleston Avenue, and Second Lieutenant William Floyd Kincaid, 2120 Twelfth Avenue. [Lieutenant Kincaid's parents are Mr. and Mrs. Emory F. Kincaid.]

Private Elza Trippett, son of Mr. and Mrs. Eugene Trippett of Glenwood, W.Va. and Private Albert Schurman, 638 Fifth Avenue, have arrived at Camp Fannin, Tex., and are taking their basic training in the 54th Battalion of the 11th Training Regiment.

Edwin Leon Dial, son of Mrs. Edgar Dial, 1005 Minton Street, has received a spot promotion from the Navy for especially meritorious conduct in action. He has been advanced ... to the rating of gunner's mate (first class), USNR.

Major Arthur E. Chambers, husband of Mrs. Bernice E. Chambers, 1009 West Third Street, is stationed in Puerto Rico with the AAF Caribbean Division of the Atlantic Transport Command. Major Chambers has spent 16 months overseas in the European theatre of operations and wears the ETO ribbon with five Bronze battle stars. He attended Chicago University and was a buyer for the Lewis Furniture Company before entering the service.

Glenna: *August 12th Sunday — Very hot. Rupert's birthday. He would have been 37 years old. I went to Sunday School at morning, baptizing at the river at 4 o'clock, and church at night.*

Rupert: *I went to Sunday school. I went to a bap—itisin.*

"West Virginia's great schoolboy sports spectacle—the North-South football game—will be witnessed by the largest crowd in its 12-year history next Friday night at Laidley field ... highlighted by fireworks and other special arrangements in keeping with the United Nations' ending of World War II."[433]

From Washington: "The Second World War entered its final hours tonight as the 'Big Four' accepted Japan's offer of unconditional surrender with a provision that Emperor Hirohito rule under the control of the supreme commander of the Allied occupation army..."[434]

> Glenna: *August 13th Monday – Very hot. I washed. Didn't feel very well. Ausley Pratt had appendix operation.*

> Rupert: *I discovered a new program on the radio. Its name is "Count of Mont Cristo."*

The radio programs, especially the fifteen-minute continuing adventures of various superheroes, were an important part of my life. "Superman," "Hop Harrigan," and "Jack Armstrong" come to mind, although there were several others.

Another local hero was honored: "The Silver Star Medal for gallantry in action during the Italian campaign has been awarded Private (First Class) Fred W. Maier, son of Mrs. Mildred Maier, 319 Twenty-fifth Street, the Army announced yesterday. Private Maier served in the Fifth Army front in the 350th 'Battle Mountain' Regiment of the 88th 'Blue Devil' Division."[435]

"Private (First Class) William Perkey, the son of Mrs. Goldie Perkey, 37 West Fifth Avenue, was in the military police escort which accompanied President Truman from Antwerp, Belgium, to Brussels, he told his mother in a letter received this morning. The escort met the President when he debarked from his ship at the Belgium port prior to the Potsdam Conference. The Huntington MP was with the Anti-Aircraft until V-E Day. He has been in service for three years."[436]

Paris: Nearly all twenty-four jurors in the treason trial of Marshal Petain reported death threats, some receiving as many as twelve letters that threated death to any who voted against Petain. The jury had been hearing final defense pleas.[437]

"WITH THE COLORS":

Huntington GIs who have high point ratings for discharge are Sergeant Charles E. Ward, 4751 Bradley Road, and Corporal Norman L. Johnson, 2737 Highlawn Avenue. Both soldiers fought with the Second Infantry Division in Normandy, Northern France, Ardennes, the Rhineland and Central Europe and wear five battle stars. Both have been overseas since October 1943.

First Sergeant Donald J. Smith, 3602 Brandon Road, is the ranking non-commissioned officer of the 26th Special Service Company, 15th Corps for over a year. The company recently received the Meritorious Service Unit Plaque. A former platoon staff sergeant, the Huntington soldier was promoted to his present rank two weeks ago and has been awarded the Bronze Star Medal.

First Lieutenant Robert E. Stalnaker, son of Mrs. A. J. Wilkinson, 6396 Pea Ridge Road, has recently been transferred to Chatham Field, Savannah, Ga. where he is serving as an instructor at the B-29 combat crew training base. Lieutenant Stalnaker served overseas with the 306th Bombardment Group from June 1944, to October, 1944, and wears the Purple Heart Ribbon.

Seaman (Second Class) Louis Alton Workman, husband of Mrs. Emily Louise Workman of Russell, Ky., served aboard the USS *Rudyard Bay* in three major Pacific operations, including the Okinawa campaign, Iwo Jima and the invasion of the Philippines.

Fireman (First Class) James B. Graham, son of Mr. and Mrs. L. T. Graham, 2608 Fourth Avenue, is serving aboard a destroyer in the Formosa, Luzon, French-Indo-China, Tokyo Bay, Iwo Jima, Okinawa, and Kyushu campaigns, a Navy release disclosed today.

Electrician's Mate Seward S. Price Jr., son of Mr. and Mrs. S. S. Price, of Ona, Route 1, is serving on an escort carrier in the Pacific and wears the American Defense ribbon, the Asiatic-Pacific ribbon with five battle stars and the Philippine Liberation ribbon with one battle star.

Captain Matthew Freed, husband of Mrs. Louise Freed, 2527 First Avenue, has recently been awarded the Bronze Star Medal for meritorious service in connection with military operations against the Germans as commanding officer of a medical battalion company in Germany.

Private (First Class) Robert B. Earl, 316 North Cedar Street, who served in Germany with the medical detachment of the 65th Armored Infantry Battalion for six months, is in the embarkation staging area at Le Havre, France, awaiting shipment to the United States. A former student at West Virginia College and Marshall College, he holds the Combat Medical Badge.

Private Joseph K. Lantz, 2041 Fifth Avenue, and Private (First Class) David W. Phippo, 1637 Fifth Avenue, are in the Newton D. Baker General Hospital at Martinsburg, W.Va. for treatment. Private Lantz served overseas with the Third Army nine months, and wears the Good Conduct Medal and the Combat Infantryman's Badge. His parents, Mr. and Mrs. F. J. Lantz live in Huntington. A brother, Sergeant Frank J. Lantz, is home on furlough. Private Phippo, who served in Europe with the Third Army also wears the ETO Ribbon with three battle stars, the Purple Heart with Oak Leaf Cluster and the Good Conduct Medal.

Corporal Theodore Stamper Jr., husband of Mrs. Dorothy Patterson Stamper of Huntington, is en route home with the Thirty-fifth "Santa Fe"

Division, which in ten months fought its way to within 42 miles of Berlin. The Thirty-fifth landed on Omaha Beach on July, 1944.

Private Clarence H. Parsons, 1345 Eighth Avenue, served with the 125th Anti-Aircraft Artillery Battalion, which scored more than 700 direct hits and 200 more crippling blows on the German V-1 buzz bombs in England and Belgium. The 125th is now patrolling traffic in the assembly area.

Corporal Ervin Napier of Huntington is with the 772nd Tank Destroyer Battalion waiting in the assembly area in France for shipment to the United States...

Corporal Harry S. Edwards, 1936 Buffington Avenue, is a member of an Ordnance Maintenance Company which has arrived at Camp Baltimore in France to be redeployed directly to the Pacific. Members of the company wear three battle stars.

Corporal Thomas J. Goodwin, 33, the husband of Mrs. Marie Goodwin, 16 Twenty-seventh Street, has returned after three months as a rifleman in Europe and is being processed through the Army Ground and Service Forces Redistribution Station at Miami Beach, Fla... He wears two battle stars on his European theatre ribbon.

Private Clarice Ruth Whittle, daughter of Mr. and Mrs. Clarence M. Whittle, 320 Thirty-fourth Street, has completed training in the clerk's course at the First Woman's Army Corps Training Center at Fort Des Moines, Ia.

West Virginians homeward bound from the European theatre of operations ... include Private (First Class) Holly R. Shamblin of Milton.

Corporal Harry K. Parcell, son of Mrs. Jessie Parcell, 239 Fifth Avenue, is serving as a stenographer with the 16th Medical General Dispensary in the base section of the India-Burma theatre at Calcutta, India. Corporal Parcell, who has been in the India-Burma theatre since last May and in the Army since May, 1944 is married and his wife lives at 794 Roby Road.

W. R. Lewis Jr., instructor in aerial gunnery, has returned to his base at Pensacola, Fla after spending a 15-day leave with his parents, Mr. and Mrs. W. R. Lewis of 1226 Union Street.

Lieutenant (j. g.) Clarence E. Morrison, son of Mr. and Mrs. W. B. Morrison of Kenova, was home on leave last week from Chapel Hill, N.C. Naval pre-flight school.

Sergeant Gilbert M. Jarrell, husband of Mrs. Alyene Jarrell, 611 Wetzel Court, has served overseas two years with the AAF and is now stationed at the Ninth Air Force service command base in Belgium...

Lieutenant Clarence Shain of Huntington was a member of the 33rd graduating class whose members received commissions as bombardiers or navigators at the bombardiers-navigator school of the Central Flying Training Command, Childress Army Air Field, Childress, Tex., last week. Lieutenant Shain is the son of Mr. and Mrs. C. E. Shain, 621 Sixteenth Street.

Seaman (Second Class) Billy Winn, son of Mrs. Frances Winn, 234 Sixth Avenue, has returned home with a medical discharge after serving for 16 months in the Navy, He spent seven months in the South Pacific and participated in the invasion of Okinawa.

Private (First Class) Charles J. Hahnert, son of Mrs. Altia Hahnert, 255 Oakland Avenue, has recently been awarded the Combat Infantryman's Badge in Germany where he is stationed with an Infantry regiment of the 90th Division.

Private (First Class) Marion F. Hammonds, son of Oscar R. Hammonds of Ashland, who is stationed at an Air Transport Command base at El Aquina, Tunis, Tunisia, will leave soon for the United States. Private Hammonds has been serving overseas for 18 months.

Gerald B. Wright, 812 Marcum Terrace, has been promoted to private (first class) in the North Atlantic where he is on duty as an Army Airways Communications System radio operator.

Private (First Class) Norman Bexfield, son of Mr. and Mrs. C. H. Bexfield, 2839 Overlook Drive, recently underwent an operation in Nance, France. He is stationed with the Rail Operations Battalion at Hanau, Germany. Private Bexfield has been in the service since November, 1942 and has been overseas 26 months. He has seen action in Africa, Italy, Sicily, France and Germany.

Sergeant Lawrence Ousley of Huntington was recently awarded the Bronze Star Medal for heroic achievement in Italy where he served on the Fifth Army front in the 135th Infantry Regiment of the 34th "Red Bull" Division.

Glenna: *August 14th Tuesday — Very hot with wind. I ironed and patched. Strong talk of peace all day. At 7 o'clock news came of peace with Japan. Such rejoicing has never been known.*

Rupert: *The japs have surrendered. The war is over.*

"*Domel,* Japanese news agency, said in a broadcast recorded by the FCC today that 'on Aug. 14, 1945, the Imperial decision was granted' and that weeping people had gathered before his palace and 'bowed to the very ground' in their shame that their 'efforts were not enough.'"[438]

"WITH THE COLORS":

Technician (Fifth Grade) John B. Johnson, husband of Mrs. Mary M. Johnson, 1328 Twenty-fifth Street, is en route home from Europe with the five-star "Santa Fe" Division, which in 10 months battled across the Elbe River to within 42 miles of Berlin. Corporal Johnson wears the Combat Infantryman's Badge and four stars on his campaign ribbon.

Staff Sergeant Jack W. Porter, husband of Mrs. Francis Porter, is home on a 30-day furlough after serving 18 months in the South Pacific with the 239th Army Engineers. Sergeant Porter is the son of Mr. and Mrs. John Byron Porter, 63 Adams Avenue.

Technician (Fifth Grade) Lloyd L. Fetty, 28, 2037 Fourth Avenue, who served overseas for 18 months in the European theatre of operations with the 77th Quartermaster Battalion where he was awarded four battle stars for his campaign ribbon, recently returned to the United States as one of the 30,000 returnees flown from Europe to the Miami Army Air Field each month by the Air Transport Command.

The U.S. 45th Infantry Division, of which Staff Sergeant Edgar E. Edwards, 1418 Lynn Street, is a member, is returning to the United States after playing a major part in the downfall of the aggressor nations in Europe. Sergeant Edwards wears the Bronze Star Medal, the Good Conduct Medal, the European theatre of operations ribbon with three battle stars, and the Combat Infantryman's Badge.

Ship's Cook (Third Class) Hilbert A. Moore of Culloden, has been awarded the Purple Heart Medal for wounds received during action in the Iwo Jima campaign last February. He was employed by glass companies around Dunbar and Culloden before entering the Navy.

Sergeant Maxine Lewedag, who is currently stationed at Arlington, Va., with the Marine Corps Women's Reserve, is spending a furlough with her parents, Mr. and Mrs. H. B. Lewedag of Jefferson Avenue.

Corporal William E. Guthrie, son of Mrs. Eleanor Guthrie of Proctorville, Ohio, who has been serving in Europe for over three years, is one of the men remaining in the European theatre of operations as part of the air transport program established by the Ninth Air Force Service Command.

Master Sergeant Roscoe E. McDaniel, 1938 Tenth Avenue, has been awarded the Bronze Star Medal for meritorious achievement in the Luzon campaign.

Private (First Class) Robert W. Staley, son of Mr. and Mrs. Charles Staley, 134 Fourth Avenue,

returned to this country yesterday aboard the hospital ship *Ernestine Koranda,* which docked at New York. The Huntington soldier was wounded twice while serving with the infantry in Europe.

Petty Officer Ralph Jordan has returned to the West Coast after spending a 27-day leave with his wife, Mrs. Sylvia Jordan of Rosalind Road. He served in the Pacific 14 months aboard the flagship, USS *Mt. McKinley.* He holds seven battle stars on his Asiatic-Pacific campaign ribbon for participation in many major battles. He formerly worked at the International Nickel Co. here.

Three GIs from the tri-state area met in Regensburg, Germany before participating in a Third Army stab across the Danube River. They are Hoot Jarrell, Huntington; Private (First Class) Melford Smoot, Chesapeake, Ohio, and Andy H. Wise, Huntington. The three soldiers are members of the 71st Division, 14th Infantry, Company D of the Third Army. They met at Fort Benning, Ga. 30 months after being inducted on February 6, 1941 and have been serving together since then.

Private Kenneth C. Waldo, 19, 2976 Staunton Road, has returned to Miami, Fla. aboard an Air Transport Command plane, after serving in Italy with the Infantry for four months.

Technician (Fourth Grade) Keene Bartley, husband of Mrs. K. L. Bartley, 1712 Fifth Avenue, is awaiting shipment to the United States at Le Havre, France. Technician Bartley served in the European theatre of operations with the 138th Ordnance Battalion for six months and has been in the Army almost three years.

Pilot of a B-17 Flying Fortress, William T. Pinson, 28, husband of Mrs. Marguerite Pinson, 2006 Marcum Terrace, was recently promoted from second to first lieutenant at an AAF air base in France. Lieutenant Pinson entered the service in March, 1943.

Corporal Michael Kozma Jr., son of Mr. and Mrs. Michael Kozma, 703 Twelfth Avenue,

ATOMIC BOMBS, JAPAN SURRENDERS

has recently been transferred to Newport News, Va. from Fort Lewis, Wash.

Corporal Whitley M. Tabor, son of Mr. and Mrs. E. B. Tabor, Yawkey, W.Va., is serving with the 113th Engineer Combat Battalion, engineer unit of the 38th (Cyclone) Infantry Division on Luzon. Corporal Tabor has seen duty in Hawaii, New Guinea and Leyte before serving on Luzon. Prior to his induction at Fort Thomas, Ky. in March 1942, he was employed as drilling contractor at Allen, Ky...

Second Lieutenant Leonard N. Seldomridge, 708 30th Street, a member of a Signal Light Construction Battalion, now being processed in Reims, France, for direct shipment to the Pacific, is currently stationed at Camp Philadelphia, one of the 18 camps in the Assembly center for troops on the continent.

Staff Sergeant Robert N. Burley, 130 Fourth Avenue, has reported to the AAF Redistribution Station at Atlantic City, N.J., after serving for 16 months in the European theatre of operations as a radio-operator and gunner on a bomber. Sergeant Burley, a wearer of the Air Medal, is the son of Mrs. Della Burley of Huntington.

Glenna: *August 15th Wednesday – Peace with Japan was celebrated all day. V.J. Day. Rain. I went to prayer meeting that night.*

Rupert: *People selbrates the end of war.*

The few simple words we wrote in our diaries didn't do justice to the intense feelings of relief we were experiencing. "Peace with Japan" wasn't as much about a far-away war as about the joy within nearly every family we knew; their loved ones were safe and finally coming home.

"Huntington, still joyous over victory in history's cruelest war, but weary from celebrating into the late hours last night, today was enjoying the first of a two-day holiday proclaimed by Governor Meadows. The governor's proclamation followed one made by President Truman shortly after the flash of Japan's surrender came."[439]

Charleston, West Virginia, August 15: "Business was at a virtual standstill throughout the state in the wake of rejoicing over the Japanese surrender and the most popular places in any city were the churches, which began to fill early..."[440]

"WITH THE COLORS":

A veteran of five major campaigns in Europe, Private (First Class) Kenneth E. Wilks, 21, son of Mr. and Mrs. E. E. Wilks, 2037 Fourth Avenue, has returned to this country for a 30-day furlough. Private Wilks was wounded while serving with the 28th Infantry Division near Percy, France. He spent 22 months in the European theatre of operations.

Private (First Class) Jack M. Waldeck, son of Mr. and Mrs. Jack Waldeck, 1004 Madison Avenue, has been stationed near Linz, Austria, since the end of the European war. He has visited Berchtesgaden, where he saw Hitler's "Eagle Nest" hideout, and seen the homes of Herrmann Goering and other Nazi leaders. During the war he served with the Third Army, but is now in General Mark Clark's occupational forces. He wears the Combat Infantryman's Badge and the ETO ribbon with two battle stars.

Hospital Apprentice (First Class) Katherine Lloyd, USNR, reported recently for duty in the Hawaiian Islands. She is the daughter of Mr. and Mrs. F. Lloyd, 416 Twenty-ninth Street. A graduate of Huntington High School, she entered the service in May, 1943. She was stationed at Ottumwa, Ia., before going overseas.

Private Lindsey P. Riggs, 625 Second Street, was in a recent shipment of men who were returned to the United States from the European theatre of operations, via Miami, by planes of the Air Transport Command. Private Riggs spent 40 months overseas with the 5th

257

Infantry Division and is looking forward to a furlough at home.

Seaman (First Class) Clayton Minor, 35, Thirty-seventh Street, fought aboard the destroyer USS *Russell* during the bombardment and invasion of Okinawa. The *Russell* has been in action 32 months.

Fireman (Second Class) Billy Gene Hite, who recently spent a furlough here with his wife, Mrs. Billie Hite and parents, Mr. and Mrs. Carl Hite, 210 Baer Street, was transferred from the U.S. Naval Training Station at Great Lakes, Ill. to Shumaker, Calif. for advanced training.

Lieutenant Nick Anest, 27, 815 Ninth Street, is serving aboard a submarine in the Pacific which has damaged and sunk many Jap vessels. He has been in the Navy almost four years and was formerly in the Maritime Service.

Private Lucian Spiller, 1610 Ninth Avenue, is with the 318th Quartermaster Service Company, which is now guarding hundreds of German prisoners of war who are turning out clothing for thousands of Reich soldiers in Germany.

Harry N. Davis, son of Mrs. Alberta Davis, 1229 ½ Third Avenue, has been recently promoted to the rating of master technical sergeant in the U.S. Marine Corps. Sergeant Davis also received a commendation from the Army for duty during the Okinawa campaign.

Corporal Robert R. Edwards, son of Mr. and Mrs. Clarence Edwards, 2463 Collis Avenue, is currently serving with an engineer battalion somewhere in Germany. He is the husband of Mrs. Virginia Edwards of Baltimore and has been in the service for more than two years.

A sailor and a marine from the Huntington area are serving aboard the 31-year-old battleship USS *Texas* in the Pacific... On board are Seaman (First Class) O. C. Watkins, 21, of Lackey, Ky., and Private (First Class) Russell D. Stowers, 20, son of Mr. and Mrs. Mack Stowers of Culloden.

Private (First Class) George L. Douglas, 711 Thirty-first Street, recently entered Berlin with elements of Major General Floyd L. Park's First Airborne Army, occupying what remains of the once beautiful German capital...

Corporal James R. Blake Jr., husband of Mrs. Clara Blake who resides at 1527 Sixth Avenue, is stationed at the Allied Headquarters in Rome. Corporal Blake saw 10 months action with the 34th Infantry Division of the U.S. Fifth Army in Italy before the fall of the Axis nations in Europe. He participated in the drive up the Po Valley and took part in several other major campaigns in Northern Italy where he was awarded two bronze battle stars for his campaign ribbon and the Combat Infantryman's Badge. After graduating from Huntington High School and attending Marshall College, Corporal Blake entered the Army in January 1944, received his basic training at Camp Blanding, Fla., and was at once sent to the European theatre of operations. He has a brother, Homer Blake, who is serving with the Merchant Marines in the Pacific.

Glenna: *August 16th Thursday – Clear and cooler. The world still celebrating V.J. Day. I canned beans all day.*

"The world still celebrating V.J. Day" and "I canned beans all day." What a contrast. Everyday life went on in Salt Rock, as it did in all parts of our country. Somehow, that is comforting.

Rupert: *People still selbrateing.*

Charleston, West Virginia: Two cases of infantile paralysis (polio) was reported by Marmet Hospital. A third case in a milder form was reported in Charleston.[441]

Winston Churchill delivered a warning that an "iron curtain" was falling across Europe.[442]

"Scattered fighting continued in northern Luzon's mountains today. American commanders spurred efforts ... to inform all isolated Japanese of Emperor Hirohito's surrender and to persuade them to lay down their arms..."[443] Emperor Hirohito announced that he would send "members of the imperial family to the various fighting fronts to assure that his orders to 'cease fire' are carried out."[444] In related news, Hirohito appointed General Prince Naruhiko Higashi-Kuni , a cousin, to form a post-war government.[445]

"WITH THE COLORS":

Raymond McKenzie, son of Mrs. Ann McKenzie, Route 4, Huntington, has recently been promoted to private (first class) in recognition of proven ability with an infantry division headquarters company in the Pacific. Private McKenzie is a member of General Paul J. Mueller's 81st "Wildcat" Infantry Division, which last fall wrested the Palau and other Western Caroline Islands from the Japanese.

Lieutenant William M. Daniel, son of Mr. W. H. Daniel, 1615 Crestmont Drive, is currently stationed in Puerto Rico with the AAF Caribbean Division of the Air Transport Command. Lieutenant Daniel has spent 16 months overseas in the European theatre of operations and wears the ETO ribbon with five battle stars, and the American theatre ribbon. He attended Marshall College and was a machinist apprentice before entering the service.

Private Lindsey Riggs, 625 Second Street, a veteran infantryman with 40 months overseas, has returned to the United States and is at the Miami Air Field, Fla.

Sergeant Paul V. Leitch, husband of Mrs. Josephine G. Leitch of Huntington, is home on furlough from the Pacific theatre of operations where he served for 30 months.

Newly arrived at Randolph Field, Tex., Lieutenant William F. Kincaid, son of Mr. and Mrs. Emory F. Kincaid, 2120 Twelfth Avenue, is in training as a flight engineer member for a B-29 Superfortress crew.

Private (First Class) Arnie M. Davis, son of Mrs. B. F. Davis of Huntington, is serving with the 21st Infantry Regiment of the famed 24th "Victory" Infantry Division as a mortar-man.

Private (First Class) Lawrence F. Lakin, son of Mr. and Mrs. J. F. Lakin of Fort Gay, has arrived at Wakeman Convalescent Hospital at Camp Atterbury, Ind. after spending a 51-day furlough with his parents. Private Lakin, a paratrooper, was wounded in action on Luzon last March 13.

Glenna: *August 17th Friday – I went to Huntington. Took Rupert to his Grandma Pratt's. Went to St. Mary's Hospital to see Ausley.*

Rupert: *I went to my Grandma Pratt's.*

My Pratt grandparents lived on Roby Road in Huntington. They would later rent a house on 28th Street and eventually buy a home in Guyandotte.

Paris, August 17: General de Gaulle commuted Marshal Petain's death sentence to life imprisonment.[446] (Petain died in prison in 1951.)

Mar Del Plata, Argentina, August 17: A German submarine surrendered to Argentina's navy. "The 600-ton craft carried the number *U-977* and a complement of 32, including four officers, one of whom was Commander Heinz Schasser." *U-530* had surrendered to Argentina on July 10.

San Francisco, August 17: General Prince Naruhiko Nigashi-Kuni became Japan's new premier.[447]

Glenna: *August 18th Saturday – I cleaned the house at evening. Went down to Joe Dick's. Pretty day.*

Rupert: *I went to the show.*

I had a lot of freedom when I visited my Pratt grandparents in Huntington. City busses carried me anywhere I wanted to go.

A Wayne County site for the construction of the proposed tri-state airport had come under consideration. The 700-acre site, "if selected, lies approximately three miles south of Kenova at Sweet Run about three-fourths of a mile south of State Route 75."[448]

San Francisco, August 18: "The Japanese people, treated heretofore to a series of face-saving, evasive explanations of their surrender, were told flatly today by one of their top-flight leaders they are a beaten people and must pay the price for an imperialistic dream bubble that burst in the blast of atomic bombs."[449]

Chungking, August 18: "The Chinese First Army, veterans of the Burma campaign, entered Canton today and will accept formal surrender of Japanese forces in south China tomorrow, and plans were under way for overall surrender of Japanese troops in China."[450]

Glenna: *August 19th Sunday – I went to Sunday School. Wink Finley ate dinner with us. We had fried chicken. Very pretty day. Thelma Lucas Sergent's girl baby was born. Its name is Shirley Ann.*

Wink Finley was the brother of Catherine, Freer Morrison's wife. Wink was a farm hand who did periodic work for Freer and for us at busy times of the year.

Rupert: *I went to two shows today.*

Glenna: *August 20th Monday – Gaynelle's birthday. I washed. Very pretty day.*

Rupert: *I came home today.*

Marshall College Registrar Luther E. Bledsoe announced that freshman orientation would run from 10 A.M. Monday, September 10 through Wednesday, September 12.[451]

The latest national weekly traffic death count increased from fifteen to fifty-four, and was assumed to be a result of the end of gas rationing and elimination of the 35 mile-per-hour speed limit.[452]

Hollywood, August 20: "Actor-Singer Dick Powell and June Allyson ... were married last night in an informal ceremony at the home of Composer and Mrs. Johnny Green..."[453]

"WITH THE COLORS":

Private (First Class) Arna R. Neal, son of Mrs. Edith Neal, 1648 Doulton Avenue, a holder of five battle stars, is en route home from the European theatre of operations with the 5-star 32nd "Santa Fe" Infantry Division, which in 10 months battled across the Elbe River to within 42 miles from Berlin.

Staff Sergeant Kenneth D. Wickline, husband of Mrs. Lucille D. Wickline, 2642 Guyan Avenue, wound up another campaign with the 136th Field Artillery Battalion, with the completion of fierce fighting in Cagayan Valley, Luzon Philippine Islands, by the veterans of the 37th Infantry Division. Sergeant Wickline, an original member of the battalion which went overseas 38 months ago, saw action in New Georgia and Bougainville of the Northern Solomon campaign, as well as the Luzon campaign, where they took part in the battles of Manil and Baguio. The sergeant was awarded the Bronze Star Medal for heroic achievement during the Northern Solomon campaign.

Seaman (First Class) Charles William Trisler of Milton, who survived the sinking of two minesweepers off Borneo, is spending a 30-day furlough with his family. Both minesweepers were sunk by enemy mines during a routine pre-invasion sweep at Balikpapan.

Charles M. Maddox, son of John Maddox of Gallipolis, O., has been promoted to private (first class) while stationed at Pope Field,

Fort Bragg, N.C. His wife, Mrs. Ruby Maddox, resides at Salt Rock, W.Va.

Private Lawrence W. Stephenson, son of Mr. and Mrs. Clifford B. Stephenson of Huntington, was graduated this week from the AAF Training Command's basic airplane and engine mechanics course at Keesler Field, Biloxi, Miss.

Technician (Fifth Grade) Ernest F. Galloway, son of Mr. and Mrs. John Galloway, 306 Sixteenth Street, and husband of Mrs. Mary Ann Galloway of the same address, is currently stationed at the army Ground and Service Forces Redistribution Station at Fort Oglethorpe, Ga... Corporal Galloway was recently returned to the States after having served for 36 months in the European theatre of operations... He holds the Good Conduct Medal, the Pre-Pearl Harbor ribbon, and the ETO ribbon with three bronze campaign stars.

Private Elmer Baisden, son of Mrs. Ethel Baisden, 1667 Fourteenth Avenue and Private (First Class) Charles Richardson, son of Mrs. Goldie Hill, 232 Richmond Street, are members of the 361st Infantry Regiment's Third Battalion...

Second Lieutenant Charles M. Stroud, husband of Mrs. Elanor J. Stroud, 1035 Twentieth Street, was recently assigned to the Bomber Barons, a B-24 Liberator group currently serving with the 13th AAF in the Philippines.

Private (First Class) Elza White of Kenova, a member of the 326th Glider Infantry in France, recently visited northern France, Luxembourg and southern Germany on a GI tour which included the forts at Metz, portions of the Maginot Line fortifications and Worms, Germany, where the Third and Seventh Armies crossed the Rhine.

Private (First Class) John B. Hensley, 727 Thirty-first Street, is attached to the 264th Ordnance Evacuation Company now at an assembly area command in France awaiting shipment to the United States.

Private (First Class) Elmer Sites, husband of Mrs. Lolarose Sites of Chesapeake, O., is a member of a mortar squad with the veteran 32nd "Red Arrow" Division engaged in patrolling the Caraballo Mountains. Private Sites has been overseas since January, 1945.

Technical Sergeant James A. Chambers of Huntington, holder of the European theatre of operations ribbon with four battle stars, a Good Conduct ribbon, and the American Defense ribbon, returned home recently after serving overseas since February 7, 1944 with the 203rd Battalion of the Seventh Armored Division. He has been for several months at the Ashford General Hospital at White Sulphur Springs, W.Va.

Glenna: *August 21st Tuesday – I ironed and mended. Dawson is on a 2 ½ weeks' vacation starting at midnight of the 17th.*

Rupert: *I read a lot.*

"The signing of Otterbein College [Westerville, Ohio] to open West Virginia University's football season at Morgantown September 22 was announced today by Athletic Director Roy M. Hawley." Other scheduled games were with Pittsburgh, Syracuse, Temple, Maryland, Virginia, Kentucky, and Ohio University.[454]

London, August 21: The Russian-Japanese war, one of the shortest wars in history between major powers, ceased in Manchuria.[455]

Moscow, August 21: The Soviets ratified the United Nations Charter.[456]

Manila, August 21: General MacArthur announced he "would soon relinquish command over the area south of the Philippines to Britain. British and Australian commanders would be responsible for the surrender of Japanese forces there."[457]

"WITH THE COLORS":

Seaman (First Class) James Franklin Smith, USNR, is spending a leave home with his father, J. F. Smith of Huntington after serving 15 months aboard a destroyer escort in the Pacific. He has taken part in seven major engagements, including the Okinawa campaign, Saipan, Iwo Jima and Leyte.

Staff Sergeant Gus E. Collins of Huntington has been awarded the Bronze Star Medal for heroic achievement while serving with the 179th Engineer Combat Battalion in Germany. The citation said he neutralized two dynamite charges [in] an enemy pillbox which had been firing upon him and his men during a ferrying operation on the Saar River. His action was with disregard for personal danger, the citation added. He is the son of Mr. and Mrs. Marshall Collins, Rear 2556 Collis Avenue.

Private (First Class) Jeanne L. Parker, daughter of Mr. and Mrs. Albert Albertsen, 206 West Eighth Avenue, is a member of the clerical staff of the adjutant general's office at General MacArthur's headquarters in Manila. She has been overseas more than a year and served on New Guinea before going to Manila.

Buster Wallen, 22, son of Mrs. Polly Ann Wallen of Melvin, Ky., has been advanced to the rating of machinist's mate (second class) in the U.S. Navy. Machinist Wallen has served aboard a destroyer escort since May, 1944. His ship participated in the Luzon, Iwo Jima, and Okinawa campaigns and was credited with the destruction of two Jap torpedo planes off Luzon.

Technician (Fifth Grade) William T. Bunn of Williamson is stationed at Fort Oglethorpe, Ga., pending his new assignment in the United States. Technician Bunn, who served for 17 months in the European theatre of operations, a member of the medical corps, holds the Good Conduct Medal and the ETO ribbon.

The unit to which Technician (Fifth Grade) Richard Hensley of Barboursville is attached in New Caledonia has been awarded the Meritorious Service Unit Plaque for "superior performance of duty." Technician Hensley is the son of Mrs. Alma Hensley who resides in Barboursville.

Machinist's Mate (Second Class) William F. Bratton of Russell, Ky. has recently been commended by his commanding officer for "exceptional skill and initiative" in the repair of a damaged destroyer escort, one of Admiral T. C. Kinkaid's Seventh Fleet units.

Electrician's Mate (Third Class) Jonnie Whittaker, 20, of Auxier, Ky., is serving aboard the USS *Solace* which evacuated and treated wounded at Tarawa, Eniwetok, Kwajalein, the Admiralties, Saipan, Guam, Pelefu, Iwo Jima and Okinawa...

Corporal Glenn Raymond Branaman, son of Mr. and Mrs. G. W. Branaman, 306 West Eleventh Avenue, is spending a 30-day furlough with his parents after having served as an Army Air Force ground radio operator in a reconnaissance group headquarters in France since before February. Before entering the Army two and a half years ago, Corporal Branaman, a graduate of Huntington Central High School, attended Marshall College and later received a Bachelor of Science degree in business administration from the Wharton School of Finance at the University of Pennsylvania in Philadelphia.

Motor Machinist's Mate (Third Class) Richard G. Thompson has returned to the East Coast following a 10-day leave with his mother, Mrs. Mayme Thompson, 2564 Collis Avenue. He is stationed aboard the USS *Lejeune*, engaged in transporting troops home from the European theatre.

Among personnel of the ordnance maintenance company assigned to disarm more than 350,000 Germans in Norway are Technician (Third Grade) John W. Gold, 138 Norway Avenue, and Technician (Fourth Grade) Harold Holcomb, 1426 Third Avenue.

Glenna: *August 22nd Wednesday – I canned tomatoes all day. That night I went to prayer meeting. Chicken for supper. Very hot.*

In the intense heat, Mother "canned tomatoes all day" and still cooked the evening meal.

Rupert: *I helped in the hay.*

I enjoyed freedom of the open fields and loading of the horse-drawn wagon with soybeans or timothy, but putting the hay in the barn was a hot and dusty job. I coughed up black "stuff" for days afterward.

Huntington area residents were advised to mail Christmas gifts to overseas service members before October 15.[458]

"Three sons of Mrs. Helen George, 612 Trenton Place, have been or are ... stationed in the Pacific theatre of operations. Marine Private Louis S. George, 17, who was wounded on Okinawa, has recently returned to the Norfolk, Va. Naval Hospital. Overseas ... are two other sons. Private (First Class) Julius S. George, 20, is a member of a B-29 pioneer group... Overseas 18 months in the China-Burma-India theatre, he wears five battle stars and is now stationed at Saipan. Seaman (First Class) Emile Ralph George, 18, has served in the Pacific aboard an LST for eight months." [459] (Mrs. George must have suffered great anxiety. The "Greatest Generation" encompassed not only the warriors, but those waiting at home.)

Moscow, August 22: "Soviet relations with Bulgaria advanced another step today with the announcement that Stepan Paviovich Kirsanov had been appointed as Russian minister to Sofia. Bulgaria appointed Prof. Dmitry Mikhalchev, well known in his own country as a scientist and philosopher, as minister to Moscow." The U.S. did not consider Bulgaria's government as "representative of all the democratic elements in the country."[460]

"WITH THE COLORS":

Staff Sergeant Forrest E. Goodman, 24, husband of Mrs. Elphia Goodman, 428 Sixth Street, has arrived in the United States from Europe with 103 points to his credit. He served overseas for nine months and holds battle stars for the Ardennes, Central European and Rhineland campaigns, and in addition to the Good Conduct Medal, was awarded the coat of arms of the city of Colmar, France, for participating in liberating the Alsace capital.

Private (First Class) Eli N. Painter, 2751 Fourth Avenue, is en route home from Europe with the five-star 35th "Santa Fe" Division. He was formerly a member of the Eighth Armored Division which supported the 35th in the battle for Rheinburg and other cities in the drive to the west bank of the Rhine River.

Sergeant Carl B. Saxton, son of Mrs. Rachel R. Saxton of Huntington, has been awarded the Bronze Star Medal for routing a German strongpoint and capturing several Nazis by advancing ahead of his squad and setting fire to a building with incendiary bullets.

Lieutenant (Junior Grade) Robert B. Burke, USNR, 431 Eleventh Avenue, is spending a leave with his patents, Mr. and Mrs. E. M. Burke. Lieutenant Burke served on Guam for nine months.

Staff Sergeant Everett E. Meadows, 2934 Eighth Avenue, has been in the Assembly Area Command in France with the 45th Infantry Division awaiting transportation elsewhere... Sergeant Meadows wears the Purple Heart, the Combat Infantryman Badge, the ETO ribbon with three battle stars, and the good Conduct Medal.

Private (First Class) Robert W. Lemley, son of Mr. and Mrs. C. A. Lemley, Proctorville, O., is en route home from Europe with the 35th "Santa Fe" Division. He wears the Combat Infantryman Badge and the ETO ribbon with two battle stars.

Seaman (First Class) Richard C. Strong, son of Mr. and Mrs. William Strong of Burlington,

O... has returned to the U.S. Naval Training Station at Great Lakes, Ill. where he will receive advanced training. Seaman Strong recently returned to the United States from Europe where he served for several months.

Lieutenant William Macdonald, 411 Sixteenth Street, has been promoted to the rank of lieutenant commander in the U.S. Naval reserve... He has been assistant supervisor of construction for the Higgins Boat Co., New Orleans, since 1942. He is a brother of F. A. Macdonald, 2188 Washington Boulevard.

Corporal Robert D. Martin, 340 Marshall Street, and Private (First Class) Paul Noe of Welch, W.Va. are members of Battery "D" 125th Anti-Aircraft Artillery Battalion, now on military police duty near Chalons, France...

A professional entertainer for 11 years before entering the service, Corporal Harold F. Hawkins, son of Mr. and Mrs. Alex Hawkins, 851 Adams Avenue, now spends much of his time furnishing music for the men of an engineer maintenance company awaiting redeployment at a staging area near Marseille, France. Corporal Hawkins is a former broadcaster for station WSAZ.

Among the first troops to enter Berlin and take up occupation duties in the American sphere with the First Airborne Army was Private Perison Goodson, 1843 Eighth Avenue.

Among West Virginians awaiting redeployment to the Pacific at [an] assembly area in France when news of our victory over Japan was announced were Lieutenant Mildred P. Knight, 928 Madison Avenue; Staff Sergeant Clarence E. Burns, 2625 Chesterfield Avenue; Corporal Robert L. Stephens, 1006 Marcum Terrace; Corporal Mount O. Holley, 4220 Riverside Drive and Corporal Billie J. Napier, Kenova.

Private (First Class) Regina M. Derda, 1630 Charleston Avenue, is stationed at St. Germain EnLaye, France, aiding in the redistribution of thousands of aircraft, motors and replacement parts which poured into Europe for the Eighth and Ninth Air Forces.

Sergeant Roy T. Bruce, who has been spending a 15-day furlough with his wife, Mrs. Mary Jo Bruce, 2804 ½ Marcum Terrace, has returned to Camp Callan, Calif. for further assignment.

Private Ray Rose has returned to Fort Meade, Md. for further assignment after spending a 12-day furlough with his mother, Mrs. Garfield Rose, 213 Fifth Avenue, Guyandotte.

Sergeant Charles Arthur and Mrs. Arthur arrived yesterday from St Joseph, Mo. for a furlough visit with his parents, Mr. and Mrs. Boone B. Arthur, 1123 Jefferson Avenue. Sergeant Arthur, of the Army Air Force, will occupy the pulpit of Madison Avenue Christian Church Sunday evening. His brother Burrell is serving with the Navy, a brother Neal is with the Army in the Philippines, while brother Fred is with the AAF in England.

Seaman (First Class) Pearl W. Donally, USNR, son of Mr. and Mrs. Edgar Ray Donally, Patriot, Ohio, was among crew members of the USS *English* which fought smoke, flames and exploding shells for three hours when the *English*, a destroyer, went to the aid of the carrier USS *Bunker Hill* after it had been attacked by Japanese suicide pilots on May 11. The *English* also transported Admiral Marc A. Mitscher and his staff from the Bunker Hill to a new flagship.

Private (First Class) Edward L. Chaffin, 1360 Adams Avenue, is at the Assembly Area Command in France awaiting transportation elsewhere...

Private (First Class) Charles E. Pratt, Route 3, Huntington, has been serving in Europe with forces engaged in redeploying Army Air Forces personnel and supplies to the Pacific. His wife, Mrs. Helen Wray Pratt, lives at New Malden, Walden, Surrey, England.

First Lieutenant William H. Forester, husband of Mrs. Joyce Morgan Forester, 424 Washington Avenue, and son of Mr. and Mrs. John Hamp Forester, 246 Eighth Avenue, has been awarded the Combat Infantryman Badge for the satisfactory performance of duty in ground combat in recent operations in the Palau Islands...

Private (First Class) Albert H. Duty of North Kenova, O. has left Antwerp, Belgium for the United States... He was a graduate of Chesapeake High School in 1936. He entered the Army on January 8, 1942 and has been serving with the 424th Infantry of the 106th Division. His wife, Mrs. Ruby Duty, lives in Burlington, O.

Private (First Class) Charles E. Money, 1639 Jefferson Avenue, is currently stationed at Camp Cleveland in the Assembly Area Command near Reims, France, awaiting transfer to the United States.

Private (First Class) Fred Z. Rust, husband of Mrs. Nannie Rust, 203 Thirty-third Street, and Private Raymond J. Poteet, son of Mrs. John L. Poteet of Huntington, Route 2, are serving at the 104th General Hospital at Kingswood, Hants, England, which has treated more than 8,000 American Soldiers during one year of operation.

Private Loren M. Rucker, 1826 Sixth Avenue, is one of 57 former combat men now helping to entertain troops being returned to the United States through the Assembly Area Command at Camp Chicago, near Reims, France.

Seaman (First Class) Carl West of Huntington is spending a 24-day furlough with his mother, Mrs. E. H. West, who resides at 2540 Collis Avenue. He has been on duty for 16 months in the Atlantic, serving in the armed guard of a Liberty ship. At the end of his brief leave he will report to New Orleans for reassignment.

Glenna: *August 23rd Thursday – I canned corn and beans. Have a very bad cold. Mowed at the graveyard. Rainy.*

Rupert: *I helped get in hay.*

San Francisco, August 23: "Japanese Red Cross delegates and aides from Swiss and Swedish legations will proceed on Friday to all of Japan's seven main prisoner-of-war camps to assist in evacuating prisoners of war and civilian internees to embarkation points."461

"WITH THE COLORS":

Private (First Class) Al J. Jessup, who served in the Pacific for 26 months, is visiting his mother, Mrs. Al Jessup, 2609 Fifth Avenue. His father, who was a police officer here, is deceased. He will return to Parris Island, S.C. after his leave.

Captain Clark M. McGhee, son of Mr. and Mrs. E. F. McGhee of Hurricane, has been appointed executive officer of the 522nd Fighter Squadron, a unit of the 27th Fighter Group that saw action in Northern Africa, Sicily, Italy, France and Germany and is now located at Sandhofen, Germany. Prior to his appointment he was the squadron intelligence officer. Captain McGhee has served overseas for more than 30 months and wears the Distinguished Unit Badge, four Oak Leaf Clusters, and has participated in eight major campaigns.

Corporal Bernard L. Riggs, 23, has returned to Cherry Point, N.C., after a visit with his mother, Mrs. Wayne Riggs of Kenova. A graduate of Ceredo-Kenova High School, Corporal Riggs entered the service in May, 1942. He received his training at Parris Island, S.C., and Jacksonville, Fla. A veteran of 19 months service on Bougainville, New Guinea and Guam, he wears the presidential unit citation and four battle stars.

Raymond W. Bertram, son of Mr. and Mrs. Willard E. Bertram, 2754 Emmons Avenue, has recently been promoted from corporal to second lieutenant in the 12th Army Air Forces in Italy... He holds the Silver Star Medal for gallantry, the Presidential Unit Citation and six battle stars. He has been doing photographic work and for some time was on detached duty with the First Armored Division.

Seaman (Second Class) Harold M. Saunders, son of Mr. and Mrs. Everett Saunders, 529 Buffington Street, is serving aboard the USS *Independence*, one of the Navy's front line aircraft carriers which played a major part in the aerial onslaught on Tokyo.

Private Herbert H. McDaniel, 32, husband of Mrs. Marguerite McDaniel, Chesapeake, O., is at the Army Ground and Service Forces Redistribution Center at Miami Beach, Fla., and will be given a new assignment. A veteran of nine months service as a rifleman in the European theatre of operations, he holds the Purple Heart, the European campaign ribbon with two battle stars and the Combat Infantryman Badge.

Miss Mary K. Casella of Huntington has been appointed a second lieutenant in the Army Nurse Corps, the War Department has announced.

Technician (First Grade) John Grassi of Huntington, a veteran of 16 months of overseas service, has returned to the United States from the European theatre of operations, via Miami, by planes of the U.S. Transport Command.

Watertender (First Class) Clyde Workman, husband of Mrs. Alice Workman of Harts, W.Va., is currently stationed aboard the USS *English*, one of the ships that went to the aid of the USS *Bunker Hill* when the carrier was attacked by suicide planes on May 11.

Radio Technician (Second Class) Homer Douglas Wells, 21, USNR, husband of Mrs. Shirley Marie Wells of Blaine, Ky., served recently in a bombardment staged by the USS *Iowa* ... with other Third Fleet units on Honshu 70 miles from Tokyo. The *Iowa* sent more than 200 tons of projectiles at war factories on the main Japanese island.

Gunner's Mate (Third Class) John W. Cooney has recently returned to New York City after spending a 30-day furlough with his mother, Mrs. Zella Cooney who resides in Kenova. He has been in the Navy for over 30 months and has seen 25 months sea duty aboard numerous merchant vessels.

Walter D. Nunley Jr., son of Mr. and Mrs. W. D. Nunley, 405 Cabell Court, has been promoted to the rank of sergeant. Now stationed in the Philippines with the Crusaders medium bomber group of the 13th Army Air Force, Sergeant Nunley has served overseas for 20 months in the Hebrides and Russell Islands and on New Guinea. Sergeant Nunley is a ground

station radio operator. Enlisting in May, 1941, he received training at Scott Field, Ill.

Glenna: *August 24th Friday – Rainy day. Cleaned house.*

Rupert: *I sprayed the house to kill the flys.*

Flies in summer were loathsome pests and we dealt aggressively with them. Flypaper on the porches caught a portion, but some got through the screen doors and into the house. I'm sure whatever chemical we used to kill them is now banned.

Another West Virginia service member received the nation's highest military award: "Technical Sergeant Bernard Bell, 34, a native of Point Pleasant, W.Va. and graduate of the high school there, was among 28 recipients of the Congressional Medal of Honor in ceremonies yesterday at the White House. President Truman made the awards."[462]

Tokyo radio announced that, due to radiation, the death rate has doubled since the atomic bomb explosions that destroyed two Japanese cities.[463]

"Four sons of Mr. and Mrs. R. D. Blake of Richmond Street are serving in the U.S. Armed forces. They are ... Clifford A. Blake, serving aboard an auxiliary destroyer in the Pacific; ... Fire Controlman (First Class) Reuben D. Blake, also serving aboard a destroyer in the Pacific theatre; ... Harold Lee Blake, a member of the U.S. Navy Supply Corps in the Pacific, and Private Earl Sheldon Blake of the U.S. Army, stationed in Washington. Two of the brothers, Clifford and Reuben, recently spent several weeks together in the Philippines."[464]

"WITH THE COLORS":

First Lieutenant Kathryn L. Byers of Huntington was recently promoted to her present rating in the Army Nurses Corps... Lieutenant Byers is a graduate of the nursing school at the St. Mary's Hospital, Covington, Ky. She is the daughter of Mr. and Mrs. J. C. Byers of Huntington.

Technician (Fifth Grade) Carl D. Meadows, 41, 1816 Fifth Avenue, has arrived at Miami, Fla. via air from the European theatre where he served with the anti-aircraft artillery. Technician Meadows, who was overseas for 22 months, wears four battle stars.

Commander Ray R. Gentry, son-in-law of Mr. and Mrs. H. K. Eustler of 520 Thirteenth Street, is visiting his family here while on leave before going overseas.

Flight Officer Edwin W. Webb, son of Mr. and Mrs. W. E. Webb, 403 Adams Avenue, has entered a five-weeks training course at the AAF Training Command's B-29 Transition school at the Roswell, New Mexico Army Air Field to become a co-pilot of one of the new sky dreadnaughts.

Six more fighting men from the Huntington area were discharged from the armed services Tuesday at the Camp Atterbury, Ind. Separation Center in accordance with the Army regulation releasing service men with 85 points or more ... included Private (First Class) Harsie G. Bolen, Huntington, Route 2; Staff Sergeant Leo F. Pearson, 911 Sixteenth Street; Staff Sergeant Rupert A. Altizer, Man; Sergeant Delbert C. Chapman, Milton; Sergeant Billie W. Dickerson, Kenova, and Private (First Class) George W. Brightwell of Teays.

Lieutenant (j. g.) Harry P. Henshaw Jr., son of Mr. and Mrs. H. P. Henshaw, 330 Woodland Drive, Private (First Class) Willis L. Wilson, USMC, of Huntington Route 4, and Seaman (First Class) Virgil E. Darling of Kenova Route 1, who are serving aboard the USS *Astoria*, have helped the light cruiser avenge her namesake, a heavy cruiser which was sunk by the Japs off Guadalcanal in 1942. After she entered Jap waters eight months ago, the ship participated in action at Iwo Jima, Okinawa, in the China Sea and off Tokyo, and

succeeded in bringing down 13 Jap planes and crippling numerous others.

Glenna: *August 25th Saturday – Hot. I baked a cake. Dawson made chicken.*

Rupert: *Larry Gill came over to stay all night.*

Larry and I exchanged visits often. We played Monopoly, a game he always managed to win.

From NEA Sports Editor, Harry Grayson: "Convinced by what Army, Notre Dame and others accomplished with it, Navy has switched from the single wing to the modern T [football formation] with man-in-motion."[465]

New York, August 25: "Rocky Graziano, a Brooklyn toughie with the kick of a mule in his right hand, is boxing's latest million-dollar baby. He zoomed into the big money class last night by again knocking out Welterweight Champion Freddie ('Red') Cochrane in the 10th round of their return non-title bout at Madison Square Garden."[466]

Bulgaria postponed elections. The United States and Britain expressed the negative opinion that ... "all democratic elements in Bulgaria would not be able to participate."[467]

Fort Leavenworth, Kansas: "Stoical, and still allegiant to a Nazism they refused to believe was beaten, seven German prisoners of war—former members of wolf-pack submarine crews—died early this morning on the gallows for the 'traitor slaying' of a fellow-prisoner."[468]

Typhoons in the Pacific caused postponement of Allied landings in the Tokyo area and the formal Japanese surrender ceremonies.[469]

Manila, August 25: "Japanese imperial headquarters notified General MacArthur today that four Japanese submarines are missing and may have been sunk..."[470] In similar news, the U.S. Navy announced that all United States submarines "not previously reported lost or missing" were accounted for.[471]

"WITH THE COLORS":

Sergeant John E. Wellman, former Marshall College student, has returned to the United States after 27 months overseas and is spending a 30-day furlough with his grandmother, Mrs. Mary Burdette of Hurricane, and his uncle and aunt, Mr. and Mrs. Clyde Harbour, 1105 Ninth Avenue. A waist gunner on a B-17 Flying Fortress, Sergeant Wellman holds the Air Medal with one Oak Leaf Cluster, the European theatre ribbon with six battle stars and the Presidential Unit Citation with one Oak Leaf Cluster. He has 95 service points to his credit and at the end of his brief furlough he will report to Fort Meade, Md., for dischargement [Not a word, but makes perfect sense.]. His brother, Corporal Forrest B. Wellman is serving with the 504th Parachute Division in Germany.

Pharmacist's Mate (Third Class) Lewis B. Clelland, who has completed 14 months in the South Pacific, is visiting his parents, Mr. and Mrs. W. H. Clelland, 837 Ninth Street. Pharmacist's Mate Clelland was assigned to the escort carrier USS *Sargent Bay* when it was commissioned in January, 1944, and wears six combat stars on his campaign ribbons for participation in the liberation of the Philippines and other operations in the Asiatic-Pacific theatre, He will return to his base next week after a 24-day leave.

Fireman (Second Class) Hugh Jerome Evans, husband of Mrs. Kathryn Evans, 159 Cedar Street, is serving aboard the USS *Walker* in the Pacific. The ship's battle record includes major operations at Tarawa, Wotje, Hollandia, Saipan, Tinian, Guam, Leyte, Okinawa and Kyushu.

Ship's cook, (First Class) Charles Edward Chapman, son of Mr. and Mrs. Burl Chapman, 219 ½ Fourth Avenue, was aboard the USS *Iowa* when she and other U.S. Third Fleet cruisers, battleships and destroyers staged a midnight bombardment of Industrial targets on the main Japanese island of Honshu, only 70 miles from Tokyo.

Corporal James E. Owens, 856 Washington Avenue, has reported to the "Green Project," an Air Lift Distribution Center at Camp Blanding, Fla., after spending 16 months in Europe.

Private (First Class) Charlie D. Watson, son of Mr. and Mrs. Clarence Watson of Branchland, is currently stationed at Camp Shelby, Miss. where the 95th Division is awaiting further assignment. Private Watson served for 12 months in Belgium, France, Holland and Germany with a field artillery unit and participated in three major campaigns. He wears the European theatre of operations ribbon and was awarded the Good Conduct Medal and the Combat Infantryman's Badge.

Technical Sergeant F. Neel Appling Jr., who has served in ground personnel work in the Pacific for the past 34 months, is on his way home, according to word received by his wife, the former Miss Louise Biddle of this city, who resides with his parents at 128 Ninth Avenue.

Corporal Stover McCoy Helser, son of Mr. and Mrs. Ted Helser, 203 West Ninth Avenue, who served 26 months in India with a communications division, is now stationed at Columbus, Miss. with the Army Air Forces.

Lieutenant (j. g.) William K. Gibson Jr. of Huntington figures in an article in the current issue of Liberty magazine, recounting the sinking of the Jap Battleship *Yamato...*

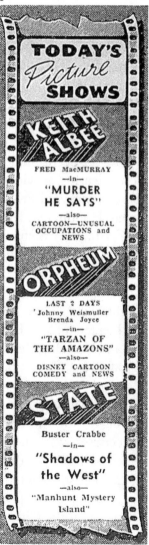

The son of Mr. and Mrs. W. K. Gibson, 104 Washington Boulevard, was a member of group of carrier-based torpedo bombers which scored direct hits on the *Yamato* with 12 of the 13 torpedoes which they released.

Sergeant John E. Jones, 915 Tenth Street, is a member of an Army detail which has been checking shoes in the clothing breakdown at the Sissonne warehouse near Reims, France. This warehouse supplies Camp Chicago, one of the many camps speeding the redeployment of American troops who have fought in the European theatre of operations.

Private (First Class) Ellis N. Napier, 1914 Maple Avenue, is now at Camp New York in the Assembly Area Command of France, awaiting transportation to the United States. Private Napier is attached to the 878th Signal Company Depot of the U.S. Ninth Air Force...

Among the 48 West Virginians discharged from the Army at the Camp Atterbury, Ind. Separation Center last Thursday in accordance with the Army regulation releasing all men with 85 points or more were four from this area. They were Private (First Class) William P. Hightower of Kenova; Private (First Class) John B. Adkins of Vivian; Private (First Class) Frank L. Orrison of Havaco and Technician (Fifth Grade) Joe B. Evans of English.

Seeing the sights of Paris recently with a pass group from the 45th "Thunderbird" Division at an Assembly Area Command near Reims, was Private (First Class) George E. Mills of 913 West Twelfth Street.

Private (First Class) William Berry, 3009 Sixteenth Street Road, is an ammunition bearer with the 80th "Blue Ridge" Infantry Division's Second Battalion of the 318th Infantry Regiment...

With three months experience behind them in handling supplies, a Quartermaster Service Company is now at Camp Cleveland, Assembly Area Command, being processed preparatory to being shipped to the Pacific. Private (First Class) Dan Chisholm, 1140 Seventh Avenue, is a member.

Corporal James M. Clark, Huntington Route 4, a member of the 45th "Thunderbird" Division, is currently stationed at an assembly Area Command in France, awaiting shipment to the United States. He is the holder of the Good Conduct Medal and the European theatre of operations with two battle stars.

Glenna: *August 26th Sunday – Went to church and Sunday School. Cool and very pretty.*

Rupert: *I went to church.*

The summer ensemble of the Huntington Sympathy held a concert in the Ritter Park amphitheater. About one thousand persons heard a program of popular numbers.[472]

Manila: "General MacArthur notified Japanese headquarters that United States Fleet ships would enter Sagami Bay, south of Tokyo, as scheduled, but there was no announced change about the 48-hour postponement for the first troop landings in Japan, postponed because of typhoons."[473]

Glenna: *August 27th Monday – Washed all day. In evening Mrs. Rousey came up and I wrote a letter for her.*

Rupert: *I went over to Larry Gills.*

Guam: B-29s dropped food to Allied prisoners of war at Weihsien, China.[474]

"WITH THE COLORS":

Private (First Class) Charles W. Thompson, son of Mr. and Mrs. Jasper Thompson, 559 West Third Avenue, has returned home from Germany after seeing 12 months of active duty in the European theatre. Private Thompson will report to Camp Shelby for reassignment after his leave terminates.

Aviation Machinist's Mate (Third Class) Clovie Adkins, son of Mrs. Sadie Adkins, 2334 Railroad Avenue, has returned to the United States after serving for four months with a Navy search plane squadron on Pacific Combat patrol. After entering the Navy in January, 1943, he flew 35 missions as a mechanic and gunner on a Mariner.

Yeoman (Third Class) William C. Dials of Huntington served aboard the destroyer escort USS *Wintle* which is undergoing repairs in the naval drydock on the West Coast after 125,000 miles and 22 months of battle duty in the Pacific.

Fireman (Second Class) Delmar E. Keenan, 317 Sixth Avenue, was aboard the escort carrier USS *Sangamon* when it was struck by a Japanese suicide plane in a recent operation in the Pacific. Fireman Keenan was below deck when the plane hit and escaped injury. The *Sangamon* limped home and is now being repaired at the Norfolk, Va. Navy Yards.

Seaman (Second Class) Charles William Trisler of Milton survived the sinking of the minesweeper *YMS 39* blown apart when a Japanese mine exploded beneath her on June 26 during pre-invasion minesweeping operations off the coast of Balikpapan.

Lieutenant William J. Little, son of Mr. and Mrs. W. J. Little, 2731 Collis Avenue, returned to the United States from the European theatre of operations where he served with the First Army in Germany. For the past three months Lieutenant Little has been attending an officer's training school just outside Paris.

Technical Sergeant Billy S. Marcum, son of Mr. and Mrs. W. R. Marcum, 2844 Overlook Drive, is spending a 30-day furlough with his parents. Sergeant Marcum served with the 13th Armored Division while in Germany and fought in the Ruhr pocket. After his leave he will report to Fort Meade, Md. for reassignment.

Staff Sergeant William G. Mitchell, 28, husband of Mrs. Lynn Mitchell, 1034 Seventh Street, has returned to the United States after 32 months service as a platoon sergeant in the European theatre of operations, [and] is at the Army Ground and Service Forces Redistribution Station at Miami Beach, Fla. He wears the Purple Heart and the ETO ribbon with one battle star. Sergeant Mitchell was inducted April 16, 1941.

Private (First Class) Lloyd W. McCorkle, son of Mr. and Mrs. H. C. McCorkle, 807 West Eleventh Street, has been awarded a bronze service star for participation in the Western Pacific campaign... A former railroad clerk, Private McCorkle entered active duty December 7, 1942, and has been serving as a clerk at the Guam Air Depot.

Private (First Class) Mary Jane Mackinnon, daughter of Mrs. Willie S. Milton, 1812 Marcum Terrace, has been awarded the Good Conduct Medal at Will Rogers Field, Oklahoma City, Okla.

Seaman (Second Class) James Arthur Sexton of Huntington was recently transferred to the USS *Amsterdam* as his first assignment since boot training. He is the son of Mrs. Nellie Sexton of Huntington, Route 2.

Corporal Patsy Hager, daughter of J. P. Hager, 401 West Whitaker Boulevard, and Corporal Frances Hopson, daughter of Mr. and Mrs. C. D. Cooper, 4420 Hughes Branch Road, are serving in the Women's Army Corps at Cincinnati, O. Corporal Hager is assigned to the statistical control section and Corporal Hopson to the air inspector of Headquarters Ferrying Division, Air Transport Command. Corporal Hager and Corporal Hopson entered the WAC in August, 1944 and received their basic training at Fort Des Moines, Ia. Before enlistment, both were employed at the Owens-Illinois Glass Co.

Louis Fridinger of Huntington has been promoted to the rank of sergeant in Headquarters Company, Fourth Engineer Special Brigade, at Manilla. P. I. Sergeant Fridinger is serving with the Army as an information and education non-com and is also doing public relations work. The husband of Mrs. Helen Virginia Fridinger, 1001 Eleventh Avenue, and son of Mrs. C. L. Fridinger, Washington, D.C., he entered the Army November 29, 1943. He is a former employee of the tax department of the Chesapeake and Ohio Railway Co. He was active in professional baseball, playing in the Mid-Atlantic League.

Corporal Mildred Hager, daughter of Mrs. Adeline Hager, 1837 Madison Avenue, is stationed at George Field, Lawrenceville, Ill., a U.S. Troop Carrier Command base. Corporal Hager has been in the Woman's Army Corps for 28 months and was formerly stationed at Alliance, Neb. She has three brothers in the service, one in the U.S. Engineers, one in the infantry and a third brother in the Air Corps.

Seaman (First Class) Everett Holderby, 21, son of Mrs. Georgia Holderby of Proctorville, is stationed with detachments of the U.S. Navy in Borneo. Seaman Holderby entered the service in July 1943, trained at the U.S. Naval Training Station at Great Lakes, Ill., and was then sent to the Pacific in March 1944, where he saw action off New Guinea and Mortal. His brother, Seaman (Second Class) Harry Holderby, is now home on leave after receiving nine weeks "boot training" at Great Lakes.

Glenna: *August 28ᵗʰ Tuesday – I ironed and mended and canned apples. Got all my jars filled up now.*

It was a major accomplishment to fill hundreds of canning jars with fruit, vegetables, and meat; Mother took great pride in the full shelves of the cellar. I eventually used many of her jars to can produce from my upstate New York garden.

Rupert: *We dug the potatoes.*

Potatoes were also stored in the cellar, which was cool and dry.

Sagami Bay, Japan, August 28: "Admiral Nimitz, commander of the Pacific Ocean areas, will arrive tomorrow and make the battleship *South Dakota* his flagship, it was announced today."[475]

"American airborne troops—the first conquerors ever to set foot on Japan—took command of Tokyo's Atsugi airfield today, simultaneously with the careful but dramatic entry of the Third Fleet's special advance squadron into Tokyo Bay."[476]

"Two Huntington men serving with the India-China Division of the Air Transport Command have been awarded the Distinguished Flying Cross upon completion of 500 hours of operational flight in transport aircraft. They are Sergeant William T. Dulaney, aerial radio operator, 1666 Eleventh Avenue, and Second Lieutenant Harlowe H. Huddleston, pilot, 1741 ½ Sixth Avenue..."[477]

"WITH THE COLORS":

Seaman (First Class) David M. Brown, husband of Mrs. Stella Brown, 4528 Ohio River Road, is now serving aboard the USS *Zaurak* in the Pacific, which recently successfully withstood 39 Jap air attacks during one major operation.

Aviation Machinist's Mate (Third Class) William Arthur Rowe of Kenova and Fire Controlman (Third Class) Johnny Walker Jr., 1245 Adams Avenue, are serving aboard the aircraft carrier USS *Santee*, which is the only carrier to take a Japanese suicide plane through her top and a torpedo through her side in the same action without halting operations.

Aviation Radioman (Third Class) Robert S. Betz, 20, son of Mr. and Mrs. Max Betz of Gallipolis, O., has returned to the United States after flying 26 combat sorties on an Avenger torpedo bomber during 70 days of combat operations off Okinawa.

Technician (Fifth Grade) Julius D. McGhee, son of Mrs. John L. McGhee, 1549 Seventh Avenue, and the late Mr. McGhee, has returned home having been discharged from the Army in accordance with regulations releasing men with 85 points or more. Corporal McGhee served as a medical technician in the Canal Zone from December 1941 to May 1944, and was later transferred to Bronx Area Hospital, New York.

Storekeeper (Second Class) James E. Tackett, 4338 Auburn Road, recently has been engaged in taking inventory of clothing and fighting gear aboard an escort aircraft carrier in the Pacific. He was employed by the Jewel Tea Co. in Huntington for nine years prior to entering the Navy two years ago...

Floyd E. McMillian, son of Mr. and Mrs. Floyd N. McMillian, 2044 Eighth Avenue, has been promoted from the rank of sergeant to that of staff sergeant. Staff Sergeant McMillian is a telephone and teletype maintenance worker in the 92ⁿᵈ Bombardment Group of the Eighth Air Force, now flying ground troops from an airfield near Marseille, France to Casablanca, French Morocco, on the first lap of their flight home. A graduate of Milton High School with the class of 1940, Sergeant McMillian was employed by the Chesapeake and Potomac Telephone Co. before entering the service in January, 1940.

First Lieutenant Thomas C. Hamill, who recently returned from service with the 15ᵗʰ Air Force in Italy, is spending a 30-day furlough with his parents, Mr. and Mrs. C. A. Hamill, 6 Willow Glen. Lieutenant Hamill wears the Air Medal with three Oak Leaf Clusters, the Distinguished Flying Cross and seven battle stars.

Glenna: *August 29ᵗʰ Wednesday – Rupert, Gaynelle, Don, and myself went to Ashland Ky. and stayed all day. I had my new teeth made there at Dr. Compton's office. We came back to Huntington at 6 o'clock and went to a show. Saw "Something to Sing About" and "Resurrection, a Russian Story." Got home at 11:30 o'clock at night.*

Rupert: *We went to Ashland Kentucky. I saw a "Lil Abner" show.*

A big movie day for me. Ashland was almost an hour's bus ride from Huntington, and it was probably there that I saw "Lil Abner" with Gaynelle and Don while Mother was at the dentist.

An airport was an important goal for Huntington government leaders. The *Huntington Herald-Dispatch* reported "Air passenger and express service will be restored promptly to Huntington after the new airport on the Wayne County site is completed, Mayor Fiedler predicted today... Huntington has been without air passenger and express service since American Airlines Inc. suspended the service last spring on the grounds of asserted unsatisfactory surface and length of runway at Huntington-Ironton-Chesapeake airport."[478] (The Huntington Tri-State Airport, also now known as the "Milton J. Ferguson Field," took longer to construct than anticipated and was not dedicated until 1952.)[479]

Student enrollment in Cabell County schools was expected to reach 20,000 for the coming school year, an increase of about 500 from the previous year.[480]

"Red Cross Field Director Otto A. (Swede) Gullickson, former professor of physical education at Marshall College, will land in Japan with General MacArthur's occupation forces... Dr. J. D. Williams, president of Marshall College, who had requested Mr. Gullickson's return to the college faculty, said he received a letter from the Red Cross the other day stating since the war has ended he prefers to stay overseas and await his turn in being sent back to the States. Mr. Gullickson resides at 1141 Edwards Street."[481] (When I was a freshman at Marshall in 1951, Mr. Gullickson was one of my physical education instructors.)

Three surrendered Japanese submarines have been given American crews. "The largest, a double decker with a crew of 170 men and 20 officers, was capable of handling a catapult plane and of extended overseas operations..."[482]

Major Gregory (Pappy) Boyington was alive and being released from a Japanese prison camp. The fighter ace, one of the most decorated of the war, had disappeared on January 23, 1944, while in a dogfight with Japanese fighter planes.[483] (Boyington's exploits inspired the movie, *Baa Baa Blacksheep*.)

Tokyo Bay (Aboard the USS *South Dakota*), August 29: "Admiral Nimitz said tonight that the Yokosuka naval base will become the first Allied shore base in Japan. It is to be occupied by U.S. Marines tomorrow morning (Wednesday evening, U.S. time)."[484]

"WITH THE COLORS":

Private Norman Damron, 307 West Seventeenth Street, is at the Newton D. Baker General Hospital at Martinsburg, W.Va. for treatment after serving for 11 months in France, Italy and Germany with the 70th Infantry Division. Private Damron wears the Combat Infantryman's Badge.

Technician (Fifth Grade) George Robinson, 23, 552 Hite Street, a paratrooper with the 82nd Airborne Division, recently returned to Miami, Fla... Technician Robinson wears the Bronze Invasion Arrowhead and five battle stars on his campaign ribbon.

Chief Warrant Officer William T. Ellis, 25, son of Mr. and Mrs. W. L. Ellis of Jefferson Drive, a veteran of almost seven years in the U.S. Navy, has been transferred from a submarine tender to the USS *Akutan*, an ammunition ship.

Electrician's Mate (Second Class) B. H. Lovett, 21, who has been serving aboard the small aircraft carrier, USS *Shipley Bay* in the Pacific since Last October has arrived in Huntington to spend a 21-day leave with his wife, the former Miss Janet King of this city, and their two-year-old son Timmy. His wife and mother, Mrs. B. H. Lovett Sr., 813 Seventh Street, met him in Cincinnati and accompanied him here yesterday. A brother, Private William Lovett, is serving with the Army at Fort Riley, Kan.

Captain Icia Perry, U.S. Army Nurses Corps, recently arrived in Huntington for a 30-day furlough after serving for 27 months overseas... While serving overseas Captain Perry served with the 3rd General Hospital in North Africa, Italy and France.

Roland G. Lillegraven, son of Mr. Louis Lillegraven of Huntington, has recently been promoted from private (first class) to technician (fifth grade) while serving with the 32nd "Red Arrow" Division on Northern Luzon... He fought with the 32nd Division during action on Luzon, and holds the Medical Badge, the Asiatic-Pacific theatre ribbon and the Philippines Liberation Medal.

Marine Corporal Carter B. Ward, 20, of Huntington, who flew 52 missions against the Japs in the Southwest Pacific as a tail gunner on a Mitchell medium bomber, has returned to the Marine Air Depot at Miramar, Calif., for leave and reassignment... Corporal Ward enlisted in the Marine Corps in March 1943 following his graduation from Huntington High School. He is the son of Mr. and Mrs. C. B. Ward of 51 Adams Avenue."

Machinist's Mate (First Class) Hansford Dooley, 20, USNR, son of Mr. and Mrs. Harrison Dooley, Louisa Route 1, is serving aboard the aircraft carrier USS *Essex* in the Pacific which steamed close to the shores of Tokyo with Task Force 38 to launch her planes against the remaining strength of the enemy in the final days of the war.

Private (First Class) Eugene H. Ramsey, son of Mr. and Mrs. H. E. Ramsey, Rear 2736 Fourth Avenue, is serving with the Seventh Traffic Regulation Group at Southampton, England, and has been cited by his commanding officer, Colonel George E. Ramey, for his excellent service record. Private Ramsey, who wears the Good Conduct Medal, has been in the Army for over a year and a half and was employed at a shipyard in Lorain, O. prior to his entering the service.

Quartermaster (First Class) Elmer F. Arrington, son of Mrs. Cora S. McCarley of Gallipolis, O., recently spent a short leave with his mother after more than two years' service in the South Pacific. Quartermaster Arrington entered the service in October, 1940, and is currently stationed at Columbus, O. awaiting reassignment.

Francis A. Akers, son of Mr. and Mrs. J. A. Akers of Dwale, Ky, has been advanced to the rating of gunner's mate (second class) at the

Naval Armed Guard Center, New Orleans, La. He enlisted in the Navy in July, 1942 and has served for 32 months aboard merchant vessels visiting ports in three continents.

Private James A. Prichard, son of Mr. and Mrs. Hal Prichard of Hubball, W.Va., is serving with the 3044th Graves Registration Company near Leghorn, Italy. Private Prichard has been in Italy and North Africa for 17 months and wears the Combat Infantryman's Badge and the Purple Heart Medal.

Private (First Class) Kirby I. Hager, 38, husband of Mrs. Violet Hager, 1151 Spring Valley Drive, is serving with the armed forces in the Hawaiian Islands. Private Hager was formerly employed by the Huntington Water Corp. before entering the service about a year ago. He has served overseas for four months.

Lieutenant (j. g.) and Mrs. James A. Farley of Huntington are visiting their parents, Mrs. T. J. Farley of 800 Memorial Park Drive and Mr. and Mrs. W. L. Emmert who reside at 239 Main Street, before going to Little Creek, Va. where Lieutenant Farley will receive advanced training before being assigned to a ship of the Atlantic Fleet. For several months the lieutenant has been serving as a resident doctor at the U.S. Naval Hospital in San Diego, Calif. Lieutenant Farley graduated from Huntington Central High School and Marshall College, and attended the Medical College of Virginia before entering the Navy about two and a half years ago. A brother of Mrs. Farley, First Lieutenant Richard Emmert, who is serving as a dentist with the U.S. Army Medical Corps overseas, is currently stationed on Mindanao in the Philippines.

Lieutenant (j. g.) William H. Tidman, USNR, has arrived here to spend a 30-day leave with his family at 836 Eighth Street, before reporting to Washington, D.C. for further orders. He has served in the Pacific for more than a year as commander of a yacht personnel vessel.

Aviation Machinist's Mate (Second Class), Dowl M. Daniels, USNR, of Gallipolis, Ohio, a Navy gunner, had returned to the United States from a tour of duty aboard a Navy Mariner patrol plane which scourged the Japs during a 10-month stay in the forward Pacific battle area.

Glenna: *August 30th Thursday – At home. Very hot. So tired I'm sick and can't work.*

Rupert: *Mother and I are feeling sick.*

A British naval fleet under the command of Rear Admiral C. H. J. Harcourt occupied Hong Kong.[485]

After years of bitter fighting in the Pacific area, joyful and prideful accounts of the occupation came at a fast pace: "General MacArthur arrived in Japan and set up headquarters in Yokohama as Nippon's military ruler today amidst the first alien armed forces ever to occupy the sacred islands. Paratroopers and seaborne Marines and sailors ... swarmed out of the skies and in from the sea in an unbroken stream."[486] Yokosuka: "U. S. Marines of the Fourth Regiment ... waded ashore past wreckage of Japanese warships that symbolize a fallen empire... 15 Japanese officers and 15 interpreters stood in two lines at stiff attention, to turn over the base and its ruined warships to the Americans."[487]

Tokyo Bay: "Major Gregory (Pappy) Boyington, U.S. Marine flying ace missing more than 16 months, was among 500 prisoners of war—the first liberated on Japan—evacuated today from a hospital described as a 'hell hole' by Navy rescuers."[488]

Manila: "Lieutenant General Jonathan M. Wainwright, pale from his years in enemy prison camps, stepped from his plane today en route from Chungking to Tokyo to witness Japan's surrender."[489]

"WITH THE COLORS":

Baker (Second Class) Osburn W. Day, husband of Mrs. Grayce Day, 550 Second Street, is a crew member of the destroyer escort *Bowers*, damaged by a Kamikaze attack and now being repaired at the Philadelphia Naval Yard, where she is the first Pacific ship to enter for repairs since the return of the USS *Bolse* in 1942.

Private (First Class) James W. Carroll, husband of Mrs. Henrietta Carroll, 12 B Street, is at a United States Staging Area in France awaiting shipment to the United States under the Army Redeployment Program. A former student at Huntington High School, Private Carroll entered the Army in March 1944 and saw action in the Battle of the Bulge and the Battle of the Rhineland with the 409th Quartermaster Co. The veteran of seven months overseas duty in the European theatre wears the Good Conduct Medal and two battle stars on his campaign ribbon.

Private (First Class) George A. Messer, 32, 1244 Third Avenue, a veteran of 30 months service in the Mediterranean theatre of operations with the180th Signal Co. of the U.S. Signal Corps, arrived at the Miami Army Field from Europe last Monday... The veteran signal corpsman wears four battle stars on his campaign ribbon.

Technician (Fifth Grade) Lionel M. Sizemore, husband of Mrs. Lola Sizemore, 1016 Rear Twenty-sixth Street, and son of Mrs. D. C. Sizemore of Huntington, is serving with a supply battalion on Iwo Jima. Technician Sizemore has been overseas for about six months and before entering the service a year and a half ago he was employed by the C. & O. railroad shops.

Roy H. Blain Jr., son of Mr. and Mrs. Roy H. Blain, 229 Indiana Street, who is serving aboard the USS *Ticonderoga* in the Western Pacific, has recently been advanced to the ranking of radioman (third class).

Private (First Class) Charles V. Stiltner, son of Mrs. Martha Stiltner of Eighteenth Street, has returned home after 14 months active duty in the European theatre of operations. Private Stiltner crossed the Rhine with the 80th 'Blue Ridge' Division of General Patton's U.S. Third Army shortly before the fall of Germany.

Staff Sergeant Arnold E. Sutherland, husband of Mrs. Georgianna Sutherland and son of

Mr. and Mrs. A. E. Sutherland, 152 Sixth Avenue, who recently returned to the United States after 17 months of duty in the European theatre with the Eighth and Ninth Air Forces, has been admitted to the Army Air Forces Convalescent Hospital, Pawling, N.Y. for treatment and rest. Sergeant Sutherland attended Huntington High School, prior to his entering the service in May, 1942.

Glenna: *August 31st Friday – Cleaned house. Feel real bad. Very hot and dry.*

Rupert: *Larry came over.*

This August 31 AP article from Southampton, England is a reminder of the unanticipated consequences of war, even after victory: "There was a queer, quiet, and somehow sad homecoming at Southampton today. More than 70 British children, sent to America five years ago to escape German bombs, returned to England—returned, some of them, almost like strangers. Mothers and fathers crowded the wharf where their ship, the *New Amsterdam*, docked... But the youngsters stood silently, almost apathetically. And when they talked it was not of England, but of Newton, Mass., Rochester, N.Y., and Wyoming, Pa."[490]

President Truman sent a letter to British Prime Minister Clement Attlee asking that he send 100,000 European Jews to British controlled Palestine.[491]

Yokohama: "American troops moved up to the southern edge of Tokyo today in their second day of a bloodless occupation... They then shifted on north through the Kawasaki area looking for more prisoner-of-war camps and moved up to positions on the south bank of the Tama River, which winds along Tokyo's southern outskirts."[492]

"WITH THE COLORS":

Gunner's Mate (Third Class) Willford C. Geer, 19, son of Covington Geer, 143 ½ Davis Street, is serving aboard the PT boat, *"The Peacock Lounge,"* which made 35 combat patrols in the Southwest Pacific. The Huntington sailor manned a 20-mm cannon aboard his craft when the Seventh Fleet PTs entered Brunel Bay, Northwest Borneo, the day before the Allied invasion and took up hazardous patrol to prevent Jap reinforcement of evacuation. He also saw action in the Philippines, having entered the Navy in November, 1943.

Two Huntington men and two from Olive Hill, Ky., are serving aboard the battleship USS *North Carolina.* They are Radioman (Third Class) John D. Bartholomew, 20, son of Mrs. N. B. Bartholomew, 2112 Seventh Avenue; Seaman (Second Class) Joseph R. Follrod, 20, son of W. W. Follrod, 260 Walnut Street; Seaman (Second Class) James M. Hillman, 20, son of Mrs. G. J. Hillman of Olive Hill, and Seaman (First Class) Ray Baker, 19, son of Mr. and Mrs. Lloyd Baker of Olive Hill.

Corporal Edward Koehler, son of Mrs. Inez Koehler, 13 Northcott Court, is serving his 31st month overseas as a member of the 21st Aviation Engineer Regiment stationed in Italy. He entered the Army June 3, 1942, and participated in the Tunisian, Naples-Foggia and Rome-Arno campaigns to earn three battle stars... He has earned 89 service points and is awaiting transfer to the United States.

Tony J. Magariello, 21, husband of Mrs. Jean Treese Magariello of 1123 Eleventh Street, and son of Mr. and Mrs. A. Magariello, who reside at 2808 Highlawn Court, has recently been promoted to staff sergeant while serving with the 13th Air Force in the Philippines... The former Huntington High School graduate saw action as a radio operator on New Guinea and was awarded the Air Medal with one Oak Leaf Cluster.

Dallas Godby, son of Mr. and Mrs. Clayton Godby of Huntington, has been promoted to the rating of Petty Officer (third class) while serving with the Navy in the Southwest Pacific. He has been serving overseas for over 11 months.

Master sergeant Vernon R. Prichard, 25, 431 Thirty-first Street, a veteran of 17 months overseas with the 160th Armored Signal Company in the European and Central Pacific theatres, recently arrived at the Miami Army Air Field ... and is now en route to Camp Blanding, Fla. The Huntington veteran wears the European theatre ribbon with one battle star and the Asiatic-Pacific theatre ribbon with one battle star.

Machinist's Mate (Third Class) Forest Sperry Jr., husband of Mrs. Jennie Shirlene Sperry, 818 Washington Avenue, is serving as a crew member aboard the destroyer escort USS *Bowers,* which was recently damaged by a Jap Kamikaze attack and is being repaired at the Philadelphia Navy Yard.

Major Arthur E. Chambers, whose wife, Mrs. Bernice Chambers, resides at 426 Washington Avenue, is stationed with the Army Air Forces Caribbean Division of the Air Transport Command in Puerto Rico. Major Chambers has been serving overseas for 16 months in the Mediterranean theatre of operations as executive officer of a heavy bombardment group... He wears the Distinguished Unit Citation badge with one Oak Leaf Cluster, the European theatre of operations ribbon with nine battle stars, the Victory ribbon (World War I) and the Mexican campaign ribbon.

First Lieutenant Frank Blood, 35, son of Ralph E. Blood, 403 Thirtieth Street, is assigned to the Army Air Force Redistribution Station 4 at Santa Ana Army Air Base in California. Lieutenant Blood, a glider pilot with the Ninth Air Force, who has three aerial invasions to his credit, entered the AAF in January, 1941 and went overseas in October of '43. He has been awarded the Purple Heart Medal with two Oak Leaf Clusters, the Distinguished Unit Citation and the European theatre of operations ribbon with seven battle stars.

September

THANKS AND PRAISE, OCCUPATION

GLENNA: SEPT. 1ST SATURDAY – VERY HOT AND DRY. I BAKED A BANANA
cake. Rained a little and cooler that night. Armistice signed that night. War completely over. Got my new false teeth.

Rupert: *I read a lot of Life Magazines. Tonight the Armistice was signed.*

Uncle Cline subscribed to *Life Magazine* all during the war years and stacked them on shelves in a root cellar on the riverbank. I often sat on a rock wall there reading the magazines.

Charleston, West Virginia: "Ten cases of rabies have been uncovered in West Virginia so far this month through the examination of heads of animals by the State Health Department and West Virginia University laboratories ..."[493]

Yokohama, September 1: "Approximately 4,200 Allied prisoners of war remain to be evacuated from Japanese camps in the Tokyo-Yokohama area, Cmdr. Harold Stassen reported today. More than 1,490 have already been moved to hospital ships and transports in Tokyo Bay."[494]

"IN THE SERVICE":

Sergeant Fred H. Turley, son of James H. Turley of Ona, and Technician Fifth Grade Vernon G. Ward, grandson of Mr. and Mrs. H. F. Nunley of Ashland, are members of the 2265th Quartermaster Truck Company which will be returning home shortly after service in North Africa and Italy.

Master Sergeant Vernon R. Prichard, 25, a veteran of 17 months in the European Theatres, has arrived at Miami, Fla... He served with the 160th Armored Division Signal Company and wears a battle star on each of his theatre ribbons.

Corporal James F. Harris, son of Mrs. J. F. Harris, 2215 Eighth Avenue, and hundreds of other enlisted men at B-29 bases in the Marianas have been commended by their commanding General of the Twentieth Air Force. Corporal Harris is a member of the ground crew which kept the Superfortresses in condition to bomb the Japs night and day.

Thomas P. Smythe, son of Mr. and Mrs. W. T. Smythe, 906 Thirteenth Avenue, was recently promoted to the rank of technician fifth grade. Technician Smythe entered the Army in May, 1944, and has been stationed in San Juan, Puerto Rico.

Corporal Edward Koehler, son of Mrs. Inez Koehler, 13 Northcott Court, has been overseas for 31 months and wears three battle stars on his European theatre ribbon. He is serving with the 21st Aviation Engineer Regiment ... and expects to return to this country soon.

Glenna: *Sept. 2nd Sunday – We all went to the Baptist Association at Guyan Valley.*

Rupert: *I went to the Association today.*

Known locally as "The Association," it was an annual Baptist event widely attended by people regardless of religious affiliations. It was a day of preaching and singing, but for me, it was a time to enjoy the enormous variety of food and drink from dozens of booths set up outside the church.

In Tokyo Bay, on board the USS *Missouri,* Japanese officials formally surrendered to the Allied Forces.[495] "The entire world is quietly at peace," said General MacArthur at the end of capitulation ceremonies... "A new era is upon us."[496]

Ho Chi Minh, the Vietnam nationalist leader, proclaimed the country's independence from France.[497]

"WITH THE COLORS":

Fireman (First Class) Donald Elmore, son of Mr. and Mrs. Harry Elmore, 1807 McVeigh Avenue, has returned to Norfolk, Va. for reassignment after spending a 30-day leave with his parents here. He recently returned from 14 months overseas service on an LCI. He has two battle stars, the Elbe and Southern France.

Lieutenant Fleming Suiter of Chesapeake, will leave Sept. 17 after a 90-day furlough for Miami, Fla., where he will be stationed for three weeks. He had been held in a German prison camp but is in good health.

Staff Sergeant James O. Williams, cavalry was awarded the Bronze Star for heroic achievement in connection with military operations against the enemy at Luzon, Feb. 12... His wife, Mrs. Edna Mae Williams, resides at 1140 Washington Avenue.

A Huntington father and son recently met for the first time in 17 months. Seaman (First Class) William Cupp, 38, U.S. Seabees, husband of Mrs. Mable Cupp, 229 Richmond Street, and his son Seaman (First Class) Robert L. Cupp, 19, USN, spent the day visiting aboard the destroyer USS *Strong,* on which Seaman Bob Cupp has been serving for four months. Seaman William Cupp, who has been in the Seabees for 18 months, 16

of which have been spent overseas, was stationed until recently on Guam.

Second Lieutenant John J. Albright is now completing his training at the Clovis, N.M. Army Air Field as a flight engineer aboard a B-29 Superfortress. His wife, Mrs. Catherine Ann Albright, resides at 1015 First Street.

Seaman (Second Class) Lee Woodruff returned to Norfolk, Va. after spending a nine-day leave with his parents, Mr. and Mrs. H. K. Woodruff of Chesapeake. Returning to Norfolk after a similar leave is Seaman (Second Class) Bob Shamblin, [who] lives in Gallipolis.

Private Fred E. Pinar, stationed at Fort Meade, Md., and his wife ... [at] 222 Main Street, are spending the weekend in Washington, D.C.

Lieutenant Anne Sweeny, Army Nurse Corps, who recently arrived in the United States after serving in England, is spending the weekend with Mrs. Stanley Brzezinski, 215 Main Street.

Glenna: *Sept. 3rd Monday – Labor Day. Very hot. I washed and cleaned everything.*

Rupert: *I went to see Larry today.*

Baguio, September 3: "Gen. Tomoyuki Yamashita, no longer the conqueror, unconditionally surrendered remnants of his once great Philippines army to the slender hero of Bataan and Corregidor, Lt. Gen. Jonathan M. Wainwright of the U.S.A. today."[498]

Yokohama, September 3: "Thirty minutes after Japan signed the surrender on the Battleship Missouri at (8:18 A.M. Saturday, EWT), a 42-ship convoy steamed into Tokyo Bay and began disgorging troops."[499]

"IN THE SERVICE":

Sergeant Ballard B. Mills, who was overseas for two and a half years, has returned to his station in California after spending a furlough with his mother, Mrs. Mary Mills, and sister, Miss Evelyn Mills, 943 Ninth Avenue. Sergeant Mills saw action in North Africa, Sicily and Italy as an aerial engineer ... Brothers in the armed forces are Staff Sergeant Evan Mills in the AAF in New Guinea and Private Claude Mills, a paratrooper in France.

Lieutenant Gordon A. Baker Jr., 127 Fourth Avenue, is serving with the service force supply ship, USS *Talita*, which participated in the campaign of Guadalcanal, New Georgia, Rendova, Bougainville, Guam, Saipan, Leyte and the Palaus.

W. W. Hensley, who served for 28 months in the South Pacific with the 59th Naval Construction Battalion, is spending a leave with his wife and son, Ronald, at their home, 1695 Charleston Avenue.

An itinerary which included 5,500 miles of travel has been covered by five-months-old David Lewis Porter so that he might be with his sailor dad, Seaman Lewis Porter of the Navy, the son of Mr. and Mrs. J. W. Porter of Wayne. David is the great grandson of the Rev. B. E. Perry of Missouri Branch, W.Va.

Private Arvel L. White, 20, of Raysal, W.Va., a rifleman in the 327th Glider Infantry Regiment of the 101st Airborne Division was recently awarded the Bronze Star Medal for heroic action during the Christmas week siege of Bastogne. On December 26, during a counterattack by his company to obtain a position, Private White found a heavy machine gun which had been abandoned. Realizing the fire power of the weapon, he manned the gun and delivered heavy supporting fire for one of the assault platoons. According to the citation, his accurate fire enabled the platoon to take the sector which had been lost. Private White also participated in the Airborne invasion of Holland and the final mop-up fighting in Alsace and Southern Germany. He wears the Combat Infantryman Badge.

Technician Fifth Grade Ogal C. Cornes, 1941 Sixth Avenue; Sergeant Cass L. Sizemore, 406 West Fifth Avenue, and Private First Class Joseph B. Hicks of Davy, W.Va., have been discharged from the Army at the Camp Atterbury, Ind. Separation Center under the point system.

Commander Albert C. Ingles of Gallipolis, O. has been presented the Commendation Ribbon "for outstanding service in the line of his profession" while serving as a gunnery officer on a cruiser...

Machinist's Mate Second Class George W. Trainer, 24, of Vinton, O. is serving on the USS *Idaho*, which is part of the Pacific Fleet completing the first stages of the occupation of Japan.

Water Tender Third Class James P. McCoy of Altizer Addition, is serving on the USS *Quincy* and Gunner's Mate Third Class Eustice L. Gothard of Eureka, O., is serving aboard the USS *Alabama* in Tokyo Bay.

Glenna: *Sept. 4th Tuesday – I ironed. Dawson went back to work after a three weeks vacation. Rupert started back to school. Very hot.*

Yokohama: "U. S. troops, crossing the Tama River just outside of Tokyo, spread their occupation zone over 720 square miles today and took over four air fields, one of them only two miles from the ruined capital of the wrecked empire... General MacArthur still had given no signal for the entry into Tokyo."[500]

Tokyo Bay: "Hundreds of Allied prisoners from Northern Japan streamed toward Yokohama today, where Army authorities drew up lists of Japanese war criminals based on stories of the liberated that their prison camps were 'a living hell.'"[501]

Glenna: *Sept. 5th Wednesday – Finished making my dress. Went to prayer meeting that night. Ercell Hutchinson was there. Jaruel Porter was the leader.*

Rupert: *Today we got started in our books.*

Marshall College announced a clinic designed to build a "well rounded" athletic program at Marshall, and is inviting all junior high and high school coaches and assistants in the Tri-State to attend. Marshall Coach Cam Henderson, "considered one of the outstanding authorities in the country on football and basketball," will be in charge.[502]

Tokyo Rose was arrested in Yokohama, Japan.[503] Iva Toguri D'Aquino, a Japanese American trapped in Japan at the beginning of the war, became a broadcaster with the name, "Orphan Annie." When D'Aquino returned to the United States after the war she was tried for treason and sentenced to ten years, but released after six.[504] (President Gerald Ford pardoned her in 1977.)

"Diamond Dust": "The sun was bearing down furiously. There wasn't a spot of shade as big as home plate to be found anywhere as the Huntington Pony Express and the Huntington East Highlanders,—Cross Town' football—rivals scampered through their pigskin paces yesterday at their respective practice fields... I am inclined to think that coaches H. C. (Twenty) Lantz and Ray (The Real) McCoy, will have their pigskin pupils honed as sharp as grandpa's razor when they face the opening k. o. (kick-off) Friday night under the lights at Fairfield Stadium, despite the fact that the weather has been hotter than a four-alarm fire."[505]

"The Congressional Medal of Honor citation [given posthumously] says the greengrocer from West Virginia was a soldier of 'superb courage.' ... He was Staff Sergeant Jonah E. Kelley, 21, who lived at Keyser and managed the produce department of a store... The sergeant's mother, Mrs. Rebecca Kelley, Orchard Street, Keyser, will be given the medal later."[506]

"IN THE SERVICE":

Sergeant Morris Willoughby, son of Mr. and Mrs. E. H. Willoughby, 1180 Norway Avenue, was recently awarded the Bronze Star Medal for heroism against the enemy on Luzon in the Philippines. Sergeant Willoughby entered the service four years ago and has been in the Pacific for two years. He recently met his brother, Corporal Ray Willoughby, who is with the engineers in Manila after a year in the European theatre.

Berlin M. Steinespring, son of Mrs. Irene Steinespring, 2127 Fourth Avenue, ended the war in the Pacific with a promotion from technical sergeant to warrant officer (j. g.) in headquarters 31st Infantry Division on Mindanao. Before induction, he was office manager for the American Guild of Variety Artists in Cincinnati.

Wallace F. Rood, seaman first class, husband of Mrs. Ruth Hartzell Rood, 323 West Third Avenue, and son of Frank Rood of that address, received an honorable discharge from the Navy after serving for a year and a half. He served as a member of an armed guard crew aboard a merchant ship for 11 months and made a trip around the world.

Private First Class Charles W. R. Bledsoe, 32, 1827 Ninth Avenue, wearing the Combat Infantryman Badge and two battle stars, has returned to this country. He served for a year in Italy with the 88th Infantry Division.

Sydney J. Snair, seaman first class, son of Mrs. G. N. Vernon, 1647 Washington Avenue, has been seeing action in the Pacific aboard a Coast Guard-manned invasion transport. Seaman Snair graduated from Central High School in 1941 and worked in Bridgeport, Conn. prior to enlisting in the Coast Guard.

Gunner's Mate First Class A. C. Notter, 149 Oney Avenue, the son of S. F. Notter, a former Huntington policeman, has been honorably discharged from the Navy. He served in the regular Navy before the war and was at Pearl Harbor during the initial attack by the Japs.

Wearing the Distinguished Flying Cross and the Air Medal, Technical Sergeant Harry E. Schrader, son of Mr. and Mrs. W. M. Schrader of Barboursville, left Miami Wednesday for the separation center at Fort Devans, Mass. where he will be discharged under the point system. He entered the Army in December, 1940 and served for 17 months in India with the Air Forces.

Sergeant Leo Gibson, son of Mr. and Mrs. John Gibson of Docks Creek near Kenova was recently advanced to that rank from corporal while serving with the Second Signal Battalion in Germany.

First Sergeant Edward Forest Bellville, son of Forest Bellville, 303 Prospect Street, who holds the Bronze-Star Medal, has been serving in the European theatre for 11 months... He also has the Combat Infantryman Badge and the Good Conduct Medal.

Glenna: *Sept. 6th Thurs. – I went back to Ashland Ky. to have my new teeth worked on. Rupert was real sick when I got home.*

Rupert: *I had to miss part of school. I was sick.*

"IN THE SERVICE":

Thomas William Tanner, 25, seaman first class (radar striker), son of Mr. and Mrs. J. E. Tanner, 2824 Oakland Avenue, is serving aboard a destroyer in the Pacific. He is the husband of the former Miss Freda Pearl Cooper of Bradley, W.Va. Seaman Tanner is a graduate of Central High School and worked at the International Nickel Co. before entering the Navy.

Sergeant Clovis E. Simpkins, son of Mr. and Mrs. Ezra Simpkins, 1900 Washington Boulevard, has been assigned to the Cazes Air Base at Casablanca with the Air Transport Command's North African Division. Sergeant Simpkins has been overseas for nine months at Cairo and has been in the service for two and

a half years. He is the husband of Mrs. Elda Mary Barnett Simpkins of Canton, O.

The promotion of Eston P. Covington Jr., son of Mr. and Mrs. Eston Covington, 303 ½ Fifth Avenue, from private first class to corporal has been announced by the Air Transport Command's West Coast Wing at Hamilton Field, Calif. Corporal Covington entered the Army on October 8, 1943 and has been at Hamilton Field since last May.

Petty Officer Second Class Theodore R. Spaulding has returned to the Naval hospital at Bainbridge, Md. after spending a 30-day furlough with his wife, Mrs. Pearl Spaulding of Salt Rock, and his parents, Mr. and Mrs. W. T. Spaulding of Kenova. Petty Officer Spaulding served for 20 months overseas and was with the 105th Naval Seabee unit to arrive in the Philippines.

Glenna: *Sept. 7th Friday – Rupert was real sick all day. Mrs. Rousey was here. I didn't feel well myself. Very hot and sultry.*

Rupert: *I am in bed with a feaver.*

I don't remember my "feaver," but the fact that we were in a heat wave must have made it an extremely uncomfortable time.

Prague, September 6: "Dr. Joseph Pfitzner, mayor of Prague under the German occupation, was hanged in Pankrac prison square at 6:30 P.M. today ... guilty of treason and other charges. Pfitzner was the first of thousands of collaborators to face the Czech people's court."[507]

More Hitler conspiracy theorists of the era geared up, as shown in an AP article from Hamburg: "A mysterious, handsomely-appointed 90-foot yacht is being widely sought in the belief that Adolf Hitler might be aboard it. The search ... got new impetus ... as British security police took official cognizance of persistent rumors that Hitler and his deputy fuehrer,

Martin Bormann, were in the Hamburg area in early May."

"Wearing the Distinguished Flying Cross with an Oak Leaf Cluster, First Lieutenant Gibbs, son of Mr. and Mrs. Samuel Gibbs of Syracuse, O. has arrived here to spend a 30-day leave with his wife, the former Miss Jeanne Roller, 929 Seventh Street. He served with the 20th Air Force in the Pacific for 16 months and survived a B-29 crash landing, which took the lives of three of his mates 200 miles off Japan..."[508] (This article, published as a graphic, did not include Lieutenant Gibbs' first name and I found no cross references that would reveal the exclusion.)

"IN THE SERVICE":

Seaman First Class Cline R. Moses, 31, husband of Mrs. Evelyn Daley Moses, 538 Roby Road, has been serving aboard the jeep carrier USS *Steamer Bay*... [He] saw action at Okinawa ... and is the father of two children, Peggy Lou, 8, and Janet, 6.

Staff Sergeant Leo B. Freyer, Formerly of Huntington, husband of Mrs. Alma Freyer, daughter of Ira McGinnis of Culloden, is en route home from the European theatre after serving there for 22 months with the 63rd Division ...

Captain Wyatte J. Gay, husband of Wanda M. Gay of Milton, has been awarded the Oak Leaf Cluster to the Air Medal ... Captain Gay, who was recently freed from a Jap prison camp after being reported missing in action, has been overseas for 16 months and a member of the AFF for more than six years.

Private Harold L. Johnson, 24, husband of Mrs. Dorothy Johnson, 1634 Charleston Avenue, has been returned to this country at Miami, Fla. after 14 months as a rifleman in the European theatre. He wears the Purple Heart medal and the Combat Infantryman Badge and a battle star on his campaign ribbon ...

Staff Sergeant Jesse J. Bias, son of Mrs. Mary Bias, 403 ½ Fourth Avenue, is serving at a station hospital on Luzon... His wife, Doris, and eight-months-old daughter live in Jackson, Miss.

Frank D. Hager, ship's serviceman third class, was serving aboard the USS *England,* a destroyer-transport, when she was hit by a Jap-suicide plane last May 8 off Okinawa.

First Lieutenant William J. Hatch, son of Mrs. Charles Hatch, 529 Twelfth Street ... [is with] a bomber group of the Eighth AAF in France... [He] wears the Air Medal and two battle stars.

Yeoman First Class Norman W. Raies of Huntington, son of Mr. and Mrs. William Raies of Mount Hope, W.Va., is serving at Pearl Harbor as a war orientation side to the educational services officer. Yeoman Raies was graduated from Davidson (N.C.) College and entered the Navy more than three years ago.

Gunner's Mate Third Class Ralph J. Adkins, son of Mrs. Della Mae Adkins of Gimlet Hollow, participated in the invasion of Okinawa. Mate Adkins has been in the Navy for two years and has been serving in the South Pacific aboard an LST for over a year. A brother, Private First Class Cledith C. Adkins, served in the Panama Canal Zone for more than 30 months and is now at Camp Butner, N.C. He has been in the infantry for four years and recently was awarded the Good Conduct Medal.

The mother of the late Petty Officer Vance D. Stonestreet, who was drowned in the Pacific, has received a letter from some of his friends aboard the USS *Portland* commending him on his excellent work and the spirit with which he performed it... Mrs. Stonestreet lives at 640 First Street. His wife, the former Miss Janie Skeans of Huntington, is making her home in California.

Petty Officer First Class Vernon S. Hatcher of the Navy, is spending a leave with his parents, Mr. and Mrs. E. G. Hatcher of Merrill Avenue. A machinist's mate, Petty Officer Hatcher was serving in the North Atlantic when Pearl Harbor was attacked. Since then he has served aboard a submarine chaser which convoyed troops to the Southwest Pacific and the European, Africa and East Asian areas. He has been in service four years.

Corporal Harold E. Morgan, 3326 Crane Avenue, a member of the 58th Bombardment Wing of the 20th AAF, was ... awarded the Air Medal at a base on Tinian Island...

The Meritorious Unit Citation badge has been presented to Private First Class Walter A. Caldwell of Huntington and Lesage for exceptional service at the Guam Air Depot. He is the husband of Mrs. Barbara Caldwell, 2781 Collis Avenue. His parents, Mr. and Mrs. J. C. Caldwell, live at Lesage.

Bobby N. Tucker, seaman second class, of Ward, W.Va. is serving with a Seabee detachment in the Philippines. His unit is the second oldest organized construction battalion in the Navy.

Lieutenant W. L. Burdette, son of Mrs. Olive C. Burdette of Logan, and Albert D. Steede, 624 West Third Avenue, are serving on a destroyer in the Pacific which has been in nine battles without suffering any casualties or damage.

Lawrence E. Boyd, radioman first class, 1705 West Fifth Avenue, is aboard the USS *Bowie* in the Pacific.

Palmer Williams, seaman second class, of Ivel, Ky., celebrated the surrender of Japan aboard the battleship USS *Nevada* as she rested at anchor in Leyte Gulf, after a 32-day mission in the China Sea.

Corporal Margaret F. Yeager, a hospital technician at Finney General Hospital, Thomasville, Ga., is spending a 15-day furlough here with her mother, Mrs. Della T. Irvine, 1604 Sixth Avenue.

Seaman First Class Stanley M. Carroll, son of Mrs. S. M. Carroll, 2961 Staunton Road, arrived here yesterday to spend a nine-day furlough after completing his basic training at Great Lakes, Ill.

Private First Class Aubrey Earl Stephenson, son of Mr. and Mrs. Lovic Stephenson Sr. of Barboursville Route 2, recently returned to Fort Meade Md. for reassignment after spending a 30-day furlough with his parents. Private Stephenson served in Europe with the 13th Army from February until July and was awarded two battle stars. Another son of Mr. and Mrs. Stephenson, Sergeant Lovic Stephenson Jr., also returned to the United States from Europe in July... Sergeant Stephenson, husband of Mrs. Kathleen Stephenson, formerly of Huntington, served with the 44th Mechanized Calvary... [He] was awarded three battle stars. His combat experience included the Battles of the Bulge, the Ruhr and Rhine.

Glenna: *Sept. 8th Saturday — Very hot and sultry. Rupert got up but still isn't well.*

Rupert: *I am better today.*

The high school football season was underway and Tri-State schools of West Virginia, Ohio, and Kentucky were fielding their 1945 teams. The area was a hotbed of rivalries, many of which continue today. Huntington High School won the Friday night football game, 26–0 over Huntington East High School.

Atlantic City: "Bess Myerson, five-feet, ten-inch tall college graduate, tonight was crowned 'Miss America' of 1945."[509]

The U.S. started sending troops to South Korea.[510] The Soviet Union had early on rushed their troops into Korea. An agreement soon stopped the Russians at the 38th parallel, which divided the country in half.[511]

"IN THE SERVICE":

Private First Class Edward Felix of Horton Street is taking a course in radio at Foxhole University at Ledo, Assam, India while awaiting his return to the United States. Foxhole

University is one of the Armed Force Institute's world-wide chain of schools.

Lieutenant Virginia Garren, 307 Thirty-second Street, is an Army Nurse stationed at a hospital in Calcutta, India.

Private Mildred Davis, 949 West Third Street, for 20 years an art teacher in West Virginia, is now a WAC on duty at the Convalescent Hospital at Camp Butner, N.C. Private Davis recently took a four-weeks course in occupational therapy at the Halloran General Hospital at Staten Island, N.Y.

Charles E. France, son of Mr. and Mrs. C. W. France, 327 Thirty-third Street, has been advanced to fireman first class aboard a cruiser in the Pacific. Fireman France has served aboard the cruiser for 17 months and took part in several bombardments of Jap territory.

A going-home party for some of the members of the 38th Infantry Division at a night club in Manila turned into a victory celebration when the surrender of Japan was announced. Corporal Arville F. Harber, son of Mr. and Mrs. A. F. Harber of Proctorville, O. attended the party. He is a member of the 32nd Division Quartermaster Company of the 38th Division.

Private First Class Homer W. Edwards, son of Mr. and Mrs. H. W. Edwards, 2760 Fifth Avenue, is presently spending a 15-day furlough at his home. Private Edwards is a student at the Army Air Forces Training School at Perrin Field, Sherman, Texas...

Raymond Shato, baker first class, husband of Mrs. Jewell Shato of Gallipolis, O., is a member of a Naval Construction Battalion in the Philippines attached to the service force of the Pacific Fleet. It is the second oldest Seabee battalion in the Navy.

Glenna: Sept. 9th Sunday – Very, very hot. Went to Sunday School that day. Stayed home and rested. At night went to church.

Rupert: I missed Sunday school. Mother went.

Washington, September 9: "Key legislators reported today a definite trend on Capitol Hill toward more power for Congress, less for the president." During the war, the president had "far-reaching" authority, and the mood was to cut back on that.[512]

"WITH THE COLORS":

Radioman (Second Class) Allan Robert Diehl, son of Mr. and Mrs. I. R. Diehl of First Avenue, left last night to return to his Naval station at Miami, Fla. after spending a leave with his parents. He returned to the United States in June after 16 months aboard a U.S. sub chaser.

Sergeant C. V. Henderson Jr. is spending a 30-day furlough with his wife, Mrs. Anna Louise Billups Henderson of 1705 Pine Street, Kenova, and his parents, Mr. and Mrs. C. V. Henderson, 4802 Brandon Road. He served for two years with the Eighth Air Force.

Sergeant Robert C. Dilley, who recently spent a 30-day furlough with his parents, State Police Sergeant and Mrs. R. C. Dilley of Barboursville, is now stationed at Camp Chaffee, Ark. He served with the Seventh Army in France, Germany and Austria.

Private James Drummond has arrived at the Army redistribution station, Fort Oglethorpe, Ga., after serving 26 months in the ETO. He is the son of Charles Drummond, 151 Baers Street, and the husband of Mrs. Hilda Drummond, 309 Twenty-fifth Street.

Private George I. Roberts, son of Mrs. Clara Roberts of 404 Thirty-first Street, is serving with the 184th Infantry Division at Cebu in the Philippine Islands. A graduate of Huntington Central High School, Private Roberts was employed by the Owens-Illinois Glass Co. before entering the service Dec. 2, 1944.

Corporal Charles E. Moore, stationed at Camp Joseph T. Robinson, Little Rock, Ark., arrived home Tuesday to spend a 12-day furlough with his parents, Mr. and Mrs. J. T. Moore, 917 Twenty-fourth Street.

Private First Class and Mrs. Robert Osburn have spent a ten-day delay en route with Mrs. Osburn's son, Private Darrell D. Dick, who recently completed his recruit training at Camp Robinson, Little Rock, Ark. He has returned to Fort Meade, Md. accompanied by his mother. Mrs. Osburn is chauffeur for the Army Service Forces at Camp Holabird Signal Depot, Baltimore, Md., where Private Osburn was stationed since his return from 15 months duty in the ETO. He is being transferred to Seattle, Wash. for military police duty.

Captain Elbert L. Bias of Washington, formerly of Huntington has been awarded the Distinguished Service Cross for heroism in leading his company near Nurnberg, Germany last April. A member of the 180th Infantry Regiment, 45th Division, Captain Bias is in England, awaiting his return to the United States.

Lieutenant Homer P. Hagaman, son of Mr. and Mrs. H. P. Hagaman, 624 South Terrace, has been transferred from India to China. He went overseas last November and is serving with a signal battalion. His wife, the former Miss Frances Logan, daughter of Mrs. S. S. Logan, 226 Twelfth Avenue, and the late Mr. Logan, is with Walter Reed Hospital in Washington.

First Lieutenant Mary E. Leaberry, Army Nurse Corps, has arrived in Huntington after serving 13 months in the ETO, to spend a 20-day leave with her mother, Mrs. E. F. Leaberry, 313 West Twenty-second Street. One brother, Cpl. Ernest Leaberry, USAAF, arrived Friday for a 15-day furlough from San Angelo, Tex. Another brother, Aviation Machinist's Mate (Second Class) Jack Leaberry, who is serving aboard the carrier USS *Bennington*, reported in Tokyo Bay for the occupation landings. Lieutenant Leaberry has orders to report to Fort Dix, N.J.

October 5, when she will be assigned to Camp Sibert, Ala., for further duty.

Glenna: *Sept. 10th Monday – Very hot. Washed and worked all day.*

Rupert: *We took Gem today. I played baseball today.*

Vidkun Quisling, former Norwegian premier, was found guilty of treason.[513] (He was executed on October 24.)

Singapore, September 10: "Admiral Lord Louis Mountbatten was en route to this key base today to accept the surrender of Japan's southern armies in a ceremony designed to humble the conquered enemy and restore Britain's 'face' throughout all Asia."[514]

"IN THE SERVICE":

Captain Roy H. Cunningham Jr., husband of Mrs. Mary Alice Cunningham, 2951 Staunton Road, has reported to the AAF Redistribution Station at Greensboro, N.C. where he is going through a military processing procedure following his return from 21 months of service as a gunnery officer in Europe.

Seaman First Class Ward H. Willis Jr., son of Mrs. Florida Allen of Mount Gay, W.Va., is a crew member on a flagship which lists no casualties or damage after taking part in nine sea strikes in the pacific from the Central Kurils to the Aleutian Islands...

Private Austin Caudill, son of R. L. Caudill of Barboursville, has returned to the United States after serving as a rifleman in Europe for 19 months. While there, he was awarded the Combat Infantryman Badge and the European campaign ribbon with two battle stars.

Private First Class William T. Bowen, 2951 Hughes Street, was one of 57 enlisted men and seven officers of the 318th Infantry Regiment, 80th Division, who were recently awarded the Purple Heart Medal for wounds received in action in Europe.

Marine Corporal Merril F. Smith, son of Mr. and Mrs. Hamlet Smith of Shoals Route 1, has arrived at Guam after spending four months on Okinawa where he participated in the initial invasion. He has been overseas for 13 months and is a member of the Third Amphibious Corps.

Graduating at Hondo Army Air Field, Hondo, Tex. last Monday as B-29 flight engineers were Flight Officer E. C. Maynor, 1205 Sixth Avenue; Second Lieutenant Donald E. Wilson, 581 Reld Avenue and Second Lieutenant Edward E. Kirk of Logan.

Private Charles H. Littleton of Proctorville, O., has arrived at Fletcher General Hospital at Cambridge, O., where he will receive treatment after serving in Germany with the 72nd Anti-Aircraft Battery.

Glenna: *Sept. 11th Tue. – I ironed and mended. Much cooler.*

Rupert: *I played football today in Gem.*

We played "touch football." Myron Drummond, our new principal, brought his own brand of organized sports to Salt Rock Elementary. It was a big change from the former "free for all" recesses where we simply "chose up" sides and went at it. (That's not to say we completely abandoned those impromptu sessions when adults weren't looking.) Thirteen years later, when I taught at Peyton Elementary School in Huntington, my basketball team played against Myron's team. We exchanged some memories after the game.

Former Japanese prime minister, Tojo Hideki, tried to kill himself to escape arrest.[515] (He survived, but was executed by the U.S. in 1948.)

Large numbers of freed Allied prisoners of war told of having suffered terrible hardships. Many were going home by boat, but those too ill to stand the ocean trip were being flown to a hospital on Guam.[516]

"IN THE SERVICE":

Lieutenant Jack C. Apperson of Hurricane, who spent three years and eight months in the South Pacific and was in Hawaii on December 7, 1941, has returned to Fort Benning, Ga., after 30 months as a paratrooper in Europe. While in Europe, he met his half-brother, Don A. Kapp of Hurricane, whom he had not seen for seven years. Lieutenant Apperson enlisted in the Army when he was 17.

Charles L. Bandy, son of Mrs. Samantha L. Bandy, 1512 Seventh Avenue, has been promoted from corporal to sergeant in the 121st Field Artillery Battalion of the 32nd Infantry Division. Sergeant Bandy has been overseas since October, 1943, and wears three battle stars on his Pacific theatre ribbon.

Thomas P. Hackney Jr., machinist's mate third class, son of Mr. and Mrs. T. P. Hackney, 2143 Eighth Avenue, is now stationed on Iwo Jima where he was commended for bomb disposal work after the invasion of the island. He has been in the Navy for 18 months and overseas for 13 months. He is a former machinist for the Chesapeake & Ohio Railway Co.

Dallas E. Adkins, seaman second class, 508 Buffington Street, is a member of a Naval Construction Battalion rehabilitating Okinawa.

Navy Lieutenant R. D. Ettinger of Huntington piloted one of two planes which helped rescue an Army Air Forces pilot 28 miles west of Tokyo in Sagami Bay shortly before the end of the war... Lieutenant Ettinger holds the Air Medal with Oak Leaf Cluster and flew 25 missions against the Japs. He is the son of Mrs. C. D. Ettinger of New York City.

Charles H. Parker, storekeeper second class of Kenova, serves at the Naval Service Force organization at Pearl Harbor.

Corporal Stuart L. Morton, husband of Mrs. Ann B. Morton of Park Hill, recently spent two weeks at the U.S. Rest Camp at Khanspur, in the northwestern Himalayas of India near the Khyber Pass.

Captain Richard Emmert, son of Mr. and Mrs. W. L. Emmert, 239 Main Street, and husband of Mrs. Dorothy Ann Emmert, 3134 Third Avenue, is serving with the Army Dental Corps in the Philippines and was recently promoted...

Staff Sergeant Richard Preston, husband of Mrs. Helen Preston, is en route home after 14 months duty in Europe, where he took part in the Battle of Germany. He has been in the Army over five years and is eligible for discharge under the point system.

Ernest W. Topping, 25, husband of Mrs. Elizabeth Topping, 4122 Four Pole Road, recently completed an intensive course of fire control training at Great Lakes, Ill.

Sergeant Garrett D. Nunley of Catlettsburg and his nephew, Private First Class James E. Deal of Huntington met recently at a rest camp at Starnberg, Germany. Sergeant Nunley is with a mobile repair unit, while Private Deal is with the 14th Infantry Regiment of the 71st Division.

Technician Fourth Grade Hiram Wellman Jr. of Fort Gay was one of the eight soldiers of the 40th Infantry Division reconnaissance company who watched Japs communication personnel use the radio in the Americans' scout car to transit a surrender message to their headquarters on Panay in the Philippines.

Glenna: *Sept. 12th Wed. – Much cooler. I made some stuffed peppers. Went to prayer meeting at night. Ercell led. It seemed just like old times.*

Ercell Hutchinson had been one of my Sunday teachers when I was younger. Out of the Army and back at his duties as postmaster at Salt Rock, he talked freely with us about his service experiences and the importance of keeping faith. Ercell was one of those proverbial "pillars" of our church.

Rupert: *I played base ball.*

The United States Senate approved a bill that gave cities $75,000,000 a year for five years to build airports and fix others. States and cities were to match the federal funds.[517] (Welcome news to Huntington since they were already planning the Tri-State Airport.)

"IN THE SERVICE":

First Lieutenant Eleanor N. Winberg, who recently returned to the United States after serving overseas for 30 months with the Army Nurse Corps, is expected to arrive in Huntington today to visit her brother and sister-in-law... Lieutenant Winberg served for 20 months in the Aleutian Islands and 10 months in the Philippines.

Staff Sergeant B. N. Maguet, son of Mr. and Mrs. S. N. Maguet, 1105 Spring Valley Drive, has been honorably discharged from the Army at Fort Lewis, Washington. He has recently been assigned to the Army Air Base at Mountain Home, Idaho. He entered the service in June, 1941 and served in the European-African-Middle Eastern theatres and wears five battle stars on his campaign ribbon.

James M. Dempsey, ship's cook second class, son of Mr. and Mrs. J. J. Dempsey, 305 West First Street, served aboard the aircraft carrier USS *Enterprise*, now back in the states for repairs after being hit by a Jap suicide plane on May 14.

Hanaford McCallister, ship's serviceman third class, of Salt Rock, served aboard the USS *Nitro*, a Navy ammunition ship, in the Pacific...

Second Lieutenant Richard F. Gray, son of Mr. and Mrs. N. M. Gray, 200 Walnut Street, who served as a fighter pilot in Europe for eight months, is now at the AAF Redistribution Station at Greensboro, N.C. undergoing a military processing procedure.

Private Kenneth Suiter, son of Mr. and Mrs. Roscoe Suiter of Chesapeake, O., recently received the Bronze Star Medal for service in China with the Army Air Forces. A brother, Lieutenant Fleming W. Suiter, AAF, will report to San Antonio, Texas, and another brother, Seaman Second Class Darby Suiter, is stationed with the Navy at Shumaker, Calif.

Seaman Second Class Hobert Callicoat of Huntington is now stationed at San Diego, Calif. where he is attending a ship repair school. He will be joined next week by his wife, Mrs. June Callicoat, and his son, Hobert Jr. [residing at 2 Ferrel Court], who will make their home in California while he is stationed there...

Private Leonard Scott, 22, son of Mr. and Mrs. W. A. Scott, 658 Marion Court, received a medical discharge from the Army last Saturday at Camp Atterbury, Ind. He served in Europe for two years with an anti-aircraft battalion.

Steve Gross, seaman first class, son of Mr. and Mrs. Joe Tarach of Holden, W.Va., and R. W. Clay, seaman first class, son of Mr. and Mrs. V. L. Clay, 2487 Collis Avenue, celebrated victory over the Japs aboard the USS *Intrepid* in the Pacific.

Private First Class William C. Lockhart, 38 [husband of Mrs. W. C. Lockhart], 1836 Fourth Avenue, was recently flown to Miami, Fla. from the Pacific where he served for three months with the Sixth Air Force.

Petty Officer Second Class William R. Crofts Jr., son of Dr. and Mrs. W. R. Crofts, 1540 Madison Avenue, was recently advanced to the rating aboard the USS *Baxter*, a troop transport.

Sergeant Robert Pullen, son of Mrs. Eugene Brown, 2124 Fifth Avenue, has been on special guard duty at General Eisenhower's headquarters since V-E Day. He is a veteran paratrooper and saw action in Italy and southern France, participating in five major battles.

Coxswain J. M. Farley, 21, of Kenova is serving aboard the destroyer USS *Shulbrick* in the Pacific.

Glenna: *Sept. 13th Thursday – I went to Huntington. Had my hair cut. Got a new pair of shoes, pretty hose, bloomers, and small things. Got back at six o'clock*

"Hose" and "bloomers" are not wardrobe words you hear much now. Regardless, reading this, I felt a bit of satisfaction that my mother was able to escape, even if for a brief time, to attend to feminine things.

Rupert: *We didn't have Gem today.*

Word came from Washington that rationing of new automobiles and shoes would soon end.[518]

"IN THE SERVICE":

A paratrooper veteran of the Normandy invasion, the Holland invasion, the Battle of Bastogne, and the Central European campaign, Second Lieutenant C. Carwood Lipton, husband of Mrs. Jo Anne Lipton, 519 Elm Street, is due to arrive in the United States soon. He is a member of the 194th Glider Infantry of the Airborne Division and has been awarded the Bronze Star medal with an Oak Leaf Cluster, the Purple Heart with two clusters, the Presidential Unit Citation with a cluster, the Belgian Croix de Guerre with Palm, the Invasion Arrowhead, and the Combat Infantryman Badge.

Private First Class Glenn F. Banks, 2 Hills Court, is a member of the First Battalion, 134th Infantry Regiment of the 35th Division, now in Germany...

Private First Class Callie V. Lee, WAC, sister of Mrs. Lottie Smith, 1615 Artisan Avenue, and stationed at Davis-Monthan Field, Ariz., was recently given the Good Conduct Medal. She entered the service in May, 1944.

Sergeant Raymond A. Hitchcock, son of Mrs. Charles Broughman, 1008 Ninth Avenue, was presented with the Bronze Star Medal for meritorious service in action in Europe. He entered the Army three years ago and is now in the Army of Occupation.

Lieutenant Betty Davis, Army Nurse Corps, 257 Locust Street, is serving at an evacuation hospital in Germany with the Army of Occupation.

Private First Class Charles F. Greer, son of Mr. and Mrs. William Greer, 1906 Artisan Avenue, has completed a four-week term at the Mediterranean theatre's university study center at Florence, Italy.

Staff Sergeant John R. Rota, son of Mr. and Mrs. James Rota of Shinnston, W.Va., a veteran of 39 months with the AAF in North Africa and Italy, recently visited Mr. and Mrs. John Kuper, 658 Marion Court while on a 17-day furlough. He has been in the service for about four years and wears the Presidential Unit Citation and four campaign stars on his theatre ribbon. Sergeant Rota, who has four brothers in the service, expects to be discharged after completing his furlough.

Staff Sergeant George A. Lorman, 28, whose wife and small son live on Huntington Route 3, is a platoon leader at the 29th Replacement Depot at Manila and now holds 61 service points...

Three men from the Huntington area who are members of the 17th Airborne Division, are expected to arrive home soon, after participating in the European campaign. They are: Corporal Eugene E. Dodd, son of Mrs. G. L. Worley, 1302 West Fifth Avenue; Corporal Hobart J. McComas of Midkiff, W.Va., and Sergeant Eslie Bills of Sheridan, W.Va.

Glenna: *Sept. 14th Friday – Rained hard all day. I went down to Mrs. Rousey's and wrote a letter for her. Cleaned my house.*

Rupert: *It has rained all day.*

Poona, India, September 14: "The All-India Congress Party working committee rededicated itself to the goal of independence tonight on the eve of the return of Lord Wavell, viceroy for India, and voted to contest all elections in India."[519]

"IN THE SERVICE":

Ralph Kenneth Campbell, 34, 1818 Nineteenth Street, son of D. F. Campbell, 1217 Manchester Avenue, has been advanced to machinist's mate third class aboard a destroyer tender in the Pacific. He is married to the former Miss Mary L. Irvin, 443 Thirty-first Street, and is the father of two children.

Having completed 23 months of duty in Europe, including time in a German prison camp, Staff Sergeant Teamus Bowling, 316 Elaine Court, has arrived at an AAF Redistributing station in San Antonio, Tex. for processing and reassignment. He wears the Air Medal with two Oak Leaf Clusters.

Corporal Harry E. Danford Jr., 923 Eleventh Avenue, is a member of the 347th Ordnance Automobile Maintenance Company, which has been inspecting and reconditioning vehicles in Europe since February, 1944. He is now at an assemble area in France.

Private First Class Robert A. Wettling, 2633 Fourth Avenue, has won the Combat Infantryman Badge after participation in the Okinawa campaign, serving with the 77th Division as an automatic rifleman. He is the son of Mr. and Mrs. J. A. Wettling.

Private Alaska C. Houston, WAC, sister of Miss Dimpa Clary, 822 ½ Sixth Avenue, was recently transferred from the WAC Training Center at Fort Des Moines, Ia. to Fort George Wright, Wash.

After 15 months in Italy, Flight Officer Ray Simpkins, 1115 Walnut Street, is now at San Antonio being processed and reassigned. He was recently released from a prison camp in Germany.

Otto A. (Swede) Gullickson, on leave from the faculty at Marshall College to serve with the Red Cross, was recently praised by Major General William C. Chase, commanding general of the First Cavalry Division for his services. Mr. Gullickson is now in Japan."

Technical Sergeant Robert L. Casey, 24, son of Mike Casey, 110 Pogue Street, recently received the Distinguished Flying Cross and Air Medal from the commanding officer of the Fourth Ferry Group of the Air Transport Command at Memphis, Tenn. Sergeant Casey was a member of the Canadian Army in 1941 and served in England and Scotland. He served in China with the Ferry Command.

Sergeant Charles W. Withrow, 29, 3608 Third Avenue, has arrived at Miami, Fla., from Italy... He served with the 332nd Air Service Group for 31 months overseas and wears five battle stars.

Private First Class Jack M. Noel, son of Mr. and Mrs. J. M. Noel, 1929 Doulton Avenue, is spending a 30-day furlough at home after serving in England for 25 months with the Eighth Air Force. A brother, Private Forrest J. Noel, served for 20 months in Europe and is now in the Philippines.

Walter D. Roush, coxswain, son of Mr. and Mrs. E. E. Roush, Middleport, O., and Verne E. Harrison, radioman first class, son of Mr. and Mrs. Fred Harrison of Mercerville, O., celebrated victory over Japan aboard the aircraft carrier USS *Intrepid*...

Staff Sergeant Edward L. VanHoose, 21, will arrive home next week, according to word received by his mother, Mrs. Beulah Keyser, 324 Marcum Terrace. He served in Europe for 16 months with the Third Army.

After three years in the AAF as an electrician, Corporal George I. Waters, 825 Twenty-third Street, was recently discharged at Fort Sam Houston, Tex. Separation Center. He served for 17 months in New Guinea and is a former employee of the International Nickel Co.

Private First Class Lee Ratcliff, son of Mrs. Mahalla Ratcliff of Pikeville, Ky., was recently awarded the Philippines Liberation Ribbon with one campaign star for his participation in the Leyte campaign. He entered the Army in October, 1943, and has been in the Philippines for seven months.

Second Lieutenant Lester N. Frantz, AAF, 928 Eleventh Street, was recently inactivated at Camp Atterbury, Ind...

Private First Class Brookie S. Hester, WAC, on furlough from Camp Pinedale, Calif., is visiting her uncle, W. H. Shaffer, 4060 Riverside Drive, and Mr. and Mrs. G. M. Burdette, 326 Thirteenth Street.

Seaman First Class James R. McComas, 19, son of Mr. and Mrs. I. M. McComas of Greenwood, W.Va., is with the Seabees in the Philippines. He has been overseas for two and a half years.

Chief Radioman John R. Beckett, USN, husband of Mrs. Betty Ann Beckett and son of Mr. and Mrs. R. F. Beckett of Eutaw Place, is en route home from the Pacific to spend a leave before going to Dearborn, Mich. to enter Navy radio school.

Staff Sergeant Virgil Hicks, son of Mrs. Nora Hicks, 1696 West Road, a veteran of 30 months in Egypt, is spending a 30-day furlough here. After his furlough, he reports to Nashville, Tenn.

Glenna: *Sept. 15th Saturday – Cool weather. Rupert went to Huntington. Larry went along.*

Rupert: *Larry and I went to town. We saw "Ernie Pyle's G.I. Joe," and "Riders of the Purple Sage."*

Despite euphoria over the war's end, the whole country was affected by labor strikes, and the Tri-State was no exception. Two of the largest disputes in the Tri-State were the bus strike in its fifth day and a milk delivery strike.[520]

"IN THE SERVICE":

Yeoman Second Class John B. Preston, son of Mr. and Mrs. Jay F. Preston of Louisa, Ky., is serving aboard the cruiser USS *Phoenix* in the Pacific. He entered the Navy five years ago this month and has taken part in nearly every major operation of United naval forces in the Pacific.

Sergeant Walter D. Nunley Jr., son of Mr. and Mrs. W. D. Nunley of Huntington is returning from the Pacific theatre after 32 months with the Jungle Air Force in which he was on active duty from Guadalcanal to the Philippines. Sergeant Nunley was a member of the 13th AAF.

Marine Sergeant Julian C. Templeton, son of Mr. and Mrs. Crud Templeton of Huntington, was recently promoted from a corporal on Okinawa. He has two brothers in the service, Corporal Jack Templeton with the engineers in India and Private First Class Billy A. Templeton in Germany.

The day that President Truman announced the surrender of Japan, Abbey T. Clark Jr., radioman third class, son of Mr. and Mrs. A. T. Clark, 3710 Brandon Road, was engaged in maneuvers on an island in the Pacific. A brother, John Clark, is in the Merchant Marines, and another brother, Cumberland Clark, is a corporal in the Army.

Arthur E. Frazier, motor machinist's mate third class, husband of Mrs. Veria Frazier of Kenova, is serving at a training and repair base in the Pacific.

Fireman Second Class Clifford A. Blake, 18, son of Mr. and Mrs. R. D. Blake, 226 Richmond Street, is a member of a Navy crew which was recently awarded the Presidential Unit Citation. He has served in the Pacific for more than a year and expects to receive a medical discharge next month. His brother, Private Earl Blake, is stationed at Fort Lewis, Wash.

Corporal Robert B. Colgrove, 29, husband of Mrs. Mildred Colgrove, 5411 Brandon Road, is at the Miami, Fla. Army Ground Forces Redistribution Center after 33 months in Europe. Corporal Colgrove has been in the Army since November, 1935.

Glenna: *Sept. 16th Sunday – Cool and cloudy all day. Went to Sunday School at morning. Stayed home all evening. Dawson's 38th birthday.*

Millie and I were married on September 16th (1956) and during the two-and-one-half years we lived in Huntington, we celebrated September 16th together.

Rupert: *I went to Sunday school.*

"Private (First Class) John W. Cartwright, 20, of Huntington, who fought with the Fourth Marine Division as a member of 'Chamber's Raiders,' has been awarded the Bronze Star Medal for action at Iwo Jima last February, he was informed yesterday at the home of his parents, Mr. and Mrs. W. E. Cartwright, 318 Thirteenth Street, where he is spending a furlough. The Huntington Marine was seriously wounded in action on Iwo last February and has been undergoing treatment in Navy hospitals since that time until his recent discharge from the Naval hospital, Asheville, N.C."[521]

"Private James Harold Edwards, son of Mr. and Mrs. H. H. Edwards of West Hamlin, who was captured by the Japanese on Corregidor more than 40 months ago, has been liberated from a Tokyo prisoner-of-war camp... He was reported in good physical condition."[522]

Tokyo, September 16: "General MacArthur clamped a tight censorship on Japan's news industry today, declaring the empire was no equal of the Allies but 'a defeated enemy which has not yet demonstrated a right to a place among civilized nations.'" Also, in Japan, "all but a few of the top saber-rattling militarists" war criminals were in custody, including Lieutenant General Masaharu Homma, who had orchestrated Bataan's "death march."[523]

Rupert: *I went to school.*

"WITH THE COLORS":

Sergeant Douglas Nichols, son of Mr. and Mrs. E. W. Nichols of Route 1, Chesapeake, O., has returned to the United States and has been discharged under the Army point system. He went overseas Sept. 4, 1941 and served in General Patton's Third Army.

Pharmacist's Mate Second Class Robert Carroll Johnson has arrived in Huntington to spend a 17-day leave with his parents, Mr. and Mrs. Forrest Johnson, 924 Twentieth Street. Pharmacist's Mate Johnson has been serving aboard the USS *Bountiful*, hospital ship in the Pacific area, for the past 18 months.

First Lieutenant Tom Hagan, son of Mr. and Mrs. W. T. Hagan, 524 Twelfth Street, who is stationed at Ft. Bliss, Tex., as an instructor in the 56th Training Battalion, has been joined by his wife, the former Miss Charlotte Nix of Logan, and their son, Tommy, who left Huntington Thursday after visiting his parents here. [That was a confusing sentence.] They will reside in El Paso, Tex. Lieutenant Hagan returned to the United States last June after serving 23 months in New Guinea with an anti-aircraft unit.

PFC Earl C. Meek, son of Mrs. W. Arch Leap, 1649 Charleston Avenue, has been transferred from Guam to Japan where he is serving with occupation forces... Private John Wolfe, son of the Rev. and Mrs. Frank [E.] Wolfe, 1050 Jackson Avenue, who has been with Pvt. Meek on several stations, is in Japan with him. Pvt. Meek is the husband of the former Miss Edna Mae Shamblin of this city.

Private First Class Hildreth Frank Huff has arrived in Huntington to spend a 30-day furlough with his mother, Mrs. June Huff, 216 West Eighth Avenue. Private Huff has served overseas for 17 months in England, France, and Germany.

Glenna: *Sept. 17th Monday – Rained all day beginning the night before. I washed.*

The milk strike in Huntington was settled but the bus strike remained in deadlock.[524]

"IN THE SERVICE":

Private First Class Homer R. Easthom, son of John Easthom, 1512 Adams Avenue, has been awarded the unit Meritorious Service Wreath for performance of "exceptionally difficult tasks" in the Pacific area. Private Easthom is with an engineer aviation battalion which has gained recognition for its ability to carve airfields out of thick jungle and hard coral which are characteristic of both Guam and Okinawa, where he is now stationed. [He has been] overseas for 15 months. Private Easthom also wears the Bronze Service Star for his participation in construction of B-29 airfields on Guam.

Second Lieutenant Prichard Gray, son of Mr. and Mrs. Morba Gray, 200 Walnut Street, received the Air Medal during a recent ceremony at the AAF Overseas Replacement Depot and Redistribution Station, Greensboro, N.C. Lieutenant Gray returned to the United States in July after eight months with the Ninth Air Force in Europe.

Seaman Second Class Orville C. Pullen of Ona Route 1 is serving aboard the USS *Parks*...

Private Orville E. Woodall, husband of Mrs. Juanita Woodall of Salt Rock, is stationed at Miami Beach, Fla. after serving for 10 months in Europe as a motorman. He wears the European theatre ribbon with two battle stars.

Technician Fourth Grade Edward F. Drew, son of Mrs. Elizabeth Drew, 2500 Marcum Terrace, has been commended for the "excellent quality" of his work by Major General Paul J. Mueller, Infantry "Wildcat' Division."

Private First Class Chester E. Carroll, 34, Twenty-fourth Street was awarded the Distinguished Unit Badge at ceremonies last

Thursday at Newton D. Baker General Hospital at Martinsburg, W.Va.

Radioman First Class James M. Seale, 27, 1012 Chesapeake Court, attached to the Naval Amphibious Base at Little Creek Va., is in the process of being discharged from the Navy after 82 months of service... His military service includes four years and nine months aboard the USS *Helm*, three months aboard the USS *Hubbard*, one month aboard the *LCI-188* and eight months at Little Creek. He was at Pearl Harbor when the Japs attacked and later participated in the invasion of the Solomons, the first battle of Savo Island, the Paipuan campaign and the assaults on the Marshall and Gilbert Islands. He wears ribbons for the American and Asiatic-Pacific Theatres with five combat stars and the American Defense Ribbon with one star.

Glenna: *Sept. 18th Tuesday – Still raining. I went to see Mrs. Smith and Aunt Sallie Morris.*

"Less than one pair of nylons per woman will be available by Christmas with predicted production of 3,500,000 dozen pairs by that time, the National Association of Hosiery Manufactures said..."[525]

British authorities announced they were sending grain to western Germany to supplement food for the Ruhr and Rhine Valleys and the British section of Berlin.[526]

Tokyo, September 18: "General MacArthur ... declared today that 200,000 regular troops probably could rule Japan." An official from the State Department said that MacArthur "apparently made his statement without notifying Washington in advance."[527]

"Major General William C. Chase, former commander of the 38th Division, presented the Purple Heart Medal recently on Luzon to Sergeant James Morgan, son of Mrs. Elsie Howard of Guyandotte. He was wounded during the Luzon campaign."[528]

"IN THE SERVICE":

Lieutenant (j. g.) Robert Richard Phillips, 315 Tenth Avenue, has returned to the States on leave after six months of Pacific duty with a medium bomber squadron that took part in rocket attacks against Paramushiro and Shimushu bases.

Hospital Apprentice First Class Paul E. Bush, 202 Fifth Avenue, is serving on the USS *Aneon*, a communications ship in Tokyo Bay.

Fireman Second Class R. F. Smith, son of Mr. and Mrs. T. A. Smith, 55 Twenty-sixth Street, is serving aboard the USS *Stockton*, a destroyer which sank a Japanese submarine, helped shoot down two suicide planes, and rescued more than 150 survivors from a damaged ship.

West Virginia men recently discharged from the Army under the point system at Camp Atterbury, Ind. include Private First Class Farley R. Cash, 338 ½ Washington Avenue; Staff Sergeant Maurice C. Chambers, Kenova; Corporal Edwin Y. Hogan, Logan, and Private First Class Robert F. Auville, Iaeger.

After a brief furlough with his parents, Mr. and Mrs. G. J. Dickerson, 210 Sixth Avenue, First Lieutenant A. M. Dickerson has returned to Tinker Field at Oklahoma City, Okla.

Miss Fay Bryan of Barboursville, Red Cross field director on the U.S. hospital ship *Marigold*, which took the first Red Cross women workers into Tokyo Bay with occupation forces, had a ringside seat when the Japanese signed the surrender, she has written her mother, Mrs. Alden Bryan of Barboursville. Miss Bryan formerly taught in Cabell County schools.

Glenna: *Sept. 19th Wednesday – I ironed. Sunny most of the day. Went to prayer meeting at night. Ercell was there again. Jaruel Porter led.*

In a quiet ceremony in Hollywood, Shirley Temple married Army Air force sergeant John Agar.[529]

Washington, September 19: "Three B-29s completed tonight the first flight direct from Japan to the capital, but failed to make it non-stop because of unexpected headwinds..."[530]

Britain's government entered talks with India's Congress Party concerning Indian independence.[531]

Shanghai, September 19: "The American Navy today returned in force to Shanghai for the first time in eight years and thousands of Chinese lined the Bund, cheering and waving flags. Gray warships of Adm. Thomas C. Kinkaid's Seventh Fleet steamed 15 miles up the muddy Whangpoo and anchored in midstream."[532]

"IN THE SERVICE":

Signalman Martin Francis Deem, a native of Huntington, was recently posthumously awarded the Silver Star Medal "for conspicuous bravery in combat during which he gallantly gave his life in service to his country." His father is Everett Ezekiel Deem, Parkersburg...

Staff Sergeant William J. Trosper, son of Mrs. Minnie Trosper, 708 Washington Avenue, who has been stationed in Germany and Belgium, has written his family that he expects to return home this month.

Motor Machinist's Mate Second Class Charles B. Weekley, brother of Mrs. Cecil Evans, 4710 Piedmont Road, who has served 21 ½ months at a Navy base at Port Lyantey, North Africa, has completed a 30-day leave with his sister and has reported at the Huntington Navy station for further orders.

Private First Class Floyd "Corkie" Johnson of the 362nd Infantry Regiment, 91st Division, somewhere in Italy, will arrive in the States this month for a 30-day furlough... Private Johnson is the son of Mrs. Alma Johnson of Gimlet Road.

Major Ewen Taylor has arrived home for a 30-day leave with his wife and daughter, and parents, Dr. and Mrs. W. Taylor. He was in a hospital in Europe for more than two years, and upon the completion of his leave will go to a camp in Alabama. Major Taylor, on leave from the Welkinson Clinic, will go with his wife to Kermit today to visit her family for several days.

Private Perison Goodson, 1843 Eighth Avenue, is a member of the 3917th Quartermaster Gasoline Supply Company which joined the occupying forces as a part of the Berlin district.

Marine Private First Class Floyd S. Jordan has arrived home to spend 30 days with his wife, the former Miss Betty Lou Adkins, and his parents, Mr. and Mrs. Sanford Jordan, 2905 Auburn Road. He will return to Philadelphia for reassignment October 14.

Hospital Apprentice Tom J. Conaty, son of Mr. and Mrs. W. J. Conaty, 1411 Fifth Avenue, spent a four-day leave here with his parents. He returned Monday night to Washington D.C. where he is serving on the staff of St. Elizabeth's Hospital.

Technician Fifth Grade George [Georgia?] P. Eplin recently attained her present rank at Crile General Hospital at Cleveland, where she is serving with the WAC Medical Corps. She is the daughter of Mr. and Mrs. L. A. Fisher, 309 West Twenty-fifth Street. She recently spent a 10-day furlough here.

Lieutenant George C. Edmonds, 440 Tenth Avenue, has arrived at the Navy Staging Center at Pearl Harbor and will soon be bound for the United States to receive an honorable discharge. He has been in the Navy since 1942, and has spent 36 months overseas.

Glenna: *Sept. 20th Thursday – Mamma bought $430.00 worth of new furniture.*

Rupert: *I went to school.*

Apparently recoiling from a statement by General Douglas MacArthur, acting Secretary of State Dean Acheson said that "the United States government and not the occupation forces under General MacArthur are determining American policy toward Japan."[533]

"Dr. Maurice Trimmer, new pastor of the Fifth Avenue Baptist Church, will be the guest of honor at the monthly meeting tonight of the J. Hanly Morgan Men's Bible Class [seventy-five members]... Following the formal meeting, the class will adjourn to the Spaghetti House on Fifth Avenue for refreshments."[534]

"IN THE SERVICE":

Second Lieutenant Forest Parsons, who was a member of the 104th "Timberwolf" Division of the First Army fighting in France, Belgium, Holland, and Germany last winter, has completed a 30-day leave with his parents, Mr. and Mrs. L. A. Parsons, and his wife and daughter of Rosalind Road.

Private First Class Walter F. Green of Pineville, Ky., brother of Mrs. Addie Rollyson of the Ashworth Apartments and of P. T. Green of Madison Avenue, will sail from Marseilles, France, for the United States and a 30-day furlough, his relatives have learned.

Private First Class Norman Wray, son of Mrs. Mary G. Nelson, 2235 Third Avenue is a member of the 407th Infantry Regiment, 102nd Division, which recently saw a British circus in Germany.

Petty Officer Second Class Haven E. Fetty recently spent a 72-hour liberty here visiting his wife and a brother, Lester, whom he had not seen for two years.

Private Charles Fred Myers, 25, son of Mr. and Mrs. Mont Myers, 2135 Eighth Avenue, is spending a 10-day furlough with his parents before reporting to Fort Meade for an overseas assignment. He has been stationed at Little Rock, Ark...

Private First Class Glen W. Hackney of Huntington arrived in New York Sunday from Le Havre, France, according to a telegram received by his mother, Mrs. Irene Hackney of Laidley Hall, Marshall College. Private Hackney served for 11 months overseas and has been in the Army of Occupation since the surrender of Germany...

Glenna: *Sept. 21st Friday − Sunny and warm. I cleaned the house, later went to visit Velma Porter.*

The disagreement between MacArthur and the State Department about occupation policies in Japan was having repercussions in Washington: "In a hot debate two senators last night delayed nomination on Dean Acheson's nomination to be undersecretary of state, on the ground that he had 'insulted' General Douglas MacArthur..."[535] In the meantime, MacArthur ordered the arrest of Lieutenant General Kenji Doihara, a marauder in Manchuria who even the Japanese said was at "the bottom of their prestige."[536]

"IN THE SERVICE":

Technical Sergeant Franklin C. Hooser of the Army Air Forces has returned home from England with a discharge to visit his patents, Mr. and Mrs. C. W. Hooser, 1423 Grove Street. He survived four and a half days in a rubber life raft after his plane went down in the North Sea in freezing weather two years ago and later was thrown through the top of his plane in a crash landing in the European theatre.

Technician Fourth Class Judson H. Adkins of Salt Rock is at the Newton D. Baker Hospital at Martinsburg, W.Va. for treatment after serving 10 months with the 1005th Engineers in New Guinea and the Philippines. His wife is the former Ethel Childers.

Cadet Midshipman Paul Probst of the U.S. Maritime Service, the son of Mrs. L. J. Yates, 1916 Parkview Street, is expected to arrive in Huntington today to spend a leave with his mother. Cadet Probst, a Central High School graduate, has seen duty in both the Atlantic and Pacific and at the termination of his leave will report to Kings Point, N.Y. for further training.

Sergeant Isaac Lerner, son of Mr. and Mrs. Louis Lerner, 404 West Tenth Avenue, celebrated V-J Day at Iwo Jima where he has been stationed aboard a 10,000-ton Army Air Forces aircraft repair ship, supporting the B-29 strikes against Japan.

Fireman Second Class Thomas Judson Sasser Jr., 1142 Spring Valley Drive, participated in the surrender and occupation of Wake Island as a crew member of the USS *Greer*, destroyer escort, anchored off the island for the flag raising.

Wallace Burnette of Huntington is serving with the rating of ship's cook third class aboard a vessel in the southwest Pacific which is manned by Coast Guard personnel. Cook Burnette's home address is 2712 Latulle Avenue.

Mr. and Mrs. H. P. Henshaw have as their guests at their home, 330 Woodland Drive, Navy Lieutenant (j. g.) H. P. Henshaw Jr., his wife and their son, H. P. Henshaw III. Lieutenant Henshaw, on leave for 23 days, has been gunnery officer of the five-inch battery on the USS *Astoria*, a light cruiser, since she was commissioned May 17, 1945, at Philadelphia. He wears the Asia-Pacific campaign ribbon with four battle stars, the Philippines Liberation Ribbon with one star, and the American Defense ribbon. His wife and son have been living in Richmond Va. since he has been overseas.

Motor Machinist's Mate First Class Harold Walter Hargis, 822 Eighth Avenue, received his present rank recently at the naval Air Station at Whidbey Island, Wash. His father is T. P. Hargis.

Private First Class David W. Dabney, son of Paul Dabney of Marne Drive, is home on a two-week furlough from his station at Seattle, Wash.

Ensign Bruce Cunningham, whose ship, the USS *Yorktown*, was off the shores of Japan during the signing of the surrender, has arrived in Huntington to spend a 30-day leave with his parents, Mr. and Mrs. Roy Cunningham, 2151 Staunton Road. Ensign Cunningham has served on the Yorktown for one year, and shortly before returning home flew over Tokyo with a navy pilot based on the carrier. He wears the American Defense ribbon, the Asiatic ribbon with six battle stars, the Philippines liberation ribbon with one star and the American theatre ribbon.

Glenna: *Sept. 22nd Sat. – Cloudy and cool. Marie Porter and Hobert Gue got married. That night we went to the bell crowd at Gilbert's.*

A "bell crowd," sometimes called a "Charivari," or "shivaree," was a folk custom (originating in France) that involved a crowd of well-wishers going to the home of newlyweds to make as much noise as possible with bells and the pounding on pots and pans in a discordant manner.

Rupert: *We started to go to Walnut Grove wood but did not go.*

Mother liked to revisit the site of the former one-room Walnut Grove School where she had taught. To reach it we walked the "hard road" to the top of Salt Rock Hill and took a gas-well access road on the right that followed the ridge about half-a-mile north. Its isolation and the introduction of school bussing to Salt Rock Elementary School were probably reasons for its closing—and razing. Some children walked up to a mile to reach it. Morrisons, Hutchinsons, Dicks, Lucases, Paughs, Swanns, Porters, Snows, and Johnsons attended. Many other one-room schools in Cabell County closed about that time. Mother had taught at Upper Madison 1927–1928, Walnut Grove 1928–1929, Leith 1929–1931 (two years), Walnut Grove 1931–1932, Merritt Creek 1932–1933, and Walnut Grove again 1933–1934. I've made copies and transcripts of her registers to preserve the historical and genealogical information. It's interesting that two children who attended Walnut Grove, Frances Paugh and Kathleen McKendree, eventually became my teachers at Salt Rock Elementary.

A sampling of high school football scores: Huntington High 38–Logan 7; Ashland 7–Huntington East 0; Barboursville 64–Winfield 7; Ironton 34–Wayne 0; C-K 41–Chesapeake 0; Charleston 20–Portsmouth 19; South Charleston 20–Montgomery 7; Russell 12–Catlettsburg 6; Vinson 2–Milton 0 (Won by a safety)

Tokyo, September 22: "General MacArthur pried into Japan's greatest state secrets today by demanding an accounting of the empire's finances, including Emperor Hirohito's fortune—reputedly the world's largest."[537]

"IN THE SERVICE":

Sergeant Robert E. Elkins, son of Mr. and Mrs. B. H. Elkins, 2513 First Avenue, has been awarded the Bronze Star for his work with the anti-submarine command. Sergeant Elkins is a radio operator in the AAF, and is stationed at Walterboro, S.C. He attended Marshall College before entering service.

Sergeant Everett H. Stamper, brother of Mrs. Elmer Smith, 3629 Chase Street, is with the 531st Air Service Group of the 15th AAF in Italy.

Seaman Second Class Lloyd J. Owen, 20, son of Mr. and Mrs. John O. Lloyd of Thurman, O., is serving aboard the USS *South Dakota*, one of the first battleships to enter Tokyo Bay for the formal capitulation of Japan.

Staff Sergeant Samuel M. Gold, son of Mr. and Mrs. John W. Gold, 136 Norway Avenue, and husband of Mrs. Joan Hope Gold, 814 Marcum Terrace, has arrived at the San Antonio, Tex. District, AAF Personnel Distribution Command. He was a prisoner-of-war in Germany and served for 17 months in Europe as an armorer gunner.

Machinist's Mate Lewis Ashland Jameson, 20, husband of Mrs. Ena Jameson, 1042 Sixth Avenue, and Seaman First Class Harold R. Harper, son of Mrs. Ida Harper, 2025 Wilshire Boulevard, are serving aboard the USS *South Dakota.*

Electrician's Mate Third Class Jack W. Sabo, 922 Thirteenth Street, is serving aboard the USS *West Virginia*, which suffered its first casualties on the day of the Okinawa invasion ...

Private First Class Sidney A. Floyd, who has served overseas for two and a half years, yesterday called his mother, Mrs. E. B. (Scotty) Floyd, 419 Sixth Street, on her birthday, telling her of his arrival in New York... Private Floyd served with the Army in Germany, winning the Combat Infantryman Badge, the Bronze Star with an Oak Leaf Cluster, the Presidential Unit Citation, and the Purple Heart...

Shipfitter Second Class James Stanley North has completed a 30-day furlough with his parents, Mr. and Mrs. M. S. North, 4883 Ohio River Road, and has reported to Newport, R.I., where he is attending a school. He served for 22 months in the southwest Pacific, participating in four major battles.

Major Thomas G. Stevenson of Huntington, Route 4, was recently returned to inactive duty at the Camp Atterbury, Ind. separation center.

First Lieutenant Clarence W. Stuart, 526 Washington Boulevard was graduated from the information and education course at the School for Personnel Services at Lexington, Va. this week.

Commander Walter B. Lett, husband of Mrs. Bea Houghton Lett, 2145 Eighth Avenue, was promoted to his present rank recently aboard the USS *Duluth*, a light cruiser, in Tokyo

Bay. The first West Virginia dentist to be called to active duty in the Navy, he entered service in February, 1941.

Glenna: Sept. 23rd Sun. – Went to Sunday School and church. Bill Vernatter preached. Very hot.

Rupert: I went to Sunday school.

"Sunday School" was a church-wide event before the main service. Classes of adults and children met in several locations in the sanctuary, separated by drawn curtains that blocked sight but not sound. There was also a room in the back where younger children met. The sessions were noisy. There was more space and more privacy after the new church building was erected in 1950.

Dr. William Knox, pastor of the Seventh Avenue Methodist Church since 1939, was appointed superintendent of the Parkersburg district at the seventh annual meeting of the West Virginia Methodist Conference in Charleston. Other appointments were made by Bishop James [H.] Straughn of Pittsburgh. The Rev. H. E. Modlin, transferred from Montgomery, was to succeed Dr. Knox.[538]

DDT, "the Army's miracle insecticide" went on sale in Huntington retail stores. "The Army, in releasing it for civilian use last August 25, laid down several stipulations for the safety of the civilian population..." They declared it safe to use in homes, "providing precautions printed on the containers were followed."[539] (How wrong they were. To my knowledge, we never used DDT on our farm.)

The war had ended, but grief and pain lingered as shown in this article about one of our heroes: "Although the War Department still lists him as 'missing in action over Germany' since December 28, 1944, the surviving crewmen of First Lieutenant William E. Loflin's B-24 Liberator bomber believe he lost his life on that date, according to information received by his parents, Mr. and Mrs. William A. Loflin, 1029 Seventh Street... Lieutenant Loflin was the bombardier ... and had flown many missions over enemy-occupied Europe. He had been awarded the Distinguished Flying Cross for heroic action in removing the detonators from live bombs when they got caught in the bomb bay doors and failed to fall free of the plane on one of his early missions. Later he was awarded the Purple Heart for wounds received in action September 18, 1944 over Holland... He had been offered ground duty after he had been wounded, but he chose to fly in combat again with his crew. He was a graduate of Huntington Central High School and a member of Boy Scout Troop 7 at the First Methodist Church."[540] (Ancestry gives his death date as December 28, 1944 and burial at St Avold, France in the Lorraine American Cemetery.)

"WITH THE COLORS":

Corporal James W. Rodgers has been promoted ... to Technician Fifth Grade, Medical Corps. Corporal Rodgers is a member of the medical unit of hospital train 66 stationed in the Calais staging area, France. He has earned the Purple Heart, Combat Medical Badge and three battle stars. His wife, Mrs. Quindora Rodgers, and three children reside at 1804 Third Avenue. He is the son of Mrs. John Harbour of 612 South Terrace.

Lieutenant Donald Boyd Smith, former Marshall student, has been released from a Japanese prison camp, according to word received by his uncle, L. Roy Smith. Lieutenant Smith, who is the son of Lemotto Smith of Los Angeles, Calif., was a member of a Flying Fortress crew shot down Sept. 15, 1943, over French Indo-China.

Captain Delbert L. Gibson of Ona and Second Lieutenant James H. Rusk, 325 West

Sixth Avenue, have been released from active duty with the Army at Fort Meade, Md.

The Army Air Forces have released Sergeant Harold Lee Ayers at the separation center at Fort Bliss, Tex. He is the husband of Mrs. H. L. Ayers of Huntington.

Electrician's Mate Third Class Lloyd Curtis Dailey, 112 ½ Bridge Street, is serving aboard the destroyer USS *Wedderburn*, which led the advance unit of the Allied Naval armada to the Yokosuka Naval Base anchorage.

Lieut. John E. Swan, son of Mr. and Mrs. E. Q. Swan, 1538 Holderby Road, landed in New York this morning after serving 23 months in the European theatre of operations. He was based in England with the 357th Fighter Group...

Private First Class Charles H. Patrick, Medical Corps, of 1208 Marcum Terrace, and his brother-in-law, Private First Class Wesley H. Nethercutt of 420 First Street, have been released by the U.S. Army at Fort Meade, Md. Nethercutt is the son of Mrs. John Nethercutt, 338 Marcum Terrace.

Radioman Third Class Tony Daiyai, USNR, of Logan, W.Va., viewed the formal Japanese surrender September 3 from the USS *Ata*.

Corporal Thomas F. Vannatter, husband of Mrs. Lillian M. Vannatter of Barboursville, has been assigned to the 529th Air Service Group of the European occupational air force.

Seaman Second Class John S. Hall Jr. left Sampson, N.Y. Saturday morning for Shoemaker, Calif. for reassignment. He is the son of Mr. and Mrs. John S. Hall of Pea Ridge Road.

Mrs. Henry Pellegrin has been notified that her husband has been promoted ... to ... Technician (third grade). He is stationed in Hawaii.

Sergeant Clifford E. Hanshaw ... served with the U.S. Army for 19 months in Italy and Germany... His wife and two daughters reside at 1101 Sixteenth Street...

Glenna: *Sept. 24th Monday – I washed a big washing. Awfully hot.*

Rupert: *I went to school. I played football.*

"With the 36th Division in Germany, Private First Class Virgil L. Wagner, 29, combat medical aid man and veteran of four campaigns, may shortly be a civilian again but his last day of combat was so packed with action that he felt then he could never do it... The 7-point man whose wife, Mrs. Violet Wagner, and two children, Barbara Ann and Gary Lee, live at Barboursville W. Va., said on May 6, after liberating some high French officials and others held captive in a castle near the Austrian-German border, his company continued the attack up a narrow valley. Wagner rode a tank with 13 riflemen." They came under heavy fire that destroyed several tanks, including the one they were riding. They retreated into a creek bed. Wagner said, "... While we were reorganizing, the valley was plastered with 170 mm shells. Then my platoon was ordered to attack the small town which held the emplacements for guns, from the flank. We advanced under cover of a dense forest to a point opposite the town. We were going into formation to make a dash across the 400-yard-wide field which separated the woods from the town when a runner came up with the order to pull back and the news that the war had ended." Wagner's parents are Mr. and Mrs. A. E. Wagner of Barboursville.[541]

"IN THE SERVICE":

First Lieutenant John Hubbard, 621 Second Street, has been honorably discharged from the AAF after three years and four months in service. He served in the European theatre as a pilot of a B-24 and was awarded the Air Medal with two Oak Leaf Clusters, the ETO ribbon with four battle stars and the Unit Citation with one Cluster...

Private First Class James A. Bills of Lavalette is at the Newton D. Baker General Hospital, Martinsburg, W.Va., for treatment after having served for 25 months with the 52nd Air Service Group in India and Burma. He wears the Asiatic-Pacific ribbon and the Good Conduct Medal.

Private First Class Epperson C. Maynard, son of Mrs. Sadie Maynard, 630 West Fourteenth Street, is stationed at Fort Oglethorpe, Ga., temporarily before reporting to his new assignment in the United States. He recently returned here after serving for 20 months in Europe as a rifleman. Private Maynard's decorations include the ETO ribbon with four campaign stars, the Good Conduct Medal, the Purple Heart with an Oak Leaf Cluster and an Arrow Head.

Seaman First Class Lee Roy Calhoun, 20, son of Mr. and Mrs. L. R. Calhoun, 635 Fourth Street, and Radioman Third Class Ralph Jackson Adams, 20, son of Mr. and Mrs. Tim J. Adams, 819 Fourteenth Street, witnessed the surrender of Pagan Island's Japanese garrison while aboard the USS *Rhind* on Apaan Bay.

Seaman First Class Harold L. Raynor, 2741 First Avenue, has been serving aboard the USS *Luzon*...

Motor Machinist's Mate Second Class James P. Hall of Huntington, stationed aboard the USS *Baron*, and Radioman Third Class Earl Sorrell of Accoville, W.Va., stationed aboard the USS *Wingfield*, on September 5 participated in flag-raising ceremonies on Jallait Atoll in the Marshall group after it had been surrendered by the Japanese.

Private James A. Day, 4605 Piedmont Road, recently rejoined the 106th "Lion" Division of the Seventh Army after spending a pass in Belgium...

Seaman First Class Clenon E. Ray, son of Mr. and Mrs. Baxter Ray of Salt Rock, was completing his 25th month of sea duty on the USS *Nevada* when the Japs surrendered. In addition to Iwo Jima and Okinawa, Seaman Ray saw action in the invasions of Attu, Normandy and Southern France.

Glenna: *Sept. 25th Tuesday – I ironed and mended. Very hot. Finished making Jean a dress.*

About 150 production workers and route men for both Mootz and Heiner bakeries had been on strike since Saturday, causing a severe shortage of bread in the Tri-state area. The bakeries supplied bread to about 1,200 stores within a fifty-mile radius. "... many housewives dusted off pans preparatory to making their own."[542]

"IN THE SERVICE":

Lieutenant (j. g.) Donald Hensley, son of Mr. and Mrs. George W. Hensley, 1425 Eighth Avenue, is serving as gunnery and athletic officer aboard an escort aircraft carrier in the Pacific. He was assistant football coach at Pittsburg and Brown Universities before entering the Navy two years ago. His wife lives at Coronado, Calif.

Navy Lieutenant John Sehon, son of Mr. and Mrs. J. L. Schon, 1222 Sixth Street, is a member of an American Army mission sent to Formosa to assist in the liberation of 1,278 Allied prisoners of war on that island. Lieutenant Schon was formerly with the Associated Press in Charleston and Philadelphia.

Corporal Louis A. Mobayed, husband of Mrs. Lavella Mobayed of Latulle Avenue, is production manager of the Far East edition of *Yank* magazine. Mrs. Mobayed is an Associated Press employee here and Corporal Mobayed was a Huntington Publishing Co. photo-engraver before entering.

Watertender First Class Preston D. Hicks of Hippo, Ky. is serving aboard the USS *Wasp*, Third Fleet aircraft carrier in the Tokyo area.

Private First Class Paul E. Chadwick, son of Mr. and Mrs. Delbert Floyd Chadwick of Kenova, is stationed at the Air Transport

Command base at Tunis, Tunisia, after being for some time at the Sharjah and Bahrein Island bases in Arabia... He served as a military policeman assigned to the provost marshal's office.

Technical Sergeant John C. Frazier, 25, of Buffalo, W.Va., brother of Mrs. Henrietta Necessary, secretary to Mayor Fiedler, recently received the Bronze Star Medal in a presentation in Paris. He is attached to an occupation unit at Frankfurt, Germany.

Men from this area who were aboard the destroyer USS *Wedderburn* in Tokyo Bay when Japan surrendered were Electrician's Mate Third Class L. C. Daily, 112 ½ Bridge Street; Seaman Second Class Raymond H. Carpenter, Mount Olive, Ky., Route 2; Seaman Second Class Jack R. Stanley, Williamson, and Electrician's Mate First Class Jennings G. Scott, Hardy, Ky.

Ship's Cook Third Class Robert D. Jordan, son of Mr. and Mrs. Sanford Jordan of Auburn Road, is spending a 10-day leave with his parents. He will return to Davisville, R.I. where he has been stationed for the past five months.

Private First Class Walter L. Young, son of A. W. Young, 38 B Street, is en route home with the 70th "Trailblazer" Division from Europe.

Sergeant Richard Tackett of Hunter, Ky. attained his present rank recently with the 38th Infantry Division on Luzon. He is chief of the Howitzer section for "A" Battery, 138th Field Artillery Battalion.

The following West Virginians from this area received discharges from the Army at Fort George G. Meade (Md.) recently: Staff Sergeant John W. Rarnsey, Kimball; Private First Class William H. Thomas, Glen Jean; Private First Class Robert L. Lamb, Williamson; Corporal Robert H. Patterson, Layland; Private First Class Donald L. Robinson, 4755 Sunset Drive, Huntington; Sergeant James B. Bryant, 512 Florence Street, Huntington; Staff Sergeant Olis G. Goodman, 350 Sixth; Street, Guyandotte, and Staff Sergeant Richard J. Bias, West Hamlin.

Watertender Third Class Zernie Kincaid, son of Mr. and Mrs. L. M. Kincaid of Huntington, is serving aboard the USS *Sirona* in Tokyo Bay, his parents learned yesterday.

Glenna: *Sept. 26th Wed. – Very hot. Did some sewing. Went to prayer meeting. A big crowd was there.*

Rupert: *I went to school. I played baseball.*

President Truman announced that remnants of the German navy were to be divided among the three principal Allies.[543] Smaller nations were demanding rights, as well. "Australia's foreign minister, Herbert Vere Evatt, demanded tonight that all nations which fought against the Axis—and not merely the Big Five—be given a voice in making the final peace settlements."[544]

"IN THE SERVICE":

Captain William W. Strange of the U.S. Marine Corps, 637 Trenton Place, is stationed aboard the USS *Solace*, the hospital ship which was recently awarded the Navy Unit Commendation for outstanding work at Pearl Harbor...

Hospital Corpsman First Class James H. Traylor, 433 East Road, is a member of the crew of the USS *Europa*, the former German transport liner which has been converted into a troop transport by the Navy.

Three Huntington men are serving on the USS *Wasp* off Tokyo. They are Private First Class Charles E. Katz, U.S. Marine Corps, son of Mr. and Mrs. C. B. Katz, 324 Thirteenth Street; Aviation Ordnanceman Third Class Philip Smith, son of Mr. and Mrs. R. R. Smith, 705 Washington Boulevard, and Watertender First Class Michael B. Ferguson, whose wife resides at 3037 Brandon Road.

Watertender Second Class R. C. Morrison, whose mother, Mrs. Creed Morrison, resides at 512 ½ Fourth Street, was among the 1,200 Navy men from the Third Fleet who arrived at Puget Sound, Wash., recently...

Gunner's Mate Third Class William C. Smith of Ona is serving on the attack transport USS *Pavlic*, which was one of the first Allied ships to enter Tokyo Bay...

First Lieutenant Shirley Greene, 1035 Ninth Avenue, was among the 85 Army nurses who were the first American women to go into the Japanese homeland following the surrender.

Coxswain Denver Davis of Lesage Route 1 is serving on the USS *Arlington*, which has been a training ship for 14 months.

Flight Officer John L. Mitchell, who is stationed at Roswell, N.M., is spending a 15-day furlough with his parents, Mr. and Mrs. H. L. Mitchell, 603 Sixth Avenue, and with friends in Charleston.

Seaman Second Class C. H. Robinette of Ashland Route 1, recently received a discharge from the Navy under the point system. He had been in service since April, 1942, and for the past two years had been stationed in Hawaiian and Mariana Islands.

Staff Sergeant Ira Markham of Huntington, who is serving with the 755th Railroad Shop Battalion of the Military Railway Service in Germany, has been awarded the Bronze Star Medal.

Glenna: *Sept. 27th Thur. – Awfully hot. I made myself an underskirt out of feed sacks.*

"Staff Sergeant Paul F. Haney has been 'presumed dead' by the War Department, his widow, Mrs. Jeanne M. Haney, 111 West Eleventh Avenue, was advised yesterday. He was reported missing in action September 18, 1944, with the Army Air Forces. His parents were the late Mr. and Mrs. F. F. Haney of Clarksburg. He attended Marshall College, where he was a football player. He was a member of the Phi Kappa Nu fraternity at Marshall."[545]

Tokyo, September 27: "Emperor Hirohito, in formal morning clothes and high top silk hat, broke all precedent today by leaving his palace for a 38-minute call on General MacArthur— tieless and wearing Army khakis... The call obviously was a social one..."[546]

"IN THE SERVICE":

Second Lieutenant Roscoe C. Jennings Jr., 337 Fifteenth Street, has been released from service with the AAF at the Drew Field Separation Center at Tampa, Fla. He is the son of Dr. R. C. Jennings.

Dave Riter, son of Mr. and Mrs. Charles Riter, 1015 West Fifth Street, was recently promoted to the rank of sergeant at his station on Iwo Jima where he is a radar repairman with a bomber group. Riter, in a letter to his parents, told of witnessing the arrival of Jap envoys on their way to Manila for the first peace talks.

Glenna: *Sept. 28th Friday – Real hot. Cleaned the house. Made myself another petticoat. Went down to Mrs. Rousey's.*

Rupert: *I went to school. I played baseball.*

Washington, September 28: "Jimmy Stewart of the Air Forces and the movies ... leaves the

Army today as Col. James M. Stewart, 37 years old, with 128 points, two years of combat flying in Europe, a chest full of decorations and a desire to return to Hollywood."[547]

Washington, September 28: "A great C-54 winged away from Washington National Airport today, inaugurating 'round-the-world flight on a regular, time-table basis."[548]

Pearl Harbor, September 28: "Admiral Halsey, the Third Fleet commander who vigorously carried out his favorite motto—'kill Japs, sink ships'—announced today he had asked for retirement at 62 to make room for younger officers."[549]

Tokyo, September 28: "General MacArthur granted the Japanese permission to use raw materials for critically-needed civilian goods, including trucks for transportation, but banned such luxuries as silk and passenger automobiles."[550]

"IN THE SERVICE":

Private First Class Sam E. Brookins, husband of Mrs. Janice Brookins, 1435 Fourth Avenue, and son of Mr. and [Mrs.] Frank Brookins, 1008 Twentieth Street, is expected to return home after serving 27 months in Europe... [He] was a member of the Tiger Stripe Bomber Group of the Ninth Air Force. He wears the Good Conduct ribbon, the Presidential Unit Citation for the Battle of the Bulge, and the European theatre ribbon with six battle stars for the offensive campaigns of Europe, Normandy, Northern France, Rhineland, Ardennes and Central Europe...

Electrician's Mate Third Class Louis E. Price, of Middleport has been serving aboard the USS *Wasp* off Tokyo in the Third Fleet's victory cruise.

Sergeant James E. O'Neal, son of Mr. and Mrs. James E. O'Neal Sr., 2810 Cottage Street, and Private First Class Virgil H. Dennison, husband of Mrs. Mary Dennison of 303 Bellevue

Road, were members of the 24th Infantry on Mindanao who made an armed truce with opposing Jap forces while both sides waited for word of Japanese surrender.

Seaman Second Class Cleotis Bocook of Olive Hill, Ky. is serving on the USS *Argonne* in the Pacific...

Technician Fifth Grade Melvin C. Lockhart, 3801 Third Avenue, a former International Nickel Co. employee, is serving on Luzon.

Lieutenant Colonel James H. Beddow, son of Mr. and Mrs. W. W. Beddow, Slagle, recently received the Bronze Star medal for meritorious achievement as deputy chief engineer of the engineer section, Allied Force Headquarters, Italy.

First Lieutenant Robert O. Hall, navigator on a medium bomber in Brazil, who is the son of Mr. and Mrs. H. B. Hall, 1247 Adams Avenue, recently attained his present rank with the 91st reconnaissance group, flying photographic missions.

Aviation Boatswain's Mate James E. Cunningham, Logan, is on the USS *Chenango*, an escort carrier off Japan.

Machinist's Mate Third Class T. A. Aliff, son of Mrs. R. M. Bosworth, 702 Jackson Avenue, participated in the occupation of Japan aboard the USS *Grafflas*.

Sergeant Gerald J. McMillian, 1663 Doulton Avenue, has been awarded the Soldier's Medal while serving with the Army's Military Railroad service in Europe.

Seaman First Class Lawrence E. Might, son of Mr. and Mrs. Clarence Might of Middleport, O., was serving aboard the USS *Nevada* when the Japanese surrendered. He has seen action at Normandy, Marseilles, Toulon, Cherbourg, Iwo Jima, Okinawa and Jaluit...

Fireman Second Class Wayne M. Kennedy of Middleport, O. is serving on a destroyer off Japan as a part of the occupation force.

Technician Fifth Grade Hobart I. Thomas of Scott Depot, W.Va. was discharged from the Army at Camp Swift, Tex., September 23.

Dotson Freelin of Matewan, W.Va. recently received an honorable discharge at Fort Still, Okla.

Corporal Karl S. Herndon of Camp Wolters, Tex. is spending a 10-day furlough with his parents, Mr. and Mrs. John W. Herndon, 1101 Ninth Avenue.

The following West Virginia Army officers from this area have been returned to inactive status at Fort George G. Meade, Md.: Captain Robert W. Coplin, 28 ½ Eleventh Avenue; Second Lieutenant Clifford C. Lipton, 107 Belford Avenue and Flight Officer Frank R. Brumfield, Yawkey.

Technical Sergeant James I. Black, husband of Mrs. Dorcas Black, 3304 Fourth Avenue, has been released from the Army Air Forces at the Drew Field Separation Center, Tampa, Fla.

Technician Fourth Grade Norman Coleman of Huntington is serving in Europe with the 724th Army Railroad in Battalion.

Glenna: *Sept. 29th Saturday – Hot at morning turning real cool at night. Didn't work at anything much all day.*

Rupert: *Larry came over. We had fun.*

"The Rev. William Graham, on leave of absence from the Village Church of Western Springs, Ill. will speak at a Huntington Youth for Christ meeting tonight at 8 P. M. at the First United Brethren Church, Twenty-first Street and Fifth Avenue. Mr. Graham has traveled extensively in behalf of the Youth for Christ international group."[551] (This was only a couple of years after Billy Graham's ordination.)

"IN THE SERVICE":

Navy personnel from this area en route from Japan waters to the West Coast aboard the USS *West Virginia* include Seaman First Class Charles C. Hazelett, Midkiff; Electrician's Mate Third Class Jack W. Sabo, 922 Thirteenth Street, and Seaman First Class James W. Rose, Olive Hill, Ky.

Fireman First Class John M. Lambert of Fallsburg, Ky. is serving aboard the USS *Hudson* off Japan.

Corporal Charles K. Cox, 982 Washington Avenue, is supervising a German labor detail in France.

Technician Fifth Grade Hiram W. Fuller, 3234 Hughes Street, has been discharged from the Army at the Fort Myers, Va. Separation Point.

First Lieutenant David Fox Jr. and First Lieutenant Robert Cavendish of Huntington, both veterans with the Army Air Forces, have been given terminal leaves prior to assuming civilian status.

Technical Sergeant Hugh M. Hinshaw, 320 Norway Avenue, son of Mr. and Mrs. Clinton W. Hinshaw, has arrived at the San Antonio District, AAF Personnel Distribution Ground, as has Staff Sergeant Corney Lett of Kenova.

Technician Fifth grade Thomas P. Smythe of Huntington has been awarded the Good Conduct Medal in San Juan, Puerto Rico.

Seaman First Class Donald Wayne Johnson, son of Mrs. Audrey S. Johnson, 2236 Guthrie Court, and husband of the former Miss Naomi Smith, 2240 Tenth Avenue, is aboard the USS *Mississippi* in Tokyo Bay.

Technician Fourth Grade Winifred U. Fizer, 210 Richmond Street, has returned to the United States after 17 months of duty in Europe and is spending a 40-day furlough here.

Glenna: *Sept. 30th Sunday – Went to Sunday School. Ossie came at 12. We just talked all day. Had a good dinner. Earl Roy [Ray] died at Cincinnati Ohio.*

Ancestry Family Trees lists Frank Earl Ray as being the son of Silas Ray and Mary Frances Morrison. He was thirty-seven years old.

Rupert: *I went to Sunday school. In the evening I played ball on the school lot.*

We played on the grassy front lawn when no school authorities were around, throwing down coats or hats to mark boundaries. Those games often included older players, such as Wink Harbour and Mousey Gill, who were in higher grades or out of school. The games continued for years, even after I was in high school.

Portland, Oregon, September 30: "Charging home with a par-shattering 64 for his final round, little Ben Hogan of Hershey, Pa., won the Portland Open golf tournament today with a record score of 261 for 72 holes, in a PGA sponsored event."[552]

October

BASEBALL, FOOTBALL, REVIVAL

GLENNA: OCTOBER 1ST MONDAY – WINDY AND HOT ALL DAY. RAINED
that night and turned cool. I washed. Dawson went on Midnight [12 to 8 o'clock shift] to work.

Dawson's crew worked a shift several weeks at a time. He rode to and from work with Sherry Childers, who was in the same work crew.

Rupert: *I went to school today. We played football.*

"Diamond Dust": "My countrymen, that was a football game to end all football games. It was a honey, I mean, the gridiron tussle between the 'Ironton Tigers' and the 'Pony Express,' Friday night, on the green carpet of Fairfield Stadium... Both teams had all the burners going, and —cookin' with gas... Although the war is won [Ironton was the victor.], you wouldn't have known it if you had seen the teams coached by T. Charlton ('Shorty') Davies, the Tiger skipper, and Ray ('The Real') McCoy, of the Pony Express eleven, tangle up like Notre Dame vs Army ... Hellz-A-Poppin. It was anybody's ball game right down to the final whistle. As a matter of fact, McCoy & Company were rapping on the goal-post door, 3-yards away, when the clock ran out. I am inclined to believe that T. Charlton Davies came to town with one of the best-balanced, best drilled, smartest and fastest and slickest clubs that has performed on the sod at Fairfield Stadium in many September moons... The Pony Express went 'all-out' to win from their foemen from the Buckeye state. Coach McCoy's youngsters had already bumped off Huntington East, Beckley and Logan ..."[553]

Tokyo, October 1: "General MacArthur's troops seized 21 financial institutions, ousted their officials and crushed with one swift blow the great banking combine that exploited an empire built by armed force."[554] "The little people of Japan who crowded about the bank, fearful that their savings would be taken away, dispersed after the Americans assured them their money was safe."[555]

"IN THE SERVICE":

The following soldiers from this area were discharged from the Army last week at Fort George G. Meade, Md.: Sergeant Othar K. Browning, Sharples; Private First Class Louie Bowen, 2040 Fourth Avenue and Staff Sergeant Richard H. Preston, 2131 West Fifth Avenue.

Seaman First Class James M. Rodgers, Gallipolis, O., has reported in at the U.S. Naval Armed Guard Center, Treasure Island, San Francisco after serving for nine months as a gun crew member aboard a merchant ship.

Private First Class Donald E. Beuhring, husband of Mrs. Eloise Beuhring of Huntington Route 3, was recently discharged from the Army Air Forces at Greensboro, N.C.

Second Lieutenant Joseph W. Reeser, son of Mr. and Mrs. Edgar Reeser, 1114 Tenth Avenue, has been released from the service at the Baer Field, Ind. separation center.

Private James E. Ferguson of Kenova was among the first American fighting men to enter Japan with the 11th Airborne Division.

Corporal Edward G. Coffey, son of Mrs. Mary E. Coffey, Barboursville, has passed through the Air Lift Disposition Center at Camp Blanding, Fla.

Captain Richard H. Cartwright, 1333 Fourteenth Street, has been awarded the fourth Oak Leaf Cluster to the Air Medal for meritorious achievement while participating in sustained operational flight missions in the Southwest Pacific area.

Corporal Russell F. Locey of Proctorville, O. recently attained his present rank in the Thirteenth Air Force in the Philippines.

Corporal William K. Adkins, 1239 Eighth Avenue, has been serving on the escort carrier USS *Block Island* in the Pacific.

Musician Second Class Eugene R. Dotson, 911 Sixth Avenue, is at the U.S. Naval Hospital at Newport, R.I. awaiting discharge. Before entering the service three years ago he was employed at the Owens-Illinois Glass Co.

Ensign Myron L. Halley of Porter, O., is serving as a logistics statistician in the Advanced Base Section, Service Force, Pacific Fleet, Pearl Harbor...

Technical Sergeant Earl E. Stover, 1235 Sixth Avenue, recently received an honorable discharge from the AAF at Lowry Field, Colo.

Technical Sergeant James Stillwell, 3712 Carane Avenue, and Staff Sergeant Russell W. Johnson, 818 Twenty-second Street, are with the Army Air Forces in the Mediterranean Area.

Technical Sergeant Kelsie W. Barbour, son of Mr. and Mrs. J. H. Barbour, 534 Eighteenth Street has been ordered to Hamilton Field, Calif. for reassignment after eight months' duty in the Marianna Islands.

Watertender Third Class Nick N. Podunavac of Ethel, W.Va., is serving on the USS *Sheridan* in the Pacific.

Machinist's Mate First Class Hoke Smith, son of Mr. and Mrs. D. F. Smith, Huntington, is being discharged from the Navy at Norfolk, Va.

Glenna: *October 2nd Tuesday – Cooler after the rain. I ironed and mended. Went to Parents and Teachers meeting at 2:30 o'clock. Earl Ray was buried.*

Rupert: *They Organized the Parent and Teacher meeting at our school.*

London, October 2: "Ministers of the United States, Russia, Great Britain, France and China concluded their first peace talks in a deadlock over procedure, which authoritative circles said would have to be resolved by President Truman, Premier Stalin and Prime Minister Attlee."[556]

Northampton, Massachusetts: "The first male student in Smith College's 70-year history today [October 2] made his appearance on the campus. A veteran of two and one-half years in the Army, Meredith Stiles of Essex Falls, N. J. enrolled in several advanced Spanish courses to augment his courses at neighboring Amherst College."[557]

"IN THE SERVICE":

Private First Class Wilbert Aluise, 230 Fifth Avenue, Private Charles J. Thompson, 1530 Monroe Avenue and Max W. Workman, 437 Twenty-second Street are members of the 474th Infantry Regiment, which reached Norway as a part of the U.S. Task Force "A" under the command of Brigadier General Owen Summers.

Staff Sergeant Walter P. Miller, husband of Mrs. Betty J. Miller of Huntington, has been honorably discharged from the AAF at Maxwell Field, Ala. His mother resides at 242 West Eighth Avenue.

Dora F. McKee of Huntington has been appointed a second lieutenant in the Army Nurse Corps.

Corporal Vernon Roy Phillips, 2930 Hughes Street, attained his present rank recently with the Army Engineers on Saipan.

Aviation Ordnance Third Class Stephen K. Sturn, nephew of Mrs. Alberta Cummings of Barboursville, is serving aboard the aircraft carrier *Randolph* off Japan.

Fireman First Class Carl Martin Adkins, 32, 715 Buffington Street, who served for eight months aboard the *LSM 232* in the Pacific, has reported at Norfolk, Va. Naval Training Station to undergo instruction for duties aboard a new destroyer.

Sergeant Harold R. Davis, 944 ½ Ninth Street, has been released from the AAF at Indiantown Gap, Pa.

Seaman First Class Robert H. Schneider, 2563 First Avenue, who is stationed at Quonset Point, R.I. with the Navy, spent the weekend with his family here.

Oscar Young, of Debord, Ky., husband of Mrs. Lucie Young, was recently discharged from the Army at Fort Still, Okla.

Electrician's Mate Third Class Lloyd O. Chaney, of Ona, has been serving on the aircraft carrier USS *Wasp* off Tokyo in the Third Fleet's victory cruise.

Glenna: *October 3rd Wednesday – Cold all day. Went to prayer meeting at night. Ishmael Lucas was buried at Fall Creek.*

Ishmael Lucas, thirty-nine years old, was the son of David Lucas and Stella Winters. His wife was Opal (Midkiff) Lucas.[558]

Rupert: *I went to prayer meeting.*

"Diamond Dust": It was World Series time. "It's the Tigers Vs. the Cublets today. Hank Borowy vs. Hal Newhouser. Some of the baseball 'railbirds' are referring to the Tigers and the Cubs as the 'Cheese Champions.' Well-l-l, there have been times this season when both clubs

did look pretty awful. But, they both finished in the No. 1 spot and are now playing for the W. S. (World Series) $$$$$. My three X X X Special to star in the series—Hank Greenberg. Hank isn't supposed to be very fast. Listen, brother-r-r, when you can rap that old rutabaga against the fence—or over it—you don't have to run very hard. Look at what Hank did in the final game of the AL season against the St. Loo Browns with the 'Ducks-on-the-Pond.' A round-tripper ... Roy Cullenbine also homered. See what I mean? Those who know both Branch Rickey and Leo Durocher are willing to wager that the Lip's salary for 1945 will be closer to $30,000 than to $50,000 ... Much closer, in fact ... Eddie Mayo, who taught his baseball A-B-C's in Huntington, at old League Park. 8th Street West, has been tagged the 'Holler guy' for the American League champion Tigers... Eddie is the old pepper box. He's the first man out on the diamond every day and the last one to leave. He never quits and he won't let any of his teammates quit. Every man on the Tiger team swears by Mayo."[559] (Chicago won that first game 9–0.)

Washington, October 3: President Truman requested that Congress start a move toward development of the St. Lawrence River for navigation and power production...[560]

Lueneburg, Germany, October 3: "A series of affidavits describing mass murder, torture, brutal beatings, grotesque medical experiments, and starvation at the Belsen and Oswiecim prison camps was read today into the record of the court trying 45 Nazis for crimes there."[561]

Briefs from Last Night's Associated Press Wires: Pope Pius XII, "inaugurating the court year of the Holy Roman Rota, said that the Catholic Church was not authoritarian and asserted that democracy must be based on Christian faith." In Germany, "Twelve breweries and four malt houses have been opened in the United States zone of Germany to supply beer for American troops."[562]

"IN THE SERVICE":

Lieutenant Colonel Victor C. Simmons, son of Mr. and Mrs. C. G. Simmons, 4096 Four Pole Road, attained his present rank recently in the ordinance division, Fourth Service Command Reclamation Center at Atlanta, Ga.

Private First Class Everett R. Rayburn, husband of Mrs. Agnes Rayburn, Route 1, recently enlisted in the post-war regular Army at Caserta, Italy. His parents, Mr. and Mrs. Bailey Rayburn, live at Barboursville.

Seaman Second Class Darrius D. Bays, son of Mr. Roy Lee Bays, Hurricane, and Seaman Second Class Jessie T. Morris, son of Mrs. Sarah Taylor, Kenova, are serving aboard the USS Oakland in Tokyo Bay.

Watertender Second Class Shelley A. Wells of Huntington is serving aboard the destroyer transport USS Kephart off Korea.

Master Sergeant Elbert Swann, 1626 Thirteenth Avenue, who served for 22 months overseas, has received an honorable discharge from the Army at Capp Swift, Tex.

Second Lieutenant Charles M. Scott, 257 Gallaher Street, who served for 10 months in Europe, has arrived at the San Antonio District AAF Personnel Distribution Command.

Huntington men honorably discharged from the armed forces at Fort Lewis, Wash. Separation Center are John W. Moore, 817 Seventeenth Street; Charles T. Skeer, 1554 Third Avenue; John W. Fuller, 2807 ½ Fourth Avenue, and Millard F. Thomas, 3601 Fifth Avenue.

Thomas L. Mullins of Harts has reported to the Naval Armed Guard Center at Treasure Island, San Francisco, after serving for 10 months as a member of a gun crew aboard a merchant ship.

Private First Class Charles E. Teschler, son of Mrs. Georgeanna Teschler, 1318 Jefferson Avenue, is spending a 45-day leave here with his mother. He came from Fort Meade, Md.

Two brothers-in-law met recently at the home of Mr. and Mrs. L. A. Maclaughlin, 911 Twenty-eighth Street. They were Private Dale Maclaughlin, oldest son of Mr. and Mrs. Maclaughlin, who had reported to Fort Meade, Md. for overseas assignment, and Corporal Thomas Stevenson, who visited his wife, the former Miss Gullen Maclaughlin, and daughter Sherry Lynn. He has returned to Newport News, Va.

Mr. and Mrs. Fletcher Sellards, 2419 First Avenue, received a telephone call yesterday from their son, Sergeant William David Sellards, who has landed at Tacoma, Wash., after three years in the Pacific with General MacArthur's forces.

Glenna: *October 4th Thursday – Very cold and sunny. I went to see Velma Porter and her new baby girl.*

Rupert: *Mother went to see Velma Porter's new baby.*

The "new baby girl" was Lois. Jaruel and Velma Porter also had a son, Arthur.

Detroit Tigers won World Series game two 4–1.

Lieutenant General Lucian K. Truscott succeeded General George Patton as commander of the U.S. Third Army in Germany.

"IN THE SERVICE":

Radioman First Class Dennis C. Jones and Boatswain's Mate First Class W. E. Jones, 1844 Charleston Avenue, recently received discharges from the Navy and have returned home. The former served on the destroyer USS George K. Mackenzie, and was in the service for eight years, while the latter spent four years in service and was a crew member of the cruiser USS Helena.

Corporal James M. Stover, husband of Mrs. Dannie Stover of Apple Grove, W.Va., has been honorably discharged from the Army Air Forces at the Indiantown Gap, Pa. Separation Center.

Private First Class Carl R. Bowles of Culloden has been discharged from the Army at Fort Ord, Calif.

Coast Guard Seaman First Class Jesse F. Ferguson of Lesage has been released from the service at Detroit.

Private First Class William P. Beckett, son of Mr. and Mrs. E. Grant Beckett, 2149 Fourth Avenue and Private First Class Thomas E. Slogic of Ashland recently arrived at Camp Swift, Tex. from the European theatre.

The following men were recently discharged from the Army at Camp Atterbury, Ind.: Staff Sergeant Ira Doughton, Crum; Technician Fifth Grade John H. Block, Kermit, and Sergeant Morris C. Willoughby, 1180 Norway Avenue.

Perry Orville Wilks, son of Mrs. Alice Wilks of Chesapeake, O., is serving with the armed forces in the Philippines.

Sergeant Kenneth M. Tucker, 2958 Piedmont Road, has been awarded the Air Medal for service with the 315th Bombardment Wing on Guam.

Sergeant Ray N. Roy, 421 West Seventh Avenue, recently received the Bronze Star decoration in southern Bavaria.

Major George F. Blume, 84 Twenty-seventh Street, recently attained his present rank at Batangas, Luzon.

Private First Class Wayne S. Wright of Ashton, W.Va., is stationed in Landsberg, Germany with the 794th Air Defense Command Unit Battalion.

The following Army officers have been returned to inactive status at Fort Meade: First Lieutenant Leland Bagby, 1513 Third Avenue; Major Jess E. Hammock, 3410 Hughes Street; Captain George E. Copeland, Huntington Route 3; First Lieutenant Charles M. Pace, 510 Washington Boulevard; First Lieutenant Frederick A. Woods, 1008 Chesapeake Court, and Second Lieutenant Oscar L. Price, 319 Thirty-first Street.

The following men from this area have recently received discharges from the Army at Drew Field, Fla.: Sergeant Raymond L. LaFon, son of Mr. and Mrs. Gilbert LaFon, 463 Smith Street, and Flight Officer Harry F. Curry, 2619 Guyan Avenue.

Glenna: *October 5th Friday – Cool and cloudy. I cleaned the house good. That night was very sick with cramps.*

Rupert: *Mother was very sick at her stomac.*

"Claude Passeau, 36 year-old Lucedale, Miss. tungnut farmer, yesterday turned in the greatest pitching performance in World Series history when he held the Detroit Tigers to one single and shut them out 3–0 to give the Chicago Cubs a 2–1 edge in the series..."[563]

"IN THE SERVICE":

The following Huntington men are serving aboard the USS *Yorktown* off Japan: Aviation Machinist's Mate Second Class Allen Watson, Twenty-fifth Street; Ensign Bruce A. Cunningham, son of Mr. and Mrs. Roy H. Cunningham, 2951 Staunton Road, and Aviation Machinist's Mate First Class Frederick A. Gilbreath, 612 Third Street.

Seaman First Class Edwin Burks and Shipfitter Third Class Harry A. Burks, sons of Mr. and Mrs. Lon Burks of Barboursville, met in Tokyo Bay recently.

Quartermaster Third Class Maurice Harold Wilson, 335 St. Louis Avenue, and Boatswain's Mate Second Class Howard Frye, Accoville, are serving aboard the USS *Giansar* in the Pacific.

Machinist's Mate William A. Gannon of Lundale is serving aboard the USS *Tuscaloosa* in the Pacific.

Fireman Second Class Billy Gene Hite is aboard the USS *Terror* anchored just off the coast of Japan. He is the son of Mr. and Mrs. Carl Hite, 210 Baer Street, and his wife is Mrs. Billie Hite, 1857 Third Avenue.

Machinist's Mate Third Class William Hugh Quinn Jr., 2 ½ Northcott Court, a veteran of 24 months of duty aboard the USS *Wasp* in the Pacific, has arrived at the Naval Training Station at Norfolk, Va. for instructions for duties aboard a new destroyer or similar type vessel.

Motor Machinist's Mate First Class Eugene S. Miller, son of Mrs. Edith Miller, 2647 Guyan Avenue, has completed 32 months of service in the Pacific aboard the USS *Cobra*, a submarine.

Chief Machinist's Mate Forrest H. Clare, 1106 Washington Avenue, and Machinist's Mate Third Class Cledith Robson, 1921 Monroe Avenue, have been honorably discharged from the Navy at the Bainbridge, Md. Separation Center.

Ensign D. T. Boyd, Spring Valley Road, is serving aboard the USS *Farquhar* off Ponape Island in the Carolines.

Watertender Second Class Darrell R. Bias of Milton, and Seaman First Class Virgil Headley of Wewanta, W.Va., are serving aboard the USS *Yorktown* off Japan.

Shipfitter First Class George Edward Butcher Jr. of Kenova, has been honorably discharged from the Navy at the separation center at Bainbridge, Md.

Charles O. Gilfilen of Middleport, O. recently witnessed the surrender and occupation of Kusale Island in the Carolines from the destroyer USS *Soley*.

Forest Lee Sullivan, 410 Fifth Street, Guyandotte, has been honorably discharged from the naval service at the separation center at Bainbridge, Md.

Technician Fifth Grade Hazel B. Bower, 521 Eighth Avenue, recently attained her present rank at Vaughan General Hospital at Hines, Ill.

Seaman Second Class Ralph Richard Fulks of Huntington, a former Marshall College student, arrived here this week to do recruiting work for the Navy.

Seaman Second Class Billie Eugene Church has returned to the Sampson, N.Y. Naval Training Station after visiting his grandparents, Mr. and Mrs. C. W. Clarke, and his aunt, Mrs. H. W. Hale, 1828 Napier Street.

Staff Sergeant Andrew Jefferson of Huntington has arrived in Japan for occupation duty.

Private First Class Edward L. Harris, son of Mr. and Mrs. Joe Harris, 2215 Eighth Avenue, has been released from the hospital at Martinsburg, W.Va., and has been discharged from the Army.

Private First Class Burnie Napier of East Lynn, has been awarded the Purple Heart Medal for wounds received in action against the Japanese on Luzon in the Philippines. The award was made at McGuire General Hospital at Richmond, Va.

Glenna: *October 6th Saturday – Cool and cloudy. Am still sick. Can't work I'm so weak. Velma Adkins died, an old school mate of mine.*

Throughout the year Mother and I experienced several illnesses in addition to the flu. I wonder if proximity to our many farm animals might have been a factor.

Velma Adkins, daughter of John Kelly Adkins and Laura (Sawyer) Adkins died in Lincoln County.[564]

Rupert: *I went over to Larry's.*

Tigers 4, Cubs 1.

"IN THE SERVICE":

Staff Sergeant Charles E. Hughes, son of Mr. and Mrs. J. T. Hughes, 1639 Seventh Avenue, has been discharged from the Service at the Scott Field, Ill. AAF separation center.

Technical Sergeant Ira J. Bias Jr. of West Hamlin has arrived at the San Antonio, Tex. District AAF Personal Distribution Command.

Electrician's Mate Third Class Gilbert W. West, husband of Mrs. Duel West of

Huntington, is serving aboard the USS *Preston* in the Atlantic.

Russell L. Faulkner, whose parents live at 320 Twenty-seventh Street, is serving aboard the USS *Leon* in Tokyo Bay.

Machinist's Mate Second Class Haskell Hodge of Branchland and Sewell Kingrey, 1931 Doulton Avenue, have been honorably discharged from the Navy at Bainbridge, Md.

Private First Class Raymond L. Reynolds, son of Mr. and Mrs. W. E. Reynolds of Salt Rock, stationed with the 36th "Texas" Division in Germany, has participated in four campaigns, serving in Italy, France, Germany, and Austria.

Chief Warrant Officer Clarence D. Frizzell, husband of Mrs. Ann Gail Frizzell, 825 West Ninth Street, is en route to San Francisco from Honolulu to receive a discharge.

Private First Class Ralph W. Lewis, husband of Mrs. Elise Lewis, 413 Tenth Street, is with the 32nd Division troops in Japan.

Telegrapher Third Class J. Riley Diamond of Chesapeake, O. has been assigned to the USS *Rocky Mount* at Shanghai, China.

Corporal Walter A. Caldwell, 2781 Collis Avenue, attained his present rank at Harmon Field, Guam.

Storekeeper Third Class John H. Fetter, 1013 Monroe Avenue, has been transferred to the Norfolk, Va. Naval Receiving Station and Chief Quartermaster John W. Meadows, 540 Washington Avenue, has been transferred to Brooklyn, N.Y. Both have been serving with the local recruiting detachment.

Sergeant Ben De Rond Jr., 1927 Madison Avenue, has been discharged from service at Lincoln, Neb.

Staff Sergeant Wilber Beaty, son of Mr. and Mrs. G. W. Beaty, 54 Adams Avenue, has been honorably discharged from the Army at Lowry Field, Denver, Colo.

Glenna: *October 7th Sunday — Went to Sunday School. Took community [communion] service. Stuart and Ruby came up and spent the day with all their children. Stuart and Dawson went to Tom Johnson's funeral at Enon. Beautiful day.*

Sundays were laid-back days, a time for rest or visits with friends; No stores were open and athletic events were of the spontaneous kind. There was one exception: Many men and older boys participated in summer baseball games, part of an area-organized baseball league.

Thomas Richard Johnson, age eighty-four, was the son of Joseph William Johnson and Lucinda Anne (Bledsoe) Johnson.[565]

"WITH THE COLORS":

Private (First Class) Paul E. Chadwick, son of Mr. and Mrs. Delbert Chadwick of Kenova, was recently transferred from Arabia to the Air Transport Command Base at El Aouina, Tunis, Tunisia, where he was assigned to the provost marshal's department as a military policeman...

Chief Yeoman Howard Raymond Gould, USN, son of Mrs. Dorthea Gould, 1039 West Seventh Street, has arrived home to spend a 30-day leave with his mother for the first time in seven years... He has been in the regular Navy since July 10, 1938, and was at Manila when the Japs attacked Pearl Harbor...

Major George F. Blume, husband of Mrs. Hester S. Blume, 84 Twenty-seventh Street, has been awarded the Bronze Star Medal at Batangas, Philippine Islands, for meritorious achievement at Tacloban, Leyte and Batangas from Feb. 17, 1945 to July 9, 1945 in direct support of combat operations against the enemy. The former sales manager for Standard Brands Inc., is the son of Mr. and Mrs. Fred L Blume of Huntington.

First Lieutenant Charles M. Pace of Huntington has been released from active service by the Army Air Forces at Fort Meade, Md.

Yeoman Third Class Harry W. Smith, USNR, recently spent a 30-day leave with his wife, the former Miss Vera Wyrick, at 4295 Eighth Street Road. He had returned to the East Coast after serving 14 months aboard the USS *LCI (L) 945*, flotilla flagship in the European theatre where he participated in the amphibious assault at Southern France. He wears the European African-Middle Eastern ribbon with one battle star. Yeoman Smith attended Wayne County High School and was employed by the National Biscuit Co. in Huntington before entering the Navy in March, 1944. He is the son of Mrs. Bertie Smith, 1310 Fifteenth Street.

Corporal Leo Ferguson has returned from 25 months of service in the South Pacific and is spending a 30-day furlough with his sister, Mrs. Lonnie F. Taylor, 19A26 Charleston Avenue.

Sergeant Thomas G. Bledsoe, son of Mr. and Mrs. R. C. Bledsoe, 1601 Sixteenth Street, a cook with the 43rd Ordnance Heavy Machine Tank Company, recently spent a seven-day rest furlough in the U.S. Riviera Recreational Area at Nice, France. Sergeant Bledsoe has been overseas for 28 months and wears the European theatre ribbon with five battle stars for campaigns in Africa, Sicily, Italy and France.

Private George I. Roberts, son of Mrs. Clara Roberts, 404 Thirty-first Street, who has served with the 164th Infantry Division on Cebu, Philippine Islands, was recently transferred to a unit assigned to occupational duty in Tokyo, Japan.

Gunner's Mate Stephen Buckland, son of Mrs. America V. Buckland, 410 Thirteenth Street, has arrived home after receiving his discharge from the Navy, having served nearly four years on the battleship USS *Massachusetts*...

Technical Sergeant Richard L. Sherman of Huntington and his wife, Private (First Class) Billie Bryan Sherman, WAC, have been granted honorable discharges from Army service at California, and have returned to this city to reside at 1838 Maple Avenue. They have both been stationed at Santa Maria, Calif. Army Air Base for 19 months.

Yeoman (First Class) Robert L. Sansom, son of Otis Sansom, 1892 Marshall Avenue, has been promoted to his present rating with a night attack and combat training unit of the Atlantic Fleet on the East Coast. His wife resides at 2677 Fourth Avenue.

Private Jack H. Hardin, son of Mr. and Mrs. G. W. Hardin, 260 B Street, Ceredo, has arrived at his station at Luzon, Philippine Islands.

Corporal Helen G. Glover has been released from the Women's Army Corps at Torney General Hospital, Palm Springs, Calif., where she served as a cryptographer with the Air Transport Command. She is the daughter of Charles C. Gressang of Widen. W.Va.

Private First Class Wilber Ellis of Ethel, W.Va. has returned to this country after 34 months service in Europe and is now being discharged from the Army at Fort Meade, Md. He has earned seven battle stars and 108 points.

Private Howard Curtis was home on a nine-day delay en route from Chanute Field, Ill. He is now at Kearns, Utah awaiting orders for overseas service. The son of Mr. and Mrs. E. W. Curtis, 2447 First Avenue, he is married to the former Mrs. Nikomas Jarrell.

Technician (fifth class) Clarence S. Matthews, 27, 206 Bridge Street, a veteran of 16 months duty in the European theatre of operations, was recently granted a discharge from service at McCaw General Hospital, Walla Walla, Wash. He was wounded in both legs while serving with the 99th Division... He served in the Army four years and four months, His wife resides at the Bridge Street address.

Glenna: *October 8th Monday – I washed and cleaned up. Began raining about 2:30. Rained hard then showered all night.*

Rupert: *It rained all day.*

An Associated Press article noted failure of the "Washington conferences" to stop the suspension of a West Virginia coal miner's strike. "Saturday night at Washington, UMW Chieftain John L. Lewis refused to order an end to the strike when requested by soft coal operators, contending the international union was not responsible and that he had not called the walkout."[566]

The Cubs won the sixth game of the World Series 8–7 to even the Series with three wins each.

From Tiptonville, Tennessee, President Truman "... declared unequivocally tonight that the secrets of the atomic bomb will not be shared with additional nations..." The exceptions were Great Britain and Canada, and he said of them that he "was certain they will agree its secrets will not be shared."[567]

Tokyo, October 8: "Emperor Hirohito ... admitted today that he knew in advance of the plan to attack Pearl Harbor, but contended he understood that a declaration of war was to be made beforehand."[568]

"IN THE SERVICE":

Seaman Second Class Von Cline of Slagle served aboard an LCI in the final days of the Pacific war, patrolling the waters of the Carolines to blockade the remaining Jap garrisons.

Pharmacist's Mate Second Class Leroy J. Woodrum, 167 Davis Street, is serving on the USS *Sherburne* in Tokyo Bay.

Radioman Third Class George R. Nicholas, son of Mr. and Mrs. V. H. Holly, 922 Twenty-third Street, is serving on the USS *Mount Olympus* in Tokyo Bay.

Hospital Apprentice First Class Walden C. Chaffin, 2607 Railroad Avenue, is serving with Fleet Hospital No. 103 on Guam.

Robert C. McCormick, 2809 Third Avenue, was graduated as a flight engineer from the Hondo, Tex. Army Air Field after completing the AAF's highly technical B-29 flight engineer course last week...

Harry Scott Bartholomew, son of Mrs. Nellie Ward Bartholomew, Rear 2112 Seventh Avenue,

has been honorably discharged from the Navy at the Bainbridge, Md., Separation Center.

Glenna: *October 9th Tuesday – Ironed and went to Velma Adkins' funeral at Merritt's Creek Church. Very cool.*

Rupert: *I went to school today.*

The Detroit Tigers won the 1945 World Series 9–3 at Wrigley Field in Chicago.

"First Lieutenant Donald L. Ferguson, son of Mr. and Mrs. Walter L. Ferguson, 2502 Collis Avenue, has enrolled at Harvard University after his discharge from the Army. Lieutenant Ferguson was a navigator in the AAF and has been an instructor at San Marcos, Tex. He will take pre-law work at Harvard under the GI Bill of Rights, his father said."[569]

Pierre Laval, French collaborator, was sentenced to death by a French court.[570]

"IN THE SERVICE":

Corporal Woodrow Hughes, Army Air Forces, arrived in Glenwood, W.Va. to visit his mother, Mrs. Sarah Hughes. Corporal Hughes returned to this country last month after serving for 40 months in the South Pacific and participating in three major battles...

Captain David K. McNish, Ninth Avenue, was returned to inactive duty by the Army at Camp Atterbury, Ind. on October 5.

Gunner's Mate Third Class William C. Washington Jr., son of Mr. and Mrs. W. C. Washington of Lavalette, a veteran of 34 engagements aboard the USS *Phoenix* in the Pacific, will return to duty Friday after a 30-day furlough.

Corporal Lloyd W. McCorkle, son of Mr. and Mrs. H. C. McCorkle, 807 West Eleventh Street, attained his present rank recently with the AAF at Harmon Field, Guam.

Technical Sergeant Billy J. Estep, son of Mrs. Bertha Ridenour, 516 Wilson Street, was recently given an honorable discharge from the Army at Amarillo Army Air Field, Tex.

Technical Sergeant Shelby A. Harbour Jr., son of Mrs. Lucille Harbour, 1401 Fifth Avenue, has passed through the "Rainbow Project," Air Lift Disposition Center, Camp Blanding, Fla., on his way home.

Private William L. Gibson Jr., son of Mrs. Madeline Gibson, 2838 Eleventh Avenue, is expected to arrive here tomorrow on a 15-day furlough from Lowry Field, Colo.

Private First Class George W. Kinnaird, son of Mr. and Mrs. Lewis Kinnaird of Hogsett, recently received an AAF discharge at Kearns, Utah.

Staff Sergeant Teamus Bowling, son of Mr. and Mrs. Grover C. Bowling, 316 Elaine Court, has been honorably discharged from the AAF at San Antonio, Tex.

Glenna: *October 10th Wednesday – Cool and clear. Went to prayer meeting. Had a wonderful time. Many people there.*

Rupert: *I went to prayer meeting.*

Prayer meetings were held on Wednesday nights and often in members' homes. I probably should not have been attending meetings that preceded school days. Sessions were long; adults took turns leading prayers and giving testimony, and some members expounded in great length and detail. I avoided prayer meetings when I could. Before you judge—I was only twelve years old, and usually the only kid there.

"IN THE SERVICE":

Private First Class Robert H. Brown, son of Mr. and Mrs. W. W. Brown, 1201 Ninth Avenue, was one of a select group of marines to land with the initial occupation forces at the Yokosuka naval base in Japan... He is a member of the Sixth Marine Division and has been overseas for 11 months... He attended Central High School and was employed by the Baltimore & Ohio Railroad as a telegrapher before volunteering on May 22, 1944.

After serving for 18 months in the Navy, Howard Jennings has returned to Huntington and has resumed the directorship of the orchestra bearing his name. A former baker third class, Mr. Jennings recently received a medical discharge in California. His wife, Mrs. Emma Jennings, and twin daughters, Jean and Jane, reside at 1018 West Second Street.

Wilber E. Harens, husband of Mrs. Katie F. Harens of Huntington, and William R. Atkinson, husband of Mrs. Dorothy M. Atkinson of Leon, have been honorably discharged from the Navy at Bainbridge, Md.

Gunner's Mate First Class Edgar Maynard is serving with an underwater demolition team in the China theatre, and his brother, Staff Sergeant Jarrett B. Maynard, is en route from Europe to the Pacific, their parents, Mr. and Mrs. C. A. Maynard, 4555 Piedmont Road, said yesterday.

Lionel Darce Egnor, son of Mr. and Mrs. A. M. Egnor, 414 Thirteenth Street, has arrived at Seattle, Wash, aboard the USS *Langfitt*. His brother, Augie Edward Egnor, is with the Third Fleet in Tokyo Bay. The former's wife and two sons live at 4426 Route 60, while the latter's wife and son live at Sanysidro, Calif.

Master Sergeant Robert Wisehart, 1216 Tenth Avenue, former managing editor of the Marshall College student paper, *Parthenon*, has returned to Huntington after 29 months' service overseas with the AAF.

Glenna: *October 11th Thursday – Cool and sunshiny. Went to see Mrs. Smith, Mrs. Morris, and Dewie Jobe.*

Those visits to aged, ill, and housebound neighbors were along Salt Rock's "Alley." (Apple Maps now lists the lane as "Gill Street.") The Alley ran from Route 10 at the foot of Salt Rock Hill by Carter's grocery store back toward the river where it made a righthand bend back to Route 10 by the bridge.

"IN THE SERVICE":

The following officers from this area have been returned to inactive status by the Army at Fort George G. Meade, Md.: First Lieutenant George N. Cowden, 830 ½ Eleventh Avenue; First Lieutenant Lee R. Hornsby, Alum Creek; Major Henderson O. Webb Jr., 1029 Tenth Street; First Lieutenant William H. French, Williamson; First Lieutenant Jack L. Hagan, 1526 Sixth Avenue; First Lieutenant Ira Elliott Jr., Wayne; First Lieutenant William M. Daniel, Barboursville, and First Lieutenant Ira W. Fuller, Iaeger."

Lieutenant Raymond M. Hannan, 739 Ninth Avenue, has been returned to inactive duty by the Navy at New York City.

Seaman First Class Burgess Maynard of Holden served on the USS *Howorth*, a destroyer which was among the first warships to enter Hodadote Harbor, Hokkaido, to accept Japanese surrender and enforce the occupation.

Fire Controlman First Class Robert L. Thompson, 1217 Twenty-fifth Street, was aboard the USS *Albert W. Grant*, sailing across the international Date Line from Bering Sea for the occupation of Japan, and eliminating September 2, V-J Day, from the lives of the crew.

Coxswain Harold Kent and Gunner's Mate Second Class Rupert R. Rent of Point Pleasant were aboard the USS *Salt Lake City* which helped take over the Ominato naval base, Japanese Navy Headquarters for northern Honshu, Hokkaido, Fare Futo and the Kurile Islands.

Seaman Second Class Samuel J. Heaberlin, 121 West Second Avenue, and Fireman First

Class Charles E. France, 327 Thirty-third Street, are serving on the USS *Concord* in the Pacific.

The following men from this area served with a Navy underwater demolition team which paved the way for invasion of enemy-held beaches: Chief Pharmacist's Mate Francis Xavier Schuller and Shipfitter First Class Thurman Lee Grass of Ona and Gunner's Mate Third Class Paul Edwin Estep of Branchland.

Ensign Lewis M. Wilcox, 2122 Tenth Avenue, served on the USS *Richmond* during the occupation of northern Japan.

Gunner's Mate First Class Glen R. Wilson, 1214 Washington Avenue, served aboard the light cruiser USS *Duluth* in the Pacific...

Radarman Third Class Ermal Clay Scutchfield of West Prestonburg, Ky. served on the destroyer USS *David W. Taylor* off the coast of Japan during the Japanese surrender.

Sergeant Charles E. Bloss, 518 Eighth Avenue, was honorably discharged from the Army Air Force at Plattsburg Barracks, Plattsburg, N.Y.

James Willard Skenses, 166 Oney Avenue, has been honorably discharged from the Navy at Bainbridge, Md.

Radioman Second Class Owen Reed Booker of Huntington has been honorably discharged from the Navy at Bainbridge, Md.

Electrician's Mate Second Class George W. T. Brandt Jr., 2713 ½ Emmons Avenue, attained his present rank recently aboard the LST *1032* with the Pacific Fleet.

Private First Class Frank Ball, brother of Mrs. Gertrude Stewart, 1846 Sixth Avenue, has returned here from the Army after receiving an honorable discharge.

Glenna: *October 12th Friday – Went up to Wilma Gue's to get her to make me a dress. Cool and pleasant all day.*

Willie and Wilma Gue owned a large dairy farm on the east side of the river, south of Salt

Rock. Wilma was my father's first cousin. Later, as a teen, I worked on the farm in haying season.

Rupert: *Mother got a bucket of apples from a naibour.*

Tokyo, October 12: A typhoon had devastated Okinawa. Thirteen American sailors were dead or missing and 100 soldiers were injured. Superfortresses delivered food to isolated American troops. "Sunk, damaged or beached were 127 naval vessels, and others were unable to unload at port facilities that had become a litter of splintered wreckage."[571]

Japanese Prince Konoye said that Japan's constitution may be changed to address "women's suffrage, labor unionization, abolition of secret police systems, education improvement, and revision of monopolistic industry."[572]

"IN THE SERVICE":

Seaman First Class James H. Berry of Huntington is among the West Virginian men who are serving on board the aircraft carrier USS *Savo Island,* which is engaged in patrol work in occupied waters around Ominato, Japan. He lives at 222 Eighteenth Street.

Seaman First Class L. D. Jackson, 26 West Third Avenue, served on the USS *David W. Taylor* in Kagoshima Bay, Kyushu, during Japanese surrender ceremonies.

Captain Robert H. Love of Barboursville reported last week at Abilene Army Air Field, Tex. for duty with the AAF's single engine weather reconnaissance squadron.

Photographer Second Class Olliebelle Petrie, 111 Moore Road, proofreader for the Huntington Publishing Co. for 18 years, returned this week to her post with the Advertiser. She has spent most of her time in the WAVES in Washington. Her husband, Shipfitter First Class Ralph L. Petrie, is en route home from Tokyo Bay to receive a discharge from the Navy.

Harry I. Ferguson, 210 Adams Avenue, has been discharged from the Navy at Bainbridge, Md., after 27 months' service.

Glenna: *October 13th Saturday – Very cool and clear. Went to Huntington and bought Rupert a new pair of shoes.*

Rupert: *We went to town and I got some shoes.*

"The Barboursville Pirates scored almost at will last night on their home field as they turned in a 69–0 victory over Elkview for their sixth straight win against no losses."[573]

"Fireman Second Class Franklin Clark Beckett, liberated on September 5 after 40 months in Japanese prison camps, spent this week with his parents, Mr. and Mrs. Morris A. Beckett, 2662 Guyan Avenue. He left yesterday for Bethesda, Md. to await discharge..."[574]

"L. C. Schmidt of Fairmont, W.Va., has been awarded a contract for preparing plans and specifications for a new $800,000 science building at Marshall College..."[575] (The building had just opened in 1951 when I enrolled at Marshall. Several of my classes were in the new Science Building.)

"IN THE SERVICE":

Shipfitter Second Class Thomas H. Rice Jr. recently was promoted to that rank aboard the USS *Hancock* in the Tokyo Bay area... Shipfitter Rice, the son of Mr. and Mrs. T. H. Rice, 120B Third Avenue, expects to return to this country for Navy Day on October 27.

Flight Leader Captain Richard H. Cartwright, 1333 Fourteenth Street, has returned to the United States after a long tour of combat duty in the Pacific.

Fireman Second Class Earl D. Carter of Gallipolis, O. was aboard the USS *Pensacola* at Ominato at the time of the Japanese surrender.

Corporal Gilbert L. Beaty, 212 Adams Avenue, was recently discharged from the Army Service Forces at Fort Leonard Wood, Mo.

Naval Reserve Nurse Corps Lieutenant Bernice A. Templeton of Chesapeake, O. has been returned to inactive duty in Washington.

William L. Hubbard of Middleport, O. is aboard the USS *Steele* en route to a West Coast port for the observance of Navy Day on October 27.

Technical Sergeant William N. Branch, son of Mr. W. N. Branch, 831 Ninth Avenue, has been transferred from the South Plains Army Air Field at Lubbock, Tex. to a separation center, preparatory to being discharged.

Marvin H. Lewis, 1912 Fourth Avenue, has been discharged from the Army at Fort Sill. Okla.

Second Lieutenant Henry C. Callihan Jr., Williamson, has been returned to inactive status by the Army at Fort Meade.

Glenna: *October 14th Sunday – Went to Sunday School. Cool and cloudy all day. Went to church that night. Revival meeting started.*

Rupert: *I went to Sunday school and went home with Larry.*

Paris, October 14: "Pierre Laval will be executed at 10 A.M. (4 A.M. EST) tomorrow by a 12-man firing squad... The former French premier would not be informed of his fate until the last moment..."[576]

Glenna: *October 15th Monday – Cool and clear. I washed. Visited Galie Adkins' family and Levi Midkiff's family. Went to Revival meeting.*

Rupert: *I went to the church meeting.*

Holding two revival meetings so close together was unusual, especially since this was the third of the year.

Pierre Laval was executed by firing squad at Fresnes Prison. His wife, Madam Pierre Laval later said, bitterly, "I am not crying. One cries over little disappointments. This is too big. You would need tears of blood."[577]

San Francisco, October 15: "Admiral Halsey, like his dungareed seamen, scorned ceremonial dignity to wave an enthusiastic greeting to crowds high above as his homecoming Third Fleet flagship [*South Dakota*] steamed beneath the Golden Gate Bridge... Then, as the cheers of the waiting throng became audible, his gold-braided arm swept aloft in reply... A seaman burst forth with: 'To hell with this standing at attention!' and he and his shipmates waved too..."[578]

"IN THE SERVICE":

Private JoAnn Perry, daughter of Mr. and Mrs. Wirt Perry of 2966 Winters Road, has been transferred from the First WAC Training Center, Fort Des Moines, Iowa, to Atlanta, Ga., for duty with the Army.

Technician Fourth Grade James C. McAllister, 544 Eighth Avenue, received his discharge last week at the separation center at Fort Leonard Wood, Mo.

Lieutenant (j. g.) John M. Baysden, 1806 Twelfth Avenue was serving aboard the cruiser USS *Guam* when she led a task force of more than 50 vessels into Jinsen, Korea on September 8 to liberate the country from the Japanese.

Technical Sergeant William N. Branch, 831 Ninth Avenue, has been discharged from the Army Air Forces at the separation center at Amarillo, Tex. He has been in service for 35 months.

Herbert L. Earl, pharmacist's mate third class, of 2021 Arthur Street, was discharged October 9 at the naval separation center at Puget Sound Navy Yard, Bremerton, Wash.

Staff Sergeant Lyle Ferguson, 106 Poage Avenue, and Private William R. Herbert, 1903 ½ Buffington Avenue, have been discharged from the Army at the Miami Beach, Fla. separation center.

Sergeant Charles T. Sansom, son of Mr. and Mrs. H. L. Sansom, Wayne, has returned to the United States with the 43rd Infantry Division. He served for 24 months in [the] South and Southwest Pacific and participated in the occupation of Japan.

Ance Baldridge, seaman first class, of Prestonsburg, Ky., was serving on the USS *Rutland*, an attack transport, when the vessel entered Tokyo Bay on September 2, the day of Japan's formal surrender...

Discharged last week from the Navy at Bainbridge, Md., were Fireman First Class Gordon Ferguson, Kenova; Fireman First Class Eugene Hensley, Huntington; Quartermaster Third Class Charles F. Hite, 51 Tenth Avenue; Seaman First Class Virgil L. Grose, Ona, and Torpedoman Third Class Matthew Caudill Jr., 701 Buffington Street.

Glenna: *October 16th Tuesday – I ironed, cleaned up the house, went to Revival that night. Pretty day.*

Rupert: *I went to the meeting.*

Transportation systems were overtaxed by the volume of returning service members. An AP article from San Francisco blamed a shortage of railroad equipment for causing late departures of trains "scheduled to carry Third Fleet discharges to separation centers..."[579]

"IN THE SERVICE":

Staff Sergeant James E. Adkins, on Guam with a Quartermaster company, was recently promoted to that grade from technician fourth grade, he has informed his parents, Mr. and Mrs. Odie Adkins of 616 South High Street, Guyandotte.

Flight Officer Everett N. Thacker, son of Mr. and Mrs. P. N. Thacker of Kenova, has been placed on inactive status by the Army Air Forces at Chanute Field, Ill.

Cecil W. Endicott of Huntington has been honorably discharged by the Army Air Forces at Davis-Mothan Field, Ariz. He served as a maintenance line chief in the CBI theatre.

Sergeant Edward C. Carmichael, son of Mrs. J. H. Hunter of Huntington, has been discharged from the Army Air Forces at the Drew Field, Fla. separation center.

Master Sergeant Milford Smith, 83B Camden Road, has been discharged from the AAF after five years' service. He is the son of Mrs. Vera Fry Smith.

Staff Sergeant Jack L. Adams, son of Mr. and Mrs. C. R. Adams, 2583 Collis Avenue, has been discharged from the Army at Camp Livingston, La. The husband of Mrs. Dorothy Adams, 404 Main Street, served overseas for 29 months with the 150th Infantry of the West Virginia National Guard.

Returning home aboard the USS *Idaho*, scheduled to dock at Norfolk, Va. tomorrow are James Burks, 1210 Washington Avenue; J. F. Bowers, 901 Seventh Street, and Edward K. Allen, Barboursville. Also aboard the *Idaho*, but as ship's company, are Herschell Nichols of Kenova and Jim Perdue of Ceredo.

Lieutenant-Commander Morris C. Shewkey, son of the late Dr. M. P. Shawkey, former president of Marshall College is in Huntington on terminal leave prior to reverting to inactive status. His wife, Mrs. Helen Shawkey, resides at 1707 Ninth Avenue.

Hospital Apprentice First Class Madeline Sarver, WAVES, daughter of F. B. Sarver of Huntington, who was graduated recently at the Hospital Corps school at Great Lakes, Ill., has returned to Farragut, Idaho after visiting her cousin, Miss Elizabeth Ann Barbour, 1601 ½ Eighth Avenue.

Sergeant Guy McComas, son of Mr. and Mrs. Bryce McComas, 834 Twelfth Street, has been honorably discharged from the Marine Corps at Cherry Point, N.C. He served for 42 months, 25 overseas.

Glenna: *October 17th Wed. – I aired the clothes and put away clothes. Beautiful day. Went to Revival meeting that night.*

Rupert: *I missed the meeting.*

Japan, on this day, took several steps toward democracy: Emperor Hirohito granted amnesty to nearly one million Japanese, four major industrial companies offered shares for sale, religious laws were relaxed, and the nation's motion picture industry was freed from government control.[580]

"IN THE SERVICE":

Presentation of the Bronze Star medal to Staff Sergeant Dwight G. Hutson, son of Mrs. Martha Hutson, 629 Elm Street, was announced yesterday. Sergeant Hutson, overseas a year, was awarded the medal in ceremonies at his station with the 78th Division in Germany.

Technical Sergeant James A. Keyser, son of Mrs. Elizabeth Keyser of Kenova, has returned to New York accompanied by his wife and baby. He served overseas for 23 months, and has been discharged from the Air Forces.

Discharged this week at the Navy separation center at Bainbridge, Md., were Seaman First Class Frederick W. Klein, Boatswain's Mate Denver A. Willis, and Signalman Second Class Noah Kendall Wheeler, Huntington.

First Lieutenant William E. McCoppin, son of Mr. and Mrs. George T. McCoppin, 2641

Collis Avenue, has been released by the Army Air Forces at Patterson Field, Ohio...

Private First Class Norman F. Bexfield, son of Mr. and Mrs. C. H. Bexfield, 2839 Overlook Drive, landed Monday at an East Coast port after 29 months overseas...

Technician Fifth Grade Emery R. Berry, son of Mr. and Mrs. Carl Berry of Lesage, is serving in Manila with the 1385th Engineer Unit. He was formerly in the European theatre.

First Lieutenant Meredith P. Wiswell, son of Mrs. M. P. Wiswell, 530 Fifth Street, has been released by the Army Air Forces at Patterson Field, Ohio.

Storekeeper First Class Mary Billman, wife of O. J. Billman, 28 West Seventh Avenue, has been discharged by the WAVES at the Washington naval separation center.

Corporal Glen G. Hager, son of Mr. and Mrs. W. E. Hager of Guyandotte, has arrived in the Philippine Islands for occupation duty with the 86th Infantry Division. Corporal Hager was with the division when it fought in Europe and remained with it during re-deployment to the Pacific.

Glenna: *October 18th Thurs. – I finished airing the clothes. Went to church that night. Lucille Sansom, Viola and Juanita Morrison were saved. Grand time.*

Rupert: *I went to the meeting. Two people were saved.*

Sisters Viola and Juanita Morrison were daughters of Arnold Morrison whose house had burned. Lucille Sansom was a member of the large Sansom family that had recently settled in Salt Rock. The Sansoms later bought Childers' grocery store and the Childers family built a new store across the road. Salt Rock once had three grocery stores in the village and another across the river at the junction of Route 10 and Tyler Creek Road.

"IN THE SERVICE":

Second Lieutenant Harvey Sullivan Jr., son of the Rev. and Mrs. Harvey Sullivan, 1242 Eighteenth Street, was recently promoted to that rank from flight officer in China, where he is serving as a C-47 pilot.

William C. Varney, son of Mrs. Edna Varney, 3003 Fourth Avenue, has been discharged from the AAF after serving for 28 months in Europe.

Fireman First Class Sam Childers of Chesapeake, O. is serving aboard the USS *Taussig* with the Pacific Fleet.

A veteran of 34 months as an aerial photographer on a B-17 in Europe, Sergeant Lloyd J. Hamlin, son of Mr. and Mrs. R. J. Hamlin, 439 Smith Street, has been discharged from service.

Captain J. Houghton Nelson, Army Air Forces, is visiting his wife and sons James and Paul, 10 Oakland Road. He returned from the China-India-theatre last January and has been a patient at Walter Reed Hospital in Washington. He will report to the hospital October 24 to receive a medical discharge.

Private Jacob P. Nicely Jr., who recently returned after 18 months duty in England, France, Belgium, Holland and Germany, is stationed at the Fort Oglethorpe, Ga. Redistribution Center, He is the son of Mr. and Mrs. Jacob Nicely, 2148 Eighth Avenue.

After participating in most of the major engagements in the Pacific aboard the USS *Yorktown*, Lieutenant R. Knowleton Stuart is spending a leave with his parents, Mr. and Mrs. H. D. Stuart, 325 West Eleventh Street.

Serving aboard the USS *Montpelier* when she helped remove more than 2,600 liberated prisoners of war from Wakayama, Honshu, Japan, were Seaman First Class G. Hager, 3023 Sixteenth Street Road; Seaman First Class Claude Gilliam, 407 Adams Avenue; Seaman First Class Virgil O. Adkins, 5234 Ohio River Road; Seaman First Class Wilbur Hill, 424 Thirteenth Street, and Seaman First Class Herman S. Messinger Jr., Salt Rock.

Charles E. Money, 1639 Jefferson Avenue, has been discharged from the Army at Fort Lewis, Wash., and Robert L. Ward, husband of Mrs. Mary Ward of Huntington [and son of Edwin F. Ward], has been discharged from the Army at Camp Livingston, La.

Serving on the USS *Tuscaloosa*, a cruiser, when the vessel participated in the occupation of Jinsen, Korea, was Machinist's Mate Third Class Carl L. Coffman, 826 Twenty-third Street.

John M. Chittem, seaman first class, 150 Leeward Avenue, was serving on the destroyer USS *Metcalf* when the vessel participated in the occupation of Jinsen, Korea.

Private First Class Farley B. Hall, son of Mr. and Mrs. Boyce Hall, 633 Seventh Avenue, is receiving treatment at the Newton D. Baker General Hospital at Martinsburg following his liberation after 32 months in Japanese prison camps. Private Hall served for 51 months in the Philippine Islands with the 59th Coast Artillery.

Pharmacist's Mate Second Class Clyde C. Taylor, has been discharged from the Navy at the Charleston, W.Va., separation center.

Electrician's Mate Second Class Joseph H. Hale of Wayne has been discharged by the Navy at Bainbridge, Md. He is the husband of Mrs. Mildred Irene Hale of Wayne.

Glenna: *October 19th Friday — Another beautiful fall day. Went to church at night. Had a fine meeting. Very spiritual.*

Rupert: *A Boy at our school got his leg broke playing football.*

I wrote that casually, but I was personally involved. Naaman and Daman Stapleton were twin brothers, recently arrived from Logan County. Their older sister, Ann Stapleton, had married Darrell Harbour, one of Eddie's older brothers.

Mr. Drummond had taught us the essentials of touch football, but on this day a few of us couldn't resist the temptation to take the game to a higher level. Naaman and Daman were in on that fateful decision. Some minutes into the lunch-hour game, Daman carried the ball and Johnny Chapman and I tackled him. I heard the crack of his leg breaking. Daman hovered over Naaman, crying. Larry Gill had the composure to yell for someone go get help. Mr. Drummond called St. Mary's Hospital in Huntington to get an ambulance.

Naaman was trembling so hard his teeth chattered. Eddie had gone down the road to tell his sister-in-law what had happened and it wasn't long before Harbour family members came to the playground with blankets and comforting words. The ambulance came in half-an-hour but it was the next day before we received word that his leg had been set and he would be all right. Our reprimand was relatively mild, but that ended the season of tackle football.

"IN THE SERVICE":

Sergeant Leonard A. Lerner, son of Mr. and Mrs. L. Lerner, 404 West Tenth Avenue, was recently promoted to that rank with the Tenth Air Force in Kunming, China.

Staff Sergeant James E. Adkins, son of the Rev. and Mrs. Odie Adkins, 616 South High Street, is reported by the War Department to be confined to a Guam hospital. Sergeant Adkins has served with a quartermaster company in the Pacific for two years.

After circling the globe once and crossing the equator six times, Leonard H. Barker, son of Mrs. M. V. Barker, 1621 Sixth Avenue, was discharged this week from the Navy with 44 points.

Technician Fifth Grade Ira C. Dingess, 1502 Harrison Avenue, has been discharged from the Army at Camp Butner, N.C.

Corporal Bernard J. Akers, 601 Buffington Street, was discharged this week from the Army

Air Forces at Key Field at Meridan, Miss. He has been in the service for 36 months as a medical technician.

Motor Machinist's Mate Second Class Ellsworth J. Bowles, 2420 Ninth Avenue, was serving aboard the USS *Sibley* as the vessel participated in the occupation of Japan at Wakayama harbor. He is the husband of Mrs. Evelyn Bowles.

As a member of the victorious softball team in the European Theatre WAC softball tournament, Private First Class Sharline Reese, 2155 Fifth Avenue, was awarded a gold watch. The team represented the WAC detachment at Berlin and competed against teams from France and England on the Riviera, France.

Woodrow W. Nease, son of Mr. and Mrs. James Nease of 4802 Waverly Place, was serving on the light cruiser USS *Mobile* as a coxswain when the vessel aided in evacuating liberated prisoners of war from Nagasaki to Okinawa.

Discharged this week from the Navy at Bainbridge, Md., were Seaman First Class William Jackson, 1628 Artisan Avenue; Seaman First Class Willie W. Lowe, 1947 Jackson Avenue; Machinist's Mate Third Class William Edwin Wyle, North Kenova, and Seaman Second Class Arvil Bowen, 1856 ½ Maple Avenue.

Seaman First Class R. A. Muth, 2926 Piedmont Road, is serving on Okinawa with the 112th Seabee Battalion. The unit is continuing construction of facilities for the occupation force.

Fireman Second Class Lowell G. Chinn, son of Mr. and Mrs. Albert Chinn, 1847 Jefferson Avenue, was serving aboard the USS *Sylvania* when the vessel participated in the occupation of Wakayama, Japan.

Private First Class Everett W. Sabo, Army Medical Corps. and his brother Jack W. Sabo, electrician's mate third class, met recently in Pearl Harbor. It was their first meeting in 27 months. They are sons of Mr. and Mrs. Joe G. Sabo, 1032 Monroe Avenue.

Flight Officer Charles M. McNeely, son of Mrs. Blanche McNeely of 247 West Sixth

Avenue, was appointed to that rank after completion of pilot training at Turner Field at Albany, Ga.

Sergeant William E. Polley, son of Mr. and Mrs. D. C. Polley, 1736 Tenth Avenue, recently spent a seven-day furlough on the French Riviera at Nice. The Riviera is under U.S. supervision as a rest and recreation area.

Corporal James Hetzer, 1809 W. Fifth Avenue, is one of a three-man team producing all-soldier shows for U.S. forces still in France and Germany...

Petty Officer Haven E. Fetty of Huntington returned Wednesday to Little Creek, Va. after spending a 72-hour leave with his wife here.

Serving aboard the USS *Tollberg* during the landings at Wakayama was Seaman First Class Raymond L. Blevins of Huntington.

Glenna: *October 20th Saturday – Another beautiful day. Went to Revival meeting that night. Mrs. Matthews died.*

Rupert: *Mrs. Matthews, a teacher's mother died today.*

There were two teachers at Salt Rock Elementary School with last name of Matthews: Velma Matthews was a single first grade teacher and Thelma (Morrison) Matthews was a sixth grade teacher. The woman who died that day was Velma's mother, Ada Belle (Lyons) Matthews,[581] wife of Amos Matthews.[582]

"Coach Clay Martin's Dunbar Bulldogs stayed in the undefeated class last night at King Field, Barboursville but they had a close squeeze doing it to give Coach Jackson Stovers's Barboursville Pirates their first defeat of the season by a score of 7–0. The victory was the fifth straight for Dunbar who has also turned back Beckley, Dupont, St. Albans and East Bank."[583]

Nuremberg, Germany: "Chubby Walther Funk, Hitler's pursekeeper, broke down in tears today when he and his Nazi cohorts received their copies of the indictment for the war crimes trials in Nuremberg."[584]

Hamburg, Germany, October 20: "Three German U-boat officers were sentenced to death by a military court today for killing eight survivors of the British freighter *Peleus*, torpedoed in the South Atlantic in March, 1944." They were, U-boat commander Heinz Eck, Lieutenant August Hoffman, and Naval Surgeon Walter Weissphennig."[585]

"IN THE SERVICE":

Sergeant Earl Scites, son of Mr. and Mrs. E. P. Scites of West Hamlin, has been discharged from the Army Air Forces at Baer Field, Ind. He was overseas for 19 months with the 477th Air Service Group.

Corporal Gerald Wright, husband of Mrs. Betty L. Wright, 812 Marcum Terrace, was promoted to that rank from private first class. He is stationed at Meeks Field in Iceland as a radio operator.

Sergeant Jeffe B. Simons, 2651 Guyan Avenue, notified his family yesterday that he is en route home from Paris, France, where he had been stationed for two years with the U.S. Engineers. He is the son of Mrs. Mary Simons, 14 Twenty-seventh Street.

Technical Sergeant Jack I. Supman, son of Mrs. Sadie Goldstein, 510 West Eleventh Street, has been discharged from the AAF at Cochran Field, Ga. He is a veteran of four years' service.

Private John W. Adkins, son of Mr. and Mrs. Larkin Adkins of Huntington, is stationed at Fort Benning, Ga. following his return after 11 months overseas service. As a medical technician he saw action with the Third and Ninth Armies in the Rhineland, Ardennes and Central Germany campaigns.

David C. Smith, aviation mechanic's mate second class, was discharged this week from the

Navy at Bainbridge, Md. He is the son of Mrs. Maude Smith, 2105 James River Road.

Lieutenant (j. g.) Carter Allen, son of Dr. James E. Allen, former president of Marshall College, has been assigned to shore duty at the Norfolk, Va., naval base after 23 months duty in the Pacific aboard the destroyer USS *McDonough*. His wife, the former Miss Helen Coley of Montgomery, W.Va., is with him at his new station.

Private First Class Elmo Gooch of Huntington has been awarded the Good Conduct Medal at Camp Knight, Oakland, Calif.

Seaman First Class Major W. Garnett, 22-year-old son of A. B. Garnett of Russell, Ky., has been transferred from Atlantic destroyer USS *Gearing* to a separation center for his discharge from the Navy...

Signalman Third Class J. L. Phipps, 2639 Collis Avenue, has arrived in Huntington to spend a 25-day leave with his parents, Mr. and Mrs. J. L. Phipps.

Augie E. Egnor, barber second class, is serving aboard the carrier USS *Manila* with the Third Fleet. The carrier is now based in Tokyo Bay. He is the son of Mr. and Mrs. A. M. Egnor, 414 Thirteenth Street.

Following discharge by the Navy at Seattle, Wash., Lionel D. Egnor, a brother [to Augie], has returned to Huntington. His wife and two sons have been residing at 4426 Route 60. Mr. Egnor served aboard the destroyer USS *Langfitt*, and was in action in both the Atlantic and Pacific.

Glenna: *October 21st Sunday – Dawson, Rupert, and I went to Stuart Hutchinson's and spent the day. We came home on the bus at six o'clock. It was a beautiful day. That night we went to Revival meeting. Sylvia Johnson was saved. Rupert, Sylvia, and Viola Morrison joined the church.*

Rupert: *We went to Billy and Dencils. I joined the church.*

Although I don't remember details about joining the church, I do remember my November baptism in the creek below the church.

The Hutchinsons lived on a working farm on Sixteenth Street Road, near Huntington. Russell Hutchinson, Billie and Dencil's uncle (albeit near their age), was with us as we explored the farm.

"WITH THE COLORS":

Private First Class Norman F. Bexfield, son of Mr. and Mrs. C. H. Bexfield of Overlook Drive, will arrive home this morning from Ft. Meade, Md... after 29 months service in Africa, Italy, France, and Germany, where he earned four campaign stars and 93 service points.

Technician Third Class Floyd L. Niday Jr., son of Mr. and Mrs. F. L. Niday, 541 Twenty-second Street ... will be home from Ft. Meade, Md. with an honorable discharge in a few days. He entered the Army April 19, 1943, and went overseas the following September to serve in Africa, Sicily, Italy, France and Germany with an intelligence unit of the Army Air Forces. He holds two battle stars for air combat of the Balkans and for the air offensive of Europe.

Sergeant Ray E. Scott was discharged this week from the Army Air Forces at Truax Field, Madison, Wis. He was in the service four years, spending 32 months in India with the Tenth Air Force.

Fire Controlman First Class Charles Raymond Miller, son of Mrs. R. C. Swan of Barboursville, W.Va., docked this week at Norfolk, Va. on the USS *Missouri*. He was aboard the *Missouri* during the surrender ceremonies. He ... served more than three years in the ETO and Pacific theatres. His wife resides in Baltimore, Md.

Private First Class James L. Mynes, son of Mrs. Lillian A. Mynes, 721 Tudell Street, has returned home with an honorable discharge from the U.S. Army. He ... served in England, Belgium, France and Germany. Private Mynes holds the Good Conduct Medal, American Defense Medal, ETO and ATO ribbons, two battle stars and the Combat Infantryman's Badge.

Fireman First Class Herbert Still Jr., son of Mrs. Gertrude Still, 2033 Ninth Avenue, arrived yesterday in San Francisco aboard the USS *Bonhomme Richard...* He will be met in San Francisco by his brother, Private First Class Jack C. Still, whom he has not seen in 28 months. Private Still served overseas 20 months with the Fifth Division in General Patton's Third Army...

Private James Bill Smith is due to arrive at Boston October 24 aboard the SS *James W. Fannin* after serving 40 months overseas...

Chief Warrant Officer Clarence F. Frizzell, husband of Mrs. Ann Call Frizzell of Ninth Street, arrived Saturday from Washington with an honorable discharge ... having been in the Navy since 1940 and having served two tours of overseas duty... His parents, Mr. and Mrs. E. H. Frizzell, reside at 1923 Monroe Avenue.

Captain Lawrence L. Brown, son of Mr. and Mrs. Albert C. Brown, 2912 Merrill Avenue, and husband of the former Miss Ruth A. Pickering, was released from active service at McClellan Field, Calif. Captain Brown was a member of the 430th Bomb Squadron and was awarded the Distinguished Flying Cross, the Air Medal with one cluster and three battle stars.

Mrs. W. F. Smith, 1655 Sixth Avenue, received the Bronze Medal and Citation posthumously awarded to her son, Private First Class Walter F. Smith Jr. in an award ceremony

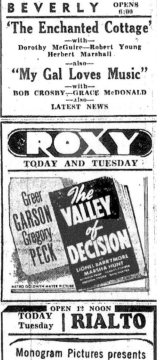

at Ashford General Hospital at White Sulphur Springs Wednesday. Private Smith, a member of the Tenth Mountain Infantry Regiment, went overseas last January. He was killed in an engagement in the Apennine Mountains.

Technician Fifth Grade Aryve Littleton, who served with the WAC for two and a half years, received a discharge at Fort Bragg, N.C. and is visiting Dr. and Mrs. Walter E. Vest of the South Side. The former WAC was with the station hospital at the Port of Embarkation at Charleston, S.C.

Air Cadet Charles Watters has arrived to spend a 17-day furlough with his parents, Mr. and Mrs. Hugh Watters, 2536 Collis Avenue. Cadet Watters has been stationed at Truax Field, Madison, Wis. since last January.

Flight Officer Frank D. McLaughlin has returned to Goose Bay Labrador after a familiarization trip to Paris, Belgium and Scotland with the Air Transport Command and a short furlough with his parents, Mr. and Mrs. J. T. McLaughlin, 5743 Pea Ridge Road. Flight Officer McLaughlin is stationed at Goose Bay as a part-time operational officer and as pilot of a C-47 flying cargo and personnel to various landing strips and weather stations in Labrador. A former Marshall College student, he enlisted in the AAF three years ago.

Corporal George Conway Eddins, son of Mr. and Mrs. George T. Eddins, 919 Ninth Street, has been transferred from Kelly Field, Tex. to Santa Ana Air Field, Santa Ana, Calif.

Master Sergeant George R. Phillips, husband of Mrs. Virginia Phillips, 809 Camden Road, has been liberated from a Japanese prisoner-of-war camp, according to the War Department list announced yesterday.

Glenna: *October 22nd Monday – Beautiful day. I washed and went to meeting that night.*

Brigadier General Armstead D. Mead Jr., son of Mrs. A. D. Mead, 5 Mortimer Place, was awarded the Distinguished Service Medal. The citation read, "General Mead's efforts contributed in great measure to the success of the Ninth Army in driving back and finally crushing large elements of the enemy's forces in Europe."[586]

"IN THE SERVICE":

Lieutenant John E. Anderson Jr., 2756 Emmons Avenue, has completed a tour of duty with 45 missions as pilot of a Navy Hellcat. Lieutenant Anderson was assigned to Fighter Squadron 87 aboard the Carrier *Ticonderoga*, which arrived in San Francisco harbor last week from the Pacific...

Machinist's Mate Second Class Karl Lee Stewart, husband of Mrs. Mary Stewart, 514 Jefferson Avenue, and son of Mr. and Mrs. C. L. Stewart, 1846 Sixth Avenue, has been discharged from the Navy after serving aboard the USS *Augusta* in the Atlantic for two years and on the USS *Hancock* in the Pacific for 18 months.

Boatswain's Mate Second Class James C. Duke of Huntington Route 2 served on the USS *Alaska* when the battle cruiser, as a part of a task force, sailed into Jinsen, Korea...

Seaman First Class John Hereford Saltsman, son of Mrs. Louise Pearl Saltsman, 313 Adams Avenue, has been serving aboard the heavy cruiser USS *Wichita*, now at Sasebo, Japan since December 7, 1943...

Fireman First Class Russell Allen Gwilliams, son of Mr. and Mrs. William Lloyd Gwilliams, 523 Smith Street, and Chief Warrant Officer Julius Richard Earl, 2911 Bradley Road, are serving together at Wakayama, Honshu, Japan.

Private Willa F. Mathews, daughter of Mr. and Mrs. Carol Mathews, Huntington Route 1, recently left Fort Des Moines, Iowa, for duty with the WAC at Letterman General Hospital in San Francisco.

First Sergeant Eugene F. LeMaster, 1644 Charleston Avenue, who for the past five years has been serving in the Army, was discharged from service Oct. 16.

Lieutenant Leon S. Wiles, 250 Roland Park drive, who served 44 months in the Navy, has been released from active duty.

Glenna: *October 23rd Tuesday – Rainy all day. I ironed and put flowers on Rupert's grave. Didn't go to church.*

Montreal, October 23: "The first Negro player ever to be admitted to organized baseball was signed tonight by the Brooklyn Dodgers for their International League farm club, the Montreal Royals. Jackie Robinson, one-time UCLA halfback ace and recent shortstop of the Kansas City Negro Monarchs, put his signature on a contract calling not only for a regular player's salary, but also for a bonus for signing."[587] In a related AP article by Gayle Talbot, Ricky Branch, Brooklyn Dodgers president ... is reported to have said, "I never meant to be a crusader, and I hope I won't be regarded as one. My purpose is to be fair to all people, and my selfish objective is to win baseball games."[588]

"IN THE SERVICE":

Miss Zeda Davis, a club director for the American Red Cross, has arrived at an air base in India, her mother, Mrs. J. H. Barbour, 534 Eighteenth Street, has been informed. Miss Davis served in India for two years and was in Huntington last June and July. She is a graduate of Central High School, attended Marshall

College, and taught in the Wayne County schools for nine years.

Corporal Ray Willoughby and his brother, Sergeant Morris Willoughby, sons of Mr. and Mrs. E. H. Willoughby, 1180 Norway Avenue, met recently on Luzon Island in the Philippines. It was their first meeting in four years.

Lieutenant Shirley Grace Greene, daughter of Mr. and Mrs. David Greene, 1035 ½ Ninth Avenue, has arrived in a West Coast city en route home. An Army dietitian, she was among the first 85 nurses to enter Japan...

Fireman First Class Arlie V. Pack, son of Mrs. Fern Pack, 20 Twenty-fourth Street, was serving aboard the troop transport USS *Sumpter* when the vessel landed occupation troops on Honshu Island, Japan.

Private First Class John S. Bellomy of Lesage has been discharged from the Army at Fort Rosecrans, Calif. following 35 months' service...

Discharged this week at Camp Atterbury, Ind. were Technician Fifth Grade William M. Hunt, Panther; Corporal Bethel D. Godby, Midkiff; Technical Sergeant Russell Warden, Huntington; Private Orval V. Cox, Point Pleasant; Sergeant Henry M. McCoy, Garretts Bend; Sergeant Max H. Homewood, Hurricane; Private William V. Christian, Yukon; Private First Class Archie H. White, Pecks Mill; Private First Class Earnest J. Adkins, Fort Gay; Technician Fourth Grade Harold F. Smith, 1824 Midway Avenue; Private First Class Lonnie R. Frye, Leet and Private [First] Class Leo Perry, Huntington.

Corporal Don A. Kapp has returned to his home at Hurricane following his release from the Army at Fort George G. Meade, Md. He is a veteran of 30 months' service in North Africa, Sicily, Italy and England.

Corporal William M. Marks Jr., 514 Bridge Street, has enrolled in the American Technical School at Warton, England, which is part of the Army education program. Corporal Marks, enrolled in a class of aircraft maintenance, is a member of the 142nd Infantry Division.

In their first meeting in three years, Sergeant Dewey Powell and Sergeant Robert Powell, sons of Mrs. Robert Powell of Kenova, were together recently in Manila.

Private First Class Bernard T. Tomlinson, son of Mrs. B. T. Tomlinson, 154 Cedar Street, has arrived in the Tokyo area as a member of the Army of Occupation. Private Tomlinson expects to enroll in college in Japan this fall.

Private James R. Deering, son of Mrs. Nettie Deering, 1526 Madison Avenue, has been discharged at Patterson Field, O. He served for 14 months in the Southwest Pacific as aerial gunner aboard a B-24 Liberator bomber and flew 64 combat missions.

Glenna: *October 24th Wed. – Cloudy all day. I went to revival meeting that night. Had a grand time. Dick Jenkins preached.*

Rupert: *I went to school and to church.*

The charter for the United Nations was ratified by its permanent members, United States, Britain, France, China, and the Soviet Union.[589]

"Diamond Dust": "There is no joy in Columbus, Ohio today. The Downtown coaches at Broad and High Streets are still punch-drunk from watching Bob De Moss peg passes to Billy Canfield. A week ago the O. S. fans were wishing Army was on the 'Bucks' schedule so its guys could claim the national title. Today they are more let down than an elevator jockey ... ; False or True: That H. C. (Twenty) Lantz has signed a 4-year contract at Huntington East High? Ans.—Just another rumor. Coaches, as well as teachers are only signed to 1-year contracts ... ; We don't claim to be football experts. In fact, we don't know from nothing. But we can't help but think that Notre Dame will lick either Army or Navy this Fall ... ; Jockey Eddie Arcaro says he may retire after this season. If I know my Eddie, he won't retire until he hears Gabriel blow that trumpet."[590]

"IN THE SERVICE":

Petty Officer Edmund L. Dickson, son of Mr. and Mrs. Walter Dickson, 207 Buffington Street, is spending a 35-day leave with his parents after 24 months of overseas service. He holds the Purple Heart, the European theatre ribbon, the Asiatic-Pacific ribbon and the American Defense ribbon.

Sergeant John Owens, son of Mr. and Mrs. J. L. Owens of Kenova, has been transferred to Korea from the Philippine Islands. He ... has been overseas 38 months.

Corporal Russell Meadows Leroy, son of Mrs. Hattie Fields, 604 Buffington Street, and Sergeant Wetzel C. Jobe, son of Mr. and Mrs. Fred Jobe of Salt rock will be discharged this week from the Army at Fort George G. Meade, Md. Corporal Leroy served overseas for 16 months with the AAF, and Sergeant Jobe served 14 months overseas with the AAF.

Carpenter's Mate John H. Singer, son of Mr. and Mrs. A. R. Singer, 6356 Aracoma Drive, was serving aboard the USS *Mifflin* when the transport landed occupation troops on southeastern Japan near the inland cities of Kobe and Osaka.

Gladys Lucille Watts, WAVES seaman first class, daughter of Mrs. Maggie Watts, 1436 Seventh Avenue, has been discharged by the Navy in Washington.

Corporal Merlin J. Roberts, 528 ½ First Street, has returned to his station with the 121st General Hospital at Bremen, Germany. He spent a seven-day furlough in Denmark, three days of which were in the capital, Copenhagen.

Corporal Paul B. Flaherty, son of Mrs. Katherine Flaherty, 1304 Tenth Avenue, has been discharged from the AAF at Andrews Field, D.C. A graduate of St. Joseph's High School, he entered service in 1943 and served overseas for 15 months as an aviation engineer.

Seaman First Class Betty J. Warlick, daughter of Mrs. Beulah Sinnock, 2499 Third Avenue, is being discharged from the WAVES at the Naval Air Technical Training Center at Memphis, Tenn. after two years' service. Her husband, Lieutenant (j. g.) Wilber W. Warlick, is stationed at Corpus Christi, Tex.

Master Sergeant James M. McQuinn, son of Mrs. Dollie B. McQuinn, 550 Second Street, is being discharged from the Army at Fort George G. Meade, Md. He ... served for 37 months overseas. He holds the European theatre ribbon with six campaign stars and the American Defense and Good Conduct ribbons...

Lieutenant (j. g.) Clarence E. Morrison, son of Mr. and Mrs. W. B. Morrison of Kenova, has been spending a leave with his parents prior to reporting to St. Mary's College, Calif., where he will instruct in meteorology.

Private Donald W. Kyle, grandson of Mrs. John Kyle, Ohio River Road, is spending a 30-day furlough with his grandmother prior to reporting to Camp Pickett, Va.

Seaman First Class Feely Frater of Hippo, Ky. and James R. Osborne of McDowell, Ky., veterans of 19 months on Pacific battlefronts, are among the sailors sightseeing in Tokyo and Yokohama. They are stationed aboard the USS *Benham*.

Seaman First Class O. C. Meade of Prestonsburg, Ky. returned to the United States from Tokyo aboard the battleship USS *Wisconsin*.

Glenna: *October 25th Thursday – Partly cloudy. Went to revival meeting that night.*

Rupert: *I went to church again.*

Dr. Robert Ley, Nazi Labor boss scheduled to go on trial for war crimes, committed suicide in his Nuremberg jail cell.[591]

"IN THE SERVICE":

Bill F. Williams, seaman second class, son of Mr. and Mrs. R. C. Williams, 3618 Piedmont Road, is serving aboard the transport USS *Henrico* in the South Pacific area. Seaman Williams is a graduate of Vinson High School and has been overseas since late August. His brother, Private Holly Williams is serving with the Army in the Philippine Islands.

Lieutenant Tom True, 724 Twelfth Avenue, husband of the former Miss Hazel Sergeant, has been released from active duty with the Army and is spending his terminal leave at his home. Lieutenant True entered service in January, 1941 and served overseas for 32 months with the 13th Air Force in the South Pacific. He participated in the invasion of New Georgia Island in the Solomons group.

Technician Fifth Grade Jesse B. Maynard, son of Mr. and Mrs. J. T. Maynard, 234 Staunton Street, is spending an 82-day furlough at the home of his parents following his return from overseas service with the Seventh and Third Armies in Europe.

John Bates, formerly coach at the Chesapeake, O. High School, is serving aboard the cargo vessel USS *Towner*, now stationed in the Japanese home waters...

Coxswain Keith Kearns, son of Mr. and Mrs. L. H. Kearns of Huntington, has reported to his new station at Miami, Fla. following a 30-day leave at his home. Coxswain Kearns served aboard the USS *Argonne* in the Pacific for two years.

After serving in Europe for 18 months, Lieutenant Colonel Harry C. Brindle, who commanded a cavalry squadron of the Sixth Armored Division of the Third Army through five campaigns in Europe, is spending a 30-day leave with his wife, the former Miss Sara Gibson, and three children at 1570 Washington Boulevard. Lieutenant Colonel Brindle wears the Silver Star, the Bronze Star Medal and the French Croix de Guerre.

Technical Sergeant Harry D. Turner, son of Mrs. Ethel Turner, 4410 Auburn Road, was discharged this week from the AAF at Hunter Field, Savannah, Ga. Sergeant Turner had served with the 455th Bomb Group in Italy.

Corporal Carl D. Thacker of Chesapeake, O. was discharged last week from the AAF at drew Field, Fla. He served 28 months overseas with an engineer company. He is the son of Noah Thacker and the husband of Mrs. Fleeta Thacker of Chesapeake.

Sergeant Kenneth Jordan, husband of Mrs. Helen Jordan, 2906 Eighth Avenue, has been awarded the Bronze Star Medal for meritorious service in the Philippines. Sergeant Jordan is a member of the 383rd antiaircraft artillery battalion and has been overseas for 23 months.

Private First Class James C. Fannin of Ashland will return to the United States soon with the 31st "Dixie" Division ... He has been overseas since March, 1944, and has participated in the campaigns of Dutch New Guinea, the Netherlands East Indies and the Philippines. He is the husband of Mrs. Rosalie Fannin, 1229 Eighth Street, and the son of Mrs. J. T. Fannin of Ashland.

Walter K. Cooper, watertender second class, 2615 Adams Avenue, was serving aboard the destroyer USS *Melvin* when the vessel accompanied the North Pacific Force in the occupation of Northern Japan...

Donald F. Nossett, aviation machinist's mate second class, 2524 Fourth Avenue, was aboard the USS *Matanikau*, an escort carrier, when the vessel entered Ominato Harbor on Honshu as part of the occupation force.

Gunner's Mate Second Class James B. Bias, 1345 Jackson Avenue, was serving aboard the attack transport *Hampton* when the vessel landed occupation troops on the beaches of Aomori, in Northern Japan.

Walter S. Montague, chief motor machinist's mate, 811 West Eleventh Street, is aboard the transport *Fillmore*, en route to San Francisco...

Ship's Cook Third Class Major V. Long of Guyandotte was serving aboard the LST *838* when the vessel unloaded men and equipment at Yokohama Naval Base for the Army of Occupation.

Seaman First Class William S. Hamlin, 439 Smith Street, was serving on the minesweeper *Diploma* when it helped clear mines from the Tsugaru Straits...

Lieutenant Commander William L. Neal, son of Dr. and Mrs. W. E. Neal, 611 Fifth Street, has recently been promoted to that rank ... at the U.S. Naval Hospital, Long Beach, Calif., where he has been a member of the medical staff for the past year.

Staff Sergeant E. W. Wingfield, son of Mr. and Mrs. H. M. Wingfield, 808 ½ Thirteenth Street, is expected home next week... He has served for nine months in the Philippines...

Private Howard A. Neff of Huntington was discharged this week from the AAF at Patterson Field, Ohio. Private Neff has been stationed at the Marianna Army Air Base, Fla. prior to receiving his discharge and was engaged in combat crew training in the A-26 "Invader," a light bomber.

First Lieutenant James R. Green, son of Mr. and Mrs. W. A. Green, 1417 Sixth Avenue, was released from active duty this week by the AAF at Drew Field, Fla. He served overseas for 10 months with the 57th Fighter Group and completed 87 missions before returning to the United States in August of this year. He holds the Distinguished Flying Cross and the Air Medal with three Oak Leaf Clusters.

Glenna: *October 26th Friday – Beautiful day. I cleaned everything. Went to Revival meeting.*

Rupert: *I went to school. We started the red cross.*

In a preliminary to Saturday's Navy Day celebration, more than 1,500 youngsters inspected the *LSM 110*, moored at the foot of Tenth Street in Huntington.[592]

"IN THE SERVICE":

Private First Class Harrison Mitchell, son of Mr. and Mrs. Stanley Mitchell of Parkersburg, formerly of Huntington, is recuperating at Newton D. Baker Hospital at Martinsburg, W.Va., following his release recently after three years and five months in a Japanese prison camp. En route home he met a brother, Corporal John Mitchell, who was stationed in the Philippines. They are grandsons of Mrs. C. J. Mitchell, 1617 Sixth Avenue.

Lieutenant Commander Harry Scherr Jr., 1655 Fifth Avenue, has been released from duty on the USS *Las Vegas* in the Marshall Islands and expects to return to the United States and be released from active duty by December, according to his parents, Mr. and Mrs. Harry Scherr Sr.

Lieutenant James F. Via, son of Mr. and Mrs. William A. Via, 1539 Madison Avenue, has been released from active duty with the Army at Fort George G. Meade, Md.

Casto E. Granville of Huntington has been discharged from the Army at Fort Sill, Okla. after 47 months service. He is a veteran of 21 months overseas service.

Flight Officer Clarence S. Nelson Jr., son of Mr. and Mrs. Clarence S. Nelson, 2768 Emmons Avenue, has arrived in Karachi, India, en route to his new station in China. Pilot of a C-47 transport, he was a student at Marshall College before entering the service in April, 1943.

Corporal Louie A. Hughes, 4747 Bradley Road, was recently advanced to that rank ... at Camp Croft, S.C. He is a veteran of the European theatre and holds the ETO ribbon with three stars and the Combat Infantryman Badge. A brother, Corporal William E. Hughes, is with the Army of Occupation in Korea.

Private First Class Ted Johnson, son of Mrs. J. I. Wiley, 800 Jefferson Avenue, is stationed in Berlin with the 82nd Airborne Division, now doing guard duty. Private Johnson participated in the airborne bridgehead on the Rhine River and in the Ardennes campaign. He wears the ETO ribbon with five stars, the Combat

Infantryman Badge, the Distinguished Unit Citation and an invasion Bronze Arrowhead.

... Marine Sergeant Amos L. Ratcliffe, son of Mrs. Laura Ratcliffe of Huntington, has received a letter of commendation from Major General G. B. Erskine. The presentation was made by Colonel William C. Hall at the Philadelphia, Pa. Navy Yard. Sergeant Ratcliffe, a marine for five years, was a member of the Third Division and a veteran of Guam and Iwo Jima. He also served in Iceland.

Sergeant Clyde A. Holston, 4340 Riverside Drive, Technician Fifth Grade Sherman Copley, Crum, and Corporal Charles B. Jameson, 1906 Third Avenue, were released this week from the Army at Camp Atterbury, Ind.

Staff Sergeant Jack Henderson, son of Mr. and Mrs. John Henderson, 620 Thirteenth Street, arrived home this week for a visit with his parents before re-enlisting. He received his discharge October 20 after returning to the United States October 9 from the South Pacific where he participated in the campaigns of New Guinea and the Philippines. Sergeant Henderson, a veteran of 12 months service overseas duty, originally enlisted in November, 1939.

Staff Sergeant Frank E. Ball, son of Mr. and Mrs. K. G. Ball of Sharples and Private First Class Donald R. James, son of Heber C. James of Hartford, have returned to the United States. They were members of the 19th "Victory"Division in the Philippines.

Seaman Second Class William Chapman, son of Mrs. Lucy C. Belengee of Huntington, is on sea duty following his transfer from his California Station.

Marine Private First Class Charles E. Kautz of Huntington will participate in Navy Day ceremonies tomorrow aboard the carrier *Wasp*, now in an East Coast port. Private Kautz pursued the carrier from the Yokosuka Naval Base on Honshu Island to Pearl Harbor in order to rejoin it for the return to the United States.

Corporal William E. Steele of Barboursville was discharged this week from the Army at Maxwell Field, Ala., after almost three years' service...

Glenna: *October 27th Saturday – Big frost. Real cold. Rupert went to town and got a new coat. Went to church that night. Cline Porter was saved. Had a grand time.*

Rupert: *I went to town and got a coat. It cost $11.17.*

It appears I could choose some of my own clothing. I remember, vaguely, a "coat of many colors."

Cline Porter and his family lived on Madison Road by the river. Porter land, settled by Patrick Porter late in the eighteenth century, once covered a wide area from the river all the way west to the ridge that divides the Guyan Valley from Smith Creek. The original homestead cabin was located where Salt Rock Elementary School now sits. Four Porter brothers, John, Gilbert, Cline, and Jaruel, descendants of Patrick, still lived on land that had belonged to their forefathers. The farm owned by my grandfather, Lucian Adkins, which we now farmed, had been part of the Porter property. Grandpa purchased it from a widow of an earlier generation. The Cabell County Board of Education, by the law of eminent domain, took part of Grandpa's land in 1938 for the school.

Lyles Branch and Buckhorn Creek were named for slaves whose cabins sat on their banks. Below my boyhood home and garden was a square plot of ground Mother said was a slave graveyard. There were no markers, but she knew some of the names. If I had had any sense of history I would have recorded those names. I do remember three—"Peggy," "Lyle," and "Buckhorn."

As an aside, I eventually became owner of most of my grandfather's property through inheritance and purchase from other family members. Mother died in 1978, and in 1979

I sold a small section of bottom land that included our two houses and the entire hill to Michael Porter, Cline Porter's son. I sold the rest in 1997 to a developer who subdivided it. The bottom land now contains houses, a post office, and a public library.

Navy Day observations "ranged from a presidential review in New York to a free beer party in London as tribute was paid to the men and ships who downed the Japanese."[593]

"IN THE SERVICE":

After serving for 18 months in the Pacific and spending an eighteen-day leave with his parents, Mr. and Mrs. D. W. Lemon, 2946 Seventh Avenue, Seaman First Class Harvey L. Lemon will return to his ship, the USS *Storm King* at Oakland Calif., on November 1... He wears the American theatre ribbon, the Asiatic-Pacific ribbon with four battle stars, the Philippine liberation ribbon with two stars and the Victory Medal.

Captain Andrew D'Antoni of Mullens, former football star at Marshall College, visited friends here yesterday following his return from Europe, where he had been on detached duty with the Air Forces for three months...

Yeoman First Class Jack H. Painter, 1051 Fourteenth Street, recently piloted the first U.S. Navy men to travel the Chinese Yangtze and Whangpoo Rivers in eight years.

Coxswain William K. Terry, son of Mr. and Mrs. Victor Terry, 1841 Buffington Avenue, has been transferred from the USS *Indiana* to a shore station for discharge.

Corporal John R. Ballangee, son of Mr. and Mrs. J. O. Ballangee, 1544 Washington Avenue, has been discharged from the AAF at Lowry Field at Denver. He is the husband of Mrs. Mayme F. Ballangee, 1692 Wiltshire Boulevard.

Discharged from the Army at Fort Knox, Ky. were Technician Third Grade Henry G. Satterwhite, 1940 Military Road; Private

First Class Linzie Vance and Private Harry M. Mathews, Mount Gay; Private Hobert W. McComas, Ona, and Technician Fifth Grade Paul S. Henderson, Panther.

Hospital Apprentice First Class Richard L. Hamilton recently attained his present grade as an honor student from Cal. Naval Hospital Corps School. He has returned to San Diego after spending a 30-day leave with his parents, Mr. and Mrs. A. C. Hamilton, 422 Thirteenth Street. His brother, Chief Specialist John W. Hamilton is expected home soon from service with the Navy in the South Pacific.

Radioman Third Class Hansford J. Patterson of Huntington was promoted to that grade ... at his station at Floyd Bennett Field, N.Y.

Discharged this week from the Navy at Bainbridge, Md. were Gunner's Mate Second Class Charles E. Frye, Wayne; Seaman Second Class Charles B. Ferguson, 410 Twenty-second Street; Gunner's Mate First Class Norman E. Holderby, 2752 Fifth Avenue; Seaman Third Class Jack P. Dillon, 606 Marcum Terrace and Seaman First Class Joseph C. Bias, Salt Rock.

Glenna: *October 28th Sunday – Went to church. Had a grand time. Later a baptizing. Cline Porter, Viola Morrison, and Sylvia Johnson were baptized. All the children of Jaruel and Cline Porter were sprinkled. Went to Revival that night. Beautiful day.*

Immersion baptisms in our area took place in the river and streams without allowances for the season. Normally, whole congregations would witness the event. I still hear in my mind's ear the hymn, "Shall We Gather at the River."

Rupert: *I went to church. Larry came and stayed all day.*

Huntington had celebrated Navy Day. "A colorful parade of bands and uniformed organizations formed in Government Square at 11

A.M. to march through the downtown streets as an opening to the main event of the day at the scene of the LSM at the Tenth Street pier." The parade, with American Legion Post 16 in charge and led off by a Marine Corp marching band, had Robert O. Ellis [Naval flyer, later to become mayor of Huntington] as parade marshal. Area high school bands taking part were: Huntington East, Central, Vinson, Douglas, Dunbar, Barboursville, Milton, Ceredo-Kenova, Wayne, and Buffalo. Also participating were the bands of the State Guard and Salvation Army. Other organizations taking part were the Veterans of Foreign Wars, Navy Mothers, State Guard Regiment, and the Junior Chamber of Commerce. Army trucks, motorized equipment, and the city's fire engines were in the line of march. "The parade closed when the bands assembled on the river bank at Tenth Street to play 'Anchors Aweigh,' opening formal ceremonies aboard *LSM 110*."[594]

Glenna: *Monday October 29th – Beautiful day. I washed. Went to church that night. Elmer Indicott and wife Frances were saved.*

Rupert: *I went to school. I went to church.*

Civil war in China looked like a possibility: Communist forces had rejected a Central Government compromise and wide-spread fighting had broken out between government and Communist troops.[595]

"IN THE SERVICE":

Sergeant Henderson Ferguson, son of Mr. and Mrs. J. M. Ferguson of Wilsondale, was recently promoted to that grade from corporal at his station with the Air Transport Command at Manila. His wife resides at Chesapeake, Ohio.

Corporal Millard G. Rorrer, 851 Bronson Court, will be discharged this week from the Army at Seymour Field, N.C...

Sergeant John E. Jenkins Jr., son of J. E. Jenkins of the Park Terrace Apartments, was promoted to that grade from corporal at his station in the Canal Zone with the 153rd Army Airways Communication System Squadron.

Corporal Willard L. Wells of Huntington has been discharged from the AAF at Drew Field, Fla.

Corporal Warren D. Ray, brother of Mrs. Clyde Chapman, 85 Twenty-seventh Street, has been discharged from the Army at Drew Field, Fla.

Sergeant Campbell J. Hage, 1107 Tenth Avenue, was discharged last week from the Army at Fort Sill, Okla. He is the husband of Mrs. Martha Hage of Huntington.

Discharged from the Navy at Bainbridge, Md., were Fireman Second Class Hilbert L. Harrison, 2130 Madison Avenue; Fireman Second Class James P. Boley, 3431 Bradley Road; Ship's Cook Second Class George A. Baise Jr., 1333 West Fifth Avenue; Pharmacist's Mate Second Class Moses S. Adkins of Huntington, and Seaman First Class Richard B. Kinkhead, 923 Twenty-second Street.

Staff Sergeant Clifford C. Stevens, son of Mrs. Marie Stevens, 1011 ½ Sixth Avenue has been discharged from the AAF at Patterson Field, Ohio.

Sergeant William S. Smith of Huntington is en route home from Tokyo where he was stationed with the First Calvalry Division, Fifth Regiment, as a machinegun squad leader. He is a veteran of four campaigns in his 20 months overseas. He is the son of William M. Smith of Huntington.

Discharged from the WAVES in Washington were Lieutenant (j. g.) Jean Johnson Slutz, 1236 Fifth Avenue; Mailman Second Class LaNora Wylie Bell, 524 Eleventh Street, and Yeoman First Class Catherine Riley Costa, Braeholm.

Discharged last week from the Army at Camp Atterbury, Ind. were Private First Class Abe J. Hage, 1628 Seventh Avenue; Technician Fifth Grade Reth Long, Midkiff; Master Sergeant Conrad L. Davis, Mason; Private First

Class Hershell A. Martin, Sharples; Private Enoch J. Dailey, Milton; Private First Class Donald R. Byrd, Hurricane, and Staff Sergeant Marion E. Thackston, 2916 Staunton Road.

Glenna: *October 30th Tuesday – Beautiful day. I ironed. Went to revival that night. Elmer Sergeant was saved and joined the church.*

Rupert: *I went to school. We went to church tonight.*

"IN THE SERVICE":

Sergeant Marion E. Thackston, son of Mr. and Mrs. Marion Thackston, 2916 Staunton Road, has returned home following his discharge by the AAF at Camp Atterbury, Ind. Sergeant Thackston received a wound in his thigh during a bombing mission over Shanghai in July and was forced to bail out when his B-24 Liberator bomber was badly damaged, Chinese guerillas aided his escape from capture by Japanese.

Motor Machinist's Mate Second Class Charles E. Young, 1933 Seventh Avenue, is spending a 30-day leave with his parents after 25 months duty in the South Pacific.

Calvin Porter, a former sergeant with the AAF, has been discharged after six years of service. He saw action in North Africa with the 1085th Engineer company. His wife is the former Miss Catherine Bailey of Packsville.

Lieutenant John J. Bates, USNR, former physical education instructor at Milton High School, is serving aboard the USS *Towner,* en route to China. He is the husband of Mrs. Ruth Bates, 1889 Marshall Avenue.

Technical Sergeant Dana A. Sidebottom, son of Mr. and Mrs. J. R. Sidebottom of West

Hamlin, has been discharged after more than five years' service. He served for 10 months overseas with the 39th Aviation Engineer Squadron.

Anna Belle Hopkins, daughter of Mr. and Mrs. H. F. Chapman, 1324 Madison Avenue, has been discharged from the WAVES in Washington... Her husband, Cagle T. Hopkins, resides at Lake Worth, Fla.

Lieutenant George I. Neal Jr. summoned home by the serious illness of his father, Colonel George I. Neal, 1112 Sixth Avenue, will arrive home today from Camp Kilmer, N.J. He landed at an East Coast port yesterday.

William Thomas Bennett, 2539 Third Avenue, has been promoted to the rating of aviation metalsmith first class at Quonset, R.I.

Private Frank L. Legge of Guyandotte has been discharged from the Army at Camp Livingston, La.

Glenna: *October 31st Wed. – Beautiful day. I didn't work. Went to revival meeting. No one saved.*

Rupert: *I went to school. We went to church*

Four thousand Greyhound Bus Line workers were on strike. Last minute attempts at a settlement had failed.[596]

"IN THE SERVICE":

Coxswain Third Class Harley Kelson Black, son of Mr. and Mrs. John F. Black of Milton, will report today in Boston for a discharge after serving in the Navy since 1943. He has been visiting his parents and wife, Mrs. Dorothy Black, for 35 days. Coxswain Black served for 21 ½ months in the Pacific as a gunner on a PT boat...

Corporal Cyrus V. Young Jr., 24, of South Charleston, nephew of S. H. Young, 213 Tenth Avenue, has arrived at Ashford General

Hospital at White Sulphur Springs, W.Va. for rest and treatment following 40 months internment by the Japs in the Philippines.

Lieutenant Charles B. Hedrick, son of Professor and Mrs. C. E. Hedrick, 1671 Fifth Avenue, has arrived in Huntington [from the South Pacific] to visit his wife, the former Miss Mary Jo Locke.

The following men recently received Navy discharges at Bainbridge, Md.: Quartermaster First Class Robert G. Russell, 2204 ½ Marcum Terrace; Machinist's Mate Third Class Thomas A. Alliff, 1447 Eleventh Avenue; Radioman Third Class Venable W. Patterson, 839 Seventh Avenue, and Machinist's Mate Second Class Clifford Clay, 411 West Fourteenth Street.

Private First Class Arlynn "Pete" Wilcox, son of Mrs. Peggy Wilcox of McVeigh Avenue and Arlynn Wilcox of Merrill Avenue, is expected home soon after serving for 33 months in the Pacific in the AAF Engineers. His brother, Donald "Boots" Wilcox, is near Tokyo with an infantry regiment.

Master Sergeant Charles H. Buxton, husband of Dorothy Buxton, 328 Washington Avenue, has been discharged from the Army at Torney General Hospital, Palm Springs, Calif.

Private First Class Herman McQue, 2105 Seventh Avenue, and Staff Sergeant Edward V. Lee, son of Mr. and Mrs. L. E. Lee, 3010 Augurn Road, recently were discharged at Patterson Field, Ohio.

Charles W. Gibbs Jr. of Huntington, a field engineer for the Radio Corp. of America, has arrived on the West Coast from the South Pacific. He is a former radio engineer for WSAZ in Huntington and WCHS in Charleston.

Captain Larry Kinsey, former terminal manager for the O-K Trucking Co. here, arrived yesterday on terminal leave with the Army Corps of Engineers in Europe.

November

FLU, MONOPOLY

Rupert: *I went to school. We got ready for the social.*

The "social" was a school money-raising event that featured booths in classrooms and hallway for sale of food and novelty items. There were also games of chance and skill, raffles, and auctions throughout the evening. Children helped decorate the booths and install decorations and signs. Socials were well-attended.

"IN THE SERVICE":

Technical Sergeant Joe Levitsky, husband of Mrs. Mabel B. Levitsky, 628 Twentieth Street, has received a discharge from the Army at Indiantown Gap, Pa.

Chief Electrician William E. Graham of Charleston, cousin of Mrs. J. A. Green, 1610 Charleston Avenue, has returned to this country from the Pacific.

Gunner's Mate Second Class Charles W. Green arrived Wednesday to visit his uncle and aunt, Mr. and Mrs. E. S. Moyer, 705 Eighth Avenue, and will leave Sunday for Washington, D.C. He served with the Navy in China and India.

Motor Machinist's Mate Second Class Leonard J. Love, husband of Mrs. Mary Dawson Love, Rosalind Road, has returned to his submarine, the USS *Cobra*, at Staten Island, N.Y. after a visit here.

The following men have received discharges from the Army at Fort Knox, Ky.; Private First Class James I. Sparks, Staff Sergeant Jont Cornett, and Private First Class Melvin Riley, all of Harlan; Technician Fourth Grade Warren R. Martin, 424 California Street; Corporal Morton V. Smith, Mayberry, and Technician Fifth Grade Orville W. Adkins, Ranger.

Corporal Floyd Haynes, son of John M. Haynes, and Corporal John G. Edwards, husband of Mrs. Mary E. Edwards, 1839 Tenth Avenue, have been discharged from the Army at Patterson Field, O.

Second Lieutenant Charles A. Scrivner, son of Mrs. C. G. Serivner, 1737 Sixth Avenue, has been honorably discharged from the Army Air Forces at Barksdale Field, La.

Private First Class Reva Lee Courts, daughter of Mr. and Mrs. Lonnie E. Turley, Hamlin, has been promoted to corporal at Pine Bluff, Ark.

Hospital Apprentice First Class Betty Jane Follrod, 124 Sycamore Street, has been discharged from the WAVES in Washington.

Private First Class Robert V. Bolling, 824 Washington Avenue, has been discharged from the Army at Camp Lee, Va.

Three Huntington men who took part in the San Francisco Navy Day celebration aboard the new Battleship *Indiana* were seaman Second Class Charles B. Ferguson, 410 Twenty-second

Street; Coxswain William K. Terry, 1841 Buffington Avenue and Boilermaker Third Class Kenneth R. Smith, 1624 Seventh Avenue.

The following men have been discharged from the Navy at Bainbridge, Md.: Henry H. Reeder, Rear 831 Ninth Avenue; Clarence Hiram Allen, Rear 1133 Eighth Avenue; Lloyd Allen Hamilton, 516 Twenty-seventh Street; Morgan Wilkins Cochran, 1123 Madison Avenue; Jimmie Warren Spurlock, 1606 Thirteenth Avenue, and Robert C. McCoy, Huntington Route 4.

Glenna: *November 2nd Friday – My birthday. I am 38 today. Rain and bad [weather]. I went to revival meeting in rain, later to social at the school house. Had a nice time.*

Rupert: *I went to the social. I spent $1.50.*

Tokyo, November 2: "Three suspected executioners of Doolittle fliers and the head of Japan's Gestapo were jailed today in a day which also saw General MacArthur freeze security transactions of the 15 greatest financial houses in the empire."[597]

"IN THE SERVICE":

Private First Class Sam H. Wheeler Jr., son of Mr. and Mrs. S. H. Wheeler of Glen View, is stationed in Linz, Austria with the 79th Fighter Group of the Ninth Air Force. Private Wheeler has almost two years overseas duty behind him, and formerly served with the 85th Infantry Division at Cassino.

Sergeant John Mandt Jr., son of Mrs. Sallie Payne Mandt, 501 Fifth Avenue, was discharged this week from the Army at Bowman Field, Ky. A veteran of 45 months in service, he served overseas for 27 months.

Coxswain John T. Waters, 2941 Piedmont Road, was discharged this week from the Coast Guard at St. Louis, Mo.

Technical Sergeant George H. Carter, husband of Mrs. Velma K. Carter, 1522 Washington Avenue, has been transferred to the 26th Division at Linz, Austria to await return to the United States. He is a veteran of two years overseas service.

Commander Kenneth Heyl, USNR, son of Mr. and Mrs. D. W. Heyl, 448 Sixth Avenue, was recently promoted to that rank from lieutenant commander... Heyl is stationed at Norfolk, Va., as head of the Fifth Naval District Rehabilitation program for Maryland, Virginia, West Virginia and North Carolina.

Sergeant Maxie Webb, son of Mr. and Mrs. Carnie Webb of Fort Gay, has arrived at Drew Field, Fla. for separation from the Army.

Discharged this week from the Navy at Bainbridge, Md. were Earl J. Harper, 745 Jefferson Avenue, and James A. Freeman, 1528 Washington Avenue.

Fireman Second Class Darrell F. Smith, 1032 Seventh Street, is serving aboard the destroyer *Landsowne*, now in Japanese waters.

Seaman First Class Earl E. Burks, son of Mr. and Mrs. Lon Burks of Barboursville, has been discharged from the Navy at Bainbridge, Md. His brother, Harry, also with the Navy, is home on a 21-day leave. They met while their ships were in Tokyo Bay.

Corporal James H. Ramey, son of Mr. and Mrs. Fred Ramey, 133 Eighth Avenue, has been discharged from the Army at Will Rogers Field, Okla.

Private Charles E. Smith, son of Mrs. Garnett [Elsewhere listed as "Georgia"] Smith, 325 West Ninth Street, has been discharged from the Army. He is the husband of the former Miss Dorothy Porter of Huntington and Detroit.

Second Lieutenant James E. Morrison Jr., son of Mr. and Mrs. J. E. Morrison, 1305 Eighth Avenue, recently received his commission at the Officer Candidate School at Fort Benning, Ga. He is a graduate of Central High School and attended Ohio State University before entering the Army in October, 1944.

Private First Class Ecopra Hale of Holden has been discharged from the AAF at Hill Field, Utah. He is the son of Mrs. Ginny Hale of Holden.

Seaman First Class William H. Hastings, son of Mr. and Mrs. T. Hastings, 613 South Terrace, is spending a 30-day leave with his parents. He is a veteran of 16 months' service on Hawaii.

Discharged this week from the Army at Fort Knox, Ky. were Private Herman H. Phillips, 215 Twentieth Street; Private Alvery Adkins, Ranger; Staff Sergeant Cecil W. Estep, Salt Rock; Private First Class Troy Hatfield, Wharncliffe, and Technician Fifth grade Clarence W. Cassell, Yolyn.

Glenna: *November 3rd Sat. – Cool all day. Stayed at home. At night we went to revival meeting. Elija [Elijah] Stevens came down and helped out. No one saved. Revival ended. It has been a grand meeting.*

Rupert: *Larry came over. We played Monopoly.*

My Monopoly set was Aunt Gaynelle's gift from the previous Christmas. Larry had taken to it and wanted to play every time he visited. His better organized strategies gave him the edge. Larry eventually became CEO of a company in Ohio and later started and managed his own businesses. We talked about those Monopoly games at our high school class reunions. Larry died in 2017. I would gladly sit down again with him for another shellacking.

Glenna: *November 4th Sunday – Went to Sunday School and church. Had a new speaker. Rev. Lombardy and wife were there. Rev. Lombardy spoke on "Moses and the Burning Bush." At 2:30 in the evening*

a baptismal service was held and Rupert Carroll, Elmer Indicott and wife Frances were baptized. Roy Midkiff brought us home.

Rupert: *I was babatised today. [Photo below]*

The baptism by the Reverend Horace Midkiff, and assisted by Jaruel Porter, took place near the mouth of Tyler Creek where it flows into the Guyandotte. The water was cold and I was pampered afterward. Even at twelve, the event was a powerful one for me.

The Tri-State is known for its glass products. Blenko Glass at Milton is one of the best-known. Two new glass plants, the Huntington Glass Manufacturing Company and the James G. Gill Glass Company were under construction in Ceredo and Kenova.[598]

"WITH THE COLORS":

A veteran of 18 months overseas, Corporal James T. Ball of Huntington is on his way home from Germany to spend a 90-day furlough in the United States. A member of the Ninth Air Defense Command, Corporal Ball has enlisted in the regular Army and will return to his old station in Germany upon completion of his furlough.

Staff Sergeant Fisher Watts who has served seven months in the European Theatre and who was awarded the Air Medal, the ETO Ribbon with three battle stars and the Distinguished Unit Citation Badge, was recently discharged from the AAF at Patterson Field, O. He is the son of Mrs. Vicie A. Watts, 1909 Jefferson Avenue.

Ship's Service Mate (Third Class) Wesley Simmons was recently discharged from the Navy at Bainbridge, Md. He is the son of Mr. and Mrs. Ollie Simmons, 2664 Harvey Road.

A veteran of 20 months with the North Atlantic Division of the ATC on Newfoundland, Technical Sergeant William K. Harrah, husband of Mrs. William K. Harrah, 1600 Charleston Avenue, has been honorably discharged from the AAF. He is the son of Mrs. Ola M. Harrah of 1246 Fifth Avenue.

Private Noah F. Keller, a member of the Fourth Air Force, has been discharged from the AAF at Patterson Field, O. He served in the African, Sicilian, Italian and Southern France campaigns, He is the son of Mrs. Nannie Keller of Sixteenth Street Road.

Seaman (First Class) Raymon C. Hitchcock served aboard the destroyer *Waller*, when that ship aided in the disarming of Jap soldiers on the isolated islands off the China coast. His home is at 808 Twelfth Street.

Chief Pharmacist's Mate Robert H. Biagi, 616 Fourth Street and Seaman (Second Class) Thomas H. Rice Jr., 1208 Third Avenue, are serving on the aircraft carrier USS *Hancock* now in a United States port after 10 months in the battle zones.

Seaman (First Class) W. D. Fought is serving with the Navy Supply Corps in The Marshall Islands, where he has been for several months on Kwajalein. (His aunt is Mrs. Sadie Hector, 2421 Third Avenue.)

Private James H. Worden, son of Mr. and Mrs. C. A. Worden of 2609 ½ Eighth Avenue ... has reported at Camp Blackstone, W.Va. From there he expects to go overseas...

Ship's Barber Lance Chapman, son of Mr. and Mrs. Aubrey Chapman of Barboursville, has returned to his ship after spending a 30-day leave with his wife and son, Lance Allen. He is stationed aboard the USS *Stanly*.

Glenna: *November 5th Monday – Beautiful day. I washed.*

Rupert: *I went to school today. It was a pretty day.*

"IN THE SERVICE":

Charles H. Smith, husband of Mrs. Vivian Smith of West Ceredo, has been discharged from the Navy at Bainbridge, Md.

First Lieutenant Chancey W. Caldwell, 648 Eighth Avenue, will revert to inactive status December 25 at Camp Croft, S.C.

Sergeant Maxie Webb, Fort Gay, has been released from the Army at Drew Field, Fla.

Watertender Third Class Lewis Marion Wamsley, 1700 Marcum Terrace, and Seaman Second Class Roy B. Draper of Caretta have been discharged from the Navy at Nashville, Tenn.

Private Roy M. Roy, brother of Mrs. Mona Swanson of Huntington, is a section leader with the 187th Company of the Fifth Replacement Depot, a unit of the Replacement Command, AFWESPAC at Manila. Of his brothers, Ray is in the paratroopers, Wilburn is in the glider troops, and Glen is in the infantry. Private Roy went overseas with Private Junior James of Huntington.

Staff Sergeant Ira H. Markham, 1618 Sixteenth Street, a member of the 755th Railway Shop Battalion, recently received the Bronze Star Medal in Europe.

Technical Sergeant John D. Ross, husband of Mrs. Edna Ross of Catlettsburg and Technical Sergeant Ernest C. Nicolls, son of Mrs. Albert Nicolls of Salt Rock, have been discharged from the AAF at Patterson Field, O.

Second Lieutenant George A. Cline of Huntington has been granted terminal leave from the Army at Camp Butner, N.C.

Private First Class James M. Stark, 1318 ½ Fourth Avenue, has been discharged from the Army at Fort Knox, Ky.

First Lieutenant Martha Ann Purtell, daughter of Mr. and Mrs. Michael J. Purtell, 1613 Montgomery Avenue, Ashland, has been awarded the Bronze Star Medal for meritorious achievement against the enemy in New Guinea. First Lieutenant Purtell is serving with the Army Nurses Corps on Luzon. After graduation from the nursing school at St. Mary's Hospital, Rochester, Minn., Lieut. Purtell was on the nursing staff at St Mary's Hospital in Huntington for two years.

Fireman Second Class Gene A. Cobb, son of Mr. and Mrs. Thomas D. Cobb Sr., 4176 Four Pole Road, is home on leave from Great Lakes Naval Training Station.

Technician Third Grade Howard S. Peters of Huntington is attending Shrivenham American University in England.

The following men from this area are members of the Sixth Traffic Regulation Group of the Army Transportation Corps, recently awarded the Meritorious Service Unit Plaque: Private First Class Charles W. Woody, 331 Walnut Street; Captain Edward G. Kelly, Huntington; Sergeant Beauford R. Blevins, Logan, and Technical Sergeant Merrield A. Scherer, Welch.

Glenna: *November 6th Tue.– Partly ironed. Went to "Parents and Teachers" meeting at the school. Mr. Fannin was there and talked. A very beautiful day.*

Rupert: *I went to school. It was a pretty day.*

"More than 31,000 veterans of the European theatre are scheduled to arrive at three East Coast ports, while on the West coast 14 troop-carriers from the Pacific are due at four West Coast ports."[599]

Russian Foreign Commissar V. M. Molotov stated that the atomic bomb "cannot be kept secret." He promised that Russia will have "atomic energy and many other things." He warned against the use of atomic energy being employed in a political way.[600]

"IN THE SERVICE":

Major R. H. F. Parsley, husband of Mrs. Kay R. Parsley of Kenova, has arrived home following a tour of duty with the Ninth Air Force in Europe where he was senior intelligence officer of the 391st Group, an A-26 Invader unit.

Staff Sergeant John H. Metz, son of Mr. and Mrs. H. L. Metz, 2819 Staunton Road, is en route to a separation center in the United States from Hawaii after 35 months overseas duty. Sergeant Metz supervised four Army bakeries during the building of the Alaska highway, and was later transferred to New Caledonia as a baker's instructor.

First Lieutenant James W. Hunter, son of Mr. and Mrs. Arch J. Hunter, 317 Twenty-fifth Street, landed last week at Mather Field, Calif. for reassignment and possible discharge. A veteran of 23 bombing missions aboard a B-29 Superfortress ... Lieutenant Hunter wears the Distinguished Flying Cross and the Air Medal with four Oak Leaf Clusters.

Master Sergeant Robert R. Hoover, son of Mr. and Mrs. William Hoover of Athalia, O., directed the installation of telephone service for U.S. Forces in Pusan, Korea... Sergeant Hoover has been overseas since August, 1942, and has been stationed at Hawaii, New Britain, Guadalcanal, Luzon and Panay.

Staff Sergeant Mattie H. Johnson Jr., son of Mr. and Mrs. M. H. Johnson of West Hamlin, was promoted recently to that grade in the Panama Canal Zone with the 902nd Antiaircraft Artillery Battalion. Sergeant Johnson has been in the Canal Zone since January, 1943.

WAC Private First Class Callie V. Lee, 1822 Tenth Avenue, has been discharged from the Army at Fort Des Moines, Iowa.

Discharged from the Navy last week at the Puget Sound Navy Yard, Bremerton, Wash. were

Howard E. Carr, 530 ½ Sixteenth Street, and Julian E. Estep, Barboursville.

Yeoman Second Class Ada E. Harvey, wife of Bill L. Harvey, 3318 Riverside Drive, was discharged this week from the WAVES in Washington. She is the daughter of Mrs. J. N. Anderson, also of Riverside Drive.

Discharged from the Navy this week at Bainbridge, Md. were Chief Machinist's Mate Delbert Wayne, 924 ½ Sixth Avenue; Seaman First Class Charles Jarrell, 1927 Virginia Avenue; Electrician's Mate Third Class Ray E. Holly, 214 Short Street; Watertender Second Class John L. Bailey, 2115 Third Avenue; Seaman Second Class Edward M. Burner, 1832 Third Street and Painter Second Class Clayton L. Hall, 545 Sixth Avenue.

Private First Class Rutherford B. Cline, son of Mrs. Sarah Cline of Wharneliffe, has been discharged from the AAF at San Bernardino, Calif.

Technician Fifth Grade Ralph E. Rogers, 1328 Enslow Boulevard, has been discharged from the Army at Camp Cooke, Calif.

Technical Sergeant Jasper H. Hatfield of Kenova has been discharged from the AAF at Richmond, Va.

Reverting to inactive [duty] at Fort George G. Meade, Md. were First Lieutenant Naaman J. Aldredge, Logan; Captain Howard V. Crews, Huntington, and First Lieutenant Gerald B. Howes, 503 Washington Avenue.

Lieutenant Colonel George E. Gross, 714 West Fourth Street, was promoted to that grade recently.

First Lieutenant Sallie F. Miller, WAC, 4462 Auburn Road, recently was promoted to that rank.

Discharged from the Army at Camp Atterbury, Ind. were Technician Third Grade Robert D. Carter, Huntington; Staff Sergeant Ernest Whitaker, Newhall; Private First Class William T. Rogers, Keyser; Corporal Austin C. Napier Jr., Omar; Technician Fourth Grade Darrell J. Clay, Pecks Mill; Staff Sergeant John D. Lee, 1706 Third Avenue; Private First Class James C. Poe, Newhall; Technician Third Grade

Allen L. Wallace, Guyandotte; Corporal Elbert F. Hurt, Yukon; Sergeant Curtis E. England, Davy, and Private First Class Ira Chatterton, 603 Washington Avenue.

Glenna: *November 7ᵗʰ Wednesday – Beautiful day. I finished ironing. Mended all the clothes and went to prayer meeting at night.*

Rupert: *I went to school. Kermet Bledso got his finger broke.*

Educators released from service were reclaiming their professions: In Cabell County, Lowell Childers, the first teacher from the county to leave for military service, returned to Sky High School (an elementary school), and Wayne Swartzwalder returned to West Junior High. Kenneth K. Loemker, former dean of men at Marshall College, was returning to the college as head of the psychology department.[601]

An AP article from Cleveland quoted Haylm Greenberg, editor of the *Jewish Frontier* as saying, "Only the British government can bring about peace and order in Palestine... But to do this, they will have to employ a forgotten weapon; its name is justice."[602]

"IN THE SERVICE":

Private First Class Roy J. Thomas, who served for 26 months in Italy, France, Germany and the Azores as a radio operator mechanic with the Army Air Forces, is visiting his mother, Mrs. Roy Thomas, Rear 2009 Tenth Avenue, and his wife, the former Miss Gladys Armstrong, 2222 Fourth Avenue... With five other men on a B-17, he experienced his fifth crash, landing at St. Lo, France, when both wings and most of the tail of the ship were destroyed by enemy fire... Private Thomas received the Air Medal and three bronze battle stars...

Corporal Clyde E. Nelson, 1950 ½ Eighth Avenue, is a member of the service battery of the 921ˢᵗ Field Artillery Battalion, now in the Philippines...

First Sergeant Charles E. Goodall of Chesapeake, Ohio is awaiting discharge from the Army at Indiantown Gap, Pa., after landing Friday at New York. He is the son of Mr. and Mrs. Iven Goodall of Chesapeake. Sergeant Goodall served for 23 months overseas.

Private First Class James E. Robinette, son of Mr. and Mrs. M. L. Robinette of Ashland, has been discharged from the Army. A veteran of 15 months in the European theatre, he saw action throughout Europe and participated in the Battle of the Bulge.

Staff Sergeant Michael P. Labus of Milton was discharged from the Army recently at Patterson Field, Ohio.

First Lieutenant Frederick A. Woods, husband of the former Miss Agnes Keesee, 310 Twelfth Avenue, has been released from active duty with the Army and has resumed his studies in electrical engineering at Harvard University. He is the son of Mr. and Mrs. J. B. Woods, 1008 Chesapeake Court.

Glenna: *November 8ᵗʰ Thursday – Beautiful day. Papa moved the table down and I cleaned and straightened up that night. We went to Lower Madison to church. Went with Jaruel Porter and Velma.*

Rupert: *I went to school. Larry and I planned a trip to Huntington to see the ship the L.S.T.*

"IN THE SERVICE":

First Lieutenant Harold L. Willey, son of Mr. and Mrs. Alrie Willey of Pine Grove, W.Va., and former Marshall College football and basketball star, has been discharged from the Army at Mitchel Field, N.Y. after 31 months' overseas

service. He was with the Fifth Air Force in Australia, New Guinea, Dutch Guinea, Leyte and Mindoro.

Chief Aviation Radioman Ferris A. Gribble, 1105 Tenth Avenue, is stationed in Hawaii as radioman aboard a Navy Avenger torpedo plane. He has been awarded the Air Medal and completed seven missions over Japan.

Major Walter E. Vest Jr., son of Dr. W. E. Vest of Huntington, has been promoted to that rank at Camp Chaffee, Ark. He is the husband of the former Miss Maria White of Huntington.

First Sergeant James L. Moreland, 2742 Oakland Avenue, has been awarded the Silver Star for gallantry in action in Italy... Sergeant Moreland, while leading a patrol near the Arno River, captured singlehandedly a house held by 15 Germans and gained information which enabled his company to continue to advance.

Award of the Bronze Star Medal for meritorious service to Sergeant Jack M. Shinkle, 501 Fifth Avenue, was reported yesterday in a letter to Mrs. Shinkle. He is with the 36ᵗʰ "Texas" Division.

Private First Class Jack F. Triplett, son of Patrolman and Mrs. J. E. Triplett, 2445 First Avenue, arrived home Saturday after being discharged from the Army at Camp Pickett, Va. A veteran of 30 months, he served in Europe for more than a year. He wears the Purple Heart with one Oak Leaf Cluster, the Distinguished Unit Badge and the European theatre ribbon with three stars, A brother, Ben E. Triplett, in London for shore duty, was recently promoted to gunner's mate third class.

The following Huntington men have been discharged from the Navy at Bainbridge, Md.: John C. Leaberry, 315 West Twenty-second Street; Donald L. Crank, 1401 Eighteenth Street; Robert L. Brown, 408 Third Street; James L. Sedinger, 207 ½ Main Street; Wesley Simmons, 2644 Harvey Road; Alvin H. Richards, 609 West Tenth Avenue; Edward H. Wright, 4524 Auburn Road, and Arnold V. Hensley, 2418 Third Avenue.

Gunner's Mate Third Class Paul A. Franz, son of Charles Franz of Russell, Ky., has been promoted to that grade aboard the heavy cruiser *Louisville*, now at Jinsen, Korea.

Lieutenant (j. g.) Pauline F. Coyer, USNR, flight nurse, daughter of Mrs. W. P. Coyer of Prestonsburg, Ky., is serving with an air evacuation squadron of the Naval Air Transport Command on Guam. She enlisted in February, 1944.

Radioman Third Class John T. C. Betts of Gallipolis, Ohio, is serving on the *Appalachian* in Tokyo bay...

Fireman First Class Kenneth G. Wells of Gallipolis, Ohio, and Shipfitter Second Class James L. Shepherd of Russell, Ky. are serving aboard the cargo attack ship *Tabors*, now at Wakayama Harbor, Japan.

Private Charles E. Hughes, son of Mr. and Mrs. B. E. Hughes, 3810 Fourth Avenue, has returned to Camp Pickett, Va. after a furlough.

Seaman First Class H. D. Hughes, 1008 Ninth Street, served aboard the assault transport *Broadwater* in the Pacific for six months.

Radioman Second Class Charles D. Irby, 536 West Tenth Avenue, has been discharged from the Navy at Bremerton, Wash. and is expected to arrive in Huntington next week. He served aboard an Atlantic Fleet minesweeper as radar specialist.

Lieutenant (j. g.) William C. Baumgardner, 1420 Charleston Avenue, son of Mr. and Mrs. C. A. Baumgardner, arrived in Huntington Tuesday on terminal leave... He is a veteran of 63 carrier-based missions against the Japanese.

Motor Machinist's Mate Third Class William R. Miller, 207 Thirty-seventh Street, is aboard the destroyer escort *McClelland* in Japanese waters.

Sergeant Frank Grant, 624 Sixth Street, has been discharged from the army at Camp Perry, Ohio.

Sergeant Robert T. Garrett, son of Mrs. Meggie Garrett, 1636 Eighth Avenue, reenlisted in the Army last week at Topeka, Kan., where

he is stationed as a cook. He will be granted a 90-day furlough prior to reassignment.

Albert J. Thomas of Huntington has been discharged from the Navy at Great Lakes, Ill.

Aviation Machinist's Mate First Class Dan B. Capehart, son of Mr. and Mrs. T. E. Capehart of New Haven, has been discharged from the Navy at Memphis, Tenn. He is the husband of Mrs. Clariece Capehart of Huntington.

Two Huntington officers have been placed on inactive status by the Army. First Lieutenant Edward A. King, 1668 Eleventh Avenue, was released through Camp Atterbury, Ind., and First Lieutenant George B. Richmond, 1123 Twelfth Street, was released through Fort George G. Meade, Md.

Glenna: *November 9th Friday – Rainy. Rupert, Nona Gill, Larry, Buddy and June and myself went to Huntington to see the ship docked at 10th St. The L.S.T. was fine.*

Rupert: *Mother, Larry, his brother and sister, his mother, and I went to see the L.S.T. It was a real event.*

The war was still on our minds as we explored the landing craft docked on the Ohio River bank. Nona's brother, James Queen, had been killed in the Pacific the year before.

Tokyo: "Japan's new Liberal Party plunged today into the empire's first peace-time election campaign with a platform calling for a 'Democratic system' under Emperor Hirohito..."[603]

"Private James H. Roberts Jr., 21, son of Mr. and Mrs. J. H. Roberts, 1676 Twelfth Avenue, died October 14 as the result of illness while serving in Italy with the 179th Railroad Battalion... A veteran of 32 months, Private Roberts had served for 26 months in North Africa and Italy. His battalion supplied front-line troops by rail. Private Roberts attended elementary schools in Huntington, completing his education in Columbus, Ohio before his family returned to Huntington. His father is also a veteran of this war, serving with the 737th Railway Operating Battalion until his discharge in April. Surviving in addition to his parents, are a sister, Miss Anna June Roberts, at home, and his paternal grandfather, Floyd Roberts of Marietta, Ohio."[604]

"IN THE SERVICE":

Sergeant R. J. Nichols is expected to arrive in Huntington today after being discharged from the Army at Fort Devens, Mass. He has been in the service two years and eight months and was overseas for two years. He and his wife, Mrs. Helen Gentry Nichols, and their daughter, Betty Jean, plan to go to their home in Portland Ore., about December 1. Mrs. Nichols and her daughter have been making their home with Mrs. Nichols' parents, Mr. and Mrs. Sam Gentry, 1461 Edwards Street.

After serving for 36 months in the South and Central Pacific areas, Captain Andrew K. Faller, a member of the 374th Troop Carrier Group, has arrived in Huntington to visit his parents, Mr. and Mrs. Harold Faller, 206 Twenty-eighth Street... He will report in 60 days to Fort Knox, Ky.

Private First Class Emmette M. Haynes, 427 East Third Street, was discharged this week from the Army at Fort Knox, Ky.

Ernest D. Wright, 1755 Fifth Avenue, a World War II veteran, and Chester H. Donahoe of Barboursville, have enlisted in the regular Army at the Huntington Army Recruiting Station. Wright selected the Army Air Forces in Europe while Donahoe enlisted unassigned.

After serving overseas with the 42nd "Rainbow" Division, Staff Sergeant Robert O. Scanlon, 329 Twenty-third Street, has been honorably discharged from the Army at Shepard Field, Tex.

Clifford S. Stewart of Ceredo, husband of Mrs. Mildred Marie Stewart, has received his discharge from the Navy at Bainbridge, Md.

Corporal Frank D. Beale Jr., son of Mr. and Mrs. F. D. Beale of New Brunswick, N.J., formerly of Huntington, has been discharged at Fort Myer, Va. after serving with the 104th Infantry Division in Northern France, Belgium, Holland and Germany. He was taken prisoner by the Germans in November, 1944 and released last May. His wife, the former Miss Virginia Anne Kane resides in New Brunswick.

After spending a furlough with his parents, Mr. and Mrs. C. C. Fisher, 1136 Spring Valley Drive, Lieutenant Carl F. Fisher has reported to his station at Coco Solo, Panama.

Glenna: *November 10th Saturday – Rainy. Stayed home and cleaned, baked cookies, etc.*

Rupert: *Larry and I played a game of Monopoly when he came after a saw.*

"Diamond Dust": "Coach Oscar Hagberg, the West Virginia boy who is head skipper of the Navy football team says 'I suppose Michigan will beat us today by two or three touchdowns. In fact, we'll be lucky if we score' ... Tsk, tsk, Coach Hagberg, don't be so modest. Can you spare an oak, Mate? . . . So, some of the experts think Notre Dame will slip up and stampede the Army today. I don't believe it. Glenn Davis and 'Doc' Blanchard will take care of the Irish. This pair are as powerful as two drops of Dotty Lamour's perfume.". . . Every football expert in West Virginia will tell you that Coach Stewart Way, who teaches the Pony Express backs their A-B-C's has the g-r-e-a-t-e-s-t combination of leather luggers in the Mountain State. As a matter of fact, Way has eight backfield runners who can really gallop with the old leather potato, viz:—Dave Green, Dick Bentine, Tom Dandelet, Co-captain Ray Simmons (everybody's all-state halfback), Jim Clary, Jimmy Mott, Bill Gerhold, etc. etc., . . . They can't all play at the s-a-m-e time. But no football team is any stronger than its replacements. (Did all of that come out of me?)"[605]

"The Barboursville Pirates powered their way to a 20–0 victory over Ceredo-Kenova last night in a muddy battle on the Kenova field... Max Clay put across the first Barboursville touchdown... Foster Bowen climaxed another... Gene Groves counted the final touchdown and Ben Wookey ran the ball over for the extra point. One of the features was the fine punting of Ray Rardin whose kicks kept the powerful Pirates in trouble most of the second half."[606]

A few other high school scores: Douglas 7–Liberty 0; Dupont 7–Mount Hope 0; Beckley 18–Welch 6; East Bank 7–St. Albans 0; Point Pleasant 20–Mason City 0; Williamson 7– Logan 0; Montgomery 14–Oak Hill 0; Portsmouth 18–Ironton 12; Ashland 38–Catlettsburg 6.

"IN THE SERVICE":

Sergeant Ernest McMullen, son of Mrs. Margaret Jane Ripley, 629 Sixth Street, has been discharged from the Army at the Greensboro, N.C. Army Air Base. He is a veteran of 20 months service with the Eighth Air Force in Europe.

Staff Sergeant John B. Mays Jr., son of Mr. and Mrs. J. B. Mays of Barboursville, has been discharged from the AAF at Randolph Field, Texas. He is the husband of Mrs. Betty Sue Mays of Barboursville.

Corporal Claude Baisden, son of Mrs. Betty Baisden of Kermit, will soon return to the United States with the 37th "Buckeye" Division, which is now on Luzon in the Philippines. A veteran of 37 months overseas, he wears the Combat Infantryman Badge, the Bronze Star Medal, the Asiatic-Pacific ribbon with two stars and the Philippine Liberation ribbon with star.

Private Edgar Walker, son of Mr. and Mrs. Dave Walker of Huntington, has been discharged from the Army at Fairfield, Ohio. He is the husband of Mrs. Jane Walker of Ceredo.

Private First Class Hence Jones, 442 West Fifth Street, has been discharged from the Army at Camp Perry, Ohio.

Raymond Miller of Barboursville, formerly a fire controlman first class aboard the battleship *Missouri*, returned to his home recently with an eye-witness account of the surrender ceremonies... Mr. Miller entered the service in July, 1942, and was aboard the destroyer *Maddox* when it was sunk in the Mediterranean in July, 1943.

Seaman First Class Cecil M. Hickman and Ship's Cook Third Class John E. Lott of Huntington, and Boatswain's Mate Second Class Luther L. Varney of Louisa, Ky., are returning to the United States aboard the attack transport *Tulagi*. They will be sent to a Naval separation center for discharge.

Technical Sergeant Frank Appling Jr., 128 Ninth Avenue and Private First Class Harlan Hazelett, 322 Tiernan Street, are returning to the United States for discharge. They are aboard the LST *30*, due to dock soon at San Francisco.

Corporal Floyd Hayner of Leet, has been discharged from the AAF at Patterson Field, Ohio. He is the son of John M. Hayner of Leet.

First Lieutenant William Steinbrecher, 285 Main Street, has been placed on inactive duty by the AAF and is spending his terminal leave at home...

Harry Bastianelli, lieutenant, USNR, recently placed on inactive duty, has returned to Huntington and is associated with the Parker Jewelry Co. Mrs. Bastianelli, former Miss Mary McLaughlin of Huntington, accompanied her husband here. They have made their home at 121 Tenth Avenue.

Lieutenant Junior grade Edward Kufahl of Kenova is serving aboard the USS *Phobos*, a Pacific fleet supply ship stationed at Pearl Harbor...

Glenna: *November 11th Sunday – Went to Sunday School. Rainy and cool. In evening Mrs. Rousey came up. That night went to West Hamlin to church. Jaruel, Velma and children and Uncle Bob, Rupert and myself.*

Rupert: *I went to Sunday school today. Larry's brother got his head cut. Larry and I played a game of Mon. [Monopoly]*

"WITH THE COLORS":

Private (First Class) Cecil Adkins, USMC, husband of Mrs. Edith Adkins, 2812 Eighth Street, is on his way home after 15 months of service in the South Pacific, according to his mother, Mrs. Sarah Johnson, 325 Nineteenth Street.

Lieutenant L. Reese, USNR, has been released from active duty with the Navy after 37 months in the service. He is the vice-president and general manager of the Armstrong Products Corp., First Street and Seventh Avenue.

Second Lieutenant Ralph H. Hall, husband of Mrs. Kathleen Hall of 519 Thirtieth Street, has been placed on inactive duty at Patterson Field, O., having won the Air Medal with two battle stars as a navigator in the Eighth Air Force.

Private (First Class) Roy L. Hysell, 1340 Jefferson Avenue, is now serving in the American occupied zone of Germany.

Fireman (First Class) Walter W. Chapman, son of Mr. and Mrs. Ivan C. Chapman, Madison Avenue, has been relieved of his duties on the USS *Turner* and has been sent to the separation center at Bainbridge, Md... His wife lives in Sanford, Fla.

Staff Sergeant John L. Wheeler, 122 Francis Street, who served for 25 months as an armorer-gunner in the ETO with the Eighth Air Force, has been discharged from the AAF at San Antonio, Tex.

Sergeant John Hite, 408 Thirty-first Street, formerly stationed with the 356th AAA battalion in the Philippines, has arrived at Fletcher General Hospital, Cambridge, O.

Sergeant E. S. Chandler Jr., son of Mr. and Mrs. E. S. Chandler of 2807 Elmwood Avenue, arrived Saturday morning at Vancouver, Wash. after 23 months of service with the Army Air Forces, where he was attached to the 13th Emergency Rescue Group. His brother, Private (First Class) Kenneth W. Chandler, USMC, is on Okinawa.

Hospital Apprentice (First Class) Paul E. Bush, son of Mrs. Clara T. Bush, 2025 Fifth Avenue, arrived home Friday after receiving his discharge from the Navy at Shelton, Va.

Seaman (First Class) Eunice Hazel Grass, WAVES, daughter of Mr. and Mrs. John Hodges, 1822 Monroe Avenue, received her discharge from the Navy this week at the separation center, Washington, D.C.

Richard E. Johnson, 620 Trenton Place, was discharged from the Army at Borden General Hospital, Chickasha, Okla., after two months of hospitalization.

Corporal E. Raymond Henderson has received his discharge from the AAF at Camp Beale, Calif., having served 26 months in England. He is visiting his mother, Mrs. W. F. Henderson, and sister, Mrs. Dewey Bias, in San Francisco, Calif.

Private (First Class) Kenneth B. Suiter, son of Mr. and Mrs. R. W. Suiter of Chesapeake, is seriously ill in the 142nd General Hospital in Calcutta, India. The nature of his illness is not known. His brother, Darby Suiter, has been promoted to seaman (first class) and is stationed at Shoemaker, Calif. with the Fleet Band. Another brother, Lieutenant Fleming Suiter, AAF, has been transferred from San Antonio, Tex. to Luke Field, Phoenix, Ariz. He was a German prisoner for 18 months.

Glenna: *November 12th Monday – Beautiful day. I washed up everything.*

Rupert: *We celebrated Armistice day today. There wasn't any school.*

Troops were coming home in great numbers. Nearly 7,000 from Europe were to land at three East Coast ports on this day. On the

West coast 21,400 were expected to arrive on sixteen vessels.[607]

President Truman, Prime Minister Attlee, and Prime Minister King of Canada were making progress in discussions toward a joint atomic bomb policy, but with some disagreement. Mr. Truman had suggested outlawing the atomic bomb while Mr. Attlee wanted to put it under United Nations control.[608]

"Major Raymond V. Humphreys, Coast Artillery Corps, of Huntington, has been awarded the Bronze Star Medal for meritorious achievement against the enemy in the southwest Pacific where he served as special service officer and education officer of a major anti-aircraft command. He is the son of Mr. and Mrs. Edward Humphreys, 903 Twenty-eighth Street, and was in the insurance business before entering the service."[609]

"Colonel Bertram A. Holtzworth of Huntington has been assigned as executive officer of the Armored Replacement Training Center at Fort Knox, Ky. as his first post following his recent return from the European theatre... Colonel Holtzworth served in headquarters of the 12th Army Group in Europe and was awarded the Legion of Merit, Bronze Star, French Legion of Honor and French Croix de Guerre."[610]

"IN THE SERVICE":

Private First Class Sanders A. Bloss, 1940 Eighth Avenue, member of the 87th Air Service Group of the famous 58th Bombardment Wing, is en route to the United States.

Chief Specialist Edwin Marco Handley, 1633 Washington Avenue, Sonarman Second Class Robert Forest Murdock, 2716 Guyan Avenue, and Carpenter's Mate First Class Elmer Jackson Brinker, New Haven, have been discharged from the Navy at Puget Sound Navy Yard, Bremerton, Wash.

Second Lieutenant Ralph H. Hall, 519 Thirtieth Street, has been honorably released from the AAF at Patterson Field, O.

Corporal Homer W. McCoy, 417 ½ Third Avenue, has been discharged from the Army at Camp Butner, N.C.

Private Orville Nameth, 217 West Second Street, is serving with a chemical warfare unit near Manila.

Private First Class Charles R. Morrison, 1045 Ninth Avenue; Private Johnny D. Thompson, Route 3, a veteran of nine months overseas with the 1934th MPs, Military Guards, and Sergeant Sherill Brookover of Hamlin, a veteran of 44 months with the 21st Pursuit Squadron, AAF, in the Philippines and China, have arrived at Newton D. Baker General Hospital at Martinsburg, W.Va.

Seaman First Class Anna Norma Meadows Thornburg, Gallipolis, O., and Seaman First Class Jean Dingess Ward, 4031 Auburn Road, have been discharged from the WAVES in Washington.

Shipfitter Third Class Frank A. Cheesebrew of Middleport, O. is a member of the 127th Naval Construction Battalion which recently won a commendation from the brigade to which it was attached for work in the Philippines.

Cadet-Midshipman Robert Hendrix, 839 Twelfth Avenue, has reported to the U.S. Merchant Marine Cadet Basic School at Pass Christian, Miss.

Technical Sergeant Henry A. Nickell, 86 Washington Avenue, has reenlisted in the Army for three years and has left his base at Lawrence, Ill. for a 90-day furlough.

Private Daniel M. Whitley, 631 Norway Avenue, was revealed this week to have been connected with the Manhattan Engineer District, the organization responsible for development of the atomic bomb.

Fireman First Class Alonzo Bailey, 429 California Street, a veteran of 18 months with the Navy in the South Pacific, returned to Huntington yesterday after receiving his honorable discharge on the West Coast. He is a former employee of the West Virginia Steel & Manufacturing Company.

Glenna: *November 13th Tuesday – Cool and rainy. I ironed. Mrs. Rousey came up again.*

Rupert: *I went to school. Eddie Harbour came home with me.*

The war was over, but hopeful families were still receiving grim news. "First Lieutenant Jack Brower, son of Mr. and Mrs. L. C. Brower, who has been missing in action since May 12, 1944, has been declared dead... Lieutenant Bower, piloting a P-47 Thunderbolt of the 15th Air Force, failed to return from a bomber-escort mission to the Ferrara-Bologna area of Italy. A graduate of Central High School in 1937, he attended Marshall College for two years before enlisting in the Army Air Forces in January, 1941."[611]

Charles de Gaulle was named president of France's provisional government.

Chungking: Unofficial sources reported, "Chinese Nationalist forces have wrested Shanhaikwan, coastal gateway through the Great Wall into Manchuria, from Chinese Communist defenders." Official dispatches, however, "told of Communist victories in other civil war-torn North China provinces... "[612]

"IN THE SERVICE":

Lieutenant (j. g.) Victor B. Varney, USNR, son of Mrs. Edna Varney, 3003 Fourth Avenue, has been placed on terminal leave by the Navy prior to release from active duty on December 12. He served for 43 months, three on sea duty in the Atlantic.

Recently discharged from the Navy at Bainbridge, Md. were Aviation Machinist's Mate Third Class Orville A. Dean of Ceredo

and Seaman First Class William A. Casey of Huntington.

D. L. Goss, fireman first class, of Huntington is serving with the Navy at Espiritu Santo, New Hebrides...

Jack R. Wright, 2716 Third Avenue, and Leland M. Chapman, 612 Third Avenue, are serving with the 115th Naval Construction Battalion on Luzon...

First Lieutenant George M. Dugan, son of M. W. Dugan, president of Emmons-Hawkins Hardware Co., arrived Sunday at Portland, Ore. aboard the USS *Marine Falcon*. His wife, formerly Miss Charlotte Burns, and son, James S. Dugan, reside at 1026 Eleventh Street.

Ensign William B. Gibson, 1122 Ninth Avenue, has been placed on terminal leave from the Navy at Seattle, Washington, prior to release from active duty.

Thomas C. Foster, 1723 Virginia Avenue, a veteran of 39 months service, has been discharged from the Army at Fort Sill, Okla. He served 22 months overseas.

Glenna: *November 14th Wed. – Rained all day. I didn't accomplish much.*

Rupert: *I went to school. we had a cookie sale.*

"IN THE SERVICE":

Staff Sergeant Chauncy S. Elkins Jr., son of Mr. and Mrs. C. S. Elkins of Huntington, returned this week to Newton D. Baker General Hospital at Martinsburg, W.Va. following a 50-day furlough at the home of his parents. He returned to the United States September 6 after 15 months overseas with the Fifth Air Force. He was injured on Blak Island in the South Pacific. Two brothers who have recently been discharged from the service were also at home — Corporal Charles Elkins, discharged after four years, nine months with the AAF, and Machinist's Mate Second Class Frederick Elkins, discharged after 40 months with the Navy.

Seaman Second Class Nelson Boyd, son of Mr. and Mrs. Harry Boyd, 320 West Sixth Avenue, has arrived in Huntington to visit his parents following his discharge from the service at Toledo, Ohio. His wife and three children have been making their home with his parents during his tour of active duty...

Sergeant Robert Hastings, son of Mr. and Mrs. Robert Hastings, 702 ½ Washington Avenue, recently discharged from the Army, is visiting his parents after returning from more than three years of duty with the Ninth Air Force in Europe. Sergeant Hastings was married in Europe to WAC Private Elizabeth Hotchkiss of Stamford, Conn. Mrs. Hastings is expected to return soon from Europe and Sergeant Hastings will join her at Stamford.

Technician Fourth Grade Paul D. Bailey, son of Mrs. Blanche Bailey, 909 Eleventh Street, has arrived in Japan for occupation duty with the Twenty-fifth Infantry Division. He entered the Army in 1943 after his graduation from Central High School and is a radio operator...

Private James Porter, son of Mrs. Mattie Porter of Branchland, has reenlisted in the Army for one year at the 24th Replacement Depot on Luzon. Private Porter, inducted earlier this year, has been overseas since October 17.

Sergeant Carl J. Mannon, son of Mr. and Mrs. W. M. Mannon, 2059 Donald Avenue, is en route to the United States from Tinian for discharge from the 58th Bombardment Wing, He was a supply clerk with the 589th Material Squadron.

Staff Sergeant Chester W. Lewis, son of Mrs. Minnie Lewis, 2459 Collis Avenue, has been discharged from the Army at Gowen Field, Boise, Idaho. He has been in service since July, 1940.

Private First Class Billy M. Estep, USMC, son of Mrs. Lily Skaggs, 1131 Sixth Avenue, has returned to the Cherry Point, N.C. Marine base following a 15-day furlough at home.

Discharged from the Army at Camp Atterbury, Ind., were Sergeant Stewart Hall, Williamson; Technician Fifth Grade William H. Wallace Jr., Point Pleasant; Technician Fifth Grade Charles T. Crawford, 138 Washington Avenue; Technician Fifth Grade Wayne J. Sammoms, Wilkinson; Sergeant Gordon S. Ware, 223 West Seventh Avenue; Private Junior E. Baisden, Branchland; Private Loval Arrington, Bradshaw...

Glenna: *November 15th Thur. — Mended, had a bad cold. Very cool day.*

Rupert: *I went to school. We had a new teacher.*

Frankfurt, Germany, November 15: Eva Braun's newly discovered treasure chest contained "dozens of photographs showing family pictures of her and Hitler and a mysterious baby girl called 'Uschi.'"[613] (Other sources have said Uschi was the daughter of Eva's best friend, Herta Schneider.)

Jerusalem, November 15: "Reports from Tel Aviv early today said two Jewish youths were killed, seven were seriously wounded and about 50 slightly injured yesterday in street rioting during a 12-hour general strike protesting new British proposals for settlement of the Palestine problem."[614]

"IN THE SERVICE":

Lieutenant Commander W. Alexander Hunter of Ashton, W.Va., and Huntington ... the son of Mr. and Mrs. J. E. Hunter of Ashton was with the first Americans to land in Japan. He entered the service three and a half years ago and has served half of that overseas... Commander Hunter was graduated from Ohio State University and taught at Point Pleasant

High School. A brother, Lieutenant Randall Hunter, USNR, is in the Pacific.

Lieutenant (j. g.) Hugh H. Wilks, USNR, formerly athletic coach at Chesapeake, O., and Hamlin, has been discharged at the Naval Air Station at New Orleans. He is the son of Mrs. E. E. Wilks of Chesapeake. He entered the Navy in April, 1942, and has served for 19 months overseas as a communications officer. Lieutenant Wilks graduated from Marshall College in 1936.

Seaman First Class William O. Curley, son of Mr. and Mrs. J. A. Curley, 630 ½ Eighth Avenue, has been discharged from the Navy at Mechanicsburg, Pa.

Corporal Robert L. Simms, son of Mrs. Verba Simms of Hurricane and husband of Mrs. Phyllis Simms of Huntington, has been promoted to that grade at his station in Korea where he is serving with the Seventh Infantry Division. A radio operator in the 32nd Regiment, he wears the Purple Heart for wounds received on Okinawa.

Petty Officer First Class W. V. Christian Jr., recently discharged from the Navy after 22 months service in the Pacific, is visiting his parents, Mr. and Mrs. W. V. Christian, 2714 Highlawn Avenue.

Corporal Kermit Byrd, son of Patrolman and Mrs. W. R. Byrd, 814 Roby Road, has been discharged from the Army and has returned to Huntington... He has been in service since July, 1942.

Claude and Clay Beheler, twin sons of Mr. and Mrs. M. G. Beheler, 1421 Beech Street, are en route to the United States for discharge... They enlisted together in 1942, Claude in the Seabees and Clay in the Army Air Forces. One other brother is also in the service, Everett, a captain in the Coast Guard.

Maurice Kaplan, formerly a staff photographer for the Huntington Publishing Co., is en route to the United States for discharge... He is the son of Mr. and Mrs. Hyman B. Kaplan, formerly of Huntington.

Captain Joseph Greene, accompanied by his wife, and Lieutenant Shirley Greene, a sister, have arrived in Huntington to visit their parents, Mr. and Mrs. David Greene, 1035 Ninth Avenue. Lieutenant Greene recently arrived on the West Coast from Japan and has been discharged after three years' service. She was an Army dietician and among the first 85 nurses to land in Japan. Captain Greene has been stationed at Fort Baker, Calif., as an Army surgeon after returning from action in Africa.

Staff Sergeant William R. Perdue, 527 Elm Street, has reenlisted in the regular Army after eight years of service. He is the son of Mrs. Grace Perdue, who was chosen Huntington's Infantry Mother during a previous War Bond campaign. He has four brothers serving with the Armed forces and another was killed in action... His wife is Mrs. Lavon Perdue and they have a son, Roscoe, 5. Sergeant Perdue, overseas 22 months as a member of the 241st Field Artillery Battalion, wears the Bronze Star, European Theatre ribbon with five stars, and the American defense ribbon. The Bronze Star award was made on September 23 for "heroic achievement in military operations against the enemy near Herborn, Luxembourg."

Technician Fifth grade Frederick W. Wallace, a former employee of the Huntington Publishing Co., arrived in New York yesterday aboard the SS *John Brown*.

Glenna: *November 16th Friday – Cool and clear. Cleaned the house. Nothing happened.*

Rupert: *I went to school. The new teacher is still there.*

"The SS *Marshall Victory*, named in honor of Marshall College, is now used to ferry home the troops from the European theatre, carrying 1,940 troops per trip"[615]

"IN THE SERVICE":

Corporal Norman L. Johnson, son of Mr. and Mrs. J. C. Johnson, 1237 Eighteenth Street, arrived in the United States Wednesday for discharge... He is the husband of Mrs. Virginia Johnson of Highlawn Avenue. Corporal Johnson served overseas for 25 months with the 12th Field Artillery in France, Belgium, Germany and Czechoslovakia...

Technician Third Grade Lawrence G. Arbaugh, son of Mr. and Mrs. Robert C. Arbaugh, 1501 Fourth Avenue, was recently promoted to that grade with the Army Signal Corps in Washington. A graduate of Central High school in 1940, he has been in service for 30 months. Technician Arbaugh attended Marshall College for one semester before entering the service. His wife, the former Miss Betty Harper, 3602 Third Avenue, is with him in Washington.

Sergeant Anne O. Spurlock, 2616 Orchard Avenue, has been discharged from the WAC at Fort Des Moines, Iowa.

Private First Class Homer Davis, whose wife resides at 521 Seventh Avenue, has been discharged from the Army at Camp Selbert, Ala. after 25 months service. He served for 14 months with the First Army as a truck driver. He has been awarded the Purple Heart and the ETO ribbon with two stars.

Private First Class Robert L. Hancock of Dunbar, W.Va., formerly of Huntington, has been assigned to headquarters of the Eighth Army in Yokohama, according to his grandmother, Mrs. William Clark of Huntington. Private Hancock entered the Army in November, 1941, and participated in the campaign on Luzon.

Technical Sergeant and Mrs. Harold K. Thomas of Goldsboro, N.C. are visiting his parents, Mr. and Mrs. Everett C. Thomas, 1033 W. Sixth Street. Sergeant Thomas has recently returned to the United States after 22 months in Europe. A brother, Private Edward C. Thomas, is expected home soon after serving for 28 months in Italy and the Pacific with the Army engineers.

Storekeeper Third Class Ralph E. Hilleary, 1937 Adams Avenue, is serving with Squadron 12 of the Naval Air Transport Service Command, which is returning liberated soldiers to the United States.

Private First Class Joseph A. Mays, son of Mr. and Mrs. Walter A. Mays, 261 Davis Street, and husband of Mrs. Doalie Mays, 139 Francis Street, has arrived at Fort Oglethorpe, Ga. for redistribution. He served for eight months in Europe and wears the Purple Heart, the Combat Infantryman Badge and three stars to the ETO ribbon.

Discharged from the Army at Fort Knox, Ky. this week were Technical Sergeant Joseph M. Muth, 1032 Twenty-second Street; Private Franklin B. Phillips, 630 Thirteenth Street; Private First Class Ivan H. H. Raby, 1533 Sixth Avenue; Technician Third Class William R. Mayberry, Rita, and Private Herman A. Napier, Roderfield.

Seaman Second Class Earl Perdue, son of Mrs. Grace Perdue, 527 Elm Street, is with a training unit at Bremerton, Wash. He enlisted at the age of 17 and recently completed his training at Great Lakes, Ill. He is the sixth son of Mrs. Perdue to enter service...

Corporal James B. Humphreys, son of Mr. and Mrs. H. G. Humphreys, 941 Eleventh Avenue, was home recently on a short furlough...

Seaman Second Class Curtis W. McCoy, son of Mrs. Florence Turner, 1626 Commerce Avenue, has been assigned to the Norfolk, Va. Navy Yard for further training.

Discharged this week from the Navy at Bainbridge, Md. were Machinist's Mate Third Class Lewis A. Jameson, 638 Fifth Avenue; Machinist's Mate Third Class Edwin N. Foster Jr., 1133 Minton Street; Ship's Cook Adolphus W. Pike, 1828 Wiltshire Boulevard; Gunner's Mate Third Class Ray Wright, Huntington; Machinist's Mate Second Class Jack H. Ramsey, 1925 Buffington Avenue; Aviation Machinist's Mate Second Class William C. Brown, 408

Third Street; Seaman First Class Charles H. Byran, Huntington, and Watertender Third Class Orvil W. McCallister, Barboursville.

Glenna: November 17th Sat. – *Rainy, didn't do much. Mamma was sick. Went to Enon to revival meeting with Cline Porter and Edith.*

Rupert: *Larry came over and got me. I took my Mopoly set over there.*

West Virginia reportedly had the wettest September on record. Average rainfall of 7.18 inches was 1.22 inches more than the record high of 5.96 in 1924.[616]

Josef Kramer, the "Beast of Belsen," and twenty-nine of his associates in crime were convicted, but fourteen other defendants, including five woman, were acquitted.[617] Other sources said Kramer, Irma Grese, and nine members of their staff were sentenced to be hanged.

Glenna: *November 18th Sunday – Went to Sunday School. Beautiful day. Went to graveyard. At night went to Enon to church. Dorcie Hicks' wife was saved.*

Rupert: *I went to sunday school. Later I went over to larrys.*

"WITH THE COLORS":

Telegrapher Second Class Elizabeth Jeanne Hopkins, daughter of Mr. and Mrs. Walter H. Mynes, 924 Twenty-seventh Street, and wife of Harold L. Hopkins, USNR, received her discharge from the WAVES November 16 at the Naval Personnel Separation Center, U.S. Naval Barracks, Washington, D.C. Mrs. Hopkins, formerly employed as a teletype operator in the Huntington office of the Associated Press, entered the service September 23, 1943...

Lieutenant Commander W. S. Daniels, USNR, arrived at Seattle, Wash., yesterday aboard the USS *Noble*... Commander Daniels entered the service January 1, 1941, and his first tour of duty was with the Marine Corps on Guadalcanal as medical officer. For his work he received a special presidential citation. His last tour was aboard the USS *Kermit Roosevelt* as head medial officer. Commander Daniels will resume his practice in Huntington as general practitioner and surgeon, a practice he had for six years prior to his entrance into the Navy. His wife, Mrs. Minnie Lou Daniels and three children, David, Billy and Joanne, reside at 3601 Piedmont Road.

Private Clifford S. Napier Jr., son of Mrs. Helen M. Napier, 1418 Fourth Avenue, will complete a 60-day furlough here this week and report to George Field, Ill. for reassignment. He was honorably discharged September 21, and has reenlisted in the regular Army.

First Lieutenant Arnold C. Castle, son of Mr. and Mrs. Frank E. Castle, formerly of Huntington, and First Lieutenant George M. Brown, son of Mr. and Mrs. J. H. Brown, 951 Madison Avenue, have been placed on terminal leave at the Lincoln, Nebr. Army Air Field prior to release from active service.

Baker Third Class George A. Harbour, Barboursville, has received his discharge from the Navy at the Separation Center, Shoemaker, Calif.

Private First Class Otis Ramey, son of Mr. and Mrs. Jack Ramey, Lundale, W.Va., is now on duty as a personal clerk in headquarters of General George C. Kenny's Far East Air Force.

Private First Class Charles Teschler, son of Mrs. Georgeanna Teschler, 1418 Jefferson Avenue has arrived at [an unnamed redistribution center. He] is a veteran of eight months service in the ETO and wears the ribbon for that area with three battle stars, the Purple

Heart and the Combat Infantryman's Badge. A brother, Max L. Teschler, was discharged from the Navy this week.

Private Daniel B. Wheeler, husband of Mrs. Lorena Wheeler, 4281 Sixteenth Street, has received his discharge from the AAF at the Amarillo, Tex., Army Air Field...

Private William Ryalls, whose wife resides at 512 ½ Bridge Street, has reported to Camp Pickett, Va., for an overseas assignment. While on furlough in Huntington he met his brother, Robert Ryalls, recently discharged after two years of service in Italy.

Technical Sergeant John M. Morris, USMC, son of Mrs. John Morris, 627 Division Street, arrived at San Diego, Calif., November 12, aboard the USS *Maryland*.

Staff Sergeant W. L. Plymale, formerly attached to the Third Marine Air Wing in the Pacific, has received his discharge from the Marine Corps. He is the son of Mr. and Mrs. J. B. Plymale, 404 West Twenty-fourth Street.

Private First Class Charles H. Stewart, United States Army, and Shipfitter Third Class Wilson M. Stewart, USNR, sons of Mr. and Mrs. Shirley Stewart, Spring Valley Drive, have received their discharges from the services. A brother-in-law, Private Curtis Nicely, has arrived overseas and is stationed with the 507th Anti-Aircraft Artillery near Manila.

Seaman First Class William C. Casto Jr., Russell, Ky., and Seaman First Class Alonzo Burton, Louisa, Ky., served as shipmates aboard the seaplane tender USS *Hamlin* in the Pacific.

Sergeant Frank K. Orr, whose wife, the former Miss Violet Burdette, resides at 632 ½ Twentieth Street, has been transferred from Harmon Field, Guam, to a personnel center in the United States.

Technical Sergeant Ira J. Bias Jr., whose parents reside in West Hamlin, has been discharged from the AAF at San Antonio, Tex. A veteran of 29 missions as a radio operator on a B-17, Sergeant Bias wears the Purple Heart and the Air Medal with three Oak Leaf Clusters.

Ensign David Estler, son of Mr. and Mrs. Irving Estler, 420 Holswade Drive, received his commission at Fort Schuyler, N.Y...

Cecil Adkins, son of Mr. and Mrs. Henon Adkins, 2233 James River Road, has entered the Marine Corps...

Lieutenant Kermit Yeater, USNR, commanding officer of an LST (tank landing ship) in the Pacific, and former principal of Altizer School in Huntington, has ... been overseas 19 months, and his ship is now operating between Manila and Japan. His wife, Margaret, and son, Larry, live in Highlawn.

Glenna: *November 19th Monday – Rained all day. I washed. Mamma was real sick.*

Rupert: *I went to school. The old teacher came back.*

I think by the third month of the school year I should have come up with something better than "old teacher." I was in sixth grade and Thelma Matthews was my teacher that year.

"IN THE SERVICE":

Private First Class Floyd S. Jordan, USMC, son of Mr. and Mrs. Sanford Jordan, 835 Washington Avenue, has been discharged from the service at Quantico, Va. He is the husband of the former Miss Betty Lou Adkins of Huntington.

Staff Sergeant Edward L. VanHoose, son of Mrs. Beulah Keyser of Huntington, has been discharged from the Army at Fort George G. Meade, Md. He is the husband of the former Miss Elizabeth Desmond of Huntington.

Seaman First Class Belva Downey Futch, daughter of Mr. and Mrs. C. R. Ridgway, 826 Eleventh Street, has been discharged from the WAVES at Memphis, Tenn. She will rejoin her husband, Edward E. Futch of Fort Lauderdale, Fla.

Sergeant Charles L. Tyree, son of Mr. and Mrs. C. L. Tyree, 1131 Sixth Avenue, has been discharged from the AAF at Sheppard Field, Texas. He entered the Army in February, 1942.

Lieutenant John C. Ensign, USNR, 55 Foster Road, has been released from active duty after 38 months service. He is the son of Mrs. John W. Ensign, 1934 S. Englewood Road, and the husband of the former Miss Anne Jarrett.

Second Lieutenant Robert K. Flanagan, son of Mr. and Mrs. R. K. Flanagan, 1556 Sixteenth Street, has been released from active duty with the AAF at Lincoln, Nebraska. He entered the service in February, 1943, and was a navigator with the air force.

First Lieutenant George G. Urian, 2804 Oakland Avenue, has been released from active duty with the AAF at Lincoln, Nebraska. He entered service in August, 1941, and served as radar officer with the 380th Bomb Group on Mindoro and Okinawa.

Technician Fifth Grade Harry C. Ferguson, 2010 Madison Avenue, has been discharged from the Army after 46 months service. He was overseas 15 months.

Russell G. Jarrell, electrician's mate first class, of Kenova, is serving on the U.S. Navy's tuna fishing fleet off Saipan. The fleet supplies fresh fish for service personnel throughout a large area.

Seaman First Class Norman L. Arthur, 106 Whittaker Hill, is undergoing training at Norfolk, Va. for duty aboard a destroyer. He is a veteran of 25 months of sea duty and wears the Asiatic-Pacific ribbon with three stars, the Purple Heart and the Philippines Liberation ribbon with star.

Fireman First Class Charles E. France, 327 Thirty-third Street and Seaman Second Class Samuel J. Heaberlin, 121 W. Second Avenue, are en route to the United States aboard the light cruiser *Concord*.

Chief Machinist's Mate Clarence E. Powers, 1048 Madison Avenue, is serving at Espiritu Santo in the New Hebrides Islands. He is a member of the 1029th Naval Construction Detachment.

Gunner's Mate Second Class James B. Bias, 1345 Jackson Avenue, is serving aboard the transport *Hampton*, now engaged with returning veterans to the United States.

Master Sergeant Robert W. Napier of Logan has been promoted to that grade at his station in Korea where he is serving with the 184th Regiment of the Seventh Division. He wears the Purple Heart, Bronze Star and the Asiatic-Pacific ribbon with two stars. His wife, the former Miss Marion Donohoe, is a member of the Logan High School faculty.

Machinist's Mate Third Class Gray W. McClary, son of Mr. and Mrs. Samuel W. McClary of Lesage, is en route to the United States for discharge.

Glenna: *November 20th Tue. – Cool and sunny at morning. Papa killed a pig.*

Rupert: *I went to school. We are talking about changing rooms.*

Huntington: Contract negotiations between the International Nickle Company and the union had failed. The number of local workers on the picket line was estimated at three hundred.[618]

The Nuremberg trials of Nazi war criminals by a tribunal of Allied jurists began on this day.[619]

Japanese army commander Baron Gen. Shigeru Honjo killed himself after he learned of his impending arrest. He was accused of causing the Mukden incident which led to the Japanese conquest of Manchuria.[620]

Washington, November 20: "President Truman today designated General Dwight D. Eisenhower and Admiral Chester W. Nimitz to head the Army and Navy…"[621]

"IN THE SERVICE":

Two sons of Mrs. H. A. Plants, 1803 Fourth Avenue, met recently in the Philippines after being separated 17 months. Staff Sergeant L. D. Plants, assigned to duty in Yokohama with the 238th Chemical Service Unit, was granted special permission to make the transfer from his Philippine station aboard the USS *Elkhart* on which his brother, Pharmacist's Mate Third Class Forrest M. Plants, was serving.

Corporal Hayward L. Morris, son of Mr. and Mrs. H. H. Morris of Clothier, is on occupation duty with the Seventh Infantry Division in Korea. Corporal Morris has been in service 18 months. A brother, Paul Morris, is also on occupation duty in Germany.

Aviation Machinist's Mate Second Class Lloyd G. Harless of Huntington arrived in San Francisco last week aboard the USS *Breton*.

Arriving in San Francisco last week aboard the USS *Doyen* were Private First Class Crystal C. Sullivan, USMC, husband of Mrs. Edna L. Sullivan, 2818 Staunton Road, and Technical Sergeant Charles A. Smith, USMC, husband of Mrs. Mary Smith, 1333 ½ Eighth Avenue.

Yeoman First Class Herman H. Appledorn, 1814 Eighteenth Street, has been discharged from the Navy at the Bremerton, Wash. Navy Yard.

Private First Class Kenneth L. Marple, USMC, 835 ½ Twelfth Avenue, is spending a furlough in Huntington. He recently returned from Pearl Harbor, where he had been stationed with a torpedo squadron for five months.

Discharged from the Navy at Bainbridge, Md. last week were Clarence McKinney, seaman first class, Decota; William Travis, boatswain's mate second class, Ceredo; Lowen H. Wentz, chief carpenter's mate, Barboursville; James P. Wright, boatswain's mate third class, 619 Thirty-first Street; James L. Patterson, coxswain, 2977 Bradley Road; Morris E. Simmons, petty officer third class, 2648 Harvey Road;

Bernard L. Hamlin, ship's cook third class, 1835 Maple Avenue, and Boyd L. McCallister, ship's fitter first class, 108 Green Oak Drive.

Seaman First Class Allen L. Steele, son of Mrs. S. H. Steele, 2502 Smith Street, has been assigned to duty on the USS *Princeton*, a new Essex-class carrier soon to be commissioned. Seaman Steele is at the Newport, R.I. Naval training station.

Private Edwert Ramey, son of Mr. and Mrs. H. J. Ramey, 1368 Thirteenth Street, is spending a furlough with his parents before reporting to the Greensboro, N.C. Army Air Base...

Second Lieutenant Dan Brower, son of Mr. and Mrs. L. C. Brower, 1244 Fifth Avenue, arrived in Huntington Saturday to spend a 14-day leave with his parents. Lieutenant Brower has qualified with the Army Air Forces as a navigator, bombardier and radar specialist. He is stationed at Victorville, Calif.

Coxswain Malcolm F. Johnson of Olive Hill, Ky. was serving aboard the USS *Sierra*, a Pacific fleet destroyer tender, when the vessel was commended for repairing 65 ships in nine days.

Glenna: *November 21st Wed. – Cool, turning to rain about 2 o'clock. Dawson and Wink killed one of our hogs.*

Rupert: *I went to town and saw "Tom Sawyer." It was so good I bought a "Tom Sawyer" book.*

A strike by 325,000 General Motors Corporation workers was set to begin at 11 a.m.[622]

"IN THE SERVICE":

First Lieutenant Charles F. Dodrill, son of Mr. and Mrs. Charles T. Dodrill, 606 Twelfth Avenue, has been released from active duty with the Army Air Forces at Patterson Field, Ohio after 40 months of service. He wears the Distinguished Flying Cross, the Air Medal with four Oak Leaf Clusters, the Distinguished Unit Badge, and the European theatre ribbon with four stars. Lieutenant Dodrill has recently returned from the Pacific where he served as pilot on a C-54 transport plane.

Staff Sergeant Cecil E. Romine, son of Mrs. Henry C. Romine, 913 Twenty-eighth Street, has been discharged from the AAF at the Greensboro, N.C. base. He is a veteran of 29 combat missions in the West Indies and wears the Air Medal with one Oak Leaf Cluster.

Staff Sergeant A. Raymond Wiseman, son of Mrs. A. L Wiseman, 1248 Sixth Avenue, has been discharged from the Army after three years' service. A veteran of 26 months in the European theatre, he formerly operated with his mother at the Wiseman School of Business.

Corporal Clifford Howard, 120 Twenty-fourth Street, has been discharged from the Army at March Field, Calif. He wears the ETO ribbon with four stars.

Marine Corporal Tom Newsome, a paratrooper, has been discharged from service. A son of Mr. and Mrs. W. H. Newsome, 2978 Winters Road, he completed two tours of duty in the Pacific, including the Solomon Islands campaign.

First Lieutenant Russell Dunbar, son of Mrs. J. L. Dunbar, 236 Fifth Avenue, is visiting his mother and wife, the former Miss Helen Sikes, 414 Twelfth Avenue, while on leave from the Greensboro, N.C. Army Air Base. A veteran of 35 bombing missions over Japanese territory with the Twentieth Air Force, he will return to Greensboro on December 16 for probable release. He wears the Distinguished Flying Cross, the Air Medal with four Oak Leaf Clusters, and the Asiatic-Pacific ribbon with four stars.

Machinist's Mate First Class Joe L. Handley, husband of Mrs. Jessalee Handley, 529 Bridge Street, is serving in the Philippines with a Naval Construction Battalion.

Lieutenant William A. Wulfman, USNR Medical Corps, is spending a leave in Huntington. He is a member of the medical staff of the Naval Training Station at Notre Dame.

The following Huntington men have been discharged from the Navy at Bainbridge, Md.: Clyde B. Ross, fireman first class, 2 ½ Washington Avenue; Paul D. Duncan, electrician's mate second class, 1228 Eighteenth Street; Evert Stanley Jr., shipfitter first class, 540 West Tenth Avenue; and Walter S. Montague, chief motor machinist's mate, 811 West Eleventh Street.

Glenna: November 22nd Thurs. – *Mamma still sick. Frosty and cold. Cline made our sausage. Dawson and me made lard. I canned 7 quarts of sausage.*

Home canning of meat was a common method of preservation.

Rupert: *We only had cake and berries today, but we were thankful.*

It was Thanksgiving, and I remember elaborate Thanksgiving meals in my childhood, so I'm not sure why there were only cake and berries. We were very busy, so we probably celebrated another day.

"IN THE SERVICE":

Released this week from duty with [the] Navy in Washington were Specialist Second Class Elizabeth Doreene Eckley and Lieutenant (j. g.) Anna Gordon Miles. Miss Eckley, daughter of Mr. and Mrs. Roy Eckley, 619 Elm Street, entered the WAVES in July, 1943 and served at the Navy Hydrographic Office at Suitland, Md. Mrs. Miles entered service in June, 1943, and as a nurse, served in the U.S. Naval Hospital, Oakland, Calif. She is the wife of John Norman Miles of Huntington.

Staff Sergeant E. A. Maynard, husband of Mrs. Opal Perry Maynard of Wilsondale, was discharged from the Army last week at the Greensboro, N.C. separation center. A veteran of 14 combat missions in the Pacific Theatre, he wears the Air Medal with one Oak Leaf Cluster.

Seaman Second Class Joe J. Rowe, 1144 Jefferson Avenue, and Seaman Second Class Bernard R. Jones, 809 Twenty-seventh Street, participated in four European invasions aboard the USS *Anne Arundel*.

Radioman First Class Raymond Merrell Bosworth, 702 Jackson Avenue, was serving on the USS *Grarfia* when the vessel entered Nagasaki Harbor soon after Marine occupation troops.

Corporal Donald Lewis, son of Mr. and Mrs. Claude Lewis of Huntington, has been awarded the Silver Star for gallantry in action in the European theatre, his wife, Mrs. Helen Lewis, 518 Eighth Avenue, has been notified. Corporal Lewis has previously been awarded the Bronze Star and the Purple Heart with one Oak Leaf luster...

Corporal Jeanne L. Parker, daughter of Mr. and Mrs. A. W. Alterston, 206 West Eighth Avenue, notified her parents yesterday from San Francisco that she has arrived in the United States and expects to come to Huntington soon. She was formerly a clerk in General MacArthur's Philippine headquarters." [In another entry for Corporal Jeanne L. Parker, her parents last name is spelled "Albertsen."]

Seaman Second Class Hobart Adkins, son of Mr. and Mrs. Lloyd Adkins of Barboursville, has returned to Great Lakes, Ill. after spending a leave with his parents.

Private App F. Cobley, brother of Jink Cobley, 1510 Third Avenue, has been assigned to duty with the 13th Airborne Division after completing advanced paratrooper wings after training at Fort Benning, Ga.

Private Leon Gillenwater and a half-brother, Private First Class Donald E. Broce, sons of Mrs. Julia Broce, 340 Twenty-second Street, met recently in Manila. Private Gillenwater was en route from Mindoro to Yokohama and stopped in Manila to see his half-brother. Another son, Robert A. Broce, has notified his mother that he will leave Germany this month to return to the United States.

Glenna: *November 23rd Friday – Very cold. Snowing lightly. Zella Hutchinson, Frances Paugh, and myself went to town to do the Xmas shopping for the Sunday School. Cline Porter took us in his car. Also, Helen, Gaynelle, and Dawson went. We got along pretty well. We all went to St. Mary's Hospital to see Cora Gill and Maurice Mann.*

Rupert: *Mother went to town. A strange thing happened, it snowed all day.*

Mrs. Ernie Pyle, age 44, died in Albuquerque, New Mexico. She had been ill since her husband's death but the immediate cause of her death was influenza.[623]

Revealed at the Nuremberg trials: "Adolf Hitler told his generals 10 days before the invasion of Poland that he had given orders 'to kill without mercy all men, women and children of the Polish race or language.' ... The brutal words of the Fuehrer ... so delighted Reichsmarshal Hermann Goering that he leaped on a table 'and danced like a savage...'"[624]

"IN THE SERVICE":

Staff Sergeant James R. Searls, husband of Mrs. Lucy Searls, 3905 Crane Avenue, has been discharged from the Army at Gulfport, Miss. He entered the service in July, 1942 and served with the Eighth Air Force in England.

Second Lieutenant Joe L. Winter, husband of Mrs. Lucille Winter, 1710 Eighteenth Street, has been released from active duty with the

Army Air Forces at Randolph Field, Tex. He entered service in August, 1943.

Glen Edward Gifford, seaman second class, 1306 Fifth Avenue, is serving aboard the tanker *Raccoon*, a mobile fueler which supplied fuel to ships in harbor.

Specialist Second Class Erma Louise Adkins, daughter of Mr. and Mrs. F. M. Adkins of Barboursville, has been discharged from the WAVES in Washington. She entered the service in February, 1943.

Boatswain's Mate Second Class Donald L. Crank, 1401 ½ Eighteenth Street, was serving aboard the destroyer *Laprade* in the Okinawa area when the Japanese surrendered.

Glenna: *November 24th Sat. – Still cold. I canned 7 more qtrs. of sausage. Mamma still sick. At night I went to Enon to Revival meeting. Donovon Porter went to the alter.*

Rupert: *We went to Enon Church.*

Glenna: November 25th Sun. – *Went to Church and Sunday School. Pearl Porter joined the church. Donovon was at the altar. In evening we went to the church house to practice for the Xmas program. At night went to Enon to revival. Donovon and Chapman boys went to the alter. Dick Chapman's wife was saved. Donovon was saved that night after he got home. Others were saved later. Mamma went to Doctor.*

Donovon Porter was the oldest son of Gilbert and Ever Porter. Donovon, his wife Pearl and their daughter Dottie, lived up Lyle's Branch not far beyond his father's farm. (Two other children, Danny and Kathy, were born later.) Donovon and Pearl became active members of Salt Rock Methodist Church. When the new church building was erected in 1950, Donovon led the construction crew and laid blocks for the walls. I remember it well because

I worked that summer mixing mortar for laying the blocks. I was going into my senior year at Barboursville High School and worked until football practice started in mid-August.

Rupert: *I went to practice for a Christmas program after church*

Hermann Goering, on trial in Nuremberg, Germany, said through his lawyer that he planned to call Charles A. Lindbergh as a witness. Lindbergh, from his home in Fairfield, Connecticut said, "I have received no such request... The information I obtained on my trips through Germany is in War and State department reports..."[625]

"WITH THE COLORS":

Staff Sergeant Thomas M. Griffith, son of Mr. and Mrs. H. R. Griffith of 450 Adams Avenue, has been discharged from the AAF after 32 months of service. Sergeant Griffith is the recipient of the Air Medal, Good Conduct Medal, Victory Medal, African-European theater ribbon with two battle stars and the Purple Heart for wounds received after capture by the Germans. [Sergeant Griffith, a turret gunner, escaped injury when his bomber crashed in Germany in May, 1944[626]] Also visiting at the Griffith home is Corporal James E. Davis of the Sixth Marines, who saw action on Okinawa. He is on a seven-day furlough visiting his wife, the former Miss Eleanor Griffith and their three children, James, Robert Lee and Judy Kay. The Davises live in Dundee, Mich., but during Corporal Davis' absence have been making their home in Huntington.

Seaman First Class A. James Mays Jr. is visiting his parents at 2935 Hughes Street on leave from San Diego, Calif. Seaman Mays, who served on the USS *Edmonds*, destroyer, wears the Philippine Invasion ribbon with one star, the Asiatic-Pacific ribbon with three stars, the Okinawa ribbon with one star, and the American Defense and Victory ribbons.

Machinist's Mate First Class Jack Chapman and brother Jimmy, sons of Mrs. H. C. Chapman, 3618 Waverly Road, met in Nagoya Harbor, Japan, after two and a half years of separation. Two other brothers, Clifton and Joe, have received their discharges from the Army services.

Private Roy Allen, husband of Mrs. Virginia Allen, has recently been sent to Yokohama, Japan for duty with the army of occupation. Private Allen has been in service for 25 months and has been overseas 12 months with the engineers. Having served in Europe also, he wears the ETO ribbon and the Asiatic-Pacific ribbon with two battle stars. The son of Mr. and Mrs. James Allen of Columbus, O., Private Allen was formerly employed by the American Car and Foundry Co. here.

Electrician's Mate Third Class J. Kenneth McDaniel is spending a 30-day leave with his parents, Mr. and Mrs. J. O. McDaniel, 901 Twenty-eighth Street. A former electrician's apprentice with the Chesapeake and Ohio Railway Co., he has been stationed for the past 27 months on the Kwajalein Atoll in the Marshall Islands. A brother, Private William McDaniel, is stationed with the AAF at Keesler Field, Miss.

Private First Class Howard Kennedy will return from the Marcus Islands to the bedside of his father, Clarence E. Kennedy, who lies ill in Pinecrest Sanitarium, Beckley, W.Va. Private Kennedy is with the military police, USMC, and has been in service two and a half years, serving the last seven months overseas.

Private First Class Paul D. Smith, son of Mr. and Mrs. Stanley Smith, 315 West Eleventh Street, and Private Harold Arnold, 204 Main Street, husband of the former Miss Eva Marie Damron of Huntington, have arrived at the Newton D. Baker General Hospital in Martinsburg, W.Va. for treatment. Private Smith, former employee of the Owens-Illinois Glass Co., served nine months in Africa with the 1262 Base Unit, AAF. Private Arnold, a student at Huntington High School before entering the Army, served eight months in France, Germany and Holland with the 101st Paratroop Infantry, Airborne Division. He wears the Purple Heart, the Bronze Star and two battle stars in his ETO ribbon.

Glenna: *November 26th Mon. – Clear and sunny. I washed.*

Rupert: *We drew names at school. I got larry's*

President Truman flew to Missouri last night on his airplane, the "Sacred Cow," to surprise his mother on her birthday. When asked if such no-advance-notice trips were to be a precedent, Truman said, "No, it was just a case of a man spending a couple of hours with his mother. I had a notion to do this and I did it."[627]

"IN THE SERVICE":

First Lieutenant Donald L. Miller, 1116 Tenth Avenue, has been awarded the Distinguished Flying Cross in Calcutta, India. Lieutenant Miller is stationed there with the India-China Division of the Air Transport Command.

Corporal Harold H. Craft, son of Mr. and Mrs. Melvin Craft of Huntington and husband of the former Miss Gladys Mullens of Wayne, has been discharged from the Army at Patterson Field, Ohio. He had been in service since October, 1942.

Staff Sergeant M. F. Short Jr., son of Mr. and Mrs. M. F. Short of Louisa, Ky., has landed at an eastern port and is en route to Fort Knox, Ky., where he will be discharged. He has served 50 months in the Army, 36 of which were spent in the Mediterranean theatre with the 12th Air Force.

Private First Class Raymond Hicks, son of Mr. and Mrs. Vernial Hicks, 526 Buffington Street, has reported for separation at Camp Cooke, Calif. He has served for 30 months and has been assigned to the 835th Quartermaster Co. since last May. He wears the ETO ribbon with three battle stars, a bronze invasion arrowhead, and the Distinguished Unit Citation.

Sergeant Phillip J. Marshall, son of Mr. and Mrs. Eugene Marshall of Wayne, has been released from the Army Air Forces at Drew Field, Tampa, Fla. after 43 months service. His wife, the former Miss Hattie Casey, and son, Billie, also reside at Wayne.

Specialist Third Class Kathleen R. Kingery, wife of Thomas B. Kingery of Hamlin, has been discharged from the WAVES in Washington after 21 months service...

Discharged at Patterson Field, Ohio last week was Staff Sergeant Gerald G. Runyon, son of Mrs. Alvin T. Runyon, 1036 W. Sixth Street. He has served 44 months and was a chief clerk with the aviation engineers of the Army Air Forces, at Geiger Field, Spokane, Wash.

First Lieutenant Elmer E. Howard, 1940 Fourth Street, has been placed on terminal leave at Camp Atterbury before returning to inactive duty.

Technical Sergeant Thaddeus D. Kauffelt, 1329 Madison Avenue, and Sergeant Albert A. Cook, 1811 Madison Avenue, were discharged last week from the Army at Fort Knox, Ky.

Glenna: *November 27th Tue – I ironed but was sick all day. Papa took Mamma to Dr. again. She is very sick. Rain.*

Rupert: *Mama was sick. She went to the Dr.*

The fact that my grandmother went to see a doctor shows the seriousness of her illness; my grandparents were not "doctor-going" people.

West Hamlin had two doctors, Dr. George McClellan and Dr. George W. Walden.

A document revealed at the Nuremberg trials showed Germany had made preparation for war as far back as the end of World War I, and that Hitler's intent to make Germany a world power "probably could not be 'achieved by peaceful means.'"[628]

"IN THE SERVICE":

Discharged from the Navy at Bainbridge, Md. were Roy Bentley, quartermaster second class, 4645 Piedmont Road; Frank L. Nowlin, steward third class, 1683 Eighth Avenue, and Arceidus B. Jones, seaman first class, 1838 Artisan Avenue.

Private First Class Percy Ross of Salt Rock was discharged last week from the Army at Coral Gables, Fla. after 45 months' service, including 27 in the CBI theatre. A son of Mrs. Nancy Ross of Salt Rock, he served as a telephone lineman with the signal Corps attached to the Tenth Air Force.

Irvin R. Gebhardt, painter second class, of Lesage was discharged last week at Miami, Fla. He entered the service in November, 1943, and served 15 months overseas.

Private First Class Kermit G. Johnson, son of Mr. and Mrs. Mack Johnson of Salt Rock, was discharged recently from the Army at Fort George G. Meade, Md., after three years' service. Private Johnson was in action in Normandy, Northern France and Germany.

Chief Signalman M. L. Kessinger, son of Mr. and Mrs. Harlan Kessinger, 54 West Sixth Avenue, is spending a two-month leave with his parents. He is a veteran of actions in the New Hebrides, Marshall and Gilbert Islands.

Petty Officer Bill Newman, son of Mr. and Mrs. J. H. Newman, of Huntington, has arrived at his Navy station in North China, his parents were informed recently.

Seaman Second Class Vernon L. Wilson, 42 Twenty-seventh Street, has been discharged from the Navy at Bainbridge, Md.

Second Lieutenant Robert D. Hippert, son of Mr. William L. Hippert, 128 West Tenth Street, has reported for duty at the Portland, Ore. Army Air Base. A graduate of West Point, he received his commission in the regular Army Air Forces last June 5.

Chief Carpenter's Mate Adolphus D. White, 1301 Jefferson Avenue, has been discharged from the Navy in Washington.

Glenna: *November 28th Wed – Rainy and cool. Mamma is still real sick. Went to prayer meeting. I led.*

Rupert: *We went to prayer meeting. Mother led.*

"The Community Players will open their season with the presentation of 'Blithe Spirit,' Noel Coward's 'improbable farce,' tonight at 8:15 P. M. in the Marshall College auditorium..."[629]

Moundsville, West Virginia: "All schools in Marshall County were ordered closed for one week by Superintendent Lewis R. Potts today after an outbreak of influenza, colds, and a few scattered cases of scarlet fever. About 1,200 students were absent."[630]

"Navy Lieutenant Willis Hertig will return Monday to his duties as head coach at Barboursville High School, School Superintendent Olin C. Nutter said last night, and his return will bring about two additional changes in placement of school personnel... Jackson Stover, former head coach at Milton High School, and for three years acting head coach at Barboursville, will become acting principal at Milton High School. G. A. Schwartz, originally assigned this year to be permanent principal of Simms School but temporarily assigned as principal of Milton High School, will return to Simms School."[631] (Willis Hertig was

still coach at Barboursville High School when I entered in 1948, but that was his last year there. He eventually became an administrator in the Cabell County Schools district. Ed Smith succeeded him as head coach at Barboursville.)

Nuremberg: "Heinrich Hoffman, Hitler's personal photographer, says that Martin Bormann had him falsely labeled as a typhus carrier last January in order to prevent him from going to Hitler to 'tell him the truth' about Germany's approaching doom. He said he finally saw Hitler, but that Hitler's 'mind was gone.' ..."[632]

"IN THE SERVICE":

Corporal John N. Weeks, son of Mr. and Mrs. James M. Weeks, 312 College Apartments, who has been serving with the 79th Fighter Group at Linz, Austria as a photographic laboratory technician, is on his way home. Corporal Weeks graduated from Central High School in 1941 and was employed by the Chesapeake & Ohio Railway before he enlisted in the Air Forces in December, 1942. He has served for 20 months overseas and wears the ETO ribbon with five battle stars.

Technical Sergeant Patrick S. Macri, son of Mr. and Mrs. James Macri, 1617 Seventh Avenue, recently spent a seven-day furlough at the Riviera Recreational Area at Nice, France. Sergeant Macri has spent 36 months in the Army and has been overseas 27 months, serving in France, Holland, Belgium, Germany and Austria. He wears the ETO ribbon with four battle stars and a bronze arrowhead, Bronze Star, Parachutist Wings, Unit Citation with one Oak Leaf Cluster and the Belgian Fourragere.

Sergeant Mount O. Holley, husband of Mrs. Geraldine Holley, 3836 Crane Street, is enrolled in journalism courses at the University of Biarritz in France while awaiting redeployment to the United States. Sergeant Holley served with the 371st Engineer Battalion in the northern France,

Ardennes, Rhineland and central European campaigns.

Seaman First Class Lester Lee Estep of Barboursville has been discharged from the Navy at Bainbridge, Md.

Ship's Cook Second Class James Marion Dempsey, 305 West First Street, has been discharged from the Navy at Bremerton, Wash.

First Lieutenant George M. Dugan, son of Mr. and Mrs. M. W. Dugan, 1124 Sixth Avenue, and husband of the former Miss Charlotte Burns of Huntington, is on terminal leave after 29 months of duty with the 33rd Infantry Division in the Pacific. He has been awarded the Bronze Star, Combat Infantryman Badge, Asiatic-Pacific ribbon with two battle stars, Philippine Liberation ribbon, American Defense ribbon and the Victory ribbon.

Corporal Everett B. Singer, son of J. Singer of Proctorville, O. has been discharged from the Army Air Forces at Patterson Field, O. His wife is the former Miss Frances Plylon of Proctorville.

Staff Sergeant Charles A. Davis, 1640 Sixth Avenue, is spending a 10-day furlough here before being discharged. Sergeant Davis was engaged in personnel work at the Air Transport Command's Casez Army Air Base near Casablanca.

Gunner's Mate Second Class Earl Edward Dorsey, son of Mr. and Mrs. M. L. Dorsey, 2100 Sycamore Street, Kenova, has been discharged from the Navy at St. Louis after serving for four years and five months in the Pacific.

Technical Sergeant J. Penbrooke Woods Jr., son of Mr. and Mrs. J. P. Woods, 1008 Chesapeake Court, has been discharged from the Army at Amarillo, Tex. after four years' service. Sergeant Woods has returned to Huntington with his wife, the former Miss Ruth McInroy of Wellsboro, Pa., and their 18-month-old son, J. P. Woods III.

Glenna: *November 29ᵗʰ Thur. – Still rainy and cold. Mamma still sick.*

Rupert: *I got my grade card.*

No bragging. I wonder why.

Philadelphia, November 29: Army was a 27-point favorite over Navy in Saturday's game.[633] (Army won the game 32–13.) Army would become the "consensus" national champions, having gone undefeated and scoring 412 points in a nine-game schedule, while giving up only 46 points.[634]

"'I looked down and saw the city—and when the bomb exploded I couldn't see a thing. Debris and a huge mushroom-shaped cloud filled the sky,' Captain James F. Van Pelt, a navigator on both the atomic bombing attacks on Japan, thus described the first—the blow that leveled Hiroshima. The 27-year-old Oak Hill, W.Va., airman arrived here early yesterday with his wife and two children to visit his aunt, Mrs. J. G. Ramsey, 515 South Boulevard."[635]

"IN THE SERVICE":

Marine Sergeant Franklin R. Jackson, husband of Mrs. Maxine J. Jackson, 287 Gallaher Street, is en route to the United States aboard the USS *Munda*. Upon arrival from Pearl Harbor, Sergeant Jackson will go directly to a separation center for discharge.

Damron E. Jay, aviation machinist's mate third class, 172 Davis Street, was discharged this week from the Navy at Shoemaker, Calif.

The Army announced yesterday that three men from this area have been assigned to the Olie Military Police Training School at Romilly, France. They are Private Henry O. Morgan of Welch, Private Clarence H. Parsons, Rear 932 Seventh Avenue, and Private First Class H. S. Scites, 219 Davis Street. After an eight-day course they will be assigned to duty as MPs.

Technician Fifth Grade Hiter Melton, 152 Wilson Court, is spending a 30-day furlough with his wife after serving overseas for a year, He was formerly stationed at Frankfurt, Germany, at the American Military Government headquarters.

Yeoman Second Class Bully J. Holtzworth, son of Mr. and Mrs. R. H. Holtzworth, 1611 Sixth Avenue, has returned to Huntington following his discharge from the Navy. He was accompanied here by his wife, the former Miss Phyllis Saunders of Huntington, and their four-year-old daughter, Josette Dawn. Mr. Holtzworth was formerly scoutmaster of the First Methodist Church.

Private First Class Edward K. Ferrell of Huntington has been promoted to that grade at his station on northern Luzon with the 2835th Quartermaster Company.

Private Hampton Thomas, son of Mrs. Grace Farrar, 2131 Tenth Avenue, is serving at Manila with the 499th Engineer Company. He has been overseas since August.

John G. Bing, aviation radio technician third class, of Huntington, is at the Naval Staging Center at Pearl Harbor awaiting shipment to the United States for discharge.

V. A. Holley Jr., son of Mr. and Mrs. V. A. Holley, 707 Buffington Street, is spending a 30-day leave with his parents following his return to the United States after 30 months in the Pacific with a naval construction battalion.

Sergeant Bill B. Sams, son of Mr. and Mrs. C. W. Sams, 1961 Underwood Avenue, has been discharged from the AAF at Sheppard Field, Texas. A graduate of Central High School, he has been in service four years.

The following men from this area were discharged this week from the Navy at Bainbridge, Md.: Virgil Beals, aviation ordnanceman third class, Lesage; David M. Brown, seaman first class, Huntington; James A. Bellomy, carpenter's mate second class, 326 Willard Court; Hartsel T. Adkins, shipfitter second class, 1830 Marshall Avenue; Frederick L. Kidd, yeoman first class, 2153 Adams Avenue; Charles F. Holley, painter third class, 1821 West Fifth Avenue; Homer G. Bellomy, seaman first class, 1542 Jefferson Avenue, and Albert R. Hensley, seaman second class, Barboursville.

The Camp Atterbury, Ind., separation center released the following list of men discharged this week: Private First Class Charles A. Clay, Huntington; Private First Class William R. Hysell, 2151 ½ Third Avenue; Sergeant Paul R. Bell, Culloden; Technician Fifth Grade John Crockett, Wayne; Technician Fifth Grade Wallace Carver, Kenova; Staff Sergeant Lillard L. Rose, Chattaroy; Private First Class Willis Porter, Barboursville; Private Carl E. Chittum, Milton, and Private First Class Martin D. Grimmette, Gilbert.

Charles E. Nelson, son of Mr. and Mrs. C. S. Nelson, 2768 Emmons Avenue, left last week for Great Lakes, Ill. where he will enter training with the Navy. A brother, Clarence S. Nelson, stationed in Shanghai, China, is a pilot on a C-47 transport plane.

Private First Class William L. Gibson Jr., Army Air Forces, is visiting his mother, Mrs. Madeline Gibson, 2038 Eleventh Avenue. He will leave Sunday for Greensboro, N.C. for overseas assignment. Private Gibson was in service a year before he recently reenlisted.

Glenna: *November 30th Friday – Still misting rain, partly snow. I am hoarse. Have an awful bad cold. I cleaned up the house and churned. Mamma still sick.*

Rupert: *Mother is feeling awful bad.*

Stockholm, November 30: Mass suicides began when Swedish authorities began putting German and other military internees, some twenty-seven hundred in number, onto trains bound for a Russian deportation ship at Tralleborg.[636]

"IN THE SERVICE":

Private Oscar P. Pardue, son of Mr. and Mrs. J. F. Pardue, 2937 Seventh Avenue, is serving on Hokkaido Island in the Japanese homelands with the Army of Occupation. He recently informed his parents that he has visited Tokyo, Yokohama and an unnamed scene of an atomic bomb explosion. A brother, Herman Pardue, is stationed at San Francisco with the Navy.

Seaman First Class Arthur W. Speaks, son of Mrs. Mable Speaks, 733 Eighth Avenue, is en route to San Francisco from Guam aboard the carrier *Yorktown*. He is scheduled to arrive tomorrow and will be sent to a separation center.

Lieutenant (j. g.) Maston L. Gray, son of Mrs. I. R. Gray, 806 Sixth Street, has been placed on inactive duty at New Orleans, La. A graduate of Marshall College in 1939 and the Medical College of Virginia at Richmond, Lieutenant Gray served as medical officer aboard the attack-transport *Lenawee* and the LST *929* during the invasions of Okinawa and Iwo Jima.

Private Edward C. Thomas, son of Mr. and Mrs. E. C. Thomas, 1033 West Sixth Street, arrived at a West Coast port last week and has been ordered to report to Camp Atterbury, Ind. for separation from the service. Private Thomas, serving in Italy and the Pacific with an engineer battalion, has been awarded five stars to the ETO ribbon, the Asiatic-Pacific ribbon and the Philippine Liberation ribbon.

Machinist's Mate Third Class Homer J. Jordan, husband of Mrs. H. J. Jordan, 1947 Ninth Avenue, is stationed with the Navy in China. He is the son of Mr. and Mrs. Robert Jordan of Huntington.

Private First Class Virgil H. Dennison, son of Mr. and Mrs. Fred Dennison, 318 Tiernan Street, is serving at Matsuyama, Japan with the Army of Occupation. His wife, and son, Ralph E. Dennison, reside at 303 Bellvue Road.

Yeoman Third Class James A. Gibson, son of Mr. and Mrs. Delbert Gibson of Huntington is spending a 30-day leave with his parents. He returned recently from 18 months duty on New Guinea.

Second Lieutenant Hager A. Porter, son of Mrs. W. F. Porter of Chesapeake, Ohio, was commissioned Tuesday after successfully completing the officer candidate course at the Fort Benning, Ga... He is a graduate of Vinson High School.

Corporal Roderick Buffington, son of Mr. and Mrs. E. R. Buffington, 921 Jefferson Avenue, has been discharged from the Army at Fort Meade, Md. after serving for 43 months. He has been stationed in Iceland, England, France and Belgium.

December

TROOPS HOMEWARD BOUND

GLENNA: DECEMBER 1ST SATURDAY – COLD AND DAMP. RUPERT AND I
went to town and did our Xmas shopping. I was sick with a cold.

Rupert: *We went to town to do our Xmas shoping.*

Charleston, West Virginia, December 1: "Sportsmen began moving into West Virginia's deer territory [into 24 of the state's 55 counties] tonight in preparation for the opening of a deer season..." It was expected to be a good season, exceeding the 2,051 bucks kill of 1944.[637] (Some southern counties, including Cabell, Wayne, and Lincoln had no deer season, but hunters from those counties could go to counties with open seasons.)

"IN THE SERVICE":

Captain Edward M. Selfe Jr., son of Mr. and Mrs. Edward M. Selfe, 1409 Fifth Avenue, was promoted to that rank November 1... Captain Selfe commands an infantry rifle company with the Ninth Infantry Division now stationed with the Third Army occupation troops in Bavaria... He went to France in July 1943. Captain Selfe holds the ETO ribbon with five battle stars, Purple Heart, Bronze Star Medal and Silver Star. He was graduated from Presbyterian College, Clinton, S.C. magna cum laude in April, 1943. [Next entry is for the same family.]

Sergeant Richard J. Selfe, 1409 Fifth Avenue, has returned home after receiving a discharge at Patterson Field, O. He holds the American

Theatre ribbon, Asiatic-Pacific ribbon with one battle star, Good Conduct Medal and the Victory Medal. He served as a meteorologist in Alaska and the Aleutians.

Yeoman Third Class Ruth Louise Lilly, daughter of Mr. and Mrs. Jason G. Lilly, 518 Eighteenth Street, has been discharged from the WAVES. She enlisted July 27, 1944, and has been stationed at Anacostia, D.C.

Staff Sergeant Glenn H. Hager, son of Mrs. Thelma Wilson, 42 Twenty-seventh Street, has been released from the Air Forces at Gowen Field, Boise, Idaho.

The following men have been discharged from the Navy at Bainbridge, Md.: Walter S. Myers, 1502 Fourth Avenue; Charles W. McGraw, 238 Main Street; William Cupp, 229 Richmond Street; Otto C. Ball, 166 Oney Avenue; James L. Scaglion, 2117 Fourth Avenue and Clarence Rookstool, 1727 Virginia Avenue.

Staff Sergeant Curtis L. Nelson, husband of the former Miss Beulah Brown, 2536 Ninth Avenue, has been discharged from the Army at Fort Douglas, Utah.

Private First Class George T. McCoppin Jr., son of Mr. and Mrs. G. T. McCoppin, 2641 Collis Avenue, has arrived home following his discharge at Sacramento, Calif. Private McCoppin served with the Fifth Infantry Division in France, Luxembourg and Germany.

Private James M. Donohoe Jr., son of Mr. and Mrs. J. M. Donohoe, 1428 Seventh Avenue, has been discharged from the Army at Camp

Beale, Calif., and is home after a two and a half years' service. He was with the infantry in Europe until his capture. He was liberated from a German prison camp last Spring.

First Lieutenant William H. Forester, 424 Washington Avenue, is spending a 45-day leave with his wife, the former Miss Joyce Morgan. He returned this week after two years' service in the Pacific.

Staff Sergeant Arthur B. Fuller, son of Mr. and Mrs. G. V. Fuller, of Huntington, is at the redistribution station at Fort Oglethorpe, Ga. after eight months service as a squad leader in New Guinea and the Philippines...

Robert T. Barrett, 1416 Belmont Street, Ashland, a veteran of World War I, is seriously ill at the Veterans' Hospital here.

Major and Mrs. G. T. Aldridge and their three-year-old daughter, are spending a leave with his parents, Dr. and Mrs., J. E. Aldridge of Ohio River Road. Major Aldridge will report to the Greensboro, N.C. Army Air Base after January 1. He served 29 months in Europe and Panama.

Glenna: *December 2nd Sunday – I was sick and didn't go to Sunday School. That evening I went to Xmas party at the church but couldn't hardly sit up.*

Rupert: *I went to church. later we went back to practice.*

"The Elks Medal of Valor ... will be presented by George W. Osgood, exalted ruler, to B. Frank Miller Sr. in memory of his son Boyda F. Miller Jr., who died June 16 in the service of his country; presentation will be made today at 3 P. M. at the First Methodist Church with the Rev. Arthur Beckett, host pastor, delivering the eulogy 'Lest We Forget.'"[638]

"WITH THE COLORS":

M. Sgt. F. B. Amburgey, brother of Mrs. J. O. Cappellari, 312 West Tenth Avenue has returned to this country after serving in Italy for the past two and a half years... He is the son of Mr. and Mrs. Jesse Amburgey of Bath, Ky.

Machinist's Mate Second Class Walter F. Myers Jr., whose parents reside at 2135 Eighth Avenue, received his discharge from active service with the Navy at Bainbridge, Md.

Private First Class David Dunfee received his discharge from the Army last week at Camp Atterbury, Ind. Private Dunfee, a tank driver, served 18 months in California before going to the Panama Canal Zone...

Henry B. Wilkes of Huntington is serving with the Air Transport Command Squadron 12 of the Naval Air Transport Service in the Pacific.

Lieutenant Charles B. Hedrick, son of Professor Charles E. Hedrick of Marshall College, 1671 Fifth Avenue, has received his release from active service at the Naval Separation Center, Washington, D.C.

Private First Class Verlin E. McClellan, son of Mr. and Mrs. Charlie McClellan of Branchland, is now on guard duty at Kyoto, Honshu, Japan. His brother, Technician Fifth Grade Harley J. McClellan has been transferred to the General Hospital at Temple, Tex.

Lieutenant James A. Patterson, USNR, who has been spending a furlough with his parents, Mr. and Mrs. H. B. Patterson, 18 West Fourth Avenue, left yesterday for San Diego, Calif. where he will be assigned to the aircraft carrier *Cape Gloucester.*

Master Sergeant Donald E. Morrison, whose wife resides at 1604 Madison Avenue, has reenlisted in the Army Air Forces at the Army Recruiting Station here. A veteran of 26 missions over Japan as a B-29 flight engineer with the 20th Air Force, Sergeant Morrison served three years and 10 months before being granted a discharge from the AAF November 7.

First Lieutenant Max E. Weeks, son of Mr. and Mrs. E. F. Weeks, 1213 Fourth Avenue, has arrived in Huntington on furlough from Fort Monroe, Va., accompanied by his wife, the former Miss Betty Donahue, daughter of Mr. and Mrs. Dan L. Donahue of this city.

Private Clyde Swiney, son of Mr. and Mrs. Everette Swiney of McConnell, W.Va., is now doing guard duty at Trieste, Italy. His brother, Boyd Swiney, was recently discharged from the Army.

Pharmacist's Mate Tom Conaty has returned to his station at St. Elizabeth's Hospital, Washington, D.C. after spending a five-day leave with his parents, Mr. and Mrs. W. J. Conaty, 1411 Fifth Avenue.

Sergeant W. L. Wheeler, son of Mrs. M. Wheeler, 423 Eighth Avenue, has received his discharge from the active service with the AAF at the Chico, Calif., Army Air Field. Sergeant Wheeler graduated from Huntington High School and was employed by the American News Co. before entering the service.

Glenna: December 3rd Monday – *I am still sick but I washed. Dawson killed the other hog. Cline made our sausage.*

Rupert: *I went to school but was so sick that I came home.*

"Canned food for the peoples of war-dev-astated nations throughout the world will be collected by Catholic churches the week of December 9–16 and the Rev. Sylvester W. Staud, assistant pastor of St. Joseph's Catholic Church, has been named to head the collection in the Huntington deanery... The most Rev. John J. Swint, bishop of the Wheeling diocese [in a letter to Huntington], called upon all members of his faith and those of other denominations to contribute to the cause."[639]

"IN THE SERVICE":

Yeoman Laundle Barnett, son of Rev. and Mrs. L. M. Barnett, 5747 Pea Ridge Road, is expected home December 20 for a 30-day fur-lough... He has been in service for 30 months and has served in South America and in Pacific areas. Yeoman Barnett formerly played football at East High School and Wayne High School.

Privates Edwert J. Ramey and Charles M. Harrison left yesterday for the Greensboro, N.C. Army Air Force Depot after spending 14-day furloughs with their parents. Private Ramey is a son of Mr. and Mrs. H. J. Ramey, 1368 Thirteenth Street, and Private Harrison is a son of Mr. and Mrs. E. S. Harrison, 522 Sixth Street.

Staff Sergeant James H. Blackburn, son of Mrs. Cecil Hite of Huntington, was discharged last week from the Army at Lowry Field, Colo. He has been in service since January, 1942, and at the time of his discharge was a photographer.

The following Army officers from this area were placed on inactive status last week at Fort Meade, Md.: First Lieutenant Frederick W. Muckenfuss, Welch; First Lieutenant Richard D. Graham, Huntington; First Lieutenant James C. Leake, 1010 Euclid Place; Captain Lake Polan Jr., 910 Thirteenth Avenue; First Lieutenant James T. Poindexter, 2751 Highlawn Avenue, and First Lieutenant Dee E. Worrell, 812 Third Street.

Technician Fourth Grade Mary E. King, WAC. 2765 Riverview Avenue, was promoted to that grade last week at the Vaughn General Hospital at Hines, Ill. where she is serving as a hospital technician.

Bruce A. Floyd, motor machinist's mate first class, 1610 Commerce Avenue, was discharged last week from the Navy at the separation center at Shoemaker, Calif.

Technician Fourth Grade James E. Hines, 2967 Staunton Road, was promoted recently to that grade at Fort Jackson, S.C. He is a member of the headquarters company of the First Training Regiment with the Army Service Forces Personnel Replacement Depot.

Mrs. Helen Shriver Carter, storekeeper second class, wife of Robert D. Carter of Huntington, was discharged last week from the WAVES at Washington. Mrs. Carter, a daughter of Mrs. A. D. Shriver of Elkview, entered service in November, 1942...

Glenna: *December 4ᵗʰ Tuesday – We made lard and I canned sausage. Still don't feel well. Rupert is real sick in bed. Came home from school sick on Monday. Mamma is getting better.*

Rupert: *I am still sick in bed.*

The flu bug was making its way through my family.

Striking International Nickel Company employees returned to work ... with assurance of the Department of Labor that U.S. conciliators would sit in on negotiations between Union and company.[640]

Washington: "The government may turn over surplus buildings to the states without cost to meet the housing emergency ... houses to be rented first to veterans and after that to the general public..."[641] (After my discharge from the Air Force in January 1957, Millie and I took up residence at Donald Court, Marshall College's veterans housing complex.)

Stuttgart, Germany, December 4: "The United States will import food into Germany to raise the German food ration effective Jan. 1, Lt. General Lucius D. Clay said today in declaring that 'hunger and starvation have never been the United States' objective.'"[642]

"IN THE SERVICE":

Specialist Second Class Ruby Lucas Calder and Yeoman First Class Aurora Flaugher Lillie were discharged this week from the WAVES in Washington. Mrs. Calder, wife of Humphrey Calder of Huntington and daughter of Mrs. Rosa Lucas, 1666 Charleston Avenue, entered the service in February, 1943. Mrs. Lillie, wife of Robert D. Lillie, 1750 Eleventh Avenue, entered the service in April, 1943. She is the daughter of Mr. and Mrs. L. K. Flaugher, also of Eleventh Avenue.

Staff Sergeant and Mrs. Norvel W. Moore of Little Rock, Ark., will return to their home there after visiting Sergeant Moore's parents, Mr. and Mrs. J. H. Moore of Milton. Sergeant Moore was recently discharged from the Army after four years' service. He served for 16 months in Europe with the First Armored Division, and has been awarded the Combat Infantryman Badge and the ETO ribbon with two stars.

Private James E. Porter, son of Mr. and Mrs. James W. Porter of Huntington, was recently discharged from the Army at Sheppard Field, Tex. A brother, Lewis E. Porter, baker third class, is with the Navy at Norfolk, Va.

George Donall, of Midkiff, husband of the former Miss Marie Reynolds of Barboursville, has been discharged from the Navy at Bainbridge, Md. after 40 months' service. He is the son of Mr. and Mrs. Phillip Donall of Midkiff.

Staff Sergeant Alton M. Evans, son of Mr. and Mrs. J. R. Evans, 1310 Tenth Avenue, recently discharged from the Army at Fort Meade, Md., returned to Huntington Sunday. The husband of the former Miss Rebecca Dobbins of Huntington, he served for three years, 22 months of which were with the 97ᵗʰ Infantry Division in the European theatre. He wears the Purple Heart with one Oak Leaf

Cluster, the Combat Infantryman Badge and the ETO ribbon with four stars.

Lieutenant L. Poe Leggette, USNR, former Marshall College speech instructor and director of the College Theatre, arrived in Huntington yesterday for a brief visit. He recently returned after 29 months' overseas service. Lieutenant Leggette left last night for his new assignment in the office of the chief of naval operations in Washington.

Captain George S. Wallace Jr., son of Colonel and Mrs. George S. Wallace of Huntington, recently placed on inactive duty by the Army at Fort Meade, Md., is visiting his parents. He was joined by his wife, the former Miss Betty Coniffe of Evansville, Ind. Captain Wallace served in Europe with the First and Third Armies. He entered the service in 1940.

Staff Sergeant Walter A. Lusk Jr., son of Mr. and Mrs. Walter A. Lusk, 2514 Smith Street, was discharged last week from the Army at Patterson Field, Ohio. He was formerly a B-17 Flying Fortress gunner in the European theatre and has been awarded the Distinguished Unit Citation and the Air Medal.

Technician Fifth Grade Jeanne L. Parker, daughter of Mr. and Mrs. A. W. Albertsen, 206 West Eighth Avenue, has been discharged from the WAC after serving at Supreme Allied Headquarters in Manila. [In another entry Jeanne L. Parker's parents are listed as "Mr. and Mrs. A. W. Alterston."]

Lieutenant Colonel Michele A. Depietro Jr. of Logan, Corps of Engineers, was released from active duty at Camp Atterbury, Ind. on December 1.

The following men have been discharged from the Navy at Bainbridge, Md.: Boyce T. Worley, soundman first class, Culloden; James C. Brumfield, radioman third class, 2966 Piedmont Road; Lloyd C. Dailey, electrician's mate third class, 2645 Fourth Avenue; James D. Phipps, seaman first class, 39 Lower Terrace; Bob S. Mathews, coxswain, 1934 Eleventh Avenue; and Robert C. Traub, motor machinist's mate second class, 334 Highland Street.

Glenna: December 5th Wed. – *I ironed, finished canning sausage. Rupert still sick. Snowed all day. Everything looks white.*

Rupert: *I am still sick don't expect to be up by Saturday.*

Five inches of snow covered the area that afternoon, closing some schools and snarling downtown Huntington traffic.[643]

Five Navy torpedo bombers went missing in the Caribbean Ocean. (This was the tragic incident that set off the Bermuda Triangle legend which persists to this day.)

"IN THE SERVICE":

Private First Class Robert A. Williamson, son of Mrs. C. W. Williamson, 1119 Ninth Street, was discharged from the Army at Fort Douglas, Utah after serving for 51 months. When he entered the service in August, 1941, he was a student at West Virginia University.

Private First Class Donald I. Pennington and Earl A. King are eligible for 30-day reenlistment furloughs in the United States before going to the European theatre, it was announced this week from Luzon Island, where they are stationed. Private Pennington is a son of Mrs. Ruby M. Pennington, Rear 4960 Sunset Drive, and Private King is a son of Mr. William B. King of Milton. Both signed up for three years in the regular Army.

Major Robert S. Barrett, 806 West Eleventh Street, former Air Forces flight surgeon, has returned to Huntington on terminal leave before being placed on inactive duty. Major Barrett served for more than five years with the Air Forces and spent 13 months in Iceland with the Air Transport Command.

Corporal Fayette H. Meehling, son of Mr. and Mrs. Charles H. Meehling of Salt Rock, has been discharged from the Army at Kearns, Utah. He had served for more than three years, his last assignment being at the Kearns overseas replacement depot.

First Lieutenant James W. Bowermaster, son of Mr. and Mrs. O. J. Bowermaster, 712 ½ West Fourth Street, has recently been designated Personal Affairs Officer at his station at Fort Lewis, Wash. He is a veteran of eight years' service, including five as an enlisted man. Commissioned in September, 1942, he served for two years overseas with the First Armored Division and the 24th General Hospital. He was awarded the Silver Star for work in evacuating wounded under heavy artillery fire while with the First Armored.

Lieutenant Commander Ralph E. Grimmett, USNR, 301 West Eighth Street, has been placed on inactive duty in Washington.

Corporal George Eddins, son of Mr. and Mrs. George Eddins, 919 Ninth Street, has been discharged from the Army at Santa Ana, Calif. He served for 29 months in England, France and Germany as a truck driver.

Radioman Third Class Kenneth Langdon, 1544 Monroe Avenue, was discharged this week from the Navy at Great Lakes, Ill.

Private First Class Clarence N. Hill Jr., son of Mr. and Mrs. C. N. Hill, 426 ½ West Fourteenth Street, was discharged from the Army last week at Patterson Field, O. after three years' service. He was in northwest Canada and Alaska for 28 months.

Glenna: *December 6th Thursday – Still got a cold. Rupert is still sick at home. I am not working. Snow is melting some. Mamma is better.*

Rupert: *A little better today but still sick.*

Salt Lake City, December 6: "Shirley Temple, back in Salt Lake City to see her husband, Sgt. John Agar whenever she can, commented today

that 'a lot of publicity doesn't go so well on John because he isn't used to it.'"[644]

"IN THE SERVICE":

Commander Willard F. Daniels, USNR, 3601 Piedmont Road, was promoted to that rank this week and was next day placed on inactive status by the Navy at Washington... In service for five years as a surgeon, he returned to the United States in November after more than 20 months in the Pacific and China.

Private First Class William H. Ramsey Jr., son of Mr. and Mrs. W. H. Ramsey of Cyclone, has been transferred from Fort Bragg, N.C. to a separation center for discharge. He served in Europe a year as an ammunition bearer with the infantry, He served in Belgium, France and Germany, participating in the battles of the Rhineland, Ardennes and Central Germany.

Major George McTigue Jr., 2104 Wiltshire Boulevard, has been awarded the Bronze Star Medal at Calcutta. India. He is with the Air Transport Command.

Hospital Apprentice First Class Katherine Lloyd, daughter of Mr. and Mrs. F. Lloyd of East Lynn, has been discharged from the WAVES at Washington. She entered the service in June, 1943 and was last stationed in the Hawaiian Islands.

Captain Joseph E. O'Dwyer, 522 Fourteenth Street, has been awarded the Air Medal at the Calcutta, India, base of the Air Transport Command where he is stationed as a pilot.

Technician Fifth grade William T. Graveley, 925 Sixteenth Street, and Private First Class Otha H. Smith of Kenova have reenlisted in the regular Army at Fort George G. Meade, Md.

Private First Class Willie Yates, son of Mrs. Nancy Yates of Huntington, has enlisted in the regular Army at his station on Luzon in the Philippines. He will receive a 30-day furlough before returning to the West Pacific with the airborne infantry.

Machinist's Mate Second Class Donald C. Woods of Huntington is at Pearl Harbor awaiting transportation to the United States for discharge from the Navy.

Private First Class Raymond Arnold, a nephew of Mrs. Omer Arnold of Barboursville, is stationed in France with the 122nd Ordnance Company. He has been overseas since September, 1943, and was stationed in England before going to the continent.

Sergeant A. Clyde Beveridge Jr., son of Mr. and Mrs. A. Clyde Beveridge, 929 Twelfth Street ... expects to return soon to the United States. Overseas for 19 months, he has been stationed in England, France, Belgium and Germany, and has been awarded five stars to the ETO ribbon.

Lieutenant Colonel Thomas J. Riggs Jr., son of Mr. and Mrs. T. J. Riggs, 207 West Eleventh Street, has been assigned to duty as engineering officer at Camp Swift, Tex. Colonel Riggs, a former football star at the University of Illinois, was captured by the Germans last year during the Battle of the Bulge. He later escaped and fought with the Russian forces before rejoining his own outfit.

Aviation Cadet Roger S. King, son of Mr. and Mrs. Harry G. King, 301 Wilson Court, returned to Huntington this week after being discharged from the Army at Patterson Field, O. He had been in service for three years.

Staff Sergeant Curtis L. Nelson, son of Mr. and Mrs. Sawyer H. Nelson of Seth, formerly employed by the International Nickel Co., has been discharged from the AAF after three years' service.

Glenna: *December 7th Friday – Still cold. Rupert is sick yet in bed. Everybody is sick with colds and flu.*

Rupert: *I'm still in bed. This is Perl Harbor day.*

Miami: "A dawn to dusk search of a vast Atlantic area by a rescue armada failed to turn up a single clue today to the disappearance of five Navy torpedo bombers and a big PBM that went out to hunt them." The six planes had twenty-seven men on board.[645]

Manila, December 7: "Lt. General Tomoyuki Yamashita, Japanese commander in the Philippines, today was convicted of condoning atrocities by his troops and sentenced to death by hanging..."[646]

"IN THE SERVICE":

Elmer A. Kitchen, motor machinist's mate second class, 3005 Fourth Avenue, was discharged last week from the Navy at Bainbridge, Md. A veteran of 26 months in the service, he was aboard the LST *921* which was sunk during the invasion of Southern France. For heroism in that action, he was awarded a special citation. He wears the Purple Heart for wounds received in the sinking, and the American and European theatre ribbons.

Chief Petty Officer and Mrs. Fred A. Thompson visited Mrs. Cecil Hite of Spring Valley Drive recently. The officer, a brother of Mrs. Hite, is stationed at Nero Beach, Fla., and has reenlisted for a two year period.

Sergeant Richard N. Smith, 1505 Third Avenue, has been discharged from the Army at Miami Beach, Florida.

Carlton L. Ward, 84 Sycamore Street, has been discharged from the Army at Fort Sill, Okla.

The following men from this area have been discharged from the Army at Camp Atterbury, Ind.: Staff Sergeant George R. Estep, Hurricane; Technician Fifth Grade Roy B. Plummer, Huntington Route 2; Staff Sergeant Charles E. Garrett, 210 Chestnut Street and Staff Sergeant Charles E. Tyler, Logan.

Private First Class Ernest H. Collins, 630 ½ Nineteenth Street, has reenlisted in the Army at Fort George G. Meade, Md.

Glenna: *Saturday December 8th – Some warmer. Sun is shining but wind is cold. Rupert got up but didn't go out. I didn't work much all day.*

Rupert: *I am better today but weak. I have just taken a bath.*

A bath was not an easy undertaking. Well-water was heated and poured into a washtub for stand-up bathing. It was another six years before our new house with modern conveniences made things easier.

"Led by scoring charges of Bill Hall and Andy Tonkovich, Marshall's Big Green basketball team chalked up their third straight victory of the 1945–46 season last night at the East High School gymnasium when they trounced Georgetown College Tigers 69 to 27."[647]

The search for twenty-seven missing Navy fliers continued over the ocean and Florida swamps between Orlando and Melbourne where an Eastern Airlines pilot said he had spotted red flares.[648]

Tokyo: "The United States today formally charged Japanese Lt. Gen. Masaharu Homma, conqueror of the Philippines, with permitting the death march of Bataan and other atrocities against Filipinos and Americans."[649]

"IN THE SERVICE":

Technician Fourth Grade Charles K. Hibner, Ona, has been discharged from the Army at Fort Leonard Wood, Mo.

Private First Class James W. Bryan, son of Mr. and Mrs. W. M. Bryan of West Hamlin and a veteran of the European war, is now serving in the South Pacific. His brother, Seaman First Class William M. Bryan Jr., recently attained his present rank in the South Pacific.

First Lieutenant Addie Frances Short, daughter of Mr. and Mrs. M. F. Short of Louisa, Ky., has landed at a West Coast port from the Pacific theatre. Since V-J Day she has been stationed on Luzon. She is a graduate of Memorial Hospital's school of nursing in Williamson, W.Va. and received her basic training at Camp Atterbury, Ind.

Sergeant Jere P. Corkran, son of Mr. and Mrs. J. P. Corkran, 606 Tenth Avenue, has been discharged from the Army Air Forces at Seymour Johnson Field, N.C.

The following men have been discharged from the Army at Camp Atterbury, Ind.: Technician Fifth Grade Herschell E. Ellis, 306 West Twenty-second Street; Corporal Gordon L. Minnich, Huntington; Technician Fourth Grade Edgar W. York, Iaeger and Sergeant Charles T. Sansom, Wayne.

The following Huntington men have been discharged from the Navy at Bainbridge, Md.: Machinist's Mate Third Class Lloyd E. Craig, 632 Ninth Street; Seaman First Class Cecil Wallace, Huntington; Firecontrolman First Class Frank F. Richards, 1643 Twelfth Avenue; Storekeeper Second Class Charles B. Lewis, 1221 ½ Nineteenth Street; Seaman First Class Edgar A. Lindsey, 341 Twenty-second Street; Machinist's Mate Second Class Alvin C. Rice, 651 Thirty-first Street, and Gunner's Mate Second Class Irl E. Carroll, 36 West Third Avenue.

Seaman First Class Edgar Augustus Lindsey, son of Mr. and Mrs. E. A. Lindsey, 321 Twenty-second Street, a veteran of 16 months service on a destroyer in the South Pacific, is stationed at the Charleston, S.C. Navy Yard.

Sergeant Billy L. Beckett, 421 ½ Fourteenth Street, is serving with the 26th Replacement Depot near Calcutta, India.

Sergeant Paul Miros, son of Mr. and Mrs. Michael Miros, 618 South High Street, recently attained his present rank with the Army Airways Communications System at Naples, Italy.

Coxswain James Robinson of Prestonsburg, Ky., served aboard the USS *Bennington* in the attack on Japan.

Lieutenant Peter H. Baer, 1666 Fifth Avenue, and Commander William C. Nelson of Huntington, have been placed on inactive duty by the Navy in Washington.

Lieutenant William E. McCoppin, 2641 Collis Avenue, accompanied by First Lieutenant Urban L. Drew of Detroit, arrived in Huntington Thursday...

Glenna: *December 9th Sunday – We went to Sunday School. Stuart, Ruby, and children came home with us and stayed until church at night and we went to church. Pretty day.*

Rupert: *I went to church. All the Hutchinsons came home with us.*

Maiden Form Brassiere Company of Bayonne, N.J. purchased the former Casey Jones overall factory at 2311 Adams Avenue. It was estimated that next year the company would need a "working force" of 350 to 450 Huntington women.[650]

The Stella Fuller Foundation "... Announced that more toys are needed to meet the demands of Huntington underprivileged children. Toys of any type and in any condition are being repaired for the settlement by the members of the fire department, and toys are to be taken to the Central fire station."[651]

"WITH THE COLORS":

Sergeant Maurice J. Flynn, son of Mrs. Maurice S. Flynn of 539 Eleventh Avenue, received an honorable discharge last Friday at Camp Selby, Miss., and returned to Huntington last Saturday. He holds the American Theatre Medal, the European Theatre Medal with two battle stars representing action in Central Europe and the Rhineland, the Good Conduct Medal, the Purple Heart with one Oak Leaf Cluster and the Combat Infantryman's Badge. He was a member of the 95th Infantry Division.

Master Technical Sergeant T. A. Ward Jr., U.S. Marine Corps, stationed in Maryland, arrived yesterday to spend a few days with his parents, Mr. and Mrs. T. A. Ward of Green Oak Drive. He has been in the Marine Corps 29 months.

Staff Sergeant Marshall L. Faulkner, son of Mr. and Mrs. W. L. Faulkner, 4332 Ohio River Road, has been discharged from the Army at Fort Meade, Md... He served 14 months with the First and Third Armies in France, Belgium, Germany and Holland. He is a graduate of Barboursville High School and was employed at the International Nickel Co. before entering the service December 5, 1942. He is married and he and Mrs. Faulkner are the parents of a daughter.

Private Lewis Fredman Jr., son of Mr. and Mrs. Lewis Fredman Sr. of 1492 ½ Washington Avenue, has returned home after serving two years and 10 months with the U.S. Engineers in the 341st Division. He participated in the invasions of Normandy, France, Ardennes, Rhineland and Central Europe. He holds two battle stars, the Good Conduct Medal and World War II Victory ribbon.

Master Sergeant Harvey N. Davis, USMC, will arrive in the United States Dec. 10 after having spent 12 months overseas where he saw action in the Marshall Islands, Okinawa, Saipan and Japan. Sgt. Davis received a special commendation for skill and bravery beyond the line of duty which was presented to him by the Commander-in-Chief of the Pacific Fleet.

Chief Yeoman Leon Edwin Dunfee of Chesapeake, O. and Washington, D.C. has been placed in charge of foreign communications at the American embassy at Havana, Cuba. He is a graduate of Marshall College, where he majored in Spanish and commerce...

Petty Officer (First Class) W. R. Rideout, son of Mr. and Mrs. Otto Rideout, recently spent a 30-day leave with his parents. He served 19 months overseas with the Amphibious Receiving Base in Plymouth, England. He arrived in New York Oct. 27 and reached Huntington on the 28th. He has been in the Navy two years and 11 months.

Seaman (First Class) William H. Brown and Corporal Samuel A. Brown, sons of Howard Brown, 1029 West Thirteenth Street, were discharged and are now at home. Seaman Brown served two years and one half in the service and 25 months overseas in the Pacific. He wears the Asiatic Ribbon and the American Theatre Ribbon with three invasion stars. Corporal Brown spent four years in the Army and 35 months overseas.

Seaman (First Class) William Clinton Skeens, Jr., son of Mrs. Clinton Skeens, who has been serving aboard the [USS *Helm*], is now spending a 30-day leave at home...

Wearing the Bronze Star Medal and the Purple Heart, Sergeant Ira Hill, formerly of the Tanks Destroyer Corps, is visiting his uncle and aunt, Mr. and Mrs. Harlan Kessinger, 54 West Sixth Avenue. In service for the past five and a half years, he has been on duty in France, Belgium, Germany and Austria.

Yeoman (Second Class) John J. Baker, 404 Ninth Avenue, served aboard torpedo boat USS *Hilo* during the South Pacific campaigns. A converted yacht, the *Hilo*, took part in the "Battle of the Bismarck Sea."

Serving aboard the USS *Register* is Signalman (Third Class) Keith Dean, son of Mr. and Mrs. Levi J. Dean, 2748 Guyan Avenue. He has been overseas 10 months and wears the American Theatre Ribbon, the Philippine Liberation Ribbon, and the Asiatic-Pacific Ribbon.

... Private (First Class) Edward K. Ferrell, son of Amanda Ferrell [Huntington Route 2], at his base at San Fernando, Luzon. A former student at Barboursville High School, he serves as a depot checker with the 3835th Quartermaster Gas Supply Co.

Private Glenn Moore of Camp Blanding, Fla., who is now home on furlough, is visiting his wife and baby who reside with Mrs. Moore's mother, Mrs. Zeba Adkins of 2233 James River Road.

Seaman (First Class) Joseph N. Elkins left Guam November 25 and is scheduled to arrive in San Francisco today. He is the husband of Mrs. Goldie M. Elkins, 719 West Third Avenue. Upon arrival in the U.S. he will report to a separation center to receive his discharge.

Glenna: *December 10th Monday – I washed. It is snowing again. Very cold and disagreeable. I'm not very well.*

Rupert: *I went to school. we got our Xmas tree today.*

Business was coming alive: "An ultra-modern two-story office building will be erected on the northeast corner of Fourth Avenue and Tenth Street next year to replace the Miller-Ritter Building, which was destroyed in one of Huntington's costliest and most spectacular fires on February 13, 1944." President William R. Ritter of the Frederick Holding Company, which owns one-half of the corner, made the announcement. The other half of the corner belongs to C. L. Ritter, father of William R. Ritter.[652]

"IN THE SERVICE":

Lieutenant Ernest C. Lawson Jr., 749 Twelfth Avenue, last week was released from active duty with the Navy in Washington.

WAVES from this area who were discharged in Washington recently include Seaman First Class Mary Frances Lewis, 2814 Elmwood

Avenue; Lieutenant Frances Jeanne Childers, 1806 Sixth Avenue and Specialist First Class Frances Louise Whitt, Bellaire.

Private First Class Jesse L. Belville, son of Mr. and Mrs. William L. Belville, 3616 Fifth Avenue, is serving with 835th Ordnance Base Depot in Japan. Private Belville also served in England and France.

Yeoman Second Class Herman L. Smith, 1041 Eighth Avenue, was one of 38 enlisted men and women who helped establish the Naval Personnel Separation Center at the Jacksonville, Fla. Naval Air Station, and who received a letter of commendation from the separation center commanding officer last Wednesday.

Mr. and Mrs. Hamlet Smith of Buffalo have as their guest their son, Captain James C. Smith, who served for 42 months with the Army Air Forces in Africa. He will return to his duties January 10.

Glenna: *December 11th Tuesday — Very cold all day. I ironed but didn't do much. Everybody in our family feeling better.*

Rupert: *I went to school today. It was awful slick.*

A great step forward: "The site for Huntington's proposed new airport yesterday was approved by R. J. Sutherland of New York, assistant district engineer of the Civil Aeronautics Authority, following an inspection of the 700 acre tract in Wayne County."[653]

"IN THE SERVICE":

Captain James Mowery, son of Mrs. Frank Mowery, 1212 Seventeenth Street, has arrived home for a 45-day leave after which he will report for duty to Camp McClelland, Ala. Captain Mowery served for 25 months overseas

with the 111th Infantry and returned to this country last month from Palau.

Fireman First Class Ray D. Garrett, husband of Mrs. Velma R. Garrett, Rear 295 Oakland Avenue, has left Okinawa aboard the USS *Lucretia* and is expected to arrive in San Francisco today.

Electrician's Mate Second Class Melvin E. Deaton of Huntington and Storekeeper Second Class Parry F. Tanner, 312 Elaine Court, are expected to arrive at San Diego tomorrow aboard the USS *Block Island* from Saipan.

Scheduled to arrive in the United States aboard the USS *Haskell* from Okinawa are Machinist's Mate Second Class Cesco H. Barnett, 1006 ½ Twenty-fifth Street; Seaman Second Class John W. Kimbrough, 1341 Madison Avenue; and Metalsmith Third Class Benjamin F. Lambert, 3746 Norwood Road.

Sergeant Jesse M. Norris of South Point, O., has been discharged from the AAF at Drew Field, Tampa, Fla. after 24 months service as an MP.

Gunner's Mate Third Class Ralph G. Bias, 419 Twenty-sixth Street, has been discharged from the Navy at the Charleston, S.C. separation center after 19 months' service. He last served on the USS *Solomons*.

Private First Class James B. Conner, son of Appeline Conner of Huntington, was sworn into the Regular Army recently at Batangas, Luzon, in the largest mass recruiting ceremony to be held in peacetime. More than 1,000 other Pacific veterans took the oath at the same time and all are expected to return to overseas duty after furloughs home.

The following men have been discharged from the Army at Fort Knox, Ky. separation center: Technician Fifth Grade Charles Arix Jr., Branchland; Staff Sergeant Charles R. Clemons, Filbert; Private First Class Charlie Peters, Rear 728 Tenth Avenue; Private First Class Jesse J. Knapp, 301 Washington Avenue; Private First Class Donald Cresong, Lyburn; Technician Fifth Grade William G. Beavers, Logan; Private First Class Willie Justice, Matewan; Sergeant

Lonnie Stanley, Six; Master Sergeant Thurman F. Fry, Stiltner; Private First Class Irian R. Maynard, Webb; Technician Fifth Class Mello Azzaea, Williamson, and Staff Sergeant Frank A. Cecil, Williamson.

Glenna: *December 12th Wed. – Still cold and sunny. I visited Aunt Sallie Morris and Mrs. Smith. At night I went over to Gilbert Porter's. Ever, George, and the little twins are sick.*

Rupert: *We visited Gilbert Porter's foaks. They have the flew.*

Gilbert and Ever Porter had a wide age-span of children, all sons except for one daughter, Marie. Donovon, the oldest son, lived farther up Lyle's Branch with his own family. Cledith was recently discharged from the Army. Shirrell was at home and helped work the farm. George was a few years younger than me. The infant twins Greg and Gary seemed to be having a rough start in life.

"A gray fox has been added to the list of wild animals killed or captured inside the Huntington city limits, ... Ray Lambert, field and stream editor of The *Herald-Advertiser*, expressed the belief that wild life was invading the city because it had become so plentiful during the war." He attributed that to farm youths being away in the armed services and the curtailment of fur trapping.[654]

Nuremberg: "Six leading Nazis were accused today by their own documents of engineering the brutal, sub-human enslavement of more than 6,500,000 foreign workers through ruthless manhunts, arson and murder."[655]

An AP release from Heidelberg, Germany stated that "... The condition of Gen. George S. Patton Jr. 'remains good,' and Mrs. Patton, after seeing her husband again today, declared herself 'not the least worried.'" Patton was paralyzed as a result of a December 9 auto accident.[656]

"IN THE SERVICE":

Major Walter Greenwood Jr., husband of the former Miss Mary Logan Jones of Huntington, has been assigned to the G-1 Personnel section at Headquarters of the Army Ground Forces in Washington. Major Greenwood, a native of East Orange, N.J., is a graduate of numerous Army schools and served overseas for seven months, He participated in the Rhineland and Central Europe campaigns.

Mrs. Elizabeth Lester Derbaum, daughter of S. L. Lester of Kenova, was discharged from the WAVES this week in Washington. The wife of Fred C. Derbaum of Tampa, Fla., she held the ratting of seaman first class. She was stationed at the Navy Signal and Code Laboratory in Washington.

Frank S. Mayberry, aviation radioman third class of Scottown, Ohio, was discharged this week from the Navy at Jacksonville, Fla.

Sergeant James F. Brumfield, son of Mrs. Mattie M. Brumfield of Kenova has been discharged from the Army at Patterson Field, Ohio. He entered the service in 1942.

Major Frederick A. Fitch Jr., former Marshall College physical instructor, has been placed on terminal leave and has returned to Huntington. He served in the Pacific for 35 months with the Air Forces in administrative, intelligence and plan-training capacities. He has been awarded the Asiatic-Pacific ribbon with three stars, the Distinguished Unit Citation and the Philippine Liberation ribbon.

Seaman First Class G. A. Mills Jr., 1234 Ninth Street, has been discharged from the service at the Naval Separation Center at Great Lakes, Ill.

Seaman Second Class Samuel E. Haworth, son of Mrs. S. V. Haworth, 1107 West Fifth

Street, is stationed at Camp Bright, Guam, with the Seabees.

Mr. and Mrs. Paul Duncan of Huntington are visiting friends and relatives at Princeton [WV] and Bluefield. He was discharged recently from the Seabees after serving for 32 months in the Pacific.

Major Stanley J. Smith, son of Mr. and Mrs. J. N. Smith, 514 West Eleventh Avenue, returned home Monday after 27 months' service with the faculty of the Command and General Staff School in Kunming, China.

Jack Bobbitt, son of Dr. and Mrs. R. M. Bobbitt, 2104 Wiltshire Boulevard, spent last week-end at home. Also here were Majors, Thomas W. Wolfe and George J. McTigue, sons-in-law of Dr. Bobbitt.

Technician Fourth Grade Ralph Pennywitt, grandson of Mr. and Mrs. Z. P. Pennywitt, 1905 Foster Avenue, is visiting in Huntington before reporting to the separation center at Fort Knox, Ky. A former student at Marshall College, he entered the service in 1942. He has served for 26 months in the Pacific with the Fifth Air Force, and wears four stars on the Asiatic-Pacific ribbon, and one star on the Philippine Liberation ribbon.

Glenna: *December 13ᵗʰ Thurs. – Cold and cloudy. Old Lady Ida Dial Ferrel got killed by a truck at Merritts Creek at 10 o'clock. Pearl Porter was here.*

Ida Ferrell, seventy-five years old, was the daughter of Tassel and Bromlette Keyser.[657]

Rupert: *Eddie came out and we road our sleds.*

Eddie's sled was a large monstrosity clobbered together with rough lumber from his family's sawmill. It was basically a little house nailed onto a wooden platform with no way to steer. He sat inside and looked out a knothole.

I helped pull it up the hill on the Lucas farm next to our pastureland. The hill was steep, but leveled off at the bottom where there was a barbed-wire fence. The sled picked up speed before crashing through the fence and sliding down into a little creek where it broke through the ice and submerged Ed up to his knees. He dried out in our house.

"Some 85 members of the staff of the O. J. Morrison department store here attended the firm's annual Christmas banquet last night at the Hotel Frederick. John L. Henry acted as toastmaster and messages were read from Carroll Morrison, manager of the store now on leave with the Navy, and from O. J. Morrison of Charleston, head of the company."[658]

Kwajalein: "Three Japanese officers were sentenced to the gallows today for the slaying of three American airmen on Jaluit atoll in March 1944... On Tuesday six other Japanese were sentenced to hang for beheading five Americans whose bombers crashed on Mill atoll."[659]

"IN THE SERVICE":

Flight Officer Euveldia C. Maynor, son of Mr. and Mrs. E. D. Maynor, 1320 Fifth Avenue, has been placed on terminal leave from the AAF at Andrews Field in Washington. He entered the service in February, 1942. He received his appointment and his wings as a flight engineer on a B-29 Superfortress. He had previously served as an aircraft mechanic and as a gunnery instructor.

Private First Class Oscar H. Scott, son of Mrs. O. H. Scott, 1326 Fourth Avenue, was discharged from the Army last week at Fort Meade, Md. after three years' service. He served in Africa, Italy and Austria with a 105mm howitzer gun crew and wears four stars to the ETO ribbon.

Private Jack E. Scott, son of Mr. and Mrs. C. W. Scott, 1326 Fourth Avenue, is serving in Japan with the Army of Occupation at the Tateyama Air Base.

Robert McDermott, pharmacist's mate second class, son of Mr. and Mrs. H. A. McDermott of Ona, is spending a leave with his parents after returning from the South Pacific area where he served with the Marine Corps...

George F. Gross, aviation machinist's mate third class, 1425 Third Avenue, has been discharged from the Navy at Charleston, S.C. He served for 33 months and was last stationed at Vero Beach, Fla.

Private Charles L. Weakley of Barboursville has been discharged from the Army at Fort Hayes, Columbus, Ohio.

Marine Sergeant J. Edward Bailey and Staff Sergeant Howard L. Bailey, sons of Mr. and Mrs. Carl F. Bailey of Park Hills, were reunited this week for the first time in four years as they returned to Huntington for the Christmas holidays. Marine Sergeant Bailey has been discharged after three years in the service, and 27 months overseas. He wears two stars on the Asiatic-Pacific ribbon. Army Sergeant Bailey is home on furlough from the Army hospital at Staunton, Va., where he has been receiving treatment, He has been in service for four years and was with the Army which was charged with the security of atomic bomb research.

Dr. Francis A. Scott, a lieutenant commander in the Naval Reserve, and Dr. J. Russell Cook, a major in the Army Medical Corps Reserve, have received their releases from active duty. Dr. Scott, an orthopedic surgeon, will resume his Huntington practice soon. Dr. Cook has already returned to Huntington and his private practice.

Major Willis S. Morgan, brother of J. Hanley Morgan, 535 Thirteenth Avenue, is visiting in Huntington on terminal leave before reverting to inactive status. A former physician at Paris, Ky., he served for 33 months in the Pacific and wears two stars to the Asiatic-Pacific ribbon.

Seaman First Class Sheldon Levine, son of Milton Levine, 1116 Eighth Street, has been

promoted to that grade aboard the LST *863*. He has served for 19 months in the South Pacific.

Lieutenant (j. g.) Irvin Dugan Jr., son of Mr. and Mrs. Irvin Dugan, 2609 Fourth Avenue, left this week to rejoin his ship, the SS *Park Victory* at Baltimore... Lieutenant Dugan is navigation officer of the ship.

Corporal Yvonne Van Valkenburgh, daughter of Mr. and Mrs. P. K. Van Valkenburgh, 1235 Eighth Street, has been discharged from the Marine Corps Women's Reserve after 32 months of service.

Lieutenant (j. g.) Charles R. Vose, son of Mrs. C. R. Vose, 1715 Fifth Avenue, is spending a 30-day leave with his mother. He has been serving in the Pacific aboard a troop transport.

Eugene Hughes, seaman first class of Omar, and John W. Affolter, radioman third class of Teays, were discharged from the service this week at Charleston, S.C.

Emory C. Raines, machinist's mate first class, Frank A. Coulter, machinist's mate second class, and Tracy L. Terrell, machinist's mate third class, all of Huntington, were scheduled to arrive this week at San Francisco aboard the carrier *Saratoga*.

Glenna: December 14th Fri. – *Cold and cloudy. Cline is sick with the asthma. School let out for Xmas holidays.*

Rupert: *We gave our preasents at school. I got a pincel box.*

"The sharpest rise in influenza cases since the epidemic of 1943 was reported today by United States Public Health officials."[660]

Lt. General James H. Doolittle, at a reunion in Miami Beach, Florida with his flyers said, "We're here for two purposes: to pay tribute to those of the original 80 who lost their lives—and for a comradely get-together."[661]

"IN THE SERVICE":

Marine Private Clemith Ellis, son of Mr. and Mrs. Harry Brook, is spending a 12-day furlough with his parents at 1836 Maple Avenue and will report back to Camp Peary, Va. December 22 for assignment to foreign duty.

Seaman First Class Charles Edward Wolfe, 614 Sixth Street, has been discharged from the Navy at Shoemaker, Calif.

Boatswain's Mate Second Class Freddie M. Miller of Barboursville, has been discharged from the Navy at Bainbridge, Md. He wears the Navy Unit Commendation Ribbon, the American and Asiatic-Pacific theatre ribbons, and the Philippine Liberation Bar.

Major Carl L. Tankersley of Wheelwright, Ky., and Captain Lee E. Nelson, husband of Mrs. Mary E. Nelson, 1219 Tenth Street, are returning from the Pacific area under the Thirteenth Army Air Force deployment system.

Captain Lawrence E. Forman, whose wife resides at 1112 Ninth Street, has been discharged from the Army at Camp Breckinridge, Kentucky.

Second Lieutenant Glenn G. Geddis, son of Mr. and Mrs. George F. Geddis, 2201 Adams Avenue, has been released from the Army Air Forces at Randolph Field, Tex.

Parachute Rigger Third Class Ann Elizabeth Colebank, daughter of Mrs. Teresa Arpp, 816 Twenty-fifth Street, has been discharged from the WAVES in Washington.

Glenna: *December 15th Sat. – Cold and clear. Nothing unusual happened. I made some chocolate candy. At night made some Xmas candy. Big snow blizzard before nine o'clock. Dawson ...* (The end of this entry was unreadable. It's likely she noted that Dawson was late or did not come home because of the storm.)

"Chocolate candy" was fudge filled with black walnuts or hickory nuts from our own trees. "Xmas candy" was a soft white goodie we called "foam candy."

Rupert: *They have been blasting out rock up the hollow all day.*

I'm not sure what the blasting was about, but a gas well about a half-mile up Lyle's Branch required constant road repair.

"Approximately 15 members of the Cincinnati Symphony Orchestra will appear with the Huntington Orchestra in its Christmas concert at 3:30 P. M. tomorrow in the City Auditorium. They will remain in the city for the Cincinnati Symphony concert Monday night, an attraction of the Marshall College Artists Series."[662]

Charleston, West Virginia, "December 15: The South Charleston Black Eagles, undefeated and untied in 11 games this season, were named the West Virginia scholastic football champions of 1945... The proteges of Coach Bill Weber nosed out the Elkins Tigers and the Weirton Red Riders for the honor, won last year by the Williamson Wolfpack."[663]

"IN THE SERVICE":

Corporal Donald A. Green, 2759 Highlawn Avenue, and 12 other West Virginians were guests at a recent "state" party given by the Red Cross in Calcutta in honor of servicemen from Virginia, West Virginia and Maryland...

Returning to the United States for discharge via the Navy's "Magic Carpet" fleet are Sergeant Milton J. Dickerson, Huntington; Technician Fourth Grade Raymond Scarberry, Huntington and Corporal Paul F. King, son of Mrs. Reba L. King, 418 Eighteenth Street, all of the Army; and Machinist's Mate Second Class Vergil K. Kincaid, 617 ½ Sixteenth Street; Pharmacist's Mate Second Class Horace L. Haun, 303 Sixth Avenue, and Machinist's Mate Third Class Paul C. Wolfe, Huntington, all of the Navy.

Seaman First Class Joseph B. McClelland, 1404 Twelfth Street, is serving aboard the Destroyer *Gridley* in the Mediterranean after seven months in the Pacific. His wife, Mrs. Margaret L. McClelland, and daughter Pattie Jo, are residing in Huntington.

Master Sergeant Robert C. Hilsheimer, with his wife and daughter Judy, is visiting J. E. Hilsheimer, 929 Twenty-fourth Street following his discharge from the AAF at Chanute Field, Ill. After the holidays he will return to Chicago to resume his position with the Chesapeake & Ohio Railway Co. Sergeant Hilsheimer has served more than four years in the armed forces.

Seaman Second Class Eugene N. Brackman, 1404 Marcum Terrace, who served with Air Transport Squadron 12 of the Naval Air Transport Service, and Water Tender Third Class W. F. McAllister, 1705 Fifth Avenue, who served aboard the destroyer USS *LaVallette*, have been detached recently to await transfer to the United States and subsequent discharge.

Coxswain Woodrow W. Nease, 4802 Waverly Road, has been discharged from the Navy at the Shoemaker, Calif. separation center.

Baker Second Class Alvin E. Spurlock, stationed at Banana River, Fla., recently spent a short leave with his parents, the Rev. and Mrs. A. E. Spurlock, 210 Bridge Street.

Flight Officer Wilber H. Barker, 1028 Eleventh Avenue, has been awarded the Air Medal by Brigadier General Charles W. Lawrence, commanding officer of the India-China Division Air Transport Command.

Glenna: *December 16th Sunday – Very, very cold. We went to Sunday school later to practice on the Xmas program. Cline is real sick with asthma.*

Rupert: *I went to sunday School. Later we went to practice for the Xmas program.*

From Tokyo: "General MacArthur today ordered state Shintoism abolished in Japan to destroy the compulsory religious ideology which his staff asserted led the nation into war— and defeat..." Allied officers explained that the action "... does not affect the sect of Shinto which, in 1941, had an estimated 17,000,000 adherents."[664]

"WITH THE COLORS":

Staff Sergeant John T. Moore, 917 Twenty-fourth Street, has returned home following his discharge from the AAF. After the holidays, Mr. Moore will return to his former occupation as a mimeograph salesman for the Swan-Morgan Co.

Jack D. Petit, son of Mr. and Mrs. C. N. Petit, 2982 Fourth Avenue, has been discharged from the Army after serving 26 months in Alaska. Petit plans to enroll in Marshall College next semester.

After 27 months of service, Petty Officer (Second Class) Haven E. Fetty of Huntington has received his discharge from the Navy. Fetty is a graduate of Huntington High School and was formerly employed by the Germann Bros. Freight Co.

William J. Adkins, AMM 1c, of Salt Rock, has received his discharge from the Navy at Nashville, Tenn.

Cpl. John B. Short, son of Mr. and Mrs. Lee Roy Short, Route 10, Davin, W.Va. has been assigned to Headquarters Panama Canal Department Squadron, Albrook Field, Canal Zone. He will serve in the Sixth Air Force as an airplane crew chief. He has been with the AAF since March, 1943.

W. F. McAllister, W T 3c, of 1705 Fifth Avenue, recently returned to the United States. He served aboard the destroyer *Lavallette*...

Lieutenant R. Knowleton Stuart, communication officer at the Naval station at Nashville, Tenn., will arrive here next Sunday to spend the

Christmas holidays with his parents, Mr. and Mrs. H. D. Stuart, 325 West Eleventh Avenue.

Lt. (j. g.) Mary Ruth Woodyard, after two and one half years serving in the WAVES, has been discharged from the Navy. Miss Woodyard is the daughter of Mr. and Mrs. R. B. Woodyard, 221 West Tenth Avenue. She was last on duty at the Naval Air Facility, Weeksville, Elizabeth City, N.C.

Claude Jackson Park Jr., son of Mr. and Mrs. C. J. Park, 2561 Collis Avenue, was recently discharged from the AAF after one and one half years of service. Park is now attending the West Virginia Institute of Technology at Montgomery. W.Va...

Michael Kozma Jr. has been advanced to the rating of sergeant, according to word received by his parents, Mr. and Mrs. Michael Kozma Sr. of 703 Twelfth Avenue.

Corporal Don Beckett of Chapmanville, W.Va. has received his discharge from the AAF at Patterson Field, O. He served as a motion picture projectionist and was last stationed at the Chico, Calif. Army Air Field.

James W. Lipscomb of Madison Avenue, after completing his engineering training at Penn State College, has been transferred to Camp Crowder, Mo.

First Sergeant James E. Legg, 409 Water Street, has reenlisted in the Regular Army at Fort George G. Meade, Md.

Watertender (Second Class) Charles R. Pettus, son of J. R. Pettus, 826 Twenty-second Street, is home on a 30-day leave. A graduate of East High School, he spent 21 months in the Pacific serving aboard the USS *Benham*, a destroyer. He wears the Asiatic-Pacific ribbon with seven battle stars, the Philippine Liberation ribbon with two stars, the Victory ribbon with one star. He will go to Seattle, Wash. for reassignment.

Glenna: *December 17th Monday – Clear and warmer. I washed and cleaned up.*

Rupert: *It was cold today. In the evening Genell [Gaynelle] and Don came up.*

"The temperature headed last night toward a predicted low of zero in Huntington, and there was no relief from the cold wave which struck here almost a week ago..."[665]

Newark, New Jersey, December 17: "The motorman of a Hudson & Manhattan tube train was crushed to death and 46 passengers were injured here tonight when the train, loaded with home-bound commuters, crashed into the east end of a Passaic River lift bridge between Harrison and Newark at about 6:27 P.M." It took three hours for railroad crews, in near-zero temperatures, to rescue the trapped conductor and two passengers. "Their cries for help could be heard at the Harrison tube station 500 feet up the track."[666]

General George S. Patton's doctors in Heidelberg, Germany said he was getting well "like a house afire."[667]

Glenna: *December 18th Tuesday – Snowed hard all day. I ironed. Dawson didn't come home. Cline still real sick.*

Rupert: *It has snowed all day. I got my Christmas tree today.*

Our Christmas trees were small cedars cut from our property. Their fragrance filled the house like no other evergreen.

"Diamond Dust": "Alva 'Bo' McMillin, Head Man at Uni. of Indiana, has been voted 'The Coach-of-the-Year' by 55 coaches throughout the U.S. & A. Bravo. Bravo ... Scoopie ... The West Point football team, Felix Blanchard, Glenn Davis & Company, more worried about their exams than they were about Navy. H-mmmm... Joe DiMaggio sez: 'I don't like to be referred to as a 'returning veteran.' (I don't blame DiMagg.) He is still a young man. Gosh, Joe was born in Frisco in 1914. That makes him only 31. He weighs 195 pounds and stands 6 feet 2. If DiMaggio doesn't hit .315 next Summer I'll be a monkey's uncle..."[668]

"Marshall's Big Green basketball team headed East yesterday for ... a nine-game trip which opens tonight at Charlottesville." They were also to play at the Army War College and the University of Maryland. Coach Cam Henderson named his starting lineup as, Bill Hall, Pete Petrone, Joe Rodak, Andy Tonkovich, and Ed Little."[669]

Fifty-four ships carrying homebound troops were to arrive on this day, twenty-seven with 17,800 veterans aboard at three East Coast ports, and 24,000 other returnees docking from 26 ships.[670] Another bleak AP report stated that 82,000 Army GIs on the Pacific Coast would have to spend Christmas in ports there awaiting transportation; the Navy situation was no better.[671]

Glenna: *December 19th Wednesday – Snowing and turning colder.*

Rupert: *It has snowed all day. I finished a book called Crime Fighter in the Land of No Man.*

Crime Fighter in the Land of No Man was my creation of the day, or week—not sure of the timeline. I still have that cardboard bound thirty-two-page narrative, along with two previous Crime Fighter novels. My cartoon strips, found tucked away in a wooden chest, reveal the influence of comic characters of that era.

"Influenza and pneumonia accompanying the most severe December weather in years have stricken nearly 400 persons in rural Cabell County," reported Dr. Raymond H. Curry, County [Cabell] Health Officer.[672]

"IN THE SERVICE":

Technician Fifth Grade Oscar McCoy, 38 A Street, has been discharged from the Army at Fort Sill, Okla.

The following men have been discharged from the Army at Camp Atterbury, Ind.: Technical Sergeant Charles R. Thacker, Scott; Private First Class E. J. Simpkins, East Lynn, and Private First Class Henry Preace, Williamson.

The following officers have been placed on inactive status by the Army at Camp Atterbury: Captain Patrick J. Urse, Huntington, and First Lieutenant James W. Stone, Gary.

Technician Fourth Grade Joseph C. Lambert, son of Mrs. C. E. Waugh, 226 Fourth Avenue, is a member of a company which recently received the Army Meritorious Service Award for outstanding service on Lete and Okinawa.

First Lieutenant Joseph A. Silverman, 110 Belford Avenue, has been discharged from the Army Air Forces at Scott Field, Ill.

"IN THE SERVICE":

Private Thomas J. West, 402 West Eighteenth Street, is returning to this country from Naples, Italy after 33 months in the Mediterranean theatre.

Staff Sergeant Davis R. Smith, son of former mayor and Mrs. Porter W. Smith, 620 Fifth Avenue, recently attained his present rank at Hakodoto [Hokodate?], Japan.

Private First Class Richard S. Maxwell, son of Mr. and Mrs. Hugh Maxwell, 5693 Ohio River Road, has been discharged from the Army and arrived in Huntington Monday after two years of overseas duty with the 1937th Aviation Engineers.

Technician Fourth Grade Lewis A. Miller Jr. of Miller, O. and Technician Fifth Grade Herbert L. Miller, 547 Ninth Avenue, Huntington, not related, have returned home after three years and five months together in the service. They had identical assignments beginning at the Huntington induction station and continuing to Fort Hayes, O., thence to the Ordnance

Department at Camp Forrest, Tenn., to Capp Pickett, Va., to Fort Dix, N.J., to Casablanca, Naples and back to the United States.

Maurice Kaplan, Huntington Publishing Co. staff photographer who has been on leave for more than three years for military service, returned to Huntington yesterday after being discharged from the Army. He saw long service in Italy and was wounded. He expects to rejoin the publishing company after January 1.

Aviation Machinist's Mate Third Class George F. Gross and his wife, the former Marian Ferene Forester, 1425 Third Avenue, are both civilians now, she having recently been discharged from the WAVES and he from the Navy.

Staff Sergeant James D. Tipton, whose wife lives at 240 Washington Boulevard, recently attained his present rank with the 97th Infantry Division in the area northwest of Tokyo.

Glenna: *December 20th Thursday – Bitter cold and snowy. Dawson went to Ashland. Cline still real sick.*

Rupert: *I have sleigh rode all day.*

"Diamond Dust": "Fortunately, most of my Christmas shopping is finished. As a matter of fact, I haven't even started. Yet, I'm not forgetting that this is the first PEACEFUL Yuletide since 1941 when Herr Hitler busted loose from his monkey house... Judging by the manner in which Uni. of Virginia put the basketball bee on Marshall's Thundering Herd, (56–39) the 'Cavaliers' are in like cats on a wet night... Hank Greenberg's motto is: 'Out of the Boob Traps and into a Florida Training Camp by Christmas.' ...Coach Herbert C. (Twenty) Lantz & Company will break bread tonight at the Hotel Frederick in their annual pigskin party. Bernard Shively, head football coach at the U. of Kentucky, will be the guest speaker of the evening. Shively usually has a lot to say about football and knows h-o-w to say it..."[673]

Washington: Price Administrator Chester Bowles announced the end of tire rationing.[674]

"Sergeant Frank W. Plunkett, a former Marshall College student, son of Mr. and Mrs. John B. Plunkett of Barboursville, has been declared dead by the War department... He had been missing since October 5, 1942. As a gunner on a B-17 Flying Fortress, Sergeant Plunkett's ship was last seen on a bombing mission on Rabaul, New Britain. He entered the service in the fall of 1939 and was at Hickam Field in Hawaii in December, 1941. He was awarded the Silver Star for action at the Battle of Midway. He was a graduate of Central High School and attended Marshall College where he was a member of Kappa Alpha Order."[675]

"IN THE SERVICE":

Seaman First Class Milton Supman, son of Mrs. Felix Goldstein, 510 West Eleventh Avenue, arrived in Seattle on board the USS *Randall* with a load of returning servicemen this week.

Private First Class Roy Thomas, son of Mr. and Mrs. Roy L. Thomas, has been honorably discharged from the Army Air Forces. He is a former employee of the Transcontinental and Western Airlines.

Glenna: *December 21st – Friday – Turning some warmer. Jaruel Porter, Rupert, and myself got out and gathered up the money to buy our preacher a suit for Christmas. That night we had $40.00.*

Rupert: *Mother went with Pearl Porter to get money for the preacher's Xmas present.*

It is likely that two separate groups went out at separate times to collect funds with Mother in both groups.

Heidelberg, Germany, December 21: "America's great master of tank warfare, Gen. George S. Patton Jr., died peacefully in his sleep today of a blood clot which developed gangrene in his lungs and weakened his warrior heart." Mrs. Patton made a quick decision that Patton would be buried in Europe. "The acid-tongued general, one of the greatest in American history, died at 5:50 P.M. (11:50 A.M. Eastern Standard Time) twelve days after a hunting trip accident."[676]

"IN THE SERVICE":

Radioman Third Class Walter F. Tabor, son of Mrs. Georgia F. Tabor, recently discharged from the Navy at Bainbridge, Md. is visiting his parents. His nephew, Private Glenn F. Banks, has reenlisted in the Army and will go to the Pacific.

Seaman Second Class Paul L. Carter, 208 Staunton Street, has been discharged from the Navy at Jacksonville, Fla.

Private First Class Homer C. Perry Jr. is serving with the Eighth Special Service Company in Manila as a truck driver.

The following men have been discharged from the Army at Camp Atterbury, Ind.: Private First Class Charles E. Blake, 3430 Chase Street; Private First Class William E. Climer, Point Pleasant; Private First Class Hyland J. Purdy, Sod; Sergeant Floyd Webb Jr., Kermit; Technician Fourth Class Paul H. Gabbell, Keystone, and Private First Class Hiram McCoy, Amherstdale.

Seaman First Class Howard H. Daniel of Huntington is en route to the United States from the Pacific theatre on the USS *Calvert*.

Glenna: *December 22nd Saturday – Jaruel Porter, Zella Hutchinson, Frances Paugh, Gaynelle, and myself went to Huntington to*

get the preacher's suit. When we left Salt Rock we had $42.00.

Rupert: *Mother went to town today.*

From Heidelberg, Germany, it was announced that General Patton, "... one of the most vivid figures in American military history, will be laid to rest Christmas Eve in a military cemetery at Hamm, Luxembourg, in soil hallowed by the blood of his fellow fighting men in the gallant U.S. Third Army..."[677]

President Truman directed entry of European war refugees into the United States at the rate of about 39,000 a year, most from central and eastern Europe and the Balkans.[678]

"IN THE SERVICE":

Second Lieutenant Elbert Shields Alston, 1814 Doulton Avenue, recently received the Army Ordnance Association Award at Aberdeen Proving Ground, Md. The son of Mr. and Mrs. Rhoden D. Alston is a graduate of West Virginia State College at Institute and studied at New York University. The award is presented to the outstanding member of each graduating class at the Ordnance School.

The following men have been discharged from the Navy at Bainbridge, Md.: Chief Pharmacist's Mate Norman Lee Winkler, 2519 Third Avenue; Carpenter's Mate George W. Britton, 2704 Emmons Avenue; Aviation Radioman Third Class James F. Duty, 528 West Twenty-sixth Street; Seaman First Class Willard Wells Umstead, 746 Washington Avenue; Seaman First Class Lawrence Troy Rood, 119 Third Avenue, and Aviation Machinist's Mate Second Class Charles Randall Mullins, 1214 Jackson Avenue.

Chief Radioman Eugene E. Bailes of Nitro and Signalman Benjamin H. Maynard, 3326 Auburn Road, served on the USS *Paul Hamilton*, which spent 14 consecutive months in the thick of the fighting in the Pacific.

Seaman Second Class Raymond C. Gould, 1022 Jefferson Avenue, served aboard the USS *Botanin* which transported more than 60,000 men to battle at Bougainville, Peleliu, Saipan, and Okinawa.

Aviation Machinist's Mate Second Class Markus O. Adkins of Huntington Route 4 has been discharged from the Navy at Jacksonville, Fla.

First Lieutenant John E. Swan, who served more than two years with the Eighth Air Force, is spending a leave with his parents, Mr. and Mrs. E. Q. Swan, 1538 Holderby Road.

Coxswain Clifford James, son of Mr. and Mrs. John James, 509 North High Street, is expected to arrive in the United States from Hawaii late in January.

Glenna: December *23rd Sunday – Went to Sunday School and church. That evening I baked a fruit cake and put flowers on Rupert's grave.*

The previous day was the thirteenth anniversary of my father's death.

Rupert: *I went to Sunday School. Later we went back to Practice.*

AP Report: "The worst traffic jam in history spread throughout the nation last (Saturday) night as servicemen, civilians and brand-new discharges surged into trains, buses and planes in a gigantic home-for-Christmas movement..."[679]

Washington officials expressed hope the tactics adopted in recognition of the new Yugoslav republic headed by the regime of Marshal Tito might also work in recognizing the Balkan countries of Romania and Bulgaria. The process of diplomatic relations with the provisional governments of Romania and Bulgaria was slow, for the U.S. had "indicated several times that it regards both regimes as Russian-sponsored and Communist-dominated."[680]

"WITH THE COLORS":

Sergeant James F. Harris, 21, son of Mr. and Mrs. Joe Harris, 2215 Eighth Avenue, and a Huntington East High School football player prior to his enlistment in the Army three years ago, is on his way home from Japan... His brother, Edward Harris, 26, was discharged from the Army last September 23 after three years of service, most of it in the European theatre of operations.

Captain Robert C. Rosenheim, son of Mrs. W. S. Rosenheim and the late Dr. W. S. Rosenheim, has been separated from the Army. Captain Rosenheim has been stationed at the Headquarters Second Air Force, Colorado Springs Calif. where he was chief of operations of the training statistics section...

Lt. (j. g.) Clara E. Closterman, daughter of Mrs. C. H. Closterman, 1025 Ninth Avenue, has been discharged from the WAVES at Washington, D.C.

First Lieutenant Leonard N. Seldomridge of Huntington has recently been discharged from the Army.

Ensign Robert T. Conaty and Pharmacist's Mate Thomas J. Conaty, are spending Christmas leave with their parents, Mr. and Mrs. W. J. Conaty, 1411 Fifth Avenue.

Private First Class Jack Still, son of Mrs. Gertrude W. Still, has been discharged from the Army at San Francisco, Calif. Pfc. Still entered the service in March 1943 and served in the European theatre of operations. His brother, MM 3-C Herbert Still Jr. is on duty with the Navy in the Pacific.

According to ... Mr. and Mrs. A. A. DeHart of 208 First Street, Lt. C. B. Dehart has been on temporary duty, assigned to Hq. Africa Middle East Theatre at Cairo, Egypt. Now assigned to the command of the Headquarters and Service

Co. of the 390ᵗʰ Engineer Regiment, stationed near Paris. Lt. DeHart expects to return to this country late in December.

Sgt. Laurence Morrison, son of Mrs. Mollie Morrison of 1604 Madison Avenue, was recently discharged from the Army at Camp Atterbury after 41 months of service in the Pacific. He served in the Army Ground Forces, attached to an antiaircraft unit.

Lieut. Joe S. Hazelett, son of Mr. and Mrs. H. H. Hazelett, 2161 Spring Valley Road, is home on leave for the holidays from his station at Selman Field, Monroe, La.

Ensign Rodney Jean Taylor, son of Mr. and Mrs. Sam Taylor of Barboursville is serving aboard the aircraft carrier *Wasp*. Ensign Taylor received his commission in the U.S. Naval Reserve at the Naval Academy, Annapolis, Md. August 24, 1945.

First Lieutenant George B. Brown, son of Mr. and Mrs. J. H. Brown of 951 Madison Avenue, has been released from active duty with the AAF at Lincoln, Neb. Lieut. Brown entered the service January 29, 1943, and received his commission and wings February 8, 1944, at Lubbock, Tex. as an AAF pilot. With his wife, and daughter, Barbara Helen, he is residing at the above address and has returned to his former employment with the fire department.

Glenna: *December 24ᵗʰ Monday – I washed and cleaned up. At night Rupert and I went to the Xmas program and Xmas tree at Salt Rock Church. We had a very good time.*

Rupert: *To [Today] is the day for the program.*

The church "program" was a huge success. Recent revivals had added faces and commitment to Salt Rock Methodist Church and the zeal showed in the work that had gone into the "Christmas Carol" type play with modern characters. Jaruel Porter played the lead and gave an "Oscar" performance.

The President granted "a full pardon" to thousands of ex-convicts who "had lost their civil rights because of convictions for violating federal laws, but who had served honorably in the armed services for a year or more after July 29, 1941."[681]

From Moscow: "The United States, Russia and Great Britain have agreed on the procedure for the peace treaties for the defeated nations of Italy, Romania, Bulgaria, Hungary and Finland, an official announcement of foreign ministers said tonight." The treaties for Romania, Bulgaria, and Hungary would be drawn up by Russia, the United States, and Great Britain. Finland's peace treaty would be drawn up by England and Russia.[682]

"IN THE SERVICE":

Private First Class Willard Coates, a member of the 93ʳᵈ Bomb Group at Pratt, Kan., arrived in Huntington Saturday to spend a seven-day furlough with his mother, Mrs. Ethel Coates, 715 Court Street. Private Coates has been in service since December 13, 1943. A brother, James Coates, is taking his Navy boot training at Camp Peary, Va.

The following men are en route home from the Pacific: Corporal Charles R. Brown, 1653 Artisan Avenue; Corporal Lloyd N. Richmond, son of Mrs. Lucy Richmond, 4511 Bradley Road; Pharmacist's Mate Third Class Bennie Abshire, 2702 ½ Oakland Avenue; Walton V. Beekner, husband of Mrs. Mary E. Beekner, 614 Sixth Street; Seaman First Class Robert P. Jarrell, 43 B Street; Gunner's Mate Third Class Roscoe E. Smith, 774 Roby Road, and Fireman First Class James H. Chapman, 3618 Waverly Road.

Sergeant Sherill Brookover of Hamlin, who was interred in a Japanese prison camp for almost three years, is spending Christmas at Newton D. Baker General Hospital at Martinsburg, W.Va.

The following officers have been returned to inactive duty by the Army at Fort Meade: First Lieutenant Don C. Hinchman, 2724 Fifth Avenue; Captain William T. Boone, 835 Eighth Street; Second Lieutenant Harold E. Mullins, Logan, and Second Lieutenant Robert L. Harmon, 908 Fifteenth Street.

Staff Sergeant Robert Lee Olaker of Glenalum has reenlisted in the Army at Fort Meade.

Petty Officer Third Class Paul E. Mays, son of Mr. and Mrs. Paul E. Mays, 602 Hagen Street, has arrived in Huntington after spending 20 months with the Navy where he served in the western New Guinea, Luzon, Leyte, Philippine liberation and Terakan operations, being entitled to wear eight bronze stars and five overseas stripes. He will be home January 7...

Glenna: *December 25ᵗʰ Xmas – Nice and warm. We got many presents and had a good Xmas dinner. I got a pair of slippers, petticoat, two towels, a heart pin, a blouse, a box of cakes, a nice purse and vanity, a billfold. Rupert got many things. It was a joyful Christmas.*

Rupert: *Today is Christmas. I got books, mickscrop set, traveling kit, and lots of things.*

The microscope was from Aunt Gaynelle.

San Francisco, December 25: "Many thousand Americans who fought in foreign and strange lands and won, spent Christmas Day on their native soil today thankfully and joyously although still far from their homes and families." On the Pacific Coast Army, Navy, and Marine service personnel became special guests in private homes, clubs, and lodges.[683]

"IN THE SERVICE":

Private Verlin Harless, Rear 133 Eighth Avenue, has been honorably discharged from the Army at Fort Lewis, Wash.

Captain Don C. Hinchman, son of Mr. and Mrs. Don Hinchman, 2724 Fifth Avenue, arrived here yesterday after spending three years overseas in Ireland, England, France, Belgium and Germany.

Captain Thomas J. Eastes, 419 Nineteenth Street, has been returned to inactive duty by the Army at Camp Atterbury.

Private First Class Wayne Smith, son of Mr. and Mrs. W. M. Smith, 2320 Twenty-eighth Street Road, has arrived here for a 60-day furlough.

Sergeant John C. Sublett Jr., who has served two and a half years in Europe with the Ordnance Depot, has arrived in Boston, Mass., and will spend the holidays with his wife and parents, Mr. and Mrs. J. C. Sublett Sr., 235 Eighth Avenue.

The following men have been discharged from the Navy at Shoemaker, Calif.: Storekeeper Third Class John R. Roach, 419 Thirty-first Street, and Coxswain Eugene L. Easter, Welch.

Glenna: *December 26ᵗʰ Wed – I ironed. Wasn't very cold. Uncle Kiah took bad and was taken to the hospital.*

Rupert: *Uncle Cire got sick. They took him to the hospital.*

My phonic spelling (with a hard C) shows how the family pronounced Kiah's name. Hezekiah (Kiah) Adkins was my Grandmother Adkins' brother. He and his family lived at Lesage, West Virginia. Grandma's maiden name was Adkins; she and Grandpa were distant cousins. Grandma's family had thirteen children: Her other five brothers were, Sterling, Volney, Elijah, Melvin, and Stewart. Her sisters were Chestina, Sarah, Lucinda, Lola, Minnie, and Okley.

The Associated Press reported a mine disaster in Pineville, Kentucky: "Although rescue workers late tonight had dug their way to a point approximately 4,000 feet from where 30 to 50 coalminers were entombed, workers and relatives alike held little hope that any of the men would be found alive. Trained mine rescue squads were balked at every step of the way by flames, gas fumes and fallen debris..."[684]

President Truman "laughed off the suggestion that he go back to Washington by train." Harsh winter conditions had some worried for his safety. Lieutenant Colonel Henry T. Myers, pilot of the presidential plane, "the Sacred Cow," declared that President Truman "took no undue risk in his flight from Washington yesterday."[685]

Another tragic consequence of war was reported from Portland, Oregon: "Two trainloads of silent Japanese arrived today from the Tulelake, Calif. camp to board a ship that will take them back to Japan." The 1,800 men, women, and children, were going to Japan either by deportation orders or by their own requests. Most "stood expressionless as customs officials examined their baggage in the embarkation depot." One boy, when asked if he would rather have remained here, "stared quickly down at his sports shoes... 'No, no,' he muttered, 'I don't want to go to Japan.'"

Glenna: *December 27ᵗʰ Thur. – Clear and sunny. Gaynelle and I went to St. Mary's Hospital to see Uncle Kiah. I stayed and sat up all night with him.*

Rupert: *Mother is going to see Uncle Cire. I am going to stay at Mama's.*

The Big Three, United States, Britain, and Russia proposed that the United Nations undertake the elimination of "atomic weapons and all other major weapons of mass destruction."

"IN THE SERVICE":

Private Lawrence Robertson, son of Mr. and Mrs. Frank Robertson, 1460 Van Buren Avenue, has been discharged from the Army after 39 months' service...

Private First Class Tom Pelfrey of Kenova, last stationed in Japan with the 97ᵗʰ Infantry Division has 64 service points, making him eligible for discharge... Private Pelfrey formerly served in Europe with the division and accompanied it when the unit was redeployed to the Pacific. He participated in action in the Ruhr and in Czechoslovakia.

Lieutenant William Arnett, husband of Mrs. Anne Arnett, 127 Locust Street, has been assigned to duty with a maintenance unit of the Fifth Air Service Command at Manila. A son of Mr. Frank E. Arnett of Inwood, he served in the western Pacific Theatre for seven months as a pilot. In service 36 months, he wears the western Pacific ribbon with three stars, the American theatre ribbon, the Philippines Liberation ribbon, and the Victory ribbon.

Technician Fifth Grade Douglas C. Page, husband of Mrs. Ruth Page, 2751 Latulle Avenue, was promoted to that grade at his station in Japan with the 97ᵗʰ Infantry Division.

Mail Clerk First Class Lowell Chandler, and his wife, Mail Clerk Third Class Virginia Menter Chandler, are visiting his parents, Mr. and Mrs. A. O. Chandler, 4502 Auburn Road. Both are stationed at Seattle, Wash.

Glenna: *December 28ᵗʰ Friday – Cloudy. I came home from the hospital at seven o'clock in the morning and rode the bus home. Ossie came a few minutes later and stayed until the next morning. Uncle Kiah died at 5 o'clock in the evening.*

Rupert: *Uncle Cire died today at five o'clock P.M.*

Pineville, Kentucky, December 28: "Eight men carried out alive tonight from the tunnel of a coal mine here where they had been trapped by an underground explosion since early Wednesday, were removed to a Pineville hospital. Rescue crews found a ninth man alive, but he died before removal from the tunnel. The fate of the remaining estimated 22 was undetermined..."[686]

Glenna: *December 29th Sat – Sunny and warm. I went to Elsie's [Uncle Kiah's daughter] Sat. night where Uncle Kiah's body is until burial. Came home on 11:15 bus.*

Rupert: *Mother is going to town. I'll stay at Mama's again.*

Pineville, Kentucky, December 29: "Weary rescue workers late tonight found four more bodies of the miners entombed by an explosion in the coal mine near here, raising to six the number known dead in the disaster..."[687]

"IN THE SERVICE":

Granville P. Vallandingham, former mayor of Barboursville, received his discharge from the Navy at Shoemaker, Calif. this week. He held the rating of pharmacist's mate third class. Mr. Vallandingham entered the service while serving as mayor...

Dewey L. Bocook, fireman first class; Ray D. Garrett, fireman first class, and Walden C. Chaffin, hospital apprentice first class, all of Huntington, were discharged this week from the Navy at Bainbridge, Md.

Quartermaster Second Class Oscar J. Lunsford, 1037 West Seventh Street, has been discharged from the Navy at the Bremerton, Wash. Navy Yard.

Sergeant Ray Willoughby, son of Mr. and Mrs. E. H. Willoughby, 1180 Norway Avenue, is spending a 30-day furlough with his parents following his return from Japan. He was a member of the 1303rd Engineer Regiment, and also served in Europe and the Philippines.

Cecil P. Varney, specialist (aviation gunnery instructor) second class, 1121 Fifth Avenue, was discharged from the Navy this week at Shoemaker, Calif.

"IN THE SERVICE":

Yeoman First Class Charles C. Lane, son of Mr. and Mrs. Oscar Lane, 926 Twenty-fourth Street, recently was advanced to that rank on Guam. He enlisted on December 7, 1942, and served with the Navy in the European theatre for 19 months, participating in invasion operations at Sicily, Salerno and southern France, and was transferred to the Pacific last March.

Lieutenant Shelba Glenn Pew, USNR, daughter of Mr. and Mrs. W. C. Pew of Ona, was released from active duty with the WAVES this week in Washington.

Master Sergeant William E. Black of Hamlin has been awarded the Bronze Star Medal for meritorious service while serving as motor sergeant of a field artillery battalion of the 98th Infantry Division, a part of the Sixth Army.

Technician Fourth Grade Earle F. Umstead, son of Mrs. Earle F. Umstead, 2538 Fifth Street, has been awarded the Bronze Star Medal for meritorious achievement in connection with military operations on Luzon. He is now in Japan.

Private First Class Ralph Lewis, husband of Mrs. Elsie Lewis, 120 Berry Street, is with the 32ⁿᵈ Red Arrow Infantry in Japan.

Private First Class Thomas Foxx of Huntington is serving with the 719ᵗʰ Medical Sanitation Company in Korea.

Dorsel L. Black and James W. Black, sons of E. L. Black of Milton, are en route to the United States after two years overseas.

Private First Class David A. Foard Jr., son of Mr. and Mrs. D. A. Foard, 51 Oakwood Road, has arrived at Newport News, Va. after 21 months overseas with the 689ᵗʰ Ordnance Company.

Aviation Machinist's Mate Third Class Eugene C. Rood, 630 Thirteenth Street, has been discharged from the Navy at Great Lakes, Ill.

Lieutenant (j. g.) Homer M. Jones, USNR, has arrived in Huntington to spend a 30-day leave with his wife, the former Miss Ruth Ellen Sarver, and his parents, Mr. and Mrs. C. C. Jones, all of 3524 Third Avenue, after serving for 21 months in the Pacific.

Private Claude R. Sullivan, son of Mr. and Mrs. Martin Sullivan, 2103 Johnstown Road, arrived in the Philippines in September, and is now serving with the 32ⁿᵈ Red Arrow Infantry Division in Japan.

Major David C. Boy Jr., USAAF, and Lieutenant Commander John Boy, USNR, sons of Mr. and Mrs. D. C. Boy, 2120 Cherry Avenue, have arrived in Huntington to spend the holidays with their parents. Both officers have been released from active duty and are on terminal leave. They entered the service in 1941.

Glenna: *December 30ᵗʰ Sun. – Went to Uncle Kiah's funeral at Salem Church on Bowens Creek at 2 o'clock. Weather cloudy and not very cold. Large crowd there. Burial was at Winslow.*

Rupert: *I went to Sunday School. Mother and Dawson went to Uncle Cire's furneral.*

Pineville, Kentucky, December 30: "The death toll in the mine disaster mounted to at least five today as one of the men carried out alive Friday died this afternoon. Weary rescue crews continued to search for 19 or more miners still unaccounted for in the wrecked tunnel of the Kentucky Straight Creek Coal Co.'s Number One mine..."[688] (There were I believe, in the final count, eight survivors.)

"WITH THE COLORS":

Tech. Sgt. James J. Bragg, son of Mr. and Mrs. Hobart Bragg of Proctorville, Staff Sgt. William Max Cartwright, son of Mr. and Mrs. W. T. Cartwright, 622 Thirty-first Street, Huntington, and Sgt. Edmond Wickline of Hurricane, W.Va. are on occupation duty in Onimichi, Japan...

M. Sgt. Clarence A. Black, recently returned from the South Pacific, is spending a 90-day furlough with his parents, Mr. and Mrs. C. E. Black of Ona, W.Va. Attached to the AAF, Sgt. Black has reenlisted in the AAF for three years and after the termination of his leave, will proceed to the European Theatre of Operations for occupation duty.

Lewis E. Porter, baler (third class), son of Mr. and Mrs. James W. Porter, Johnstown Road, was recently discharged from the Navy after serving 38 months...

Lieut. (j. g.) Michael J. Healey, 232 Carrington Court, and Lieut. Van Meter Love, 1217 Sixth Avenue, were released to inactive duty at the Naval Separation Center, Washington, D.C.

Marine Private A. D. Preston of Huntington expects to receive his discharge this week from the Great Lakes Naval Training Center, Great Lakes, Ill... Private Preston served overseas and took part in the battle of Iwo-Jima and returned to the United States in November.

Frank Appling Jr., husband of Mrs. Louise Appling, 128 Ninth Avenue, has received a promotion to technical sergeant. Appling is serving in the Far East Air Service Command and is attached to the 374th Troop Carrier Group based in the Philippines.

Lieut. (j. g.) Beatrice Vandament Lewis, daughter of Mr. and Mrs. H. L. Vandament, 47 Fairfax Court, has received her discharge from the WAVES.

First Lieut. Carroll Emerson, son of Mr. and Mrs. B. C. Emerson, 1212 Seventh Street, is now taking treatment in the Newton D. Baker General Hospital, Martinsburg, W.Va. Lieut. Emerson served overseas with the 11th Air Group, Seventh Air Force, based in Guam, Okinawa and Japan.

Ship's Serviceman (Second Class) James E. Kitchen, of 1760 Madison Avenue, has returned to the United States for discharge from the Navy after serving on the PT tender, USS *Wachapreague*.

Sgt. Dale Fahrenz, grandson of Mrs. C. J. Henderson, 2747 Emmons Avenue, has been discharged from the Army after 55 months of service with the 38th "Cyclone" Division. Sgt. Fahrenz had two years of overseas service and participated in the Leyte, New Guinea and Luzon campaigns.

Pfc. Richard D. Spurlock, 2521 Adams Avenue, returned home Saturday. Spurlock has been in the Army three years and four months, serving one year in Burma and China. He is the holder of the Air Medal with two clusters and three battle stars.

Pfc Lloyd Stickler has returned to his post in Orlando, Fla. after spending a ten-day leave with his mother, Mrs. Claire Stickler, 2125 Seventh Avenue.

William Womack, S-2-C, of Arlington, Va., spent Christmas with his parents, Mr. and Mrs. W. W. Womack, 2976 Third Avenue.

Col. George Graves Dixon, supervision surgeon of the 37th General Hospital at Naples, is the guest of his aunt, Mrs. Frank Mann of Fifth Avenue and his cousin, Mrs. Ernest J. Adams of Twelfth Avenue. He is en route to his home in New York City where he will resume his practice in medicine. He is also head of the 37th General Hospital in Africa.

Fred T. Hall, with the 69th Infantry Signal Corps in Frankfurt, Germany for several months, has been flown home on emergency furlough because of the serious illness of his father, Fred Hall, 418 Tenth Avenue, who is in St. Mary's Hospital.

Glenna: *December 31st Mon. – I washed and cleaned up. Cold and snowing. At 10 o'clock Rupert and I went to the church to a watch meeting. We saw the old year out and the new year in by praying. 35 people were there ... We got home at 12 minutes until one o'clock. Very cold.*

Rupert: *We are going to a watch meeting.*

"IN THE SERVICE":

Captain Francis A. Scott, USNR, Medical Corps, a Huntington Orthopedic surgeon, has been placed on inactive duty after 48 months service. He was last stationed at the Naval Hospital at Brooklyn, N.Y., and was relieved of duty at the naval separation center in New York.

The following Huntington Army Officers have been placed on terminal leave at the Fort Knox, Ky. separation center: Captain Ross Dodson, 134 Ninth Avenue; First Lieutenant Lawrence G. Barbour, Huntington: First Lieutenant Roy E. Thacker, 528 Fifth Street, and Second Lieutenant Donald R. Hart, 1116 Tenth Street.

January 1946

A NEW YEAR FREE OF WAR.

GLENNA: JANUARY 1ST 1946 – I IRONED. VERY COLD AND SNOWING SOME.

Rupert: *Today is new year's day. I go to school tomorrow.*

The end of World War II truly was a turning point in the history in our country—and in the world. An AP article from Washington displays an awareness of that evolution: "The advent of 1946 finds the United States, once aloof from foreign troubles, now playing an active part in settling problems in other countries, great and small, all over the world... The war had been a world war and the U.S. had become tied up for keeps with the world...".[689]

Japanese Emperor Hirohito addressed his subjects to tell them he is not a divine being, but a man after all.[690]

On the home front: "Lieutenant (j. g.) Andrew B. Dorsey, 1653 Doulton Avenue, has been placed on inactive status by the Navy in Washington" and "Technician Fifth Grade Aaron Fizer of Culloden is en route to the United States from Pearl Harbor aboard the USS *Tyron*...".[691]

"IN THE SERVICE":

James B. Christian, 2714 Highlawn Avenue and Robert W. Gibson of West Hamlin have been discharged from the Navy at Great Lakes, Ill.

Private First Class Herbert E. Richards, 520 Sunset Drive, is en route to the United States from Guam aboard the USS *Lander*...

Seaman First Class Joseph N. Elkins of Huntington is stationed at Guam aboard the LST *803*.

Woodrow W. Jackson, 4217 Magazine Avenue, was scheduled to arrive at San Pedro, Calif. this week aboard the USS *Guilford*. He was formerly stationed at Saipan.

Coxswain John D. Crossley of Huntington and Chief Boatswain's Mate Ray Nicely, 331 First Street, are serving on the submarine net tender *Terebinth*.

George D. Blair, Harold M. Bias and Harold C. Layman of Huntington were scheduled to arrive this week at San Pedro, Calif. aboard the USS *Texas*.

Walter E. Ray, watertender third class, 3246 Hughes Street; Robert P. Holley Jr., signalman second class, 1016 Sixth Avenue, and Ray C. Humphrey, carpenter's mate first class, 1202 Marcum Terrace, were discharged from the Navy at Bainbridge, Md.

First Lieutenant Basil Bennett, 2833 Collis Avenue, and Captain Paul R. Baker, 315 Eleventh Avenue, were placed on terminal leave this week at Fort Mead, Md.

Staff Sergeant Jack Henderson, son of Mr. and Mrs. John Henderson of Sixth Avenue is a patient at the Veterans Hospital here. He returned recently from Manila and Tokyo where he had been serving with the Army Medical Corps.

First Lieutenant Russell F. McCallister, husband of Mrs. R. F. McCallister, 1714 Crestmont Drive, arrived at Newport News, Va. yesterday aboard the SS *William Evarts*. He had served in the European theatre for a year.

Captain Basil Dennett, 2633 Collis Avenue, who recently was returned to inactive duty by the Army, is visiting in New York City. He was promoted to his present rank effective December 25.

Chief Boatswain's Mate Jasper Popp Jr. is spending a 60-day leave with his wife, Mrs. Lorraine McCallister Popp, and their 14-month-old son, Larry Jay, at their home, 2501 Twelfth Avenue. Chief Popp has been in the Navy eight years and was overseas for 19 months. During that time he participated in the battles for Leyte, Iwo Jima and Okinawa.

Glenna: *January 2ⁿᵈ 1946 – Cold and sunny. Took down the Xmas tree. School started up again.*

Rupert: *I started back to school today.*

Nuremberg, January 2: "Hulking, scar-faced Ernst Kaltenbrunner, head of the dread Nazi security police, was accused before the international military tribunal today of ordering entire communities exterminated and of personally watching concentration camp victims die in a gas chamber..."

Glenna: *January 3ʳᵈ Thursday – Cloudy and cold. I made a sack sheet.*

The testimony of SS Major Dieter Wisliceny (hanged in 1948) highlighted the "Nazi lust for blood." Wisliceny bragged that he had, himself, "prepared vast shipments of Jews" to German murder camps. He quoted Adolf Eichmann as declaring that he was "much pleased to have five million people on my conscience." Eichmann was, at that time, sought the by Allied authorities.[692] (Eichmann was caught in 1960 by Israeli agents in Argentina and hanged in Israel in 1962.)

"IN THE SERVICE":

Sergeant Herman S. Rhodes, son of Mr. and Mrs. W. H. Rhodes, 425 Water Street ... has been in The Marine Corps for over two years and is now stationed at Vero Beach, Fla. with a Marine night fighter squadron. His wife, the former Miss Marguerite Sharp of Huntington, is at Vero Beach with him.

Private First Class Donald A. Wilson, who became seriously ill while spending a furlough with his parents, Mr. and Mrs. R. A. Wilson, 823 Twenty-second Street, is a patient at the Veterans Hospital. Private Wilson is stationed at Camp Lee, Va. He was wounded in Germany last March and had been in an Army hospital until shortly before Christmas when he was transferred to Camp Lee.

Private Edwin L. Kaiser, son of Mr. and Mrs. L. B. Kaiser of Athalia, O. is visiting his parents. Upon termination of his holiday furlough, he will return to his station at Sheppard Field, Tex.

Captain Basil Bennett, 2833 Collis Avenue, who last week was placed on terminal leave at Fort Meade, Md., is now visiting in New York City.

Glenna: *January 4ᵗʰ Friday – Sunny and warm. I made 2 pillow cases. Dawson bought cable to wire the house for electricity.*

Rupert: *I went to school. We played guns.*

"IN THE SERVICE":

Watertender Third Class William McAllister, son of Mr. and Mrs. W. D. McAllister, 1725 Fifth Avenue, was promoted to that grade recently at his station at San Diego, Calif. He entered the service in July, 1943, and was formerly on active duty in the Pacific.

Corporal Marshall W. Burkhamer, son of Mrs. O. A. Burkhamer, 321 Thirteenth Street, landed at New York, New Year's Day and is expected to arrive in Huntington next week. He is a veteran of 25 months in the China-Burma-India theatre with the 1875th Aviation Engineer Battalion.

Lieutenant Harvey Sullivan Jr., son of Mr. and Mrs. Harvey Sullivan, 1242 Eighteenth Street, has arrived at Santa Ana, Calif... He had been stationed in India and China with the Army Transport Command. He expects to report to Fort Knox, Ky. for release from active duty.

Corporal Julius A. Curry, son of Mrs. Nora Payne, 521 ½ Eighth Street, has been relieved of duty with the Eighth Army's Eleventh Airborne Division at Sendal, Japan and transferred to a replacement depot for return to the United States. A veteran of the Luzon campaign, he wears the Distinguished Unit Citation, the Combat Infantryman Badge, the Philippine Liberation ribbon and the Asiatic-Pacific ribbon with one star. He entered service in March, 1942, and went overseas in May, 1945.

Lieutenant Ray Argabrite, USNR, formerly manager of the McCrory Co. store here, has returned to the position after two and a half years with the Navy...

Jack Budnick of Keystone, W.Va., former announcer with station WSAZ under the name of Jack Bradley, has returned to his position here after three and a half years' service with the Navy. He served in the Pacific for 18 months.

Lieutenant Colonel Douglas C. Tomkies, former Huntington attorney, arrived in Huntington this week to spend a 45-day leave with his wife and two sons at their home on Woodland Drive... Colonel Tomkies has been assigned for duty with the general staff of the Army Service Forces in Washington, with the Chinese Combat Command and with the Fourteenth Air Force in China. He wears the Legion of Merit, the Bronze Star Medal with three Oak Leaf Clusters, two Chinese decorations and two stars on the Asiatic-Pacific ribbon...

Glenna: *January 5th 1946 Saturday – Warm sunny day with much wind. I went down to Mrs. Rousey's and stayed a long time with her. The preacher came while I was there and we had prayer meeting.*

Rupert: *Eddie, Astin [Austin Wagoner,] and I went on a hike.*

A "hike" was a frequent occurrence, sometimes with other boys when they were available, or more often alone. I had an intimate relationship with the hilly landscape surrounding Salt Rock.

"IN THE SERVICE":

Technical Sergeant George J. Kliegel, husband of Mrs. G. J. Kliegel, 448 West Twenty-second Street, is en route to the United States aboard the SS *Young America* from New Caledonia.

Sergeant Bill Cummings, formerly with the Army Transportation Corps, has arrived in Huntington to visit his mother, Mrs. R. B. Cummings, 1042 Fifth Avenue...

Private First Class R. Wayne George and Private Everett W. Wray of Huntington recently spent furloughs at Nice, France. Private George, son of Mr. and Mrs. Russell W. George, 406 West Tenth Avenue, has been in service for 15 months, 10 of them in the European theatre as a member of the 755th Field Artillery Battalion.

Private Wray, 816 Twelfth Street, has been in service 29 months, and overseas 16 months. He is a member of the 764th Railway Shop Battalion. Mrs. Kathy Wray, his wife, resides at Jamestown, N.Y.

Private First Class David A. Foard Jr., son of Mr. and Mrs. D. A. Foard, 51 Oakwood Drive, arrived in Huntington this week after receiving a discharge at Fort Meade, Md. He had been in service three years, and was in Europe for 22 months.

Private First Class Robert G. Smith, son of Mr. and Mrs. J. W. Smith, 1126 Sixth Avenue, is stationed at Hokkaido, Japan with the 307th Airborne Infantry Regiment.

Corporal Ben McClellan of Huntington was recently promoted to that grade in the Marianas Islands where he is serving as an automotive mechanic. His wife, Mrs. Grace M. McClellan, and child, reside at 2133 Third Avenue.

A brother-sister reunion after a separation of 14 years took place in Huntington yesterday when Corporal Eugene Hull of Columbus, O. arrived for a visit with another sister, Mrs. B. F. Markin, 1044 Sixteenth Street and found his youngest sister, Eula Faye, 19, residing there. Corporal Hull, who came here with his wife, the former Miss Betty May Kirk of Huntington, was discharged last week from the Army after two years overseas service.

Seaman First Class Erma Frances Miller Shell, daughter of Mrs. Edith Miller, 2647 Guyan Avenue, was discharged from the WAVES this week in Washington after 14 months service. Her husband, Richard N. Shell, resides in Washington, where she was stationed.

Glenna: *January 6th Sun. – I went to church and Sunday School. Uncle June came up and told us about Martha Berry being dead. Beautiful day.*

Martha Berry, 61 years old, was the wife of Smith Berry and daughter of Jerry and Anna (Childers) Adkins. She was buried at Barboursville.[693]

Rupert: *I went to sunday school. Later, Astin [Austin Wagoner,] Eddie, Larry, Buddy [Larry's brother], and I went hiking.*

I remember that day. We walked up the railroad tracks and onto the fields by Gue's dairy farm. We visited the "Indian Carving Rock" not far below the tracks; a large boulder held the image of a lengthy snake, an eagle (or turkey), and several other markings.

On a historical note, the Guyan Valley had been a popular route for traveling Native American tribes, and I believe the level bottom where Salt Rock sits was the site of a permanent camp. All the farm land near our house produced artifacts after spring plowing, and I even found arrowheads by the house where water from the roof eroded the soil. On the edge of a bank just west of the Porter Cemetery where a large black walnut tree once stood, we found flint shavings, failed arrowheads, and broken fragments of ancient tools. Years later, Julian Forbush, my Aunt Gaynelle's second husband and Native American artifact hobbyist, declared the spot a toolmaker's site. I have axes, spearheads, arrowheads and drills collected by Julian, and Uncles Cline and Milo.

Inside the Gill Cemetery on the hill east of the river and railroad, there is a Native American burial mound which predates later tribes. My Grandmother, Jennie Adkins, told a story about a professor from a "big university" (she could not remember the name) coming to Salt Rock when she was a child. He stayed at their home on River Road while he excavated the mound.

Glenna: *January 7th Mon. – Raining hard. I washed.*

Rupert: *I went to school today. We ate hot lunch.*

The hot lunch program had moved from the old school building to the new one, possibly during Christmas vacation.

Glenna: *January 8th Tuesday — Still raining. Flood coming up. Papa, Mamma, and myself went to Martha's funeral and Mamma got sick and we left.*

Rupert: *I went to school. I ate hot lunch again.*

Floodwaters were rising throughout the area. In Huntington, the Ohio River was expected to reach 39 feet, a crest well below the official flood stage of fifty feet.[694]

Glenna: *January 9th Wed — I ironed and mended at night. Rupert and I went to prayer meeting. Flood still high.*

Rupert: *I went to school. Mother and I went to prayer meeting.*

Glenna: *January 10th Thur. — Still drizzling rain. I went to visit Mrs. Smith and Aunt Sallie Morris.*

Rupert: *I went to school. Mr. Drumond built a jumping rack.*

Myron Drummond enlisted the boys' help, not only in making an outdoor basketball court that would serve the community for many years, but also building athletic equipment. The "jumping rack" was a big hit with Eddie and me and we spent hours high-jumping.

The Ohio River continued to rise and approached 50 feet in Huntington, but was slowing. Across several southeastern states, the death toll from flooding reached 22.[695]

Glenna: *January 11th Friday — Cold with misty rain. Awfully muddy. I cleaned up the house, went down to Mrs. Rousey's.*

Rupert: *I went to school. The boy that got his leg broke came back. Eddie and me can jump higher than our heads.*

In Huntington, the Ohio River crested at 47.2 feet and was falling.[696]

Glenna: *January 12th Sat. 1946 — Cold with misty rain. I have baked a cake, ironed a few things, patched, and one thing after another as usual.*

This ends my diary of 1 year and 12 days. It's been a great year full of happenings.

Rupert: *I am awful sore over jumping.*

Just like that, Mother stopped writing in her diary and I have no evidence she ever again wrote a diary entry. I'm happy I discovered her diary and was able to save the little snippets she recorded of her busy and sometimes difficult life.

I continued for a couple more years to make entries in my leather-bound five-year diary, but less often as I grew into my teen years. After eighth grade at Salt Rock, I entered junior high school at Barboursville, and later Barboursville High School, where sports became important. Nevertheless, in those transition years I continued to read books and write stories. I still do.

This ends my recordings and narrative of the extraordinary year of 1945.

ADDENDUM

ALL IMAGES, ARTICLES, AND STORIES IN THIS BOOK, UNLESS OTHER-wise noted, are from the 1945 and January 1946 *Huntington Herald-Dispatch* or *Huntington Herald-Advertiser,* now part of *HD Media Company, LLC.*

Writing styles have changed over the past seventy-five years. I made no attempt to modernize the excerpts from articles and columns, and made no changes except to correct obvious typos or blatant spelling errors. I did shorten some entries that contained redundant or insignificant text but made it obvious when I did so.

Except for excerpts from the "In the Service" and "With the Colors" columns, I followed no plan for inclusion except to record what seemed timely and appropriate. Newspapers were crowded with news of the day that could have fitted in nicely, but the choices were mine alone.

The seven military service members on the front cover are, left to right, Hansel H. Adkins, Eileen Virginia Wooddell, Max Crawford, John W. Cartwright, Jacob Rone Jr., Clarence E. Hysell, and Raymond V. Humphreys.

As stated in the foreword, it's the "little stories" I most wanted to preserve. I encourage local historians to take up the task of saving such stories or vignettes from the other years of World War II. Daily editions of both newspapers are on microfilm in the Cabell County Library in Huntington, West Virginia.

On a personal note, I feel privileged for God's gift of a long life and good memory. My generation understands how faith and commitment brought us through the worst of times. God gifted us with the spirit for that. He will again, should the need arise.

ABOUT THE AUTHOR

RUPERT PRATT GREW UP IN A THREE-MEMBER FAMILY ON A FORTY-ACRE farm in Salt Rock, West Virginia, with an extended family of grandparents, uncles, aunts, and cousins nearby. As an only child he had time to pursue his interest in writing. Adventure-packed stories were told through penciled cartoons on lined notebook paper and in cardboard-bound "novels."

Not unlike other area residents in the agrarian and small village setting, Pratt's community activities centered around church and school. Salt Rock Methodist Church was the family place of worship. He attended Salt Rock Elementary School and Barboursville junior and senior high schools. In January 1951, with suffcent academic high school credit, he enrolled at Marshall College in nearby Huntington, West Virginia.

In March 1953, he left school to join the United States Air Force. That four-year stint took him through basic training at Sampson Air Force base in Geneva, New York, to Fort Wadsworth on Staten Island, New York for training in petroleum analysis, to Ladd Air Force Base in Fairbanks Alaska, and finally to Stewart Air Force Base at Newburgh, New York.

In September 1956, Pratt married Mildred Mereness of Schenectady, New York. On discharge from the service in January 1957, the couple moved to Huntington, where he earned his BA degree at Marshall College and taught two years at Peyton Elementary School while earning an MA degree in school administration. During that time Millie worked as a billing clerk at the Foster-Thornberg warehouse in Huntington. From Huntington they moved to Schenectady, where he took a teaching position in the Schenectady City School District. Millie enrolled at Albany State University in business education, leading to her own teaching career.

Son Gregory was born in 1970 and son Jonathan in 1972. Through the busy teaching and child-rearing years, Pratt continued leisure writing, as well as reading, gardening, camping, hiking, and church work. The proud parents saw both sons graduate from college, Greg from RIT and Jon from Princeton. Pratt retired in 1995 and Millie in 2000. They traveled, visiting Canada, England, Bulgaria, and Alaska. Grandchildren inspired frequent trips to Berkeley, California, Portland, Oregon, and Hamilton, New York.

In 1996, Pratt spearheaded a reunion at Dayton, Ohio of the survivors of an Air Force C-47 crash in the mountains of Alaska, a disaster he had survived. *People* Magazine attended the reunion and did a two-page story in their September 23, 1996 issue. In 2006, Pratt published *Touching the Ancient One*, the story of that accident and the relationships it generated.

After Millie's death in 2013, he began planning *Tri-State Heroes of '45*. Although he has lived most of his life in Upstate New York, his West Virginia roots run deep. His and his mother's long-forgotten diaries had stirred up vivid memories of 1945, a time when the world was in great turmoil. It became his purpose to honor the men and women of the Tri-State area of West Virginia, Ohio, and Kentucky who served during World War II.

Rupert Pratt lives in retirement overlooking the Mohawk River in Cohoes, New York. He travels often to West Virginia to visit relatives and friends and to New Jersey to see sons Greg and Jon, their respective spouses Purvesh and Bobbi, and grandchildren Lizzie, Nathan, and Andy.

INDEX OF PEOPLE

THIS INDEX CONTAINS THE FULL NAME OF PERSONS MENTIONED IN this book. An exception is where "Mr. and Mrs." precedes the husband's name and the wife's first name is not given. All names are referenced to days within a month rather than to specific page numbers.

Adkins, Evie–March 16

Adkins, Ezra–July 30

Adkins, Ezra L.–July 30

Adkins, F. M.–Nov 23

Adkins, Frederick–June 15

Adkins, G. O.–Aug 3

Adkins, Galie–Oct 15

Adkins, Garnet–Feb 19, April 20

Adkins, Glen–July 25

Adkins, Greta Porter–April 23

Adkins, H. B.–April 2

Adkins, Hansel H.–Feb 13, May 17

Adkins, Hartsel T.–Nov 29

Adkins, Hatten–March 16

Adkins, Henon–Nov 18

Adkins, Herman–March 16

Adkins, Herman L.–June 14

Adkins, Heron M.–March 21

Adkins, Hettie–July 25

Adkins, Hobart–Nov 22

Adkins, Isaac–March 21

Adkins, J. B.–May 17

Adkins, J. S.–April 2

Adkins, J. W.–June 22

Adkins, James E.–Oct 16, Oct 19

Adkins, James J.–June 23

Adkins, Jennie–Jan 12, March 14, 20, 24, 27, April 29, May 16, 18, 30, June 16, 23, July 3, 11, 22, 26, 28, Sept 20, Nov 19, 22, 24, 25, 27, 28, 29, 30, Dec 4, 6, Jan 6, 1946, Jan 8, 1946

Adkins, Jerry–Jan 6, 1946

Adkins, Jerry Lynn–July 8, 13, 14, 15, 24, 26, 27,

Adkins, Jesse–March 16

Adkins, Johanna–April 9

Adkins, John B.–Feb 13, May 17, Aug 25

Adkins, John Kelly–Oct 6

Adkins, John W.–Oct 20

Adkins, Jonnie L.–Aug 8

Adkins, Judson H.–Sept 21

Adkins, Julia–July 4

Adkins, Junius–July 6, 22

Adkins, Kiah–Dec 26, 27, 28, 29, 30

Adkins, Larkin–Oct 20

Adkins, Laura (Sawyer)–Oct 6

Adkins, Lee–Jan 10

Adkins, Lloyd–Nov 22

Adkins, Lola–Dec 26

Adkins, Lorena–Aug 1

Adkins, Louise–Feb 23

Adkins, Lucian–Jan 12, 23, Feb 10, 17, March 14, 20, 24, April 19, 27, 29, May 16, 17, 18, 30, June 16, 23, July 3, 11, 22, 26, 28, 30, Oct 27, Nov 8, 20, 27, Jan 8, 1946

Adkins, Lucinda–Dec 26

Adkins, Markus O.–Dec 22

Adkins, Marvin–June 23

Adkins, Maxine Lewis–Feb 25, March 12, May 16, 19, June 18, 20, 21, 26, July 22, Aug 2, 8

Adkins, Melvin–Dec 26

Adkins, Millard–Jan 16

Adkins, Milo–Feb 25, March 12, May 16, 19, June 18, 20, 21, July 22, Aug 8, 9, Jan 6, 1946

Adkins, Minnie–Dec 26

Adkins, Mose–July 9

Adkins, Moses S.–Oct 29

Adkins, Myrtle Ellen–July 8

Adkins, N.–March 16

Adkins, Norman B.–April 23

Adkins, Odie–Oct 16

Adkins, Okley–Dec 26

Adkins, Orin E.–June 23

Adkins, Orville W.–Nov 1

Adkins, Ottie–Aug 8

Adkins, Pat–April 8

Adkins, Patrick–July 6

Adkins, Paul P.–Jan 16

Adkins, Pharoah–Jan 16

Adkins, Ralph J.–Sept 7

Adkins, Raymond–July 9

Adkins, Raymond H.–Jan 10

Adkins, Rev. Odie–Oct 19

Adkins, Robert W.–July 12

Adkins, Rose M.–June 15

Adkins, Sadie–Aug 27

Adkins, Samuel R.–July 9

Adkins, Sarah–Feb 3, Dec 26

Adkins, Shelby Jean–Jan 23, March 4, May 30, Sept 25,

Adkins, Shirley–Feb 23

Adkins, Sterling–Dec 26

Adkins, Stewart–Dec 26

Adkins, Sybil–July 24

Amburgey, Cullen O.–Jan 31
Amburgey, F. B.–Dec 2
Amburgey, Jesse–Dec 2
Amick, Ray S.–April 4
Anderson, Brooks D.–April 19
Anderson, Burtis W.–May 3, June 26
Anderson, Charles W.–July 3
Anderson, E. J.–July 3
Anderson, Edwin H.–July 15
Anderson, John E. Jr.–Oct 22
Anderson, Lane S.–April 26
Anderson, Mrs. J. N.–Nov 6
Anderson, W. W.–May 3, June 26
Anderson, William–July 15
Andes, Bessie–Feb 17, May 6, July 1
Andes, Mrs. E. C.–Jan 12
Anest, Nick–Aug 15
Angel, A. B.–April 12
Angel, Henry–April 12
Ansara, Lewis–April 21
Appeldorn, H. J.–April 17
Appeldorn, Henry–March 9
Appeldorn, Philip–April 17
Appeldorn, Philip L.–March 9
Apperson, Jack C.–Sept 11
Appledorn, Herman H.–Nov 20
Appling, F. Neel Jr.–Aug 25
Appling, Frank Jr.–Nov 10, Dec 30
Appling, Louise–Dec 30
Aquino, Iva Toguri D'
Toyko Rose–Sept 5
Arbaugh, Floyd–April 24
Arbaugh, Francis–April 24
Arbaugh, Lawrence G.–Nov 16
Arbaugh, Mrs. L. Glen–Jan 29
Arbaugh, R. C.–July 15
Arbaugh, Robert C.–Nov 16
Arbaugh, Robert E.–Jan 29
Arcaro, Eddie
Jockey–June 8, Oct 24
Archer, Myrtle–July 11
Archer, William R.–July 11
Argabrite, Ray–Jan 4, 1946
Arix, Charles–June 24
Arix, Charles Jr.–June 24, Dec 11
Arix, Earl Rex–June 24

Arix, Paul–June 24
Arix, Robert–June 24
Armstrong, Gladys–Nov 7
Armstrong, H. F.–March 29
Armstrong, Irvin D.–May 9, May 10
Armstrong, John–March 29
Arnall, Ellis
Governor of Georgia–June 27
Arnett, Anne–Dec 27
Arnett, David W.–March 29
Arnett, Frank E.–Dec 27
Arnett, William–Dec 27
Arnold, Harold–Nov 25
Arnold, Mrs. Omer–Dec 6
Arnold, Raymond–Dec 6
Arpp, Teresa–Jan 5, Dec 14
Arrington, Betty–March 14
Arrington, Elmer F.–Aug 29
Arrington, Loval–Nov 14
Arrington, T. E.–March 14
Arrowood, Albert–July 25
Arrowood, Estill D.–July 25
Arrowood, Imogene–July 25
Arthur, Boone B.–Aug 22
Arthur, Brady–March 14
Arthur, Burrell–Aug 22
Arthur, Charles–Aug 22
Arthur, E. F.–March 8
Arthur, Florine–April 14
Arthur, Fred–Aug 22
Arthur, Gloria Jean–March 14
Arthur, Herbert D.–June 2
Arthur, L. M.–March 8
Arthur, Lee–Feb 21
Arthur, Leo–March 6
Arthur, Lloyd–June 2
Arthur, Mrs. J. D.–April 9
Arthur, Neal–Aug 22
Arthur, Norman L.–Nov 19
Arthur, Oman–March 6
Arthur, Ruth Thelma–March 14
Arthur, Verlin J.–March 14, June 4
Arthur, Willie–April 14
Arthur, Woodrow–Feb 21
Asbury, Claude–July 4
Asher, Marguerite–Jan 9

Baker, Nathan–July 1
Baker, Omer E.–Feb 24, May 10
Baker, Paul R.–Jan 1, 1946
Baker, Ralph–June 21
Baker, Ray–Aug 31
Baker, William L.–Feb 24, May 10
Bakhaus, Earleen–March 1
Bakhaus, Orville F.–March 1
Baldridge, Ance–Oct 15
Ball, Chester–July 28
Ball, Frank–July 28, Oct 11
Ball, Frank E.–Oct 26
Ball, Imogene–May 10
Ball, James T.–Nov 4
Ball, K. G.–Oct 26
Ball, Lewis–May 6
Ball, Margaret–May 10
Ball, Otto C.–Dec 1
Ball, R. Harry–July 28
Ball, Robert B.–July 28
Ballangee, J. O.–Oct 27
Ballangee, John R.–Oct 27
Ballangee, Mayme F.–Oct 27
Ballard, Arnold L.–May 8
Ballard, Flora–July 22
Ballard, Shirley–May8
Ballengee, Carl B.–June 21
Bandy, Charles L.–June 10, Sept 11
Bandy, Samantha–June 10
Bandy, Samantha L.–Sept 11
Banks, Glenn F.–Sept 13, Dec 21
Barber, L. E.–March 27, Aug 6
Barber, Leonard E.–March 27, Aug 6
Barbour, Claude U.–Feb 13
Barbour, Elizabeth A.–Feb 1
Barbour, Elizabeth Ann–Oct 16
Barbour, F. U.–Feb 13
Barbour, J. H.–May 22, Oct 1
Barbour, Kelsie W.–Oct 1
Barbour, Lawrence G.–Dec 31
Barbour, Lloyd D.–May 22
Barbour, Mrs. J. H.–Oct 23
Barcello, Manuel–Aug 11
Barcello, Rosemary–Aug 11
Barclay, Don
Artist and caricaturist–April 23

Barcus, L. M.–May 2
Barcus, Leslie Morton Jr.–May 2
Barker, J. W.–April 7
Barker, John W.–Feb 1
Barker, Kessel L.–March 1
Barker, Leonard–April 6
Barker, Leonard H.–June 29, Oct 19
Barker, Mrs. M. V.–Oct 19
Barker, Virgil W.–June 29
Barker, W. H.–April 7
Barker, Wilber H.–Dec 15
Barker, Wilbur H.–Feb 1
Barlow, Vera J.–Feb 14
Barner, Arthur P.–July 12
Barnett, Alice–Feb 28
Barnett, Cesco H.–Feb 28, Dec 11
Barnett, Laundle–Dec 3
Barnett, Rev. L. M.–Dec 3
Barnett, S. L.–Feb 28
Barnhart, Alma–June 29
Barrett, Mrs. Dean–Jan 24
Barrett, Mrs. Tom–Feb 19
Barrett, Robert S.–Dec 5
Barrett, Robert T.–Dec 1
Barrett, Roy E.–Feb 19
Barrett, Vernon J.–Feb 14
Bartholomew, Harry Scott–Oct 8
Bartholomew, John D.–Aug 31
Bartholomew, Mrs. N. B.–Aug 31
Bartholomew, Nellie Ward–Oct 8
Bartlett, Ann Steele–Jan 31
Bartlett, Thomas B. Jr.–Jan 31
Bartley, Keene–Aug 14
Bartley, Mrs. K. L.–Aug 14
Bartram, Betty–March 13
Bartram, Doris–June 5
Bartram, Fritz A.–July 22
Bartram, Harold M.–June 5
Bartram, Juanita M.–June 5
Bastianelli, Harry–Nov 10
Bates, Earl–March 24
Bates, James–March 24
Bates, John–Oct 25
Bates, John J.–Oct 30
Bates, Ralph W.–April 9
Bates, Ruth–Oct 30

Bellomy, Homer G.–Nov 29
Bellomy, James A.–Nov 29
Bellomy, John S.–Oct 23
Bellville, Edward Forest–Sept 5
Bellville, Forest–Sept 5
Belville, Jesse L.–Dec 10
Belville, William L.–Dec 10
Benhoing, V. E.–Feb 23
Bennett, Basil–Jan 1, 3 1946
Bennett, Charles G.–Feb 5
Bennett, Elaine–June 17
Bennett, Kathleen–Feb 5
Bennett, William Thomas–Oct 30
Bentine, Dick
Huntington High football player–Nov 10
Bentine, John L.–April 5
Bentine, Mrs. J. L.–April 5
Bentley, Basil N.–March 24
Bentley, Roy–Nov 27
Berry, Bessie–June 19
Berry, Carl–Oct 17
Berry, Charles–June 19
Berry, Emery R.–Oct 17
Berry, James H.–June 19, Oct 12
Berry, Martha–Jan 6, 1946
Berry, Roy E.–June 19
Berry, Smith–Jan 6, 1946
Berry, Vernon–March 11
Berry, Willa–June 19
Berry, William–Aug 25
Bertram, Raymond W.–July 4, Aug 23
Bertram, W. E.–July 4
Bertram, Willard E.–Aug 23
Bertucci, Clarence–July 9
Bertucci, Clarence V.–July 10
Beseler, Mrs. P. C.–July 15
Beseler, Peter C.–July 15
Bess, Demma–May 24
Bethel, Barnette D.–Feb 5
Bethel, Helen D.–Feb 5
Betts, Fred–June 9
Betts, John T. C.–Nov 8
Betz, Max–Aug 28
Betz, Robert S.–Aug 28
Beuhring, Donald E.–Oct 1
Beuhring, Eloise–Oct 1

Beveridge, A. Clyde–Dec 6
Beveridge, A. Clyde Jr.–Dec 6
Beveridge, Clyde–Jan 12
Bexfield, C. H.–Aug 13, Oct 17, 21
Bexfield, Norman–Aug 13
Bexfield, Norman F.–Feb 4, Oct 17, 21
Biagi, Robert H.–Nov 4
Bias, Agnes V.–March 26, April 21
Bias, B. S.–Feb 4
Bias, Berkie W.–May 28
Bias, Darrell R.–Oct 5
Bias, Doris–Sept 7
Bias, E. D.–Feb 21
Bias, Elbert L.–Feb 21, Sept 9
Bias, Eldora–April 24
Bias, Ever–Feb 4
Bias, F. W.–April 25
Bias, Harold M.–Jan 1, 1946
Bias, Ira J. Jr.–Oct 6, Nov 18
Bias, James B.–Oct 25, Nov 19
Bias, Jesse J.–Sept 7
Bias, Joseph C.–Oct 27
Bias, Kermit Lowell–April 25
Bias, Mary–Sept 7
Bias, Maxine–May 28
Bias, Mrs. A. M.–May 24
Bias, Mrs. Dewey–Nov 11
Bias, Mrs. Tennyson–June 6
Bias, Ralph G.–Dec 11
Bias, Richard J.–Sept 25
Bias, Robert–Jan 11
Bias, Violet Joyce–May 10
Bias, Vivian–Jan 11
Bias, Vivian McCorkle–March 26
Bias, W. H.–Jan 11
Bias, Walter–Feb 24
Bias, William Everett–Jan 11
Bias, William H.–March 26
Bias, William J.–Feb 24
Bias, William L.–Jan 11
Bias, William Leroy–March 26
Biddle, Louise–Aug 25
Biern, Samuel Jr.–Feb 21
Biggs, Dennie B.–June 1
Biggs, Helen–June 1
Biggs, Kelsie R.–June 1

Blevins, Madeline–June 10
Blevins, Mary–Feb 3
Blevins, Ralph–June 10
Blevins, Raymond L.–Oct 19
Block, John H.–Oct 4
Blood, Frank–May 5, August 31
Blood, Ralph E.–Aug 31
Bloss, Charles E.–Oct 11
Bloss, Earl–May 1
Bloss, Rebecca–May 1
Bloss, Sanders A.–Nov 12
Blue, Carlotta Hutchinson–April 8
Blume, Fred L.–Oct 7
Blume, George F.–Oct 4, Oct 7
Blume, Hester S.–Oct 7
Bobbitt, Betty A.–July 21
Bobbitt, Dr. R. M.–Dec 12
Bobbitt, Evelyn–April 23
Bobbitt, Jack–Dec 12
Bockway, Mildred–June 15
Bockway, Mrs. Frank–June 15
Bockway, William C.–June 15
Bocook, Cleotis–Sept 28
Bocook, Dewey L.–Dec 28
Bohl, Betty–April 27
Bohl, Harold C.–April 27
Bolen, Harsie G.–Aug 24
Boley, James P.–Oct 29
Boling, C. L.–Feb 21
Boling, Carl L. Jr.–Feb 21
Bolling, Anna–April 7
Bolling, Anna Marie–Jan 5
Bolling, Carl–Jan 28, 31
Bolling, Carl L.–April 7
Bolling, K.–Jan 28
Bolling, Richard–Jan 31
Bolling, Richard N.–Jan28
Bolling, Robert V.–Nov 1
Bond, Carol–May 24
Bond, Jeanne M.–June 13
Bond, Ruth N.–June 13
Bonecutter, Ernest–March 9
Bonecutter, George–March 9
Bonham, Edna–July 13
Bonham, Paul W.–March 24, April 24, 25, July 13

Bonhoeffer, Dietrich–April 9
Booker, Owen Reed–Oct 11
Boon, Audrey O.–Jan 18
Boon, Howard D.–Jan 18
Boone, William T.–Dec 24
Booten, F. H.–Aug 9
Booten, Freelin H. Jr.–Aug 9
Booth, Frank–June 24
Booth, Frank Jr.–June 24
Booth, Nancy–March 2
Booth, Robert E.–April 23
Booth, William E.–March 2
Boothe, Mrs. Charles A.–March 19
Boothe, Nancy–Feb 20
Booton, W. T.–Jan 27
Booton, Woodrow H.–Jan 27
Border, Clinton L.–April 19
Bormann, Martin
    Hitler's deputy fuehrer–Sept 7, Nov 28
Borowy, Hank
    Baseball–Oct 3
Boster, Bettie M.–June 29
Boster, Betty–Feb 16
Boster, Daniel–Feb 16
Boster, David–Feb 16
Boster, Elizabeth–March 20
Boster, Fay–Feb 16
Boster, Howard E.–June 29
Boster, Jonathan–Feb 16
Bostic, Raymond A.–June 1
Bostick, Mrs. Thomas–March 24
Bosworth, Mrs. R. M.–Sept 28
Bosworth, Raymond Merrell–Nov 22
Bottoms, Ruth Pennington–April 20
Bottoms, Thomas H.–April 20
Boudreau, Lou
    Cleveland Indians' manager–Feb 25
Bowden, John B.–July 28
Bowen, Arvil–Oct 19
Bowen, Betty Jo–March 25
Bowen, Clive E.–April 5
Bowen, Clyde M.–April 5
Bowen, Foster
    Barboursville football player–Nov 10
Bowen, Foster–April 5
Bowen, French–Feb 17

Brookins, Frank–Sept 28
Brookins, Janice–Sept 28
Brookins, Sam E.–Sept 28
Brookover, Sherill–Nov 12, Dec 24
Brooks, Charles–July 12
Brooks, Frank E. (Ted)–July 12
Brooks, Marguerite–March 15
Broughman, Mrs. Charles–Sept 13
Brower, Dan–Nov 20
Brower, Jack–Nov 13
Brower, L. C.–Nov 13, 20
Brown, Albert C.–Oct 21
Brown, Andy H–April 30
Brown, Barbara Helen–Dec 23
Brown, Beulah–Dec 1
Brown, Charles R.–Dec 24
Brown, Charles S.–Aug 6
Brown, David M.–Aug 28, Nov 29
Brown, Dossie E.–June 9
Brown, E. E. Sr.–Aug 2
Brown, Ermalee H.–April 30
Brown, Everett E. Jr.–Aug 2
Brown, G. T.–July 7
Brown, George B.–July 22, Dec 23
Brown, George M.–Nov 18
Brown, Howard–Dec 9
Brown, J. H.–Nov 18, Dec 23
Brown, Jack H.–April 4
Brown, Kathie Sue–March 29
Brown, Lawrence L.–Oct 21
Brown, Louise–June 13
Brown, Luther R.–June 13
Brown, Mrs. C. C.–Aug 6
Brown, Mrs. Eugene–Sept 12
Brown, Paul E.
NFL football coach–May 5
Brown, Robert H.–Oct 10
Brown, Robert L.–March 29, Nov 8
Brown, Sam–July 26
Brown, Samuel A.–Dec 9
Brown, Stella–Aug 28
Brown, W. W.–Oct 10
Brown, William C.–Nov 16
Brown, William H.–Dec 9
Brown, Willie E.–May 23
Brown, Willie W.–June 9

Browning, Clayton C.–June 18
Browning, Donald W.–July 18
Browning, George–June 18
Browning, Iva–July 18
Browning, Mrs. Hallie–July 18
Browning, Mrs. Iley–Feb 7
Browning, Othar K.–Oct 1
Bruce, C. E.–May 25
Bruce, Leonard C.–Feb 13, May 25
Bruce, Mary Jo–Jan 28, Aug 22
Bruce, Roy G.–Jan 28
Bruce, Roy T.–Aug 22
Bruce, W. S.–Jan 28
Brudine, Cecil A.–April 27
Brumfield, A. S.–Jan 19
Brumfield, Donald Lee–Aug 2
Brumfield, F. B.–Aug 11
Brumfield, Frank R.–Sept 28
Brumfield, Harry E.–Jan 19
Brumfield, James C.–Dec 4
Brumfield, James F.–Dec 12
Brumfield, Mary–May 28
Brumfield, Mary Jewell–Aug 2
Brumfield, Mary M.–July 23
Brumfield, Mattie M.–Dec 12
Brumfield, Paul V.–Aug 11
Brumfield, Virgil–May 28, July 23
Brumfield, Virgil Jr.–May 28
Brunty, Carl C.–Jan 12
Brunty, Clarice–Jan 12
Bryan, Buford C.–Jan 14
Bryan, Ethel–Jan 12
Bryan, Fay–Sept 18
Bryan, Homer P.–Jan 14
Bryan, James W.–Dec 8
Bryan, Mrs. Alden–Sept 18
Bryan, Paul M.–Feb 5
Bryan, Thomas E.–Jan 12
Bryan, W. M.–May 3, 23, Dec 8
Bryan, William M. Jr.–May 3, Dec 8
Bryant, Aubrey C.–June 7, Aug 2
Bryant, E. O.–June 5
Bryant, George–May 12
Bryant, James B.–Sept 25
Bryant, John B.–May 10
Bryant, Lee–Feb 26

Butts, Howard A.–Feb 4
Buxton, Charles H.–Oct 31
Buxton, Dorothy–Oct 31
Byers, J. C.–Aug 24
Byers, Kathryn L.–Aug 24
Byran, Charles H.–Nov 16
Byrd, Aubrey C.–July 19, Aug 11
Byrd, Donald R.–Oct 30
Byrd, Kermit–Nov 15
Byrd, Mrs. William R.–July 19
Byrd, W. R.–Nov 15
Byrd, William R.–July 19
Byus, Mrs. Elvis–March 19
Byus, William J.–March 19

C

Calder, Humphrey–Dec 4
Calder, Ruby Lucas–Dec 4
Caldwell, Barbara–Sept 7
Caldwell, Chancey W.–Nov 5
Caldwell, Clyde R.–May 2
Caldwell, Elizabeth E.–May 2
Caldwell, J. C.–Sept 7
Caldwell, Mrs. Dabney–Jan 9
Caldwell, Nick–March 10
Caldwell, T. J. F.–Jan 9
Caldwell, Walter A.–Sept 7, Oct 6
Calhoun, L. R.–Sept 24
Calhoun, Lee Roy–Sept 24
Callicoat, Helen M.–Jan 13, June 26
Callicoat, Hobert Jr.–Sept 12
Callicoat, June–Sept 12
Callicoat, Raymond–Jan 13
Callicoat, Raymond A.–June 26
Callicoat, Hobert–Sept 12
Callihan, Henry C. Jr.–Oct 13
Calvin, John–July 12
Camp, Andrew C.–June 1
Camp, Eloise–April 21, 25
Camp, J. M.–June 1
Campbell, A. L.–July 26
Campbell, Alfred L.–Feb 23
Campbell, D. F.–Sept 14
Campbell, Dr. Carl–July 26
Campbell, Herschel–May 7
Campbell, Herschell–May 6

Campbell, Kenneth–Sept 14
Campbell, Owen R.–May 6
Campbell, Robert–July 4
Campbell, Russell V.–May 6
Campbell, Russell V. Jr.–May 6
Campbell, William C.–May 1
Canfield, Billy
Football player–Oct 24
Canter, James E.–May 18
Cantrell, Alfred T.–July 28
Capehart, Clariece–Nov 8
Capehart, Dan B.–Nov 8
Capehart, T. E.–Nov 8
Cappellari, Mrs. J. O.–Dec 2
Carey, Fred–July 4
Carico, Martha–April 3
Carico, Willard Woodrow–April 3
Carmichael, Edward C.–Oct 16
Carpenter, Aubrey T.–Jan 16
Carpenter, Raymond H.–Sept 25
Carper, E. V.–May 24
Carper, Frank E. V.–May 24
Carr, Carrie–Jan 22
Carr, Howard E.–Nov 6
Carrico, Chester L.–May 20
Carrico, Edward T.–May 20
Carroll, Chester E.–Sept 18
Carroll, Helen–June 15
Carroll, Henrietta–Aug 30
Carroll, Irl E.–Dec 8
Carroll, James W.–Aug 30
Carroll, Mrs. S. M.–Sept 7
Carroll, Stanley M.–Sept 7
Carter, Earl D.–Oct 13
Carter, Edna J.–March 4
Carter, F. G.–May 5
Carter, Froud–May 5
Carter, George H.–Nov 2
Carter, Helen B.–May 31
Carter, Helen Shriver–Dec 3
Carter, Leslie E.–July 30
Carter, Oxford–May 31
Carter, Paul L.–Dec 21
Carter, Robert D.–Nov 6, Dec 3
Carter, Robert E.–May 31
Carter, Velma K.–Nov 2

Chapman, Jack–March 13, Nov 25
Chapman, James G.–Aug 8
Chapman, James H.–Dec 24
Chapman, Jimmy–Nov 25
Chapman, Joe–Nov 25
Chapman, Johnny–Oct 19
Chapman, Lance–Nov 4
Chapman, Lance Allen–Nov 4
Chapman, Leland M.–Nov 13
Chapman, Louis–June 28
Chapman, Morris–Jan 25
Chapman, Mrs. C. W.–April 23
Chapman, Mrs. Clyde–Oct 29
Chapman, Mrs. H. C.–Nov 25
Chapman, Ray A.–June 28
Chapman, W. L.–Aug 8
Chapman, Walter H.–Aug 1
Chapman, Walter W.–June 14, Nov 11
Chapman, William–Oct 26
Chapman, William J.–Jan 11, May 8
Chapman, William L.–June 2
Chappell, J.–March 4
Chappell, Russell E.–March 4
Charles, Addie–Jan 7
Charles, William O.–Jan 7
Charter, M. D.–June 6
Charter, Milford D. Jr.–June 6
Charter, Richard L.–June 6
Chase, William C.
Major General Chase–Sept 14, 18
Chatterton, Ada L.–Feb 19
Chatterton, Ira–Nov 6
Chatterton, John W.–Feb 19
Chee, Woo Yon–Jan 9
Cheesebrew, Frank A.–Nov 12
Chennault, C. L.
Major General Chennault–May 15
Cheuvront, Mrs. Obie–Feb 5
Childers, Arnie–June 2
Childers, Avnel E.–June 5
Childers, Elsie–July 7
Childers, Elson–June 2
Childers, Ethel–Sept 21
Childers, Frances Jeanne–Dec 10
Childers, Janet–June 2
Childers, John T.–June 2

Childers, Johnny–June 2
Childers, Kathryn–June 2
Childers, Ladoskia–June 2
Childers, Laura–March 29
Childers, Lowell–Nov 7
Childers, Maggie–Jan 5, 7
Childers, Mrs. Oscar–June 5
Childers, Mrs. W. J.–March 26
Childers, Norma–July 6
Childers, Perlina Ann–Feb 18
Childers, Sam–Oct 18
Childers, Sherry–Oct 1
Childers, Thurman–April 27
Childers, Tilmon–June 2
Childers, Waitman B.–March 29
Childers, William J.–March 26
Childs, Sallee–Jan 22
Childs, William A.–Jan 22
Childs, William A. Jr.–Jan 22
Chinn, Albert–Oct 19
Chinn, Harry A.–March 31
Chinn, Lowell G.–Oct 19
Chisholm, Dan–Aug 25
Chittem, John M.–Oct 18
Chittum, Carl E.–Nov 29
Christian, Arnold–June 24
Christian, Charles–Feb 5
Christian, James B.–May 17, Jan 1, 1946
Christian, Joe Shelby–Feb 5
Christian, Joyce–May 28
Christian, Lulu Dyer–June 24
Christian, Mary DeBord–Feb 5
Christian, Mrs. E. E.–June 12
Christian, Thomas Elwood–May 28
Christian, W. V.–May 17, Nov 15,
Christian, W. V. Jr.–Nov 15
Christian, William V.–Oct 23
Christopher, Elliot C.–July 1
Christopher, Robert–July 1
Christy, Orlando–April 1
Christy, Sidney–April 1
Chuikov, Vasily
Soviet General–May 2
Church, Billie Eugene–Oct 5
Church, Eugene D.–April 20
Church, Lawrence–Feb 4

Cobb, Artemis H.–Feb 13
Cobb, Gene A.–Nov 5
Cobb, Kathryn–Feb 13
Cobb, Thomas D. Sr.–Nov 5
Cobley, App F.–Nov 22
Cobley, Jink–Nov 22
Cochran, Elda Marion–April 24
Cochran, Jack C.–Jan 27
Cochran, Jack M.–April 13
Cochran, Maude–April 13
Cochran, Morgan Wilkins–Nov 1
Cochran, Mrs. M. C.–Jan 14
Cochran, Thomas C.–April 24
Cochrane, Freddie ('Red')Boxer–Aug 25
Coffey, Edward G.–Oct 1
Coffey, John R.–June 29
Coffey, Mary–June 29
Coffey, Mary E.–Oct 1
Coffman, Carl L.–Oct 18
Cogan, Bruce G.–July 2
Cogan, Martin Lewis–July 2
Cogar, Inez–April 27
Cogar, Jack–June 29
Cogar, John O.–April 27
Cogar, Mrs. T. J.–June 29
Cohen, Charles–April 6
Cohen, David–July 31
Cohen, James–April 28
Cohen, Joseph–April 6
Cohen, Sarah–July 31
Colbert, Bertie–Jan 11
Colbert, Selma–Jan 11
Colbert, Willard–Jan 11
Cole, Charles G.–July 31
Cole, Della Ohnalene–Feb 1
Cole, Ernest W.–Feb 1
Cole, Ezra Jr.–Aug 6
Cole, J. W.–Feb 1
Colebank, Ann Elizabeth–Dec 14
Colebaugh, Anne E.–Jan 5
Coleman, Beuford–May 6
Coleman, Dennis–June 18
Coleman, Norman–Sept 28
Coleman, Norman L.–June 5
Coleman, Raymond–April 9
Coleman, Thurmond–July 12

Coley, Helen–Oct 20
Colgrove, Mildred–Sept 15
Colgrove, Robert B.–Sept 15
Collier, Preston A.–Jan 20
Collins, Carl–April 2
Collins, Charles F.–June 2
Collins, Ernest H.–Dec 7
Collins, Gus E.–Aug 21
Collins, John M.–Jan 18
Collins, Marion–April 2
Collins, Marshall–Aug 21
Collins, Mrs. Ollie–Feb 5
Collins, Mrs. Zena–March 16
Collins, Roe M.–Feb 5
Collins, Ruth–June 2
Collins, Tommy L.–April 16
Colloway, Tom–April 29
Combs, Catherine–Feb 23
Combs, Harry E.–Feb 23
Conard, Elza L.–April 12
Conard, Mrs. Eora E.–April 12
Conaty, Robert C.–June 28
Conaty, Robert T.–Dec 23
Conaty, Thomas J.–April 29, June 28, Dec 23
Conaty, Tom–Dec 2
Conaty, Tom J.–Sept 19
Conaty, W. J.–June 28, Sept 19, Dec 2, 23
Conaty, Walter–April 29
Coniffe, Betty–Dec 4
Conley, James E.–March 9, June 22
Conn, Billy
Boxer–April 3
Conner, Appeline–Dec 11
Conner, Charles Bert–Jan 31
Conner, James B.–Dec 11
Conrad, Della–June 1
Conrad, Ernest L.–June 1
Conrad, Harold–June 1
Cook, Albert A.–Nov 26
Cook, Dr. J. Russell–Dec 13
Cook, George T.–July 12
Cook, Gladys–March 20
Cook, J. E.–March 20
Cook, James–March 20
Cook, Mrs. C. E.–Jan 31
Cook, Norman D.–Jan 31

Crawford, Lake E.–Feb 24
Crawford, Lucille–Feb 24
Crawford, Max–May 27
Creagor, Luther–May 27
Cregan, Norma J.–Aug 7
Cregan, William J.–Aug 7
Cregger, Flossie–Feb 26
Cregger, Hugh C.–Feb 26
Cregut, E. D.–May 20
Cregut, Eddie D. Jr.–May 20
Cremeans, Allen–July 24
Cremeans, Allen J.–July 24
Cremeans, C. C.–Jan 27
Cremeans, Carlie–May 13
Cremeans, Clayton–March 26
Cremeans, Clifford–April 18
Cremeans, Cuma–April 3
Cremeans, Dixie–May 8
Cremeans, Dorcas Ellen–April 3
Cremeans, Elizabeth–July 14
Cremeans, Ernest A.–June 12
Cremeans, Grant–Jan 30
Cremeans, H. G.–April 10, Aug 11
Cremeans, H. G. Sr.–April 10
Cremeans, Henry G.–Aug 11
Cremeans, Henry G. Jr.–April 10
Cremeans, Joe–July 28
Cremeans, L. P.–April 24
Cremeans, Maxine–April 24
Cremeans, Mrs. Ervin–Jan 19
Cremeans, Rev. and Mrs. Richard–April 18
Cremeans, Thurman T.–Jan 27, April 3
Cremeans, Vernon L.–June 12
Cremeans, Walter M.–Jan 30
Cremeans, Warren L.–July 28
Cremeans, Wed–April 8
Cremeans, William L.–March 26
Cresong, Donald–Dec 11
Creuch, A. C.–Feb 23
Creuch, Arthur E.–Feb 23
Crews, Cara E.–June 26
Crews, Dr. A. W.–June 26
Crews, Howard V.–Nov 6
Crickmer, Robert C.–July 30
Crickmer, Robert E.–May 23
Crickmer, Vera–July 30

Cridlin, E. J.–Jan 11
Cridlin, E. J. Jr.–Jan 11
Cridlin, T. J.–Jan 11
Criser, Mrs. Harry C.–Feb 10
Crites, Jack E.–Feb 4
Crockett, John–Nov 29
Crofts, Dr. and Mrs. W. R.–Sept 12
Crofts, Dr. W. H.–March 15
Crofts, Phillip H.–March 15
Crofts, William R. Jr.–Sept 12
Cromwell, Jack–July 28
Cross, E. H.–May 22
Cross, Elby H. Jr.–May 22
Cross, John P.–May 2
Cross, Mrs. M. V.–May 2
Crossley, John D.–Jan 1, 1946
Crouch, Clyde A.–July 15
Crouch, Mrs. C. A.–July 7
Crouch, Mrs. L. D.–Jan 16
Crouch, William C.–July 15
Crum, Irvin–Feb 19
Crum, William J.–Jan 11
Crum, William W.–Jan 11
Crum, Willis–April 20
Crumbley, Cecil F.–Jan 24, July 11
Cullenbine, Roy
Baseball–Oct 3
Cummings, Alberta–Oct 2
Cummings, Bill–Jan 5, 1946
Cummings, Frank B.–March 22
Cummings, Mrs. R. B.–Jan 5, 1946
Cummings, Mrs. Urna–March 22
Cummins, C. L.–Jan 1
Cummins, C. S.–Jan 1
Cunningham, Bertha E.–April 11
Cunningham, Bruce–Sept 21
Cunningham, Bruce A.–Oct 5
Cunningham, James E.–Sept 28
Cunningham, Martin–Aug 1
Cunningham, Mary Alice–Sept 10
Cunningham, Morris E.–April 11
Cunningham, Roy–Sept 21
Cunningham, Roy H.–Oct 5
Cunningham, Roy H. Jr.–Sept 10
Cupp, Mable–Sept 2
Cupp, Robert L.–Sept 2

Davis, Harvey N.–Dec 9
Davis, Homer–Nov 16
Davis, Homer P.–Jan 11, July 30
Davis, Howard Lee–April 4
Davis, Ina Mae–March 25
Davis, Jack–July 21
Davis, James–Nov 25
Davis, James E.–Nov 25
Davis, Judy Kay–Nov 25
Davis, Maggie–May 24
Davis, Marcellus L.–May 2
Davis, Mildred–Sept 8
Davis, Mrs. Arnold–March 29
Davis, Mrs. B. F.–Aug 16
Davis, Otho Jr.–July 21
Davis, Otho Sr.–July 21
Davis, Paul G.–Jan 20
Davis, Robert Lee–Nov 25
Davis, Robert M.–March 28
Davis, Ruth–Jan 14, June 20
Davis, S. A.–Feb 2
Davis, Verlin–March 22
Davis, Vernon–March 22
Davis, Vincent M.–June 19
Davis, W. L.–April 27
Davis, W. O.–July 31
Davis, Wetzel C.–July 7
Davis, William E.–April 27
Davis, William L.–April 4
Davis, William O. Jr.–July 31
Davis, Zeda–Oct 23
Dawson, Hobert E.–Feb 2, 13
Day, Earl–May 22
Day, Grayce–Aug 30
Day, James A.–Sept 24
Day, Mrs. George–Jan 19
Day, Osburn W.–Aug 30
de Gaulle, Charles
General de Gaulle–March 26, Aug 17, Nov 13
De Moss, Bob
Football player–Oct 24
De Rond, Ben Jr.–Oct 6
Deal, James E.–April 19, Sept 11
Dean, Elba–May 7
Dean, Ella–May 1
Dean, Elmer H.–July 16

Dean, Frank–April 20, July 24
Dean, Hal
Foorball player–May 5
Dean, Hiram R.–May 1
Dean, John J.–May 7
Dean, John T.–May 11
Dean, Keith–Dec 9
Dean, Levi J.–May 8, Dec 9
Dean, Loren–May 2
Dean, Madge–May 2
Dean, Mary–July 24
Dean, Orville A.–Nov 13
Dean, Sebren B.–May 8
Dean, Tolbert B.–May 11, July 23
Deardorff, H. C.–July 14
Deardorff, Nancy C.–July 14
Dearnell, Elbert–May 22, June 6
Dearnell, Thomas D.–May 22, June 6
Deaton, Melvin E.–Dec 11
Debarr, Rev. W. A.–Feb 22
Deem, Everett Ezekiel–Sept 19
Deem, Martin Francis–Sept 19
Deerfield, Louise–June 26
Deerfield, W.–June 26
Deering, James R.–Oct 23
Deering, Nettie–Oct 23
DeHart, A. A.–Dec 23
Dehart, C. B.–Dec 23
Deihl, Gary Carlos–July 13
Deihl, Tillie–July 13
Dejarnette, Madeline–Feb 7
Dejarnette, Scott–Feb 7
Delancy, Bonita–July 28
Deline, Andrew J.–Aug 1
Deline, Mae–Aug 1
Demmler, Bessie L.–Jan 14, April 21, June 6
Demmler, William–Jan 14
Demmler, William E.–April 21
Demmler, William F.–June 6
Dempsey, Clyde Harold–Feb 13
Dempsey, Edna–Jan 11
Dempsey, J. J.–Sept 12
Dempsey, Jack
Boxer–May 5
Dempsey, James M.–Sept 12
Dempsey, James Marion–Nov 28

Dillon, Roy C.–Jan 14
Dillon, Virginia F.–May 11
Dillworth, Dickie–July 8
Dillworth, Lora Helen–July 8
Dillworth, Mrs. Richard–July 8
DiMaggio, Joe
Baseball player–Aug 5 , Dec 18
Dingess, Ansel–July 18
Dingess, Ira C.–July 18
Dingess, J. M.–July 2
Dingess, Roscoe–Feb 23
Dingess, Roscoe Jr.–Feb 23
Dingess, Thomas T.–July 2
Dingess, Virginia–July 18
Dishman, Cass–Jan 14
Dishman, Cecil–Jan 14
Dixon, Carl–March 15
Dixon, George Graves–Dec 30
Dixon, Glenn–March 15
Dixon, Manford–March 15
Dixon, Paul–March 15
Dixon, William T.–March 15
Dobbins, Rebecca–Dec 4
Dober, Gerald–July 21
Dodd, Eugene E.–Sept 13
Dodge, Roy L.–May 15
Dodrill, Charles F.–Nov 21
Dodrill, Charles T.–Nov 21
Dodson, Ross–Dec 31
Doihara, Kenji
Japanese Lieutenant General Doihara–Sept 21
Dolin, John–Jan 10
Donahoe, Bernard–April 2
Donahoe, Chester H.–Nov 9
Donahoe, Cleve–April 2
Donahoe, Irene–April 2
Donahue, Betty–Dec 2
Donahue, Dan L.–Dec 2
Donaldson, J. Harold–Feb 3
Donaldson, R. W.–Feb 3
Donall, George–Dec 4
Donall, Phillip–Dec 4
Donally, Edgar Ray–Aug 22
Donally, Pearl W.–Aug 22
Dönitz, Karl
German Grand Admiral–May 1, 4, 8, 23

Donohoe, J. M.–May 19, June 13, Dec 1
Donohoe, James M. Jr.–May 19, June 13, Dec 1
Donohoe, Marion–Nov 19
Dooley, Hansford–Aug 29
Dooley, Harrison–Aug 29
Doolittle, James H.
Lt. General Doolittle–April 21, Dec 14
Dorsey, Andrew B.–Jan 1, 1946
Dorsey, Earl Edward–May 27, Nov 28
Dorsey, Lee–May 27
Dorsey, M. L.–Nov 28
Doss, Herman D.–Feb 21, June 13
Doss, Mrs. G. B.–Feb 21, June 13
Doss, N. V.–April 3
Doss, Nettie L.–June 13
Dotson, Charmaine–June 2
Dotson, Eugene R.–Oct 1
Doughton, Ira–Oct 4
Douglas, George L.–Jan 23, Aug 15
Douglass, Mrs. J. P.–Feb 21
Douglass, Richard B.–Feb 21
Douglass, Robert W. Jr.
US Major General–Feb 21
Douthitt, Carl C.–March 6
Douthitt, Hugh W.–March 6
Downey, Fan–May 12
Downey, Robert–June 17
Downey, Robert L.–Aug 2
Doxey, Lloyd G.–April 28
Doxey, Mrs. Lloyd–April 28
Draper, G. E.–March 5
Draper, Roy B.–Nov 5
Draper, William F.–March 5
Drew, Edward F.–Sept 17
Drew, Elizabeth–Sept 17
Drew, Urban L.–Dec 8
Drexler, Arthur A.–Feb 4
Drexler, Robert B.–Feb 4
Drummond, Charles–Sept 9
Drummond, Hilda–Sept 9
Drummond, James–Sept 9
Drummond, Myron
Salt Rock Elementry School principal–Sept 11,
Oct 19, Jan 10, 1946
Dudleston, H. S.
Ceredo-Kenova Chamber of Commerce–Aug 11

Eck, Heinz
U-boat commander–Oct 20
Eckley, Doreene–Feb 7, April 13
Eckley, Elizabeth Doreene–Nov 22
Eckley, Jo Ann–Feb 28
Eckley, Leroy E.–May 17
Eckley, Roy–Feb 7, April 13, May 17, Nov 22
Eddins, George–Aug 4, Dec 5
Eddins, George Conway–Oct 21
Eddins, George T.–Oct 21
Eddins, Mr. and Mrs. George–Dec 5
Eddy, A. R.–Jan 19, April 12
Eddy, Asa C.–Jan 19
Eddy, Ruth J.–April 12
Edmonds, George C.–Sept 19
Edmondson, Charles L.–Jan 23
Edmondson, Dorothy Jean.–Jan 23
Edmondson, Frank–May 3
Edmondson, Russell–May 3
Edwards, Bertram E.–Feb 23
Edwards, C. R.–Feb 23
Edwards, Clara–Feb 23
Edwards, Clarence–Aug 15
Edwards, Edgar E.–March 7, Aug 14
Edwards, H. H.–Sept 16
Edwards, H. W.–Sept 8
Edwards, Harold–Feb 23, Sept 16
Edwards, Harry S.–Aug 13
Edwards, Homer H.–March 7
Edwards, Homer W.–Sept 8
Edwards, James C.–Feb 23
Edwards, James H.–March 7
Edwards, John G.–Nov 1
Edwards, Joseph–June 1
Edwards, Lynal–Feb 23
Edwards, Mary E.–Nov 1
Edwards, Robert R.–Aug 15
Edwards, Virginia–Aug 15
Edwards, William H.–March 7
Edwards, Willie F.–Feb 23
Effingham, Bernice–Feb 9
Effingham, Clifford–Feb 9
Effingham, Mrs. Ervin–Feb 9
Egnor, A. M.–Oct 10, 20
Egnor, Augie E.–Oct 20
Egnor, Augie Edward–Oct 10

Egnor, Lionel D.Oct 20
Egnor, Lionel Darce–Oct 10
Eichelberger, Robert L.
Lieutenant General Eichelberger–July 23
Eichmann, Adolf–Jan 3, 1946
Eisenhower, Dwight David
General Eisenhower–March 18, May 10, 23, 27, June 12, 19, 20, Nov 20
Elkins, B. H.–Sept 22
Elkins, Bessie–July 29
Elkins, C. S.–Nov 14
Elkins, Charles–Nov 14
Elkins, Chauncy S. Jr.–Nov 14
Elkins, Dorsey Darrell–Aug 1
Elkins, Ernest H.–June 29
Elkins, Ernest R.–July 29
Elkins, Ernest Sr.–July 29
Elkins, Frederick–Nov 14
Elkins, Goldie M.–Dec 9
Elkins, Hazel V.–Aug 1
Elkins, Joseph N.–Dec 9, Jan 1, 1946
Elkins, Norman R.–Jan 29
Elkins, Robert E.–Sept 22
Elkins, Rosa Nell–Jan 29
Elkins, Roy J.–July 29
Elkins, Rush E.–Jan 9, May 18
Elkins, Vivian–July 2
Elkins, Winnie–Jan 9
Elliott, Ira Jr.–Oct 11
Elliott, Mrs. Rufus–March 30
Elliott, Richard A.–March 30, May 2
Elliott, Rufus–May 2
Ellis, Barbara–April 8
Ellis, Clemith–Dec 14
Ellis, Clifton D.–Jan 14, Feb 11, June 10
Ellis, Edward C.–June 3
Ellis, Herschell E.–Dec 8
Ellis, Mervin C.–Feb 14
Ellis, Mrs. Ezra–June 18
Ellis, Myrtle–Feb 11, June 10
Ellis, Myrtle M.–Jan 14
Ellis, R. O.–June 9
Ellis, Robert E.–April 28
Ellis, Robert O.–Oct 28
Ellis, Robert O. Jr.–June 9
Ellis, Vina–July 22

Forester, Marian F.–Feb 11
Forester, Marian Ferene–Dec 19
Forester, Raymond–Feb 11
Forester, William H.–March 24, Aug 22, Dec 1
Forman, Lawrence E.–Dec 14
Forman, William M.–June 5
Forsythe, Abe Jr.–March 16, Aug 1
Fortner, George B.–April 4
Fossum, Kyle K.–July 6
Fossum, Mrs. Jessi H.–July 6
Foster, Charles A.–Feb 6
Foster, Charles W.–July 31
Foster, Charles William–July 19
Foster, Edwin N. Jr.–Nov 16
Foster, James L.–June 19
Foster, Mrs. C. D.–June 19
Foster, Thomas C.–Nov 13
Fotos, C. P.–Feb 14
Fotos, George P.–Feb 14
Fought, W. D.–Nov 4
Fountain, Joseph C.
Catholic Welfare Council–Aug 1
Fowler, James V.–Feb 6
Fox, Betty–Jan 18
Fox, Carl L.–April 7, July 11
Fox, Carl V.–Jan 18
Fox, David–July 10, 14,
Fox, David Jr.–March 24, Sept 29
Fox, Mr. and Mrs. Era–June 3
Foxx, Thomas–Dec 29
Fraley, C. B.–Jan 9
Fraley, Cecil–Jan 24
Fraley, Edwin J.–Jan 24
Fraley, James L.–Jan 9
Fraley, Lyle–Jan 9
Fraley, Paul J.–Jan 24
Fraley, Ruth–Jan 9
Fraley, Wilma–Jan 24
Frampton, William E.–April 9
France, C. W.–Sept 8
France, Charles E.–Sept 8, Oct 11, Nov 19
France, Mary J.–May 5
France, Russell P.–May 5
Francis, W. G. Sr.–June 22
Francis, Walter G. Jr.–June 22
Frank, Karl Hermann

Butcher of Lidice–July 24
Franklin, Oscar–July 19
Frantz, Lester N.–Sept 14
Franz, Charles–Nov 8
Franz, Paul A.–Nov 8
Franzello, Arty J.–Jan 16
Frater, Feely–Oct 24
Frazier, Arthur E.–Sept 15
Frazier, Bonnie R.–April 24, June 1
Frazier, Elwood–Jan 24
Frazier, Fred L.–June 1
Frazier, H. G.–May 5
Frazier, H. P.–Feb 11
Frazier, Harold H.–Jan 24
Frazier, John C.–Sept 25
Frazier, Olene–Jan 24
Frazier, Paul–April 1
Frazier, Paul E.–May 5
Frazier, Rachael–April 1
Frazier, Robert E.–Feb 11
Frazier, Sherman J.–April 24, June 1
Frazier, Veria–Sept 15
Fredman, Lewis Jr.–Dec 9
Fredman, Lewis Sr.–Dec 9
Freed, Louise–June 20, Aug 13
Freed, Matthew–June 20, Aug 13
Freelin, Dotson–Sept 28
Freeman, James A.–June 9, Nov 2
Freeman, James O.–April 23, Aug 9
Freeman, W. E.–April 23
Freeman, Willard–June 9, Aug 9
French, William H.–Oct 11
Freyer, Alma–Sept 7
Freyer, Leo B.–Sept 7
Fricker, Henry F.–March 4
Fridinger, Helen Virginia–Aug 27
Fridinger, Louis–Aug 27
Fridinger, Mrs. C. L.–Aug 27
Frisby, Betty Lou–March 8
Frisby, Carl E.–March 8
Fritz, Frank–Feb 1, March 10, Aug 10
Fritz, Martha–March 10
Fritz, Mrs. Fred–Feb 1
Frizzell, Ann Call–Oct 21
Frizzell, Ann Gail–Oct 6
Frizzell, Clarence D.–Oct 6

Gay, A. L.–March 1, 7
Gay, A. L.–March 1, 7
Gay, Wyatte J.–March 1, 7, Sept 7
Gaylord, Edith
AP Correspondant–April 17
Gearhart, C. F.–Jan 14
Gearhart, Robert M–Jan 14
Gebhardt, Charles R. (Buzz)–June 13
Gebhardt, E. S.–June 13
Gebhardt, Grover C.–June 13
Gebhardt, Homer–Feb 18
Gebhardt, Irvin R.–Nov 27
Geddis, George F.–Dec 14
Geddis, Glenn G.–Dec 14
Geer, Covington–Aug 31
Geer, Willford C.–Aug 31
Gentry, Ray R.–Aug 24
Gentry, Sam–Nov 9
George, Edward–May 18
George, Emile Ralph–Aug 22
George, Helen–Aug 22
George, Jean–July 22
George, Julius S.–Aug 22
George, Louis S.–Aug 22
George, Mrs. Charles–May 18
George, R. Wayne–Jan 5, 1946
George, Russell W.–Jan 5, 1946
Gerhold, Bill
Huntington High football player–Nov 10
Gesner, Mort–Feb 4
Gesner, Robert A.–Feb 4
Geyer, Bob–March 20
Gibbs, Charles W. Jr.–Oct 31
Gibbs, Edward C.–May 8
Gibbs, Georgia–March 23
Gibbs, Lester N.–Aug 7
Gibbs, Lieutenant–Sept 7
Gibbs, Samuel–Sept 7
Gibson, Alex–April 25
Gibson, Anyce V.–March 4
Gibson, Boyd–April 25
Gibson, Charles H.–June 1
Gibson, Delbert–Nov 30
Gibson, Delbert L.–Feb 1, June 2, Sept 23
Gibson, E. G.–May 23
Gibson, E. G. Jr.–Jan 13

Gibson, Ed G.–April 17
Gibson, Fanny–Jan 17
Gibson, George N.–March 4
Gibson, J. E.–Feb 1
Gibson, James–Jan 27
Gibson, James A.–Nov 30
Gibson, James M.–May 18
Gibson, Jess E.–June 2
Gibson, John–Sept 5
Gibson, Joseph–April 10
Gibson, Juanita–May 18
Gibson, Leo–Sept 5
Gibson, Madeline–April 4, Oct 9, Nov 29
Gibson, Mrs. Lewis–March 15
Gibson, Mrs. Lovell–June 2
Gibson, Nancy–May 23
Gibson, Robert W.–Jan 1, 1946
Gibson, Sara–Oct 25
Gibson, Silas–June 9
Gibson, Thomas–April 10
Gibson, Virgie–May 5
Gibson, W. K.–June 9, Aug 25
Gibson, Wilber–April 10
Gibson, William B.–Nov 13
Gibson, William K. Jr.–June 9, Aug 25
Gibson, William L. III–April 4
Gibson, William L. Jr.–Oct 9, Nov 29
Gibson, William M.–Jan 17
Gifford, Glen Edward–Nov 23
Gilbreath, Frederick A.–Oct 5
Gilfilen, B. O.–July 28
Gilfilen, Charles O.–July 28, Oct 5
Gill, A. H.–July 21
Gill, Albert–May 8
Gill, Bud–Nov 9, 11, Jan 6, 1946
Gill, Charles E.–May 8
Gill, Cora–Nov 23
Gill, Deedy–March 4
Gill, Eddie
Douglas High School football scholarship–May 13
Gill, Ever Leona Bias–Feb 4
Gill, June–March 4, Nov 9
Gill, Larry–Feb 25, March 4, 10, April 18, 19, Aug 25, 27, 31, Sept 3, 15, 29, Oct 6, 14, 19, 28, Nov 3, 8, 9, 10, 11, 17, 18, 26, Jan 6, 1946,

Grassi, John–Aug 23

Graveley, William T.–Dec 6

Gray, Brinton O.–April 17, July 22

Gray, Charles S.–June 3, 25

Gray, Comkolane–Feb 23

Gray, Frank B.–June 26

Gray, Harry C.–June 3

Gray, Marion–Feb 23

Gray, Maston L.–Nov 30

Gray, Morba–Sept 17

Gray, Mrs. I. R.–Nov 30

Gray, N. M.–Sept 12

Gray, Pete–March 20

Gray, Prichard–Sept 17

Gray, Richard F.–Sept 12

Grayson, Harry

NEA Sports Editor–Aug 25

Graziano, Rocky

Boxer–Aug 25

Green, Carl R.–March 6

Green, Charles W.–Nov 1

Green, Clarkson E.–Aug 1

Green, Culver A.–April 24

Green, Dave

Huntington High football player–Nov 10

Green, Donald A.–Dec 15

Green, James R.–March 28, Oct 25

Green, Johnny

Composer–Aug 20

Green, Mrs. J. A.–Nov 1

Green, Mrs. Jessie–Feb 17

Green, P. T.–Sept 20

Green, W. A.–Oct 25

Green, Walter F.–Sept 20

Green, Warren–March 28

Green, William Edward–Feb 17

Greenberg, Hank

Baseball–Oct 3, Dec 20

Greenberg, Haylm

Editor of the Jewish Frontier–Nov 7

Greene, David–May 8, Oct 23, Nov 15

Greene, Joseph–Nov 15

Greene, Joseph L.–May 8

Greene, Shirley–Sept 26, Nov 15

Greene, Shirley Grace–May 8, Oct 23

Greenhill, Benjamin P.–May 23

Greenhill, Harriett–May 23

Greenwell, Donald H.–April 6

Greenwell, Mrs. O. W.–April 6

Greenwood, Walter Jr.–Dec 12

Greer, Charles F.–Sept 13

Greer, Donald

Douglas High School basketball scholarship–May 13

Greer, Frieda–April 13

Greer, William–Sept 13

Gregory, Mrs. L. E.–Jan 10

Greig, Arthur D.–Feb 9, April 12

Greig, Dorcas D.–Feb 9

Greig, John D.–Feb 9, April 12

Grese, Irma

Nazis horror camp specialist–Nov 17

Gressang, Charles C.–Oct 7

Grew, Joseph

Secretary of State–July 11

Grews, Benjamin–Jan 27

Gribble, Ferris A.–Nov 8

Griffin, Fred C.–April 24

Griffith, Almita Mae, 14

Griffith, Eleanor–Nov 25

Griffith, Fred E.–Jan 6, 13, 19, May 1

Griffith, H. R.–March 22, Nov 25

Griffith, John H.

Lieutenant Colonel Griffith–April 1

Griffith, Thomas M.–March 22, Nov 25

Griffith, Woodrow M.–Jan 19

Griffiths, Betty White–Feb 21

Griffiths, G. R.–March 12, May 24

Griffiths, Val S.–Feb 21, March 12, May 24

Griffiths, Virginia–March 12

Grimmett, Ralph E.–Dec 5

Grimmette, Martin D.–Nov 29

Grose, Samuel S.–Feb 14

Grose, Virgil L.–Oct 15

Gross, Alfred–March 13

Gross, Elizabeth March 13

Gross, George E.–Nov 6

Gross, George F.–Dec 13, 19

Gross, Steve–Sept 12

Grove, Douglas C.–Feb 28

Grove, Mrs. W. F.–Feb 28

Groverman, William H.–July 17

Halfhill, Wayne E.–June 3
Hall, Ann–Jan 19
Hall, Bill
Marshall Basketball Player–Dec 8, 18
Hall, Boyce–March 2, Oct 18
Hall, Bud Clarence–Jan 19
Hall, C. J.–Feb 11
Hall, Charles E.–July 23
Hall, Clayton L.–Nov 6
Hall, Farley B.–Jan 13, Feb 2, March 2, Oct 18
Hall, Frank E.–July 5
Hall, Fred–Dec 30
Hall, Fred T.–Dec 30
Hall, George B.–May 18
Hall, H. B.–Sept 28
Hall, Hillman–Jan 19
Hall, James P.–Sept 24
Hall, John J.–March 24, June 2
Hall, John R.–Jan 29
Hall, John S.–July 3, Sept 23
Hall, John S. Jr.–July 3, Sept 23
Hall, Kathleen–May 18, Nov 11
Hall, Laura–Jan 25
Hall, Lenorah–Jan 19
Hall, Mar. A.–June 7
Hall, Mildred L.–Jan 29, March 24
Hall, Mrs. Boyce–Feb 2
Hall, Mrs. John R.–June 2
Hall, Oliver–June 2
Hall, Paul–Jan 19
Hall, Price W.–March 20
Hall, Ralph H.–May 18, Nov 11, 12
Hall, Rena K.–March 20
Hall, Robert E.–May 5
Hall, Robert O.–Sept 28
Hall, Ruth E.–May 5
Hall, Selma–Jan 19
Hall, Stewart–Nov 14
Hall, Strother (Todd)–Jan 19
Hall, Troy–July 23
Hall, Willard C.–Jan 29, Feb 11, March24
Hall, William C.
Colonel Hall–Oct 26
Hall, William Wallace–July 23
Halley, Eloise–May 11
Halley, Floyd–May 11

Halley, John W.–July 18
Halley, Myron L.–Oct 1
Halley, R. S.–May 13
Halley, Robert S. Jr.–May 13
Halsey, William F.
Admiral Halsey–July 14, Sept 28, Oct 15
Hamill, C. A.–Aug 28
Hamill, Thomas C.–Aug 28
Hamilton, A. C.–Oct 27
Hamilton, John W.–Oct 27
Hamilton, Lloyd Allen–Nov 1
Hamilton, R. L.
Mayor of Chesapeake OH–Aug 9
Hamilton, Richard L.–Oct 27
Hamlin, Bernard L.–Nov 20
Hamlin, Charles–Feb 25
Hamlin, E. J.–Jan 17
Hamlin, Hazel–May 10
Hamlin, Helen–Feb 25
Hamlin, Keith J.–Feb 25
Hamlin, Lloyd J.–Jan 17, Oct 18
Hamlin, R. J.–Oct 18
Hamlin, Robert–May 10
Hamlin, Tom C.–Feb 25
Hamlin, William S.–Oct 25
Hamm, C. E.–June 23
Hamm, Wilford–June 23
Hammock, Jess E.–Oct 4
Hammond, Walter C.–March 15
Hammonds, Caroline–May 9
Hammonds, Marion F.–May 9, Aug 13
Hammonds, Marion Kay–May 9
Hammonds, Mary Catherine–May 9
Hammonds, Oscar–May 9
Hammonds, Oscar R.–Aug 13
Hampton, Gid–June 28
Hancock, Charles C.–July 27
Hancock, James–July 27
Hancock, Mrs. H. V–July 27
Hancock, Robert L.–Nov 16
Handley, Edwin Marco–Nov 12
Handley, Jessalee–Nov 21
Handley, Joe L.–Nov 21
Haney, F. F.–Sept 27
Haney, Jeanne M.–Sept 27
Haney, Paul F.–Sept 27

Hartz, Leonard–July 14
Hartz, S. K.–July 14
Harvey, Ada E.–Nov 6
Harvey, Barbara Woodrum–Ackmowledgments
Harvey, Bill–April 8
Harvey, Bill L.–Nov 6
Harvey, Harriet P.–Feb 1
Harvey, Mary–July 14
Harvey, Mrs. T. W.–May 12
Harvey, Thomas William Jr.–May 12
Harvie, William Lewis–March 4
Hash, Garrett–July 15
Hash, O. T.–July 15
Haskins, Wanda–May 17
Hastings, Robert–Nov 14
Hastings, T.–Nov 2
Hastings, William H.–Nov 2
Hatch, Mrs. Charles–June 2, Sept 7
Hatch, William J.–June 2, 9, Sept 7
Hatcher, E. G.–May 6, June 18, Sept 7
Hatcher, Vernon S.–May 6, June 18, Sept 7
Hatfield, Claude–May 30
Hatfield, Erskine H.–Jan 6, Feb 17
Hatfield, Jasper H.–Nov 6
Hatfield, Marion W.–Feb 24
Hatfield, Mary–April 3
Hatfield, Mrs. Lucian M.–Feb 24
Hatfield, Robert A.–March 14
Hatfield, Ruth–May 21
Hatfield, T. F.–Feb 17
Hatfield, Thomas R.–Feb 14
Hatfield, Troy–Nov 2
Hatmaker, James W.–May 1
Hatmaker, Jerry–May 1
Hatten, Bert–Feb 5
Hatten, John W.–April 13
Hatten, Loren L.–Feb 12
Hatten, Mr. and Mrs. Alva–April 13
Hatton, Julia Anne–Feb 2
Hatton, Robert E.–Feb 2
Haun, Horace L.–Dec 15
Hawes, Mrs. Sylvia–Jan 12
Hawkins, Alex–Aug 22
Hawkins, Clarence Jr.–April 10
Hawkins, H. B.–July 17
Hawkins, Harold F.–Aug 22

Hawkins, James Marshall–July 17
Hawley, Roy M.
West Virginia University Athletic Director–Aug 21
Haworth, Mrs. S. V.–Aug 2, Dec 12
Haworth, Sam–Aug 2
Haworth, Samuel E.–Dec 12
Haws, Julia–July 4
Hay, Wetzel–May 25
Hay, Wetzel Sr.–May 25
Hayes, Eloise–July 1
Hayes, George W.–July 1
Hayes, James R.–July 28
Hayes, Julie–Aug 11
Hayes, Mabel V.–April 3
Hayes, P. M.–July 1
Hayes, Sidney
Manager, Hotel Governor Cabell–July 7
Hayes, Tommy–Aug 11
Hayes, W. S.–July 28
Hayes, William W.–April 3
Hayner, Floyd–Nov 10
Hayner, John M.–Nov 10
Haynes, Emmette M.–Nov 9
Haynes, Floyd–Nov 1
Haynes, John M.–Nov 1
Hayton, Ezra–April 12
Hayton, Mark–April 12
Hazapis, Thomas–May 24
Hazeldine, Henry–June 27
Hazeldine, Norman P.–June 27
Hazelett, Charles C.–Sept 29
Hazelett, Ernest W.–March 7
Hazelett, George W.–July 4
Hazelett, H. H.–July 4, Aug 2, Dec 23
Hazelett, H. T.–Jan 28
Hazelett, Harlan–Nov 10
Hazelett, Harold Golden–Aug 6
Hazelett, James–March 26
Hazelett, Joe S.–Jan 28, Dec 23
Hazelett, Joseph–July 4
Hazelett, Joseph S.–Aug 1
Hazelett, Lillian L.–July 4
Hazelett, Pearlie–Aug 6
Hazelett, Robert A.–March 7
Hazelwood, Floyd T.–July 5

Herndon, J. H.–July 14
Herndon, John–March 14
Herndon, John W.–Feb 2, Sept 28,
Herndon, Karl S.–Sept 28
Herndon, Mack–Feb 2
Herold, Moser B.–Jan 20
Herold, William C.–Jan 20
Herrenkohl, Beulah Cremeans–April 7
Herrenkohl, Charles Thomas–April 7
Hertig, Willis
Barboursville Coach–Nov 28
Hess, Eva–Feb 5
Hester, Brookie S.–Sept 14
Hetzer, Elouise–July 1
Hetzer, James–Oct 19
Hetzer, James T.–July 1
Hetzer, T. A.–July 1
Hewitt, Cecil A.–June 4
Heyl, D. W.–Nov 2
Heyl, Kenneth–Nov 2
Hibbard, William E.–Feb 14
Hibner, Charles K.–Dec 8
Hickman, Cecil M.–Nov 10
Hickman, James F.–Feb 16
Hickman, Naomi–Feb 16
Hicks, Chauncey–May 15
Hicks, Clarence–March 20, 29, May 15
Hicks, Dorcie–Nov 18
Hicks, Joseph B.–March 14, Sept 3
Hicks, Mrs. Oscar–March 29
Hicks, Nora–Sept 14
Hicks, Preston D.–Sept 25
Hicks, Raymond–Nov 26
Hicks, Vernial–Nov 26
Hicks, Virgil–Sept 14
Hideki, Tojo
Former Japanese prime minister–Sept 11
Higashi-Kuni, Naruhiko
Japanese prince–Aug 16
Hightower, William P.–Aug 25
Hilbert, Mary E.–May 8
Hill, Barrner M.–July 14
Hill, C. N.–Dec 5
Hill, Clarence N. Jr.–Dec 5
Hill, Ernest–July 12
Hill, Goldie–Aug 20

Hill, Ira–Dec 9
Hill, Wilbur–Oct 18
Hilleary, Ralph E.–Nov 16
Hillery, Edward V.–June 29
Hillman, James M.–Aug 31
Hillman, Mrs. G. J.–Aug 31
Hilsheimer, J. E.–Dec 15
Hilsheimer, Judy–Dec 15
Hilsheimer, Robert C.–Dec 15
Himmler, Heinrich
Gestapo Chief–April 23, 24, May 23
Hinchman, Don–Dec 25
Hinchman, Don C.–Dec 24, 25
Hinerman, A. B.–April 23
Hinerman, Elvin L.–March 14
Hinerman, Jack E.–March 14
Hinerman, Maurice E.–April 23
Hinerman, Walter F.–March 14
Hines, James E.–Dec 3
Hines, James F.–May 11
Hines, Lucille L.–May 11
Hines, Opal Fraley–April 13
Hines, Raymond–April 13
Hinshaw, C. W.–Feb 20
Hinshaw, Clinton W.–Sept 29
Hinshaw, Hugh M.–Sept 29
Hinshaw, W. K.–Feb 20
Hippert, Robert D.–Nov 27
Hippert, William L.–Nov 27
Hirby, George W.–Jan 6
Hirohito, Emperor–June 10, Aug 10, 12, 16,
Sept22, 28, Oct 8, 17, Nov 9, Jan 1, 1946
Hitchcock, Chaplain O. V.–July 27
Hitchcock, Raymon C.–Nov 4
Hitchcock, Raymond A.–Sept 13
Hite, Billy G.–March 28
Hite, Billy Gene–Aug 15, Oct 5
Hite, Blanche O'Brien–Jan 7
Hite, Carl–Aug 15, Oct 5
Hite, Charles F.–Oct 15
Hite, Elza–Jan 7
Hite, F. E.–May 9
Hite, John–Nov 11
Hite, Mrs. Billie–Aug 15, Oct 5
Hite, Mrs. Cecil–March 17, Dec 3, 7
Hite, Mrs. W. F.–April 23

Holtzworth, Richard–Feb 8
Homewood, Max H.–Oct 23
Homma, Masaharu
Japanese general–Sept 16, Dec 8
Honacker, Luther M.–June 8
Honacker, Sarah–June 8
Honaker, Gerald L.–May 19
Honaker, J. C.–May 19
Honjo, Shigeru
Japanese army commander–Nov 20
Hooser, C. W.–Sept 21
Hooser, Franklin C.–Sept 21
Hoover, Robert R.–Nov 6
Hoover, William–Nov 6
Hopkins, Anna Belle–Oct 30
Hopkins, Cagle T.–Oct 30
Hopkins, Earl E.–Feb 17
Hopkins, Elizabeth Jeanne–Nov 18
Hopkins, Harold L.–Nov 18
Hopkins, Lula–Feb 17
Hopson, Frances–Aug 27
Horn, Thomas M.–April 14
Hornsby, Lee R.–Oct 11
Hoscar, Charles E.–Jan 5
Hotchkiss, Elizabeth–Nov 14
Houston, Alaska C.–Sept 14
Houston, John W.–Jan 23
Houston, William H.–Jan 23
Houvouras, Mrs. Tom–April 19
Houvouras, Nick–June 10
Houvouras, Ted–June 10
Howard, Alfred E.–March 1
Howard, Clifford–Nov 21
Howard, Edward–Feb 26
Howard, Elmer E.–July 12, Nov 26
Howard, Elsie–Sept 18
Howard, George W.–March 1
Howe, Jack Lee–Feb 3
Howe, Mary–Feb 3
Howell, Carroll L.–June 24
Howell, Clarence–June 12
Howell, Clarence Jr.–June 12
Howell, Clyde W.–June 9
Howell, Donald L.–Feb 1
Howell, Elouise E.–Feb 1
Howes, Charles C.–June 26

Howes, Gerald B.–July 16, Nov 6
Hubbard, Ethel–Feb 28
Hubbard, John–Sept 24
Hubbard, William L.–Oct 13
Huchock, Alexander–Feb 20
Huddleston, Harlowe H.–Aug 28
Huddleston, Roy L.–March 7
Hudson, Clement–July 18
Huff, Hildreth Frank–Sept 16
Huff, June–Sept 16
Huffman, Brilliant J.–April 17
Huffman, C. C.–June 8
Huffman, Ferrell–June 8
Huffman, Jack–June 8
Huffman, Kenneth R.–July 14
Huffman, Mrs.–July 14
Huffman, Viola–April 17
Hughes, B. E.–Nov 8
Hughes, Charles–March 23
Hughes, Charles E.–Oct 6, Nov 8
Hughes, Charles F.–Jan 9
Hughes, Dewey–Jan 9
Hughes, Donald Lee–March 16
Hughes, Elsie–Jan 9
Hughes, Eugene–Dec 13
Hughes, H. D.–Nov 8
Hughes, Hurley–Jan 9
Hughes, J. M.–March 16
Hughes, J. T.–March 23, Oct 6
Hughes, Louie A.–Oct 26
Hughes, Sarah–Oct 9
Hughes, William E.–Oct 26
Hughes, Woodrow–Oct 9
Hull, Eugene–Jan 5, 1946
Hull, James R.–Aug 2
Humphrey, Ray C.–Jan 1, 1946
Humphreys, Edward–Nov 12
Humphreys, Gordon–April 29
Humphreys, H. G.–Nov 16
Humphreys, James B.–April 29, Nov 16
Humphreys, Raymond V.–Nov 12
Hundley, Edwin G.–Feb 4
Hundley, T. E.–Feb 4
Hunt, Amelia F.–June 12
Hunt, Bernard Ray–April 3
Hunt, Clyde–July 4

Jackson, William–Oct 19
Jackson, Woodrow W.–Jan 1, 1946
Jacobs, Henry–Jan 24
Jacobs, James H.–Jan 24
James, Clifford–Dec 22
James, Donald R.–Oct 26
James, Heber C.–Oct 26
James, John–Dec 22
James, Junior–Nov 5
James, Rebecca–Jan 23
Jameson, Charles B.–Oct 26
Jameson, Ena–Sept 22
Jameson, Lewis A.–Nov 16
Jameson, Lewis Ashland Sept 22
Jarrell, Alyene–Aug 13
Jarrell, Charles–Nov 6
Jarrell, Clifford–Jan 6
Jarrell, Forrest D.–Jan 5
Jarrell, Gilbert M.–Aug 13
Jarrell, Homer C.–July 22
Jarrell, Hoot–Aug 14
Jarrell, Mrs. Nikomas–Oct 7
Jarrell, Nora Mae–Jan 6
Jarrell, Robert P.–Dec 24
Jarrell, Russell G.–Nov 19
Jarrett, Anne–Nov 19
Jarvis, Albert J.–March 16, July 2
Jarvis, Lucille–March 16, July 2
Jarvis, Okey A.–July 2
Jay, Damron E.–Nov 29
Jeffers, Cora E.–May 15
Jeffers, Sherma L.–May 15
Jeffers, Walter Glen–May 15
Jefferson, Andrew–Oct 5
Jefferson, John–May 30
Jefferson, Mrs. John–April 1
Jefferson, Wallace G.–March 31, May 30
Jeffrey, Millard–April 8
Jeffrey, Opal S.–April 8
Jeffrey, Raymond R.–April 8
Jeffrey, Robert Paul–April 8
Jeffrey, Roy L.–April 8
Jeffrey, Stacy E.–April 8
Jeffrey, Thomas M.–April 8
Jeffrey, Vivian L.–April 8
Jeffrey, Wylie Jack–April 8

Jenke, Marie
　German Doctor–June 16
Jenkins, Dick–Oct 24
Jenkins, Evelyn–Jan 28
Jenkins, George–Jan 28, Feb 25
Jenkins, Harrison–March 16
Jenkins, J. E.–Oct 29
Jenkins, John E. Jr.–Oct 29
Jenkins, Leroy–Jan 28, Feb 25
Jenkins, Opal Maddox–March 16
Jennings, Dr. R. C.–Sept 27
Jennings, Emma–Oct 10
Jennings, Howard–Oct 10
Jennings, Jane–Oct 10
Jennings, Jean–Oct 10
Jennings, Roscoe C. Jr.–Sept 27
Jessup, Al J.–Aug 23
Jessup, Mrs. Al–Aug 23
Jobe, Dewie–Oct 11
Jobe, Fred–Aug 2, Oct 24
Jobe, Grace–June 4
Jobe, Wetzel C.–Aug 2, Oct 24
Jodi, Gustav
　Nazi high command–July 22
Johnson, Alma–May 27, Sept 19
Johnson, Anna Mae–July 3
Johnson, Anna Marie–Feb 5
Johnson, Arnold–July 5
Johnson, Arnold D.–April 14
Johnson, Betty W.–Jan 29
Johnson, Charles–May 1
Johnson, Charles R.–Feb 5
Johnson, Clifton V.–March 12
Johnson, Clovis D.–Jan 30, May 21
Johnson, Dale–March 31
Johnson, David–April 14
Johnson, Donald B.–Jan 29
Johnson, Donald Wayne–Sept 29
Johnson, Dorothy–May 2, Sept 7
Johnson, Ella–June 19
Johnson, Emery C.–July 29
Johnson, Everett–May 10
Johnson, Floyd 'Corkie'–Sept 19
Johnson, Forrest–Sept 16
Johnson, Garland–March 1
Johnson, Georgia B.–March 13

Kinnaird, George W.–Oct 9
Kinnaird, Lewis–Oct 9
Kinsey, Larry–Oct 31
Kinzer, Mrs. W. B.–April 27
Kinzer, William B.–Feb 26
Kirk, Betty–May 10
Kirk, Betty May–Jan 5, 1946
Kirk, Chester–June 18
Kirk, Edward E.–Sept 10
Kirk, Harold E.–July 30
Kirk, Harry–July 30
Kirk, Lan J.–June 18
Kirk, Norman
U. S. Ambassador to Italy–April 6
Kirk, Ray–July 30
Kirk, Ruby–May 19
Kirkland, Alpheus–Jan 5
Kirsanov, Stepan Paviovich
Russian minister to Sofia, Bulgaria–Aug 22
Kirsh, Mrs. Paul–Jan 30
Kitchen, Elmer A.–Dec 7
Kitchen, G. A.–Jan 16
Kitchen, Gilba–Feb 3
Kitchen, Gilba A. Jr.–Feb 3
Kitchen, Greene–Jan 24
Kitchen, J. S.–June 29
Kitchen, James E.–Dec 30
Kitchen, James H.–June 29
Kitchen, M. T. Sr.–April 21
Kitchen, Martin T. Jr.–April 21
Kitchen, Minnie L.–Jan 24
Kitchen, Shannon E.–Jan 14
Kitchen, Stanley D.–Jan 14, May 9, June 13
Kitchen, Wilford–Jan 14, June 13
Kitts, Mrs. Charles–July 25
Klein, Frederick W.–Oct 17
Klein, H. S.–June 1
Klein, Robert E.–June 1
Kliegel, George J.–Jan 5, 1946
Kliegel, Mrs. G. J.–Jan 5, 1946
Klumpp, James S.–Aug 6
Knapp, Clarence W. Jr.–July 5
Knapp, Jesse J.–Dec 11
Knapp, W. F.–March 4
Knight, Edward W. Jr.–March 28
Knight, Mildred P.–Aug 22

Knight, Vick–March 23
Knox, Dr. William
Seventh Avenue Methodist Church–Sept 23
Koehler, Edward–June 13, Aug 31, Sept 1
Koehler, Inez–June 13, Aug 31, Sept 1
Koehler, Sadie–June 13
Koiso, Kuniaki
Japanese Premier Koiso–March 19
Konoye, Fuminaro
Japanese Prince–Oct 12
Koontz, Elmer R.–May 2
Koontz, Fern B.–June 14
Koontz, Fern Black–May 2, 30
Koontz, Raymond–May 30
Kopp, A. A.–June 14
Kopp, Florine–June 14
Kopp, Robert A.–June 14
Kozma, Michael–Aug 14
Kozma, Michael Jr.–Aug 14, Dec 16
Kozma, Michael Sr.–Dec 16
Kramer, Josef
Beast of Belsen–Nov 17
Krantz, J. M.–Jan 9
Krantz, Joseph M. Jr.–Jan 9
Kufahl, Edward–Nov 10
Kuhn, Forest B.–March 22
Kuhn, G. C.–Jan 17
Kuhn, Marjorie–March 22
Kuhn, Ralph M.–Jan 17
Kuper, John–Sept 13
Kyle, Donald W.–Oct 24
Kyle, Mrs. John–Oct 24

L

Labus, Michael P.–Nov 7
Lacock, Henry T.–April 28
Ladd, Jesse A.
Brigadier General Ladd–Aug 4
LaFon, Gilbert–Oct 4
LaFon, Raymond L.–Oct 4
Lahue, Dean–March 13
Lahue, Paul D.–March 13
Laishley, Charles G.–Feb 17
Laishley, Lawrence W.–Feb 17
Lake, Avie Jr.–April 6
Lakin, Ferguson–May 19

Legg, Clyde E.–July 31
Legg, Edward–July 31
Legg, James E.–July 7, Dec 16
Legge, E. J.–Jan 9
Legge, Frank L.–Oct 30
Legge, Lowell E.–Jan 9
Leggette, L. Poe–Dec 4
LeGrand, Claud–Aug 1
LeGrand, Donald–Aug 1
Leighty, Edward–March 28
Leighty, Eugene O.–March 28
Leitch, Josephine G.–Aug 16
Leitch, Paul V.–Aug 16
Leith, Jean–Feb 3
Leith, John W.–March 20
LeMaster, B. E.–May 19, June 23
LeMaster, Charles E.–April 26
LeMaster, D.–April 26
LeMaster, Eugene F.–Oct 22
LeMaster, Irvin J.–April 26
LeMaster, Julia Kathryn–June 23
LeMaster, Norman–June 23
LeMay, Curtis
General LeMay–July 30
Lemley, C. A.–Aug 22
Lemley, Mrs. G. D.–June 26
Lemley, Robert W.–Aug 22
Lemley, William V.–June 26
Lemon, D. W.–Oct 27
Lemon, Harvey L.–Oct 27
Leonard, Etta M.–Jan 29
Leonard, Wendell–Jan 29
Lerner, Isaac–Jan 13, Sept 21
Lerner, L.–Oct 19
Lerner, Leonard A.–Oct 19
Lerner, Louis–Jan 13, Sept 21
Leroy, Russell Meadows–Oct 24
Lester, Frederick L.–July 1
Lester, Holt–Feb 18
Lester, M. E.–July 1
Lester, M. H.–July 1
Lester, Max E.–June 14
Lester, P. J.–June 14
Lester, Phillip J.–June 14
Lester, S. L.–Dec 12
Lett, Bea Houghton–Sept 22

Lett, Corney–Sept 29
Lett, Sarah–July 27
Lett, Wallace H.–July 27
Lett, Walter B.–Sept 22
Levine, Milton–Dec 13
Levine, Sheldon–Dec 13
Levitsky, Joe–Nov 1
Levitsky, Mabel B.–Nov 1
Lewedag, H. B.–Aug 14
Lewedag, Maxine–Aug 14
Lewis, Alice M.–March 6, 21
Lewis, Alta–Jan 17
Lewis, Alva V.–Jan 17, 24, Feb 2
Lewis, Beatrice Vandament–Dec 30
Lewis, C. W.–July 17
Lewis, Chaplain Norman R.–April 9
Lewis, Charles B.–Dec 8
Lewis, Charles E.–Jan 28
Lewis, Charles H.–April 24
Lewis, Chester W.–Nov 14
Lewis, Claude–Nov 22
Lewis, Delano–June 26, Aug 2
Lewis, Donald–Nov 22
Lewis, Earl–June 26
Lewis, Elise–Oct 6
Lewis, Elsie–Jan 7, July 17, Dec 29
Lewis, George–March 21
Lewis, George R.–March 6
Lewis, Helen–Nov 22
Lewis, Henry T.–Jan 8
Lewis, James D.–Aug 6
Lewis, Jesse O. D.–March 24
Lewis, John F.–July 2
Lewis, John L.
UMW Chieftain–Oct 8
Lewis, Lenora
Douglas High School music scholarship–May 13
Lewis, Lowell–July 2
Lewis, Marvin H.–Oct 13
Lewis, Mary Frances–Dec 10
Lewis, Mildred–July 2
Lewis, Milford–April 24
Lewis, Minnie–Nov 14
Lewis, O. D.–March 24
Lewis, Oscar L.–May 22
Lewis, R. C.–April 9

Lovely, Evelyn E.–July 31
Lovely, Robert L.–July 31
Lovett, B. H.–Aug 29
Lovett, Mrs. B. H. Sr.–Aug 29
Lovett, Timmy–Aug 29
Lovett, William–Aug 29
Lovins, B. B.–Jan 12
Lovins, James H.–Jan 12
Lowe, Ervin–June 29
Lowe, Herman–Jan 27
Lowe, James H.–June 12
Lowe, May W.–April 6
Lowe, Riley W.–April 6
Lowe, Robert E.–June 29
Lowe, Willie W.–Oct 19
Lubin, Dora–June 27
Lubin, John David–June 27
Lucas, Burt–Feb 20
Lucas, David–Oct 3
Lucas, Gladys B–Feb 18
Lucas, Glenn A.–Feb 18
Lucas, Herman H.–June 26
Lucas, Irving–Jan 12
Lucas, Ishmael–Oct 3
Lucas, Mary J.–Feb 20
Lucas, Opal (Midkiff)–Oct 3
Lucas, Rosa–June 26, Dec 4
Lucas, Vernon–April 10
Lucas, Vinson–April 10
Lunsford, Oscar J.–Dec 28
Lusher, E. L.–July 31
Lusher, Lyle D.–July 31
Lusk, A.–April 21
Lusk, Mrs. Joe–Feb 10
Lusk, Walter A.–March 2, 6, July 9, Dec 4
Lusk, Walter A. (Tom)–April 21
Lusk, Walter A. (Tom) Jr.–July 9
Lusk, Walter A. Jr.–March 2, 6, Dec 4
Luther, Mrs. Erie–July 4
Lycan, Donald C.–April 14
Lyle
A slave of mid-1800s–Oct 27
Lynch, E. A.–May 17
Lynch, Jean E.–May 17
Lynch, Wilbur E.–May 17
Lyng, Bill I.–May 6

Lyng, Henry I.–May 6
Lyon, Mrs. Thomas R.–Aug 4
Lyon, Thomas R. Jr.–Aug 4
Lyons, Lee M.–Jan 8
Lyons, Rev. Ira–March 25

M
MacArthur, Douglas A.
General MacArthur–Feb 19, April 3, Aug 4, 21, 26, 30, Sept 2, 16, 18, 21, 22, 28, Nov 2, Dec 16,
Macdonald, F. A.–Aug 22
Macdonald, William–Aug 22
Mace, Herman Edward–May 7
Mace, Thelma–May 7
MacKenzie, DeWitt
Huntington columnist–Aug 7
Mackey, Dr. W. K.–Feb 7
Mackey, Joseph–Feb 7
Mackinnon, Mary Jane–Aug 27
Maclaughlin, Dale–Oct 3
Maclaughlin, Gullen–Oct 3
Maclaughlin, L. A.–Oct 3
MacRae, Miriam W.–May 25
Macri, James–Nov 28
Macri, Patrick S.–Nov 28
Maddox, Charles M.–Jan 22, Aug 20
Maddox, John–Jan 22, Aug 20
Maddox, Ruby–Aug 20
Maddox, Ruby Adkins–Jan 22
Magariello, A.–Aug 31,
Magariello, Anthony–May 19, June 26
Magariello, Jean Treese–Aug 31
Magariello, Tony J.–May 19, June 26, Aug 11, 31
Maguet, B. N.–Sept 12
Maguet, S. N.–Sept 12
Mahan, C. E.–June 21
Mahan, Robert R.–June 21
Maier, Ann–Mach 19
Maier, Fred W.–Mach 19, Aug 13
Maier, Frederick W.–Feb 19
Maier, Mildred–Mach 19, Aug 13
Maier, Sharon–March 19
Malcolm, Archie C.–March 28
Malcolm, Donald–March 4
Malmquist, Betty Klein–Jan 11
Malmquist, Tord V.–Jan 11

Matthews, Joseph O.–June 28

Matthews, O. W.–June 28

Matthews, Thelma–Feb 28

Matthews, Thelma (Morrison)–Oct 20

Matthews, Velma–Jan 2, Oct 20

Mautz, Albert F.–March 2

Mautz, Lloyd–March 2

Mautz, Richard M.–March 2

Mautz, Virgil–March 2

Maxwell, Alan B.–June 27

Maxwell, Allen B.–March 28

Maxwell, E. B.

Lieutenant Colonel Maxwell–July 12

Maxwell, Hugh–March 11, Dec 19

Maxwell, Hugh L.–June 27

Maxwell, Richard S.–Dec 19

May, Edgar–June 22

May, Waldeck–June 22

Mayberry, Frank S.–Dec 12

Mayberry, William R.–Nov 16

Mayenschein, Eugene–March 7

Mayenschein, Iris Augusta–March 7

Mayenschein, Iris Eugenia–March 7

Mayenschein, Mary Lou–March 7

Mayenschein, Sadie–March 7

Mayes, Elizabeth–Jan 17

Mayes, Howard G.–Jan 17

Mayes, John William–Jan 17

Mayes, Robert A.–Jan 17, Aug 8

Maynard, Benjamin H.–Dec 22

Maynard, Benjamin T.–Feb 16, Match 30, April 15

Maynard, Burgess–Oct 11

Maynard, C. A.–Oct 11

Maynard, Charles L.–Feb 20

Maynard, Curtis E.–Jan 29

Maynard, Dennis–April 15

Maynard, Don–Jan 9, 30

Maynard, E. A.–Nov 22

Maynard, Edgar–Oct 11

Maynard, Epperson C.–Sept 24

Maynard, Fayette–July 15

Maynard, Frank–Jan 9, 31

Maynard, Harold–April 25

Maynard, Irian R.–Dec 11

Maynard, J. T.–Oct 25

Maynard, James–March 30, April 15

Maynard, Jarrett B.–Oct 11

Maynard, Jesse–April 15

Maynard, Jesse B.–March 12 , Oct 25

Maynard, Joe–Aug 1

Maynard, McKinley–Feb 20

Maynard, Noah–April 25

Maynard, Ollie–Jan 29

Maynard, Opal Perry–Nov 22

Maynard, Russell T.–March 23

Maynard, Ruth–Jan 9, 30

Maynard, Sadie–Sept 24

Maynard, Stella–Feb 16

Maynor, E. C.–Sept 10

Maynor, E. D.–Jan 26, Dec 13

Maynor, Euveldia C.–Dec 13

Maynor, Fuveldia C.–Jan 26

Mayo, Betty–Feb 5

Mayo, C. C.

Captain–Huntington Fire Department–June 20

Mayo, Earl–Feb 5, May 23, June 4

Mayo, Eddie

Baseball–Oct 3

Mayo, Edward C.–Jan 5, June 20

Mayo, Elizabeth M.–March 16

Mayo, Mary–Jan 5

Mayo, Paul J.–March 16

Mayo, Thomas–Feb 5

Mayo, William O.–March 16

Mays, A. James Jr.–Nov 25

Mays, Betty Sue–Nov 10

Mays, Doalie–Nov 16

Mays, E.–June 3

Mays, Elmer E.–Feb 4

Mays, J. B.–Nov 10

Mays, John B. Jr.–Nov 10

Mays, Joseph A.–Nov 16

Mays, Lloyd R.–May 5

Mays, Mildred–June 3

Mays, Paul A.–Feb 4

Mays, Paul E.–Feb 4, Dec 24

Mays, Shelby–Feb 14

Mays, W. A.–Feb 14

Mays, Walter A.–Nov 16

Mays, Walter H.–Feb 14

Mazo, Mrs. Harry–Jan 30

Mikhalchev, Dmitry
Bulgarian Professor- Minister to Moscow–Aug 22
Miles, Anna Gordon–Nov 22
Miles, John–March 24
Miles, John Norman–Nov 22
Miles, Leslie R.–March 24
Miles, Leslie R. Jr.–March 24
Miller, B. Frank Sr.–Dec 2
Miller, Betty Dailey–Feb 8
Miller, Betty J.–Oct 2
Miller, Boyda F. Jr.–Dec 2
Miller, Charles P.–Feb 8
Miller, Charles Raymond–Oct 21
Miller, Charles S.–April 16
Miller, Donald L.–Nov 26
Miller, Edith–Jan 26, Feb 4, Oct 5, Jan 5, 1946
Miller, Erma Frances–Jan 26, Jan 5, 1946
Miller, Ernest–Jan 24
Miller, Eugene S.–Oct 5
Miller, Eva–Feb 8
Miller, Freddie M.–Dec 14
Miller, Golden R.–March 4
Miller, Guy–Jan 20
Miller, Hassel–May 15
Miller, Hassel L.–May 15
Miller, Herbert L.–Dec 19
Miller, Herman E.–Jan 24
Miller, Hilda B.–May 17
Miller, Irma F.–Feb 4
Miller, J. P.–Jan 12
Miller, J. Price–Aug 6
Miller, La Vern–May 17
Miller, Lewis A.–June 8
Miller, Lewis A. Jr.–June 8, Dec 19
Miller, Mrs. Irie–April 16
Miller, Mrs. Ottie–Aug 1
Miller, Naomi–May 4
Miller, Pauline–July 15
Miller, Raymond–Nov 10
Miller, Sallie F.–Nov 6
Miller, Victor–Jan 20
Miller, Victor Guy–July 15
Miller, W. M.–Jan 12
Miller, Walter P.–Oct 2
Miller, Wanda–July 19
Miller, William–Aug 8

Miller, William R.–Nov 8
Mills, A. W.–Feb 21
Mills, A. W. Jr.–Feb 21
Mills, Ballard B.–Sept 3
Mills, Claude–Sept 3
Mills, Dorothy–Jan 31
Mills, Dorothy M.–May 31
Mills, Edmond–Jan 31, May 31
Mills, Evan–Sept 3
Mills, Evelyn–Sept 3
Mills, G. A. Jr.–Dec 12
Mills, George E.–June 23, Aug 25
Mills, Mary–Sept 3
Mills, Wilber C.–June 1
Milton, Mrs. Willie S.–Aug 27
Milum, James F.–Feb 11
Minnich, Gordon L.–Dec 8
Minor, Clayton–Aug 15
Minton, Albert N.–April 3, May 2
Minton, Carolyn V.–April 3, May 2
Minton, E. U.–May 2
Minton, Emile U.–April 3
Miros, Michael–June 1, Dec 8
Miros, Mike–Jan 26
Miros, Mike Jr.–Jan 26
Miros, Paul–Dec 8
Miros, Paul I.–Jan 26
Miros, Paul T.–June 1
Mitchell, Eva–April 10
Mitchell, H. L.–Sept 26
Mitchell, Harrison–Oct 26
Mitchell, Harry L.–April 9
Mitchell, Herbert–Jan 12
Mitchell, James–March 11
Mitchell, John–Oct 26
Mitchell, John L.–April 9, Sept 26
Mitchell, Lawrence–May 19
Mitchell, M. Lawrence–Feb 4
Mitchell, Mrs. C. J.–Oct 26
Mitchell, Sibyl–May 19
Mitchell, Sibyl Lynn–Aug 27
Mitchell, Stanley–Oct 26
Mitchell, Sybil–Feb 4
Mitchell, William–Feb 4
Mitchell, William G.–May 19, Aug 27
Mitscher, Marc A.

Napier, Robert W.–Nov 19

Napier, W. F.–March 24

Narcise, Mr. and Mrs. Patsy–April 11, July 19

Narcise, Rocco–April 11, July 19

Nash, Herbert–April 27

Nason, Evelyn–June 3

Naylor, George Lee–July 8

Naylor, Marjorie–July 8

Neace, John H.–Aug 6

Neal, A. R.–June 26

Neal, Arna R.–May 2, Aug20

Neal, Dr. W. E.–Oct 25

Neal, Edith–Aug 20

Neal, Elliot–July 22

Neal, George I.–Oct 30

Neal, George I. Jr.–Oct 30

Neal, Kathleen–July 22

Neal, Richard E.–June 26

Neal, William L.–Oct 25

Neale, Eugene L.–June 20

Neale, John (Jack)–June 20

Nease, J. W.–May 11

Nease, James–Oct 19

Nease, Rosa–July 29

Nease, Spicie–May 1

Nease, Walter P.–May 1

Nease, Woodrow–July 29

Nease, Woodrow W.–Oct 19, Dec 15

Nease, Woodrow Wilson–May 11

Necessary, Henrietta–Sept 25

Neel, Harriet A.–April 20

Neel, J. S.–Jan 28

Neel, John S.–Jan 28

Neel, John S. Jr.–April 20

Neel, R. T.–May 4

Neel, Rudd C.–May 4

Neff, Howard A.–Oct 25

Neilson, Alexander M.–April 6

Nelson, Andrew C.–May 21

Nelson, Billie E.–June 8

Nelson, Bryan

Golfer–March 21

Nelson, C. P.–Feb 7

Nelson, C. S.–Aug 7, Nov 29

Nelson, Charles E.–Nov 29

Nelson, Clarence S.–Feb 11, 21, Nov 29

Nelson, Clarence S. Jr.–Feb 21, Aug 7, Oct 26

Nelson, Clarence S. Sr.–Feb 11

Nelson, Clifford T.–March 13

Nelson, Clyde E.–Nov 7

Nelson, Curtis L.–Dec 1, 6

Nelson, Earl E.–Jan 13

Nelson, Edwin–Feb 7

Nelson, George W.–May 21

Nelson, Irene–April 6

Nelson, J. H.–Feb 7

Nelson, J. Houghton–Oct 18

Nelson, James–Oct 18

Nelson, Joe

Barboursville High School–May 13

Nelson, Lee E.–April 19, Dec 14

Nelson, Mary E.–April 19, Dec 14

Nelson, Mary G.–Sept 20

Nelson, Mrs. F. B.–Jan 13

Nelson, Mrs. Marion–Jan 24

Nelson, Paul–Oct 18

Nelson, Sawyer H.–Dec 6

Nelson, T. A.–April 19

Nelson, Wanda–March 13

Nelson, William C.–Dec 8

Nethercutt, Mrs. John–Sept 23

Nethercutt, Wesley H.–Sept 23

Newcomb, Rt. Rev. James F.

Monsignor Newcomb–May 23

Newcomb, Vida–March 15

Newhouser, Hal

Baseball–Oct 3

Newlon, C. L.–Jan 27

Newlon, Erma–Jan 27

Newlon, Robert H.–Jan 27

Newman, Bill–Nov 27

Newman, Billy Jack–July 22

Newman, Charles L.–April 9, May 24

Newman, Elmer C.–Jan 12, April 24

Newman, J. H.–July 22, Nov 27

Newman, Josephine–Jan 12

Newman, Josephine C.–April 24

Newman, Mildred–April 9, May 24

Newsome, Thomas–April 6

Newsome, Tom–Nov 21

Newsome, W. H.–Nov 21

Newsome, William H.–April 6

Penhorwood, Marion–June 5
Penhorwood, Richard J.–June 5
Penix, Roscoe H.–March 16
Pennington, Donald I.–Dec 5
Pennington, Faye–May 23
Pennington, Floyd A.–March 24
Pennington, G. O.–Feb 28, May 23
Pennington, Ida–March 24
Pennington, James C.–July 27
Pennington, James Lee–Feb 28
Pennington, R. M.–Feb 28
Pennington, Ruby–July 27
Pennington, Ruby M.–Dec 5
Pennywitt, Ralph–Dec 12
Pennywitt, Z. P.–Dec 12
Perchu, Hillie–June 14
Perdue, Ann Katherine–July 13
Perdue, Carl C.–Jan 27, Feb 20
Perdue, Earl–Nov 16
Perdue, Grace–Nov 15, 16
Perdue, J. W.–July 13
Perdue, Jesse H.–Jan 27, Feb 20
Perdue, Jim–Oct 16
Perdue, John R.–July 13
Perdue, Mrs. Lavon–Nov 15
Perdue, Omer J.–Jan 23
Perdue, Roscoe–Nov 15
Perdue, William R.–Nov 15
Perkey, Goldie–Aug 13
Perkey, Mrs. Goldie–March 10, April 25
Perkey, William–April 25, Aug 13
Perkey, William D.–March 10
Perkins, Frank–March 7
Perry, Allan Scott–March 15
Perry, Anna–Aug 9
Perry, Bob–March 24
Perry, Brady–Feb 28
Perry, C. E.–March 20
Perry, Cedric E.–March 12
Perry, Charles F.–Aug 9
Perry, Dennie C.–May 8
Perry, Essie–March 12
Perry, Frank–March 24
Perry, Grover F.–Jan 26, July 14
Perry, Homer C. Jr.–Dec 21
Perry, Icia–Aug 29

Perry, Icia M.–March 16
Perry, J. G.–June 23
Perry, James G. Jr.–June 23
Perry, Joan–July 31
Perry, JoAnn–Oct 15
Perry, Laura–July 14
Perry, Leo–Oct 23
Perry, R. J.–March 31
Perry, Rev. B. E.–Sept 3
Perry, Richard–March 31
Perry, Russell D.–March 20
Perry, Ruth–Feb 26
Perry, Wirt–July 31, Oct 15
Persinger, Avanelle–June 21
Persinger, Carl M.–June 21
Persinger, Frank–July 31
Persinger, Harold L.–July 31
Persinger, J. E.–June 21
Petacci, Clara
Mistress of Benito Mussolini–April 28
Petain, Henri Philippe
Marshal Petain–July 23, 24, Aug 17
Peters, Charlie–Dec 11
Peters, Donald V.–Jan 8
Peters, Francis W.–Jan 8
Peters, Howard S.–Nov 5
Peters, James P.–Feb 24, April 6
Peters, Oswald–March 31
Peters, R. L.–April 6
Peters, Rufus M.–Feb 24
Peters, Sam–Jan 8
Peters, W. C.–Feb 5
Petit, C. N.–Dec 16
Petit, Jack D.–Dec 16
Petit, Richard P.–Jan 28
Petrie, Olliebelle–Oct 12
Petrie, Ralph L.–Oct 12
Petrone, Pete–Dec 18
Petterson, Paul A.–Jan 27
Petterson, Peter N.–Jan 27
Pettus, Charles R.–Dec 16
Pettus, J. R.–Dec 16
Pew, Shelba Glenn–Dec 29
Pew, W. C.–Dec 29
Peyton, Ardrey Vernon–July 2
Peyton, Charles Jr.–June 29

Porter, Edith–March 25, July 19, Nov 17
Porter, Emogene–July 14
Porter, Ever–Nov 25, Dec 12
Porter, Frances H.–Jan 26
Porter, Frank W.–July 5
Porter, Frank W. Jr.–July 5
Porter, G. A.–July 5
Porter, Gary–Dec 12
Porter, George–Dec 12
Porter, Gertie Waddell–Jan 31
Porter, Gilbert–Feb 10, Sept 22, Oct 27, Nov 25, Dec 12
Porter, Greg–Dec 12
Porter, Hager A.–Nov 30
Porter, J. W.–Sept 3
Porter, Jack W.–Jan 26, Aug 14
Porter, James–Nov 14
Porter, James E.–Jan 11, Dec 4
Porter, James W.–Dec 4, 30
Porter, Jarrette–April 5
Porter, Jaruel–March 17, 25, April 11, May 20, July 25, Sept 5, 19, Oct 4, 27, 28, Nov 4, 8, 11, Dec 21, 22, 24
Porter, Jimmy–July 14
Porter, John–March 25, Oct 27
Porter, John Byron–Jan 26, Aug 14
Porter, Kathy–Nov 25
Porter, Lewis–Sept 3
Porter, Lewis E.–Dec 4, Dec 30
Porter, Lois–Oct 4
Porter, Lucretia–May 17
Porter, Marie–Sept 22, Dec 12
Porter, Mattie–Nov 14
Porter, Michael–Oct 27
Porter, Mrs. Francis–Aug 14
Porter, Mrs. W. F.–Nov 30
Porter, Orlene–Jan 31
Porter, Patrick
Early Salt Rock settler–Oct 27
Porter, Pearl–Nov 25, Dec 13, 21
Porter, Roy
National Broadcasting Co.–July 24
Porter, Sam–Jan 31
Porter, Sam Jr.–Jan 31
Porter, Shirrell–Feb 10, Dec 12
Porter, Velma–May 20, Sept 21, Oct 4, Nov 8

Porter, Willis–Nov 29
Poteet, Mrs. John L.–Aug 22
Poteet, Raymond J.–Aug 22
Potter, Hiram E.–March 16
Potts, Lewis R.
Marshall County WV school superintendant–Nov 28
Poulton, David–Jan 11
Poulton, Mrs. C. A.–Jan 11
Powell, Dewey–Oct 23
Powell, Dick
Actor-Singer–Aug 20
Powell, Mrs. Robert–Oct 23
Powell, Robert–Oct 23
Powers, Arnold–July 22
Powers, Clarence E.–Nov 19
Powers, Floyd E.–Aug 9
Powers, Ralph E.–April 24
Pratt, Alie–March 7
Pratt, Ausley–July 14, Aug 13, 17
Pratt, Bessen Rupert
Author's father–Jan 1, April 7, July 14
Pratt, Charles E.–Aug 22
Pratt, Gregory–Aug 4
Pratt, Hattie–Jan 3, March 7, Aug 17
Pratt, Helen Wray–Aug 22
Pratt, Jenoise Kimes–Jan 25
Pratt, John Aubra–Jan 25
Pratt, Jonathan–Aug 4
Pratt, Maxwell–July 14
Pratt, Mildred Mereness
Author's wife–May 19, August 4, Sept 16, Dec 4
Preace, Henry–Dec 18
Precce, Joe–June 24
Precce, W. M. Z.–June 24
Preston, A. D.–Dec 30
Preston, Arthur–Jan 13
Preston, Dorothy–Jan 13
Preston, Frank H. Jr.–March 24
Preston, Frank Jr.–April 25
Preston, Helen–May 15, Sept 11
Preston, Herman A.–Jan 13
Preston, Jay F.–Sept 15
Preston, John B.–June 26, Sept 15
Preston, Richard–Sept 11
Preston, Richard H.–May 15, Oct 1

Preston, William C.–July30
Price, J. E.–Aug 11
Price, John W.–May 13
Price, Leslie E.–Aug 11
Price, Louis E.–Sept 28
Price, Mrs. Charles A.–Jan 7
Price, O. L.–May 8
Price, Oscar L.–Oct 5
Price, Oscar L. Jr.–May 8
Price, S. S.–Aug 9, 13
Price, Seward S.–Aug 9
Price, Seward S. Jr.–Aug 13
Prichard, Hal–Aug 29
Prichard, James A.–Aug 29
Prichard, Vernon R.–Aug 31, Sept 1
Priddy, W. C.–May 6
Priddy, William W.–May 6
Pridemore, Daniel–Aug 11
Pridemore, Joson–Aug 11
Prillman, Clifford A.–Jan 27
Prince, Earl–April 14
Prince, Isaac C.–Feb 16
Princess Elizabeth–April 21
Pritt, Clifford Allen–April 15
Pritt, Henry–April 15
Probst, Paul–Sept 21
Prout, William E.–March 4
Pryor, Mary–May 3, June 26
Pullen, Orville C.–Sept 17
Pullen, Robert–Sept 12
Purdue, Mrs. E. E.–Jan 23
Purdy, Hyland J.–Dec 21
Purtell, Martha Ann–Nov 5
Purtell, Michael J.–Nov 5
Puryear, Adrian–Jan 20
Pygman, Chlovis C.–March 31
Pygman, Welford R.–March 31
Pyle, Ernie–March 14, April 18
Pyle, Mrs. Ernie–Nov 23
Pyles, Charles Jr.–May 28, June 4
Pyles, Jamison T.–March 5
Pyles, Martha–March 5

Q

Queen, Ada–May 11
Queen, Albert–Jan 21

Queen, Arden–May 30
Queen, Billy S.–March 22
Queen, Clifford E.–Jan 13
Queen, Dallas–May 13
Queen, Emma–March 9
Queen, Galen B.–Jan 13
Queen, H. S.–March 9
Queen, Hasten–May 11
Queen, J. A.–May 30
Queen, Jack–May 30
Queen, James–Nov 9
Queen, John–June 14
Queen, Marie–Jan 21
Queen, Mary–March 22
Queen, Opal–May 13
Queen, W. D.–Jan 13
Quickle, James Francis–July 9
Quinlan, M. I.–June 9
Quinlan, M. R.–June 9
Quinn, Andrew T.–March 30
Quinn, Lois–March 30
Quinn, William Hugh Jr.–Oct 5
Quisling, Vidkun
Norwegian premier found guilty of treason–Sept 10
Quitmeyer, Charles L.–June 21
Qulia, A. J.–Jan 24
Qulia, Frank–Jan 24

R

Raby, Ivan H. H.–Nov 16
Raies, Norman W.–Sept 7
Raies, William–Sept 7
Raines, Emory C.–Dec 13
Rainey, Ralph G.–July 4
Rainey, T. H.–July 4
Rainey, Thomas J.–July 4
Rains, Marguerite–April 20
Ramey, Audie–March 26
Ramey, Edwert–Nov 20
Ramey, Edwert J.–Dec 3
Ramey, Fred–Nov 2
Ramey, George E.–Aug 29
Ramey, H. J.–Feb 26, April 17, Nov 20, Dec 3
Ramey, Henry J. Jr.–Feb 26, April 17
Ramey, Jack–Nov 18

Ramey, James–March 26
Ramey, James H.–Nov 2
Ramey, Lettie–March 26
Ramey, Mrs. G. A.–June 6
Ramey, Otis–Nov 18
Ramsey, Charlene–June 13
Ramsey, Eugene H.–Aug 29
Ramsey, H. E.–Aug 29
Ramsey, Harold E.–March 9
Ramsey, Jack H.–Nov 16
Ramsey, Mrs. J. G.–Nov 29
Ramsey, Paul E.–June 13
Ramsey, W. H.–Dec 6
Ramsey, Walter–March 9
Ramsey, William H. Jr.–Dec 6
Rapp, Bob–April 8
Rardin, F. M.–June 17
Rardin, J. Fred–June 17
Rardin, Ray
C-K football player–Nov 10
Rarnsey, John W.–Sept 25
Ratcliff, A. G.–March 1
Ratcliff, A. J.–March 20
Ratcliff, Cora Blair–March 1
Ratcliff, George–March 1, 20
Ratcliff, James–March 1, 20
Ratcliff, John A.–June 13
Ratcliff, John P.–June 13
Ratcliff, Lee–Sept 14
Ratcliff, Mahalla–Sept 14
Ratcliffe, Amos L.–Oct 26
Ratcliffe, Laura–Oct 26
Ray, Baxter–March 22, June 20, Sept 24
Ray, Charles–Jan 14, March 22
Ray, Charles A.–Jan 26
Ray, Charles E.–June 20
Ray, Clenon E.–Sept 24
Ray, Earl–Oct 2
Ray, Frank Earl–Sept 30
Ray, Silas–Sept 30
Ray, W. M.–Jan 26
Ray, Walter E.–Jan 1, 1946
Ray, Warren D.–Oct 29
Rayburn, Agnes–Oct 3
Rayburn, Bailey–Oct 3
Rayburn, Everett R.–Oct 3

Rayburn, James H.–July 23
Raynor, Harold L.–Sept 24
Reckard, Charles H.–June 7
Reckard, Lois–June 7
Ree, Leo
Steward, Hotel Frederick–July 7
Reed, J. A.–Jan 13, July 19
Reed, John W.–April 13
Reed, Virginia–Jan 13, July 19
Reed, Wallace–April 13
Reed, Warren–July 19
Reed, Warren A.–Jan 12
Reede, Lewis–July 16
Reede, Octavia–July 16
Reeder, Elmer B.–March 5
Reeder, Henry H.–Nov 1
Reese, L.–Nov 11
Reese, Mrs. T. L.–April 9
Reese, Sharline–April 9, Oct 19
Reeser, Edgar–Oct 1
Reeser, Joseph W.–Oct 1
Reeves, Dr. W. C.
Pastor- Highlawn Baptist Church–May 20
Reid, Henry C.–Jan 9
Reid, Ida–Jan 9
Rencsok, Dave–April 25
Rencsok, Steve–April 25
Rent, Rupert R.–Oct 11
Reynolds, Arvel C.–Jan 9
Reynolds, Betty Jo–June 15
Reynolds, Earl B.–Jan 9, March 24
Reynolds, G. E.–May 2
Reynolds, James W.–July 3
Reynolds, John F.–May 2
Reynolds, Marie–Dec 4
Reynolds, Marshall–June 15
Reynolds, Raymond L.–Aug 4, Oct 6
Reynolds, W. E.–Aug 4, Oct 6
Reynolds, Wallace–June 15
Rhodes, Herman S.–Jan 3, 1946
Rhodes, Mrs. W. H.–Jan 3, 1946
Rice, Alma E.–Jan 12
Rice, Alvin C.–Dec 8
Rice, Carl Melvin–July 2
Rice, Darrell–July 19
Rice, Donald L.–Feb 11, Aug 3

Sams, Bill B.–Nov 29
Sams, C. W.–Nov 29
Sanford, Mrs. Leon–March 27
Sanford, Robert B.–March 27
Sanford, Steven D.–March 27
Sansom, Charles T.–Oct 15, Dec 8
Sansom, H. L.–Oct 15
Sansom, Lucille–Oct 18
Sansom, Otis–Oct 7
Sansom, Robert L.–Oct 7
Sarver, F. B.–Jan 16, Feb 1, Oct 16
Sarver, Madeline–Jan 16, Feb 1, Oct 16
Sarver, Mrs. F. B.–Jan 16, Feb 1
Sarver, Ruth Ellen–Dec 29
Sassaman, Rev. John–March 25
Sasser, T. J.–Jan 26
Sasser, Thomas J. Jr.–Jan 26
Sasser, Thomas Judson Jr.–Sept 21
Satterfield, Charles C.–June 26
Satterfield, Mrs. H. A.–June 26
Satterwhite, Henry G.–Oct 27
Saul, Calvin E.–June 5
Saul, July A..–June 5
Saunders, Everett–Aug 23
Saunders, Everett W.–Feb 24
Saunders, Harold M.–Feb 24, Aug 23
Saunders, Jack–Jan 20
Saunders, Jack L.–March 25
Saunders, Phyllis–Nov 29
Saurborne, George F. Jr.–April 24
Saurborne, George P.–Feb 1
Sawyer, Edith L.–April 13
Sawyer, George N.–April 13
Sawyer, William–June 28
Sawyer, William F.–June 28
Saxton, Carl B.–Aug 22
Saxton, Rachel R.–Aug 22
Sayre, Hubert J.–March 5
Sayre, John H.–March 5, April 24
Sayre, Lynette F.–April 24
Scaggs, Fred C.–March 4
Scaglion, Charlotte–May 25
Scaglion, James L.–May 25, Dec 1
Scanlon, Robert O.–Nov 9
Scarberry, Grover Russell–April 29
Scarberry, Raymond–Dec 15

Schasser, Heinz
U-Boat Commander–Aug 17
Scheifly, John E.–June 24
Scheifly, Luke–June 24
Scherer, Merrield A.–Nov 5
Scherffius, Barbara–Feb 21
Scherr, Harry Jr.–Oct 26
Scherr, Harry Sr.–Oct 26
Schmauch, Arthur–June 9
Schmauch, Arthur H.–June 9
Schmauck, Arthur–May 5
Schmauck, Arthur H.–May 5
Schmeling, Max
Boxer–May 22
Schmidt, L. C.–Oct 13
Schneider, Mrs. F. W.–March 28
Schneider, Robert H.–Oct 2
Schoenbaum, Emil–March 13
Schoenbaum, Raymond–March 13
Schoew, Frederick W.–June 5
Schoew, Mrs. F. L.–June 5
Schon, J. L.–Sept 25
Schrader, Harry E.–April 12, Sept 5
Schrader, W. M.–April 12, Sept 5
Schuller, Francis Xavier–Oct 11
Schultz, George E.–May 25
Schultz, O. J.–May 25
Schurman, Albert–Aug 11
Schurman, C. R.–June 6
Schurman, Jack C.–June 6
Schwartz, G. A.–Nov 28
Scites, Donald–April 24
Scites, E. P.–Oct 20
Scites, Earl–Oct 20
Scites, Emma–April 24
Scites, H. S.–Nov 29
Scott, C. B.–June 21
Scott, C. W.–Dec 13
Scott, Charles B.–Feb 17
Scott, Charles M.–June 21, Oct 3
Scott, Charles Marshall–Feb 17
Scott, Dr. Francis A.–Dec 13
Scott, Edgar–June 2
Scott, Francis A.–Dec 31
Scott, Harry R.–April 24
Scott, J. R.–June 10

Shepherd, James L.–Nov 8
Sheppard, Raymond–July 21
Sheppard, W. M.–July 21
Sheppe, Dr. and Mrs. A. H.–Jan 26
Sheppe, Joe–Jan 26
Sherman, Billie Bryan–Oct 7
Sherman, Billie R.–April 17, Aug 1
Sherman, Richard L.–Oct 7
Sherwood, Rev. J. H.–March 25
Shewkey, Morris C.–Oct 16
Shinkle, Jack M.–Nov 8
Shipe, Chester L.–April12
Shires, Al G.–Aug 4
Shiveley, J. C.–April 29
Shiveley, Joe–April 29
Shively, Bernard
U. of Kentucky head coach–Dec 20
Shively, Ethel–June 4
Shively, Robert W. Jr.–May 9, 30
Short, Addie Frances–Dec 8
Short, Denver E.–March 27
Short, John B.–Dec 16
Short, Lee Roy–Dec 16
Short, M. F.–Nov 26, Dec 8
Short, M. F. Jr.–Nov 26
Short, William Jr.–May 2
Short, William Sr.–May 2
Shriner, Frederick F.–Feb 19, May 24
Shriner, Mrs. V. V.–Feb 19, May 24
Shriver, Mrs. A. D.–Dec 3
Shuff, Ewell F.–May 5
Shuff, Lester–July 15
Shy, Addie–Jan 11, June 17
Shy, Avanel M.–June 13
Shy, Robert A.–June 13
Sibley, S. E.–July1
Sidebottom, Dana A.–Oct 30
Sidebottom, J. R.–Oct 30
Sidebottom, John–May 4
Sidebottom, Robert S.–May 4
Sigler, E. A.–April 17
Sigler, Edward A Jr.–April 17
Sikes, Helen–Nov 21
Silas, Wayne–Aug 1
Silverman, Joseph A.–Dec 18
Silvey, V. E.–May 15

Simmons, C. G.–Oct 3
Simmons, James E.–Jan 31
Simmons, Morris E.–Nov 20
Simmons, Ollie–Nov 4,
Simmons, Ray
Huntington High football player–Nov 10
Simmons, Victor C.–Oct 3
Simmons, Wesley–Nov 4, 8
Simms, Anna M.–July 11
Simms, Cecil Jr.–July 11
Simms, Clarence E.–Jan 13, July 3
Simms, Dorothy P.–Aug 2
Simms, J. H.–June 1
Simms, Phyllis–Nov 15
Simms, Robert L.–Aug 2
Simms, Robert L.–June 1, Nov 15
Simms, Verba–Nov 15
Simons, Betty Jane–June 8
Simons, Jeffe B.–Oct 20
Simons, Mary–Oct 20
Simpkins, Clovis E.–Sept 6
Simpkins, E. J.–Dec 18
Simpkins, Elda Mary Barnett–Sept 6
Simpkins, Ezra–Sept 6
Simpkins, Ray–Sept 14
Simpson, J. M.–Jan 27
Simpson, James Madison Jr.–Jan 27
Simpson, Jean–Jan 27
Sindell, Helen Eugenia–April 26
Singer, A. R.–Oct 24
Singer, Everett B.–Nov 28
Singer, J.–Nov 28
Singer, John H.–Oct 24
Singleton, Mrs. Maude–March 4
Singleton, Paul Clifford–March 4
Sinnett, Barr–March 25
Sinnett, Barr Jr.–March 25
Sinnock, Beulah–Oct 24
Sisk, Foster M.–March 27
Sites, Elmer–Aug 20
Sites, Lolarose–Aug 20
Sizemore, Cass L.–Sept 3
Sizemore, James F.–July 21
Sizemore, Lionel M.–Aug 30
Sizemore, Lola–Aug 30
Sizemore, Mrs. D. C.–Aug 30

Skaggs, Easter M.–April 30
Skaggs, Eugene–Aug 8
Skaggs, Evertt M.–April 30
Skaggs, Lily–Nov 14
Skaggs, Mrs. Lenny–April 30
Skaggs, R. H.–Aug 8
Skeans, Janie–Sept 7
Skeens, Clinton–June 24
Skeens, Mrs. Clinton–Dec 9
Skeens, William C. Jr.–June 24
Skeens, William Clinton Jr.–Dec 9
Skeer, Charles T.–Oct 3
Skenses, James Willard–Oct 11
Slattery, Thomas J.–June 20
Slaughter, Rev. C. A.–March 25
Slogic, Thomas E.–Oct 4
Slone, Alka–June 15
Slone, Bertha–June 3
Slone, Clifford–May 15, June 3
Slone, Denver R.–July 7
Slutz, Eugene Kelly–May 28
Slutz, Gene Kelly–April 7
Slutz, Jean Johnson–Oct 29
Smarr, Cary M.–June 21
Smith, Alma–May 19, July 14
Smith, Alvin–April 28
Smith, Alvin D.–July 7
Smith, Arthur W.–March 26
Smith, Bluford–July 27
Smith, C. J.–July 19
Smith, Caleb–July 4
Smith, Charles–March 26
Smith, Charles A.–Aug 10, Nov 20
Smith, Charles E.–Aug 6, Nov 2
Smith, Charles H.–Nov 5
Smith, Clair S.–Feb 19, July 23
Smith, Clinton L.–Feb 11
Smith, Clyde–March 9
Smith, Covy L.–Aug 6
Smith, D. F.–Oct 1
Smith, Darius–May 25
Smith, Darrell F.–Nov 2
Smith, David C.–July 9, Oct 20
Smith, Davis R.–Dec 19
Smith, Dona–May 24, June 9
Smith, Donald Boyd–Sept 23

Smith, Donald J.–May 22, Aug 13
Smith, Donald L.–May 1
Smith, Donald W.–June 8
Smith, Dorothy–June 14
Smith, Dorothy May–March 26
Smith, Doyle E.–March 26
Smith, Drucilla–May 1
Smith, E. H.–Aug 10
Smith, Earl W.–May 1
Smith, Ed
Barboursville 1949–50 head coach–Nov 28
Smith, Edgar–Feb 5
Smith, Edith F.–April 12
Smith, Elden E.–April 24
Smith, Everett R.–Jan 11
Smith, Florence A.–May 24, June 9
Smith, Floyd E.–March 24
Smith, Floyd F.–Feb 28
Smith, Garnett–Nov 2
Smith, George–April 4, 24
Smith, Georgia–Jan 21, Aug 6
Smith, Hamlet–Sept 10, Dec 10
Smith, Harold F.–April 12, Oct 23
Smith, Harry F.–March 24
Smith, Harry W.–Oct 7
Smith, Helen V.–July 27
Smith, Henry–July 19
Smith, Herman–Aug 6
Smith, Herman L.–Dec 10
Smith, Hoke–May 25, Oct 1
Smith, Isabell–May 13
Smith, Ivan J.–Jan 12
Smith, J. F.–Aug 21
Smith, J. N.–Dec 12
Smith, J. W.–May 1, Jan 5, 1946
Smith, James Bill–Oct 21
Smith, James C.–March 26, Dec 10
Smith, James Franklin–Aug 21
Smith, James H.–May 19, July 14
Smith, Juanita Freda–Jan 11
Smith, Kendall W.–June 19
Smith, Kenneth H.–June 14
Smith, Kenneth R.–Nov 1
Smith, Kimball Lee–March 24
Smith, L. Roy–Sept 23
Smith, Lemotto–Sept 23

Smith, Lindsey–April 4, June 8
Smith, Lloyd K.–June 4
Smith, Lola Mae–Jan 29
Smith, Lottie–Sept 13
Smith, Luther–June 8
Smith, Mabel–April 4
Smith, Mary–Nov 20
Smith, Maud E.–July 9
Smith, Maude–Oct 20
Smith, Maxine–June 27
Smith, Merril F.–Sept 10
Smith, Milford–Oct 16
Smith, Morris W.–May 2
Smith, Morton V.–Nov 1
Smith, Mrs. A. A.–March 26
Smith, Mrs. Albert–June 19
Smith, Mrs. Bertie–Oct 7
Smith, Mrs. Elmer–Sept 22
Smith, Mrs. James–May 20
Smith, Mrs. Lou B.–March 6
Smith, Mrs. O. F.–May 2
Smith, Mrs. W. F.–Oct 21
Smith, Myrtie Anise–May 26
Smith, Naomi–Sept 29
Smith, O. J.–Feb 28
Smith, O. M.–Aug 1
Smith, Otha H.–Dec 6
Smith, Paul D.–Nov 25
Smith, Philip–Sept 26
Smith, Porter W.
Former Huntington mayor–Dec 19
Smith, R. F.–Sept 18
Smith, R. R.–Sept 26
Smith, Ralph G.–April 20
Smith, Richard N.–Dec 7
Smith, Robert G.–Jan 5, 1946
Smith, Robert Lee–June 5
Smith, Rosa Hall–April 20
Smith, Roscoe E.–May 2, Dec 24
Smith, Ross W.–June 19
Smith, Roy–Jan 21
Smith, Ruth Johnson–March 22
Smith, Stanley–Nov 25
Smith, Stanley J.–Dec 12
Smith, T. A.–Sept 18
Smith, Vera Fry–Oct 16

Smith, Veta–Jan 9
Smith, Violet–Feb 18
Smith, Vivian–Nov 5
Smith, W. F.–Feb 28
Smith, W. M.–July 7, Dec 25
Smith, W. Z.–June 8
Smith, Waldo W.–June 9
Smith, Walter F.–May 6
Smith, Walter F. Jr.–Feb 28, May 6, Oct 21
Smith, Walter H.–July 6
Smith, Wanda M.–Aug 6
Smith, Wayne–April 28, Dec 25
Smith, Wayne M.–April 28
Smith, William–April 28
Smith, William C.–Sept 26
Smith, William C. Jr.–July 9
Smith, William C. Sr.–July 9
Smith, William H.–June 27, Aug 2
Smith, William Howard–June 17
Smith, William M.–Oct 29
Smith, William R.–March 6
Smith, William S.–Oct 29
Smoot, Melford–Aug 14
Smythe, Thomas P.–Sept 1, 29
Smythe, W. T.–Sept 1
Snair, Sydney J.–Jan 19, July 4, Sept 5
Snead, Sam–Jan 14
Snead, Sammy
Golfer–March 21
Snider, C. W.–July 14
Snider, Robert J.–July 14
Snyder, Mamie–May 13
Snyder, Richard H.–Jan 30
Sollazzo, John–July 12
Sorrell, Earl–Sept 24
Sowards, Cecil V.–Jan 19
Sowards, John S.–March 28
Sowards, Leuvenia–Jan 19
Sowards, William C.–May 7
Spalding, Jack W.–Jan 1
Sparks, Benjamin–Jan 16
Sparks, Elizabeth–Jan 16
Sparks, James I.–Nov 1
Sparks, Walter R.–Jan 16
Spaulding, E. R.–Jan 1
Spaulding, Nora–May 6

Stephens, Floyd Ray–May 6
Stephens, Lucian–May 27
Stephens, Robert L.–Aug 22
Stephenson, Aubrey Earl–Sept 7
Stephenson, Clifford B.–Aug 20
Stephenson, Jack Laverne–July 20
Stephenson, Kathleen–Sept 7
Stephenson, Lawrence W.–Aug 20
Stephenson, Lovic Jr.–Sept 7
Stephenson, Lovic Sr.–Sept 7
Stephenson, Lovie–July 20
Stephenson, Mary H.–Feb 11
Stepp, Mr. and Mrs. William H.–Feb 24
Stepp, Mrs. William H.–Feb 3
Stepp, William H.–Feb 3, Feb 24
Stepp, William H. Jr.–Feb 3
Stettinius, Edward R.
Secretary of State–June 18
Stevens, Ben–July 24
Stevens, Bernard S.–July 21
Stevens, Betty–April 5
Stevens, C. L.–April 5
Stevens, Clifford–July 24
Stevens, Clifford C.–Oct 29
Stevens, Clyde–April 25
Stevens, Elijah–Nov 3
Stevens, James C.–April 5
Stevens, Judge–June 23
Stevens, Lucian–April 1
Stevens, Marie–Oct 29
Stevens, Martha–April 25
Stevens, Mary Lou–Aug 6
Stevens, Mrs. B. W.–April 25
Stevens, Ruth–April 25
Stevens, Virginia–July 21
Stevens, William V.–Aug 6
Stevenson, Mary–Aug 3
Stevenson, Sherry Lynn–Oct 3
Stevenson, Thomas–Oct 3
Stevenson, Thomas G.–Feb 23, Sept 22
Stewart, Anna Fay–Feb 4
Stewart, C. L.–Oct 22
Stewart, Charles–June 18, 28
Stewart, Charles H.–Nov 18
Stewart, Claude Wilmer–Jan 1
Stewart, Clifford S.–Nov 9

Stewart, Curtis–July 27
Stewart, E. L.–Jan 22, July 7
Stewart, Eyster L. Jr.–July 7
Stewart, Gertrude–Oct 11
Stewart, Harvey–June 28
Stewart, Jimmy
Actor–Sept 28
Stewart, Karl L.–June 18
Stewart, Karl Lee–Oct 22
Stewart, Mary–Oct 22
Stewart, Mildred Marie–Nov 9
Stewart, Mr. and Mrs. Shirley–Nov 18
Stewart, Richard–Feb 4
Stewart, Ruth
New York soprano–April 16
Stewart, Shirley–June 28
Stewart, W. P. Jr.–March 10
Stewart, Welden–July 27
Stewart, William E.–Jan 22, July 7
Stewart, William Price III–March 10
Stewart, Wilson M.–Nov 18
Stewart, Wilton–June 28
Stickler, Claire–Dec 30
Stickler, Cloie–Jan 25
Stickler, Lloyd–Jan 25, Dec 30
Stidd, Billy L.–June 15
Stidd, Imogene–June 15
Stidham, Dean L.–June 8
Stiff, Lindell–Feb 14
Stiles, Meredith–Oct 2
Still, Gertrude–Oct 21
Still, Gertrude W.–Dec 23
Still, Herbert Jr.–Oct 21, Dec 23
Still, Jack–Dec 23
Still, Jack C.–Oct 21
Stillwell, James–Oct 1
Stiltner, Charles V.–Aug 30
Stiltner, Martha–Aug 30
Stiltner, Pauline–March 28
Stimson, Henry L.
Secretary of War–Aug 6
Stinson, Donald S.–Feb 6
Stinson, W. L.–Feb 6
Stombock, Alma B.–June 5
Stombock, David B.–June 5
Stone, J. W.–May 11

Thompson, Mayme–Aug 21

Thompson, Mrs. Mack–Jan 12, 20

Thompson, Mrs. R. J.–April 7

Thompson, Mrs. Robert J.–Feb 19

Thompson, Paul

Vinson HS Tigers coach–Jan 13

Thompson, Pearl T.–Feb 19

Thompson, Richard G.–Aug 21

Thompson, Robert L.–Oct 11

Thompson, Viola–June 21

Thompson, Wayne G.–April 7

Thompson, William–May 12

Thompson, William Jr.–July 10

Thompson, William Sr.–July 10

Thompson, Woodrow L.–July 18

Thornburg, Anna Norma Meadows–Nov 12

Thornburg, C. W.–April 27

Thornburg, Charles I.–April 27

Thornburg, Charles William–April 27

Thornburgh, Hugh Warren–March 28

Thornton, Billy–Feb 25

Thornton, Earl B.–July 28

Thornton, Earl S. E.–April 29

Thornton, J. P.–Feb 25

Thornton, Jimmy Jr.–Feb 25

Thornton, Naomi–Feb 25

Thornton, S.–July 28

Thornton, S. E.–April 29

Threlkeld, Lillian–July 4

Threlkeld, Marvin C.–May 28, July 4, 23

Threlkeld, R. A.–May 28, July 23

Thuotte, Joan–Acknowledgments

Tidman, Lola–Jan 25, July 11

Tidman, William H.–Aug 29

Tidman, William Haskell–Feb 2

Tignor, Douglas W.–May 4

Tipton, James D.–Dec 19

Titler, George J.

United Mine Workers District 19 president–April 26

Tito, Marshal–Dec 23

Toler, Drewey H.–April 20

Toler, William H.–July 14

Tomkies, Douglas C.–Jan 4, 1946

Tomlinson, Bernard T.–Oct 23

Tomlinson, Gerald–March 29

Tomlinson, Mrs. B. T.–Oct 23

Tonkovich, Andy

Marshall basketball player–Dec 8, 18

Tooley, Guy T.–March15, May 11

Tooley, Mary B.–May 11

Tooley, Wilburn.–May 11

Toothman, Bill

Marshall basketball player–Jan 13

Topping, Elizabeth–Sept 11

Topping, Ernest W.–Sept 11

Totten, Alonzo–March 10

Totten, David R.–May 2

Trainer, George W.–Sept 3

Trainer, George W. R.–June 4

Traub, Robert C.–March 7, Dec 4

Trautner, William–May 22

Trautner, William H.–May 22

Travis, William–Nov 20

Traylor, Bobby–July 2

Traylor, Earl–July 2

Traylor, Earl M.–Jan 7

Traylor, J. W.–Jan 7, July 2

Traylor, Jack E.–July 2

Traylor, James–July 2

Traylor, James H.–Sept 26

Trent, Herman–June 29

Trimmer, Dr. J.

Fifth Avenue Baptist Church–Aug 1

Trimmer, Dr. Maurice

Fifth Avenue Baptist Church–Sept 20

Triplett, Ben E.–Nov 8

Triplett, Howard–Aug 9

Triplett, J. E.–Nov 8

Triplett, Jack F.–Nov 8

Triplett, Otho B.–Feb 6

Triplett, Wilson–Aug 9

Trippett, Dock–April 15

Trippett, Elza–Aug 11

Trippett, Eugene–Aug 11

Trippett, Lola–April 15

Trippett, Roy–April 15

Trippett, William–Feb 23

Trisler, Charles William–Aug 20, 27

Trogdon, Eula Mae–Feb 28

Trogdon, Pat H.–Feb 28

Trosper, Minnie–Sept 19

Watts, Vicie A.–Nov 4
Waugh, Emery–May 13
Waugh, Mrs. C. E.–Dec 18
Wavell, Lord
British Viceroy for India–June 27, Sept 14
Wayne, Delbert–Nov 6
Weakley, Charles L.–Dec 13
Weaver, Mrs. J. S.–Feb 10
Webb, Chester W.–May 1
Webb, Christine V.–May 27
Webb, Clarence–June 12
Webb, Dorothy–June 12
Webb, Edwin W.–Aug 24
Webb, Effie–July 24
Webb, Floyd Jr.–Dec 21
Webb, Henderson O. Jr.–May 27, Oct 11
Webb, Lilyan–Jan 1, April 21
Webb, Lottie–July 28
Webb, Maude–Feb 1
Webb, Maurice E.–Aug 2
Webb, Maxie–Nov 2, 5
Webb, Mr. and Mrs. Carnie–Nov 2
Webb, Mrs. Mattie–June 22
Webb, Paul H.–Feb 1
Webb, Roy E.–July 28
Webb, Tommie–June 22
Webb, W. E.–Aug 24
Webb, William–April 21
Webb, William W.–Jan 1
Weber, Bill
South Charleston football coach–Dec 15
Wechsler, George W.–June 8
Weekley, Charles B.–Sept 19
Weeks, E. F.–Feb 8, Dec 2
Weeks, James M.–Nov 28
Weeks, John N.–Nov 28
Weeks, Max E.–Feb 8, Dec 2
Weeks, Max Edwin–July 21
Weeks, Robert L.–Feb 8
Weeks, William F.–Feb 8
Weider, Dr. Don F.–Jan 12, April 29
Weider, Frank–Jan 12
Weider, Frank E.–April 29
Weidling, Helmuth
German General–May 2
Weiseman, Donald N.–March 28, June 14

Weiseman, Frederica–March 28, June 14
Weissphennig, Walter
Nazi Naval Surgeon–Oct 20
Wellman, Forrest B.–Aug 25
Wellman, Hiram Jr.–Sept 11
Wellman, John E.–Aug 25
Wellman, Martin–May 8
Wellman, W.–May 8
Wells, Anne Virginia–March 29
Wells, Dr. J. C.–March 29
Wells, Homer Douglas–Aug 23
Wells, Kenneth G.–Nov 8
Wells, Lorraine–Jan 1
Wells, Shelley A.–Oct 3
Wells, Shirley Marie–Aug 23
Wells, Verlin E.–Jan 1
Wells, Willard L.–Oct 29
Wentz, Lowen H.–Nov 20
Wess, Hollie P.–Feb 4
West, Carl–Aug 22
West, Fenton T.–July 4
West, Gilbert W.–Oct 6
West, Illiff–July 4
West, Mrs. Duel–Oct 6
West, Mrs. E. H.–Aug 22
West, Mrs. J. C.–Aug 7
West, Rachel Frances–May 5
West, Thomas J.–Dec 19
Westfall, Everett C.–May 12
Westfall, Mary–May 12
Wetherall, C. E.–March 7
Wettling, J. A.–Sept 14
Wettling, Robert A.–Sept 14
Whaley, Harlan C.–Jan 13
Whaley, T. E.–Jan 13
Wheatley, Jane–April 8
Wheatley, William H.–Jan 9
Wheeler, Daisie A.–Aug 1
Wheeler, Daniel B.–May 27, Nov 18
Wheeler, Earl Robert–July 9
Wheeler, Georgia Hutchinson–July 9
Wheeler, John L.–Nov 11
Wheeler, Joseph C.–June 9
Wheeler, Lorena–May 27, Nov 18
Wheeler, Mrs. M.–Dec 2
Wheeler, Mrs. Weltha–April 10

Wilkes, John F.–June 2
Wilkes, R. L.–Feb 23
Wilkes, S. O.–July 4
Wilkes, Samuel O.–July 4
Wilkinson, Mrs. A. J.–Aug 13
Wilkinson, Richard–May 20
Wilks, Alice–Oct 4
Wilks, Carroll E.–May 27
Wilks, E. E.–Aug 15
Wilks, Faye–June 12
Wilks, Hugh H.–Nov 15
Wilks, James F.–June 12
Wilks, Kenneth E.–Aug 15
Wilks, Mrs. E. E.–Nov 15
Wilks, Perry–May 27
Wilks, Perry Orville–May 27, Oct 4
Wilks, William V.–May 27
Will, Hope–Jan 29
Will, Orville O.–Jan 29, May 19
Willey, Alrie–Nov 8
Willey, Harold L.–Nov 8
Willey, S. S.–Jan 20
Williams, Antionette T.–May 1
Williams, Bill F.–Oct 25
Williams, Cecil–March 1
Williams, Charles Thomas–March 13
Williams, Clarence–July 17
Williams, Donald–March 1
Williams, Dr. J. D.
  Marshall College president–Aug 1, 29
Williams, Edna Lynn–June 24
Williams, Edna Mae–Jan 28, Sept 2
Williams, Ester–Aug 2
Williams, Everett A.–March 26
Williams, Henry–July 4
Williams, Holly–Oct 25
Williams, J. J. Sr.–May 1
Williams, James–Jan 28
Williams, James O.–Sept 2
Williams, Jesse J. Jr.–May 1
Williams, Jimmy–Jan 28
Williams, Louise B.–Jan 22
Williams, Mrs. C. M.–July 17
Williams, Mrs. E. E.–Jan 11
Williams, Mrs. J. G.–April 18
Williams, Mrs. James–Jan 28

Williams, Mrs. Jesse–March 26
Williams, Mrs. W. A.–March 13
Williams, Palmer–Sept 7
Williams, R. C.–Oct 25
Williams, Rev. Oma–Feb 27
Williams, Richard–Jan 22
Williams, Russell–Jan 7
Williams, William E.–Jan 11
Williams, William K.–Jan 7
Williamson, L. Mae–Aug 6
Williamson, Mrs. C. W.–Dec 5
Williamson, Paul E.–Aug 6
Williamson, Robert A.–Dec 5
Willingham, Dr. E. B.
  Fifth Avenue Baptist Church–Aug 1
Willis, Arnold Jr.–April 5
Willis, Denver A.–Oct 17
Willis, Dr. C. A.–April 21
Willis, Henry B.–April 20
Willis, James S.–April 21
Willis, Nancy J.–April 20
Willis, Sarah–April 5
Willis, Thomas–May 5
Willis, Ward H. Jr.–Sept 10
Willoughby, E. H.–Sept 5, Oct 23, Dec 28
Willoughby, Morris–Sept 5, Oct 23
Willoughby, Morris C.–Oct 4
Willoughby, Ray–Sept 5, Oct 23, Dec 28
Wilmink, Robert C.–Feb 4
Wilson, A. B.–July 31
Wilson, B. L.–June 18
Wilson, Curtis W.–April 7
Wilson, Cyril F.–April 10
Wilson, Donald A.–Jan 3, 1946
Wilson, Donald E.–Sept 10
Wilson, Glen R.–Oct 11
Wilson, Kermit R.–July 17
Wilson, L. L.–April 12
Wilson, Louis L. Jr.–April 12
Wilson, Mary E.–July 17
Wilson, Maurice Harold–Oct 5
Wilson, Mrs. C. H.–June 29
Wilson, Nan–May 5
Wilson, Ottis G.
  Marshall College dean–March 24
Wilson, Paul H.–May 5

Woodrum, Darlene–July 15
Woodrum, Gerald P.–June 5
Woodrum, Leroy J.–Oct 8
Woodrum, P. D.–June 5
Woods, Donald C.–Dec 6
Woods, Erma Lee–July 30
Woods, Frederick A.–Oct 4, Nov 7
Woods, Galway–Aug 1
Woods, Georgie–March 15
Woods, Howard L. H.–July 30
Woods, J. B.–Nov 7
Woods, J. P.–Nov 28
Woods, J. P. III–Nov 28
Woods, J. Penbrooke Jr.–Nov 28
Woodward, Charles E.–April 27
Woody, Charles W.–Nov 5
Woody, George–May 6
Woodyard, Frances–Jan 1
Woodyard, Mary Ruth–Dec 16
Woodyard, R. B.–Dec 16
Wookey, Ben
Barboursville football player–Nov 10
Wooten, Gordon–April 9, June 24
Wooten, Gordon D. Jr.–June 24
Worden, C. A.–Nov 4
Worden, James H.–Nov 4
Workman, Alice–Aug 23
Workman, Clyde–July 30, Aug 23
Workman, Clyde H.–Feb 16
Workman, Ellen–July 9
Workman, Emily Louise–Aug 13
Workman, Ethel–Feb 13
Workman, Floyd J.–June 2
Workman, James B.–June 20
Workman, John–Feb 16
Workman, Louis Alton–Aug 13
Workman, Louis W.–June 21
Workman, Max W.–Oct 2
Workman, Thelma–June 20
Workman, Truman–July 9
Workman, Wallace–July 30
Worley, Boyce T.–Dec 4
Worley, Mrs. G. L.–Sept 13
Worley, William Gerald–Feb 2
Worrell, Dee E.–April 5, Dec 3
Worrell, E. E.–April 5

Worrell, Rodney E.–April 5
Wray, Eugene R.–Jan 24
Wray, Everett–March 8
Wray, Everett W.–April 30, Jan 5, 1946
Wray, Kathy–Jan 5, 1946
Wray, Norman–Sept 20
Wray, W. L.–March 8
Wright, Albert A.–Feb 13, May 17
Wright, Betty L.–Oct 20
Wright, E.–June 12
Wright, Edward H.–Nov 8
Wright, Emmette L.–April 5
Wright, Ernest D.–Jan 12, Nov 9
Wright, Gerald–Oct 20
Wright, Gerald B.–Aug 13
Wright, H. V.–Feb 13, May 17
Wright, Hilary Ann–Jan 12
Wright, Jack R.–Nov 13
Wright, James P.–Nov 20
Wright, Ray–Nov 16
Wright, Roy O.–April 5
Wright, Stanley–May 22
Wright, Wayne S.–Oct 4
Wulfman, William A.–Nov 21
Wyant, George A.–Aug 1
Wyant, Mildred F.–Aug 1
Wyle, William Edwin–Oct 19
Wylie, S. W. 'Buster'–March 13
Wyrick, Vera–Oct 7
Wysong, Frances–March 15
Wysong, Frances Burly–March 21
Wysong, J. M.–March 15, March 21
Wysong, James–March 15, March 21
Wysong, Linda–March 21
Wysong, Robert–March 21

Y

Yamashita, Tomoyuki
Japanese commander in the Philippines–
Sept 3, Dec 7
Yates, Joseph Jr.–Feb 25
Yates, Joseph O. Sr.–Feb 25
Yates, Mrs. L. J.–Sept 21
Yates, Nancy–Dec 6
Yates, Willie–Dec 6
Yeager, Alice–June 22

ENDNOTES

1 Farrar, Harry T., Trade Winds, Huntington Herald-Dispatch, Huntington, West Virginia, January 6, 1945

2 Ridgley, Duke, Diamond Dust, Huntington Herald-Dispatch, Huntington, West Virginia, January 1, 1945

3 Stone, David J., World War II Chronicle, Legacy Publishing, Lincolnwood, IL, 2007, p 406

4 Briefs from Last Night's Associated Press Wires, Huntington Herald-Dispatch, Huntington, West Virginia, January 6, 1945

5 Associated Press Report, Huntington Herald-Dispatch, Huntington, West Virginia, January 6, 1945

6 Huntington Herald-Dispatch, Huntington, West Virginia, January 9, 1945

7 Associated Press Report, Huntington Herald-Dispatch, Huntington, West Virginia, January 9, 1945

8 Huntington Herald-Dispatch, Huntington, West Virginia, January 10, 1945

9 Huntington Herald-Dispatch, Huntington, West Virginia, January 13, 1945

10 Pittman, Frank, Huntington Herald-Advertiser, Huntington, West Virginia, January 14, 1945

11 Cussler, Clive & Craig Dirgo, The Sea Hunters: True Adventures with Famous Shipwrecks, Simon & Schuster, New York, 1996

12 Huntington Herald-Dispatch, Huntington, West Virginia, January 16, 1945

13 Stone, David J., World War II Chronicle, Legacy Publishing, Lincolnwood, IL, 2007, p 408

14 Huntington Herald-Dispatch, Huntington, West Virginia, January 19, 1945

15 Huntington Herald-Dispatch, Huntington, West Virginia, January 19, 1945

16 Associated Press Report, Huntington Herald-Dispatch, West Virginia, January 20, 1945

17 Huntington Herald-Dispatch, Huntington, West Virginia, January 23, 1945

18 Huntington Herald-Dispatch, Huntington, West Virginia, January 23, 1945

19 Huntington Herald-Dispatch, Huntington, West Virginia, January 24, 1945

20 Associated Press Report, Huntington Herald-Dispatch, Huntington, West Virginia, January 27, 1945

21 Stone, David J., World War II Chronicle, Legacy Publishing, Lincolnwood, IL, 2007, p 408

22 Huntington Herald-Advertiser, Huntington, West Virginia, January 28, 1945

23 Huntington Herald-Advertiser, Huntington, West Virginia, January 28, 1945

24 Huntington Herald-Dispatch, Huntington, West Virginia, January 29, 1945

25 Associated Press Report, Huntington Herald-Dispatch, West Virginia, January 29, 1945

26 Stone, David J., World War II Chronicle, Legacy Publishing, Lincolnwood, IL, 2007, p 408

27 Huntington Herald-Dispatch, Huntington, West Virginia, January 30, 1945

28 Huntington Herald-Dispatch, Huntington, West Virginia, January 31, 1945

29 Stone, David J., World War II Chronicle, Legacy Publishing, Lincolnwood, IL, 2007, p 414

30 Associated Press Report, Huntington Herald-Dispatch, Huntington, West Virginia, February 2, 1945

31 Hicks, Marguerite, Huntington Herald-Dispatch, Huntington, West Virginia, February 2, 1945

32 West Virginia Division of Culture and History Website, http://www.wvculture.org/vrr/va_dcdetail.aspx?Id=2735925

33 Associated Press Report, Huntington Herald-Advertiser, Huntington, West Virginia, February 4, 1945

34 Huntington Herald-Advertiser, Huntington, West Virginia, February 4, 1945

35 Stone, David J., World War II Chronicle, Legacy Publishing, Lincolnwood, IL, 2007, p 4014

36 Ancestry.com, Everett Bellomy, FHL File number 1788164

37 War in Brief, Associated Press Report, Huntington Herald-Dispatch, Huntington, West Virginia, February 6, 1945

38 Huntington Herald-Dispatch, Huntington, West Virginia, February 6, 1945

39 Huntington Herald-Dispatch, Huntington, West Virginia, February 7, 1945

40 Click, Bill, Plan Your Garden, Huntington Herald-Dispatch, Huntington, West Virginia, February 8, 1945

41 Huntington Herald-Dispatch, Huntington, West Virginia, February 8, 1945

42 Huntington Herald-Dispatch, Huntington, West Virginia, February 8, 1945

43 Huntington Herald-Dispatch, Huntington, West Virginia, February 8, 1945

44 Ridgley, Duke, Huntington Herald-Dispatch, Huntington, West Virginia, February 9, 1945

45 Stone, David J., World War II Chronicle, Legacy Publishing, Lincolnwood, IL, 2007, p 4014

46 Services in Churches Sunday, Huntington Herald-Dispatch, Huntington, West Virginia, February 10, 1945

47 Huntington Herald-Advertiser, Huntington, West Virginia, February 10, 1945

48 Associated Press Report, Huntington Herald-Dispatch, Huntington, West Virginia, February 10, 1945

49 Associated Press Report, Huntington Herald-Advertiser, Huntington, West Virginia, February 11, 1945

50 Stone, David J., World War II Chronicle, Legacy Publishing, Lincolnwood, IL, 2007, p 4014

51 Associated Press Report, Huntington Herald-Dispatch, Huntington, West Virginia, February 13, 1945

52 Associated Press Report, Huntington Herald-Dispatch, Huntington, West Virginia, February 13, 1945

53 Huntington Herald-Dispatch, Huntington, West Virginia, February 14, 1945

54 Associated Press Report, Huntington Herald-Dispatch, Huntington, West Virginia, February 15, 1945

55 Huntington Herald-Dispatch, Huntington, West Virginia, February 16, 1945

56 Huntington Herald-Dispatch, Huntington, West Virginia, February 17, 1945

57 Ancestry.com, Perlina Ann Childers, FHL File number 559883

58 Maxwell, Hugh, Huntington Herald-Advertiser, Huntington, West Virginia, February 18, 1945

59 Huntington Herald- Advertiser, Huntington, West Virginia, February 18, 1945

60 Huntington Herald- Advertiser, Huntington, West Virginia, February 18, 1945

61 Associated Press Report, Huntington Herald-Dispatch, Huntington, West Virginia, February 19, 1945

62 Associated Press Report, Huntington Herald-Dispatch, Huntington, West Virginia, February 19, 1945

63 Huntington Herald-Dispatch, Huntington, West Virginia, February 19, 1945

64 Ancestry.com, Mary J. Lucas, FHL File number 559883

65 Huntington Herald-Dispatch, Huntington, West Virginia, February 20, 1945

66 Huntington Herald-Dispatch, Huntington, West Virginia, February 20, 1945

67 Huntington Herald-Dispatch, Huntington, West Virginia, February 20, 1945

68 Stone, David J., World War II Chronicle, Legacy Publishing, Lincolnwood, IL, 2007, p 4016

69 Huntington Herald-Dispatch, Huntington, West Virginia, February 22, 1945

70 Associated Press Report, Huntington Herald-Dispatch, Huntington, West Virginia, February 22, 1945

71 War in Brief, Associated Press Report, Huntington Herald-Dispatch, Huntington, West Virginia, February 22, 1945

72 Huntington Herald-Dispatch, Huntington, West Virginia, February 23, 1945

73 Stone, David J., World War II Chronicle, Legacy Publishing, Lincolnwood, IL, 2007, p 4016

74 War in Brief, Associated Press Report, Huntington Herald-Dispatch, Huntington, West Virginia, February 23, 1945

75 Associated Press Report, Huntington Herald-Dispatch, Huntington, West Virginia, February 24, 1945

76 Associated Press Report, Huntington Herald-Dispatch, Huntington, West Virginia, February 24, 1945

77 Associated Press Report, Huntington Herald-Dispatch, Huntington, West Virginia, February 25, 1945

78 Stone, David J., World War II Chronicle, Legacy Publishing, Lincolnwood, IL, 2007, p 4018

79 War in Brief, Associated Press Report, Huntington Herald-Dispatch, Huntington, West Virginia, February 26, 1945

80 Personals, Huntington Herald-Dispatch, Huntington, West Virginia, February 27, 1945

81 Personals, Huntington Herald-Dispatch, Huntington, West Virginia, February 27, 1945

82 Associated Press Report, Huntington Herald-Dispatch, Huntington, West Virginia, February 27, 1945

83 Associated Press Report, Huntington Herald-Dispatch, Huntington, West Virginia, February 27, 1945

84 Associated Press Report, Huntington Herald-Dispatch, Huntington, West Virginia, February 28, 1945

85 Pratt, Rupert, A Teacher's Daily Register of Four County Schools in Cabell County West Virginia-1927–1934, Cohoes, New York, 2018

86 Ancestry.com, Virginia Lee Morrison, FHL File number 1953777

87 Warfront Briefs from Last Night's AP Dispatches, Huntington Herald-Dispatch, Huntington, West Virginia, March 1, 1945

88 Associated Press Report, Huntington Herald-Dispatch, Huntington, West Virginia, March 2, 1945

89 Associated Press Report, Huntington Herald-Advertiser, Huntington, West Virginia, March 4, 1945

90

Stone, David J., World War II Chronicle, Legacy Publishing, Lincolnwood, IL, 2007, p 418.

91 Huntington Herald-Dispatch, Huntington, West Virginia, March 5, 1945

92 Stone, David J., World War II Chronicle, Legacy Publishing, Lincolnwood, IL, 2007, p 418.

93 Stone, David J., World War II Chronicle, Legacy Publishing, Lincolnwood, IL, 2007, p 418.

94 Associated Press Report, Huntington Herald-Dispatch, Huntington, West Virginia, March 6, 1945

95 Stone, David J., World War II Chronicle, Legacy Publishing, Lincolnwood, IL, 2007, p 420.

96 War in Brief, Associated Press Report, Huntington Herald-Dispatch, Huntington, West Virginia, March 8, 1945

97 Huntington Herald-Dispatch, Huntington, West Virginia, March 10, 1945

98 Maxwell, Hugh, Huntington Herald-Advertiser, Huntington, West Virginia, March 11, 1945

99 Huntington Herald-Advertiser, Huntington, West Virginia, March 11, 1945

100 Frye, William, Associated Press Report, Huntington Herald-Advertiser, Huntington, West Virginia, March 11, 1945

101 Huntington Herald-Advertiser, Huntington, West Virginia, March 12, 1945

102 Click, W. D., How's Your Garden, Huntington Herald-Dispatch, Huntington, West Virginia, March 13, 1945

103 Huntington Herald- Dispatch, Huntington, West Virginia, March 13, 1945

104 Stone, David J., World War II Chronicle, Legacy Publishing, Lincolnwood, IL, 2007, p 420.

105 Warfront Briefs, Associated Press Report, Huntington Herald- Dispatch, Huntington, West Virginia, March 13, 1945

106 Huntington Herald- Dispatch, Huntington, West Virginia, March 13, 1945

107 Stone, David J., World War II Chronicle, Legacy Publishing, Lincolnwood, IL, 2007, p 422.

108 Pyle, Ernie, Associated Press, Huntington Herald-Dispatch, Huntington, West Virginia, March 14, 1945

109 Huntington Herald- Dispatch, Huntington, West Virginia, March 14, 1945

110 War Front Briefs from Last Night's Associated Press Report, Huntington Herald-Dispatch, Huntington, West Virginia, March 15, 1945

111 Huntington Herald-Dispatch, Huntington, West Virginia, March 15, 1945

112 War Front Briefs from Last Night's Associated Press Report, Huntington Herald-Dispatch, Huntington, West Virginia, March 16, 1945

113 Associated Press Report, Huntington Herald-Dispatch, Huntington, West Virginia, March 16, 1945

114 Huntington Herald-Dispatch, Huntington, West Virginia, March 16, 1945

115 War Front Briefs from Last Night's Associated Press Report, Huntington Herald-Dispatch, Huntington, West Virginia, March 17, 1945

116 Huntington Herald-Advertiser, Huntington, West Virginia, March 18, 1945

117 Associated Press Report, Huntington Herald-Advertiser, Huntington, West Virginia, March 18, 1945

118 Stone, David J., World War II Chronicle, Legacy Publishing, Lincolnwood, IL, 2007, p 422.

119 War in Brief, Associated Press Report, Huntington Herald-Dispatch, Huntington, West Virginia, March 19, 1945

120 Stone, David J., World War II Chronicle, Legacy Publishing, Lincolnwood, IL, 2007, p 422.

121 Associated Press Report, Huntington Herald-Dispatch, Huntington, West Virginia, March 19, 1945

122 Huntington Herald-Dispatch, Huntington, West Virginia, March 20, 1945

123 Associated Press Report, Huntington Herald-Dispatch, Huntington, West Virginia, March 20, 1945

124 Ridgley, Duke, Diamond Dust, Huntington Herald-Dispatch, Huntington, West Virginia, March 21, 1945

125 Associated Press Report, Huntington Herald-Dispatch, Huntington, West Virginia, March 21, 1945

126 Huntington Herald-Dispatch, Huntington, West Virginia, March 21, 1945

127 Huntington Herald-Dispatch, Huntington, West Virginia, March 22, 1945

128 Huntington Herald-Dispatch, Huntington, West Virginia, March 22, 1945

129 Associated Press Report, Huntington Herald-Dispatch, Huntington, West Virginia, March 23, 1945

130 Stone, David J., World War II Chronicle, Legacy Publishing, Lincolnwood, IL, 2007, p 424.

131 Huntington Herald-Dispatch, Huntington, West Virginia, March 24, 1945

132 Huntington Herald- Advertiser, Huntington, West Virginia, March 25, 1945

133 Huntington Herald- Advertiser, Huntington, West Virginia, March 25, 1945

134 Ridgley, Duke, Diamond Dust, Huntington Herald-Dispatch, Huntington, West Virginia, March 26, 1945

135 Huntington Herald-Dispatch, Huntington, West Virginia, March 26, 1945

136 War in Brief, Associated Press Report, Huntington Herald-Dispatch, Huntington, West Virginia, March 29, 1945

137 Associated Press Report, Huntington Herald-Dispatch, Huntington, West Virginia, March 31, 1945

138 Pyle, Ernie, Associated Press, Huntington Herald-Advertiser, Huntington, West Virginia, April 1, 1945

139 Stone, David J., World War II Chronicle, Legacy Publishing, Lincolnwood, IL, 2007, p 424

140 Huntington Herald-Dispatch, Huntington, West Virginia, April 1, 1945

141 Associated Press Report, Huntington Herald-Dispatch, Huntington, West Virginia, April 2, 1945

142 Ancestry.com, Almeda Keyser, FHL Film Number 559883

143 Claassen, Harold, Associated Press Report, Huntington Herald-Dispatch, Huntington, West Virginia, April 3, 1945

144 Ridgley, Duke, Diamond Dust, Huntington Herald-Dispatch, Huntington, West Virginia, April 3, 1945

145 Stone, David J., World War II Chronicle, Legacy Publishing, Lincolnwood, IL, 2007, p 426

146 Click, W. D., Huntington Herald-Dispatch, Huntington, West Virginia, April 4, 1945

147 Associated Press Report, Huntington Herald-Dispatch, Huntington, West Virginia, April 4, 1945

148 War in Brief, Associated Press Report, Huntington Herald-Dispatch, Huntington, West Virginia, April 4, 1945

149 Stone, David J., World War II Chronicle, Legacy Publishing, Lincolnwood, IL, 2007, p 426

150 Huntington Herald-Dispatch, Huntington, West Virginia, April 5, 1945

151 Stone, David J., World War II Chronicle, Legacy Publishing, Lincolnwood, IL, 2007, p 426

152 Associated Press Report, Huntington Herald-Dispatch, Huntington, West Virginia, April 6, 1945

153 Huntington Herald-Dispatch, Huntington, West Virginia, April 7, 1945

154 War Front Briefs from Last Night's AP Dispatches, Huntington Herald-Dispatch, Huntington, West Virginia, April 7, 1945

155 Stone, David J., World War II Chronicle, Legacy Publishing, Lincolnwood, IL, 2007, p 426

156 Some of the facts about these men were also in an article in the June 28, 2015 Charleston Gazette

157 Huntington Herald-Dispatch, Huntington, West Virginia, April 8, 1945

158 Ancestry.com, Ewell Eplin, U.S., Find A Grave Index, 1700s-Current

159 Ancestry.com, Vernon Lucas, U.S. World War II Army Enlistment Records, 1938–1946

160 Huntington Herald-Dispatch, Huntington, West Virginia, April 10, 1945

161 Stone, David J., World War II Chronicle, Legacy Publishing, Lincolnwood, IL, 2007, p 428

162 Stone, David J., World War II Chronicle, Legacy Publishing, Lincolnwood, IL, 2007, p 428

163 Associated Press Report, Huntington Herald-Dispatch, Huntington, West Virginia, April 12, 1945

164 Associated Press Report, Huntington Herald-Dispatch, Huntington, West Virginia, April 12, 1945

165 Huntington Herald-Dispatch, Huntington, West Virginia, April 12, 1945

166 Claassen, Harold, Associated Press Report, Huntington Herald-Dispatch, Huntington, West Virginia, April 14, 1945

167 Associated Press Report, Huntington Herald-Dispatch, Huntington, West Virginia, April 13, 1945

168 Huntington Herald-Dispatch, Huntington, West Virginia, April 13, 1945

169 Stone, David J., World War II Chronicle, Legacy Publishing, Lincolnwood, IL, 2007, p 428

170 Associated Press Report, Huntington Herald-Dispatch, Huntington, West Virginia, April 14, 1945

171 Ridgley, Duke, Diamond Dust, Huntington Herald-Dispatch, Huntington, West Virginia, April 14, 1945

172 Stone, David J., World War II Chronicle, Legacy Publishing, Lincolnwood, IL, 2007, p 428

173 Stone, David J., World War II Chronicle, Legacy Publishing, Lincolnwood, IL, 2007, p 428

174 Associated Press Report, Huntington Herald-Dispatch, Huntington, West Virginia, April 15, 1945

175 Huntington Herald-Advertiser, Huntington, West Virginia, April 15, 1945

176 Huntington Herald-Advertiser, Huntington, West Virginia, April 15, 1945

177 Huntington Herald-Advertiser, Huntington, West Virginia, April 15, 1945

178 Huntington Herald-Dispatch, Huntington, West Virginia, April 16, 1945

179 Stone, David J., World War II Chronicle, Legacy Publishing, Lincolnwood, IL, 2007, p 430

180 Huntington Herald-Dispatch, Huntington, West Virginia, April 17, 1945

181 Gaylord, Edith, Associated Press Report, Huntington Herald-Dispatch, Huntington, West Virginia, April 17, 1945

182 Stone, David J., World War II Chronicle, Legacy Publishing, Lincolnwood, IL, 2007, p 430

183 Huntington Herald-Dispatch, Huntington, West Virginia, April 19, 1945

184 Briefs from Last Night's Associated Press Wires, Huntington Herald-Dispatch, Huntington, West Virginia, April 20, 1945

185 Associated Press Report, Huntington Herald-Dispatch, Huntington, West Virginia, April 21, 1945

186 Briefs from Last Night's Associated Press Wires, Huntington Herald-Dispatch, Huntington, West Virginia, April 21, 1945

187 Huntington Herald-Dispatch, Huntington, West Virginia, April 21, 1945

188 Huntington Herald-Dispatch, Huntington, West Virginia, April 21, 1945

189 Stone, David J., World War II Chronicle, Legacy Publishing, Lincolnwood, IL, 2007, p 430

190 Stone, David J., World War II Chronicle, Legacy Publishing, Lincolnwood, IL, 2007, p 430

191 Huntington Herald-Dispatch, Huntington, West Virginia, April 25, 1945

192 Stone, David J., World War II Chronicle, Legacy Publishing, Lincolnwood, IL, 2007, p 430

193 Associated Press Report, Huntington Herald-Dispatch, Huntington, West Virginia, April 25, 1945

194 Briefs from Last Night's Associated Press Wires, Huntington Herald-Dispatch, Huntington, West Virginia, April 25, 1945

195 Huntington Herald-Dispatch, Huntington, West Virginia, April 26, 1945

196 Huntington Herald-Dispatch, Huntington, West Virginia, April 26, 1945

197 Associated Press Report, Huntington Herald-Dispatch, Huntington, West Virginia, April 26, 1945

198 Associated Press Report, Huntington Herald-Dispatch, Huntington, West Virginia, April 26, 1945

199 Associated Press Report, Huntington Herald-Dispatch, Huntington, West Virginia, April 27, 1945

200 Huntington Herald-Dispatch, Huntington, West Virginia, April 27, 1945

201 Stone, David J., World War II Chronicle, Legacy Publishing, Lincolnwood, IL, 2007, p 432

202 Stone, David J., World War II Chronicle, Legacy Publishing, Lincolnwood, IL, 2007, p 432

203 Huntington Herald-Dispatch, Huntington, West Virginia, April 30, 1945

204 Huntington Herald-Dispatch, Huntington, West Virginia, April 30, 1945

205 Stone, David J., World War II Chronicle, Legacy Publishing, Lincolnwood, IL, 2007, p 432

206 Associated Press Report, Huntington Herald-Dispatch, Huntington, West Virginia, May 1, 1945

207 Huntington Herald-Dispatch, Huntington, West Virginia, May 1, 1945

208 Huntington Herald-Dispatch, Huntington, West Virginia, May 1, 1945

209 Huntington Herald-Dispatch, Huntington, West Virginia, May 2, 1945

210 Huntington Herald-Dispatch, Huntington, West Virginia, May 2, 1945

211 Huntington Herald-Dispatch, Huntington, West Virginia, May 3, 1945

212 Stone, David J., World War II Chronicle, Legacy Publishing, Lincolnwood, IL, 2007, p 432

213 Stone, David J., World War II Chronicle, Legacy Publishing, Lincolnwood, IL, 2007, p 434

214 Huntington Herald-Dispatch, Huntington, West Virginia, May 4, 1945

215 Huntington Herald-Dispatch, Huntington, West Virginia, May 4, 1945

216 Associated Press Report, Harrison, Harold, Huntington Herald-Dispatch, Huntington, West Virginia, May 5, 1945

217 Stone, David J., World War II Chronicle, Legacy Publishing, Lincolnwood, IL, 2007, p 434

218 Associated Press Report, Huntington Herald-Dispatch, Huntington, West Virginia, May 5, 1945

219 Associated Press Report, Huntington Herald-Dispatch, Huntington, West Virginia, May 5, 1945

220 Associated Press Report, Huntington Herald-Dispatch, Huntington, West Virginia, May 5, 1945

221 Associated Press Report, Huntington Herald-Dispatch, Huntington, West Virginia, May 5, 1945

222 Huntington Herald-Advertiser, Huntington, West Virginia, May 6, 1945

223 Huntington Herald-Advertiser, Huntington, West Virginia, May 6, 1945

224 Huntington Herald-Advertiser, Huntington, West Virginia, May 6, 1945

225 Stone, David J., World War II Chronicle, Legacy Publishing, Lincolnwood, IL, 2007, p 434

226 Stone, David J., World War II Chronicle, Legacy Publishing, Lincolnwood, IL, 2007, p 436

227 Stone, David J., World War II Chronicle, Legacy Publishing, Lincolnwood, IL, 2007, p 436

228 Associated Press Report, Huntington Herald-Dispatch, Huntington, West Virginia, May 8, 1945

229 Wikipedia, Timeline of World War II (1945), https://en.wikipedia.org/wiki/Timeline_of_World_War_II_(1945)#May_1945

230 Associated Press Report, Huntington Herald-Dispatch, Huntington, West Virginia, May 8, 1945

231 Stone, David J., World War II Chronicle, Legacy Publishing, Lincolnwood, IL, 2007, p 436

232 Huntington Herald-Dispatch, Huntington, West Virginia, May 9, 1945

233 Huntington Herald-Dispatch, Huntington, West Virginia, May 9, 1945

234 Huntington Herald-Dispatch, Huntington, West Virginia, May 9, 1945

235 Ancestry.com, Everett Johnson, FHL File number 559883

236 Huntington Herald-Dispatch, Huntington, West Virginia, May 11, 1945

237 Associated Press Report, Huntington Herald-Dispatch, Huntington, West Virginia, May 10, 1945

238 Stone, David J., World War II Chronicle, Legacy Publishing, Lincolnwood, IL, 2007, p 436

239 Associated Press Report, Huntington Herald-Dispatch, Huntington, West Virginia, May 10, 1945

240 Stone, David J., World War II Chronicle, Legacy Publishing, Lincolnwood, IL, 2007, p 436

241 Stone, David J., World War II Chronicle, Legacy Publishing, Lincolnwood, IL, 2007, p 436

242 Huntington Herald-Advertiser, Huntington, West Virginia, May 13, 1945

243 Huntington Herald-Advertiser, Huntington, West Virginia, May 13, 1945

244 Stone, David J., World War II Chronicle, Legacy Publishing, Lincolnwood, IL, 2007, p 436

245 Huntington Herald-Dispatch, Huntington, West Virginia, May 15, 1945

246 Stone, David J., World War II Chronicle, Legacy Publishing, Lincolnwood, IL, 2007, p 436

247 Stone, David J., World War II Chronicle, Legacy Publishing, Lincolnwood, IL, 2007, p 438

248 Stone, David J., World War II Chronicle, Legacy Publishing, Lincolnwood, IL, 2007, p 438

249 Briefs from Last Night's Associated Press Wires, Huntington Herald-Dispatch, Huntington, West Virginia, May 19, 1945

250 Associated Press Report, Huntington Herald-Dispatch, Huntington, West Virginia, May 19, 1945

251 Associated Press report, Huntington Herald-Advertiser, Huntington, West Virginia, May 20, 1945

252 Johnston, Mary Weaver, Huntington Herald-Advertiser, Huntington, West Virginia, May 20, 1945

253 Stone, David J., World War II Chronicle, Legacy Publishing, Lincolnwood, IL, 2007, p 438

254 Ridgley, Duke, Diamond Dust, Huntington Herald-Dispatch, Huntington, West Virginia, May 22, 1945

255 Stone, David J., World War II Chronicle, Legacy Publishing, Lincolnwood, IL, 2007, p 438

256 Wikipedia, Timeline of World War II (1945), https://en.wikipedia.org/wiki/Timeline_of_World_War_II_(1945)#May_1945

257 Huntington Herald-Dispatch, Huntington, West Virginia, May 23, 1945

258 Associated Press Report, Huntington Herald-Dispatch, Huntington, West Virginia, May 24, 1945

259 Huntington Herald-Dispatch, Huntington, West Virginia, May 25, 1945

260 findagrave.com, Joe Cephas Duty, Find A Grave Memorial# 32080271

261 Associated Press Report, Huntington Herald-Advertiser, Huntington, West Virginia, May 27, 1945

262 Huntington Herald-Advertiser, Huntington, West Virginia, May 27, 1945

263 Huntington Herald-Advertiser, Huntington, West Virginia, May 27, 1945

264 Stone, David J., World War II Chronicle, Legacy Publishing, Lincolnwood, IL, 2007, p 438

265 Huntington Herald-Dispatch, Huntington, West Virginia, May 28, 1945

266 Huntington Herald-Dispatch, Huntington, West Virginia, May 30, 1945

267 Associated Press Report, Huntington Herald-Advertiser, Huntington, West Virginia, June 1, 1945

268 Stone, David J., World War II Chronicle, Legacy Publishing, Lincolnwood, IL, 2007, p 444

269 Huntington Herald-Dispatch, Huntington, West Virginia, June 2, 1945

270 Associated Press Report, Huntington Herald-Advertiser, Huntington, West Virginia, June 3, 1945

271 Associated Press Report, Huntington Herald-Advertiser, Huntington, West Virginia, June 3, 1945

272 Huntington Herald-Advertiser, Huntington, West Virginia, June 3, 1945

273 Associated Press Report, Huntington Herald-Dispatch, Huntington, West Virginia, June 4, 1945

274 Huntington Herald-Dispatch, Huntington, West Virginia, June 5, 1945

275 Associated Press Report, Huntington Herald-Dispatch, Huntington, West Virginia, June 5, 1945

276 Stone, David J., World War II Chronicle, Legacy Publishing, Lincolnwood, IL, 2007, p 444

277 Associated Press Report, Huntington Herald-Dispatch, Huntington, West Virginia, June 5, 1945

278 Associated Press Report, Huntington Herald-Dispatch, Huntington, West Virginia, June 6, 1945

279 Huntington Herald-Dispatch, Huntington, West Virginia, June 7, 1945

280 Stone, David J., World War II Chronicle, Legacy Publishing, Lincolnwood, IL, 2007, p 444

281 Associated Press Report, Huntington Herald-Dispatch, Huntington, West Virginia, June 7, 1945

282 Associated Press Report, Huntington Herald-Dispatch, Huntington, West Virginia, June 8, 1945

283 Ridgley, Duke, Diamond Dust, Huntington Herald-Dispatch, Huntington, West Virginia, June 8, 1945

284 Huntington Herald-Dispatch, Huntington, West Virginia, June 9, 1945

285 Ancestry.com, Manford H. Paugh, FHL File number 1983803

286 Associated Press Report, Huntington Herald-Advertiser, Huntington, West Virginia, June 10, 1945

287 Associated Press Report, Huntington Herald-Advertiser, Huntington, West Virginia, June 10, 1945

288 Associated Press Report, Huntington Herald-Dispatch, Huntington, West Virginia, June 12, 1945

289 Stone, David J., World War II Chronicle, Legacy Publishing, Lincolnwood, IL, 2007, p 444

290 Associated Press Report, Huntington Herald-Dispatch, Huntington, West Virginia, June 13, 1945

291 Associated Press Report, Huntington Herald-Dispatch, Huntington, West Virginia, June 14, 1945

292 Associated Press Report, Huntington Herald-Dispatch, Huntington, West Virginia, June 14, 1945

293 Stone, David J., World War II Chronicle, Legacy Publishing, Lincolnwood, IL, 2007, p 444

294 Associated Press Report, Huntington Herald-Dispatch, Huntington, West Virginia, June 16, 1945

295 Associated Press Report, Huntington Herald-Advertiser, Huntington, West Virginia, June 17, 1945

296 Tucker, George, Associated Press Report, Huntington Herald-Advertiser, Huntington, West Virginia, June 17, 1945

297 Associated Press Report, Huntington Herald-Advertiser, Huntington, West Virginia, June 17, 1945

298 Stone, David J., World War II Chronicle, Legacy Publishing, Lincolnwood, IL, 2007, p 446

299 Huntington Herald-Dispatch, Huntington, West Virginia, June 18, 1945

300 Associated Press Report, Huntington Herald-Dispatch, Huntington, West Virginia, June 18, 1945

301 Associated Press Report, Huntington Herald-Dispatch, Huntington, West Virginia, June 19, 1945

302 Huntington Herald-Dispatch, Huntington, West Virginia, June 19, 1945

303 Associated Press Report, Huntington Herald-Dispatch, Huntington, West Virginia, June 20, 1945

304 Associated Press Report, Huntington Herald-Dispatch, Huntington, West Virginia, June 21, 1945

305 Stone, David J., World War II Chronicle, Legacy Publishing, Lincolnwood, IL, 2007, p 446

306 Huntington Herald-Dispatch, Huntington, West Virginia, June 27, 1945

307 Associated Press Report, Huntington Herald-Dispatch, Huntington, West Virginia, June 22, 1945

308 Stone, David J., World War II Chronicle, Legacy Publishing, Lincolnwood, IL, 2007, p 446

309 Stone, David J., World War II Chronicle, Legacy Publishing, Lincolnwood, IL, 2007, p 447

310 Associated Press Report, Huntington Herald-Dispatch, Huntington, West Virginia, June 23, 1945

311 Cornell, Douglas B., Associated Press Report, Huntington Herald-Advertiser, Huntington, West Virginia, June 24, 1945

312 Associated Press Report, Huntington Herald-Dispatch, Huntington, West Virginia, June 25, 1945

313 Coons, Robbin, Associated Press Report, Huntington Herald- Dispatch, Huntington, West Virginia, June 25, 1945

314 Associated Press Report, Huntington Herald-Dispatch, Huntington, West Virginia, June 26, 1945

315 Associated Press Report, Huntington Herald-Dispatch, Huntington, West Virginia, June 27, 1945

316 Associated Press Report, Huntington Herald-Dispatch, Huntington, West Virginia, June 27, 1945

317 Stone, David J., World War II Chronicle, Legacy Publishing, Lincolnwood, IL, 2007, p 446

318 Briefs from Last Night's Associated Press Wires, Huntington Herald-Dispatch, Huntington, West Virginia, June 27, 1945

319 Huntington Herald-Dispatch, Huntington, West Virginia, June 27, 1945

320 Associated Press Report, Huntington Herald-Dispatch, Huntington, West Virginia, June 29, 1945

321 Associated Press Report, Huntington Herald-Advertiser, Huntington, West Virginia, July 1, 1945

322 Associated Press Report, Huntington Herald-Advertiser, Huntington, West Virginia, July 1, 1945

323 Associated Press Report, Huntington Herald-Advertiser, Huntington, West Virginia, July 1, 1945

324 Associated Press Report, Huntington Herald-Dispatch, Huntington, West Virginia, July 2, 1945

325 Associated Press Report, Huntington Herald-Dispatch, Huntington, West Virginia, July 3, 1945

326 Associated Press Report, Huntington Herald-Dispatch, Huntington, West Virginia, July 3 1945

327 Huntington Herald-Dispatch, Huntington, West Virginia, July 3, 1945

328 Briefs from Last Night's Associated Press Wires, Huntington Herald-Dispatch, Huntington, West Virginia, July 4, 1945

329 Huntington Herald-Dispatch, Huntington, West Virginia, July 4, 1945

330 Lochner, Louis P., Associated Press Report, Huntington Herald-Dispatch, Huntington, West Virginia, July 5, 1945

331 Associated Press Report, Huntington Herald-Dispatch, Huntington, West Virginia, July 6, 1945

332 Huntington Herald-Dispatch, Huntington, West Virginia, July 7, 1945

333 Associated Press Report, Huntington Herald-Dispatch, Huntington, West Virginia, July 7, 1945

334 Associated Press Report, Huntington Herald-Dispatch, Huntington, West Virginia, July 7, 1945

335 Hovey, Graham, Associated Press Report, Huntington Herald-Advertiser, Huntington, West Virginia, July 8, 1945

336 Whitehead, Don, Associated Press Report, Huntington Herald-Advertiser, Huntington, West Virginia, July 8, 1945

337 Huntington Herald-Advertiser, Huntington, West Virginia, July 8, 1945

338 Briefs from Last Night's Associated Press Wires, Huntington Herald-Dispatch, Huntington, West Virginia, July 9, 1945

339 Associated Press Report, Huntington Herald-Dispatch, Huntington, West Virginia, July 9, 1945

340 Associated Press Report, Huntington Herald-Dispatch, Huntington, West Virginia, July 10, 1945

341 Associated Press Report, Huntington Herald-Dispatch, Huntington, West Virginia, July 10, 1945

342 Associated Press Report, Huntington Herald-Dispatch, Huntington, West Virginia, July 11, 1945

343 Briefs from Last Night's Associated Press Wires, Huntington Herald-Dispatch, Huntington, West Virginia, July 11, 1945

344 Associated Press Report, Huntington Herald-Dispatch, Huntington, West Virginia, July 11, 1945

345 Associated Press Report, Huntington Herald-Dispatch, Huntington, West Virginia, July 11, 1945

346 Briefs from Last Night's Associated Press Wires, Huntington Herald-Dispatch, Huntington, West Virginia, July 11, 1945

347 Associated Press Report, Huntington Herald-Dispatch, Huntington, West Virginia, July 11, 1945

348 Huntington Herald-Dispatch, Huntington, West Virginia, July 12, 1945

349 Associated Press Report, Huntington Herald-Dispatch, Huntington, West Virginia, July 12, 1945

350 Huntington Herald-Dispatch, Huntington, West Virginia, July 14, 1945

351 Associated Press Report, Huntington Herald-Dispatch, Huntington, West Virginia, July 14, 1945

352 Associated Press Report, Huntington Herald-Dispatch, Huntington, West Virginia, July 14, 1945

353 Stone, David J., World War II Chronicle, Legacy Publishing, Lincolnwood, IL, 2007, p 448

354 Associated Press Report, Huntington Herald-Advertiser, Huntington, West Virginia, July 15, 1945

355 Associated Press Report, Huntington Herald-Advertiser, Huntington, West Virginia, July 15, 1945

356 Associated Press Report, Huntington Herald-Dispatch, Huntington, West Virginia, July 16, 1945

357 Associated Press Report, Huntington Herald-Dispatch, Huntington, West Virginia, July 17, 1945

358 Associated Press Report, Huntington Herald-Dispatch, Huntington, West Virginia, July 18, 1945

359 Huntington Herald-Dispatch, Huntington, West Virginia, July 19, 1945

360 Stone, David J., World War II Chronicle, Legacy Publishing, Lincolnwood, IL, 2007, p 448

361 Associated Press Report, Huntington Herald-Dispatch, Huntington, West Virginia, July 20, 1945

362 Associated Press Report, Huntington Herald-Dispatch, Huntington, West Virginia, July 20, 1945

363 Ridgley, Duke, Diamond Dust, Huntington Herald-Dispatch, Huntington, West Virginia, July 21, 1945

364 Associated Press Report, Huntington Herald-Dispatch, Huntington, West Virginia, July 21, 1945

365 Associated Press Report, Huntington Herald-Dispatch, Huntington, West Virginia, July 21, 1945

366 Huntington Herald-Advertiser, Huntington, West Virginia, July 22, 1945

367 Associated Press Report, Huntington Herald-Advertiser, Huntington, West Virginia, July 22, 1945

368 Associated Press Report, Huntington Herald-Dispatch, Huntington, West Virginia, July 23, 1945

369 Associated Press Report, Huntington Herald-Dispatch, Huntington, West Virginia, July 23, 1945

370 Associated Press Report, Huntington Herald-Dispatch, Huntington, West Virginia, July 23, 1945

371 Associated Press Report, Huntington Herald-Dispatch, Huntington, West Virginia, July 24, 1945

372 Associated Press Report, Huntington Herald-Dispatch, Huntington, West Virginia, July 24, 1945

373 Stone, David J., World War II Chronicle, Legacy Publishing, Lincolnwood, IL, 2007, p 450

374 Huntington Herald-Dispatch, Huntington, West Virginia, July 26, 1945

375 Huntington Herald-Dispatch, Huntington, West Virginia, January 27, 2020

376 Associated Press Report, Huntington Herald-Dispatch, Huntington, West Virginia, July 26, 1945

377 Associated Press Report, Huntington Herald-Dispatch, Huntington, West Virginia, July 26, 1945

378 Stone, David J., World War II Chronicle, Legacy Publishing, Lincolnwood, IL, 2007, p 448

379 Stone, David J., World War II Chronicle, Legacy Publishing, Lincolnwood, IL, 2007, p 450

380 Associated Press Report, Huntington Herald-Dispatch, Huntington, West Virginia, July 27, 1945

381 Associated Press Report, Huntington Herald-Dispatch, Huntington, West Virginia, July 27, 1945

382 Huntington Herald-Dispatch, Huntington, West Virginia, July 28, 1945

383 Gallup, George, Gallup Poll, Princeton, N.J., Huntington Herald-Advertiser, Huntington, West Virginia, July 29, 1945

384 Spencer, Murlin, Associated Press Report, Huntington Herald-Advertiser, Huntington, West Virginia, July 29, 1945

385 Faron, Hamilton W., Associated Press Report, Huntington Herald-Advertiser, Huntington, West Virginia, July 29, 1945

386 Stone, David J., World War II Chronicle, Legacy Publishing, Lincolnwood, IL, 2007, p 450

387 Associated Press Report, Huntington Herald-Dispatch, Huntington, West Virginia, July 30, 1945

388 Stone, David J., World War II Chronicle, Legacy Publishing, Lincolnwood, IL, 2007, p 450

389 Huntington Herald-Advertiser, Huntington, West Virginia, August 1, 1945

390 Buzek, Dorothy, Huntington Herald-Advertiser, Huntington, West Virginia, August 1, 1945

391 Maxwell, Hugh, Huntington Herald-Advertiser, Huntington, West Virginia, August 1, 1945

392 Huntington Herald-Advertiser, Huntington, West Virginia, August 1, 1945

393 Herald-Advertiser, Huntington, West Virginia, August 1, 1945

394 Huntington Herald-Advertiser, Huntington, West Virginia, August 1, 1945

395 Associated Press Report, Huntington Herald-Advertiser, Huntington, West Virginia, August 1, 1945

396 De Luce, Daniel, Associated Press Report, Huntington Herald-Advertiser, Huntington, West Virginia, August 1, 1945

397 Associated Press Report, Huntington Herald-Advertiser, Huntington, West Virginia, August 1, 1945

398 Associated Press Report, Huntington Herald-Advertiser, Huntington, West Virginia, August 1, 1945

399 Associated Press Report, Huntington Herald-Advertiser, Huntington, West Virginia, August 2, 1945

400 Associated Press Report, Huntington Herald-Advertiser, Huntington, West Virginia, August 2, 1945

401 Associated Press Report, Huntington Herald-Advertiser, Huntington, West Virginia, August 2, 1945

402 Stone, David J., World War II Chronicle, Legacy Publishing, Lincolnwood, IL, 2007, p 454

403 Huntington Herald-Advertiser, Huntington, West Virginia, August 2, 1945

404 Associated Press Report, Huntington Herald-Advertiser, Huntington, West Virginia, August 3, 1945

405 Associated Press Report, Huntington Herald-Advertiser, Huntington, West Virginia, August 3, 1945

406 Huntington Herald-Advertiser, Huntington, West Virginia, August 4, 1945

407 Cowan, Howard, Associated Press Report, Huntington Herald-Advertiser, Huntington, West Virginia, August 4, 1945

408 Hutcheson, James, Associated Press Report, Huntington Herald-Advertiser, Huntington, West Virginia, August 4, 1945

409 Associated Press Report, The Charleston Gazette, Charleston, West Virginia, August 5, 1945

410 Associated Press Report, The Charleston Gazette, Charleston, West Virginia, August 5, 1945

411 Associated Press Report, The Charleston Gazette, Charleston, West Virginia, August 5, 1945

412 Associated Press Report, The Charleston Gazette, Charleston, West Virginia, August 5, 1945

413 Associated Press Report, Huntington Herald-Advertiser, Huntington, West Virginia, August 6, 1945

414 Associated Press Report, Huntington Herald-Advertiser, Huntington, West Virginia, August 6, 1945

415 Huntington Herald-Advertiser, Huntington, West Virginia, August 7, 1945

416 Associated Press Report, Huntington Herald-Advertiser, Huntington, West Virginia, August 7, 1945

417 MacKenzie, DeWitt, Trends, Huntington Herald-Advertiser, Huntington, West Virginia, August 7, 1945

418 Maxwell, Hugh, Huntington Herald-Advertiser, Huntington, West Virginia, August 8, 1945

419 Associated Press Report, Huntington Herald-Advertiser, Huntington, West Virginia, August 8, 1945

420 Stone, David J., World War II Chronicle, Legacy Publishing, Lincolnwood, IL, 2007, p 454

421 Stone, David J., World War II Chronicle, Legacy Publishing, Lincolnwood, IL, 2007, p 454

422 Associated Press Report, Huntington Herald-Advertiser, Huntington, West Virginia, August 9, 1945

423 Spencer, Murlin, Associated Press Report, Huntington Herald-Advertiser, Huntington, West Virginia, August 9, 1945

424 Stone, David J., World War II Chronicle, Legacy Publishing, Lincolnwood, IL, 2007, p 454

425 FamilySearch.org, Rachel Amanda Strum, West Virginia Deaths, 1804–1999 Database

426 Associated Press Report, Huntington Herald-Advertiser, Huntington, West Virginia, August 10, 1945

427 Associated Press Report, Huntington Herald-Advertiser, Huntington, West Virginia, August 10, 1945

428 Associated Press Report, Huntington Herald-Advertiser, Huntington, West Virginia, August 10, 1945

429 Huntington Herald-Advertiser, Huntington, West Virginia, August 11, 1945

430 Huntington Herald-Advertiser, Huntington, West Virginia, August 11, 1945

431 Wiley, Bonnie, Associated Press Report, Huntington Herald-Advertiser, Huntington, West Virginia, August 11, 1945

432 Associated Press Report, Huntington Herald-Advertiser, Huntington, West Virginia, August 11, 1945

433 The Charleston Gazette, Charleston, West Virginia, August 12, 1945

434 Associated Press Report, The Charleston Gazette, Charleston, West Virginia, August 12, 1945

435 Huntington Herald-Advertiser, Huntington, West Virginia, August 13, 1945

436 Huntington Herald-Advertiser, Huntington, West Virginia, August 13, 1945

437 Associated Press Report, Huntington Herald-Advertiser, Huntington, West Virginia, August 13, 1945

438 Associated Press Report, Huntington Herald-Advertiser, Huntington, West Virginia, August 14, 1945

439 Maxwell, Hugh, Huntington Herald-Advertiser, Huntington, West Virginia, August 15, 1945

440 Associated Press Report, Huntington Herald-Advertiser, Huntington, West Virginia, August 15, 1945

441 Associated Press Report, Huntington Herald-Advertiser, Huntington, West Virginia, August 16, 1945

442 Stone, David J., World War II Chronicle, Legacy Publishing, Lincolnwood, IL, 2007, p 456

443 Associated Press Report, Huntington Herald-Advertiser, Huntington, West Virginia, August 16, 1945

444 Associated Press Report, Huntington Herald-Advertiser, Huntington, West Virginia, August 16, 1945

445 Associated Press Report, Huntington Herald-Advertiser, Huntington, West Virginia, August 16, 1945

446 Associated Press Report, Huntington Herald-Advertiser, Huntington, West Virginia, August 17, 1945

447 Associated Press Report, Huntington Herald-Advertiser, Huntington, West Virginia, August 17, 1945

448 Huntington Herald-Advertiser, Huntington, West Virginia, August 18, 1945

449 Associated Press Report, Huntington Herald-Advertiser, Huntington, West Virginia, August 18, 1945

450 Associated Press Report, Huntington Herald-Advertiser, Huntington, West Virginia, August 18, 1945

451 Huntington Herald-Advertiser, Huntington, West Virginia, August 20, 1945

452 Associated Press Report, Huntington Herald-Advertiser, Huntington, West Virginia, August 20, 1945

453 Associated Press Report, Huntington Herald-Advertiser, Huntington, West Virginia, August 20, 1945

454 Associated Press Report, Huntington Herald-Advertiser, Huntington, West Virginia, August 21, 1945

455 Associated Press Report, Huntington Herald-Advertiser, Huntington, West Virginia, August 21, 1945

456 Associated Press Report, Huntington Herald-Advertiser, Huntington, West Virginia, August 21, 1945

457 Associated Press Report, Huntington Herald-Advertiser, Huntington, West Virginia, August 21, 1945

458 Huntington Herald-Advertiser, Huntington, West Virginia, August 22, 1945

459 Huntington Herald-Advertiser, Huntington, West Virginia, August 22, 1945

460 Associated Press Report, Huntington Herald-Advertiser, Huntington, West Virginia, August 22, 1945

461 Associated Press Report, Huntington Herald-Advertiser, Huntington, West Virginia, August 23, 1945

462 Page, Fred, Huntington Herald-Advertiser, Huntington, West Virginia, August 24, 1945

463 Associated Press Report, Huntington Herald-Advertiser, Huntington, West Virginia, August 24, 1945

464 Huntington Herald-Advertiser, Huntington, West Virginia, August 24, 1945

465 Grayson, Harry, NEA Sports, Associated Press, Huntington Herald-Advertiser, Huntington, West Virginia, August 25, 1945

466 Associated Press Report, Huntington Herald-Advertiser, Huntington, West Virginia, August 25, 1945

467 Associated Press Report, Huntington Herald-Advertiser, Huntington, West Virginia, August 25, 1945

468 Swarts, Jr., James, Associated Press Report, Huntington Herald-Advertiser, Huntington, West Virginia, August 25, 1945

469 Associated Press Report, Huntington Herald-Advertiser, Huntington, West Virginia, August 25, 1945

470 Associated Press Report, Huntington Herald-Advertiser, Huntington, West Virginia, August 25, 1945

471 Associated Press Report, Huntington Herald-Advertiser, Huntington, West Virginia, August 25, 1945

472 Huntington Herald-Advertiser, Huntington, West Virginia, August 27, 1945

473 Associated Press Report, The Charleston Gazette, Charleston, West Virginia, August 26, 1945

474 Associated Press Report, Huntington Herald-Advertiser, Huntington, West Virginia, August 27, 1945

475 Associated Press Report, Huntington Herald-Advertiser, Huntington, West Virginia, August 28, 1945

476 Associated Press Report, Huntington Herald-Advertiser, Huntington, West Virginia, August 28, 1945

477 Huntington Herald-Advertiser, Huntington, West Virginia, August 28, 1945

478 Maxwell, Hugh, Huntington Herald-Advertiser, Huntington, West Virginia, August 29, 1945

479 Huntington Tri-State Airport Website, http://www.tristateairport.com/about-us/airport-history/ January 27, 2019

480 Huntington Herald-Advertiser, Huntington, West Virginia, August 29, 1945

481 Huntington Herald-Advertiser, Huntington, West Virginia, August 29, 1945

482 Associated Press Report, Huntington Herald-Advertiser, Huntington, West Virginia, August 29, 1945

483 Associated Press Report, Huntington Herald-Advertiser, Huntington, West Virginia, August 29, 1945

484 Associated Press Report, Huntington Herald-Advertiser, Huntington, West Virginia, August 29, 1945

485 Associated Press Report, Huntington Herald-Advertiser, Huntington, West Virginia, August 30, 1945

486 Associated Press Report, Huntington Herald-Advertiser, Huntington, West Virginia, August 30, 1945

487 Spencer, Murlin, Associated Press Report, Huntington Herald-Advertiser, Huntington, West Virginia, August 30, 1945

488 Associated Press Report, Huntington Herald-Advertiser, Huntington, West Virginia, August 30, 1945

489 Schedler, Dean, Associated Press Report, Huntington Herald-Advertiser, Huntington, West Virginia, August 30, 1945

490 Associated Press Report, Huntington Herald-Dispatch, Huntington, West Virginia, September 1, 1945

491 Stone, David J., World War II Chronicle, Legacy Publishing, Lincolnwood, IL, 2007, p 456

492 Associated Press Report, Huntington Herald-Advertiser, Huntington, West Virginia, August 31, 1945

493 Associated Press Report, Huntington Herald-Advertiser, Huntington, West Virginia, September 1, 1945

494 Associated Press Report, Huntington Herald-Advertiser, Huntington, West Virginia, September 2, 1945

495 Stone, David J., World War II Chronicle, Legacy Publishing, Lincolnwood, IL, 2007, p 458

496 Associated Press Report, Huntington Herald-Dispatch, Huntington, West Virginia, September 2, 1945

497 Stone, David J., World War II Chronicle, Legacy Publishing, Lincolnwood, IL, 2007, p 458

498 Associated Press Report, Huntington Herald-Dispatch, Huntington, West Virginia, September 3, 1945

499 Associated Press Report, Huntington Herald-Dispatch, Huntington, West Virginia, September 3, 1945

500 Associated Press Report, Huntington Herald-Dispatch, Huntington, West Virginia, September 4, 1945

501 Associated Press Report, Huntington Herald-Dispatch, Huntington, West Virginia, September 4, 1945

502 Burns, Fred, Huntington Herald-Dispatch, Huntington, West Virginia, September 5, 1945

503 Stone, David J., World War II Chronicle, Legacy Publishing, Lincolnwood, IL, 2007, p 458

504 Stone, David J., World War II Chronicle, Legacy Publishing, Lincolnwood, IL, 2007, p 459

505 Ridgley, Duke, Diamond Dust, Huntington Herald-Dispatch, Huntington, West Virginia, September 5, 1945

506 Associated Press Report, Huntington Herald-Dispatch, Huntington, West Virginia, September 5, 1945

507 Associated Press Report, Huntington Herald-Dispatch, Huntington, West Virginia, September 7, 1945

508 Huntington Herald-Dispatch, Huntington, West Virginia, September 7, 1945

509 Associated Press Report, Huntington Herald-Advertiser, Huntington, West Virginia, September 9, 1945

510 Stone, David J., World War II Chronicle, Legacy Publishing, Lincolnwood, IL, 2007, p 458

511 Stone, David J., World War II Chronicle, Legacy Publishing, Lincolnwood, IL, 2007, p 464

512 Associated Press Report, Huntington Herald-Dispatch, Huntington, West Virginia, September 10, 1945

513 Stone, David J., World War II Chronicle, Legacy Publishing, Lincolnwood, IL, 2007, p 458

514 Associated Press Report, Huntington Herald-Dispatch, Huntington, West Virginia, September 11, 1945

515 Stone, David J., World War II Chronicle, Legacy Publishing, Lincolnwood, IL, 2007, p 458

516 Associated Press Report, Huntington Herald-Dispatch, Huntington, West Virginia, September 11, 1945

517 Associated Press Report, Huntington Herald-Dispatch, Huntington, West Virginia, September 13, 1945

518 Associated Press Report, Huntington Herald-Dispatch, Huntington, West Virginia, September 14, 1945

519 Associated Press Report, Huntington Herald-Dispatch, Huntington, West Virginia, September 15, 1945

520 Huntington Herald-Dispatch, Huntington, West Virginia, September 15, 1945

521 Huntington Herald-Advertiser, Huntington, West Virginia, September 16, 1945

522 Huntington Herald-Advertiser, Huntington, West Virginia, September 16, 1945

523 Associated Press Report, Huntington Herald-Advertiser, Huntington, West Virginia, September 16, 1945

524 Huntington Herald-Advertiser, Huntington, West Virginia, September 17, 1945

525 Associated Press Report, Huntington Herald-Dispatch, Huntington, West Virginia, September 18, 1945

526 Associated Press Report, Huntington Herald-Dispatch, Huntington, West Virginia, September 19, 1945

527 Associated Press Report, Huntington Herald-Dispatch, Huntington, West Virginia, September 18, 1945

528 Huntington Herald-Dispatch, Huntington, West Virginia, September 18, 1945

529 Associated Press Report, Huntington Herald-Dispatch, Huntington, West Virginia, September 20, 1945

530 Associated Press Report, Huntington Herald-Dispatch, Huntington, West Virginia, September 20, 1945

531 Stone, David J., World War II Chronicle, Legacy Publishing, Lincolnwood, IL, 2007, p 458

532 Associated Press Report, Huntington Herald-Dispatch, Huntington, West Virginia, September 20, 1945

533 Associated Press Report, Huntington Herald-Dispatch, Huntington, West Virginia, September 20, 1945

534 Huntington Herald-Dispatch, Huntington, West Virginia, September 20, 1945

535 Associated Press Report, Huntington Herald-Dispatch, Huntington, West Virginia, September 21, 1945

536 Associated Press Report, Huntington Herald-Dispatch, Huntington, West Virginia, September 22, 1945

537 Associated Press Report, Huntington Herald-Advertiser, Huntington, West Virginia, September 23, 1945

538 Huntington Herald-Dispatch, Huntington, West Virginia, September 24, 1945

539 Huntington Herald-Advertiser, Huntington, West Virginia, September 23, 1945

540 Huntington Herald-Advertiser, Huntington, West Virginia, September 23, 1945

541 Huntington Herald-Dispatch, Huntington, West Virginia, September 24, 1945

542 Huntington Herald-Dispatch, Huntington, West Virginia, September 25, 1945

543 Stone, David J., World War II Chronicle, Legacy Publishing, Lincolnwood, IL, 2007, p 458

544 Associated Press Report, Huntington Herald-Dispatch, Huntington, West Virginia, September 27, 1945

545 Huntington Herald-Dispatch, Huntington, West Virginia, September 27, 1945

546 Associated Press Report, Huntington Herald-Dispatch, Huntington, West Virginia, September 27, 1945

547 Associated Press Report, Huntington Herald-Dispatch, Huntington, West Virginia, September 29, 1945

548 Miller, Paul, Associated Press Report, Huntington Herald-Dispatch, Huntington, West Virginia, September 29, 1945

549 Associated Press Report, Huntington Herald-Dispatch, Huntington, West Virginia, September 29, 1945

550 Associated Press Report, Huntington Herald-Dispatch, Huntington, West Virginia, September 29, 1945

551 Huntington Herald-Advertiser, Huntington, West Virginia, September 29, 1945

552 Associated Press Report, Huntington Herald-Dispatch, Huntington, West Virginia, October 1, 1945

553 Ridgley, Duke, Diamond Dust, Huntington Herald-Dispatch, Huntington, West Virginia, October 1, 1945

554 Associated Press Report, Huntington Herald-Dispatch, Huntington, West Virginia, October 1, 1945

555 Associated Press Report, Huntington Herald-Dispatch, Huntington, West Virginia, October 2, 1945

556 Associated Press Report, Huntington Herald-Dispatch, Huntington, West Virginia, October 3, 1945

557 Associated Press Report, Huntington Herald-Dispatch, Huntington, West Virginia, October 2, 1945

558 Ancestry.com, Ishmael Lucas, FHL Film Number 559883

559 Ridgley, Duke, Diamond Dust, Huntington Herald-Dispatch, Huntington, West Virginia, October 3, 1945

560 Associated Press Report, Huntington Herald-Dispatch, Huntington, West Virginia, October 4, 1945

561 Associated Press Report, Huntington Herald-Dispatch, Huntington, West Virginia, October 4, 1945

562 Briefs from Last Night's Associated Press Wires, Huntington Herald-Dispatch, Huntington, West Virginia, October 3, 1945

563 Associated Press Report, Huntington Herald-Advertiser, Huntington, West Virginia, October 5, 1945

564 Ancestry.com, Velma Adkins, FHL Film Number 1983804

565 Ancestry.com, Thomas Johnson, FHL Film Number 559883

566 Associated Press Report, Huntington Herald-Dispatch, Huntington, West Virginia, October 8, 1945

567 Associated Press Report, Huntington Herald-Dispatch, Huntington, West Virginia, October 9, 1945

568 Associated Press Report, Huntington Herald-Dispatch, Huntington, West Virginia, October 9, 1945

569 Huntington Herald-Dispatch, Huntington, West Virginia, October 9, 1945

570 Stone, David J., World War II Chronicle, Legacy Publishing, Lincolnwood, IL, 2007, p 464

571 Associated Press Report, Huntington Herald-Dispatch, Huntington, West Virginia, October 13, 1945

572 Associated Press Report, Huntington Herald-Dispatch, Huntington, West Virginia, October 13, 1945

573 Huntington Herald-Dispatch, Huntington, West Virginia, October 13, 1945

574 Huntington Herald-Dispatch, Huntington, West Virginia, October 13, 1945

575 Huntington Herald-Dispatch, Huntington, West Virginia, October 13, 1945

576 Associated Press Report, Huntington Herald-Dispatch, Huntington, West Virginia, October 15, 1945

577 Associated Press Report, Huntington Herald-Dispatch, Huntington, West Virginia, October 16, 1945

578 Associated Press Report, Huntington Herald-Dispatch, Huntington, West Virginia, October 16, 1945

579 Associated Press Report, Huntington Herald-Dispatch, Huntington, West Virginia, October 17, 1945

580 Associated Press Report, Huntington Herald-Dispatch, Huntington, West Virginia, October 18, 1945

581 Ancestry.com, Ada Belle Matthews, FHL Film Number 559883

582 Ancestry.com, Amos Matthews, 1920 United States Census

583 Huntington Herald-Dispatch, Huntington, West Virginia, October 20, 1945

584 Associated Press Report, Huntington Herald-Dispatch, Huntington, West Virginia, October 20, 1945

585 Associated Press Report, Huntington Herald-Advertiser, Huntington, West Virginia, October 21, 1945

586 Associated Press Report, Huntington Herald-Dispatch, Huntington, West Virginia, October 23, 1945

587 Feder, Sid, Associated Press Report, Huntington Herald-Dispatch, Huntington, West Virginia, October 24, 1945

588 Talbot, Gayle, Associated Press Report, Huntington Herald-Dispatch, Huntington, West Virginia, October 24, 1945

589 Stone, David J., World War II Chronicle, Legacy Publishing, Lincolnwood, IL, 2007, p 464

590 Ridgley, Duke, Diamond Dust, Huntington Herald-Dispatch, Huntington, West Virginia, October 24, 1945

591 Associated Press Report, Huntington Herald-Dispatch, Huntington, West Virginia, October 26, 1945

592 Huntington Herald-Dispatch, Huntington, West Virginia, October 27, 1945

593 Associated Press Report, Huntington Herald-Advertiser, Huntington, West Virginia, October 28, 1945

594 M'Coppin, Pat, Huntington Herald-Advertiser, Huntington, West Virginia, October 28, 1945

595 Associated Press Report, Huntington Herald-Dispatch, Huntington, West Virginia, October 29, 1945

596 Associated Press Report, Huntington Herald-Dispatch, Huntington, West Virginia, November 1, 1945

597 Associated Press Report, Huntington Herald-Dispatch, Huntington, West Virginia, November 3, 1945

598 Belanger, Bill, Huntington Herald-Advertiser, Huntington, West Virginia, November 4, 1945

599 Associated Press Report, Huntington Herald-Dispatch, Huntington, West Virginia, November 6, 1945

600 Associated Press Report, Huntington Herald-Dispatch, Huntington, West Virginia, November 7, 1945

601 Huntington Herald-Dispatch, Huntington, West Virginia, November 7, 1945

602 Associated Press Report, Huntington Herald-Dispatch, Huntington, West Virginia, November 8, 1945

603 Associated Press Report, Huntington Herald-Dispatch, Huntington, West Virginia, November 10, 1945

604 Huntington Herald-Dispatch, Huntington, West Virginia, November 9, 1945

605 Ridgley, Duke, Diamond Dust, Huntington Herald-Dispatch, Huntington, West Virginia, November 10, 1945

606 Huntington Herald-Dispatch, Huntington, West Virginia, November 10, 1945

607 Associated Press Report, Huntington Herald-Dispatch, Huntington, West Virginia, November 12, 1945

608 Associated Press Report, Huntington Herald-Dispatch, Huntington, West Virginia, November 13, 1945

609 Huntington Herald-Dispatch, Huntington, West Virginia, November 12, 1945

610 Huntington Herald-Dispatch, Huntington, West Virginia, November 12, 1945

611 Huntington Herald-Dispatch, Huntington, West Virginia, November 13, 1945

612 Associated Press Report, Huntington Herald-Dispatch, Huntington, West Virginia, November 14, 1945

613 Associated Press Report, Huntington Herald-Dispatch, Huntington, West Virginia, November 16, 1945

614 Associated Press Report, Huntington Herald-Dispatch, Huntington, West Virginia, November 15, 1945

615 Huntington Herald-Dispatch, Huntington, West Virginia, November 16, 1945

616 Associated Press Report, Huntington Herald-Advertiser, Huntington, West Virginia, November 18, 1945

617 Associated Press Report, Huntington Herald-Dispatch, Huntington, West Virginia, November 17, 1945

618 Huntington Herald-Dispatch, Huntington, West Virginia, November 20, 1945

619 Stone, David J., World War II Chronicle, Legacy Publishing, Lincolnwood, IL, 2007, p 464

620 Associated Press Report, Huntington Herald-Dispatch, Huntington, West Virginia, November 20, 1945

621 Associated Press Report, Huntington Herald-Dispatch, Huntington, West Virginia, November 21, 1945

622 Associated Press Report, Huntington Herald-Dispatch, Huntington, West Virginia, November 21, 1945

623 Associated Press Report, Huntington Herald-Dispatch, Huntington, West Virginia, November 24, 1945

624 Associated Press Report, Huntington Herald-Dispatch, Huntington, West Virginia, November 24, 1945

625 Associated Press Report, Huntington Herald-Dispatch, Huntington, West Virginia, November 26, 1945

626 Huntington Herald-Advertiser, Huntington, West Virginia, June 27, 1945

627 Associated Press Report, Huntington Herald-Dispatch, Huntington, West Virginia, November 26, 1945

628 Associated Press Report, Huntington Herald-Dispatch, Huntington, West Virginia, November 28, 1945

629 Huntington Herald-Dispatch, Huntington, West Virginia, November 28, 1945

630 Associated Press Report, Huntington Herald-Dispatch, Huntington, West Virginia, November 28, 1945

631 Huntington Herald-Dispatch, Huntington, West Virginia, November 28, 1945

632 Associated Press Report, Huntington Herald-Dispatch, Huntington, West Virginia, November 29, 1945

633 Talbot, Gayle, Associated Press Report, Huntington Herald-Dispatch, Huntington, West Virginia, November 30, 1945

634 Wikipedia, https://en.wikipedia.org/wiki/1945_Army_Cadets_football_team, June, 29, 2018

635 Huntington Herald-Dispatch, Huntington, West Virginia, November 29, 1945

636 Associated Press Report, Huntington Herald-Dispatch, Huntington, West Virginia, December 1, 1945

637 Associated Press Report, Huntington Herald-Advertiser, Huntington, West Virginia, December 2, 1945

638 Huntington Herald-Advertiser, Huntington, West Virginia, December 2, 1945

639 Associated Press Report, Huntington Herald-Dispatch, Huntington, West Virginia, December 3, 1945

640 Huntington Herald-Dispatch, Huntington, West Virginia, December 4, 1945

641 Associated Press Report, Huntington Herald-Dispatch, Huntington, West Virginia, December 5, 1945

642 Associated Press Report, Huntington Herald-Dispatch, Huntington, West Virginia, December 5, 1945

643 Associated Press Report, Huntington Herald-Dispatch, Huntington, West Virginia, December 6, 1945

644 Associated Press Report, Huntington Herald-Dispatch, Huntington, West Virginia, December 7, 1945

645 Associated Press Report, Huntington Herald-Dispatch, Huntington, West Virginia, December 8, 1945

646 Associated Press Report, Huntington Herald-Dispatch, Huntington, West Virginia, December 7, 1945

647 Burns, Fred, Huntington Herald-Dispatch, Huntington, West Virginia, December 8, 1945

648 Greene, Roger, Associated Press Report, Huntington Herald-Advertiser, Huntington, West Virginia, December 9, 1945

649 Associated Press Report, Huntington Herald-Advertiser, Huntington, West Virginia, December 9, 1945

650 Huntington Herald-Advertiser, Huntington, West Virginia, December 9, 1945

651 Huntington Herald-Dispatch, Huntington, West Virginia, December 9, 1945

652 Huntington Herald-Dispatch, Huntington, West Virginia, December 10, 1945

653 Huntington Herald-Dispatch, Huntington, West Virginia, December 11, 1945

654 Associated Press Report, Huntington Herald-Dispatch, Huntington, West Virginia, December 12, 1945

655 Associated Press Report, Huntington Herald-Dispatch, Huntington, West Virginia, December 13, 1945

656 Associated Press Report, Huntington Herald-Dispatch, Huntington, West Virginia, December 13, 1945

657 Ancestry.com, Ida Ferrell, FHL Film Number 1983805

658 Huntington Herald-Dispatch, Huntington, West Virginia, December 13, 1945

659 Associated Press Report, Huntington Herald-Dispatch, Huntington, West Virginia, December 14, 1945

660 Associated Press Report, Huntington Herald-Dispatch, Huntington, West Virginia, December 14, 1945

661 Associated Press Report, Huntington Herald-Dispatch, Huntington, West Virginia, December 14, 1945

662 Huntington Herald-Advertiser, Huntington, West Virginia, December 15, 1945

663 Associated Press Report, Huntington Herald-Advertiser, Huntington, West Virginia, December 15, 1945

664 Associated Press Report, Huntington Herald-Advertiser, Huntington, West Virginia, December 16, 1945

665 Huntington Herald-Dispatch, Huntington, West Virginia, December 17, 1945

666 Associated Press Report, Huntington Herald-Dispatch, Huntington, West Virginia, December 18, 1945

667 Associated Press Report, Huntington Herald-Dispatch, Huntington, West Virginia, December 18, 1945

668 Ridgley, Duke, Diamond Dust, Huntington Herald-Dispatch, Huntington, West Virginia, December 18, 1945

669 Huntington Herald-Dispatch, Huntington, West Virginia, December 18, 1945

670 Associated Press Report, Huntington Herald-Dispatch, Huntington, West Virginia, December 18, 1945

671 Associated Press Report, Huntington Herald-Dispatch, Huntington, West Virginia, December 19, 1945

672 Report, Huntington Herald-Dispatch, Huntington, West Virginia, December 19, 1945

673 Ridgley, Duke, Diamond Dust, Huntington Herald-Dispatch, Huntington, West Virginia, December 20, 1945

674 Associated Press Report, Huntington Herald-Dispatch, Huntington, West Virginia, December 21, 1945

675 Huntington Herald-Dispatch, Huntington, West Virginia, December 20, 1945

676 Associated Press Report, Huntington Herald-Dispatch, Huntington, West Virginia, December 22, 1945

677 O'Regan, Richard A., Associated Press Report, Huntington Herald-Advertiser, Huntington, West Virginia, December 23, 1945

678 Associated Press Report, Huntington Herald-Advertiser, Huntington, West Virginia, December 23, 1945

679 Associated Press Report, Huntington Herald-Advertiser, Huntington, West Virginia, December 23, 1945

680 Associated Press Report, Huntington Herald-Dispatch, Huntington, West Virginia, December 24, 1945

681 Associated Press Report, Huntington Herald-Dispatch, Huntington, West Virginia, December 25, 1945

682 Associated Press Report, Huntington Herald-Dispatch, Huntington, West Virginia, December 25, 1945

683 Associated Press Report, Huntington Herald-Dispatch, Huntington, West Virginia, December 26, 1945

684 Associated Press Report, Huntington Herald-Dispatch, Huntington, West Virginia, December 27, 1945

685 Associated Press Report, Huntington Herald-Dispatch, Huntington, West Virginia, December 27, 1945

686 Associated Press Report, Huntington Herald-Dispatch, Huntington, West Virginia, December 29, 1945

687 Vance, Kyle, Associated Press Report, Huntington Herald-Advertiser, Huntington, West Virginia, December 30, 1945

688 Associated Press Report, Huntington Herald-Dispatch, Huntington, West Virginia, December 31, 1945

689 Associated Press Report, Huntington Herald-Dispatch, Huntington, West Virginia, January 1, 1946

690 Stone, David J., World War II Chronicle, Legacy Publishing, Lincolnwood, IL, 2007, p 464

691 Huntington Herald-Dispatch, Huntington, West Virginia, January 1, 1946

692 Associated Press Report, Huntington Herald-Dispatch, Huntington, West Virginia, January 4, 1946

693 Ancestry.com, Martha Berry, FHL Film Number 559883

694 Associated Press Report, Huntington Herald-Dispatch, Huntington, West Virginia, January 8, 1946

695 Associated Press Report, Huntington Herald-Dispatch, Huntington, West Virginia, January 10, 1946

696 Huntington Herald-Dispatch, Huntington, West Virginia, January 11, 1946

CPSIA information can be obtained
at www.ICGtesting.com
Printed in the USA
LVHW061129061020
668071LV00013B/462